The Oliver Wendell Holmes Devise

HISTORY OF THE SUPREME COURT
OF THE UNITED STATES

General Editor: Paul A. Freund

THE

Oliver Wendell Holmes

DEVISE

HISTORY OF
THE SUPREME COURT
OF THE UNITED STATES

VOLUME II

THE OLIVER WENDELL HOLMES DEVISE

History of the

SUPREME COURT

of the United States

VOLUME II
Foundations of Power: John Marshall, 1801-15

PART ONE

by George Lee Haskins

MEMBER OF THE PHILADELPHIA BAR, THE MAINE BAR, AND THE
MASSACHUSETTS BAR; ALGERNON SYDNEY BIDDLE
PROFESSOR OF LAW AT THE UNIVERSITY OF PENNSYLVANIA

PART TWO

by Herbert A. Johnson

MEMBER OF THE NEW YORK BAR; PROFESSOR OF LAW
AND HISTORY AT THE UNIVERSITY OF SOUTH CAROLINA

MACMILLAN PUBLISHING CO., INC.

NEW YORK

COLLIER MACMILLAN PUBLISHERS

LONDON

Macmillan Publishing Co., Inc.
866 Third Avenue, New York, N.Y. 10022
Collier Macmillan Canada, Ltd.

Library of Congress Cataloging in Publication Data (Revised)
Main entry under title:

History of the Supreme Court of the United States.

At head of title: The Oliver Wendell Holmes Devise.
Includes bibliographical footnotes.
CONTENTS: v. 1. Antecedents and beginnings to 1801, by J. Goebel, Jr.—v. 2. Foundations of power, John Marshall, 1801–15, by G. L. Haskins and H. A. Johnson. [etc.] v. 6. Reconstruction and reunion, 1864–88, pt. 1, by C. Fairman.
1. United States Supreme Court—History. I. Title.
I. Title: The Oliver Wendell Holmes Devise.
KF8742.A45H55   347.73'26   78-30454
ISBN 0–02–541360–0

10 9 8 7 6 5 4 3 2 1

PRINTED IN THE UNITED STATES OF AMERICA

Contents

Contents

Illustrations

ILLUSTRATIONS

Foreword

THE *History of the Supreme Court of the United States* is being prepared under the auspices of the Permanent Committee for the
Oliver Wendell Holmes Devise with the aid of the estate left by Mr.
Justice Oliver Wendell Holmes, Jr. Mr. Justice Holmes died in 1935
and the Permanent Committee for the Devise was created by Act of
Congress in 1955. Members of the Committee are appointed by the
President of the United States, with the Librarian of Congress, an *ex
officio* member, as Chairman. The present volume is the fourth to be
completed and the first to appear during the tenure of the present
members of the Permanent Committee for the Devise. The Committee
hopes to complete the history expeditiously while maintaining the high
quality of the scholarship. The volumes in the Holmes Devise *History
of the Supreme Court of the United States* bring to this subject some of
the best legal scholarship of the decades since Mr. Justice Holmes'
death. They will also have such advantages (not anticipated at the
time of the Justice's death) as can be secured from a more than ample
measure of judicious deliberation. We hope that, when completed, the
series will widen and deepen our understanding of the Supreme Court
and bring honor to the memory of one of its great Justices.

Daniel J. Boorstin
LIBRARIAN OF CONGRESS

Editor's Foreword

I N THE PERIOD covered by this volume—roughly the first half of
John Marshall's Chief Justiceship—the Supreme Court faced one
or another of two dark fates. The Court might languish in benign ob-
scurity or it might go down under the lash of active contempt. How
Marshall and his colleagues were able to escape these opposing perils
and establish the authority of the Court is the pervading theme of this
richly documented and multidimensional study, which draws on manuscript sources and contemporary journals as well as official records for
an insight into this critical stage of the Court's history.

Salvation was achieved for the judges partly through external circumstances and partly by dint of their own good works. As Professor
Haskins emphasizes in his analysis of the social and political currents
of the day, the Federalists and the Jeffersonian Republicans were each
riven by internal divisions reflecting sectional and personal attachments.
These cleavages, as they affected both judicial appointments and popular response to judicial decisions, served to blunt what might have been
an even sharper political confrontation between the Court and the
national administration. Joseph Story of Massachusetts and William
Johnson of South Carolina, the two strongest side judges, both bore a
Republican-Democratic allegiance, yet they out-Marshalled Marshall
in their nationalism. And to New Englanders of that party the decision
in *Fletcher* v. *Peck*, sustaining the claims of remote purchasers of Yazoo
lands against the resistance of the State of Georgia, was no less welcome than it was to the Federalists. A binary classification scheme is
more suitable for computers than for societies or judges.

Internally, the Court came to speak ordinarily through a single
voice, rather than through seriatim opinions, and that voice was normally the Chief Justice's, magisterial yet tactful, justifying judgments
with a dialectical prowess that was extraordinary. In addition, as

xiii

Professor Johnson shows with a wealth of particulars, the Court proved itself to be a highly serviceable instrument for the settlement of controversies that did not implicate sensitive political issues: commercial disputes, conflicts over land titles, and voluminous garden-variety litigation arising in the District of Columbia. Thus the Court helped to establish itself as an arbiter of fundamental issues of governmental power by earning acceptance as a fair-minded and sagacious tribunal in the decision of legal causes that were not, to borrow Justice Holmes' phrase, "great" cases since they did not involve the Constitution or a telegraph company.

The effort to maintain the Court as a court of law, and to mark a separation between law and politics, is seen by the authors as a centrally significant undertaking in this period. Clearly they would wish to guard against delusive precision here. Judges who strive to maintain the constitutional order must possess a vision of that order and recognize that they too are engaged in a form of statecraft, of politics, if you will, in an Aristotelian sense. But there are constraints that operate on the judges in a special way. Their vision of the constitutional order must respect the "meaning" of the document: though not its time-bound denotative meaning, its enduring connotative meaning. And judges are constrained by the record before them and by the limits on jurisdiction that by law have been imposed on them. Precisely because a court, as Marshall declared in *Marbury* v. *Madison*, in the discharge of its adjudicative function has the power and duty to determine whether other branches of government have exceeded their legal bounds, the courts must be alert—and this is the corollary drawn by Marshall in that case—to remain within their own. What are the bounds, when we pass from specific positive mandates of law to a subtler focus of scrutiny and to still more philosophical criteria of the judicial domain and its relation to representative government, is an issue that has been ever more self-consciously addressed. It is not remarkable that the Marshall court did not give us clear-cut or refined answers. Our debt to that Court, of which the authors insistently remind us, is that its members, and especially its Chief Justice, perceived the question as an honest and important one. In our preoccupation with the formulation of particular constitutional and other legal doctrines in the early Marshall period we may overlook what is even more basic, as scientific method is more perduring than the particular dogmas of a science. This shaping of the judicial process, the authors tell us, is at once a clue to the survival of the early Court and a legacy that must be comprehended if it is to be possessed.

Paul A. Freund

PART ONE

By George Lee Haskins

Acknowledgments

THE INITIAL RESPONSIBILITY for preparing this volume for the Oliver Wendell Holmes Committee would probably not have been placed in my hands but for the insistent and relentless persuasiveness of the late Mr. Justice Frankfurter. Because of teaching responsibilities and several writing commitments, and also because of some protracted litigation in which I was involved as legal counsel, I did not see how I could accept the honor of joining the panel of authors assembled to write the volumes which would comprise the congressionally authorized History of the Supreme Court. Indeed, less gracefully than Caesar, the crown was "thrice refused." Gradually, over the course of several conversations, including sandwich luncheons together in his chambers, Justice Frankfurter overcame my objections and convinced me that I should undertake the so-called Marshall volume. It was a duty, he finally argued, "not only to scholarship and to history, but to *this Court*." That did it, and the decision was thus already made when he led me unexpectedly down the corridor for what he thought would be the closing argument from Chief Justice Warren, who benignly began, "You will do that volume, won't you?" To that my answer was, "Yes, Mr. Chief Justice, it has been decided."

There were many times when I later regretted that decision because of the enormous amounts of time and travel involved and because the tasks often seemed diversionary from other studies on which I was and have been engaged. Yet when it proved that I did not have to desert entirely my other legal writing, especially in American, English, and Roman history, I found the new task not only beckoning but rewarding. Judges and fellow members of the Bar were genuinely interested, inquiring, and were kind enough to insist that this Volume of the series would have particular importance. Law students were also eager to know what lay behind the formal scene of the early Court's

3

decisions. Moreover, almost at the outset, it was decided to divide the "Marshall period" chronologically between myself for Volume II (1801–15) and Professor Gerald Gunther for Volumes III and IV (1816–35). Later, as my collections of source materials grew to immense proportions, it was decided to add Professor Johnson as a co-author of Volume II, giving him responsibility for the second part, which I had tentatively sketched out as "The Business of the Court." As my own work progressed, I found that it involved meeting, almost face to face, through their writings, correspondence, and other papers, persons long since dead, who could speak for themselves and others and thus help bring the past to life. Above all, I began to understand, at first hand, the mind, personality, and achievements of one of the greatest men in the history of Anglo-American law and jurisprudence: Chief Justice Marshall.

Now that the work is ready for publication, I can feel grateful to Justice Frankfurter and even slightly embarrassed by my initial and obdurate refusal to do as I was asked. I hope that, if he were still living, he would approve and give his blessing (as his disciple Professor Paul A. Freund has given his) to what I have written. Yet I know that the real test, and an enjoyable one, would have been the rigorous cross-examination to which Justice Frankfurter would have subjected me on one topic after the other, as he meticulously read through the text and supporting notes.

A book of this sort is not easily written when major sources of time for research and composition have had to come chiefly from weekends and from summer months when the author was free of teaching and other regular academic responsibilities. Most of the archival research and specialized reading was, of necessity, done in that way; and, while it prolonged the preparation of the book, it also produced far more sources and other materials than could in fact be used, with the result that much time has been consumed in cutting out or pruning valuable letters, memoranda, and opinions of judges and political figures in order to put together a book of manageable proportions which had a central theme. Fortunately, research leaves from the University of Pennsylvania Law School greatly aided the ensuing task of composition, and I wish to thank Dean Fordham for his continuing interest in the project, and Dean Wolfman and Dean Pollak particularly for their special enthusiasm and personal encouragement in furthering it to conclusion. Those periodic leaves of absence were supported in part by the University, but chiefly through foundation subventions (the Rockefeller and Ford Foundations) arranged by the Oliver Wendell Holmes Committee. That Committee also provided an allowance for

Acknowledgments

travel and related expenses which supplemented student assistance made available by the Law School.

In providing research facilities and information relating to archival sources, gratitude is expressed for the continuing assistance provided by Mrs. Elizabeth Hamer Kegan and the other administrative officers of the Holmes Devise Committee, and especially for the courtesies extended by the Manuscripts Division at the Library of Congress. In recent months, Dr. James H. Hutson, of the American Revolution Bicentennial Office at the Library, has been especially helpful. Officials and their assistants at every archival center or institution in which I worked provided guidance and attention beyond what a researcher might normally expect. These include, in addition to the Library of Congress, particularly the Massachusetts Historical Society, the New York Historical Society, the New York Public Library, the Pennsylvania Historical Society, the Maryland Historical Society, the National Archives in Washington, the Institute for Early American History and Culture at Williamsburg, and the Southern Historical Collection at the University of North Carolina. The unfailing assistance rendered in countless ways by the staff of the Biddle Law Library at the University of Pennsylvania cannot go unmentioned, especially the cooperation of Professor Richard Sloane, Librarian, and his associates Mr. Paul Gay and Miss Nancy I. Arnold.

Four friends have been kind enough to offer criticism and to read the manuscript as it developed. Morris Duane, Esquire, of the Philadelphia Bar, went over the opening chapters with great care and made numerous suggestions which helped to clarify the theme of Part I. Professor Herbert A. Johnson, of the University of South Carolina and author of Part II, has continually shared his special knowledge of the legal and other papers of John Marshall which he has helped to edit. Professor William E. Nelson, of the Yale Law School, read through the entire final draft (originally twelve chapters, but now reduced to ten) and was especially helpful in emphasizing efforts of John Marshall and other members of the Court who were determined to establish an identifiable "rule of law." Professor Paul A. Freund, of the Harvard Law School, and Editor-in-Chief of the *History*, read not only the final draft but the final version and all footnotes, so that his careful and exacting criticisms and suggestions give me confidence that the theme of the book, as well as the story of the Court in its early years under John Marshall, is tenable and accurate.

Many of my former students, during the summer months, provided valuable memoranda on special topics or searched out needed source materials and references, and to each of them I express my thanks for their labors. In addition, during the closing months of revision and copy editing, Thomas R. Eshelman, Esquire, recently a student but now a member of the Philadelphia Bar, and his wife Dr. Nancy G. Eshelman, supervised meticulously and with vigilance the final research and the preparation of the printer's copy. Certain portions of this conscientious work devolved upon Miss Sarah Duggin, an officer of the *Pennsylvania Law Review*. Another former student, Kristin R. Hayes, whose competent work enhanced the accuracy of my research for several portions of the manuscript, has carefully supervised the final corrections in the galley proofs; for the accomplishment of those tasks particular thanks are expressed. These combined labors were supplemented by the willing and efficient assistance of Patricia M. Stolnis. Earlier, the final version and its revisions were typed by Donna C. Smith, Denise R. Hagan, and Deborah Nearey, to each of whom I am especially grateful for long hours of painstaking work.

In concluding, it is gratifying to remember how much of the writing of these chapters was done in the quiet of my down-east home on the coast of Maine, and to record the personal encouragement of those, there, who shared my eagerness to see the work completed.

G.L.H.

Philadelphia
July 1980

Preface

T HE PREPARATION of Volume II of the History of the United States
Supreme Court has proved to be an exceedingly difficult and time-
consuming task. Entitled *John Marshall: Foundations of Power*, it deals
with the history of the Court from 1801 to 1815, a period during which
the Court was enmeshed in the political strife of the conflicting ideologies and philosophies of the Federalist and Republican factions and
yet was attempting to gain for itself a sure foothold as an independent
tribunal in the constitutional pattern of government. A relatively feeble
institution during the 1790s, too unimportant to interest the talents of
two men who declined President Adams' offer of the position of Chief
Justice, it nevertheless acquired in only a few years' time, and largely
under the guiding hand of John Marshall, more power than even the
framers of the Constitution may have anticipated. It became not only
the final important seat of federal judicial power, a bulwark of an
identifiable rule of law as distinct from the accommodations of politics,
but also the embodiment of principles of judicial power that permeated
the lower federal courts and through them helped to spread nascent
ideas of a new American nationalism.

The process by which these developments took place, in the course
of direct confrontation with the executive and legislative branches of
the government, as well as through capable judicial statesmanship, is
reflected less in particular decisions than in the course of development
of legal ideas. The latter can be discerned in episodes that directly
affected the functions and power of the Court, as well as in "public"
and "private" areas of the law where it exercised jurisdiction. Partly
for this reason, partly because of the immense amount of collateral
materials (letters, journals, debates, and the like), it was decided that
this Volume fell naturally into two Parts, and that those Parts could
be more expeditiously completed by joint rather than single author-

7

ship. Hence, Part I, "Foundations of Power," became the responsibility of Professor Haskins; Part II, "The Business of the Court," that of Professor Johnson. Each author bears the sole responsibility for his respective Part only, even though each has had available the work of the other. Each Part contains each author's individual Acknowledgments.

In 1801, when Marshall was appointed Chief Justice, the Court was clearly "Federalist," both in the political makeup of the members and in attitudes formed in and inherited from the administrations of President Washington and President Adams and earlier. By contrast, the majority of both houses of Congress had become "Republican," as a result of the 1800 election, as was Thomas Jefferson, the new President. To many Republicans it was an anomaly that the third branch of the government, that is, the judiciary, should remain an entrenched vestige of the defeated Federalist power. The harmony that many eighteenth-century men felt should exist in government was broken; in addition, the new Republican plans for the conduct of government faced unforeseen obstacles from a Court now headed by one who was a renowned soldier of the Revolution, a patriot and statesman who was also a skilled lawyer of the highest reputation. That conflicts between the judiciary and the two other branches of government should arise was almost inevitable. When those conflicts turned—as they did—on efforts to establish the recognition of a rule of law, as opposed to the vagaries of political decision and indecision, and when they were nurtured by assertively strong personalities, they were exacerbated. It hardly needs stating that in a large sense, law, and particularly constitutional law, is not sealed off from social and political ideals; but the rule of law respects the division of governmental functions and stands in opposition to partisan, opportunistic, or merely expedient judicial decisions.

From certain standpoints, it is unfortunate that the harsh spotlights of reality should be turned upon a public figure who has earned the continuing admiration of so many, and in such different ways, as has Thomas Jefferson. Brilliant, versatile, ingenious, he had an innate flair for politics and political machinations. These talents and qualities he turned to the achievement of new programs and policies in which he strongly believed and to which he clung almost unwaveringly. Nevertheless, the conflicts above referred to, and others as well, clearly delineate what has been termed his "darker side."[1] It was he who, with skilled lieutenants in and outside of Congress, led the fight for repealing the 1801 Judiciary Act, pushed for the impeachment of Federalist judges

---

[1] L. Levy, *Jefferson and Civil Liberties: The Darker Side* (Cambridge, Mass., 1963).

who were to be replaced by his Republican nominees, interposed executive action over the authority of Congress in the enforcement of the Embargo Act, declared his former Vice-President, Aaron Burr, guilty of treason before he had even been tried, and subsequently guided and manipulated that trial in a way that satisfied his own sense of self-righteous convictions. With other aspects of the "darker side" (e.g., his attitudes towards sedition and libel, black slavery) this Volume does not concern itself; neither is it concerned with his many-sided gifts of learning and his imaginative contributions to the practical arts.

Several of the chapters in Part I deal with this persistent conflict, which is so prominent while Jefferson was in office but which subsided under Madison. Some effort is made to explain the sources of this conflict, other than by reference to the strong personal antagonism that had so long persisted between Jefferson and John Marshall, and to ideological convictions that obtained between extreme Republicans on the one hand and right-wing Federalists on the other.[2] A conscious effort has been made not to overemphasize some of the standard charges against Jefferson for his alleged "deviousness," "duplicity," and "prejudice" but rather to permit letters, documents, and events speak for themselves. The contradictions in Jefferson's thinking and character are so numerous and difficult to sort out, here at least, that the reader should be alerted to the problem yet be advised not always to take Jefferson's statements or accusations at their apparent face value. What in some other person could be labeled rank dishonesty or demogogical vituperation could, for Jefferson, be merely an expression of his political attitudes, wrong-headed perhaps, yet sincere.

Jefferson's party in Congress, after the 1800 election, was far less strong than many have supposed, and the Federalists, who had lost by the narrowest of margins, were hardly subdued. This fact accounts for close votes and much temporizing in the debates and resolutions in Congress. If Jefferson had strong lieutenants and adherents, not a few —particularly William B. Giles of Virginia—were little respected by either party. Yet Giles, and the more idealistic John Randolph, were successful manipulators of public opinion and masters of debate both in calumny and in insinuation, and their effect, even on middle-of-the-road Republicans in Congress, could be staggering. The party "machine," if that term is not anachronistic, that Jefferson and others had organized to gain election, and to hold power thereafter, had been and continued to be extraordinarily effective for putting new policies and programs into effect. Disenchantment was to follow during his second

---

[2] See Part I, chapter 2 infra.

term, as failures followed success and as men perceived his single-mindedness of purpose in politics and saw that, far from doing the harm it was accused of perpetrating, the Federalist judiciary was keeping within prescribed bounds and exercising appropriate self-restraint insofar as the actions of other departments of government were concerned.[3] Notwithstanding the political thrusts and opposition with which the Court was confronted, it soon became clear that the Court's outlook was fast becoming depoliticized, that it was performing its tasks in the field of law in a professional way, as were the members of the Bar who came before it, regardless of their political affinities. Most of the judges on the Court in this period saw the way of the judiciary to be separate and independent of polarized political concepts and in the direction of formulating a growing body of legal rules, usually without reference to political implications.

The period with which this Volume deals may seem unduly short for so lengthy a book. It covers less than one-half of the years during which John Marshall served as Chief Justice, but it is nevertheless so vital a period in the Court's history that the Volume bears a special subtitle. Indeed, the number of pages devoted to these years is far less than originally contemplated when fifteen chapters were outlined for Part I, and as many more for Part II. It is a source of regret that in the ultimate structure of the book it was necessary to omit special chapters on Marshall, Story, the federal Bar, and legal education. However, other recent interpretive studies, as well as standard works, such as those of Senator Beveridge and Charles Warren, can readily supply much of the broad outlines at least of those omitted chapters.

Some readers may be disappointed that John Marshall appears as less of a central figure for the period than he is cast in Beveridge's biography. Others who have been taught to revere Thomas Jefferson for his many-splendored genius may balk at the exposure of his "darker side." But this book is not written in praise, or otherwise, of famous men. There were countless others on the stage of political history at this important time, not to mention well-known judges and lawyers, who influenced or failed to influence the development of the Court's power. Marshall, like Jefferson, had been raised and nurtured in eighteenth-century thinking, but unlike Jefferson, who was some ten years his senior, he became progressively less wedded to a "consensus" theory of government, originating in traditional concepts of shared values, which presumed that all branches should cooperate to the same

---

[3] For a carefully drawn summary of Jefferson's character and ambitions, see H. Adams, *A History of* *the United States of America* (New York, 1889), I, chapter 12.

ends.[4] Marshall recognized certain ideas of natural rights as great or fundamental principles anterior to government and legislation,[5] but he proved adaptable to the necessity of re-evaluating the appropriate distribution of power among the agencies of government in light of constitutional mandates and emerging nationalism.

In law as in politics, to focus merely on the acts and decisions of the great and prominent can result in ignoring what may be less obvious. Thus, to read *Marbury* v. *Madison* without careful study of the arguments of Charles Lee can result in missing much of the thrust of Marshall's opinion. Similarly, to emphasize only the "great cases" of the 1801–15 period can distort the amount and value of the more routine business of the Court in problems relating to maritime affairs, insurance, negotiable instruments, and land titles. To describe in balance the diversities of the work of the Court, and to adumbrate the factors which moved it from relative unimportance towards greatness, has been no easy task; yet if this Volume has contributed in any significant way to an understanding of this process, its authors will feel some sense of accomplishment.

G.L.H.

---

[4] The eighteenth-century background of consensus theories of government, moral and political, has recently been explored by W. E. Nelson, "The Eighteenth-Century Background of John Marshall's Jurisprudence," *Michigan Law Review* LXXVI, 893 (1978). See generally, B. Bailyn, *The Ideological Origins of the American Revolution* (Cambridge, Mass., 1967).

[5] Nelson, "John Marshall's Jurisprudence," 932; Part I, chapter 10 infra.

CHAPTER I

The State of the Union

THE YEAR 1801 was a revolutionary one both in the history of the Supreme Court and in the history of the United States generally. It was the year in which the Federalist party, whose leaders had been chiefly responsible for welding the nation together after the Revolution, was turned out of office and the reins of government taken up by the Republicans, with Thomas Jefferson as President. It was the year in which President Adams performed "the proudest act of his life"[1] in appointing John Marshall to what Justice Holmes has described as "perhaps the greatest place that ever was filled by a judge."[2]

Almost immediately after Jefferson's inauguration the Court became embroiled in a series of political and constitutional controversies which were to continue for more than a decade; these controversies substantially shaped many of the Court's powers and numerous aspects of its jurisdiction into a recognizably modern form. During the years between 1801 and 1835, under the leadership of the new Chief Justice, the Supreme Court emerged at the head of an enormously strengthened federal judiciary, successfully asserting the power of centralized jurisdiction against the centrifugal forces of States' rights and against the visionary efforts of its political opponents of a strong national government, who sought to impose on the country many of the outmoded ideals of the previous century. Had those efforts been successful, the vigorous growth of the new nation would have been seriously retarded.

When Marshall took his seat on the Bench, few important questions of constitutional law had ever engaged the attention of the Supreme

---

[1] Adams made the remark to John Marshall's youngest son in 1825. Quoted in C. Warren, *A History of* the *American Bar* (Boston, 1966), 252, note 1.

[2] *Speeches by Oliver Wendell Holmes* (Boston, 1934), 90.

Court.[3] By 1816, several major constitutional cases had been decided; the Court had resolved important issues of substantive law, as well as significant jurisdictional and procedural questions; and the basic principle of judicial power to review and pass upon the constitutionality of acts of Congress had been established. By the close of 1835, when Chief Justice Marshall died, the Court had extended the compass of its jurisdiction into areas hardly envisaged in 1800, including, for example, those of corporations law, maritime law, and interstate commerce.

A principal share of the credit for carrying out the ideas of national unity embodied in the Constitution, expressly and by implication, as well as for ensuring that it was to be the supreme law of the land, belongs to the Court in this period and, more particularly, to the dominating influence of one of the greatest figures in American history —John Marshall. To him, more than to any other single person, belongs the credit for establishing the foundations of constitutional interpretation. His luminous exposition of the principles of the Constitution are an enduring monument not only to his own fame but to the principles of federal government. If it can be said that greatness in man results from great qualities and great opportunities, few, if any judges, in the history of the English-speaking world can be called greater than Marshall. In him were combined the wisdom, the vision, and the practicality of the statesman, together with the lucidity of exposition and the power of persuasive reasoning that characterize the eminent lawyer. If in certain aspects of his judicial work, notably in some conventional areas of the law, he may not have been the equal of Story or Kent or of Lord Eldon or Lord Mansfield, his decisions in the field of international law are of the highest calibre, and in the field of constitutional law he was preeminent. Convinced of the necessity of a strong national government to preserve the Union, Marshall insisted on constructions of the Constitution that he believed would best effectuate the original purposes of its framers. But for his brilliant expositions of constitutional principles, skillfully explained, powerfully argued, and elaborated in detail, it seems doubtful at best whether the country's political fabric would have survived the Civil War. Chief Justice Marshall's accomplishments in this area have been summarized by Lord Bryce, as follows:

> His work of building up and working out the Constitution was accomplished not so much by the decisions he gave as by the judgments in which he expounded the principles of these decisions, judgments which for their philosophical breadth, the luminous exactness of their

---

[3] See J. Goebel, Jr., *Antecedents and Beginnings to 1801. History of the Supreme Court of the United States*, ed., P. Freund (New York, 1971), I.

14

reasoning, and the fine political sense which pervades them, have never been surpassed and rarely equalled by the most famous jurists of modern Europe or of ancient Rome. Marshall did not forget the duty of a judge to decide nothing more than the suit before him requires, but he was wont to set forth the grounds of his decision in such a way as to show how they would fall [*sic*] to be applied in cases that had not yet arisen. He grasped with extraordinary force and clearness the cardinal idea that the creation of a national government implies the grant of all such subsidiary powers as are requisite to the effectuation of its main powers and purposes, but he developed and applied this idea with so much prudence and sobriety, never treading on purely political ground, never indulging the temptation to theorize, but content to follow out as a lawyer the consequences of legal principles, that the Constitution seemed not so much to rise under his hands to its full stature, as to be gradually unveiled by him till it stood revealed in the harmonious perfection of the form which its framers had designed. That admirable flexibility and capacity for growth which characterize it beyond all other rigid or supreme constitutions, is largely due to him, yet not more to his courage than to his caution.[4]

It is impossible to assess or to appreciate the work of the Supreme Court and its place in the history of the nation between 1801 and 1816 without some preliminary understanding of the state of the nation at the beginning of this period. The conditions of life, and the political and economic problems that faced the country, had a significant bearing on the cases that came before the Court and on its place and role in the government. At the turn of the new century, the United States was still in many respects hardly more than the loose federation of States that it had been when the Constitution was adopted. The fibers of union were scarcely knit and certainly not strong. Despite the ideals of federation inspired by the Revolution, by the Constitution, by the impressive leadership of Washington, and by the practical accomplishments of Hamilton, the possibilities of secession presented a continuing threat. Not only were the advocates of States' rights vociferous and powerful, but large sections of the inland populace were opposed to centralized government in any form, whether at the State or federal level.[5] Tom Paine was still one of the most widely read and admired authors of the time, and his inflammatory maxims about government as a necessary evil, continued to be quoted by the demagogues, to the enchantment of the multitudes and especially the credulous.

[4] J. Bryce, *The American Commonwealth* (London, 1891), I, 375.

[5] A. J. Beveridge, *The Life of John Marshall* (Boston, 1919), I, 288 et seq. See also O. Handlin and M. F. Handlin, *Commonwealth: Massachusetts, 1774–1861* (New York, 1947), 53 et seq., especially 92.

A. THE LAND AND THE PEOPLE
OF THE NEW NATION

In 1800 the country sprawled across three-quarters of a million square miles, much of it not even settled. The original thirteen States had been increased to sixteen by the addition of Vermont and by the formation of Kentucky and Tennessee out of the territory south of the Ohio River. Three new territories had been organized on the frontier—Mississippi, Indiana, and Northwest. The area belonging to the United States thus extended from northeastern Maine to southern Georgia, and from the Atlantic on the east to the Mississippi River on the west. The total population was only 5,308,483, most of it concentrated in farms and villages along the seacoast, with a bare six percent in urban centers.[6] Much of the land west of the Appalachians was still hostile Indian country, governed from scattered military outposts such as those in the areas that were to become the States of Indiana and Illinois. To the north the British were firmly entrenched in the Canadas, and to the south the Floridas were still in Spanish hands. To the west, thousands of square miles of prairies and forests between the Mississippi River and the Rocky Mountains belonged to France as the result of the recent retrocession from Spain. Despite earlier victories, such as that of Fallen Timbers, it seemed doubtful whether the United States Army was sufficient even to hold off the Indians, to say nothing of withstanding an incursion of British troops; similarly, the Navy was not strong enough to watch the coast, which lay virtually at the mercy of any power that might wish to attack.

East of the Appalachians dense forests still stretched for nearly a thousand miles, broken along the seaboard by bays and estuaries and, inland, by rivers and the enlarging areas of farmland. Small towns were scattered throughout the settled section along the coast and inland, and a few important cities had grown up at major seaports—Boston, Salem, New York, Philadelphia, Baltimore, and Charleston. Yet large sections of the interior one hundred miles inland were a wilderness as desolate as it was vast. Penetrated only by rivers, trails, and an occasional rough road, the interior was almost as difficult of access as it had been a century before. Although a number of communities—for example, Reading, Lancaster, and Pittsburgh—were beginning to expand and thrive on the growing traffic of the rivers and the widening tracks of

---

[6] Census of 1800, cited by H. Adams, *History of the United States of America* (New York, 1889), I, 1 (hereafter cited as Adams, *History of United States*); and *Historical Atlas of the United States* (Washington, 1914).

roads, such sparse settlements as there were in the interior consisted of primitive cabins, stump-filled fields, and acres of strangled dead trees.

Since 1790 moderate increases in population had taken place everywhere, yet it is said there were few periods in American history in which foreign immigration was so small or of such little consequence as it was between 1790 and 1815.[7] The seaboard States were well settled along the coast and tidewater regions, except in northern New England and the western part of Georgia. Recent migrations had extended into the uninhabited area, and in the course of the 1790s large numbers of settlers had poured up the Hudson River and through the Mohawk Valley, while in western Pennsylvania they had streamed west and formed an increasingly dense body of population about the place where the Allegheny and Monongahela Rivers merged to form the Ohio. Over ancient trails and over the three long wagon roads that crossed the Alleghenies, half a million persons had moved to Ohio, Kentucky, and Tennessee, and they had driven a great wedge of white settlements between the Indian tribes to the north and south. Yet, save by the main post road that ran from Wiscasset in Maine to Savannah, Georgia, the means of inland communication between the several parts of the country were still slow and primitive.

The two great groups of population, east and west of the Alleghenies, were distinct from each other not only geographically and physically but in their attitudes and interests. The principal interest of the western sector was in agriculture, whereas in the East commerce and incipient manufacturing were becoming progressively more important. Many of the western settlers were apparently emotional and quick-tempered, and often ready to take on any new project that might appear. With gambling, drinking, and wrestling as their major diversions, they believed in "easy credit and uncurbed expansion."[8] The magnitude of this division had been a source of concern to President Washington even ten years before, and in 1800 it seemed entirely possible to many that the western States and territories might form a separate confederation. Already, strong expressions of hostility towards the jurisdiction of the federal courts had been heard from beyond the Appalachians, yet the importance of knitting half a continent into one political unit did not strike even Jefferson as great. In 1804, while President of the United

---

[7] J. A. Krout and D. R. Fox, *The Completion of Independence, 1790–1830* (New York, 1944), 5.

[8] C. M. Wiltse, *The New Nation, 1800–1845* (New York, 1961), 13. The West at this time, as Professor Philbrick has observed, was a region characterized by optimism and individualism. It was less rigid in its social and economic stratification than was the East, but, by the same token, illiteracy and crude manners were more prevalent. F. S. Philbrick, *The Rise of the West, 1754–1830* (New York, 1965).

States, he wrote with apparent sincerity: "Whether we remain in one confederacy, or form into Atlantic and Mississippi confederations, I believe not very important. . . ."[9]

From a twentieth-century perspective, it is difficult to appreciate the extraordinarily regional character of the United States and its effects on the life of the people. The absence of any strong tradition of union, the physical and climatic differences, and the dissimilar backgrounds of the several sectors combined to set them apart from one another. Distance and the difficulties of travel intensified inherited sentiments of localism, and men spoke of themselves not as Americans but as New Englanders, New Yorkers, Virginians, and so on. New England was as independent of New York as both were of Virginia.[10]

New England

New England at this time was an area of compact towns, villages, and fishing settlements, with substantial farming communities developing in the western sector. In 1800 its population, primarily of English extraction, amounted to over a quarter of a million. Except in the prosperous seaports that were centers of ocean and coastal trade, lumbering, fishing, and subsistence farming provided the basis of life. Save in the fertile Connecticut valley, the country was poor and the soil grudging. Agriculture was as backward and primitive as the rude plough that turned the soil; cattle and sheep were unimproved and badly cared for, and nearly everywhere boulder-strewn fields, scrub oak, and stunted orchards met the eye. Although the farms were small generally speaking they were largely self-sufficient; many were able to produce some surplus food, wool, or linen for transportation to the port towns.

In 1801 prosperity had recently come to the Boston and Salem merchants and shipbuilders as a result of the French wars. Yet Boston, the third-largest city in the United States, resembled an English market town, with crooked, narrow, shop-lined streets, and busy wharves at the harbor's edge. Shipping and shipbuilding had also helped such smaller ports as Portsmouth, Newburyport, Hartford, New London, and New Haven to flourish. From these centers whale oil, salt fish,

---

[9] Quoted in Adams, *History of United States*, I, 73.

[10] For general descriptions of the several regions of the United States in the period, see *ibid.*, I, chapters 1–6; S. E. Morison, *The Oxford History of the United States, 1783–1917* (Oxford, 1927), I, chapters 2–3 (hereafter cited as Morison, *Oxford History of U. S.*). See also D. T. Gilchrist, ed., *The Growth of the Seaport Cities, 1790–1825* (Charlottesville, 1967).

leather, lumber, and rum were shipped abroad, and the return voyages brought manufactured goods from England, wines and spices from the Iberian Peninsula, and silks from the Near East. Coastal vessels carried these and other commodities, such as homespuns, cheese, shoes, and nails—largely the products of home industry—as far as the southern ports, while the fleets of the whaling industry supplied oil for almost the entire coast. Small-scale manufacturing enterprises had been established in many places; snuff and paper mills were to be found on several of the rivers, and in the seaports there were a few distilleries for rum. Textile mills were still in their infancy, but Arkwright's power-loom had already been pirated by Samuel Slater, and improved machines were beginning to appear, portending a new industry from the Merrimack to Pawtucket.

Throughout most of New England the stern Puritan faith was well entrenched and still nurtured the twin principles of thrift and righteousness. Most of the region's inhabitants lived frugally, and physical hardship, sickness, and recurring epidemics contributed to the grim earnestness of their outlook. The autocratic union of the Congregational clergy and the professional classes had helped to foster in politics an extreme Federalism which scorned, as much as it feared, the "Jacobinism" of Thomas Jefferson and pilloried in the press of Fisher Ames the new libertarian democracy. Conservatism dominated a relatively static social system in which "respectability, education, property, and religion united to defeat and crush the unwise and vicious."[11] Intellectual tastes were still chiefly those of the age of Queen Anne. The fashionable gentlemen of Boston, many still wearing colored coats, knee breeches, ruffled shirts, and wigs, sat at interminable state dinners at which "[t]he talk of Samuel Johnson and Edmund Burke was the standard of excellence. . . ."[12] Harvard College was still a training school for the ministry, but is said to have resembled a priesthood "holding the flickering torch before cold altars."[13] By and large, both the literature and the interests of New England reflected the concerns of the clergy and of professional men for maintaining the ancient social order that had deep roots in the Puritanism of the colonial period.

Yet there were stirrings in the air. Nearly one-half of the qualified voters were Republicans, and the public generally was becoming restive under the antiquated discipline of the pulpit and the entrenched rule of "the wise, the good and the rich." The ban on Sunday travel and amuse-

---

[11] Adams, *History of United States*, I, 108. See generally W. A. Robinson, *Jeffersonian Democracy in New England* (New Haven, 1916).

[12] Adams, *History of United States*, I, 92.
[13] *Ibid.*, 77.

ments was widely ignored, and respectable Boston had recently been scandalized by performances of Shakespeare in the theatre. The thoughts of many were turning increasingly to money-making, and already the construction of new buildings, roads, and canals foretold the coming of a commercial age.

The Middle Atlantic States

To the southwest of New England, the State of New York was still largely a frontier area, with the inhabited areas chiefly confined to the farming communities along the Hudson and Mohawk Valleys and to the shipping and commercial metropolis of New York City. A few miles distant from these settlements were forests that seemed nearly as old as the world itself. President Timothy Dwight of Yale, traveling a main inland road in 1804, found only a few lonely plantations and scattered cottages. "All else," he wrote, "was grandeur, gloom and solitude."[14] Upstate, Albany was the second-largest city, and although it contained only about five thousand inhabitants, it could berth vessels of 70 tons carrying products—chiefly lumber and potash—from Vermont and the Mohawk country. The city was one of the major gateways to the settlement of the West. Most of western New York was a wilderness, for Buffalo was not yet laid out, Rochester did not even exist, and Utica had barely fifty small and temporary houses. Primarily agricultural, the State was dominated politically as well as socially by the great patroon families of the Hudson Valley.

New York City, with its Dutch background still evident in street names and in the high yellow-brick gables of its houses, had become one of the largest and most cosmopolitan of American cities. The city, whose population had nearly doubled over the previous decade to 60,000, owed its prosperity to its unique harbor on one of the largest tidal inlets on the Atlantic seaboard; its shipping facilities were available to half of New Jersey and Connecticut, as well as to the Hudson Valley. Here, where the Battery was still a fashionable walk and Broadway a country drive, the principal commercial activity was that of merchants, warehousers, shopkeepers, and shipowners. There was little industry. New York, unlike New England, "possessed no church to overthrow, or traditional doctrines to root out, or centuries of history to disavow."[15] Society was gay and hospitable, fond of music, dancing, plays, lectures, and parades. Yet the city itself was badly paved

---

[14] F. W. Halsey, *The Old New York Frontier, 1614–1800* (New York, 1901), 384.

[15] Adams, *History of United States,* I, 110.

and undrained, and periodically it was ravaged by the dread yellow fever, which occasionally caused even the Supreme Court Justices to avoid it and postpone their circuit duties.[16]

Across the Hudson, New Jersey, then as now, was the "garden state," famed for its orchards and well-cultivated farms. Much of its produce was shipped to the New York and Philadelphia markets, as were its cattle, fattened on upland pastures. The endless pine barrens and salt marshes in the eastern and southern extremities yielded salt hay, some lumber, and a plentiful supply of bog iron; but with few towns of any size, there was little manufacturing. Consequently the foreign export of the State in 1800 was a bare $2,000, the smallest of any of the sixteen States.[17] Although several tanneries produced excellent leather, the principal source of income was the production of iron.

Pennsylvania, the second-largest State in the Union, has been described as a microcosm of America as it was to become. It was a State characterized by a wide heterogeneity of race, policy, and social structure, and the most democratic community in the Atlantic States.[18] No social hierarchy existed here as in New York. There were no Livingstons or van Rensselaers, nor does there appear to have been a single family having any extensive influence. The population was largely German, but included Scotch-Irish and the original Quaker stock as well. Hence, there was none of the homogeneity that obtained in New England. Industrially, it was the most diversified of all the States, and its products were transported to widespread destinations in great Conestoga wagons, heavy keel-boats, and coastwise sailing vessels. Robert Sutliffe, an Englishman who traveled in Pennsylvania in about 1804, remarked on the

> great numbers of wagons drawn by four or more fine fat horses, the carriages firm and well made, and covered with good stout linen, bleached almost white; and it is not uncommon to see ten or fifteen together travelling cheerfully along the road. . . . Many of these come more than three hundred miles to Philadelphia from the Ohio, Pittsburg, and other places, and I have been told . . . that more than one thousand covered carriages frequently come to Philadelphia market.[19]

---

[16] See J. Duffy, "An Account of the Epidemic Fevers that Prevailed in the City of New York from 1791–1822," *New York Historical Society Quarterly* L, 333 (1966).

[17] *American State Papers. Documents, Legislative and Executive, of the Congress of the United States,* Class IV, *Commerce and Navigation, 1789–1815* (Washington, 1832), VII, 453 (hereafter cited as *American State Papers: Commerce and Navigation*).

[18] Adams, *History of United States,* I, 114–15.

[19] Quoted in *ibid.,* 34. See generally F. Bailey, *Journal of a Tour of the Unsettled Parts of North America in 1796 and 1797* (London, 1856).

Philadelphia in 1800 was America's largest and most important city, consisting of some 70,000 inhabitants. It was not only one of the principal ports but the center of culture, intellect, and the elegancies of life. One need but mention the names of Dallas, Ingersoll, Peters, Rawle, and Tilghman (to list only some of the prominent members of the Bar) to recall how many in the legal profession—to say nothing of clergymen and physicians—left lasting records. Yet the range of intellectual interests even in Philadelphia was not wide, and in educated and literary circles next to nothing could be found that was unknown in England or France.

Like New York, Philadelphia was regularly subjected to the dread yellow fever, and partly in consequence it had been well paved, partly drained, and outfitted with a system of piped water to supply many of its inhabitants. Although no longer the nation's political capital, it continued to hold the Bank of the United States, capitalized at $10 million. In and near the city several important industries flourished, producing iron, furniture, gunpowder, paper, and other manufactured articles on a larger scale than anywhere else in the nation. There were only two other communities of any size in the State, Lancaster and Reading, with populations of about 5,000 and 2,500 respectively.

Farming was of course the principal occupation of the inhabitants of Pennsylvania, and, to use Benjamin Latrobe's expression, the labor of the hand took precedence over that of the mind. Nevertheless, more roads and canals had been built or were in progress than in any other State. The paved turnpike to Lancaster had recently been completed and was the marvel of the decade. Over that highway, from one of the most fertile areas of the United States, came cattle, wheat, and other farm products to the Philadelphia market. Along the Delaware, Schuylkill, and Susquehanna Rivers and southward into Maryland, there stretched rich farms with huge barns whose produce moved down to the coast for export at substantial profits. West of Lancaster a great wagon road, the most important artery in any State, wound through virgin forests of oak, maple, and walnut along the valley of the Juniata and up through the mountains to Pittsburgh, chief of the three inner gateways to the newly-opened western territory.

Delaware was likewise a farming State, famous for its wheat crop, the excellence of its tobacco, and the great flour mills of the Brandywine. The largest community was Georgetown, with a population of less than 3,000, whereas Dover and Newcastle had less than 2,000 inhabitants each.

Maryland was another agricultural State in which there were few manufactures except iron. Baltimore was rapidly increasing in population, and its port was becoming an important center of trade. From the great wharves and warehouses that fronted its deep harbor radiated the lanes of road and water transport that carried enormous quantities of wheat, tobacco, and corn from the hinterland as well as from central Pennsylvania. In 1800 the value of the State's exports exceeded $12 million, second only to New York,[20] and the registered tonnage of Baltimore compared favorably with that of Philadelphia.

The South

South of the Potomac lay Virginia, with a white population of roughly half a million, descendants for the most part of the same English middle-class and yeoman stock that had settled early New England. Here there were few towns and virtually no manufacturing. Economic and social life had long since settled into the stable pattern of aristocratically managed, self-contained tobacco plantations, supported by a slave population which in 1800 numbered roughly 350,000. Although Virginia was the most populous and powerful of all the States, its ideal was patriarchal and was "little likely to produce anything more practical in the way of modern progress" than the ideals of Cato or the eloquence of Cicero.[21] Its agriculture had suffered from the competition of Kentucky and Tennessee and from emigration which had drawn away at least a hundred thousand persons. Moreover, the land was fast losing its productivity, and, except in a few districts such as the Shenandoah Valley, Virginian land did not average more than eight bushels of wheat per acre despite the energetic but vain efforts of the great planters to improve their crops. Moreover, they lacked even local markets, and the machinery of production, with the notable exception of Jefferson's inventions and importations, had hardly changed since the mid-eighteenth century. The Duc de Liancourt remarked that the Virginians were not generally rich in terms of net revenue and that

one often finds a well-served table, covered with silver, in a room where for ten years half the window panes have been missing, and where they will be missed for ten years more. There are few houses in a passable state of repair, and of all parts of the establishment those best cared for are the stables.[22]

Apart from an occasional "stately aristocratic palace, with all its appurtenances, . . . almost no buildings [were] to be seen but the little smoky huts and cabins of the poor, laborious, ignorant tenants."[23]

In the tidewater region, long fingers of lowland stretched to the

---

[20] *American State Papers: Commerce and Navigation*, VII, 453.

[21] Adams, *History of United States*, I, 32.

[22] Quoted in *ibid.*, 33.

[23] W. Wirt, *Letters of the British Spy* (New York, 1832), 101–102.

sea between the wide estuaries of the Potomac, the Rappahanock, the York, and the James Rivers. Here, especially, the productivity of the soil had been exhausted by tobacco culture, country seats had been dismantled, and the old farms were fast declining as their fields were reclaimed by mournful evergreens. The population and wealth of the State now lay above the fall-line, west of a line drawn through Petersburg, Richmond, and Alexandria. This fruitful, rolling country had become the seat of the plantation system. Here nearly all the great Virginians of the era had been born or grown to manhood. Yet Richmond, the principal town and the new capital of the State, had less than 2,500 inhabitants, and, except for the great mansion houses, the appearance of the region is said to have been "slovenly in the extreme," characterized by "ill-cultivated fields, straggling fences, and dilapidated negroes' cabins."[24] Roads were poor and often impassable; bridges were few. In 1801 Jefferson complained to his Attorney-General that of the eight rivers he crossed in the hundred miles between Monticello and Washington only three had bridges or boats.[25]

Reckoned in terms of land and slaves, Virginia was rich, but its prosperity was nevertheless well on the wane. Barred by its labor system from manufactures (which Jefferson for all his liberality of mind continually discouraged), lacking shipping, and having no domestic market for skilled labor, the State's exports by 1800 amounted to less than $4.5 million.[26] Moreover, the strength of the social system had been sapped by the abolition of entailed estates as well as by other reforms of Jefferson and Madison which had tended to cripple and impoverish the gentry while doing next to nothing for the common people.[27] Small farms were

---

[24] Morison, *Oxford History of U. S.*, I, 29. A description of the decline of the tidewater region of Virginia may be found in John Randolph's Letters to Josiah Quincy, July 1, 1814, Manuscripts Division, Library of Congress. Two somewhat later descriptions, written in 1814 and 1827 respectively, may be found in J. C. Willey, ed., "Observations Made During a Short Residence in Virginia," *Virginia Magazine of History and Biography* LXXVI, 387 (1968); and R. D. Gray, ed., "A Tour of Virginia," *ibid.*, 444.

[25] Adams, *History of United States*, I, 14.

[26] *American State Papers: Commerce and Navigation*, VII, 453. For a general discussion of Virginia at this time see P. Rouse, *Planters and*

Pioneers (New York, 1968). See also D. C. Klingaman, "The Development of the Coastwise Trade of Virginia in the Late Colonial Period," *The Virginia Magazine of History and Biography* LXXVII, 26 (1969).

[27] Adams, *History of United States*, I, 137. See also R. M. Healey, *Jefferson on Religion in Public Education* (New Haven, 1962); R. McColley, *Slavery and Jeffersonian Virginia* (Urbana, Ill., 1964), chapter 1; E. D. Genovese, Book Review, *American Historical Review* LXXI, 301 at 303 (1965).

The attack by Jefferson and others on primogeniture accomplished less than has often been supposed. The system had fallen into disuse because of the abundance of land and speculation therein, with the result that only

unprofitable, and wise men had been emigrating to the fertile valleys across the mountains.

Virginia society was ill at ease. Below the "first families" of the rich planter class was a class of provincial smaller planters and an even larger class of unstable yeomen. The latter, chiefly descended from indentured servants and deported convicts, were quarrelsome, undisciplined, and illiterate. Stereotyped in character, unwilling to accept new ideas, such as the system of general education proposed by Jefferson, they were the principal sufferers from the decay of agriculture in an aristocratically managed economy. Between these people and the gentry the gap was wide, but between them and the slaves it was enormous.

Despite these societal undercurrents, the plantation owners had entrenced themselves in power by high property qualifications for voting while adopting the traditions of good breeding and public spirit of the English aristocracy. Well-educated, well-read, refined in manners, trained to administration and bred to politics, the great planters "stepped naturally and gracefully into the leadership of the nation."[28] Law and politics were the chief objects of their thought, and these men, as Henry Adams writes, "were equal to any standard of excellence known to history."[29] It was no accident, as Professor Morison wrote, that

> Jefferson of Virginia drafted the Declaration of Independence, that Washington of Virginia led the army and became the first President, that Madison of Virginia drafted the Federal Constitution, that Marshall of Virginia became the greatest American jurist, and that he and Taylor of Virginia led the two opposing schools of American political thought.[30]

North Carolina, although ranking fifth in white population with close to half a million inhabitants, was one of the poorest, most undeveloped, and backward States in the Union. Its coastal plain, a good hundred miles wide, consisted chiefly of great stands of pine and long stretches of flat, sandy land, interspersed with extensive swamps and marshes. President Washington described the region as the most barren country he had ever beheld, without "a single house of elegant appearance,"[31] and a contemporary traveler commented upon the immense

---

a small portion of land was affected when the Revolutionary era swept away the last vestiges of primogeniture. See C. R. Keim, "Primogeniture and Entailed Estates in Colonial Virginia," *William and Mary Quarterly* XXV, 545 et seq., especially 585–86 (1968).

[28] Morison, *Oxford History of U. S.*, I, 30.
[29] Adams, *History of United States*, I, 133.
[30] Morison, *Oxford History of U. S.*, I, 30.
[31] *Ibid.*, 33.

pine savannahs, the stagnant ponds, and the dark, sluggish creeks spanned by crazy rotting bridges.[32] Transportation was even more primitive than in Virginia. Long barrier beaches locked the river mouths, and the narrow wagon tracks hardly deserved the name of roads. Except in sectors adjoining Albemarle and Pamlico Sounds, where better soil and a navigable waterway were conducive to the maintenance of plantation agriculture, farming in the coastal area was next to impossible because of sand and swamps. Tar, turpentine, and pine lumber had become staple products and were already the chief sources of the State's export revenues; yet in 1800 those revenues amounted to a bare $769,000,[33] and even that was becoming endangered as Charleston, rather than the ports of Brunswick and Wilmington, began to drain the State's commerce. To the westward, however, the piedmont was an area of thriving farms where the main part of the population was chiefly concentrated, but in the absence of navigable rivers, its export produce had to be dragged overland to the markets of Petersburg or Charleston. The invention of the cotton gin in 1793, however, and the growing mechanization of spinning and weaving, were stirring both the upland farmers and the coastal planters to produce cotton on a profitable basis, and the crop had begun to hold forth the beckoning promise of prosperity.

For the most part the inhabitants of North Carolina, as uneducated as they were poor, were indifferent to their conditions. New Bern, the largest town in the State, had no more than 400 wooden houses, whereas Raleigh had merely 80, scattered over ground that might contain thousands.[34] In the Wilmington, New Bern, and Edenton areas, the planters' homes were often spacious and commodious, but the houses of small farmers were as primitive and as miserable as the few inns that dotted the crude roads.[35] Nathaniel Macon, whom John Quincy described as a man of small parts and mean education but rigid integrity, personified the upper-class North Carolinian of his day and believed that for that "meek state and just people" conditions were ideal.[36] He was as opposed to public education, internal improvements, and reform as Jefferson

[32] Adams, *History of United States*, I, 36.

[33] *American State Papers: Commerce and Navigation*, VII, 453. For a general description of North Carolina at about this time see L. Lea, *The Lower Cape Fear in Colonial Days* (Chapel Hill, N. C., 1965). Source material and data on North Carolina in this period, particularly on commerce, money, and credit transactions and on plantation and consumer supplies, may be found in W. H. Masterson, ed., *The John Gray Blount Papers* (Raleigh, N. C., 1965), III, passim.

[34] J. Morse, *The American Gazetteer* (Boston, 1804), sub. nom. New Bern and Raleigh.

[35] H. T. Lefler and A. R. Newsome, *North Carolina* (Chapel Hill, N. C., 1954), 108–10.

[36] *Ibid.*, 310–11.

was anxious to promote them. Yet if the State was backward and unambitious, landlocked from commerce, it did not suffer from the ills incident to Virginian aristocracy, such as the sense of social importance, or from the turbulence that plagued Georgia. It was a farming democracy in which agriculture was aided by rather than dependent upon slavery, with the result that North Carolina enjoyed greater freedom of political action than any other southern State.

South Carolina was also divided into tidewater and piedmont, with Charleston on the coast the gay and affable center of an established aristocracy of rice planters descended chiefly from English stock and French Huguenot émigrés. The subtropical climate of the tidewater was hot and humid. It not only bred malaria but was so unhealthy generally that white landowners purposely utilized slave labor; in Charleston, for example, Negro slaves accounted for over two-thirds of the population. Yet the plantation system was spreading inland to the populous uplands, and cotton-raising was fast competing with rice cultivation and the production of indigo as the dominant economic activity of the State. Although South Carolina had grown rich on the two latter products, the 200,000 pound cotton crop shipped in 1791 had increased a hundredfold by 1800 and was to double again by 1803.[37] Of all the southern States, South Carolina seemed to have the brightest future. In 1800 her exports exceeded $10 million, nearly equaling those of Pennsylvania or Massachusetts.[38]

Charleston was an intellectual oasis. Hospitable and cultivated, the city was a delight to foreign visitors. Its inhabitants, though conservative in politics and drawn to the Federalism of New England, were travelers and readers, and Charleston society "compared well in refinement with that of any city of its size in the world."[39] More cosmopolitan than any town south of Philadelphia, Charleston had an excellent library, a theatre, and even a jockey club. The prosperous went north to the New England States in the summer months, and they regularly sent their sons to study abroad at Westminster, Eton, and Oxford, or to read law at the Temple. With a new canal that brought the Santee River to its harbor, with a road planned to Tennessee to draw the whole interior within its reach, and with the rich trade of the West Indies close at hand, the city seemed destined to outstrip the other Atlantic ports. "Nowhere in the Union," wrote Henry Adams, "was intelligence, wealth, and education greater in proportion to numbers than in the little society of cotton and rice planters who ruled South Carolina."[40]

---

[37] Adams, *History of United States,* I, 38.

[38] *American State Papers: Commerce and Navigation,* VII, 453.

[39] Adams, *History of United States,* I, 149.

[40] *Ibid.,* 38.

Georgia, across the Savannah River, shared with South Carolina the hot, subtropical climate and a slave-supported plantation system along the coast.[41] Here rice and indigo were still the staple products and formerly accounted for most of the exports of the State. However, cotton production was on the increase, both inland and on the adjoining islands, and was fast becoming a principal source of revenue, both to the State and to its chief seaport, Savannah. Already the State's exports exceeded $2 million.[42] Behind the rice coast and a belt of infertile pine barrens were the scattered upland farms of frontiersmen—vigorous, lawless, and a continuing source of trouble to the State and federal governments.

Of the newly opened-up regions beyond the Alleghenies, the most prosperous were those of Tennessee, Kentucky, and southern Ohio. The rich bottom lands were easily cultivated, and the luxuriant soil produced the great staple crops of grain, tobacco, and cotton.[43] Prosperity was hampered and retarded by distance from eastern markets and by the difficulties of land transport, but already the inhabitants of these regions were eyeing the river system with a view to finding markets for their produce—grain, flour, hides, and cotton—in Europe and along the eastern seaboard of the United States via the Mississippi and the Gulf. By 1802 the customs house at Natchez reported that hemp, tobacco, flour, whiskey, and other commodities valued at over $1,000,000 descended the Mississippi every year.[44] The vastness and still unsettled character of this region were such that, as in other areas, there had been extensive speculation on the part of absentee proprietors and land companies of the East, and their claims had already begun to come before the federal courts, constituting a significant part of their business.[45]

---

[41] There is a contemporary description of Georgia by Nathaniel Pendleton in Pendleton Papers, Miscellaneous, New York Historical Society, New York City (courtesy of the New York Historical Society). See also Morse, *American Gazetteer*, sub. nom. Georgia.

[42] *American State Papers: Commerce and Navigation*, VII, 453.

[43] Morse, *American Gazetteer*, sub. nom. Kentucky, Tennessee. For a more recent and excellent characterization of Kentucky, see T. P. Abernethy, *Three Virginia Frontiers* (University, La., 1940); for Tennessee, see *idem, From Frontier to Plantation in Tennessee* (Chapel Hill, N. C., 1932).

[44] *American State Papers. Documents, Legislative and Executive, of the Congress of the United States*, Class III, *Finance* (Washington, 1832), II, 56–58.

[45] See chapter 4 infra. See also S. Livermore, *Early American Land Companies* (London, 1939); R. M. Robbins, *Our Landed Heritage* (Princeton, 1942); A. M. Sakolski, *The Great American Land Bubble* (New York, 1942).

B.   THE AMERICAN WAYS OF LIFE

To picture how Americans lived at the turn of the century requires considerable imagination, because the patterns of the eighteenth century still dominated most aspects of life. Nine-tenths of the population lived in rural areas—on the compact homesteads of New England, on the more extensive farms or plantations of Pennsylvania, Maryland, Virginia, and the Carolinas, and on the newly cleared tracts of the frontier beyond the Alleghenies. The inhabitants were about equally divided between the northern and southern States, but nearly one-half of those in the South were black slaves.[46] Blacks accounted for one-fifth of the total population, and of these approximately ninety percent were in the South. As discussed earlier, a scant six percent of the 5,308,483 persons listed in the 1800 census were concentrated in urban centers.[47] Of the twenty-one principal urban centers, only five had a population of over 10,000.[48] Except in the few large cities, the houses in which men lived were little different from what they had been a hundred years before, and, indeed, within a few score miles of the coast at least half were log cabins, often lacking glass windows. Clothing, food, drink, habits of life, and agricultural tools and methods (except for the cotton gin) had hardly changed during the course of the eighteenth century, and the smaller the town or the more remote the farm, the simpler were the standards of life. Rotation of crops was not scientifically practiced, and if drills, threshing machines, and other types of modern equipment were occasionally to be seen on the plantations of gentlemen farmers, they were novelties and certainly not in common use. Most of the population wore odd-shaped homespuns which produced an appearance of awkwardness and rusticity, sharply distinguishing country from town.[49]

Urban life more closely approximated that of contemporary England. In their physical aspects, the larger towns resembled those of provincial England, except that the houses were frequently of brick and in the Georgian style, surrounded on three sides by small gardens and shrubbery. Windows were unscreened and in the summer months admitted swarms of flies, as well as the mosquitoes that brought the dreaded malarial fevers to large sectors of the population. Streets were narrow, seldom paved, and nearly always cluttered with garbage, debris,

---

[46] U. S. Bureau of Census, *Negro Population, 1790–1915* (Washington, 1918), 33.

[47] *Historical Atlas of the United States* (Washington, 1914).

[48] R. B. Nye, *The Cultural Life of the New Nation, 1776–1830* (New York, 1960), 124.

[49] It is reported that many rural Americans were "contemptuous of fine clothes and polished speech." Wiltse, *New Nation*, 2.

and filth. Except for parts of New York and Philadelphia, wells and cisterns were the source of domestic water supplies, and sewage-disposal systems did not exist. Police protection was almost unknown, but watchmen with lanterns generally patrolled the streets at night on the lookout for unlocked doors and fires.

The houses of the well-to-do in city and country alike were often expensively decorated and furnished, and at night they were lit by candles or crude oil lamps. Wood ranges for cooking were a novelty, and most people still cooked on open fires. Only the rich could afford fresh meat, which seldom kept for long in any case, and the bulk of the population lived on a diet of salt pork or dried codfish, supplemented by occasional wild game and by porridge or cakes made from Indian maize. Rum, whiskey, and cider were staple beverages and were consumed in enormous quantities, especially in the South and West. Europeans traveling about the country were shocked by the excessive drinking, poor food, and low standards of cleanliness, particularly in the inns, which permitted two or three to sleep in the same bed made up with dirty sheets and provided drinks from a common glass. Privacy, by day or by night, was the exception, and letters of the period are replete with references to sharing rooms not only on a transient basis in inns but in regular lodging houses. For example, John Davis, an Englishman who traveled in America at the beginning of the century, wrote of finding only six beds for sixteen persons at one inn.[50] Another traveler reported that between Philadelphia and Baltimore he stopped at an inn where the landlord boasted that he had no less than eleven beds in one room.[51] Aaron Burr wrote to his daughter in 1805, "It is a high evidence of the barbarism of our Southern states that, in an extent of three hundred miles, filled with wealthy people, and in a hot climate, there should not be, in any one private family, a convenient bathing-room."[52]

The diversity of the American character resulted not only from regional and geographical differences, intensified by disparate cultural heritages from the colonial era, but from occupational and economic status. Wealth was unusual except among merchants, professional men, and the large planters. As Wiltse observed:

> The common man of 1800, whatever his political inclinations, was restless, curious, acquisitive, jealous of his freedom and skeptical of authority . . . . He was optimistic, confident, self-reliant, with . . . a

---

[50] J. Davis, *Travels of Four Years and a Half in the United States of America* (London, 1803), 323.

[51] Adams, *History of United States*, I, 45–46.

[52] M. L. Davis, *Memoirs of Aaron Burr* (New York, 1836), II, 366.

well-nourished hankering after this world's goods. . . . In person, save for the aristocratic few . . . the American was inclined to be ill-mannered contemptuous of fine clothes and polished speech quick to fight, ready to help a neighbor, eager to try anything that promised gain. . . . He was a hard drinker, a gambler, a brawler. He was a fierce competitor who believed in progress as surely as he believed in sin.[53]

C. TRANSPORTATION AND COMMUNICATION

Travel

Regional differences in the United States were intensified by the difficulties of travel. British policies prior to the Revolution had inhibited the carriage of articles of colonial manufacture and hence had helped to deter the development of adequate transportation facilities. Independence from Britain had hardly helped to unite the four principal regions, in part because inherited sentiments of local independence continued to deter the construction of bridges and highways. At the same time fears of legislative despotism in Congress at the expense of self-government, voiced at the ratifying conventions, persisted, and helped to dampen such interest as there was in the advancement of transportation facilities. Consequently, only the first beginnings had been made towards improving the old roads and wagon tracks that stretched from one small inland town to another and finally joined the larger highway that connected the towns and cities of the coast. Transportation was slow, laborious, expensive, and hazardous—whether by horse, stage, wagon, or vessel. The stagecoach was a rude, uncomfortable conveyance into which as many as twelve persons were crowded with bags and luggage. Departures frequently took place before dawn, and the drivers were often reckless, and the vehicles half worn out.[54] Passengers were constantly required to trim or balance the stage by leaning to one side or the other to prevent it from overturning in the deep ruts of the roads. Few enjoyed the luxury of a private carriage, much less that of the two-seated phaeton of Judge Cushing which was ingeniously fitted out with cabinets for books and food and drawn by two horses.[55]

Roads in 1800 were deplorable. It has been estimated that in that year there were barely 1,200 miles of surfaced roads in the entire

---

[53] Wiltse, *New Nation*, 2.
[54] See S. H. Holbrook, *The Old Post Road* (New York, 1962), 43. Cf. S. T. Riley, Book Review, *New England Quarterly* XL, 591 at 592 (1967).
[55] See chapter 3 infra.

country, as compared with 6,500 miles in 1815.[56] Flanked by ruts and gullies, skirting stumps, rocks, and precipices, they were frequently nothing but wide cuts in the forest. It was not unusual for stagecoach passengers to be forced to abandon a bemired or overturned vehicle, or to give up their journeys when frozen rivers blocked their passage. Even in the best of weather travelers were obliged to ferry, and even to ford, swollen streams and rivers, hoping that the horses would not drown or break their legs. Delays were incessant, and stops were frequent while horses were changed or shod, wheels and axles replaced, or harnesses repaired. Heavy rains in spring and autumn and deep snow and ice in winter made havoc of the roads, turning them into seas of mud that made travel not only dangerous but often impossible.

The hazards and accidents of road travel are a constant subject of comment in letters of the time, including those of the Supreme Court judges who were required not only to convene in Washington but to travel about the country to hold the circuit courts assigned to them. Paterson was so seriously injured in a carriage accident in 1804 that for weeks he could scarcely move and was obliged to absent himself from the Court and from circuit duties.[57] John Marshall fractured his collarbone when a stagecoach overturned near Fredericksburg, and his subsequent confinement delayed his attendance at the Court.[58] In the next year Judge Livingston wrote to Story that as a result of a bruise received in a stagecoach he was still suffering from violent pains in the head.[59] The fatigue of circuit riding for Supreme Court judges was a subject of comment by the Attorney-General as early as 1790[60] and of a memorial presented by the judges themselves in 1792. Later, in discussing with Senator John Breckenridge the problem of forming a new Circuit in Tennessee, Kentucky, and Ohio, Judge Harry Innes wrote

---

[56] U. S. Bureau of Census, *Historical Statistics of the United States, 1789–1945* (Washington, 1949), 220. For a full discussion of road, as well as water, transportation at this time, see B. H. Meyer, *History of Transportation in the United States before 1860* (Washington, 1917), chapters 1–2.

[57] W. Paterson to S. Chase, Feb. 1, 1804, Miscellaneous Manuscripts, Chase, New York Historical Society, New York City. See also Breckenridge Family Papers, Manuscripts Division, Library of Congress. In May 1800, Judge Paterson described traveling on circuit from Portsmouth, New Hamp-

shire, to Windsor, saying that the roads were so impassable that he was obliged to make a detour of 140 miles to accomplish a journey of 100. "For one-third of the way I did not go more than the rate of three miles an hour." "Extracts from Unpublished Letters of Governor Paterson," *Somerset County Historical Quarterly* II, 1 at 3 (1914).

[58] T. Todd to C. Todd, Feb. 5, 1812, Todd Manuscripts, The Filson Club, Louisville, Ky.

[59] R. Livingston to J. Story, Apr. 23, 1813, Joseph Story Papers, University of Texas.

[60] See chapter 4 infra.

that riding upward of 1,600 miles annually would "break the most robust constitution."[61] He referred to heat and exposure to the sun, lack of drinking water in many areas, deep ruts, high water, and indifferent accommodations.[62] Frequently a circuit court could not be held because the Supreme Court judge assigned was delayed or prevented from attending. The same difficulties beset litigants and witnesses who were obliged to undertake long and hazardous journeys. There is no question but that the difficulties of travel hampered the entire judicial process or that they were a principal reason for the enactment of the Judiciary Bill of 1801, designed to facilitate justice by bringing it closer to every man's door.[63]

The best section of the coastal highway was between Boston and New York, yet the journey required at least three days by light stage under favorable conditions; two more were required to Philadelphia, and often as much as another five to Baltimore. As late as 1811 Washington Irving wrote to Henry Brevoort that the road was "terrible," that the journey took three days, and that he "slept one night in a Log house."[64] From Baltimore the road to Washington was execrable, in places nothing but a track meandering through forests. Although the average speed for a stagecoach in the northern States was four miles per hour, it dropped to two or three south of Baltimore. On routes other than the main post road travel conditions were intolerable except on such newly improved roads as the Lancaster–Philadelphia turnpike. In terms of speed, however, it may be said that inland travel was hardly much better in Europe, where three days were still required to traverse by *diligence* the 150 miles from Calais to Paris.[65]

South of the Potomac, the difficulties of road travel were such that the mails were carried on horseback even on the main post road. On the best road in Virginia a journey from Williamsburg to Richmond, a distance of about sixty miles, required two days. Coaches were rarely seen in the South, and no public conveyance appears to have run in the southern States except one between Charleston and Savannah.[66] Consequently, much travel was accomplished on foot or by wagon. Travel on horseback in the Carolinas and Georgia was beset with hazards in areas where the rider could easily become lost in the dense

---

[61] H. Innes to J. Breckenridge, Dec. 20, 1804, Breckenridge Papers, Manuscripts Division, Library of Congress.

[62] *Ibid.*

[63] See chapter 4 infra.

[64] G. S. Hellman, ed., *Letters of Washington Irving to Henry Brevoort* (New York, 1918), 19.

[65] In 1809 Burr referred to a six-hour trip in Germany that covered twelve miles. A. Burr, *The Private Journal of Aaron Burr* (Rochester, 1903), I, 313.

[66] See Adams, *History of United States*, I, 12.

woods or vast pine savannahs and where inns became progressively fewer and more widely scattered as the traveler proceeded.[67]

Water travel, although more comfortable than travel by stage, had many inconveniences. The steamboat did not yet exist, sailing vessels were small and slow, and passengers were expected to provide their own bedding and supplies. River transportation, although much used for the carriage of bulk commodities—wheat, flour, and forest products—was dangerous for passengers on all save the largest streams. Coastwise travel was irregular, and, although generally safer than on the rivers, ships' passengers were subject to the hazards of storms, tides, shoals, and lack of wind. In 1810 Caesar A. Rodney, President Madison's Attorney-General, lost all his law books as well as his furniture and household effects while on a voyage down Chesapeake Bay on his way to Washington.[68] However, by 1815, the year with which this Volume closes, the steamboat was already beginning to replace the stagecoach. William Wirt, writing to his wife on December 27 of that year, expressed his delight with the "translation from the cold jolting stage, to a warm and elegant apartment in the steam-boat."[69]

The vastness of the distances, as well as the difficulties of American travel, are illustrated by the postal service at the turn of the century. On the general post route from Portland, Maine, to Louisville, Georgia, twenty days were required for the trip; Philadelphia to Lexington, sixteen days; and Philadelphia to Nashville, twenty-two days. The mails were slow at best, often delayed, lost, damaged, or tampered with. Men felt safer entrusting letters and dispatches to friends than to the Post Office. Even Supreme Court judges, John Marshall and Bushrod Washington for example, acted as couriers for friends when they rode the circuits.[70]

Expense was an additional deterrent to travel. By road, the stagecoach charges appear to have been not less than ten cents a mile, including the expenses of lodging en route. The average American—the farmer, the artisan, and the shopkeeper—could not afford to travel, and a man wishing to bring an action for wrongdoing or breach of contract had to weigh the amount of his claim against the expense of journeying with his witnesses to the next session of a court. Few had the means

[67] *American State Papers. Documents, Legislative and Executive, of the Congress of the United States*, Class VII, *Post Office* (Washington, 1834), 22. See also J. Mason, "Diary of the Hon. Jonathan ˜Mason," *Massachusetts Historical Society Proceedings*, II, 2d ser., 5 (1885).

[68] C. Rodney to A. Gallatin, Dec. 21, 1810, Gallatin Papers, New York Historical Society, New York City.

[69] Wirt Papers, Jan.–Dec. 1815, Maryland Historical Society, Baltimore.

[70] [Illegible] Hopkins to E. Haywood, Oct. 10, 1800, Nov. 21, 1800, Dec. 19, 1802, Ernest Haywood Collection, Southern Historical Collection, Chapel Hill, N. C.

to travel for curiosity, and it was chiefly those in the service of the government, or those engaged in commerce, who would undertake a journey of more than a day's length.

The cost of road transportation was an even more serious deterrent to trade and commerce, which were not carried on to any substantial extent save by vessel along the coast and on navigable riverways. Even the average seagoing vessel did not carry freight much above 250 tons, and the capacity of the largest merchant ships did not exceed 400 tons. In the South, hogsheads of tobacco could be moved reasonable distances with shafts set in their ends, but the condition of inland roads was such that commercial wagon transportation was feasible or profitable only in the environs of reasonably large towns. Road building was expensive, and incentives to build were only beginning to emerge. The absence of extensive commerce between the several regions of the country thus tended further to emphasize their isolation from one another.

Early Newspapers

The distances, the dangers, the means, and the expenses of transportation inevitably meant that except on the parts of the seaboard having easy access to the post road and coastal waters there were large clusters and sections of the population that were almost entirely out of touch with one another. In rural and frontier areas letters, newspapers, and the gossip of travelers were the primary means of communication. But with slow mails and few travelers, the trickles of news were few. Only the largest newspapers, notably those that were organs of the two political parties, circulated far beyond the place of publication, and often they carried little reliable news, much of it several weeks old and copied from other papers.

In 1800 over 200 newspapers were being published in the United States. Of these, some 178 were weeklies, 29 were semiweeklies, and 24 were dailies.[71] Most of the important papers were published in the larger cities. New York alone had 11 newspapers in 1800, and, of the 24 dailies then being published, 16 were located in the five principal cities of the Atlantic coast.[72] Of these the most important included the *Aurora*, the *Columbian Centinal*, the *National Intelligencer*, and the *Washington Federalist*. Small towns, however, were also heavily repre-

---

[71] N. E. Cunningham, *The Jeffersonian Republicans—The Formation of Party Organization, 1789–1801* (Chapel Hill, N. C., 1957), 166, note

86 (hereafter cited as Cunningham, *Formation of Party*).

[72] F. L. Mott, *American Journalism—A History, 1690–1960* (New York, 1962), 133.

sented. New York and Pennsylvania were dotted with more than twenty towns that had their own papers. New England did at least as well, and some of these—for example, the *Massachusetts Spy* (Worcester) and the *Farmer's Weekly Museum* (Walpole, New Hampshire)—were among the most important and widely circulated newspapers of the day. Of the foregoing, the *Columbian Central* in Boston was the most popular, with a circulation of 4,000. The *Aurora*, in Philadelphia, and the *Farmer's Weekly Museum* had circulations of about 1,700 and 2,000 respectively.[73] Papers also followed settlers westward. In 1800 nearly twenty were being published beyond the Alleghenies in Kentucky, Tennessee, Ohio, Mississippi, and Louisiana.[74]

Newspapers in this era were chiefly concerned either with providing the mercantile classes with information necessary for business, or with promoting a political party. Papers of the former type, however, once established, also frequently took sides in the maturing party politics of the day. The close relationship between newspapers and politics in the early years of the United States is demonstrated by a survey of 512 of the 550 papers published between 1789 and 1801. Of these it has been estimated that 260 were Federalist organs, 129 Republican, and 123 impartial or unclear as to their position.[75] Most of the political papers announced their preferences in their first number, as a matter of course.

Newspapers in 1800 were therefore more or less alike in content. The staple item was commercial advertising, including the times of ship arrivals, descriptions of cargoes, and the like.[76] The most important component of the news itself was foreign news, which was usually copied verbatim from European papers. Such news, which arrived by ship, was typically two months old when printed, and consequently a continuing problem for the editor of the day was the unpredictable delay in ship arrivals. When a ship was late, either nothing was printed or "old" news republished. Although most papers merely copied European reports, a few enterprising editors began to print summaries of items culled from several foreign papers, and these in turn were quickly copied by other papers in the exchange system, described below. Governmental news was only beginning to assume importance for the papers in 1800, but its significance was to increase markedly by 1815. Local news, especially in the smaller papers, was never given more than token space, since the focus was on world events.[77]

The remainder of the space in most papers was given over to

---

[73] *Ibid.*, 159.
[74] *Ibid.*, 142.
[75] Cunningham, *Formation of Party*, 167–68, note 89.
[76] Mott, *American Journalism*, 157–58.
[77] *Ibid.*, 114, 153–55.

"features," a miscellany comprised of essays, poetry, scientific articles, and serials of what were regarded as important books of the time. The literary output varied, and some papers published excellent work. The *Farmer's Weekly Museum*, for example, was noted for the essays of Joseph Dennie and Royall Tyler, whereas the contributions of the Hartford Wits to the paper of their town are still cited for their literary quality.[78] As early as 1796 Noah Webster began placing the first regular editorial column in his *American Minerva*. Although a few other editors had taken up that practice by 1800, the editorial as such was still a novelty, and most papers still relied on "letters" which they often composed themselves or which were supplied them to represent the views of a political party. For example, Jefferson wrote anonymous letters for several papers, the *National Intelligencer* in particular, while cautioning the editors carefully to conceal his identity.[79]

Gathering the news was accomplished primarily in two ways. Foreign news, as discussed above, was copied verbatim from European papers, or taken from American summaries of European news. In the cities, where there were almost no reporters, domestic news was gathered chiefly from rumors or from information supplied by friends, whereas in smaller towns the local papers copied the city reports and republished them. The latter practice was considered entirely proper, since the country papers subscribed to the city organs and believed that publication of important news could be effected in no other way. The postal delivery of city papers to the country was known as the "exchange" system.[80]

The time-lapse in news-reporting was notable. Foreign news, as stated above, was generally two months old when printed, and domestic news also had an appreciable lag. The death of Washington furnishes a good example of the latter. He died at Mount Vernon on December 14, 1799, and the event was first reported locally two days after the event. The news reached Winchester, Virginia, 2 days later; Philadelphia, 3 days later; New York, 5 days later; Boston, 9 days later; New Hampshire, 14 days later; Kentucky, 17 days later; and Cincinnati, 22 days after the initial publication.[81]

So polemical and vituperative were the stands of most American newspapers on political issues that they were little less than "storehouses of . . . calumny," and slight difference could be seen in the uses which the two parties made of such weapons.[82] However, this was no

---

[78] *Ibid.*, 114–15, 137–38.
[79] N. E. Cunningham, *The Jeffersonian Republicans in Power* (Chapel Hill, N. C., 1963), 225 et seq.

[80] Mott, *American Journalism*, 153–55.
[81] *Ibid.*, 154–55.
[82] Adams, *History of United States*, I, 120.

new departure brought on by the Federalist and Republican antagonisms. The patient Franklin, and even Jefferson, had excoriated the
press more than a decade earlier. Beveridge remarks that "what this
pygmy press lacked in information it made up in personal abuse. Denunciation of public men was the rule, scandal the fashion."[83] In this
respect probably the most slanderous paper in America at the turn of
the century was William Duane's violently anti-Federalist *Aurora*,
published in Philadelphia. Its influence as a party weapon, however,
was greatly diminished by the removal of the capital to Washington,
and by the establishment of the *National Intelligencer* as the unofficial
organ of the Republicans. Samuel Harrison Smith, editor of the latter
and a close friend of Jefferson, though a spokesman for the Party,
became noted for the excellence of his coverage of congressional debates; for a quarter of a century most of the nation's papers took their
news from the pages of the *Intelligencer*.

American Schools

Despite the existence of numerous newspapers, there were large
sectors of the populace who could not read or write. Noah Webster
wrote that learning was superficial in a shameful degree, that the colleges
were disgracefully destitute of books, that the three or four tolerable
libraries were extremely imperfect, and that great numbers of the most
valuable European books had not yet found their way across the
Atlantic.[84] Moreover, the educational system of the United States had
hardly advanced beyond what it had been two generations before. There
was no common school system outside of New England, and even in
Massachusetts, where primary school education had been compulsory
since the mid–seventeenth century, little change had taken place. The
few academies and colleges that existed—some of them very good, but
most mediocre—were sparsely attended, and many emphasized only
training for the ministry. In the decade preceding 1800, for example,
the average number of graduates from Harvard College was about
thirty-nine, whereas in the years 1720–30 the average number had

---

[83] Beveridge, *John Marshall*, I, 268.

[84] Adams, *History of United States*,
I, 62–63. Such schoolbooks as there
were in this period were not, generally
speaking, written by intellectuals but
by journalists, ministers, teachers, and
others in need of money. See R. M.
Elson, *Guardians of Tradition: American Schoolbooks of the Nineteenth*
Century (Lincoln, Neb., 1964).
Adams remarks that "all the public
libraries in the United States—collegiate, scientific, or popular, endowed
or unendowed—could hardly show
fifty thousand volumes, including
duplicates, fully one-third being still
theological." Adams, *History of*
United States, I, 61.

been thirty-five. With four professors, including the President, and four tutors, the instruction remained poor and the discipline indifferent.[85]

Several of the State constitutions had provided for the establishment of public schools; the most notable were those of Massachusetts and New Hampshire.[86] Early school laws, without reference to legislation relating to colleges and academies, tended to fall into three groups: first, those supporting or establishing a strong school system—notably in New England; second, those in which fixed attitudes that education was within the province of churches and of charitable organizations resulted in resistance to State interference, except for assistance in maintaining pauper schools—chiefly in the States of the old middle colonies; and third, what may be termed the "no-action" group, reflecting Anglican attitudes in Virginia and those of the "poor white" settlers of Tennessee and Kentucky.

The colonial attitude that education was a matter to be taken care of primarily by private, religious, or philanthropic effort persisted well into the early years of the Republic, despite public statements of men such as Washington and Madison, and the elaborate plan devised by Jefferson and Wythe for Virginia.[87] In spite of State efforts to make education more definitely a function of government, programs varied in pattern from one State to another and were not well systematized or sufficiently implemented. For example, New York, although a city of 60,000 in 1800, had no schools except those that were operated by private individuals or groups or by the churches.

A public school, in the early nineteenth century, denoted a free school open to all, subsidized by the State or by some State organ. Such free education, however, was generally confined to the elementary level, and, despite utterances of liberal statesmen about the national importance of education,[88] in practice children were sent to school to learn the "three Rs" for the commonplace activities of daily life. Only gradually, as the result of the publication of texts such as those of Nicholas Pike, Jedidiah Morse, and Noah Webster, were subjects like advanced arithmetic, history, and geography introduced. These free elementary schools were generally poorly housed in primitive buildings, and their teachers, with but few exceptions, possessed only meager qualifications. To education beyond the elementary level the mass of the population was almost entirely indifferent.

---

[85] Adams, *History of United States*, I, 77.

[86] E. P. Cubberley, *Public Education in the United States* (Boston, 1919), 61–64.

[87] See N. Edwards and H. G. Richey, *The School in the American Social Order* (Boston, 1963), chapter 7.

[88] Cf. Washington's Farewell Address, quoted in *ibid.*, 214.

Even as popular pro-education sentiment grew in some areas, the colonial view persisted in other parts of the country. In the South the prevailing view was that education was a personal matter and that "competent parents would see to it that their children were trained according to their proper stations in society."[89] For the well-to-do, however, this meant a good education, and as a result many private schools were founded and private tutors were widely employed. For the most part, such tutors were well-prepared and competent persons who had been trained abroad or at such colleges as William and Mary and the College of New Jersey. Tutoring was not confined to the elementary level, but was available for a great variety of subjects, such as foreign languages, mathematics, navigation, and surveying. It was often the prelude to more formal education in one of the many private academies or to study in well-established colleges. By the opening of the nineteenth century, numerous academies had sprung up in various parts of the country. They appear to have been supported generally either by land grants, subsidies, immunities given by the States, or by private endowment. Usually the academies, though independent of the colleges, sought to provide their students with a substantial education at the secondary level, whether or not they wished to go on to college, but not all by any means attained the standards of the Academies of Exeter and Andover. As in the colonial period, the large plantation-owners in the South frequently sent their sons to English, Scottish, or Continental schools and universities.

American colleges, of course, had been established in the colonial and post-Revolutionary periods—for example, Harvard, Yale, Columbia, Pennsylvania, William and Mary—and more were to appear as the nineteenth century wore on. Yet even with the expansion of the number of public and private colleges, both types of institution were very selective, in spite of increasing popular interest in higher education. As late as 1815 the number of graduates of the leading colleges remained small. For example, in that year Harvard graduated 66; Yale, 69; Pennsylvania, 15; Princeton, 40; and William and Mary, 40.[90]

The existence of formal, post-college educational facilities in 1800 was confined to only a few institutions. The first medical school had been established in connection with the College of Philadelphia in 1765, followed by the King's College Medical School in 1767, and the Harvard Medical School in 1782. Instruction in medicine was offered at Dartmouth in 1797. Law was taught, largely through lectures, at William and Mary (where the first American law professorship was established in 1779), Pennsylvania, Columbia, Princeton, and the University of

---

[89] *Ibid.*, 140.   [90] Cubberley, *Public Education*, 90.

Transylvania in Lexington, Kentucky.[91] The best-known school for legal education was that at Litchfield, Connecticut, founded in 1784, where between that date and 1833 over a thousand students were enrolled, and many of its alumni became some of the most distinguished lawyers in the nation.[92] For the most part, however, legal education took place in law offices of the larger cities or under the aegis and instruction of some member of the local State Bar.[93]

D. TURN OF THE CENTURY DEMOCRACY

Although the government of the country was democratic in form and dedicated to the principle of the consent of the governed, few of its leaders were advocates of egalitarianism. Nearly all of them were well aware of the consequences of popular license in the printing of paper money,[94] and all were aware of the effects of Shay's rebellion in Massachusetts.[95] Republicans who talked of the rights of man might mean the rights of "honest" farmers against creditors or of Virginia gentlemen against a clique of Northern businessmen.[96] All States except Kentucky and Vermont, where universal manhood suffrage prevailed, had property tests or qualifications, such as the payment of taxes, as a prerequisite to voting, and these limitations kept a large number of inhabitants from the polls.[97] Not even in congressional elections was suffrage universal because of the restrictions imposed by the Constitution. Article I, Section 2, Clause I recites that the members of the House of Representatives were to be chosen by the people of the several States, but goes on to say that "the Electors in each State shall

---

[91] Warren, *American Bar*, 343–55.

[92] *Ibid.*, 357–59.

[93] See C. Consalus, "Legal Education During the Colonial Period, 1663–1776," *Journal of Legal Education* XXIX, 295 (1978).

[94] Beveridge, *John Marshall*, I, 298–302.

[95] *Ibid.*, 295–97.

[96] Thomas Jefferson, however, vehemently opposed property qualifications on voting rights. For critical analysis and discussion of Jefferson's views on the electorate, see, in addition to his *Notes on Virginia* (London, 1787), 192–94; J. R. Pole, *Political Representation in England and the Origins of the American Republic* (New York, 1966), 296 et seq. See also *idem., The Pursuit of Equality in American History* (Berkeley, 1978).

[97] In 1799 Kentucky had specially excluded Blacks and Indians. Both Vermont and Kentucky had residence requirements. On suffrage requirements generally, see K. H. Porter, *A History of Suffrage in the United States* (Chicago, 1918), 20 et seq.; C. Williamson, *American Suffrage from Property to Democracy* (Princeton, 1960), chapters 8–9. Valuable statistics on the small percentage of qualified voters who made their way to the polls in the several States at the end of the eighteenth and in the early nineteenth century have been collected by Pole, *Political Representation*, 542–64. In this connection it may be noted that the Virginia statute for compulsory voting proved to be a dead letter. *Ibid.*, 566.

have the Qualifications requisite for Electors of the most numerous Branch of the State Legislature." Article I, Section 3, Clause I provided that Senators should be chosen by the legislature of each State.

The regionalism of the United States at the turn of the century, together with the parochialism of local life, had an inevitable effect on men's attitudes towards the federal government and the work of the courts, whether or not they had the right to vote. Taken as a whole, Americans were simple, with conservative habits of mind, frequently fostered by the general ignorance and childish credulity of the eighteenth century. Despite the enlargement of federal powers in the administrations of Washington and Adams, it seems fair to say with Beveridge that

> Generally speaking and aside from statesmen, merchants, and the veterans of the Revolution, the idea of a National Government had not penetrated the minds of the people. They managed to tolerate State Governments, because they always had lived under some such thing; but a National Government was too far away and fearsome, too alien and forbidding for them to view it with friendliness or understanding.[98]

Isolation, poverty, and temperament encouraged independence and self-reliance in both rural and frontier sectors. In newly opened-up areas the head of the family was more often than not a man with no capital or credit who had left a settled sector to take up land in an area where neither was necessary. For him a gun, a rude cabin, and a small clearing provided home, subsistence, and even the staple drink of whiskey. Men were continually forsaking the settled regions of the coast and tidewater for the more distant settlements where hardships, perils, and privations were more abundant, but where government, creditors, and taxes were remote. Houses built of logs, their chimneys of sticks, their roofs of warping clapboards with weighted traversing poles, stood in small clearings of decaying stumps and small new growth surrounded by the gloom and silence of the great forests. Woods and streams provided game and meat and the skins of animals which might be bartered to supply simple needs.

Even the second wave of settlers, who took up the abandoned farms of those who had left their debts and moved on to the frontier, were hardly less provident than their predecessors. Both groups were made up of men fired with a spirit of independence, insistent upon freedom from restraint. Rural as well as frontier life meant individual enterprise and minimal involvement in trade or contact with other communities. Consequently, large sectors of the population were im-

---

[98] Beveridge, *John Marshall*, I, 285.

provident and antisocial; they did not take kindly to any form of authority, which to them inevitably meant order, limitations on freedom of action, mutual obligations, and, worst of all, taxes.

The frontiersman, whether single or the head of a family, was a rough character at best, noted for shiftlessness and hard drinking. It is scarcely to be wondered that observers from abroad could see little to admire in the brutality and semibarbarousness of such people. Talleyrand described the down east frontiersman of Maine of this period as slothful and indolent, interested primarily in the least amount of labor needed to protect himself and his family from hunger in some miserable cabin on the edge of a clearing.[99] His observations are applicable to other outlying parts of the United States, particularly in the hinterland and beyond the Appalachians.

> Placed at a great distance from the seat of the state to which they belong, poorly supplied with public papers, little prepared to read them, they leave their opinions on men and things in the hands of a small number of men who dispose of the votes, each in his district. . . .[100]

Only in more stable rural sections and in the older settled towns did community consciousness appear much in evidence, and there, too, it was seldom strong. Nearly everywhere, save in New England and parts of the middle States, men were more interested in amusements and diversion than in hard work, thrift, or political affairs. Sports, such as hunting, shooting, boat races, handball, racing, cockfighting, and equestrian shows, were great attractions. Horse racing probably attracted the largest number of spectators.[101] Inevitably, there was widespread opposition to those whose drives led them in other directions, such as trade and the accumulation of capital. Small wonder that the principles of Jeffersonian democracy—equality, agrarianism, and tax reductions—should have had the appeal they did in the election of 1800, after demagogues had exploited such party cries by the application of every stimulant within their reach. Turbulent and changeable, gullible and naïve, coarse and often brutal, envious of those who had property, the bulk of the people had next to no comprehension of the announced goals of the Republican leaders, and it was to tax to the utmost the abilities of the new President to accommodate those ideals to the exigencies of practicality.

---

[99] H. Huth and W. J. Pugh, trans. and ed., "Talleyrand in America as a Financial Promoter," *Annual Report of the American Historical Association for 1941* (Washington, 1942), II, 82.

[100] *Ibid.*, 84. Such factors helped to nurture inherited fears of despotism from a far–removed center of government.

[101] Krout and Fox, *Completion of Independence*, 391 et seq.

E. NATIONALISM AND EXPANSION:
THE BEGINNING OF A SENSE OF UNITY

For all the diversity in the American character and in the nation itself, there were becoming apparent trends that may be identified as distinctly American patterns or ways of life and that were to become more marked as the century advanced. On the seaboard, at least, there was a strong sense of the country's past and of the union bred by war under the leadership of Washington and by adoption of a Constitution that made possible a national government. Although in many ways the States had hardly yet become a Union, there were other signs of growing nationalism. There was the earlier work of Hamilton, who had created the federal revenue system as well as a system of debt management, thereby establishing the credit of the federal government and stabilizing its securities; Hamilton had also been successful in bringing about the assumption of State debts, which had helped to further his objectives of concentrating economic and political power in the federal government by attaching the State creditors to the national government.[102] These and other factors were indicative of a spirit of improvement in the air which gave impetus to the building of roads and canals and evinced a desire to take advantage of the country's natural resources.[103] Thus, some sense of union was becoming increasingly apparent and was beginning to combat localism and the centrifugal forces that flowed from the opening up of the West. Moreover, political unity had been fostered by the peace policies of George Washington and especially of John Adams, and the beginnings of the turnpike era foreshadowed a unification of the country by transportation.

The importance to the country of improving radically the transportation system to promote commerce and political union had been perceived at an early date by President Washington and, within a decade, by the federal and State governments. Poor as the system was in 1800, the tide was beginning to turn. Although the great era of internal improvements was to begin at a later date, legislative proposals heralding a growing sense of nationalism began to mount soon after 1800. For example, a number of bills were presented in Congress to authorize the building of roads and canals to the West, and many more were to be forthcoming. The Lancaster Turnpike had recently been completed in Pennsylvania, as noted earlier, and elsewhere other roads

---

[102] See chapter 2 infra.
[103] J. Marshall, ed., *The Life of George Washington* (Philadelphia, 1836), II, 65; C. Goodrich, *Government Promotion of American Canals and Railroads, 1800–1890* (New York, 1960), 3.

and canals were projected or under construction.[104] Pursuant to an act of the Sixth Congress, new post roads were being established, and the postal system was expanding rapidly to link old States with those newly admitted to the Union. By 1801 the number of post offices had increased to 1,025 as compared with 89 ten years before, and the mileage of the post roads had increased commensurately.[105]

Such measures for the improvement of inland transportation facilities would, in time, not only help to unite the country but redound to the benefit of manufacturing and trade. In 1801, however, so little had been accomplished in that direction that American commerce was conducted chiefly by water. Impetus for the development of maritime commerce and shipping had been provided by the European wars that erupted in 1793. Although initially those wars had involved only England and France, other nations were gradually drawn in. The wartime needs of Europe, accentuated by serious crop failures, created an enormous demand for agricultural products, lumber, and naval stores. Prices for such commodities were raised to previously unknown levels. With this came a demand for shipping, and burgeoning American capital that might otherwise have gone into the promotion of manufacturing was drawn off into shipping and shipbuilding. Dockyards hummed, and world commerce began to move in increasing quantities in American vessels. By the end of the eighteenth century a substantial part of the carrying trade of Europe was in the hands of American merchantmen. Between 1789 and 1800 American merchant shipping increased from around 202,000 to more than a million tons, all built in the United States;[106] and in 1800 the net earnings of the American merchant marine are said to have approximated $32 million a year.[107] At the same time, foreign tonnage carrying American products had declined from 41.4 percent in 1790 to 15.1 percent in 1800.[108]

Great Britain was the principal customer of the United States. Of the total value of exports, over 20 percent went to that country, approximately 8 percent to north Germany, and over 28 percent to the British, French, and Spanish West Indies. New York, Maryland, Pennsylvania,

---

[104] *American State Papers. Documents, Legislative and Executive, of the Congress of the United States, Miscellaneous, 1789–1809* (Washington, 1834), I, 893. See generally letters and documents collected in ibid., 724 et seq.

[105] T. Pitkin, *A Statistical View of the Commerce of the United States of America* (New York, 1817), 378, 419.

[106] A. Seybert, *Statistical Annals: Embracing Views of the Population, Commerce, Navigation, Fisheries, Public Lands, Post–Office Establishment, Revenues, Mint, Military and Naval Establishments, Expenditures, Public Debt and Sinking Fund of the United States of America* (Philadelphia, 1818), 317.

[107] V. S. Clark, *History of Manufacturers in the United States, 1607–1860* (Washington, 1916), 237–38.

[108] Seybert, *Statistical Annals*, 319.

Massachusetts, and South Carolina accounted for over 80 percent of the value of all exports.[109] The total value of American exports rose from approximately $19 million in 1790 to nearly $71 million in 1800, and to over $94 million by 1801.[110] In addition to supplying domestic products, American merchants also became warehousers, distributors, and re-exporters of foreign merchandise, and shipments of such goods in several years were greater than those of domestic produce.[111] Re-exports in 1800 and 1801 amounted to over $39 million and $46 million respectively.[112] Export figures were to continue to make rapid gains until 1806, when they passed $108 million, only to fall to $22 million in 1807–1808 after the passage of the Embargo Act.[113]

Further benefits to the American economy had resulted from the modification of commercial restrictions embodied in the Jay Treaty of 1794, which had also enabled Britain to obtain an American market for her own manufactures—boots, shoes, cutlery, hardware, agricultural implements, and the like.[114] In 1800 the total value of foreign imports was $91 million, nearly four times what it had been in 1790, and in 1801 it was to rise to over $111 million.[115] Among the principal consequences of these commercial developments was an increase in commercial and customs litigations and the involvement of American citizens in admiralty and prize suits in the federal courts. Accordingly, they had their effect on the business of the Supreme Court.

The expansion of shipping and ocean commerce had, as indicated, no counterpart in manufacturing and domestic commerce. In fact, the new prosperity inured primarily to the benefit of the seaports, where the stimulus to foreign imports and the reservoir of foreign goods tended to discourage existing American domestic manufacturers because the carrying services of American vessels were paid for largely in foreign merchandise. Inevitably, there was no stimulus to domestic shipping, except insofar as it was required for the carriage of farm produce, lumber, and fish destined for the export trade. As in the colonial period, nearly all manufacturing at the turn of the century consisted of local industries and hand trades, and these were generally combined with farming, particularly in the Middle-Atlantic and northern States. So large was the rural population, and so difficult and costly was overland transportation, that those living in rural areas, villages, and small towns engaged in the manufacture of farm implements, utensils, clothing, and furniture primarily for the benefit of the immediate neigh-

[109] *American State Papers: Commerce and Navigation*, X, 453.

[110] Seybert, *Statistical Annals*, 142–43.

[111] *Ibid.*, 93.

[112] *Ibid.*

[113] *Ibid.*

[114] Clark, *History of Manufacturers*, 255–56.

[115] Pitkin, *A Statistical View*, 252.

borhood. Nevertheless, the textile industry had made a small beginning,[116] as had local ironworks; paper was milled in many States; and glass and other articles were manufactured in several places.

The difficulties of road transport and the relatively small amount of domestic trade and manufacture help in some measure to explain why no case involving the Commerce Clause of the Constitution,[117] in its interstate aspects, came before the Supreme Court between 1801 and 1816. Yet, curiously enough, among the most serious impediments to the expansion of the domestic economy and to internal trade generally were the restrictions that the several States imposed upon commerce. Although foreign commerce had been relieved of many of the burdens of State regulation as a result of the Commerce Clause, and although a uniform system of import duties had supplanted the diverse antecedent State systems, numerous local restraints remained. The activities of the State governments in establishing highways and in improving navigable watercourses within their borders had led to regulation of their use both to pay for the capital expenditures involved and as a source of revenue. Large and numerous toll charges were levied on both freight and passenger traffic by the States for the use of waterways and turnpikes,[118] and the legislation drew no distinction between traffic moving wholly within a State or between States. The regulation of pilotage fees, despite their intimate connection with interstate commerce, was viewed as a matter for State control,[119] as were wharfage rates and harbor dues.[120]

Even to the extent that Congress exercised jurisdiction over such rates and charges after 1800, it appears to have been limited to the District of Columbia, and there was little federal legislation relating to the rights and liabilities of persons engaged in the carrying trade. All this was left to State regulation.[121] State legislation frequently created exemptions in such a way that burdens fell only on interstate and foreign commerce,[122] and there are other instances of the exercise of State jurisdiction over vessels bound for other States and foreign coun-

---

[116] C. F. Ware, *The Early New England Cotton Manufacture* (Boston, 1931), 25, 27.

[117] For an early decision relating to the Commerce Clause, see United States v. The William, 28 F. Cas. 614 (D. Mass. 1808) (No. 16,700).

[118] See generally A. S. Abel, "Commerce Regulation Before *Gibbons v. Ogden*: Interstate Transportation Facilities," *North Carolina Law Review* XXV, 121, especially 139, 171 (1947) (hereafter cited as Abel, "Interstate Transportation Facilities"). For sam-

ple schedules of rates of toll see Meyer, *History of Transportation*, chapter 2.

[119] A. S. Abel, "Commerce Regulation Before *Gibbons v. Ogden*: Interstate Transportation Enterprise," *Mississippi Law Journal* XVIII, 335 at 337, note 5 (1947) (hereafter cited as Abel, "Interstate Transportation Enterprise").

[120] *Ibid.*, 339.

[121] *Ibid.*, 374.

[122] *Ibid.*, 361.

tries.[123] By 1800 there were numerous statutory provisions in the States declaring particular streams or parts of streams to be public highways or navigable waters,[124] as well as legislation that provided for improving waterways under both public auspices and private franchises.[125]

Of obvious importance to interstate traffic by land were bridges and ferries that connected highways interrupted by streams and watercourses. By and large, the establishment of bridges and ferries was remitted to local authorities that had discretion to grant licenses.[126] Under such diverse practices, there could naturally be no assurance that ferries would operate where needed or with any uniformity as to service or cost. The fact that post-riders were sometimes permitted to keep boats for crossing rivers in order to avoid being detained by lack of ferry service bears witness to the difficulties created by local maintenance of such facilities.[127]

Professor A. S. Abel has summarized the general situation as follows:

> Congress regulated rates and charges, pilotage, harbor control, and what have you, within the District of Columbia; it defined and provided punishments for felonies on the high seas; it regulated the lading and unlading of vessels incident to the system of customs administration; it approved state imposition of tonnage charges for the erection of marine hospitals. These matters were all relevant to the operation of the transportation enterprise but all were covered by specific constitutional language outside the commerce clause. Aside from particularized grants, federal legislation merely prescribed the minimum quality of service to be afforded by ships to passengers to or from foreign countries, expressly abdicated to the states the regulation of pilotage, and supervised the terms and enforcement of shipping articles and penalized desertion—matters connected exclusively with seafaring enterprise and, one may surmise, principally with foreign trade.
>
> The states, on the other hand, legislated freely throughout the entire range of transportation activities. Rates and charges, liabilities to travelers and shippers, accommodations of passengers and crew, the management of vehicles on land and vessels on the water, pilot qualifications and licenses, wreck, salvage, logging—whatever in the business of interstate transportation interested the states they regulated and regulated as best suited their interests, just as variously as they dealt with purely intrastate movements and with just as little apparent consciousness of constitutional guilt.[128]

---

[123] *Ibid.*, 362.
[124] Abel, "Interstate Transportation Facilities," 131.
[125] *Ibid.*, 132–33.

[126] *Ibid.*, 139.
[127] *Ibid.*, 142.
[128] Abel, "Interstate Transportation Enterprise," 379–80.

I: *The State of the Union*

Conservative habits of mind, together with prejudices such as those against banks, typified by Jefferson's hostility to all the machinery of capital, presented a continuing obstacle to the expansion of domestic business and commerce. Americans of the day were, generally speaking, simple. Skepticism about scientific inventions also deterred new enterprise as it did development of advanced agricultural techniques. For example, steam as a source of locomotive power was generally viewed as so visionary, and as involving such risks, that the energy, resources, and influence of Livingston and Fulton were required before it could be forced upon a disbelieving public. "Experience forced on men's minds the conviction that what had ever been must ever be. . . . Radicals as extreme as Thomas Jefferson and Albert Gallatin," writes Adams, "were contented with avowing no higher aim than that America should reproduce the simpler forms of European republican society without European vices."[129]

Such, briefly, was the state of the nation when John Marshall became Chief Justice at the beginning of 1801: a loosely knit federation of predominantly agrarian States, regionally separate, insisting on local independence, and, by and large, unfriendly to the forces that were attempting to expand the powers of the national government. Men of strong will and inflexible conceptions opposed national hegemony, and out of their struggles for ascendancy were to come the issues that helped to shape the destinies of the Supreme Court and the nation.

---

[129] Adams, *History of United States*, I, 72.

CHAPTER II

The Posture of American Politics in 1801: The Clash of Ideologies and the Roots of Political Allegiance

THE HISTORY OF American politics in the formative period from 1789 to 1801 consists primarily of a study in conflicting concepts of man's nature, societal goals, and governmental structure and policy. Even in 1801 the ratification of the Constitution was still a recent event, and basic questions of political and economic philosophy were as yet unresolved. The fundamental problem in the political arena of the time was to define the nature of the society that would emerge from the principles embodied in the new Constitution.[1]

The control of the national government by the Hamiltonian wing of the Federalist party in the first part of these formative years gave Hamilton and his associates the opportunity to present their solutions to the problems involved in shaping a new society. In the 1790s this dominant faction of the Federalist party was pursuing a program of economic transformation. The basically agrarian economy of the nation was to be diversified in order to develop along with it a closely-knit commercial community in which all classes would find their living standards improved. By 1800 many of the measures espoused by the Hamiltonian group had been implemented: the basic impulse was one of conserving what its members had helped to build as they sought to protect their program from the threats posed by the rising Republican party.

The growing power of the Republicans resulted, at least in part, from the negative popular reactions to Federalist policies. The progressive articulation of the alternative ideology of the Republicans grew out of the gradual alienation of the disparate elements of the Federalist

---

[1] See J. Charles, *The Origins of the American Party System* (New York, 1961), 5–6.

coalition and a reduction of the party's support to its primal elements. In response to solutions put forward by the dominant Federalist faction, the Republican party advanced its own program, which provided a different solution to the problem of societal structure and thereby gradually united the basic anti-Federalist elements into a coherent entity. The election of 1800 produced the first dramatic clash between the two ideologies.[2]

A summary presentation of the basic political principles of the contending forces in the election of 1800 is in order because it is through an examination of those philosophies that the political posture of the country in 1801—the year when the Marshall era began—may best be understood. The focus of this chapter is on the views of the Hamiltonian Federalists and the rival Republican party. In addition, this chapter will examine the beliefs of a third group—consisting of adherents to the "balance" political philosophy of John Adams—which is sometimes ignored by historians who view the party battles of this period only as a Manichean struggle between the forces of Hamilton and those of Jefferson. Much of the following discussion is familiar learning, at least to historians, but it is nonetheless necessary to the theme of this Volume. Although the Republicans were victorious in the election of 1800, Federalist ideals remained a powerful force, particularly through the influence of John Marshall. The conflict between President Jefferson and Chief Justice Marshall had its roots in the ideological struggle that came to a head in the election of 1800.

---

[2] The head-on clash of Federalist and Republican ideologies in the election of 1800 was foreshadowed by the controversy following the enactment of the Alien and Sedition Acts in 1798. The high Federalists took advantage of widespread fear of war and general anxiety over both internal and external security to push these extreme measures—even Hamilton found them somewhat shocking—through Congress. The legislation served to clamp down on opposition to the federal government and its policies. The Acts also provided a means of limiting the political power of European immigrants—particularly the Irish and the French—who were beginning to swell the ranks of the Republican Party. The Republicans responded with the Kentucky and Virginia Resolutions (see text accom-panying note 35 infra), substantially written by Jefferson and Madison. These resolutions denounced the Alien and Sedition Acts as an unconstitutional exercise of powers not granted to the federal government and asserted the right of States to nullify within their territories such unconstitutional assumptions of power.

For a discussion of the Alien and Sedition Acts, see D. Malone, *Jefferson and the Ordeal of Liberty* (Boston, 1962), 380–94; M. Dauer, *The Adams Federalists* (Baltimore, 1953), 153–67; and C. G. Bowers, *Jefferson and Hamilton: The Struggle for Democracy in America* (Boston, 1925), 374–407. The Kentucky and Virginia Resolutions are discussed in Bowers, *Jefferson and Hamilton*, 407–11, and Malone, *Jefferson*, 394–409.

A. THE COMMERCIAL WING OF THE
FEDERALIST PARTY: PRINCIPLES AND POLICIES

The early shaping of the nation was largely the work of what came to be described as the commercial wing of the Federalist party. In substantial control of the governmental appartus on the national level during Washington's tenure in office, this group, under the aegis of Hamilton, met no substantial intra-party opposition to its policies until the Adams administration presented a different stance on particular issues of the time. Since Hamilton was both its spokesman and major theorist, an examination of his thought is necessary for an appreciation of what the commercial wing was attempting to do.[3] The essence of Hamilton's political philosophy may be found in a passage contained in his speech at the Constitutional Convention on June 22, 1787:

> Take mankind in general, they are vicious—their passions may be operated upon. . . . Our prevailing passions are ambition and interest; and it will ever be the duty of a wise government to avail itself of those passions, in order to make them subservient to the public good— for these ever induce us to action. . . .[4]

The roots of Hamilton's political thought may thus be found in his conception of human nature, much of which was derived from the theories of Hume. Each man, in Hamilton's view, was possessed of, and characterized by, certain fundamental drives and desires. He further believed that these basic impulses were, in the main, uniform among men; racial or economic distinctions had no effect upon them. The essence of these impulses was a personal drive towards self-gratification; hence, if left uncontrolled, man would seek to exploit his fellowman in search of his own pleasure. In such circumstances, what we understand by the term society would be impossible.

From these psychological roots Hamilton deduced certain political implications. If social life was to be attained, the mechanism of government must be shaped so as to control basic human drives and impulses. No system, however, could hope to change human nature. The wise legislator should recognize this premise and devise a system capable of using

---

[3] This presentation of Hamilton's political thought is much indebted to C. Rossiter, *Alexander Hamilton and the Constitution* (New York, 1964), 113–225.

[4] R. Yates, *Secret Proceedings and Debates of the Convention Assembled at Philadelphia in the Year 1787, for the Purpose of Forming the Constitution of the United States of America* (Albany, 1821), 156–57, reprinted in H. Syrett, ed., *The Papers of Alexander Hamilton* (New York, 1962), IV, 216–17 (hereafter cited as Syrett, *Hamilton Papers*).

these drives to best advantage. The task of government, therefore, was to focus these human impulses for the advancement of community goals. In *The Farmer Refuted*,[5] written in 1775, Hamilton quoted the following statement by Hume:

> [I]n contriving any system of government, and fixing the several checks and controuls of the constitution, *every man* ought to be supposed a *knave*; and to have no other end in all his actions, but *private interest*. By this interest, we must govern him and by means of it *make him co-operate to public good*, notwithstanding his insatiable avarice and ambition.[6]

Every community, Hamilton reasoned, is divided into the few and the many, the rich and the poor. If government is controlled by the many, only anarchy can result, because the personal goals of a large group are too diverse for any governmental policy to bring them into a focus. The few, on the other hand, have relatively similar interests which a calculated governmental policy can advance. If the government pursues a policy favorable to the few, it can anticipate stability, for the few are the actual leaders of society, while the many are customarily too unorganized to present a substantial opposition. Yet the many cannot be exploited, for if they are, they will tend to unite and overthrow government. Moreover, the neglect of their interests will injure the welfare of the entire community. Wise policy is thus based upon pursuing the interests of the few without excessive favoritism; the successful government never overlooks the welfare of the community.

Since the health of the entire community was a prerequisite for stable, orderly government in Hamilton's system, the emphasis in his thinking about American politics was on the federal government. If policy formulation were to be left in the hands of each of the several States, community growth would be uneven, and those parts of the community that were less prosperous would be alienated from the whole. Thus, divisive sectionalism would be nurtured, and the national government would not attain a stable course. Only the overall direction of the entire community by the national government would ensure community progress and well-being as well as guarantee stable government.

If the federal government were to assume the task of formulating and implementing national policy, it would need sufficient powers to enable it to perform those duties. Concepts envisioning the federal government as a mere diplomatic assembly whose duties were limited

---

[5] A. Hamilton, *The Farmer Refuted &c.* (New York, Printed by James Rivington, 1775), reprinted in Syrett, *Hamilton Papers*, I, 81.

[6] D. Hume, *Essays and Treatises on Several Subjects*, 4th ed. (London and Edinburgh, 1753), I, 64–65, quoted in *ibid.*, 95.

to conducting foreign affairs and preventing quarrels among the several States were inadequate to meet the needs of the entire American community. The federal government must actively undertake positive programs to catalyze national economic development and to benefit the community as a whole.

Federalist policy, at least until President Adams took office, adhered fairly closely to the Hamiltonian scheme of government. The basic thrust of Hamilton's philosophy was clearly reflected in the complex economic program inaugurated during President Washington's term of office. The goals of that program were twofold: to induce the monied element of the population to support the national government, and to bring about an economic expansion benefiting all national interests. This program was to be realized through the influence and operation of a strong federal government.

One of the initial steps taken by Washington's administration was the recognition of the debt owed on government securities issued prior to the adoption of the Constitution. This action was intended to give the monied interests who held the bulk of the debt a stake in the new government. The self-interest of this wealthy group would thus be stimulated to support the national authority. From this perspective, the Madisonian plan to discriminate between original purchasers and assignees of government securities[7] was self-defeating. Madison's scheme would serve only to alienate the very interests needed to support the new government, since the obligation holders were, for the most part, no longer original purchasers but speculators and other assignees.

A second step was the assumption of State debts by the national government. This measure had the dual effect of transferring the allegiance of the State bondholders from the States to the national government, while at the same time further weakening the State governments as a rival source of authority. Anti-assumptionists voiced legitimate fears that the Hamiltonian program was "meant to aggrandize all rights of taxation to the national authority."[8]

With the support of the security holders assured to the national government, the next goal of the Hamiltonian economic system was to enlist the support of the "few"—the commercial elements of the Northeast—without alienating the "many"—the agrarian interests, represented primarily by the South. Since the leaders of commerce were also the leaders of the community in the larger and more populous States, their

---

[7] For a brief discussion of Madison's plan to discriminate among four classes of creditors, see B. Mitchell, *Alexander Hamilton: The National Adventure 1788–1804* (New York, 1962), 63–64 (hereafter cited as Mitchell, *Hamilton*).

[8] *Ibid.*, 71. For a discussion of this controversy, see Bowers, *Jefferson and Hamilton*, 58–68.

support was essential to the national government. The major planks of the economic program, geared to commercial interests, were the establishment of the first Bank of the United States and the promotion of manufactures by the granting of certain government bounties. The Bank was expected to supply currency and liquid capital for the expansion of credit—two essentials for the growth of commerce. Stimulation of manufactures would result in an expansion of domestic and foreign markets, particularly by opening up the vast avenues of European commerce to American ships and merchants. Such a program, in Hamilton's view, would also benefit agrarian interests, since the growth of commerce and manufactures would induce marginal farm workers and foreigners to move into urban areas, and thus provide successfully established farmers with a larger domestic market for agricultural products. In the future, Hamilton hoped, his economic system would realize its maximum potential through the construction of a system of roads and canals, which would unite the country by providing more rapid means of access to supply consumer demands and thereby enlarge markets at home and abroad.

Hamilton's advocacy of the economic system described above is strong proof of his belief that government was to be an active influence on a national scale. Such cornerstones as the Bank and internal improvements were not mentioned specifically in the Constitution as being within the province of the national government, but they were authorized by implication under the Hamiltonian concept of the basic functions of national government. This broad construction of national powers also appears in Hamilton's argument for the national carriage tax in *Hylton* v. *United States*,[9] and, more importantly, in the doubling of federal expenditures between 1789 and 1795.[10]

In advocating his program, Hamilton took the view that the Constitution was a flexible document which granted all powers reasonably necessary to effect the goals he envisaged. Congress must be able to read into it the grant of powers it needed to guide and benefit the community, and the executive must be strong enough to provide effective leadership. A strict construction of the Constitution, limiting the national government to specifically enumerated powers, could easily result in rendering it virtually impotent to achieve many of its most necessary goals. As Clinton Rossiter has observed, the Constitution,

---

[9] 3 Dall. 171 (1796). This measure, which levied a federal tax on carriages, exemplifies Hamilton's sweeping view of the federal taxing power. See Mitchell, *Hamilton*, 381–82.

[10] *American State Papers. Documents, Legislative and Executive, of the Congress of the United States*, Class III, *Finance* (Washington, 1832), I, 11–12, 319. For a discussion of Hamilton's influence on economic policies during his tenure as Secretary of the Treasury, see Mitchell, *Hamilton*, 351–75.

under the Hamiltonian concept of government, must be viewed as a liberal grant of powers, and not as a system of limitations upon national sovereignty.[11]

To guarantee the success of his program, Hamilton had to formulate a construction from which the power to charter a national bank and similar powers could be found in the Constitution. His success in so doing is emphasized by the tenacity with which his theory of implied powers was repeated by the Federalists even after his death. It was Hamilton whom Marshall echoed in his historic opinion in *McCulloch v. Maryland*,[12] in which the constitutionality of a national bank was upheld. Hamilton's position was clear:

> [T]his *general principle* is *inherent* in the very *definition* of government and *essential* to every step of the progress to be made by that of the United States; namely—that every power vested in a government is in its nature *sovereign*, and includes by *force* of the *term*, a right to employ all the *means* requisite, and fairly *applicable* to the attainment of the *ends* of such power. . . .[13]

> If the end be clearly comprehended within any of the specified powers, & if the measure have an obvious relation to that end, and is not forbidden by any particular provision of the constitution—it may safely be deemed to come within the compass of the national authority.[14]

On the basis of such reasoning, Hamiltonian measures not falling within the enumerated powers could still be regarded as constitutional and could thus be articulated and preserved by a Federalist Court long after the Republican accession to power.

To carry out its economic planning measures, the national government had to overcome two major obstacles. First, there was the problem of the State governments, which were widely regarded as the proper repositories for the broad powers required to implement Hamilton's program. As early as the Constitutional Convention, Hamilton had recognized that "[t]he states [would] be dangerous to the national government, and ought to be extinguished, . . . modified, or reduced to a smaller scale."[15] One way of reducing this potential threat was by the

---

[11] Rossiter, *Hamilton and the Constitution*, 189.

[12] 3 Wheat. 316 (1819).

[13] Syrett, *Hamilton Papers*, 98.

[14] *Ibid.*, 107. This statement is taken from Hamilton's "Opinion on the Constitutionality of an Act to Establish a Bank," dated Philadelphia, Feb. 23, 1791, and sent to President Washington. For a discussion of Hamilton's views on the implied powers of the federal government as later reflected in the opinions of Chief Justice Marshall, see Mitchell, *Hamilton*, 100–104; Rossiter, *Hamilton and the Constitution*, 199–208.

[15] Syrett, *Hamilton Papers*, 211.

assumption of State debts, referred to above. By 1800 the national government was exercising many of the broad State powers that Hamilton believed were required for national progress; but the Republicans were threatening, if elected to power, to reduce the federal machinery to a bare minimum, and to restore economic powers to the several State governments. At the turn of the century, therefore, the Federalists were waging a holding operation in an attempt to preserve what they had gained.

A second and more basic problem was the concept of popular sovereignty. Government, in Hamilton's view, must be for the people, but not by the people. It must advance their general well-being, but it should not cater to them subserviently lest their diversity and changing sentiments make wise planning an impossibility. National plans must be made without popular interference. Having in mind the excesses of the French Revolution as object lessons in the vices of popular rule, the Federalists manifested their position by providing for a standing army, by the quick, efficient suppression of the Whiskey Rebellion, by the enactment of the Alien and Sedition Acts, and by their propaganda attacks upon "democratic" societies, particularly in France.[16]

The essence of these policies is clear: the populace must be kept obedient to the national government, lest it rend the fabric of economic planning and endanger community welfare. The slightest resistance to the dictates of the national government must be dispersed quickly, lest that government forfeit its leadership to the States and community union become impossible. Again, the French Revolution seemed to provide an object lesson of the consequences of adopting any popular-based government.

Foreign policy presents further aspects of the Hamiltonian approach, but that policy must be viewed in the light of the two major problems it faced—the ratification of the Jay Treaty and the plan for a war with France.[17] The foundation of Hamiltonian foreign policy was a close relationship with Britain. That tie would benefit American com-

---

[16] Basic accounts of Hamiltonian policies may be found in Mitchell, *Hamilton,* 57–108, 138–53 (economic policies); 308–30 (Whiskey Rebellion); 423–73 (military policies). See also C. A. Beard, *Economic Origins of Jeffersonian Democracy* (New York, 1927), 108–64 (economic system) (hereafter cited as Beard, *Jeffersonian Democracy*). A valuable short treatment may be found in Charles, *American Party System,* 7–36, which provides an overall view of Hamilton's policies.

[17] For discussions of Hamilton's position on the Jay Treaty, see Mitchell, *Hamilton,* 331–50; and Beard, *Jeffersonian Democracy,* 268–98. An account of Hamilton's position on a possible war with France may be found in Mitchell, *Hamilton,* 423–53. See generally G. Lycan, *Alexander Hamilton and American Foreign Policy* (Norman, Okla., 1970), 226–82.

merce, which even in 1795 was still some 75 percent dependent on British trade. The treaty was designed to promote closer ties with England by removing certain popular sources of complaint against the British, notably the evacuation of the western posts. From a domestic standpoint, the fostering of British trade would guarantee a prime source of government revenue in the form of customs duties; any drastic reduction in those revenues would necessitate more internal taxes of the type that had helped to cause the Whiskey Rebellion. The popular appeal of the French Revolution and continuing antipathy to England, however, were in danger of becoming insuperable obstacles to closer British ties.

The Jay Treaty failed to change popular sentiment. Although it did preserve commercial well-being and the customs duties, new measures to effect a British alliance were thought necessary. A war with France, to be incited by publishing the XYZ dispatches and capitalizing on the moral conflict already existing between France and the United States, was Hamilton's solution. Such a war would bring a plethora of welcome effects: first, it would help to discredit the new Republican opposition which was notably pro-French; second, it would unite the country behind the new and unpopular Adams administration; third, it would dampen popular sentiment for the French; fourth, it would further aid commerce by securing the protection of the English Navy for American ships; fifth, it would effect the long-sought British entente, since England was already at war with France; and sixth, it would facilitate ultimately the expansion of United States territory to the Floridas and Louisiana, both of which were claimed by France. The aims of Hamilton's foreign policy were the same as his domestic policy: to benefit the commercial interests that formed the core of support for the national government and to unite the country behind that government in its attempt to bring about community well-being.

B.   THE MODERATE WING OF THE FEDERALIST PARTY: PRINCIPLES AND POLICIES

As the Hamiltonian faction of the party progressively ignored the noncommercial elements of Federalist support, a new type of Federalist emerged. The divergence from the Hamiltonian group was one of principle—some would call it emphasis—and was apparent in positions taken on many of the vital issues between 1796 and 1800. This departure was not to be seen in any sharply defined intra-party organization, but was characterized simply by support for the policies of President John Adams.

Hamilton and Adams had long been at loggerheads—ever since Hamilton had manipulated the electoral vote in 1789 in an attempt to discourage Adams' hopes for a national political career. This opposition reached its zenith in 1800 when Hamilton actively campaigned against Adams in an attempt to replace him with a candidate more favorable to his own views. Hamilton's fears of Adams were well-founded.

The political thought of John Adams, unlike that of Hamilton, was well, if not rigorously, defined and was familiar to the public. His *Defence of the Constitutions*,[18] written in 1787 before the Constitutional Convention, and his *Discourses on Davila*,[19] a reaction to the French Revolution, had both been serialized in popular newspapers. Adams accepted Hamilton's pessimistic view of human nature and his division of societies into rich and poor—"gentlemen and simplemen," as Adams phrased it—but he deduced different conclusions from those concepts. Since men will naturally attempt to gratify their own selfish desires at the expense of others, a careful balance between the two major divisions must be achieved in the government; if either segment were overly represented, it would exploit the other. The rich, Hamilton notwithstanding, could never govern for the community welfare if they were given greater power and further incentives to exercise it, for such power would lead them to exploit the poor. Since balance was the key to much of the Adams "system," governmental forms and apparatus were of great concern to him. Adams' focus, unlike Hamilton's, was not upon the federal-State division but rather upon the separation of powers and balance of representation at both levels. As such, his political philosophy tended to be more technical and precise, as well as more systematic, than that of Hamilton.

To Adams, the essence of good government lay in an enlightened bicameralism. Hence, a system providing for the representation of wealth in one house of the legislature, and of the masses in the other, would strike the necessary balance between those central elements. A unicameral system, he thought, could never succeed, since one element must inevitably gain the upper hand and destroy the balance. If either group should fall under the influence of a faction, the balance would be destroyed, for that faction would have an additional voice in government. To ensure a successful system, an executive independent of ties to either group and a judiciary likewise free were required. To deter the threat that either house might enact legislation that would serve only its own interests, Adams' executive would possess an absolute veto to suspend such "class" legislation. This concept of an independent

---

[18] John Adams, "A Defence of the Constitutions of Government of the United States of America Against the Attack of M. Turgot, in His Letter to Dr. Price, Dated The Twenty-second Day of March, 1778," reprinted in C. F. Adams, ed., *The Works of John Adams* (Boston, 1851), IV, 271.

[19] John Adams, "Discourses on Davila: A Series of Papers on Political History," *ibid.*, VI, 223.

executive, carefully weighing the interests of the two major groups and taking sides with neither, contrasts sharply with the Hamiltonian scheme of using the executive to lead a policy favorable to the wealthy few. Since Adams attempted to promote his concept of the executive function, his conflict with Hamilton is understandable.

Adams viewed political parties as the natural concomitants of the class division of society, and hence entirely sound and permissible. His only stricture upon parties was in Presidential selections, since he believed that the executive should not be partisan. Hamilton, on the other hand, dismissed political parties as mere factions whose only function was the negative one of opposing a wise government's policies. Finally, Adams agreed with Hamilton that the ultimate source of power in society was the people; but he went beyond Hamilton in recognizing a popular right to take part in the government. That right was not limited to the privilege of selecting the members of the lower house but extended to the point of popular removal of officials by impeachment or deposition. This sanction of popular participation in government was a further source of friction with Hamilton, as will appear.

Additional elements of Adams' political theory were only incidental to his major purposes, but they provided ammunition for his Republican critics, who contended that they revealed his "monarchism." These elements included Adams' professed admiration for the British system of government and his insistent attack upon French unicameralism as too democratic and anti-aristocratic. Another expressed element of Adams' political philosophy was the emphasis he placed upon the trappings and pomp of government and his tentative suggestion that hereditary officials might come into being in America. These, again, seemed to lend credence to the charges of "monarchism."

In sum, the major difference between Hamilton and Adams was, as Manning J. Dauer has pointed out, that the former believed that the rich had a right to rule, and that social welfare made their rule a necessity, whereas the latter believed that either rich or poor would be self-seeking if in sole control of the government, and that such a rule would inevitably end in exploitation of the unrepresented group.[20]

Since the sources of Adams' political views differed so markedly from those of Hamilton, it was natural that after Adams assumed office his policies should not infrequently diverge from those of his rival for party leadership.[21] Adams' attitude towards Hamilton's economic system

---

[20] Dauer, *The Adams Federalists*, 54. Adams' political and economic theories are well summarized in Dauer, *ibid.*, 35–77. See also Beard, *Jeffersonian Democracy*, 299–321; P. Smith, *John Adams* (Garden City, 1962), II, passim, especially 692–97, 797–802 (hereafter cited as Smith, *Adams*); Charles, *American Party System*, 54–74.

[21] The policies of the Adams administration are well covered in an

is particularly instructive. He was troubled by the grand design of favoring the commercial interests of the Northeast for two major reasons: such a policy seemed to be pure class legislation; and, even if some economic group needed to be favored in order to foster economic growth, the natural group to favor would be the agrarian. This conclusion resulted from Adams' recognition of the existence of the substantial agrarian interests in the nation and from his own acceptance of the Physiocratic concept of land as the source of all wealth. In this connection it may be noted parenthetically that Adams thought himself something of a farmer, whereas Hamilton had a large commercial law practice in New York.

Despite his objections to Hamilton's commercial policy, Adams agreed generally with the funding and assumption elements of the Hamiltonian program, probably to ensure that American credit abroad would not be harmed by any repudiation of pre-existing debts. He strongly opposed the Bank concept, however, although this opposition was more theoretical than practical, since he took no steps to defeat the plan. The whole concept of banks seemed to Adams a plan for only a few elements in the country—above all for the bankers—to enrich themselves at the expense of others. The interest of a small group would be advanced by taxes falling mainly on the agrarian and labor elements of the population, both of which would be unaided by the Bank. Bank issuance of paper money, Adams thought, was unsound and inflationary; to him specie was the only true currency. The main function of banks should be one of deposit rather than one of economic planning. He did see some promise in the idea of a national bank, however, since it could perhaps replace the several State banks and concentrate banking activities in one place, where governmental supervision might prevent misuses of the banks' apparatus which might benefit only the few.

Adams' major practical concern over the Hamiltonian program probably arose from a fear that the tax burden needed to support the plan would be too great for the mass of the people to bear, especially in light of the fact that so few would benefit from the program. Nevertheless, it should be emphasized that Adams' view of the Hamiltonian scheme was theoretical and largely post-hoc; his opposition, if it existed at the time of the enactment of the plan, was not public. This latter fact becomes more understandable when it is recalled that Adams, as Vice-President, was not then in a policy-making position.

When Adams became President, the conflict with Hamilton became more open. In addition, his basic concept of the President's

---

interpretative fashion in Dauer, *The Adams Federalists*, 120–245. See also Smith, *Adams*, 917–1056; and Bowers, *Jefferson and Hamilton*, 315–439. Charles, *American Party System*, 54–74, is especially valuable.

function as one of balancing divergent interests showed itself awkwardly in many ways. Believing the Hamiltonian program to be overly favorable to commercial interests, Adams attempted to redress the balance. He began by attempting to cut the interest rates on government bonds, which were held, for the most part, by only a small sector of the population. Adams also opposed Hamilton's elaborate War Preparations Program, with its basic element of a standing army, since he believed that the people were already being subjected to a harsh burden of taxation, and that standing armies, as history revealed, were a first step in the direction of the enslavement of the masses. It seemed to Adams that the interest of the masses had not been protected, and thus it was his duty to defend that interest by redressing the balance needed for sound government. This position helps, in part, to explain his pardoning of the rebel Fries,[22] whose assault on the tax burden was understandable to Adams. It also explains his approval of the democratic societies, which seemed to serve the useful function of interesting the masses in government in situations where their interests could be threatened by Hamiltonian policy. Needless to say, Adams' approach, especially in the two instances referred to, seemed to Hamilton a sanction of popular participation in government, a concept he viewed as a Republican heresy and a threat to sound government.

It was in the field of foreign policy, with its attendant effects upon domestic concerns, that the conflict between Hamilton and Adams became most bitter. Adams' basic stance in foreign affairs was one of neutrality, probably because of his desire to avoid entanglement in a European war. Despite his professed distaste for the French Revolution, Adams wished to remain on friendly terms with both France and England without entering into alliance with, or secretly plotting against, either. He found Jay's Treaty satisfactory since it removed numerous obstacles to British-American friendship.

The key to foreign affairs during Adams' Presidency was the question of what the American response should be to the French severance of diplomatic relations and depredations against American ships and commerce. Hamilton's resolution of this problem, as already noted, was a war with France, and he had devised a grand plan for waging it. Adams destroyed the entire plan by reducing the War Preparations expenditures and by sending a peace mission to France to reconcile the two countries. In the face of Hamilton's hopes for a

---

[22] John Fries was convicted of treason for his part in a rebellion against the imposition of direct federal property taxes. The uprising took place in Northampton, Bucks, and Montgomery counties in Pennsylvania during the late summer of 1798. For a brief description of the incident, see Dauer, *The Adams Federalists*, 207; Smith, *Adams*, 1004–1005, 1033–34.

British-American coalition for war against France, Adams wished to avoid all war. He further disapproved of the coalition because he thought that the proposed alliance was at heart merely a plan to benefit commerce and erect an even stronger commercial aristocracy which would upset his whole conception of "balance." Only in the event that a French war proved unavoidable would Adams be willing to accept the proposed alliance.

The destruction of the plan for a French war was Adams' major assault against the Hamiltonian forces. In this connection, another difference in views helps to illustrate another point of conflict between Hamilton and Adams. Because of the possibility of a French war, Adams believed that the Navy should be strengthened to protect American interests on the seas; Hamilton's position was that the Navy should be kept small, lest the situation vis-à-vis England should deteriorate. The British were already stopping American ships and removing sailors to serve in the British Navy. An enlargement of the American Navy would only encourage those actions and also operate as a further barrier to a British alliance. Adams viewed the situation in terms of domestic needs; Hamilton viewed it largely in terms of how it might affect plans for an alliance that would benefit his supporters. Adams' approach to government therefore consisted less of a program than of policies resulting from a political philosophy that accorded with his personal point of view. To his mind, the proper focus of action should not be upon specific measures to be implemented but rather upon their consequences for society. Progress was the ultimate goal, but it must be the progress of the entire community, not merely of a single class. Adams did not hope to design the shape of society; his concern was to establish a government responsive to the wishes of the community. If that were accomplished, the people could design their own society.

C. JEFFERSON AND THE RISE OF THE REPUBLICAN PARTY: THE PRINCIPLES OF REPUBLICANISM

As a political phenomenon, the Republican party arose as a challenge to the policies of a national government controlled by the commercially-minded Federalists. Although Adams seemed to offer some alternative to the hard-core Federalist position, he was still suspected of "aristocratic" leanings because of certain of his published writings. Moreover, Adams had had little effect upon the domestic policies of the Federalists and had failed to bring about any notable change in the shape or functions of the Hamiltonian governmental system. Because of a series of unpopular measures sponsored by the Adams administration, a new approach seemed necessary, and the Republican party presented new resolutions for the problems that its leaders regarded as the central issues of the time, such as high taxes and neglect of agrarian interests. Gradually, the Republican party began to break down the Federalist coalition and integrate the basic anti-Federalist elements of the population by means of a tight party organization.

Although not originally an anti-Federalist leader, Thomas Jefferson became the spokesman for Republicanism, mainly because of his opposition role in Washington's cabinet and the attacks made upon him by the various Federalist newspapers of the day. More directly concerned than either Hamilton or Adams with the form that American government and society would assume after 1789, Jefferson based his political philosophy[23] on a profound mistrust of European systems of government. He had seen Europe at first hand, as a minister negotiating commercial treaties for America, and he viewed Continental history as an endless story of corruption and exploitation of the masses. America had the opportunity to develop a new society, free from the feudal encrustations that still lay upon the countries of Europe. Jefferson's intense dislike and distrust of European governments sharply contrasted with the admiration professed by both Hamilton and Adams for the British system. The goal of the American system, in Jefferson's view, should be to put into practice a philosophical ideal—to establish the principles of "just" government.

In Jefferson's earlier thought, free society was equated with agrarian society. In a well-known passage, he praised the virtues of the farmer:

> Those who labour in the earth are the chosen people of God . . . whose breasts he has made his peculiar deposits for substantial and genuine virtue. . . . Corruption of morals in the mass of cultivators is a phaenomenon of which no age nor nation has furnished an example. . . . [G]enerally speaking, the proportion which the aggregate

---

[23] Jefferson's political thought, unlike that of Hamilton and Adams, has been exhaustively reported. See, e.g., Beard, *Jeffersonian Democracy*, 415–67; C. P. Patterson, *The Constitutional Principles of Thomas Jefferson* (Austin, 1953), passim (a States' rights tract); and A. Koch, *The Philosophy of Thomas Jefferson* (New York, 1943), 113–85. Jefferson's public speeches are especially revealing, particularly his First Inaugural Address, which is one of the many speeches, letters, and other works contained in P. L. Ford, ed., *The Works of Thomas Jefferson* (New York, 1904–1905). A convenient selection of Jefferson's writings is A. Koch and W. Peden, eds., *The Life and Selected Writings of Thomas Jefferson* (New York, 1944). Relating Jefferson's thought (as manifested in the Declaration of Independence) to the Natural Rights philosophy is C. L. Becker, *The Declaration of Independence: A Study in the History of Political Ideas* (New York, 1942), 24–79. A brief overall view of Jefferson's political thought is contained in Charles, *American Party System*, 74–90.

of the other classes of citizens bears in any state to that of its husband-men, is the proportion of its unsound to its healthy parts, and is a good enough barometer whereby to measure its degree of corruption.[24]

Industry and manufactures could only sap the agrarian virtue that formed the foundation of a free society. Commercialism was thus to be avoided, where possible.

> While we have land to labour then, let us never wish to see our citizens occupied at a work-bench. . . . [B]ut for the general operations of manufacture, let our workshops remain in Europe. The mobs of the great cities add just so much to the support of pure government, as sores do to the strength of the human body.[25]

This was Jefferson's view before the adoption of the Constitution; by 1800 he had come to recognize that commerce in its broadest sense had its place in American society, if only as the "handmaid" (as he later put it in his First Inaugural Address)[26] of agriculture. Neverthe-less, agriculture should still be the foundation of the American econ-omy. Thus, Jefferson was convinced that the Hamiltonian system was wrongly focused; commerce might be tolerated, but it should never be encouraged. Jefferson's primary fear of the Hamiltonian system was his belief that any resulting diversification of trade would involve the country in European commerce, European politics, and ultimately European wars; this would make independent development of a free society impossible.

The core of Jefferson's political thought was rooted in three funda-mental principles. First, the basis of just government is the consent of the governed; second, all men are created equal and have an equal right to participate as rulers; and, third, all men are possessed of certain basic rights *qua* men, and governments cannot infringe upon these rights save by the consent of the people. From these principles he deduced a system of government for America. Since government originates in a social compact—that is, in an agreement between men—it seemed clear to Jefferson that no government could assert jurisdiction over any man who had not signified his assent to it. Thus, constitutions could last only for the generation of the original signers.[27] If they were to last longer,

---

[24] W. Peden, ed., *Notes on the State of Virginia by Thomas Jefferson* (Chapel Hill, 1955), 164–65.

[25] *Ibid.*, 165.

[26] "Inaugural Address, March 4, 1801," in Ford, *Works of Jefferson*, IX, 198.

[27] *Ibid.*, VI, 3. Jefferson expressed his views on this subject in a letter to James Madison from Paris dated September 6, 1789. This letter is the source of the frequently quoted state-ment that:

> No generation can contract debts greater than may be paid during the course of it's own existence. At

the earth would no longer belong to the living, for generations yet unborn would be bound by a set of rules devised by their ancestors—rules to which they had never signified their assent—and such a government would obviously not rest upon the consent of the governed.

On the assumption that all men are possessed of the same fundamental rights, and are equal by birth, Jefferson concluded that majority rule was the essence of true government. Class rule to him was both anathema and political heresy. The people must always make social decisions, even to the extent of compulsory jury trial in every lawsuit. This approach presumed an intelligent populace, so that government on the local level must provide for general public education. Jefferson's concept of equality demanded religious freedom as well, and necessitated the abolition of tax-supported, established churches.

Implicit in Jefferson's social compact theory was a strict constructionist view of the Constitution; the government should be permitted to exercise only those powers specifically granted to it by the people in the original compact. Jefferson gave his view of the General Welfare Clause and the scope of congressional power as follows: "Certainly no . . . universal power was meant to be given them. It was intended to lace them up straitly within the enumerated powers, and those without which, as means, these powers could not be carried into effect."[28]

If powers not specifically enumerated in the Constitution were found necessary to perform the functions of government, they could be obtained only by popular authorization, that is, by constitutional amendment:

> I had rather ask an enlargement of power from the nation, where it is found necessary, than to assume it by a construction which would make our powers boundless. Our peculiar security is in the possession of a written Constitution. Let us not make it a blank paper by construction. . . . Let us go on then perfecting it, by adding, by way of amendment to the Constitution, those powers which time & trial show are still wanting.[29]

Thus, to Jefferson, the evil of the Hamiltonian system lay not merely in its unwise encouragement of commerce, but also in its arbitrary assumption of undelegated powers, particularly as manifested by the establishment of the Bank of the United States and the encourage-

---

21 years of age they may bind themselves and their lands for 34 years to come: at 22 for 33: at 23 for 32 and at 54 for one year only; because these are the terms of life which remain to them at those respective epochs.

Ibid., VI, 5.

[28] T. Jefferson, "Opinion on the Constitutionality of a National Bank," Feb. 15, 1791, *ibid.*, VI, 200.

[29] T. Jefferson to W. Nicholas, Sept. 7, 1803, *ibid.*, X, 10–11.

ment of manufactures. Such usurpation of power he believed to be based upon misguided and erroneous concepts. Hamilton viewed the federal government as a national planner requiring adequate powers to perform the tasks he thought belonged to it. Jefferson, on the other hand, believed, as he observed in his First Inaugural Address, that government should be "wise and frugal" and "should restrain men from injuring one another, [but] leave them otherwise free to regulate their own pursuits of industry & improvement. . . ."[30] If the Republicans were to gain control of the national government, it seemed clear that they would prune "bureaucracy" and reduce its duties.

As to the actual form of the governmental apparatus, Jefferson's plans were quite unlike those of the Federalists, although they resembled Adams' views before 1789 as represented in his *Defence of the Constitutions*, at least with respect to the concepts of division of powers between the national and State governments. Government should be partly federal and partly local. The national government should be limited to the spheres of foreign affairs and interstate relations. Its functions were thus purely negative: to prevent internal and external strife and friction. All economic planning and so-called policy decisions beyond the foregoing spheres were the province of State and local governments. Again, national government was to be small, frugal, and passive. If it were more—if, as Hamilton desired, it were to be granted powers over economic planning, for example—it would approach the systems of the strong central governments of Europe, and become an engine for the exploitation of the masses.

Jefferson accepted the national government's power to tax with reluctance and only because his ambassadorial experience had demonstrated to him that taxation powers were required on the national level to maintain foreign credit. His approach to the division of powers between the federal and State governments is perhaps best illustrated by his belief that a Constitutional Convention was unnecessary, since, with a few exceptions, such as the national taxing power, which could be cured by amendment, the government devised by the Articles of Confederation was quite suitable for American needs.

Jefferson's economic philosophy conflicted sharply with that of the commercially-minded Federalists. Here his approach was entirely antithetical to the Hamiltonian concept of government as national planner. Jefferson saw laissez-faire as the natural concomitant of social equality, and government could thus aid no occupation or industry. Land was the source of all wealth, and agriculture the most fitting occupation for free men. Agrarian virtue was the pillar of democracy,

---

[30] *Ibid.*, **IX**, 197.

whereas industry threatened degradation to its workers. Jefferson at first believed that America should follow the lead of China in spurning manufactures. Not until 1807 did he begin to see manufactures as co-equal with agriculture, commerce, and navigation as legitimate national occupations.

Jefferson's opposition to Federalist policies began when the Hamiltonian economic system was adopted.[31] Although he finally threw his support behind that system, he was to maintain later that Hamilton had tricked him into backing the program, and that his support of the system was the gravest political error of his career.[32] Funding and assumption were needed insofar as they would stabilize American credit abroad, but Jefferson thought the latter measure unnecessary to effect that end. Moreover, he perceived funding as benefiting only a small group of speculators at the expense of the nation's farmers, whose tax money provided the government with the revenue necessary to pay its bond obligations.[33] Furthermore, assumption was a gross violation of States' rights, for it effectively deprived the States of much of their tax revenue sources. Assumption was also sectional legislation, for the South had largely settled its financial affairs at home, whereas the North was in dire financial distress because of outstanding State debts. Southern tax money would thus be used to pay off Northern debts.[34] The Bank measure increased this sectional imbalance, harming the agrarian South by discouraging loans to farmers, since government bonds paid higher interest rates. The stimulation of manufactures by the grant of bounties was a further benefit to northern interests, and a violation of sound economics whose watchword should be laissez-faire. In addition, manufactures required cheap labor, and that would be supplied by European immigrants. Accustomed to political subservience, these new immigrants would serve only as instruments of the aristocracy against the basic agrarian interests of the nation.

A system of government finance based on excise and, later, land taxes further troubled Jefferson, for their incidence fell upon the agrarian community, while their expenditure benefited the commercial interests. Moreover, the size of the debt was such as to bind future generations,

---

[31] Jeffersonian responses to Federalist policies, and alternative resolutions to national problems, are well documented in Malone, *Jefferson*, passim, especially 245–506; and Bowers, *Jefferson and Hamilton*, passim. For a well-rounded interpretative biography of Jefferson, tracing his policies to their roots, see G. Chinard, *Thomas Jefferson: The Apostle of Americanism* (Boston, 1929).

[32] See T. Jefferson to G. Washington, Sept. 9, 1792, in Ford, *Works of Jefferson*, VI, 102. For a discussion of Jefferson's and Hamilton's conflicting views of assumption, see Mitchell, *Hamilton*, 79–85.

[33] See Bowers, *Jefferson and Hamilton*, 58–59.

[34] See *ibid.*, 59; Mitchell, *Hamilton*, 70.

without their consent, to repay it. To these specific objections Jefferson added an overall indictment of the Hamiltonian system, namely, that it arrogated improper functions to the national government, whose concerns, he believed, should be mainly diplomatic and passive. Active government was an invitation to dominance of one group over another, and it seemed to him that the commercial interests of the country were gaining ascendancy over the more fundamental agrarian interests. Moreover, a measure such as the establishment of the Bank violated basic political tenets, for, as it was not one of the enumerated powers, the people had never authorized it.

This opposition to active government at the national level culminated, after the excesses of the Alien and Sedition Acts, in the formulation of the Virginia and Kentucky Resolutions,[35] which asserted the rights of the several States to suspend any national legislation they deemed unconstitutional. The theory behind those Resolutions was harmonized in the Jeffersonian pattern of government by depicting the Constitution as a contract or compact among the States as agents for their citizens. Since the States were the parties to this contract, they had the right to judge when the contract was broken—for example, by governmental usurpation of undelegated powers on the national level. In sum, Jefferson distrusted the entire Federalist scheme because of its unhappy similarity to the corrupt patterns of European governments.

Jefferson's solutions to Federalist excesses were simple. Although the core of the Hamiltonian system was too deeply rooted by 1800 to permit its complete destruction, its worst aspects could be curtailed at least to some extent. Government could be reduced to negative functions, the national bureaucracy sharply cut, and expenditures reduced. With the resulting economies, the excise and land taxes could be repealed; thus the agrarian tax burden could be lightened. Furthermore, governmental favoritism of one industry over another could be ended, and all native occupations allowed to grow on their own under a system of laissez-faire. The commercial interests would be expelled from dominance in the high seats of the government and reduced to equality with their fellows. Policy decisions would be relegated to the States, and more egalitarian measures, such as trial by jury, would be implemented at all levels. As to the national judiciary, its excesses of partisanship would have to be checked by some undefined submission to popular control. All branches of government must be controlled by the entire community, and they must govern for the common good.

In foreign affairs, the obvious Federalist design for a British-American entente particularly distressed Jefferson, for it seemed to

---

[35] See note 2 supra.

augur a loss of self-determination and a forfeiture of the hope of building a new society in a new world free from the ills that plagued European systems. The adoption of the Jay Treaty seemed an attempt to undo the Revolution; it is probable that it did more to unite anti-Federalist sentiment than any other single event of the 1789–1801 period. Southerners generally were especially distressed by the Treaty, for they received no benefits equal in either kind or scope to those obtained by the commercial community of the North. Southerners also had long-standing differences with the British, particularly over the seizure of slaves without compensation after the Revolution. It may also be noted that the southern planters owed large pre-Revolutionary debts to English creditors, and that the country as a whole, at least before the XYZ disclosures, had pro-French leanings. Attempts to foment a French war also alarmed Jefferson, who feared that the war would be used as a measure to extinguish Republican opposition to Federalist policies and to provide a basis for a military dictatorship in America. The standing army policy and the muzzling effect of the Sedition Act supported that fear. Jefferson believed that foreign policy should be based upon strict neutrality and American self-determination. American independence should not be endangered, Jefferson came to believe, even to aid the French Revolution in fulfilling its promise.

In sum, the Republican opposition to Federalist policies was an opposition based upon a totally different conception of what American society ought to be. The Republican party offered an alternative resolution of the key issues with which Americans had been concerned since 1789.

D.   THE ROOTS OF POLITICAL ALLEGIANCE

Without reference to the roots of political allegiance, the dry bones of political history remain largely fleshless.[36] The appeal of a political platform is rarely an example of abstract admiration of a partisan ideology; political support is ordinarily a function of interests served by the party platform. With this in mind, a brief summary of

---

[36] Factors bearing on political allegiance are given close attention in three works already cited: Charles, *American Party System*; Dauer, *The Adams Federalists*, 3–34; and Beard, *Jeffersonian Democracy*, 1–33. The elements of support that united to secure the ratification of the Constitution are examined in J. T. Main, *The Antifederalists: Critics of the Constitution 1781–1788* (Chapel Hill, 1961), passim, especially 249–81. An incisive view of the Federalist rise and decline in New England is provided in W. A. Robinson, *Jeffersonian Democracy in New England* (New Haven, 1916).

the socio-economic background of political support from 1789 to 1801 is offered.

The core of Federalist support in those years was a congeries of the same interests that had secured the adoption of the Constitution— the so-called commercial interests typified by the shipping and trade industries of New England. Until the Adams administration, the Federalists maintained their political ascendency by adding new elements of strength to this core. Factors tending to strengthen Federalist support in the nation included the relative lack of cohesion and unity among the basic anti-Federalist elements; the strong desire for union in the early years; the appeal of the standing army policy to areas, particularly in the South, still subject to frontier fighting; the support of the religious establishment in New England; personal respect for General Washington and for the national prosperity that obtained during his tenure of office; and, finally, the support of the agrarian element producing goods for sale in the cities and abroad. The eventual decline of the Federalist party was the result of the alienation of these extracommercial elements of support from the party coalition. Manning J. Dauer has emphasized that "the history of the decline of the Federalist party is largely the history of the step-by-step loss of the agrarian elements from the party."[37]

The loss of these elements of Federalist support resulted from a series of factors: first, the generation of popular interest in government in response to the Federalist positions on foreign policy, especially on the French Revolution and the Jay Treaty; second, the organization of a tight party structure by the Republicans which capitalized upon this popular interest; third, the depiction of the Federalists as monarchists in Republican propaganda; fourth, the increasingly procommercial policy of the Federalists that further alienated agrarian support for the party and drove the agrarian population together into opposition; fifth, the tax expense of Federalist policies that bore most heavily upon agrarian interests; sixth, the death of Washington and the end of prosperity under Adams; seventh, the increasing influences of the dissenting churches in New England; and, lastly, the fear that a French war would not only destroy the Union but would require additional taxes to promote.

The Republicans' triumph in 1800 can be traced in large measure to the party platform, although it was no visionary ideal. That program was the concrete expression of a complex system of proposals geared towards a new order more beneficial to the majority of the electorate.

---

[37] Dauer, *The Adams Federalists*, 7.

For example, the predominately agrarian elements of the population were attracted by the promises of lower taxes and an unbiased national government. That these and other elements came to support the Republican party so rapidly is attributable in great part to the superior industry and system of the Republican party.[38]

By 1800 the Republicans possessed a party that was well organized under competent leaders. In a few States, like Virginia, it was tightly knit into a pyramidal system, with lines of control leading from the State committee down to party organs at the local level. One of the best examples of the party's zeal and organization was New York, where a campaign led by Aaron Burr swung that key State into the Republican column.[39] Even in other, less-organized States, the Republicans placed people responsive to popular sentiment in appropriate places and maintained strict discipline.[40] The Republicans also benefited from the zeal of party members who organized popular rallies and picnics, published stirring pamphlets and newspapers, and constantly confounded the Federalists with unorthodox methods in party battles.[41] The triumph of the party in 1800 can be traced primarily to this zeal and organization. Other factors aiding the Republicans were the rise of the dissenting churches in New England, where the established churches had become associated with Federalism,[42] and the fear for the Union among those who anticipated a French war, which was still a Federalist hope in Hamiltonian circles. At bottom, however, the Republican victory in 1800 was produced by a zealous party organization that carried its message to the electorate. The people were ready to accept new leaders whose policies promised greater benefits for all Americans through the inauguration of a new order. Political ideology had found genuine social and economic support.

The Federalists were never to regain power in the executive and legislative branches after the loss of the election of 1800, but the influence of the Hamiltonian vision was to remain alive for years to come. One month before Thomas Jefferson's inauguration, President Adams appointed his Secretary of State to the position of Chief Justice of the United States. Although John Marshall had opposed the Alien and Sedition Acts and some of the other more extreme policies of the Federalists during his brief tenure in Congress, he remained a true proponent of Hamilton's belief in a strong national government. Marshall continued to support this ideal throughout his years as Chief

---

[38] See S. E. Morison, *The Oxford History of the American People* (New York, 1965), 355–57.

[39] See N. Cunningham, *The Jeffersonian Republicans: The Forma-* *tion of Party Organization, 1789–1801* (Chapel Hill, 1957), 144–210.

[40] See *ibid.*, 177–83.

[41] See *ibid.*, 258–61.

[42] See Robinson, *Jeffersonian Democracy*, 128–33.

Justice. Thus, the clash of Federalist and Republican ideologies that produced the Revolution of 1800 did not end with the Republican victory. On March 4, 1801, when Chief Justice Marshall administered the oath of office to President Jefferson, a new phase began in the struggle between Federalist and Republican ideologies that would ultimately determine the shape of American society and its federal judiciary.

CHAPTER III

The Court in Washington

ARTICLE I, Section 8, Clause 17 of the Constitution gave Congress power "To exercise exclusive Legislation . . . over such District (not exceeding ten Miles square) as may, by Cession of particular States, and the Acceptance of Congress, become the Seat of the Government of the United States." In 1790 such a District, ten miles square and centering around what was called "Jenkins Hill," formerly property of the Carroll family, was selected as the seat of the new Government by President Washington and his adviser Major L'Enfant. Maryland, Virginia, and Congress agreed upon the site, which was named the "Territory of Columbia." The diagonal axis of the ten-mile square extended due north and placed about one-third of the District west of the Potomac in Virginia and two-thirds to the east in Maryland. The portion of the District lying west of the Potomac was shortly to be ceded back to Virginia, so that the remaining two-thirds became the District of Columbia as known today.[1]

A. THE CAPITAL CITY AT THE TURN OF THE CENTURY

The United States Government moved to Washington in the autumn of the year 1800. After the comforts and amenities of Philadelphia, the so-called Federal City, still in the early stages of construction, presented a dreary and disheartening prospect to new arrivals.[2]

---

[1] See H. H. Burton, *The Story of the Place* (Washington, 1952), 2–4.

[2] The description of Washington is based upon such contemporary accounts as those contained in H. Adams, *The Life of Albert Gallatin* (Philadelphia, 1879), 252–53; G. Gibbs, ed., *Memoirs of the Administrations of Washington and John Adams Edited from the Papers of Oliver Wolcott* (New York, 1846), II, 376–78 (hereafter cited as Gibbs,

III: *The Court in Washington*

Stretching for those several square miles across a broad plain lying between the east and west branches of the Potomac River, the city area was surrounded by an amphitheater of low hills beginning at the southeast and extending to the higher ground of Georgetown in the west. Vast stretches were still covered with great trees and alder-bushes, much was swampland, but wide footpaths and a few roads, often deep in mud, ran through the trees and blackberry brambles and had begun to connect one clearing with another. Few of the great avenues had yet been built, but their courses had been surveyed, and the stones that marked them could be seen among the bushes. Early in January of 1801 James A. Bayard of Delaware commented in a letter to Andrew Bayard of Philadelphia on the appearance of the capital city at that time. He wrote that except for a wing of the Capitol and the President's House, there was "nothing to admire but the beauties of nature." Commenting that few men brought their wives, he complained that "there is a great want of society, especially female. An invitation to dinner costs you a ride of 6 or 8 miles and the state of the roads obliging you to return before night, you have just time to swallow your meat."[3] In the same letter he said, "We have the name of a city, but nothing else." A French traveler described Washington at that time as resembling "those Russian towns, traced in the deserts of Tartary . . . naked fields, and a few groupes of houses," while another visitor ironically referred to it as the "city of magnificent distances."[4]

Prominent among the few buildings visible to the eyes of travelers were the beginnings of the Capitol, which stood on a steep hill seamed with gullies among the tangled trees and vines and surrounded by swamp on two sides. Only the North Wing (which today adjoins the central rotunda and connects it with the Senate Wing) had been completed, and that only recently.[5] It appeared as a large, square building

---

Memoirs of Washington and Adams Administrations); G. Hunt, ed., *The First Forty Years of Washington Society* (New York, 1906); D. C. Mearns and V. W. Clapp, *Some Materials for the Life of Elias Boudinot Caldwell* (typescript, 1933, Library of Congress), 62–63; W. P. and J. P. Cutler, *Life, Journals and Correspondence of Rev. Manasseh Cutler* (Cincinnati, 1888), II, 50–51; "An Account of the City of Washington," *Literary Magazine and American Register* IV, 133 et seq. (1805). See also S. D. Wyeth, *The Federal City* (Washington, 1865), 92. A vivid description of Washington at this time, also based on contemporary sources,

may be found in J. S. Young, *The Washington Community 1800–1828* (New York, 1966), 41–83.

[3] Papers of James A. and Richard H. Bayard, Manuscripts Division, Library of Congress.

[4] F. de Beaujour, *Sketch of the United States*, trans. W. Walton (London, 1814), 78. See H. P. Caemmerer, *A Manual on the Origin and Development of Washington* (Washington, 1939), 40.

[5] As recently as the preceding July, the Commissioners of Public Buildings had complained that every rain produced fresh leaks in the roof, so that the walls had been damaged and the plaster was falling off. *Docu-*

of white stone, measuring 126 by 121 feet and built in Italian Renaissance style. Simple but dignified, it was three stories high and surmounted by an imposing balustrade that concealed the chimneys and a roof of lead flats and wooden shingles. The south side was of rough brick, pending the addition of the central rotunda and dome, for which a portion of the foundation was in place. Beyond were the beginnings of the South Wing, projecting only a few feet above the ground. The whole surrounding area was covered with disorderly piles of brick, stone, lumber, and other building materials stacked beside large puddles of dirty water. Nearby were seven or eight wooden boarding-houses, a tailor shop, a shoemaker's shop, a grocery store, a dry-goods shop, a printer's business, an oyster house, and a washing-woman's establishment.[6] These were the dismal surroundings in which Congress and, a few months later, the Supreme Court first met.

To the southeast of Capitol Hill, and separated from it by swampland, were a few brick houses, many of them unfinished, and beyond stretched the wide and muddy Potomac River. To the west lay another and vaster section of swamp through which ran a sluggish creek bordered with tulip poplars. Originally known as Goose Creek, the stream had been pretentiously renamed the Tiber. This area was traversed by a primitive causeway that was to become Pennsylvania Avenue, and a mile and a half distant, with not a house intervening among the alder-bushes, tree stumps, yellow mudholes, and stagnant pools, the palatial but still unfinished house of the President rose out of a barren field. Although the building was well advanced five years earlier,[7] not a single room had yet been completed, the plastering was but half done, and even the main staircase had not been installed.[8] A rough wooden fence "not fit for a barnyard" was shortly to be erected about the premises by the new President "to gratify his republican taste."[9] Nearby were two or three new government buildings, notably the War Department and the Treasury, but the latter was apparently the only building

---

mentary History of the Construction and Development of the United States Capitol Buildings and Grounds (Washington, 1904), 91 (hereafter cited as Documentary History of U. S. Capitol). It also appeared that green timber had been used; its resultant shrinkage caused the poor carpentry work to become even more apparent. For an engraving of the Capitol at this time, see ibid., 94, plate.

[6] See A. J. Beveridge, The Life of John Marshall (Boston, 1919), III, 2.

[7] American State Papers. Documents, Legislative and Executive, of the Congress of the United States, Miscellaneous 1789–1809 (Washington, 1834), I, 142–44 (hereafter cited as American State Papers: Miscellaneous).

[8] C. F. Adams, Letters of Mrs. Adams (Boston, 1841), 434–35.

[9] W. Plumer to N. Emery, Jan. 6, 1803, William Plumer Papers, Manuscripts Division, Library of Congress.

ready for the occupancy of the executive departments.[10] Farther to the west, across the broad estuary of Rock Creek, lay the thriving port of Georgetown, which tapped a rich agricultural hinterland. Its wide anchorage, busy wharves, and warehouses provided a center for river shipping at the head of navigation, and behind, on the hill above, were the comfortable and capacious brick dwelling houses of the town.

North of the roadway that was to become Pennsylvania Avenue a few clearings had been made here and there to accommodate isolated houses in scattered chasms among the trees. Many of these were miserable huts, but others, more commodious, were still in course of construction and surrounded by lumber piles, brick kilns, tree stumps, and the temporary shacks of laborers. By the end of 1801, according to a report of the Commissioners of the City of Washington, a total of about 600 houses had been completed, of which approximately one-third were of brick and the remainder of wood.[11] A contemporary stated that there was but one church building in the city, a small frame building which had formerly served as a tobacco house. Altogether, the appearance of the city was somewhat grotesque by reason of the contrasts between plan and execution. Save for the pretentious magnificence of the few public buildings that had been completed, there was little then, or for several years to come, to indicate that the city was beginning to take shape in accordance with the grand design envisaged by Major L'Enfant. Even as late as 1818 John Quincy Adams recorded in his diary that the streets were in such condition that the carriage in which he rode had been upset and the harness broken, "and at the Treasury Office corner we were both obliged to get out of the carriage in the mud. I called out the guard of the Treasury Office and borrowed a lantern with which we came home."[12]

Living conditions within the District were primitive and expensive, and, with the exception of Georgetown, quite inelegant. The total population numbered about 3,000, a large proportion of whom were artisans and laborers engaged upon the public works; included in the figure were less than a hundred government employees and some 600 slaves.[13] Members of Congress were crowded into the boarding-houses adjacent to the Capitol, often two in a room, and many government officials had been forced to take up residence at great distances from their places of work.

---

[10] S. C. Busey, *Pictures of the City of Washington in the Past* (Washington, 1898), 74 (hereafter cited as Busey, *Pictures of Washington*).
[11] *American State Papers: Miscellaneous*, I, 256–57.

[12] C. F. Adams, *Memoirs of John Quincy Adams* (Philadelphia, 1875), IV, 74.
[13] Busey, *Pictures of Washington*, 68–69, 74.

Some indication of the cost of living may be obtained from a letter in which James Bayard wrote that for himself and a servant, in a house of about thirty, he was obliged to pay $23 a week.[14] So scarce were accommodations after Congress convened (and most members did not bring their wives) that early in 1801 Mr. Jefferson was the only one in his boarding-house who had a room to himself. Henry Adams has written that "there was nothing which wealth could buy; there were in Washington no shops or markets, skilled labor, commerce or people."[15] Despite the abundance of wood, it was difficult to find anyone to cut and haul logs for stoves and fireplaces, and coal grates were unobtainable. Meat and poultry from the nearby countryside seem to have been reasonably plentiful, but few vegetables were available closer than Alexandria. The newspapers of the day carried advertisements for staple groceries, drugs, and medicines, yet nothing, as Secretary Wolcott complained, was convenient: "there is no industry, society, or business."[16] This situation was to continue for several years. In 1803 John Lytton wrote from Washington, "The want of confidence in this place being continued as the seat of Government had nearly put a stop to building, indeed, they had pushed it so far that tennants were scarce to be had for the houses built."[17] In 1804 a bill for temporarily removing the capital from Washington to Baltimore was proposed but failed on its second reading.[18]

The Capitol building had been planned as the headquarters of the legislative branch of the government. Entrance to the ground floor of the structure as it then existed was gained through a door at the southeast corner. Inside was a vestibule, 22 by 34 feet, that opened on the right into the Senate Chamber and, straight ahead, across a small passage, into an elliptically shaped central rotunda. Here rose a magnificent double staircase, three stories high, hanging from successive galleries adjoining the second and third floors.[19] North of this rotunda was the

---

[14] The costs varied somewhat from one boarding-house to another. At Conrad's, where Jefferson boarded until his inauguration, the charge was $15 a week in 1801, including service, wood, candles, and liquor. At the Indian Queen, board was $1.50 a day, with brandy and whiskey free. See Beveridge, *John Marshall*, III, 7.

[15] H. Adams, *History of the United States of America* (New York, (1889), I, 31.

[16] Gibbs, *Memoirs of Washington and Adams Administrations*, 378. For sample advertisements, see the *Washington Federalist* for early 1801.

[17] J. Lytton to J. Blount, May 10, 1803, J. G. Blount Papers, North Carolina Historical Society, Raleigh, N. C.

[18] J. Gales and W. Seaton, comps., *The Debates and Proceedings of the Congress of the United States* (Washington, 1834–1856), XII, 282–88 (8th Cong., 1st sess.) (hereafter cited as *Annals of Congress*); Cutler and Cutler, *Rev. Manasseh Cutler*, II, 168.

[19] The description of the Capitol and the locations and measurements of its various rooms are based on contemporary drawings preserved in the Library of Congress and on re-

Senate Ante-Room, 38 feet in length and leading to the north entrance of the Wing. Along the west side were four committee rooms, 18 feet in height, opening off the central hallways. On the east side, the Senate Chamber stretched for 86 feet. Lavishly decorated and 48 feet wide, it rose two full stories to a height of 41 feet. Around the inner wall was an imposing colonnaded gallery built in a semicircle at the level of the second floor upon which it opened.

The room assigned to the House of Representatives, pending the eventual completion of the South Wing, was on the second floor. In length it extended 86 feet along the west side and hence corresponded to the upper part of the Senate Chamber on the east side. Although less elegant in its decor, the House Chamber was also two stories high, extending 36 feet to the roof. It, too, had a narrow gallery across its inner side. Access to the House Chamber, as to the Senate gallery, was gained from the elliptically shaped gallery at the head of the main staircase and from the House Ante-Room which adjoined it to the north. Off the south end of the central gallery were the offices of the Senate and House Clerks. On the portion of the third floor not taken up by the upper parts of the House Chamber and its Ante-Room were further accommodations for the clerks of the Legislature.

B. THE FIRST SESSIONS OF THE COURT IN WASHINGTON

Nowhere in the spacious halls and chambers of the Capitol had any accommodations been reserved for the Supreme Court. Despite recommendations for the construction of a building for the Judiciary made as early as 1796,[20] the government moved to Washington without having made any provision whatever for housing the Supreme Court. Perhaps this failure provides further evidence that the Court was not yet regarded as an institution of great importance in the federal system. At any rate, early in December 1800 the Commissioners of the City of Washington wrote to the Secretary of State to report that although a reservation had been made for a judiciary building in the square between D Street and G Street, and between Fourth Street and Fifth Street,

---

ports contained in *Documentary History of U. S. Capitol*, 87–89. See also G. Brown, *History of The United States Capitol* (Washington, 1900), I, 24–31 (hereafter cited as Brown, *U. S. Capitol*). The "grand staircase" was replaced after the British burned the Capitol, by the colonnade with tobacco-leaf capitals that now stands in the rotunda of the North Wing.

[20] *American State Papers: Miscellaneous*, I, 137, 143. The second recommendation proposed the expenditure of $100,000 for a building on the President's square. See also *Memorial to Congress from the Commissioners for the Federal City*, Feb. 23, 1798, National Archives, General Records Division, Legislative Branch.

N.W., no building had been proposed. Accordingly, they recommended that a committee room in the Capitol be set aside as a temporary accommodation, provided the arrangement was convenient to Congress.[21] Alternately, they proposed that the Court be accommodated in "one or two Rooms in the new Executive or War Office, and the Judges . . . with private lodgings in George Town."[22] Six weeks later, on January 13, 1801, they again wrote to the Secretary, referring to the "crowd of Business and Strangers which have lately arrived in the City," and soliciting the President's directions with respect to providing "a House for holding the Supreme Court."[23] However, not until January 20, 1801, with the convening of the Court imminent, do any arrangements appear to have been initiated. On that day, the very day on which President Adams sent to the Senate John Marshall's nomination as Chief Justice, the Speaker of the House laid before that body a letter from the Commissioners requesting that an arrangement be made for the accommodation of the Supreme Court in a room in the Capitol; this was referred to a committee headed by John Rutledge of South Carolina for report.[24] On the following day, the Vice-President communicated a similar letter to the Senate, and it was thereupon "*Resolved*, That the Secretary be directed to inform the Commissioners of the City of Washington that the Senate consent to the accommodation of the Supreme Court in one of the committee rooms, as proposed in their letter."[25] Two days later, on Friday, January 23, the House acted upon its committee report and resolved "That leave be given to the Commissioners of the City of Washington to use one of the rooms on the first floor of the Capitol for holding the present session of the Supreme Court of the United States."[26]

The room assigned to the Court pursuant to these resolutions was one of the first-floor committee rooms, the third from the north, on the west side of the North Wing, under the south end of the hall assigned to the House of Representatives. As a result of the addition of the central rotunda of the Capitol, the room later became the corner room of the North Wing. It can be identified as having looked out from the last two windows at the present southwest corner of that Wing. As of this writing, its quarters are occupied by a small committee room (Number 82) and by a storage room that adjoins the Senate Barber Shop.

It was at one time supposed, and has more than once been stated

---

[21] Papers of the Commissioners, 1773, National Archives, Interior Branch, Social and Economic Division.

[22] *Ibid.*

[23] *Ibid.*, 1798.

[24] *Annals of Congress*, X, 914 (6th Cong., 2d sess.).

[25] *Ibid.*, 734. For the Commissioners' letter, signed by William Thornton, Alex White, and W. Cranch, see *Documentary History of U. S. Capitol*, 94.

[26] *Annals of Congress*, X, 959 (6th Cong., 2d sess.).

in print, that the room first occupied by the Court was situated on the first floor under the Senate Chamber.[27] This was manifestly impossible, since such a room did not even exist; in 1801, as already explained, the floor of the Senate Chamber itself was on the ground floor. Probably the mistake resulted from assuming that in 1800 the Senate Chamber occupied the second and third stories, as it did after 1809, rather than the first and second, and from assuming that the later location of the Court was also its first.[28] Others, notably Charles Warren, have placed the first courtroom on the main floor over the basement east entrance hall.[29] This statement is equally incorrect, for in 1800 that room was assigned to and occupied by the Clerk of the Senate. Convincing proof of the actual location of the courtroom in Committee Room 2 on the ground floor is revealed by plans discovered in the Library of Congress,[30] by correspondence between Jefferson and the Architect of the Capitol, Benjamin Latrobe,[31] and by Latrobe's own drawings for a proposed remodeling of the North Wing.[32]

Structural changes since made within the Capitol make it difficult to describe the interior of the first courtroom with entire accuracy, for a partition has been added and now divides it into two rooms. The fireplaces have long since been bricked up, and the extent of the ceiling obscured by shelving and new partitions. Latrobe's drawings, however, are detailed and reveal that this first room assigned to the Court mea-

---

[27] See, H. L. Carson, *The History of the Supreme Court of the United States* (Philadelphia, 1902), I, 241; cf. Beveridge, *John Marshall*, III, 120–21, note 2.

[28] In 1808 and 1809 the level of the Senate floor was raised from the ground floor to that of the second; the gallery was raised from the second to the third story. See "Correspondence Relating to the Capitol at Washington," 2 vols., Latrobe Papers, Manuscripts Division, Library of Congress (hereafter cited as Latrobe Papers). At this time, the original joists in the North Wing were found to be rotten, decayed, or reduced to powder. See *Report of the Surveyor of Public Buildings* (Washington, 1808), 6.

[29] C. Warren, *The Supreme Court in United States History* (Boston, 1926), I, 171. Brown, *U. S. Capitol*, I, 28, places the Court room "in the room marked No. 1 [Plate 36]." This plate reproduced a drawing of the second floor on which two rooms are

marked "No. 1"—one assigned to the Clerk of the House and the other to the Clerk of the Senate. Probably, therefore, the reference was intended to be to Plate 35, which contains a drawing of the basement floor on which there were four Committee Rooms numbered 1 through 4. Even assuming that this error was not intended, a drawing contained in a letter from Latrobe to Jefferson (see note 31 infra), makes clear that the Court was assigned to Committee Room No. 2, and not to Committee Room No. 1. See also *Records of the Columbia Historical Society* (Washington, 1901), IV, plate I, where measurements of the Committee Rooms are also given.

[30] Preserved in Prints and Photo Division, Library of Congress. See also Brown, *U. S. Capitol*, I, plate 29.

[31] B. Latrobe to T. Jefferson, Aug. 31, 1805, Latrobe Papers, II.

[32] Prints and Photo Division, Library of Congress.

sured 30 feet across by 35 feet deep, that its height was 18 feet, and that it had two windows looking out to the west. The room was originally heated by a fireplace set in the corridor wall and perhaps also by one in the center of the south wall. Where the Bench was located has not been ascertained.

Here, in Committee Room 2, the Court sat from 1801 until 1808, and during at least part of that period the room was apparently shared by the District and Circuit Courts for the District of Columbia. We are told by Latrobe that even in 1808 the room was but half finished, and that it was "meanly furnished, very inconvenient."[33] Its proximity to the main staircase was manifestly a source of annoyance because, as Latrobe explained, it "[brought] the persons attending the Court in very inconvenient crowds close to the Senate chamber."[34]

In these bare and simple quarters, certainly modest by comparison with the courtroom occupied in Philadelphia, the Supreme Court convened for the first time in the city of Washington on Monday, February 2, 1801.[35] The only judge who is recorded as having been present was William Cushing. The Court *Minutes* state, "A sufficient number of Justices not being convened to constitute a quorum," the Court was adjourned until the next day at 11 o'clock.[36] Again, only Judge Cushing was present, and the Court was adjourned until February 4. On that cold and rainy morning,[37] three more were on hand—Samuel Chase, John Marshall, and Bushrod Washington. Marshall's commission, dated January 31, 1801, and signed by Samuel Dexter, executing the office of Secretary of State *pro hac vice*, was thereupon read in open court. After taking the oath of office prescribed by law, Marshall then took his seat upon the Bench.[38] Judge Paterson and Judge Moore apparently did not sit until the August term.[39]

---

[33] B. Latrobe to J. Madison, Sept. 8, 1809, Madison Papers, Manuscripts Division, Library of Congress.

[34] B. Latrobe to T. Jefferson, Sept. 2, 1807, Latrobe Papers, II.

[35] *Manuscript Minutes of the Supreme Court*, Feb. 2, 1801, National Archives, Washington (hereafter cited as *MS Minutes of the Supreme Court*). The furnishings of the Court brought from Philadelphia included records and a "large press" for books and papers. These were packaged and transported for the sum of $114. J. Steele to A. Gallatin, June 4, 1802, John Steele Papers, Folder 31, Southern Historical Collection, Chapel Hill, N. C.

For discussion and photographs of earlier locations of the Supreme Court in Philadelphia, see R. P. Reeder, "The First Homes of the Supreme Court of the United States," *Proceedings of the American Philosophical Society* LXXVI, 543–96 (1936).

[36] *MS Minutes of the Supreme Court*, Feb. 2, 1801.

[37] See Gouverneur Morris, "Diary," X, Feb. 4, 1801, Manuscripts Division, Library of Congress.

[38] *MS Minutes of the Supreme Court*, Feb. 4, 1801.

[39] See *ibid.*, Aug. 3, 1801. On February 2, Marshall wrote Paterson regretting that the latter "cannot attend this session of the supreme court and still more the cause that detains you." Paterson Papers, Bancroft Transcripts, 635, New York Public Library, New York City.

III: *The Court in Washington*

Save for the induction of the new Chief Justice, the accomplishments at the February term were few. Neither Marshall's appointment nor this session of the Court received virtually any notice in the newspapers.[40] Partly this absence of interest stemmed from the Court's lack of prestige at that time, and partly it resulted from the fact that the Court had not yet become embroiled in the factiousness of the political storms that were only beginning to brew. Moreover, at the beginning of the nineteenth century, its sessions did not attract public attention or excite admiration as did sessions of the Senate and House, where political figures and orators provided daily spectacles for the curious. Interest in the judges appears to have been chiefly confined to the Bar and to the litigants before them. The public at large had little understanding or appreciation of the judicial process or of intricate legal reasoning, and sessions of the Supreme Court did not afford the opportunities for gossip, drinking, and fighting that made attractive sessions of the State and lower federal courts. As Judge Story wrote a generation later,

> Questions of law rarely assume a cast, which introduces them to extensive, public notice; and those, which require the highest faculties of mind to master and expound them, are commonly so intricate, and remote from the ordinary pursuits of life, that the generality of readers do not bring to the examination of them the knowledge, necessary to comprehend them, or the curiosity, which imparts a relish and flavor to them.[41]

In any event, the accomplishments of the Court during its first session in Washington were in no way striking. On February 4 six men were admitted to practice as counselors,[42] and the Court then disposed

---

[40] The *Aurora*, February 3, 1801, merely noted that Marshall's nomination had been confirmed by the Senate. The leading Washington newspaper, the *National Intelligencer*, February 5, 1801, stated only that the Justices had "made a court," noting the presence of Marshall, Cushing, Chase, and Washington.

[41] J. Story, *The Miscellaneous Writings, Literary, Critical, Juridical, and Political of Joseph Story* (Boston, 1835), 195–96.

[42] They were Robert W. Peacock, Augustus B. Woodward, Philip Barton Key, John T. Mason, James A. Bayard, and A. Shaaf. *MS Minutes of the Supreme Court*, Feb. 4, 1801. The so-called *Attorney Rolls of the Supreme Court* (National Archives, Washington, 1955) is not reliable for the early years. The names are frequently not in the order of admission and the dates are often missing or inaccurate in the light of the *MS Minutes of the Supreme Court*—which appear to be accurate.

At this time a distinction was drawn between an "attorney" and a "counselor." See Rule II, promulgated Feb. 5, 1790, 1 Cranch xvi (1790), stating that for the admission of attorneys or counselors to practice in the Court, "they shall have been such for three years past in the supreme courts of the state to which they respectively belong. . . ." In August 1801, Rule XIV was adopted, ordering "that counsellors may be admitted as attorneys in this court on taking

83

of or continued three cases that had been docketed during the preceding summer.[43] Several distinguished members of the Philadelphia and Maryland Bars were present at this session,[44] and arguments were heard in *Course* v. *Stead's Exors.*[45] docketed in August 1800. An order thereon, reversing the Circuit Court for the District of Georgia, was entered the following week,[46] at which time five more cases were continued.[47] The Court adjourned for the term on February 10. The foregoing is illustrative of the type of proceedings of the Court in 1801 and the years that immediately followed. Sessions were generally short, partly because of the difficulties of travel, partly because the task of circuit-riding consumed such a large part of the judges' time and energies. When the Court was in session, cases of great constitutional import were unusual. Cases requiring interpretation of congressional legislation were almost equally rare in this period. Far more common were cases involving questions of pleading, jurisdiction, contract, insurance, bills and notes, land titles, and admiralty. With this summary of the kinds of cases that came before the Court, it is now in order to consider the judges who were members of the Court in 1801.

C. THE MEMBERS OF THE COURT IN 1801

There were at this time six judges on the Court. In order of appointment they were: William Cushing, of Massachusetts (1789); William Paterson, of New Jersey (1793); Samuel Chase, of Maryland (1796); Bushrod Washington, of Virginia (1798); Alfred Moore, of North Carolina (1799); and John Marshall, of Virginia (1801). All of

---

the usual oath." 1 Cranch xviii. See also rules of the First Circuit summarized in C. Warren, *A History of the American Bar* (Boston, 1966), 243.

[43] Talbot v. Seeman, 1 Cranch 1 (1801); Olmstead v. Clarkson (unreported); State of New York v. State of Connecticut (unreported). See *MS Minutes of the Supreme Court*, Feb. 4, 1801. Talbot v. Seeman, which was decided in August 1801, was apparently Marshall's first opinion and one in which he spoke for the entire Court.

[44] *MS Minutes of the Supreme Court*, Feb. 4, 1801. See also J. Bayard to R. Bassett, Feb. 6, 1801,

in E. Donnan, ed., "Papers of James A. Bayard, 1796–1815," *Annual Report of the American Historical Association for the Year 1913* (Washington, 1915), II, 123.

[45] Unreported case (decided in 1801).

[46] *MS Minutes of the Supreme Court*, Feb. 10, 1801.

[47] Telfair v. Stead's Executors, 2 Cranch 407 (1805); Williamson v. Kincaid (unreported); Greenleaf v. Banks (unreported); Wilson v. Mason, (decided in December 1801), 1 Cranch 45 (1801); United States v. The Schooner Peggy, 1 Cranch 103 (1801).

these men had fought or otherwise served their country in the Revolutionary period; all of them were prominent in the localities of their origins and had served the State or federal governments; and all of them were drawn from the governing class of public-spirited citizens, nurtured in the Federalism of President Washington. All were competent lawyers, and all, except Marshall, whose judicial career had barely begun, had proven to be competent judges. Of each of them except Marshall some account has already been given in the preceding Volume of this *History*, but it is nevertheless appropriate to say something here by way of recapitulation, in order to attempt an appraisal of their several personalities and their antecedent backgrounds, which had an inevitable bearing upon the work and accomplishments of the Court in the early Marshall Period. Even though the personalities, abilities, and differences of opinion of the associate judges tended to appear submerged after Marshall became Chief Justice, largely because of the abandonment of the practice of seriatim opinions and adoption of the custom whereby Marshall usually spoke for the Court, they did not become mere sounding-boards for their Chief. Not only those who were members of the Court in 1801, but others who were to succeed them—notably William Johnson and Joseph Story—were men of independence of thought with views of their own, views that appeared far more openly when they sat individually on circuit than when they sat as a united group in Washington. Their personal qualities, their backgrounds, and their contributions to the decision-making process of the Court should not be underestimated.

Before embarking on the brief appraisals that follow, it is appropriate to emphasize that, unlike the Justices of the Supreme Court today, those of the early 1800s had duties elsewhere than in Washington. They had the obligation of riding circuit and of holding court twice a year in the several districts into which the country was divided and to which they were respectively assigned. The circuit obligation proved to be their chief work at this time. It was not only onerous in that they were required to ride over vast stretches of the nation, usually on horseback and under difficult traveling conditions as noted in the preceding chapter, but it required them to spend a large part of every year on the road. Consequently, there was little opportunity to exchange ideas and communicate with one another face to face, except during the two annual sessions of the Supreme Court in Washington. On the other hand, during the early part of the nineteenth century, when the Court was in session, the judges nearly always occupied the same boarding-house, so that more intimacy for talk and consultation was possible, and more unity was fostered at such times than in later years when the judges ceased to live together.

* * *

In 1801 William Cushing was the oldest member of the Court and was already beginning to suffer from the infirmities of age.[48] Born on March 1, 1732, he was graduated from Harvard College in 1751, and, after a year of teaching, he studied law in Boston in the office of the well-known lawyer, Jeremiah Gridley. He was admitted to the Bar in 1755 and practiced law in Scituate until his appointment as register of deeds and judge of probate in the District of Maine. During these latter years he made professional appearances before the Massachusetts Superior Court at Falmouth, "where he was often associated in cases with John Adams, who traveled the Maine circuit."[49] In 1772 he succeeded his father as a judge of the Massachusetts Superior Court. Aside from his reputedly distinguished career on the judiciary and in public affairs in Massachusetts, little is known of his work on the Superior Court beyond the fact that he was noted for his accurate and extensive legal knowledge and for his competence in addressing juries, which was always favorably commented upon.

Cushing was described by a contemporary as "a sensible, modest man, well acquainted with law, but remarkable for the secrecy of his opinions."[50] Others spoke of the ceremoniousness of his deportment; he not only wore a three-cornered hat, smallclothes, and shoe buckles, but he appears to have been the last American judge to wear a full-bottomed English wig.[51] His manner is reported to have been benign and cheerful, affable and courteous in conversation. A Memoir among the Cushing Papers at the Massachusetts Historical Society refers to his general courteousness which lacked familiarity, and goes on to say of him that he was dignified without austerity and a patient listener who did not seek to elicit what in due course he might hear. In appearance he was of medium height, erect and slender, with a fair complexion, light blue eyes, and an aquiline nose.

It has been said of Cushing that nothing is more remarkable than the way in which, despite the high office he held, he was able to remain in the background during the struggles that preceded the Revolution.[52] It is possible that it was partly for that reason that when the Massa-

---

[48] The best biographical sketches of Judge Cushing are J. Dickinson, "William Cushing," *Dictionary of American Biography* (hereafter cited as *D.A.B.*) IV, 633; and A. P. Rugg, "William Cushing," *Yale Law Journal* XXX, 128 (1920). A comprehensive biography is in course of preparation by J. D. Cushing of the Massachusetts Historical Society.

[49] Dickinson, "William Cushing," 634.

[50] M. O. Warren, *History of the Rise, Progress and Termination of the American Revolution* (Boston, 1805), I, 118.

[51] Dickinson, "William Cushing," 635.

[52] *Ibid.*, 634. See also W. O'Brien, "Justice Cushing's Undelivered Speech on the Federal Constitution," *William and Mary Quarterly* XV, 74–92 (1958).

chusetts courts were reorganized in 1775, Cushing was the only one of the previous judges to be retained in the newly formed Supreme Judicial Court. In 1777 he became Chief Justice and held that position until 1789. During this period he did not desert public life but served as a member of the 1779 Convention which framed the first Constitution of Massachusetts, and he was vice-president of the State convention of 1788 which ratified the federal Constitution.

When the United States Supreme Court was organized, Cushing was the first associate judge to be appointed. At the time of Cushing's appointment, Christopher Gore had written to Rufus King without enthusiasm, saying that Cushing could not last long as an active member of the Court and that he had "new habits and new modes of legal decision to acquire."[53] His commission was dated September 1789, and he was present at the first Term of the Court, which was held in New York in February 1790. During Jay's absence in England in 1794 and 1795, he acted as Chief Justice and, on Jay's resignation in 1796, was in fact commissioned by President Washington to that position. After a week, however, he returned his commission on the ground of ill health.[54]

During the course of his twenty-one years on the Court, Cushing delivered opinions in nineteen cases, of which the most important is probably *Chisholm* v. *Georgia*.[55] Of these opinions, all of them brief, John Dickinson wrote that Cushing "concurred with the majority of the judges and did not add to their exposition of the law."[56] Probably by 1801 the brilliance of youth had somewhat abated. Senator Plumer, a few years earlier, had characterized him as having "once possessed abilities, firmness, & other qualities . . . but *time*, the enemy of man, has much impaired his mental faculties."[57] Yet a contemporary, who saw Cushing on the Bench in 1801, remarked how forcibly his youthful mind was affected by the order and perspicuity with which he performed the duties of his high office, and commented on the mild though commanding dignity with which he guided the Bar.[58] In all fairness, it must be said that although Cushing's intellectual qualities were not extraordinary, he was of all the judges a force in constitutional law. For several years before the Constitution was ratified he had occasion to interpret the Constitution of Massachusetts, which he had helped to frame, and until

---

[53] C. R. King, ed., *The Life and Correspondence of Rufus King* (New York, 1894–1900), I, 366.

[54] C. Warren, *Supreme Court*, I, 139–40.

[55] 2 Dall. 419 (1793). See also Ware v. Hylton, 3 Dall. 198 (1796); Calder v. Bull, 3 Dall. 386 (1798).

[56] Dickinson, "William Cushing," 634.

[57] W. Plumer to J. Smith, Feb. 19, 1796, William Plumer Papers, Letters 1781–1804, Manuscripts Division, Library of Congress.

[58] Quoted in H. Flanders, *The Lives and Times of the Chief Justices of the Supreme Court of the United States* (Philadelphia, 1858), II, 45.

Marshall's appointment he had met and decided questions of far-reaching importance under the federal Constitution. His mind was strong, though perhaps somewhat slow, and his legal attainments, according to Josiah Quincy, who often saw him in Court, "were of high rank. His judgment sound, his habits laborious, and devoted to the duties of his occupation and station."[59]

Cushing was a man of wide literary tastes, and he was also learned in and well acquainted with theology and current controversies related thereto. He seems, however, to have been unaspiring either in literary or political distinction. Though a strong-minded Federalist, and a friend of such men as George Washington and John Adams, he took no active part in politics, with the result that his habits of life were retired. He nearly always took his wife with him, even on circuit, when he rode in a four-wheeled phaeton, drawn by a pair of horses, and equipped with ingenious contrivances for carrying books and choice groceries. The baggage followed behind in a one-horse vehicle. It is said that Mrs. Cushing generally read aloud to him while they traveled.[60] With strong family attachments, even though he had no children, "he sought his happiness in domestic life; desirous rather to be useful than to be known."[61]

William Paterson had come to the Court in 1793 with a distinguished political and legal career in his native State behind him.[62] Born in Northern Ireland on December 24, 1745, he was now fifty-five years old. He had come to America at an early age and was graduated from the College of New Jersey at Princeton in 1763, where he was known to be popular with students; his friends included such well-known persons as Benjamin Rush, David Caldwell, and Jonathan Sergeant. Paterson had then studied law under Richard Stockton, and had become a member of the New Jersey Bar in 1769. He had served his native

---

[59] *Ibid.*, 51.
[60] *Ibid.*, 38.
[61] *Ibid.*, 51.
[62] For studies and biographies of Paterson, see J. Boyd, "William Paterson, Forerunner of John Marshall," in *The Lives of Eighteen from Princeton*, ed. W. Thorp (Princeton, 1946); W. S. Carpenter, "William Paterson," *D. A. B.* XIV, 293; L. B. Rosenberg, "William Paterson: New Jersey's Nation-Maker," *New Jersey History* LXXXV, 8 (1967) and sources cited therein; C. A. Shiner, *William Paterson* (Paterson, New Jersey, 1940); G. S. Wood, *William Paterson of New Jersey* (Fair Lawn, New Jersey, 1933). See also R. C. Hackett, "William Paterson, Counsellor-at-Law" (Ph.D. diss., Princeton University, 1952).

Mr. Hackett has commented on the unreliability of W. J. Mills, *Glimpses of Colonial Society and the Life at Princeton College, 1766–1773* (Philadelphia, 1903), a source frequently used by scholars in connection with Paterson's career. See R. C. Hackett, "Princeton Before the Revolution: Notes on a Source," *William and Mary Quarterly* VI, 90 (1949).

State as a member of the Provincial Congress, of the convention that formed the State constitution, and of the Legislative Council of the State. Elected attorney-general in 1776, he continued to serve in that capacity until the end of the Revolutionary War in 1783, when he resumed the practice of law. In his practice Paterson became principally concerned with championing the causes of well-to-do creditors who had extensive mercantile interests. Although chosen as a delegate to the Continental Congress in 1780, he declined the position because he felt the weight of his duties and had "more than once been ready to sink under it."[63]

Paterson played an important part as delegate to the Federal Convention in 1787,[64] where he advocated the creation of a strong and truly federal central government but recognized the vital importance of striking a balance between the demands for national union and a federation of sovereign States. Although the so-called New Jersey Plan, which he introduced (and which, incidentally, provided for a Supreme Tribunal to hear appeals from the State courts), was not adopted, he was sufficiently satisfied with the final version of the Constitution to be one of its signers. Later, in 1788, he was elected United States Senator from New Jersey and was appointed to the Senate committee to report a judiciary bill.[65] It is of more than passing interest to note that the first nine sections of the original copy of the Judiciary Act of 1789 are in Paterson's handwriting, with most of the remainder in the hand of the future Chief Justice of the Supreme Court, Oliver Ellsworth.[66] In 1790 Paterson was appointed Governor of New Jersey. During his tenure of office, which ended in 1792, he was authorized to collect all the English statutes in force in New Jersey prior to the Revolution, as well as all public acts prior and subsequent thereto that were still in force.[67] This work, finally published in 1800 as the *Laws of the State of New Jersey*, together with a remodeled code of the rules of practice and procedure in the common law and chancery courts, adopted by act of the State legislature, was largely accomplished while Paterson was an associate judge of the Supreme Court, and during a period when he was also spending a major part of his time in the onerous duty of circuit riding.

Paterson was appointed to the Supreme Court to succeed Thomas

---

[63] Quoted in Carpenter, "William Paterson," 293.

[64] See, e.g., M. Farrand, ed., *The Records of the Federal Convention of 1787* (New Haven, 1911–37), I, 176–79 (hereafter cited as Farrand, *1787 Federal Convention*); and a detailed discussion in Wood, *William Paterson*, 59–85.

[65] For a discussion of this period of Paterson's career, see Wood, *William Paterson*, 91–115.

[66] Carpenter, "William Paterson," 294.

[67] *Ibid.* See also E. Q. Keasbey, *The Courts and Lawyers of New Jersey, 1661–1912* (New York, 1912), II, 317.

Johnson of Maryland, who resigned early in 1793. His portrait by Sharples[68] reveals an alert intelligence, with fine eyes in a well-proportioned head. At the time of the Federal Convention, one of his colleagues, William Pierce, had said of Paterson that he was one of those men "whose powers break in upon you, and create wonder and astonishment. He is a Man of great modesty, with looks that bespeak talents of no great extent, but he is a Classic, a Lawyer, and an Orator; and of a disposition so favorable to his advancement that every one seemed ready to exalt him with their praises."[69] His distinction as a judge is attested by the high regard in which he was held not only by the Bar of New Jersey and the federal Bar but by those in the Senate who bent every effort to have him appointed Chief Justice of the Court instead of Marshall—an office that he repeatedly declared he would not accept.

As a judge, Paterson openly espoused, as did so many of his brethren on the Court, Federalist objectives in several of his opinions, particularly those aimed at increasing the power and prestige of the federal judiciary. In *Van Horne's Lessee* v. *Dorrance*,[70] for example, eight years before *Marbury* v. *Madison*, he clearly enunciated the doctrine of judicial review in his charge to the jury. His independence of mind and his courage are illustrated by the trials of Smith and Ogden,[71] in the early summer of 1806. Smith and Ogden were accused of aiding the Spanish adventurer Miranda in his attack on Caracas, Venezuela. Upon the defendants' affidavits that the testimony of the Secretaries of State, War, and Navy was necessary to their defense, the latter were called to appear in court. They refused on the ground that they had been informed by the President that their official duties could not at the time be dispensed with. After a three-day argument on a motion for an attachment to bring the Secretaries and their clerks into court, Paterson and Mattias B. Talmadge—a Jeffersonian appointee and the other judge assigned to the case—disagreed. Paterson was "of opinion, that the absent witnesses should be laid under a rule to show cause, why an attachment should not be issued against them."[72] Talmadge held otherwise. The obvious political aspects of the case, and the defiant refusal of the Cabinet officers to obey the summons of the court, together with Talmadge's disagreement, so disgusted Paterson that he immediately left the bench under plea of ill health.

In fact, Paterson had been suffering from ill health ever since he

---

[68] Reproduced in Wood, *William Paterson* (frontispiece).

[69] Farrand, *1787 Federal Convention*, III, 90.

[70] 2 Dall. 304 (C.C.D. Pa. 1795). See comment of J. Boyd, "William Paterson," 15–16.

[71] 27 F. Cas. 1186, 1192, 1233, 1246 (C.C.D. N.Y. 1806) (Nos. 16,341a, 16,342, 16,342a, 16,342b).

[72] Beveridge, *John Marshall*, III, 436, note 1.

received serious injuries early in 1804, when his carriage overturned.[73] Moreover, he was worn out by overwork and by the exhaustion of riding hundreds of miles on horseback under adverse seasonal conditions and through very rough country. He died in September of the same year. In the sermon preached at his funeral, his former pastor commented that "he possessed from nature a strong comprehensive understanding; a clear, distinguishing judgment; an elevated imagination and the power of commanding eloquence."[74]

Samuel Chase had been on the Court since 1796 and had almost reached his sixtieth birthday. Born in Maryland on April 17, 1741, his early education—chiefly in the classics—had been under his father. He studied law in the offices of Hammond and Hall in Annapolis and was admitted to practice in various Maryland courts between 1761 and 1763. In the following year he was elected to the State Assembly, a position he retained until 1784. From the outset of his membership in the Maryland Assembly, Chase engaged in riotous demonstrations against the Stamp Act, and the violence of his activities resulted in his denunciation by the local government of Annapolis as a "busy, restless incendiary, a ringleader of mobs, a foul mouthed and inflaming son of discord and faction, a common disturber of the public tranquility, and a promoter of the lawless excesses of the multitude."[75] In reply, Chase called his critics men who "sulked in . . . houses, asserting the parliamentary right and esteeming the Stamp act a beneficial law."[76] Later, as a member of both the Continental Congress and the Maryland Committee of Correspondence, he urged, at the outbreak of the Revolution, a total embargo upon trade with Great Britain, with the idea in mind that such a measure would bring that country to its knees. He opposed the suggestion of an American Navy as the "maddest idea in the world."[77]

These and similar activities would seem to justify Professor Corwin's characterization of Chase as "a born leader of insurrection."[78] Certainly he was a person of strong passions and prejudices. A man of violent opinions, overbearing manners, and fierce temper, he made enemies rapidly and easily, and he was always a center of controversy, in law as in politics. Indeed, a partisan verse of the period ended in the couplet

---

[73] See chapter 1, supra.
[74] Quoted in Wood, *William Paterson*, 197.
[75] R. T. Conrad, ed., *Sanderson's Biographies of the Signers of the Declaration of Independence* (Philadelphia, 1865), 580, 583.

[76] *Ibid.*, 583.
[77] E. S. Corwin, "Samuel Chase," *D.A.B.* IV, 34, 35. Chase later took the position that an American Navy was desirable.
[78] *Ibid.*

Cursed of thy Father, scum of all that's base
Thy sight is odious and thy name is [Chase].[79]

He had apparently been somewhat implicated with others in an attempt to corner the market on flour, on the basis of information gained in Congress, in order to raise its price for sale to the approaching French fleet.[80] Probably, Chase's activities in this respect were greatly exaggerated by his enemies[81] in order to discredit him, and his reputation "fell suddenly into shadow" towards the end of 1778.[82]

Nevertheless, there were constructive aspects to his career in this period, for, as a Maryland delegate, Chase served on twenty-one Congressional committees in 1777, and on thirty in 1778.[83] His law practice, according to Warren, established him as "one of the ablest lawyers of the State."[84] Moreover, in 1783 Chase's career brightened with his appointment to an official mission to England.[85] Three years later he moved to Baltimore, where shortly afterwards he was appointed chief judge of the Maryland General Court. In consequence of his accumulation of offices, however, Chase was later threatened by the Assembly with removal, on constitutional grounds, by a motion that failed to pass for lack of the required two-thirds majority vote.[86]

Chase had campaigned against the unconditional ratification of the United States Constitution and had been one of the eleven at the Convention to vote against it in 1788. In consequence of these and other activities, he became known as the leader of the anti-Federalists in Maryland. However, his politics were soon to change, and in 1789 he wrote to President Washington to assure him of his support, while at the same time requesting consideration for judicial appointment.[87] Professor Corwin states that "why Chase turned Federalist is something of a mystery, especially in view of his strong anti-British prejudice which he voiced as late as 1793."[88] It may be suggested, however, that Chase's opposition to the Constitution in 1787 and 1788 might have been linked to the popular opposition to ratification of the Constitution

[79] J. M. Smith, *Freedom's Fetters: The Alien and Sedition Laws and American Civil Liberties* (Ithaca, 1956), 357 (quoting the *Aurora*).

[80] Corwin, "Samuel Chase," 35. See also H. C. Lodge, ed., *The Works of Alexander Hamilton* (New York, 1904), I, 204.

[81] C. Warren, *Supreme Court*, I, 125.

[82] Corwin, "Samuel Chase," 35.

[83] *Ibid.*

[84] C. Warren, *Supreme Court*, I, 125.

[85] According to Senator Plumer, Chase was said to have received $27,000 for undertaking this mission. Plumer to J. Smith, Dec. 6, 1804, William Plumer Papers, Letters 1804–1807, Manuscripts Division, Library of Congress.

[86] Corwin, "Samuel Chase," 35.

[87] S. Chase to G. Washington, Sept. 3, 1789, Gratz Collection, Case 1, Box 19, Historical Society of Pennsylvania, Philadelphia.

[88] Corwin, "Samuel Chase," 36.

which Madison believed was based on the omission of guarantees subsequently incorporated in the Bill of Rights.[89] At any rate, in a letter to President Washington dated June 4, 1795, James McHenry, a Maryland Federalist, recommended Chase for federal office, praising his "general conduct since the adoption of our government." He went on to say,

> You know that his services and abilities were of much use to the cause . . . [during the Revolutionary period], sometimes by the measures he proposed or had influence to get adopted, and sometimes to the steady opposition he gave to the intrigues raised against yourself. . . . Sir, after having weighed all these circumstances since our conversation respecting him, after having reflected upon the good he has done and the good that he may still do; after having debated within myself whether his political or other errors (which exist no longer) have been of such a cast and magnitude as to be a perpetual bar to his holding any office under the United States, . . . I have thought it a duty to mention him as a subject of consideration for present or future attention. . . . I need not tell you that, to his professional knowledge, he subjoins a very valuable stock of political science and information, but it may be proper to observe that he has discharged the office which he fills without the shadow of imputation upon the integrity of his decisions.[90]

Apparently Washington was at first inclined to appoint Chase as Attorney-General, but on January 26, 1796, he nominated him to the Supreme Court, and the nomination was unanimously approved the next day. McHenry wrote to Washington that Chase was "extremely pleased with his appointment" and had expressly asked to have the President informed that the latter "shall never have reason to regret the nomination."[91]

From contemporary comments, it appears that Chase joined a Court which was none too enthusiastic to receive him. For example, Judge Iredell wrote that he had no personal acquaintance with the new judge, "but [was] not impressed with a very favorable opinion of his moral character, whatever his professional abilities may be."[92] Nevertheless, and despite the doubts of some as to the wisdom of the appointment, Chase's performance on the Court has been described as "the most notable of any previous to Marshall."[93] Because his was the latest

---

[89] E. L. Barrett, P. W. Bruton, J. Honnold, *Constitutional Law* (Brooklyn, 1963), 577, note 13.

[90] Quoted in C. Warren, *Supreme Court*, I, 125–26. See also *ibid.*, 126–27, note 1, with respect to an application made by Chase to Washington

in 1794 and an earlier one referred to in note 87 supra.

[91] Quoted in C. Warren, *Supreme Court*, I, 143.

[92] Quoted in *ibid.*, 143–44.

[93] Corwin, "Samuel Chase," 36.

appointment, he gave his opinion first. "This accident of position, together with the colorful quality of his judicial utterances, their positiveness of expression, their richness in 'political science' have all contributed to give his opinions predominant importance in this period."[94] His most significant decisions prior to Marshall's taking office are listed and briefly appraised by Professor Corwin.[95] Probably one of the most important of his decisions was delivered on circuit in *United States* v. *Worrall*,[96] a case involving an indictment for attempting to bribe a United States officer. In *Worrall*, contrary to the position previously taken by other judges,[97] Chase held that the courts of the United States had no jurisdiction over crimes at common law.[98] The opposing view was that "crime" must be punished, and, if Congress failed or refused to act, it was the duty of the courts to act without the authority of statute. Chase's position was later accepted by the Supreme Court in *United States* v. *Hudson and Goodwin* in 1812.[99]

Although Chase's role on the Court was to become a subordinate one after Marshall's appointment as Chief Justice, his subsequent career on the Bench continued to attest to his legal capacities, his ability, and his industry. John Marshall spoke of his strong mind and great legal knowledge. A lengthy letter written to Marshall in the winter of 1802 anent the constitutionality of the repeal of the 1801 Act is remarkable for its clarity and for its careful and perspicuous reasoning.[100] In 1804, referring to Chase's earlier conduct on circuit at the trial of John Fries,[101] Judge Richard Peters wrote to Timothy Pickering that "Mr. Chase (a few tangents excepted) . . . conducted himself to general satisfaction. His talents are indubitable."[102] In the face of such opinions, Judge Johnson's statement to Jefferson in 1822 that "Chase could not be got to think or write"[103] must be viewed as partisan.

---

[94] *Ibid.*
[95] *Ibid.*
[96] 2 Dall. 384 (1798).
[97] Warren states that Chief Justices Jay and Ellsworth and Judges Cushing, Iredell, and Wilson had all sustained indictments at common law in the United States courts. C. Warren, *Supreme Court*, I, 159, note 1.
[98] 2 Dall. at 394.
[99] 7 Cranch 32 at 32–34 (1812), per Johnson, J.:
> Although this question is brought up now, for the first time, to be decided by this court, we consider it as having been long since settled in public opinion . . . The legislative authority of the Union must first make an act a crime, affix a punishment to it, and declare the

court that shall have jurisdiction of the offence.
[100] S. Chase to J. Marshall, Feb. 24, 1802, Miscellaneous Manuscripts Marshall, New York Historical Society, New York City, reprinted in chapter 5 infra, note 182 (reference courtesy of the New York Historical Society).
[101] See text accompanying notes 101–108 infra.
[102] R. Peters to T. Pickering, Jan. 25, 1804, Pickering Manuscripts, XXVII, 44, Massachusetts Historical Society, Boston (reference courtesy of the Massachusetts Historical Society).
[103] W. Johnson to T. Jefferson, Dec. 10, 1822, Jefferson Papers, Manuscripts Division, Library of Congress.

III: *The Court in Washington*

Chase's decisions on circuit were seldom reversed, but his conduct in a number of trials was far from exemplary. Although several of the national, and even State judges, used the Bench as a political rostrum from which to lecture grand juries on religion and partisan politics,[104] it was Chase, in his zeal to enforce the Sedition Act of 1798, who earned himself the reputation of a Jeffreys, particularly in Republican circles. His overbearing manner, his immoderate language, and his tone of voice in speaking to counsel were especially evident in the sedition trials of Thomas Cooper,[105] John Fries,[106] and James Callender[107] in 1800. In the latter case he had been particularly arrogant and offensive in his constant interruptions of defendant's counsel. When, for example, William Wirt was addressing the jury, Chase ordered him to sit down, and ultimately so affronted Wirt's dignity that he abandoned the case.[108] Likewise, when George Hay (later to be the prosecutor in the Burr trial) was addressing the jury, Chase told him his statements of the law were incorrect, with the result that Hay folded his papers and refused to proceed; later, he became so indignant that he stalked from the room.[109]

"All over the country," says Beveridge, "men were being indicted and convicted for wholly justifiable political criticisms,—some of them trivial and even amusing,—as well as for false and slanderous attacks on public officers."[110] Because in the enforcement of the Sedition Act political opposition was frequently confused with sedition, there was a growing conviction among the people that it was no longer safe to criticize the government or its officers, and this popular feeling was intensified by the alarm of the Bar.[111] The attention that Chase had attracted to himself by the open political character of his conduct on the Bench when on circuit was to become a major ground for the impeachment proceedings later brought against him.[112]

At his prime, Chase was a man of imposing aspect. His face was

---

[104] Beveridge, *John Marshall*, III, 30, note 1.

[105] F. Wharton, *State Trials of the United States During the Administrations of Washington and Adams* (Philadelphia, 1849), 659–81.

[106] *Ibid.*, 610–48.

[107] *Ibid.*, 688–721. For discussion of the Cooper and Callender trials see also Smith, *Freedom's Fetters*, 307–59.

[108] Wharton, *State Trials*, 709–10. Judge Chase sarcastically called Wirt "the young gentleman," which amused the audience but so upset Wirt that

he gave up then and there. Beveridge, *John Marshall*, III, 40.

[109] Wharton, *State Trials*, 712; Beveridge, *John Marshall*, III, 40.

[110] Beveridge, *John Marshall*, II, 420–21. For a sampling of these cases see Wharton, *State Trials*.

[111] "But not only all Virginia, but the profession throughout the country, was stung to the quick." In Philadelphia, for a long time, "counsel declined to appear before the Judge who had thus violated, as they alleged, the decorum of his office." Wharton, *State Trials*, 719, note.

[112] See chapter 7 infra.

broad and of a brownish-red color that had earned him the sobriquet of "bacon-face." Over six feet in height, with a massive head, broad brow, and thick white hair, he presented an almost majestic appearance. The Reverend Manasseh Cutler said Chase was one of the largest men he had ever seen. His manners, as indicated above, were frequently coarse, and his speech often intemperate, peremptory, and ungracious, so that the impression he gave could be harsh and formidable. In 1807 Story compared him to Lord Thurlow, "bold, impetuous, overbearing, and decisive."[113] Yet elsewhere in the same letter, noting that Chase had counted nearly seventy winters, Story wrote that "he possesses considerable vigor and vivacity; but the flashes are irregular and sometimes ill-directed."[114] Story, who eventually became another admirer, wrote that

> he abounds with good humor [and] amuses you extremely by his anecdotes and pleasantry. His first approach is formidable, but all difficulty vanishes when you once understand him. In person, in manners, in unwieldy strength, in severity of reproof, in real tenderness of heart; and above all in intellect, he is the living, I had almost said the exact, image of Samuel Johnson. . . . I like him hugely.[115]

There can be little doubt as to the sincerity of such statements, but as Professor Corwin concisely concludes his article on Chase, "His intellectual grasp is fully attested by his judicial opinions; his turbulent disposition appears at every turn of his career."[116]

Bushrod Washington, nephew of President Washington, was thirty-eight years of age when the Court first convened in Washington.[117] Born in Westmoreland County, Virginia, on June 5, 1762, he was graduated from the College of William and Mary in 1778, served in the Continental Army, and after the Revolutionary War studied law in Philadelphia in the office of James Wilson. After being admitted to the Virginia Bar, he began the practice of law in Alexandria, where, thoroughly grounded as he was in the common law, he not only became a successful equity lawyer, but, in the opinion of Horace Binney, became the most accomplished *nisi prius* judge he had ever known or

---

[113] W. W. Story, ed., *Life and Letters of Joseph Story* (Boston, 1851), I, 154.

[114] *Ibid.*

[115] W. Story, *Joseph Story*, I, 167–68.

[116] Corwin, "Samuel Chase," 37. The sharpness of Chase's intellect and the quickness of his mind are illustrated by the exchanges between him and counsel in the trial of James Callender. See, e.g., J. Wood, *The Suppressed History of the Administration of John Adams* (Philadelphia, 1846), 277–78.

[117] See generally, G. W. Goble, "Bushrod Washington," *D.A.B.* XIX, 508.

could imagine.[118] In 1787 Washington was elected to the Virginia House of Delegates and later to the Virginia State Convention, where he supported the ratification of the federal Constitution.

When James Wilson's death created a vacancy on the Court, President Adams offered the position to Washington on the recommendation of Attorney-General Lee, after John Marshall had refused to accept it; Washington's appointment was confirmed and his commission sent to him on December 20, 1798.[119] He served on the Court with increasing distinction and reputation for a period of thirty-one years, until his death in 1829.

Although apparently uninterested in, as well as unfamiliar with, general literature and the arts, he was devoted and painstaking in his study of the law. Characterized as mild and conciliatory, he was nevertheless prompt and firm in decision. His calmness and courage are apparent in his actions and speech in the trial of General Bright for resisting the laws of the United States—a case that aroused great public excitement at the time.[120] Sitting as a circuit judge in Philadelphia in 1809, he fearlessly sentenced the General to fine and imprisonment despite the threat of a general rebellion in Pennsylvania if he did so.[121] Horace Binney, whose acquaintance with Washington began in 1799, referred to his powers of attention, his quickness and accuracy of apprehension, his power of logical argument, and his precise and expressive language.[122] Yet, despite his thoroughness of reasoning and clarity of thought, Professor Goble states that he was slow of mind.[123] Nevertheless, in the course of his three decades on the Court, "he rendered a number of opinions influential in the development of American law not only upon Constitutional matters where he saw eye-to-eye with Marshall, but also upon admiralty, commercial and other subjects."[124] Of these opinions the most notable in the period covered by this Volume was probably *Marine Insurance Co.* v. *Tucker*,[125] involving the legal effect on an insurance policy of altering a voyage. In 1808 Joseph Story said of Washington "[n]othing about him indicates greatness; he converses with simplicity and frankness. But he is highly esteemed as a profound lawyer, and I believe not without reason. His

---

[118] H. Binney, *Bushrod Washington* (Philadelphia, 1858), 12.

[119] His commission was first sent to him on October 6, but a recommission was sent to him after the Senate reconvened on December 20, 1798. Goble, "Bushrod Washington," 508.

[120] See chapter 10 infra, pp. 329–31.

[121] C. Warren, *Supreme Court*, I, 385–86.

[122] Binney, *Bushrod Washington*, 12, 16.

[123] Goble, "Bushrod Washington," 509.

[124] *Ibid.*

[125] 3 Cranch 357, 387 (1806).

written opinions are composed with ability, and on the bench he exhibits great promptitude and firmness in decision. It requires intimacy to value him as he deserves."[126]

Much of Bushrod Washington's contribution to the development of American law and the power of the Court is undoubtedly attributable to the appointment of, and his association with, such able judges as Marshall, Story, William Johnson, and others. At the time of his appointment in 1798, the Court was not regarded as an institution of great importance in the federal system, and the performance of Judge Chase as a member of the Court was probably the most publicized of any of the judges since the Court had been established. Yet, beginning with the appointment of Washington and the series of distinguished judges who were later to join him on the Court, that tribunal took on new dimensions in terms of its role in the governmental system and in the development of American law.

It can scarcely be doubted that, despite a few years' difference in age, the close friendship that existed between Marshall and Washington was a highly important factor in the formulation of constitutional theory and interpretation during the difficult yet formative period in the history of the United States. The two men had known each other at the College of William and Mary, and both were initiated into the Phi Beta Kappa Society in May 1780.[127] Both were elected in 1787 to the Virginia House of Delegates, and both served as members of the Virginia Convention for the ratification of the Constitution. In the practice of law, Marshall and Washington frequently argued against each other before the Court of Appeals in Richmond.

> Each had adequate opportunity to come fully to know and to appreciate the virtues and talents of the other. . . . While Marshall's practice appears to have been more active, . . . Washington's interest in the law seems to have tended toward the reflective and scholarly, for his detailed notes were published toward the end of his Virginia career. . . .[128]

According to Timothy Pickering, it was Washington's "indefatigable pursuit of knowledge and the business of his profession" that deprived him of the sight of one eye.[129] Later, in September of 1798, Marshall and Washington were both invited to Mount Vernon, and during a visit of several days they discussed the impending congressional elections with General Washington. Martin Van Buren relates that both

---

[126] W. Story, *Joseph Story*, I, 167.
[127] See L. B. Custer, "Bushrod Washington and John Marshall: A Preliminary Inquiry," *American Journal of Legal History* IV, 36, note 11 (1960) (hereafter cited as Custer, "B. Washington and J. Marshall").
[128] *Ibid.,* 40.
[129] Quoted in C. Warren, *Supreme Court,* I, 154.

lawyers were reluctant to accede to the request that had been made of them to run for office, but after the General had listened to his nephew's objections, he answered gravely and emphatically, "Bushrod, it must be done!"[130] Although the General's nephew then agreed to run for the Sixth Congress, Marshall consented only after being implored by the former President to consider the crises in national affairs that made it his duty to forego private and family concerns in favor of the public interest.[131] As events were to turn out, Washington was appointed to the Court, and Marshall succeeded in being elected to Congress.

When Marshall was appointed Chief Justice, the friendship between him and Washington grew closer, and William Johnson, who joined the Court in 1804, remarked to Jefferson in 1822 that the two men were "commonly estimated as one judge."[132] Mr. Lawrence Custer seems to have appraised the situation correctly in his statement that it was perhaps "because of their political leanings and because of their relationship both on and off the bench, [that] the two Justices from Virginia differed in opinion only three times during their twenty-nine years on the Supreme Court. . . ."[133]

Other circumstances further tended to draw the two men together —Marshall's biography of President Washington, which the latter's nephew Bushrod supervised, and similar family circumstances, for each had an invalid wife. Both shared the concern of many men of that day about the increasing number of freed slaves, with the result that both became members of the American Colonization Society, which was engaged in attempts to repatriate former slaves to Africa and whose activities resulted in the establishment of Liberia.[134]

It is one of the curious facts of history that few letters of importance exchanged by such close friends and associates as were Washington and Marshall appear to have survived,[135] although numerous letters relating to personal and judicial matters were exchanged between Marshall and Story and Story and Washington.[136] In the face of facts

---

[130] J. C. Fitzpatrick, ed., "The Autobiography of Martin Van Buren," *Annual Report of the American Historical Association for the Year 1918* (Washington, 1920), II, 178.

[131] Beveridge, *John Marshall*, II, 376–77. See also Marshall's account of this conference in a letter to J. K. Paulding, Miscellaneous Marshall Papers. Manuscripts Division, Library of Congress.

[132] W. Johnson to T. Jefferson, Dec. 10, 1822, Jefferson Papers, Manuscripts Division, Library of Congress.

[133] Custer, "B. Washington and J. Marshall," 43.

[134] In addition to Goble, "Bushrod Washington," 509, see an undated letter in the Bushrod Washington Papers, Washington State Historical Society, a copy of which I have examined through the courtesy of Senator Washington of that State's legislature.

[135] Searches in, and inquiries made of, numerous historical societies throughout the country have yielded little.

[136] See chapter 5 infra.

now known it must be supposed, as has Mr. Custer, "that important letters were destroyed by Washington and Marshall during their lives or by other persons after their deaths."[137]

In personal appearance, Washington is described as short in stature and boyish in appearance. Usually he was negligently dressed. Already, as stated, his sight was impaired by the excessive use of his eyes,[138] but a contemporary portrait reveals a handsome, if somewhat pointed, face, with the deep-set eyes and the firm, thin-lipped mouth of his uncle. Somewhat later, in 1815, George Ticknor of Boston described him as "a little, sharp-faced gentleman, with only one eye, and a profusion of snuff distributed over his face."[139] Martin Van Buren spoke of the vivacity of Washington's disposition and of the "simplicity and frankness of his manners" which "made his society peculiarly agreeable."[140] In 1824 a newspaper correspondent who attended the argument in *Gibbons* v. *Ogden* said of him that he then had "a sallow countenance, not very strongly marked, but deeply furrowed by the hand of time and bearing the marks of infirm health. He wears his dark, unfrosted hair, long and combed back from his forehead."[141]

When Judge Washington died in 1829 Story said of him,

> Few men have left deeper traces, in their judicial career, of everything which a conscientious judge ought to propose for his ambition, or his virtue, or his glory. His mind was solid, rather than brilliant; sagacious and searching, rather than quick or eager; slow but not torpid; steady, but not unyielding; comprehensive, and at the same time cautious; patient in inquiry, forcible in conception, clear in reasoning. . . . He was a learned judge. . . . He read to learn, and not to quote; to digest and master, and not merely to display. He was not easily satisfied. If he was not as profound as some, he was more exact than most men. But the value of his learning was, that it was the keystone of all his judgments. He indulged not the rash desire to fashion the law to his own views; but to follow out its precepts with a sincere good faith and simplicity. . . . He was a real lover of the Constitution . . . a good old-fashioned federalist, of the school of the days of Washington. He never lost his confidence in the political principles which he first embraced. He was always distinguished for moderation, in the days of their prosperity, and for fidelity to them, in the days of their adversity.[142]

* * *

---

[137] Custer, "B. Washington and J. Marshall," 46.

[138] See text accompanying note 129 supra.

[139] Quoted in C. Warren, *Supreme Court*, I, 466.

[140] Fitzpatrick, "Autobiography of Martin Van Buren," 177.

[141] Quoted in C. Warren, *Supreme Court*, I, 467.

[142] W. Story, *Joseph Story*, II, 30–32.

Alfred Moore, a native of North Carolina, was forty-five in 1801 and had been a member of the Court for just over a year. Descended from an ancient Irish family, he was born on May 21, 1755, educated in Boston. Moore later studied some law under his father; but he seems to have acquired most of his legal learning on his own.[143] He served as an officer in the Revolutionary War and, becoming a prominent Federalist, served in the State senate, as Attorney-General, and finally as a judge of the Superior Court of North Carolina.[144] His career as a lawyer was brilliant, equalled only by that of his contemporary, William R. Davie. Moore is spoken of as possessing a mind of uncommon strength, together with quickness of perception and great power in analysis. "A keen sense of humor, a brilliant wit, a biting tongue, a masterful logic, made him an adversary at the bar to be feared."[145] His language was always clear and concise, and his success as an advocate was complemented by his profound knowledge of the criminal law. These qualities naturally made a deep impression on his contemporaries. "No one ever doubted his learning and penetration; or that, while he enforced the law with an enlightened vigilance and untiring zeal, his energy was seasoned with humanity. . . ."[146] A contemporary, Judge A. D. Murphey, described Moore's quick perceptions and a judgment that was almost intuitive. His manner of speech was animated, and he spoke with ease and with force enlivened with flashes of wit.[147] It was undoubtedly mainly recognition of Moore's eminence at the Bar and his professional abilities that led President Adams to appoint him to the Court in December 1799, to succeed Judge Iredell. He is reported to have delivered an opinion in only one case while on the Court, that of *Bas v. Tingy*[148] in 1800, holding that a state of limited war existed with France.[149]

In appearance, Judge Moore was described as being so small in stature that at first glance he seemed only a child, for his height was about four feet five inches, and he was proportionately slender. "Probably he weighted about 80 or 90 pounds. His head was large for his body, after the manner of dwarfs, and his face . . . was fine-featured, good-humored and dark-eyed."[150] An historical address to the Bar and

---

[143] This information was supplied through the courtesy of Judge Francis O. Clarkson, of the Superior Court of North Carolina, from an undated newspaper article in the *Raleigh News and Observer*.

[144] See generally A. R. Newsome, "Alfred Moore," *D.A.B.* XIII, 112. Also, an obituary article in the *Wilmington Gazette*, of which a copy may be found, indexed under Moore, in the State Department of Archives and History, Raleigh, N. C.

[145] J. Davis, "Alfred Moore and James Iredell, Revolutionary Patriots and Associate Justices of the Supreme Court of the United States," 124 N.C. Rep. 877, 887 (1899).

[146] *Ibid.*, 889.

[147] See obituary, note 144 supra.

[148] 4 Dall. 37 (1800).

[149] *Ibid.*, 38–39.

[150] See obituary, note 144 supra.

Supreme Court of North Carolina published in the North Carolina Reports speaks of his neatness of dress, his gracefulness in manner, his dark, singularly piercing eye, and his clear sonorous voice.[151] Moore was to resign from the Court for reasons of ill health at the end of the 1804 term, and he died on October 15, 1810.

D. CHIEF JUSTICE MARSHALL

By the time of his appointment as Chief Justice in 1801, John Marshall was recognized as one of the leading citizens of the United States.[152] Born in Fauquier County, Virginia, on September 24, 1755, he was now forty-five years of age. His career had included distinguished service as an officer in the Army, a leader of the Virginia Bar, a diplomat, a statesman, and a public servant.

During the Revolution, Marshall had commanded a company of the Continental Line. He had fought in the battles of Brandywine, Germantown, and Monmouth, and had served under Washington at Valley Forge. From Washington, Marshall acquired a strong sense of nationalism and respect for discipline and authority; Washington's influence had more than once drawn Marshall from private and professional life into the broad area of national affairs.

In the difficult months after the War, Marshall had acted as an advocate of national unity through an efficient federal government. He had been a loyal supporter of Washington and Madison in a time of intense popular debate concerning the proper balance of nationalism and States' rights. His had been an impressive voice in favor of national authority and the power of the judicial branch, and he had helped stem the tide of public prejudice against those views in the Virginia convention. After notable service in the Virginia legislature, he had gone to Congress at Washington's urging.

Marshall had vigorously defended the power of the executive to negotiate the Jay Treaty with Great Britain in 1794, and his constitutional arguments on this subject were famous throughout the country. He had distinguished himself by his courage and determination in the difficult negotiations with Talleyrand and the French government in 1798. His XYZ dispatches earned him a hero's welcome upon his return to this country, and even today they stand as strik-

---

[151] Davis, "Alfred Moore and James Iredell."

[152] The standard and most detailed life of Marshall is, of course, that of A. J. Beveridge, *The Life of John Marshall* (Boston, 1919). For a recent study of the Marshall Court see W. F. Swindler, *The Constitution and Chief Justice John Marshall* (New York, 1978). See the special study, W. E. Nelson, "The Eighteenth Century Background of John Marshall's Constitutional Jurisprudence," *Michigan Law Review* LXXVI, 893 (1978).

ing examples of tact and forceful reasoning in the annals of American diplomacy.[153]

Politically, Marshall was considered a member of "that class of conservative Virginians whose devotion to President Washington, and whose education in the common law caused them to hold Jefferson and his theories in antipathy."[154] He thus incurred the enduring wrath of Virginia Republicans, whose hostility was intensified by Jefferson's own personal animosity towards the new Chief Justice. These feelings against Marshall were not to subside for more than a decade.[155]

Although President Adams later remarked that the appointment of Marshall was the proudest act of his life,[156] it was in fact the unexpected result of a somewhat complex sequence of events.[157] In December 1800 Adams had received the resignation of Chief Justice Ellsworth, who had fallen ill in France.[158] This timing was critical, because by then it seemed clear that the Republican party would come into power the following year. Moreover, the Judiciary Bill of 1801, sponsored by Federalists and designed to strengthen the role of the federal bench, was almost certain to become law the following month. One section of the Bill provided that the membership of the Court should be reduced to five after the next occurring vacancy,[159] and Adams was therefore anxious to fill the post quickly with a trusted Federalist.

His immediate choice was John Jay, whose appointment was promptly confirmed by the Senate. There was substantial doubt, however, whether he would accept the position, even though his term as Governor of New York was about to expire.[160] Alternates in Adams' mind at this time appear to have been Judge Cushing and Judge Paterson, in that order. Both were then members of the Court; Jared Ingersoll, of the Philadelphia Bar, was apparently a candidate for the resulting vacancy for an associate judge.[161]

Jay declined the appointment in a letter dated January 2, 1801.[162]

---

[153] See Beveridge, *John Marshall*, II, 296–309.

[154] Adams, *History of United States*, I, 192.

[155] See, e.g., the attack of J. Thomson, *The Letters of Curtius* (Richmond, 1804).

[156] See C. Warren, *American Bar*, 252, note 1.

[157] For an excellent and detailed account of the circumstances leading to Marshall's appointment see K. Turner, "The Appointment of Chief Justice Marshall," *William and Mary Quarterly* XVII, 143 (1960).

[158] Letters Received, Adams Papers, Massachusetts Historical Society, Bos-

ton, endorsed "Rcd. Dec. 15, 1800." (quotations from the Adams Papers are made by courtesy of the editor-in-chief and the Massachusetts Historical Society).

[159] 2 Stat. 89, Sec. 3 (1801).

[160] F. Monaghan, *John Jay* (New York, 1935), 424–25.

[161] See A. Adams to T. Adams, Dec. 25, 1800, Adams Papers, Massachusetts Historical Society, Boston.

[162] J. Jay to J. Adams, Jan. 2, 1801, in H. P. Johnston, ed., *The Correspondence and Public Papers of John Jay* (New York, 1971: reprint of 1893 ed.), IV, 284.

Meanwhile, Adams had been advised that Ingersoll had reservations about accepting a position on the Bench because of the impending legislation.[163] In light of the pressures of time, Adams apparently decided to abandon the plan of making the appointment from within the Court. Word came to him on January 19 that the Judiciary Bill would come to a vote the next day.[164] On the eve of that vote, Adams discussed the problem with Marshall, then his Secretary of State, who later recounted the episode in a letter to Judge Story:

> When I waited on the President with Mr. Jay's letter declining the appointment he said thoughtfully "Who shall I nominate now"? I replied that I could not tell, as I supposed that his objection to Judge Patteson [*sic*] remained. He said in a decided tone "I shall not nominate him." After a moments hesitation he said "I believe I must nominate you." I had never before heard myself named for the office and had not even thought of it. I was pleased as well as surprized, and bowed in silence. Next day I was nominated. . . .[165]

Only a few weeks before, Marshall had written to C. C. Pinckney that he hoped he would "never again fill any political station whatever,"[166] and curiously there is no evidence that Adams had considered Marshall at any time since Ellsworth's resignation. Subsequent efforts to persuade Adams to substitute Paterson's name were fruitless, and on January 27 Marshall's nomination was unanimously confirmed. In acknowledging his acceptance, Adams expressly asked him to continue as Secretary of State.[167]

In appearance Marshall was unquestionably a commanding figure in the courtroom. He was tall to the point of awkwardness, loose-jointed but erect, his black hair tied in a queue after the fashion of the time, but his clothes were frequently disheveled. Some of his features resembled those of his cousin Thomas Jefferson. Both in and out of court, his bearing was not that of a man impressed with his own station: William Wirt wrote that "in his whole appearance, and demeanor; dress, attitudes, gesture; sitting, standing or walking; he is as far removed from the idolized graces of lord Chesterfield, as any other

---

[163] See T. Adams to J. Adams, Dec. 28, 1800; T. Adams to A. Adams, Dec. 30, 1800, Adams Papers, Massachusetts Historical Society.

[164] B. Stoddert to J. Adams, Jan. 19, 1801, Adams Papers, Massachusetts Historical Society.

[165] J. S. Adams, ed., *An Autobiographical Sketch of John Marshall* (Ann Arbor, 1937), 30.

[166] J. Marshall to C. Pinckney, Dec. 18, 1800, Pinckney Family Papers, Manuscripts Division, Library of Congress.

[167] J. Adams to J. Marshall, Feb. 4, 1801, John Adams Letter Book, Reel 120, Manuscripts Division, Library of Congress. Marshall drew only his salary as Chief Justice during this period. Beveridge, *John Marshall*, II, 559.

gentleman on earth."[168] Judge Story described him as "not graceful nor imposing . . . his manners are plain yet dignified, . . . his language chaste but hardly elegant."[169]

Story further provides a memorable description of Marshall's judicial demeanor:

> Enter but that hall, and you saw him listening with a quiet, easy dignity to the discussions at the bar; silent, serious, searching; with a keenness of thought which sophistry could not mislead, or error confuse, or ingenuity delude; with a benignity of aspect which invited the modest to move on with confidence; with a conscious firmness of purpose which repressed arrogance, and overawed declamation. You heard him pronounce the opinion of the Court in a low, but modulated voice, unfolding in luminous order every topic of argument, trying its strength, and measuring its value, until you felt yourself in the presence of the very oracle of the law.[170]

Although his brethren on the Bench were men of intellectual independence, Marshall soon became a dominant force. Despite certain objections on the part of Judge Johnson,[171] he abandoned the custom of seriatim assignment of opinions, and became himself the spokesman of the Court. Perhaps differences among the members of the Court were usually minor and resolved in conference, but there is little evidence from which to judge.[172] His colleague Judge Story, however, has suggested that Marshall's influence was not resented by his brethren, and that the duty to write opinions in the cases in which Marshall took no part devolved upon others to their own regret in view of the difficulty of matching the quality of his analysis and insight.

Judge Story eulogized Marshall's adherence to principle as a prime trait and moving force behind his contribution to the law:

> What, indeed, strikes us as the most remarkable in his whole character, even more than his splendid talents, is the entire consistency of his public life and principles. There is nothing in either which calls for apology or concealment. Ambition has never seduced him from his principles, nor popular clamor deterred him from the strict performance of duty. Amid the extravagances of party spirit, he has stood with a calm and steady inflexibility; neither bending to the pressure of adversity, nor bounding with the elasticity of success. . . . Whatever

---

[168] W. Wirt, *The Letters of the British Spy* (Baltimore, 1811), 95.

[169] J. Story to Samuel P. P. Fay, Feb. 25, 1808, in W. Story, *Joseph Story*, I, 166.

[170] J. Story, *A Discourse Upon the Life, Character and Services of the Honorable John Marshall* (Boston, 1835).

[171] W. Johnson to T. Jefferson, Dec. 22, 1801, Jefferson Papers, Manuscripts Division, Library of Congress.

[172] See Part II of this Volume, chapter I infra.

changes of opinion have occurred, in the course of his long life, have been gradual and slow; the results of genius acting upon larger materials, and of judgment matured by the lessons of experience. The constitution, since its adoption, owes more to him than to any other single mind, for its true interpretation and vindication. Whether it lives or perishes, his exposition of its principles will be an enduring monument to his fame, as long as solid reasoning, profound analysis, and sober views of government, shall invite the leisure, or command the attention of statesmen and jurists.[173]

To this high praise must be added a brief comment on Marshall's extraordinary powers of exposition. His work was that of a lawyer who insisted that ground for every premise must be carefully prepared, every possible objection examined and answered, every conclusion clearly and concisely stated.[174] His analysis was thorough to the point of exhaustiveness.[175] His remarkable combination of eloquence and skill in argumentation contributed to the force his opinions had during his lifetime and maintain to this day:

> His power of phrase was such that today, when lawyers and judges wish to express the constitutional principles he enunciated, they revert to his own choice of words. Unpopular as most of his opinions were, Marshall's contemporary influence was immense, and he affected profoundly the political as well as the legal thinking of the bar. Because so many politicians of his day were lawyers, this means also that he affected to a substantial degree the political thinking of people at large. . . . [I]t is submitted that his influence became all-pervasive because his opinions, carefully reasoned, lawyer-like opinions, were studied generation after generation by law students, by practitioners and by judges, and his opinions therefore live almost as if they were a part of the Constitution itself.[176]

---

[173] W. Story, *Joseph Story*, I, 521–22.

[174] W. D. Lewis, ed., *Great American Lawyers: John Marshall* (Philadelphia, 1907), II, 375.

[175] *Ibid.*

[176] G. L. Haskins, "John Marshall and the Commerce Clause of the Constitution," *University of Pennsylvania Law Review* CIV, 23, 37 (1955).

CHAPTER IV

The Federal Judicial System—
1801–1802

A. THE ACCOMPLISHMENTS OF THE JUDICIARY ACT OF 1801

Until recent years, historians generally have not been kind to the accomplishments of John Adams. His personal traits, combining sternness and irascibility, were not endearing, and by the end of his term of office he was no hero with the people, with Congress, or with most of his associates in the government. As a principal leader of the Federalist party, whose political power had been shattered by the election of 1800, he has been viewed as an exponent of conservatism who did not champion the people's rights as did the "great democrat" who succeeded him. The popularity and the dramatic accomplishments of Jefferson during his first term have also helped to eclipse for generations much of the worth of what Adams did. Indeed, it is sometimes forgotten that Adams failed to win re-election by a margin of only eight electoral votes, and it may well be doubted, despite the visionary ideas that Jefferson entertained about the perfectibility of man, whether the latter "led his country or mankind any farther towards perfection than Washington and Adams had done."[1] For example, the late Samuel Eliot Morison queried whether it is not "time to admit that John Adams' defeat in 1800, and the relegation of the Federalists to an important minority status, were in the long run bad for the United States?"[2]

Among the notable accomplishments of the Adams administration, few were more important than the reorganization and extension of the

---

[1] S. E. Morison, *The Oxford History of the United States, 1783–1917* (Oxford, 1927), I, 227. To the same general effect, see idem, *The Oxford History of the American People* (New York, 1965), 359.

[2] S. E. Morison, Book Review, *New England Quarterly* XLII, 126, 128 (1969).

federal judicial system, short-lived though those innovations proved to be. At the time of Marshall's appointment as Chief Justice, Congress was at work on the final revisions of the Judiciary Bill, which was to become law on February 13, 1801, and which would introduce far-reaching changes into the judicial system as it had existed since 1789. The chief, though by no means the only, innovation affecting the Supreme Court was the reorganization of the circuit courts and the consequent abolition of circuit duty for the Supreme Court judges. Six new circuit courts were to be created; they were to be manned by sixteen new circuit judges, together with an array of clerks, United States marshals, and attorneys.[3] The close connection between the timing of Marshall's appointment as Chief Justice and the enactment of this legislation cannot be ignored,[4] and the fact that the new Act gave the outgoing President an opportunity to make a number of judicial appointments from the Federalist party had substantial repercussions on the history of the Supreme Court.

Misleading, incorrect, and intemperate charges were immediately leveled against President Adams by his political opponents as a result of the passage of the Act. Among the most vituperative were those of Jefferson, who viewed the Act not only as a final partisan outrage but also as a last-ditch effort on the part of the Federalists to seize control of the judiciary and perpetuate their influence in the national government. Much of the brunt of his attack was directed against the new judicial offices that were filled by Adams' so-called "midnight" appointments on the eve of his departure from office. Largely as a consequence of these appointments, stigmatized by Republicans with that derisive nickname from the Duke of Braintree's Midnight Judges, Jefferson pressed for immediate repeal of the 1801 Act. As J. B. McMaster has suggested, "Had the appointment of these officers been left to Jefferson, the Republicans would undoubtedly have found little fault with the law."[5]

Charges of political opportunism were not confined to the Federalists' opponents of the time but have been repeated and perpetuated by writers who have fallen under Jefferson's spell, as well as by serious historians who have castigated the law of the midnight judges, passed by the Federalist-dominated Seventh Congress, as a piece of stupendous jobbery. Claude G. Bowers, after alluding to the "transparent" purpose of the Act, wrote: "All that now remained was for Adams to pack the courts with partisans as narrow and intolerant as those who had for ten

---

[3] 2 Stat. 89–100.
[4] See text accompanying notes 76–77, 101–102 infra.

[5] J. B. McMaster, *A History of the People of the United States* (New York, 1885), II, 533.

years been delivering common party harangues from the Bench."[6] Other voices have raised similar complaints,[7] and mistaken statements of fact have increased misunderstanding.[8] Unquestionably, the Federalists took advantage of the opportunity that the Act afforded to make appointments from their own party. Henry Adams, one of the first to appraise the Act with objectivity, pointedly remarked that filling the new courts and the vacancies on the old bench with "safe men" was a natural "manoeuvre . . . to prevent the overthrow of those legal principles in which, as they believed, national safety dwelt."[9] Even in the course of the House debates on the legislation it was admitted that the passage of the Bill was highly important because "the close of the present Executive's authority was at hand, and, from his experience, he was more capable to choose suitable persons to fill the offices than another."[10]

The fact that the Act was repealed the following year, after bitter and acrimonious debates in Congress, has hardly served to enhance its reputation. Nevertheless, it was "by no means the design only of hungry politicians, or the effort of a party to entrench itself on the bench after the country has sent it into the wilderness."[11] Neither was it a "prodigal"[12] waste of public funds to expend $31,500 on the salaries of sixteen new circuit judges for a government whose income amounted to more than $10 million a year. Morever, it is not true, as has been alleged, that the Judiciary Bill was only introduced after Adams' defeat in the election of 1800.[13] Not only had congressional committees been at work

---

[6] C. G. Bowers, *Jefferson and Hamilton* (Boston, 1925), 508. See also L. G. Tyler, *Parties and Patronage in the United States* (New York, 1891), 23–24: "A systematic attempt seems to have been made by the Federalists to pack the judiciary . . . without even a feeling of shame that he was appointing men to office for life whose principles had just been condemned by the people."

[7] See, e.g., E. Channing, *Students' History of the United States* (New York, 1924), 259–60; idem, *The United States of America, 1765–1865* (New York, 1896), 157–58. Among other critical appraisals of the 1801 Act are those of M. Farrand, "The Judiciary Act of 1801," *American Historical Review* V, 682 (1900); and F. Frankfurter and J. M. Landis, *The Business of Supreme Court* (New York, 1927), 14–30.

The most comprehensive critical study to date is that of K. Turner, "The Midnight Judges," *University of Pennsylvania Law Review* CIX, 494 (1961).

[8] L. G. Tyler, for example, states that thirty-six new judgeships were created. Tyler, *Parties and Patronage*, 24.

[9] H. Adams, *History of the United States of America* (New York, 1889), I, 275.

[10] J. Gales and W. Seaton, comps., *The Debates and Proceedings in the Congress of the United States* (Washington, 1834–1856) (hereafter cited as *Annals of Congress*) X, 648 (6th Cong., 1st sess.).

[11] Frankfurter and Landis, *Business of Supreme Court*, 21.

[12] *Annals of Congress*, XI, 27 (7th Cong., 1st sess.).

[13] Tyler, *Parties and Patronage*, 24.

on a succession of legislative proposals from the time of Adams' message to Congress on December 3, 1799,[14] but two bills had been drafted many months before. One of these was strikingly similar to the bill passed in 1801 in that it abolished circuit riding for the Supreme Court judges.[15] In addition to the establishment of the new circuit courts and the abolition of circuit riding, a number of other important changes had also been proposed to extend the jurisdiction of the federal courts and to remedy certain deficiencies in the Judiciary Act of 1789 that had been evident for a decade.[16] Thus, behind the 1801 Act had been "the pressure of solid professional conceptions regarding a judicature appropriate for the new country, reinforced by defects unmistakably revealed in the workings of the initial system."[17]

B. DEFECTS IN THE JUDICIAL SYSTEM PRIOR TO THE ACT OF 1801

The organization of the federal judiciary under the Act of 1789 is familiar and has been discussed in Volume I of this *History*. That Act provided for United States district courts, each presided over by a district judge. The district courts were grouped into a second tier of circuit courts—the Eastern, Middle, and Southern Circuits—presided over (after 1793) by one Supreme Court judge and by the district judge in the district where the court sat.[18] Under the 1789 Act, which had

---

[14] *Annals of Congress*, X, 188–89 (6th Cong., 1st sess.).

[15] See *Annals of Congress*, VII, 527 (5th Cong., 1st sess.) (March 21, 1798). Although the provisions of the Bill are not reported in the *Annals*, it was introduced in the Senate and is described in a letter from Chief Justice Ellsworth to Judge Cushing, Apr. 15, 1798, preserved in the Robert Treat Paine Papers in the Massachusetts Historical Society, Boston (reference courtesy of the Massachusetts Historical Society). As well as abolishing circuit riding, the Bill proposed to create five new federal districts and to associate the district judges for the holding of the circuit courts. In April, the Senate resumed consideration of the Bill and then deferred consideration to the next session. *Annals of Congress*, VII (5th Cong., 1st sess.) (Apr. 20, 1798).

[16] On April 26, 1798, a Bill was introduced in the Senate that proposed creating four, in place of the existing three, circuits as well as adding two new judges to enable each circuit (except in the districts of Kentucky and Tennessee) to hold court semi-annually. *Annals of Congress*, VII, 549–50 (5th Cong., 1st sess.). This bill apparently passed the Senate on May 25 after several readings. *Annals of Congress*, VII, 556, 558, 559, 561, 564 (5th Cong., 1st sess.). No action concerning it appears to have been taken in the House.

[17] Frankfurter and Landis, *Business of Supreme Court*, 21. For a scholarly, comprehensive, and compressed survey of the background and purpose of the 1789 Act, including the economic forces as well as the philosophy underlying the unique American judicial experiment, see *ibid.*, 4–14.

[18] Act of Sept. 24, 1789, chapter 20, Sec. 4, 1 Stat. 74; Act of Mar. 2, 1793, chapter 22, Sec. 1, 1 Stat. 333–34.

resulted from a compromise between those who were insistent upon confining federal power within narrow limits and those who wished to implement as completely as possible the judicial authority conferred by the Constitution,[19] not only were the powers of the Supreme Court limited, and those of the other federal courts carefully circumscribed, but, except for admiralty and criminal jurisdiction, major areas of jurisdiction were allocated on the basis of concurrent jurisdiction with the State courts.[20] Thus, original jurisdiction of the circuit courts in diversity of citizenship cases was concurrent with the State courts and limited to cases where the amount in dispute was in excess of $500. Certain classes of suits involving more than $500 and begun in the State courts might be removed to the circuit courts before trial.[21] Numerous limitations of this sort were removed by the 1801 Act, and both the powers and the jurisdiction of the federal courts were greatly expanded.

Among the deficiencies of the 1789 Act, none was more prominent and deserving of rectification than the requirement that the Supreme Court judges ride circuit. As a consequence of this requirement each judge was forced to consider on appeal some of the same cases that he had helped to decide in a circuit court. In 1790, in response to the invitation of President Washington to comment on the operation of the new judicial system, the judges of the Supreme Court strongly recommended that different judges man the circuit courts and the Supreme Court.[22]

---

[19] See C. Warren, "New Light on the History of the Federal Judiciary Act of 1789," *Harvard Law Review* XXXVII, 49 (1923), and references cited therein. The issue of judicial authority had also been controversial in the State ratifying conventions. See J. Elliot, ed., *The Debates in the Several Ratifying Conventions on the Adoption of the Federal Constitution* (Philadelphia, 1896), II, III, passim.

[20] R. Peters, ed., *The Public Statutes at Large of the United States of America* (Boston, 1845), I, Secs. 9, 11, 13, 25.

[21] *Ibid.*, Sec. 12.

[22] G. Washington to J. Jay, et al., Apr. 3, 1790, and Nov. 19, 1790, in H. P. Johnston, ed., *The Correspondence and Public Papers of John Jay* (New York, 1890–1893), III, 396, 409 (hereafter cited as Johnston, *John Jay Papers*). Jay's proposed draft of a letter of reply to the President was sent to Judge Iredell on Sept. 15, 1790 and apparently to the other judges at the same time for their "alterations and corrections." G. J. McRee, ed., *Life and Correspondence of James Iredell* (New York, 1858), II, 292. For a printed version of the draft, see *ibid.*, II, 293–96. It does not appear that the draft letter was completed or sent. In any event, it is not contained in the Washington Papers. See J. C. Fitzpatrick, ed., *The Writings of George Washington* (Bicentennial ed., Washington, D. C., 1976), XXXI, 32, note 58. The first written reply from the Judges collectively appears to have been in Aug. 1792, quoted in the text accompanying note 23 infra. See, however, a reference to the subject in a letter from Jay to Washington, Sept. 23, 1791, in W. Jay, ed., *The Life of John Jay* (New York, 1833), II, 207: "The judicial system undoubtedly calls for revision. . . ."

In the summer of 1792, the Judges wrote to the President and asked him to lay their message before the Congress:[23]

Philadelphia, August 9, 1792

SIR:

Your official connexion with the Legislature, and the consideration that applications from us to them cannot be made in any manner so respectful to Government as through the President, induce us to request your attention to the enclosed representation, and that you will be pleased to lay it before the Congress.

We really, sir, find the burdens laid upon us so excessive that we cannot forbear representing them in strong and explicit terms.

On extraordinary occasions weshall [sic] always be ready, as good citizens, to make extraordinary exertions; but while our country enjoys prosperity, and nothing occurs to require or justify such severities, we cannot reconcile ourselves to the idea of existing in exile from our families, and of being subjected to a kind of life on which we cannot reflect without experiencing sensations and emotions more easy to conceive than proper for us to express.

With the most perfect respect, esteem, and attachment,

We have the honor to be, sir, your most obediant and most humble servants,

> JOHN JAY,
> WILLIAM CUSHING,
> JAMES WILSON,
> JOHN BLAIR,
> JAMES IREDELL,
> THOMAS JOHNSON.

The Chief Justice and the Associate Judges of the Supreme Court respectfully represent to the Congress of the United States:

That when the present judicial arrangements took place, it appeared to be a general and well-founded opinion, that the act then passed was to be considered rather as introducing a temporary expedient than a permanent system, and that it would be revised as soon as a period of greater leisure should arrive.

The subject was new, and was rendered intricate and embarrassing by local as well as other difficulties; and there was reason to presume that others, not at that time apparent, would be discovered by experience.

The ensuing sessions of Congress were so occupied by other affairs of great and pressing importance, that the judges thought it improper to interrupt the attention of Congress by any application on the subject.

That, as it would not become them to suggest what alterations

---

[23] *American State Papers. Documents, Legislative and Executive, of the Congress of the United States,* *Miscellaneous* (Washington, 1834), I, 51–52 (hereafter cited as *American State Papers: Miscellaneous*).

or system ought in their opinion to be formed and adopted, they omit making any remarks on that head; but they feel most sensibly the necessity which presses them to represent—

That the task of holding twenty-seven circuit courts a year, in the different States, from New Hampshire to Georgia, besides two sessions of the Supreme Court at Philadelphia, in the two most severe seasons of the year, is a task which, considering the extent of the United States, and the small number of judges, is too burdensome.

That to require of the judges to pass the greater part of their days on the road, and at inns, and at a distance from their families, is a requisition which, in their opinion, should not be made unless in cases of necessity.

That some of the present judges do not enjoy health and strength of body sufficient to enable them to undergo the toilsome journeys through different climates and seasons, which they are called upon to undertake; nor is it probable that any set of judges, however robust, would be able to support, and punctually execute, such severe duties for any length of time.

That the distinction made between the Supreme Court and its judges, and appointing the same men finally to correct in one capacity the errors which they themselves may have committed in another, is a distinction unfriendly to impartial justice, and to that confidence in the Supreme Court which it is so essential to the public interest should be reposed in it.

The judges decline minute details, and purposely omit many considerations, which they are persuaded will occur whenever the subject is attentively discussed and considered.

They most earnestly request that it may meet with early attention, and that the system may be so modified as that they may be relieved from their present painful and improper situation.

JOHN JAY,
WILLIAM CUSHING,
JAMES WILSON,
JOHN BLAIR,
JAMES IREDELL,
THOMAS JOHNSON.

.Although Warren states that no action was taken in response to this memorial,[24] in fact it resulted in the Act of March 2, 1793, which

---

[24] C. Warren, *The Supreme Court in United States History* (Boston, 1926), I, 89. Warren overlooked not only the bill that resulted in the Act of March 2, 1793 (referred to in note 25 infra), but also the President's Speech to both Houses of Congress on November 6, 1792, delivered three months after the Judges' memorial, in which he referred to the importance of "a revision of the Judiciary system" and stated that a "representation from the Judges of the Supreme Court, which will be laid before you, points out some of the inconveniences that are experienced." *Annals of Congress*, III, 608 (2nd Cong., 1st sess.).

afforded some small relief to the complaints of the judges; thereafter only one Supreme Court judge was required for each circuit, and six judges became available for the three circuits, so that each judge was called upon for circuit duty only once a year.[25] However, the almost unbearable hardships of circuit riding, which were caused in part by the scarce and primitive transportation facilities in undeveloped portions of the country, continued to result in accidents, delays, and fatigue.

John Jay felt that the office of the Judge of the Supreme Court was intolerable,[26] and later, after leaving the bench, he refused Adams' offer of the Chief Justiceship, largely because of the duty of circuit riding.[27] Distances ranged from a few to several hundred miles a year, depending on the Circuit. Moreover, as the decade wore on, the increasing volume of federal court business was to take an ever increasing toll on the time and energies of the Supreme Court judges.[28]

Contemporary letters, and even newspapers, pointed up the defects in the judicial system from the standpoint of the public. Frequently, because of bad weather, the hazards of travel, or the illness of a Supreme Court judge, a circuit court was unable to convene. This problem involved hardships as well as great expense to litigants, witnesses, and jurors, who in some States were obliged to travel as much as two or three hundred miles to attend court. On March 17, 1799, Judge Chase wrote to his brother judge William Paterson that his health was such that he could not ride in a carriage and that he was therefore obliged to "solicit the favor of you to hold the Court for me in New York,"[29]

---

[25] Chapter 22, Sec. 1, 1 Stat. 333–34. For evidence that this measure was taken in direct response to the Judges' memorial, see *Annals of Congress*, III, 616, 627, 658, 659, 675, 896 (2d Cong., 1st sess.), and President Washington's speech, note 24 supra.

[26] See E. Benson to R. King, Dec. 18, 1793, in C. R. King, ed., *The Life and Correspondence of Rufus King* (New York, 1894–1900), I, 506–507 (hereafter cited as King, *Rufus King Correspondence*).

[27] J. Jay to J. Adams, Jan. 2, 1801, in Johnston, *John Jay Papers* IV, 284.

[28] Numerous contemporary accounts and letters graphically describe the hardships of circuit riding, some of which are referred to in "Plain Truth & Algernon Sidney, A View & Vindication of the Measures of the Present Administration," a partisan pamphlet supporting the reestablishment of the old circuit system in 1802. It summarized Judge Cushing's duties as follows: holding of the three circuit courts in conjunction with the district judges, 60 days; travel (480 miles) in connection therewith, 24 days; one session of the Supreme Court, 21 days; travel (480 miles) in connection therewith, 48 days; total days "while on expense and in the public service, 153 days, or a little over five months . . . [a] less portion of time than he devoted to the public service while a judge of the state courts of Massachusetts." Pamphlet cited in Frankfurter and Landis, *Business of Supreme Court*, 23. See also the text of the Act of 1793, *Annals of Congress*, III, 1447–49 (2d Cong., 1st sess.).

[29] S. Chase to W. Paterson, Mar. 17, 1799, Miscellaneous Manuscripts, Chase, New York Historical Society, New York City (reference courtesy of the New York Historical Society).

but Paterson's own ill health prevented him from doing so. Several years earlier Rufus King had referred in a letter to his correspondent's case having been delayed in the federal court "for want of Judges to form a court."[30] The *National Gazette* for January 5, 1792, reported that at an important season for the North Carolina farmer the Circuit Court had been opened but, because of the absence of the Supreme Court judge assigned thereto, had been unable to do any business for twelve days, when it was finally adjourned for six months. Not only were the jurors and litigants greatly inconvenienced, but prisoners in jail awaiting trial were "doomed to suffer the inclemencies of the winter in a situation already shocking to humanity."[31]

The problem of the judges' correcting in the Supreme Court in one capacity errors that they might have committed in their other capacity as circuit judges is alluded to in several letters, as well as in the Attorney-General's Report. Concern also arose over lack of uniformity and predictability in the several circuits. On December 19, 1793, John Jay wrote to Rufus King:

> It has happened in more than one Instance that Questions in the Circuit Courts decided by one Set of Judges in the *affirmative*, have afterwards in the same Court been decided by others in the *negative*. As writs of Error do not reach every case, this Evil has no remedy. The natural Tendency of such Fluctuations is obvious; nor can they otherwise be avoided than by confining the Judges to their proper place, viz. the Sup. Court. . . .[32]

In February 1794 the Supreme Court judges again presented to Congress their further opinion with respect to deficiencies in the judicial system from the public standpoint and sought the interposition of the legislature:[33]

> *The chief justice and the associate justices of the Supreme Court of the United States respectfully represent to the Congress of the United States—*

> That their representation, communicated last year through the President to both Houses of Congress, and to which they refer, comprehended few other remarks than such as were suggested by the personal difficulties to which the judges were subjected.

---

[30] J. King to R. Southgate, Sept. 30, 1792, in King, *Rufus King Correspondence*, I, 430.

[31] Warren, *Supreme Court*, I, 87, note 3 (quoting *National Gazette*, Jan. 5, 1793).

[32] J. Jay to R. King, Dec. 19, 1793, in King, *Rufus King Correspondence*, I, 509.

[33] *American State Papers: Miscellaneous*, I, 77–78.

They acknowledge, with sensibility and gratitude, that the act which thereupon passed, and whereby the attendance of one judge only was made indispensable to the holding of a circuit court, afforded them great relief, and enabled them to pass more time at home and in studies made necessary by their official duties.

They think it incumbent on them to submit to the consideration of Congress, whether the sessions of the several courts, comprehended in any of the three circuits, ought to depend entirely on the health of the judge to whom either of them may be assigned; for in case, by accident or illness, his attendance should be prevented, the inconveniences and useless expenses to all the parties would certainly be great as well as obvious.

It has already happened, in more than one instance, that different judges, sitting at different times in the same court, but in similar causes, have decided in direct opposition to each other, and that in cases in which the parties could not, as the law now stands, have the benefit of writs of error. They therefore also submit to the consideration of Congress, whether this evil, naturally tending to render the law unsettled and uncertain, and thereby to create apprehension and diffidence in the public mind, does not require the interposition of Congress.

They fear it would not become them to take a minute view of the whole system, and to suggest the alterations which to them appear requisite; and their hesitation is increased by the reflection that some of those alterations would, from the nature of them, be capable of being ascribed to personal considerations.

JOHN JAY,
WM. CUSHING,
JAMES WILSON,
JOHN BLAIR,
WM. PATERSON.

This time, their pleas fell upon deaf ears: in the House, the letter was tabled; in the Senate, the committee to which it was referred recommended postponement to the next session.[34]

As early as December 31, 1790, Edmund Randolph, Washington's Attorney-General, had submitted to the House of Representatives, at its request, a report which analyzed at length and in detail what he considered to be the principal defects in the workings of the new federal judiciary system and the difficulties that he was convinced would arise thereunder. He regarded a principal defect to be the dual functions of

---

[34] *Annals of Congress*, IV, 109 (3d Cong., 1st sess.).

the Supreme Court judges under the 1789 Act. In the course of suggesting alterations in that Act, Randolph proposed that the judges should cease to act as judges of the circuit courts. Putting to one side whether, in principle, "inferior" courts should be distinct from "supreme" courts, he confined his observations "within the pale of expediency only" and summarized his arguments succinctly as follows:

> 1. Those who pronounce the law of the land without appeal, ought to be pre-eminent in most endowments of the mind. Survey the functions of a judge of the Supreme Court. He must be a master of the common law in all its divisions, a chancellor, a civilian, a federal jurist, and skilled in the laws of each State. To expect that in future times this assemblage of talents will be ready, without further study, for the national service, is to confide too largely in the public fortune. Most vacancies on the bench will be supplied by professional men, who, perhaps, have been too much animated by the contentions of the bar, deliberately to explore this extensive range of science. In a great measure, then, the supreme judges will form themselves after their nomination. But what leisure remains from their itinerant dispensation of justice? Sum up all the fragments of their time, hold their fatigue at naught, and let them bid adieu to all domestic concerns, still the average term of a life, already advanced, will be too short for any important proficiency.[35]

Randolph then went on to summarize arguments, covering several pages in small print, for and against "the separation of the supreme judges from the circuit service."[36] These arguments were not only exhaustive but prophetic in that they were to be used again and again by countless proponents of judicial reform, in congressional debates and elsewhere, in a controversy over the circuit court system which lasted some eighty years. Except for the brief period of 1801–1802, when the Supreme Court judges were relieved of circuit riding, those duties continued until 1869.[37] Hence Randolph's exposition and arguments are central to one phase of the activities and the history of the Supreme Court until after the Civil War. In a nutshell, the problem was one of the capacity of the judges to perform their duties in person both in Washington and throughout a nation whose continuing expansion of population and territory was a foregone conclusion with the advancing frontier and the opening up and settlement of the West. The problem has been pithily summarized by Frankfurter and Landis: "More terri-

---

[35] *American State Papers: Miscellaneous*, I, 23–24.

[36] *Ibid.*, I, 24–36. Subsequently, in a letter to Washington dated Aug. 15, 1792, Randolph expressed his regret that the judiciary system as a whole was "crude." J. Sparks, ed., *The Writings of George Washington* (Boston, 1836), X, 513.

[37] See Act of Apr. 10, 1869, 16 Stat. 44–45.

tory implied more circuits. More circuits meant either more circuit riding for the Justices or more Justices for circuit riding."[38]

At least two arguments later pressed with considerable urgency in favor of the judges' direct participation in the work of the circuit courts[39] were either ignored or given short shrift by Randolph. One was the contention that by direct contact with State legislators and the local Bar the judges would acquire a better understanding of State law than by reading the session laws, and they would thus contribute to the Supreme Court itself first-hand familiarity with local laws. This familiarity would enable them to enlighten their brethren and achieve greater cohesiveness in the administration of justice. Such supposed educative advantages of circuit riding, later urged, for example, by Senator Van Buren in 1826,[40] were hardly touched upon by Randolph. These contentions were tersely disposed of by Gouverneur Morris in the debate on the repeal of the 1801 Act, when he said that riding rapidly from one end of the country to the other on the highroad was not necessarily the best way to study law.[41] In the same year James A. Bayard remarked in the House that both local needs and earlier proceedings in the same case would be overlooked by rotating interpreters who seldom sat twice successively in the same district, and that law as a science was endangered as it became "less important to be skilled in the books than to be acquainted with the character of the judge who was to preside."[42] To the argument that the commingling of trial and appellate work for the same judges was based upon long-established English *nisi prius* practice (and hence presumably tested and sound), Randolph replied that the analogy was a false one, and the English system essentially different. Randolph was indeed correct, since at *nisi prius* the English judges tried only questions of fact on issues and pleadings already settled, whereas in the United States, as Webster later pointed out, "suits are brought, proceeded with, through all their stages, tried and finally determined. . . ."[43]

Randolph's attacks also focused on other features. His language merits quotation rather than paraphrase:

2. The detaching of the judges to different circuits defeats the benefit of an unprejudiced consultation. The delivery of a solemn opinion in court commits them; and should a judgment rendered by two be erroneous, will they meet their four brethren unbiassed? May

---

[38] Frankfurter and Landis, *Business of Supreme Court*, 14.

[39] See H. C. Clark, "Circuit Riding as a Former National Asset," *American Bar Association Journal* VIII, 772 (1922).

[40] *Register of Debates in Congress* (Washington, 1824–1837), II, 416.

[41] *Annals of Congress*, XI, 82 (7th Cong., 1st sess.).

[42] *Ibid.*, XI, 619–20, 621.

[43] *Register of Debates*, II, 874.

not human nature, thus trammelled, struggle too long against conviction? And how few would erect a monument to their candor, at the expense of their reputation for firmness and discernment?

3. Jealousy among the members of a court is always an evil; and its malignity would be double, should it creep into the Supreme Court, obscure the discovery of right, and weaken that respect which the public welfare seeks for their decrees. But this cannot be affirmed to be beyond the compass of events to men agitated by the constant scanning of the judicial conduct of each other.

If this should not happen, there is fresh danger on the other side, lest they should be restrained by delicacy and mutual tenderness from probing, without scruple, what had been done in the circuit courts. . . .[44]

Prophetic as his report was to prove, Randolph far from exhausted the possible arguments against the circuit system, arguments that were to appear as the judiciary was drawn into the vortex of partisan politics at the end of the Adams and the beginning of the Jefferson administrations. He did, however, feel it incumbent upon himself to rebut the assertion that the image of government in the eyes of its citizens would be favorably improved "should the most distinguished judges visit every State."[45] This he denied on the ground that the judges who had decided a case on circuit would be likely to decide it similarly on appeal, and indeed press more strongly for the earlier decision lest they be thought to have erred, and hence likely to persuade their brethren on the Court to adopt the view taken below.[46]

Randolph could not at the time anticipate certain "educative" uses to which Federalist-minded judges would put circuit court duty in the course of their jury charges towards the end of the decade. Indeed, as will appear, those charges were all too often pungent political

---

[44] *American State Papers: Miscellaneous*, I, 24.

[45] *Ibid.*

[46] Randolph wrote:
When a discomfited party looks up to the highest tribunal for redress, he is told, by the report of the world, that in it every quality is centred necessary to justice. But how would his sanguine hopes be frustrated, if, among six judges, two are most probably to repeat their former suffrages, or to vindicate them with strenuous ability; or, if to avoid this, the wisdom of a third of the number must be laid aside?

Ibid. Compare the argument against the "negative vote" in the Colony of Massachusetts Bay, where the magistrates, as members of the General Court, heard on appeal cases that they had decided in the Court of Assistants. G. L. Haskins, *Law and Authority in Early Massachusetts* (New York, 1960), 38–39; idem, "Parliamentary Aspects of Representative Government in Early Massachusetts," *Studies Presented to the International Commission for the History of Representative and Parliamentary Institutions* (Paris, 1970), 203, 215–16.

harangues, in part designed to aid the Federalist cause, with the result that the practice, indulged in by several distinguished judges, was readily condoned. Nevertheless, there can be little question that, together with other factors, those jury charges helped to consolidate Republican opposition to the judiciary, and hence to some extent were responsible for the repeal of the Act of 1801. Certainly the practice as indulged in by Judge Samuel Chase was a major factor in arousing the ire of Jefferson and of Republicans generally to the point of instigating impeachment proceedings against him.[47]

Contemporaneously with the submission of the report summarized above, the Attorney-General presented a proposed judiciary bill designed to ameliorate and correct these and other deficiencies of the federal judicial system as he saw them. His proposals included assigning the district judges of each circuit to hold the several circuit courts, so that the Supreme Court judges might remain in Washington.[48] No action was taken. In 1793, however, Congress approved a bill that reduced the number of circuit court judges from three to two—the district judge and one Supreme Court judge.[49] Under that law the circuits were thereafter assigned on a rotating basis. However, the problem of circuit riding, as such, was hardly resolved, except insofar as the Supreme Court judges made informal arrangements among themselves to change around their assigned circuits in order to alleviate the hardships of extended circuit riding.[50]

That revisions of the federal judicial organization were not more urgently pressed during the early years of the last decade of the eighteenth century is not surprising in view of the numerous foreign and domestic problems that were absorbing the full attention of Congress. Political factors, notably the wish not to arouse further enmity among those who feared incursions of federal power into the spheres of State authority through the courts, and especially the mounting opposition to the federal courts, whose decisions were running counter to the philosophy and doctrines of the Republicans,[51] also deterred judicial reform.

---

[47] See chapter 7 infra.

[48] *American State Papers: Miscellaneous*, I, 29.

[49] See note 25 supra.

[50] Several letters of the period illustrating such arrangements are still extant and may be found in the Robert Treat Paine Papers at the Massachusetts Historical Society, Boston. These are conveniently cited in K. Turner, "Federalist Policy and the Judiciary Act of 1801," *William and Mary Quarterly* (3rd ser.) XXII, 3 at 6, note 15 (1965).

[51] See J. Jay to R. King, Dec. 22, 1793, in King, *Rufus King Correspondence*, I, 509; E. Randolph to G. Washington, Aug. 5, 1792, in Fitzpatrick, *Writings of George Washington*, X, 501, in which Randolph urged that reference to judicial matters be "as mild as possible." For a sampling of the type of decision referred to in the text, see Turner, "Federalist Policy," 8, note 19.

IV: *The Federal Judicial System—1801–1802*

It has been accurately stated that "[n]ot until the desire of leading Federalists to extend federal jurisdiction converged with professional dissatisfaction was change seriously contemplated."[52] This change was not to occur until the final years of the Adams administration, when peace with France was in the offing, and when the political interests of the Federalists were being threatened by the party machinery of the Republicans.[53] Much of the impetus for judicial reform was generated during the year 1799 by such men as Alexander Hamilton,[54] Theodore Sedgwick,[55] Oliver Wolcott,[56] and, most importantly, by President Adams in his message to Congress on December 3 of that year.[57]

General familiarity with the history of the time, together with those aspects that have been emphasized above, makes it apparent that among the leading factors favoring judicial renovation were, first, the pressure of sound, unbiased professional opinions and conceptions with respect to an appropriate system of national courts, and, second, newly-shaped Federalist policies that favored the extension and popularization of the federal courts to combat local prejudices interfering with the enforcement of federal laws. The Federalists were seeking viable means to strengthen the web of government by binding more closely the threads of national union. As Oliver Wolcott wrote to Fisher Ames on December 29, 1799, "It is impossible, in this country, to render an army an engine of government, and there is no way to combat the state opposition but by an efficient and extended organization of judges, magistrates, and other civil officers."[58] Some fourteen months later, Gouverneur Morris was to write to Robert R. Livingston that the new judiciary act

---

[52] Turner, "Federalist Policy," 7.

[53] See generally N F. Cunningham, Jr., *The Jeffersonian Republicans—the Formation of Party Organization, 1789–1801* (Chapel Hill, 1957), chapters 7–9; J. M. Smith, *Freedom's Fetters: The Alien and Sedition Laws and American Civil Liberties* (Ithaca, 1956).

[54] A. Hamilton to J. Dayton, 1799, in H. C. Lodge, ed., *The Works of Alexander Hamilton* (New York, 1904), X, 331 et seq. Sedgwick, at the time, was on the Senate committee responsible for judicial revision and Dayton was Speaker of the House.

[55] T. Sedgwick to R. King, Nov. 15, 1799, in King, *Rufus King Correspondence*, III, 146–47.

[56] On February 20, 1799, "in obedience to the command of the President," Wolcott submitted a number of observations that included the following: "To give energy to the government, it appears indispensible that the judicial system of the United States should be revised." G. Gibbs, ed., *Memoirs of the Administrations of Washington and John Adams Edited from the Papers of Oliver Wolcott* (New York, 1846), II, 299 (hereafter cited as Gibbs, *Memoirs of Washington and Adams Administrations*).

[57] *Annals of Congress*, X, 188–89 (6th Cong., 1st sess.).

[58] O. Wolcott to F. Ames, Dec. 29, 1799, in Gibbs, *Memoirs of Washington and Adams Administrations*, II, 316. Wolcott had been strenuously opposing Hamilton on the Army issue and recommending very limited military preparedness. S. G. Kurtz, *The Presidency of John Adams* (Philadelphia, 1957), 323.

"answers the double purpose of bringing *Justice* near to Men's Doors and of giving additional fibres to the Root of Government."[59]

Finally, with the passage of time, the weaknesses of the circuit system which Randolph had criticized in 1790 became increasingly apparent because the volume of appellate and circuit court business became greater and hence increased the drain on the time and energies of the judges. Influential opinion clearly favored a more comprehensive federal judiciary.

C. THE DEVELOPMENT OF THE JUDICIARY ACT OF 1801

Professor Kathryn Turner Preyer, in her study of the Judiciary Act of 1801,[60] has succinctly described the course of the bills and debates that immediately preceded the enactment of that law, and little further is required by way of amplification other than to summarize her conclusions, with certain appropriate additions and comments. Although, as stated above, early in 1798 two judiciary bills were introduced in the Senate—one relieving the Supreme Court judges of circuit duty, and another increasing the size of the federal judiciary and assigning two judges to each circuit—no action was taken in the House on either bill.[61] It was not until President Adams prodded the Sixth Congress in his opening Message in December 1799 that decisive steps were taken, and both the Senate and the House appointed committees to consider judicial revision. It is not without interest that Adams' recommendation was made in almost the same words as those used by Oliver Wolcott in writing to the President on February 20, 1799, when he said:

> To give energy to the government, it appears indispensible that the judicial system of the United States should be revised. It cannot but happen that numerous questions respecting the interpretation of the laws and the rights and duties of officers and citizens must arise in this extensive country; on the one hand it is necessary that the laws should be executed; on the other, that individuals should be guarded against oppression; neither of these objects can be assured under the present organization of the judicial department.[62]

Immediately it became apparent that radical changes in the organization of the circuit courts and their jurisdiction were contem-

---

[59] G. Morris Papers, Letter Book 5, Manuscripts Division, Library of Congress.
[60] See Turner, "Federalist Policy."

[61] See notes 15 and 16 supra.
[62] Gibbs, *Memoirs of Washington and Adams Administrations*, II, 299 (quoted in part in note 56 supra).

plated,[63] and the extent of those changes became clear in the bill introduced by Robert Goodloe Harper on March 11, 1800.[64] The bill was not published in the *Annals of Congress*, but it was printed by order of the House, and a copy has been preserved in the Library of Congress.[65] Among the numerous innovations proposed, one of the most radical was the abolition of the existing district courts, which were to be replaced by courts having only admiralty jurisdiction.[66] Another was the division of the country into twenty-nine districts, organized in turn into nine circuits. A circuit judge was to be appointed to each of the new districts within the particular circuit.[67] The bill also provided for radical changes with respect to the jurisdiction of the federal courts. These changes have been competently summarized by Professor Preyer as follows:

> In a startling abandonment of the concept of sovereign immunity, it gave the Supreme Court jurisdiction over suits in tort or contract against the United States by "any state, body politic or corporate, company or person." It extended the jurisdiction of the circuit courts to include "all actions or suits, matters or things, cognizable by the judicial authority of the United States," thus giving these courts, for the first time, the federal question jurisdiction which they had not been given in 1789. The amount necessary to give jurisdiction was reduced from five hundred to one hundred dollars and jurisdiction over cases involving title or bounds of land was specifically unrestricted by the value of the lands in question. The limitation as to venue which the Act of 1789 placed on the parties in diversity suits was abandoned and no "assignee clause" was included. Jurisdictional amount for removals was reduced to one hundred dollars and here, too, suits involving land titles were exempt from the qualification. Furthermore, removal *after* trial was authorized when judgment had been given in a state court for a sum exceeding one hundred dollars against a defendant (in the specified classes of suits) who had not been

---

[63] Both houses of Congress at once appointed committees to report revisions of the judiciary system. *Annals of Congress*, X, 15, 197–98 (6th Cong., 1st sess.). For a list of members see Turner, "Federalist Policy," 10. Turner also notes that the all-Federalist composition of the House committees was identical with that engaged simultaneously in preparing the first national bankruptcy act and suggests that the formation of those two committees may not have been fortuitous. *Ibid.*, 10, note 33.

[64] *Annals of Congress*, X, 623 (6th Cong., 1st sess.).

[65] "A Bill to Provide for the Better Establishment & Regulation of the Courts of the United States, 11th March, 1800," 6 HIR 135 and 6 HID 521, Rare Book Room, Library of Congress.

[66] *Ibid.*, Secs. 27, 28, 32. It was provided that the district judges then in office should act as judges in admiralty until death or resignation, when judges in admiralty should be appointed in their stead.

[67] *Ibid.*, Secs. 10, 11.

personally served with process or who had not appeared. And finally, the proposed legislation empowered the circuit courts to issue writs of prohibition, supersedeas, mandamus, or certiorari to the state courts to compel removal whenever the latter should refuse to permit it. The Supreme Court became the only appellate court in the federal system; the avenue to review at this level widened through a reduction of jurisdictional amount to five hundred dollars instead of the two thousand formerly required.[68]

Clearly, the bill had been drawn with great care and had behind it the almost unanimous voice of the Bar. Its heart lay in the provisions for the twenty-nine districts and the new circuit courts. Despite the strong support of Harper and a lengthy defense by John Marshall, who was then a member of the judiciary committee,[69] the key section was narrowly defeated in the House.[70] Four days later Harper presented an amended bill[71] in which the only significant changes were the reduction of the number of districts to nineteen and the number of circuits to six. After what has been described as a "warm and lengthy" debate, a Republican motion to postpone until the next session was carried by a margin of two votes on April 14, 1800.[72] Nevertheless, another bill was reported by Harper from the same committee on May 1, and this was ordered to be printed.[73] Apparently, no further effort was made in the Senate during this session to effect a complete revision of the judiciary.[74]

Pending the convening of the forthcoming session of Congress, Harper was not idle. In the course of a long printed report sent to his constituents and dated May 15, 1800, he emphasized the efforts that

---

[68] Turner, "Federalist Policy," 11–12.

[69] *Annals of Congress*, X, 197, 646 (6th Cong., 1st sess.). Beveridge fails to mention either of these important facts.

[70] *Ibid.*, 646.

[71] *Ibid.*, 650. See Bill 6 HID 52.1, Rare Book Room, Library of Congress.

[72] *Annals of Congress*, X, 665–66 (6th Cong., 1st sess.).

[73] "Report of the Committee To Whom was referred So Much of the President's Speech as relates to 'A revision and amendment of the Judiciary System,' 1st May, 1800," 6 HIR 135, Rare Book Room, Library of Congress.

[74] Judge Sitgreaves of North Carolina wrote to John Heywood on April 29, 1800, that:

The alteration proposed in the Judiciary system of the United States was pregnant with many objections of a general as well as private nature in my Opinion but the inconvenience it would occasion to me were unworthy of consideration compared with the enormity of unnecessary Expense to the public— it was generally disapproved in the House & I now observe its further Consideration postponed till next session—.

University of North Carolina Papers, University Archives, Chapel Hill, N.C. Sitgreaves was subsequently advanced by Adams from the federal district court to one of the new circuit judgeships.

had been made in Congress to increase the number of federal courts to "render the administration of justice more effectual and less burthensome."[75] Referring to the inconvenience and expense caused litigants and their witnesses by attendance at a federal court held at great distances from their homes, he stated that such circumstances had "a strong tendency to bring the laws of the United States into neglect and disrepute, by deterring people from prosecuting offenders against them." He also referred to the "immense labor," fatigue, and time-consuming duties of the existing circuit system, which obliged the Supreme Court judges "to travel perpetually from one end of the continent to the other . . . and prevents them from giving that application to the study of the law which is necessary. . . ." Other members of Congress appear to have been more concerned, for the time being, with the crucial problem of the forthcoming election; consequently, during the summer recess of 1800, the most important effort to effect reform of the judiciary system was probably the preparation of Adams' address to be delivered to Congress later that year. The drafting of that speech became the task of John Marshall, who prepared it in its entirety for Adams to deliver, incorporating with only slight changes in wording the substance of a letter of advice that Marshall had sent to Adams[76] (at the President's request) the previous September.[77] In this speech Marshall stressed, in words far stronger than those Adams had used in 1799, the vital necessity of reforming the judicial system.

In the next session of Congress, after only a short period of work that involved virtually no revision of the preceding bill, the new House judiciary committee presented what was substantially the Judiciary Bill of 1801. Without pursuing the course of the debates, which Professor Preyer has summarized,[78] suffice it to say that, after considerable wrangling, but with few amendments, the Bill passed through the House in fifteen days by a vote of ·51-43 on January 20, 1801, and then went on to the Senate.[79] There, without the revisions for which some Federalists hoped,[80] the committee to which the Bill was referred re-

---

[75] Original copies, from which the quotations in the text are taken, may be found in Robert G. Harper Papers, Manuscripts Division, Library of Congress, and in Bayard Papers, Maryland Historical Society, Baltimore. For a reprinted text, see E. Donnan, ed., "The Papers of James A. Bayard," *Annual Report of the American Historical Association for the Year 1913* (Washington, 1915), II.

[76] J. Marshall to J. Adams, Nov.

22, 1800, in C. F. Adams, ed., *The Works of John Adams* (Boston, 1854), IX, 143.

[77] J. Adams to J. Marshall, Sept. 27, 1800, *ibid.*, IX, 85.

[78] Turner, "Federalist Policy," 15–19. See also Frankfurter and Landis, *Business of Supreme Court*, 24–25, note 66.

[79] *Annals of Congress*, X, 912, 915 (6th Cong., 1st sess.).

[80] See the letters from Senator Bingham of Pennsylvania to Richard

ported it without amendment,[81] lest it be returned to the House and defeated by a change in the narrow vote by which it had passed. The Bill was rushed through the Senate without a single amendment, and on February 11 was passed by a vote of 16-11.[82] It was signed with obvious distaste by Thomas Jefferson, the Senate's presiding officer,[83] and became law on February 13, 1801.[84]

D. THE FEDERAL JUDICIARY AND PARTISAN POLITICS

With the enactment into law of the 1801 Bill, the federal judiciary was drawn more irresistibly than ever into the vortex of politics, and for the next eight years, while the implacable Jefferson was in office as President, the judiciary's history was an inextricable part of the fierce party strife that raged between Republicans and Federalists both in and out of Congress. There were several causes for this persistent struggle between the two rival groups. In the first place, as previously noted, the federal courts had become unpopular with large sectors of the population in the early 1790s because of the nationalistic principles for which they stood.[85] That unpopularity had increased for a number of reasons, including the supposed invasions of States' rights,[86] the suspected anti-French sentiment of the Federalist judges,[87] the prosecutions under the Sedition Act,[88] and the Federalist-oriented jury charges of the judges.[89] Reference has already been made to the vituperations that Republicans began to heap upon the Act—the "law of the midnight judges"—as they became aware that it put into the hands of the outgoing Federalist President the opportunity to name sixteen federal judges to the new circuits. In addition to the appointments made possible by the Act, others were afforded by the enactment of legislation creating a court for the District of Columbia. This Act became law on February 27, four

Peters, Feb. 1, 1801, Peters Papers, Pennsylvania Historical Society, Philadelphia; J. Marshall to W. Paterson, Feb. 2, 1801, Paterson Papers, Bancroft Transcript, New York Public Library, New York City.

[81] *Annals of Congress*, X, 737 (6th Cong., 1st sess.).

[82] *Ibid.*, 741–42. Senator Mason of Virginia wrote to John Breckenridge on Feb. 12 that the judiciary bill "has been crammed down our throats without a word or letter being suffered to be altered." Breckenridge Papers, Manuscripts Division, Library of Congress.

[83] See T. Truxton to A. Hamilton,

Mar. 26, 1802, J. C. Hamilton, ed., *Works of Alexander Hamilton* (New York, 1851), VI, 535.

[84] 2 Stat. 89.

[85] See the letter of Chief Justice Jay, note 51 supra.

[86] See Warren, *Supreme Court*, I, 156–67.

[87] See, e.g., Bas v. Tingy, 4 Dall. 37 (1800), and newspaper comment thereon cited in Warren, *Supreme Court*, I, 157 et seq.

[88] See Smith, *Freedom's Fetters*; A. J. Beveridge, *The Life of John Marshall* (Boston, 1919), III, 29–43.

[89] See chapter 7 infra.

days before the close of the Adams administration, and provided for the appointment of three more judges having the powers of circuit judges, together with appointments of numerous marshals, clerks, attorneys, and justices of the peace.[90]

Republicans generally began to view these two Acts only as iniquitous party measures designed by the defeated Federalists to entrench themselves and their discredited political doctrines in the judiciary—a measure "as good to the party as an election."[91] Other related charges also helped to widen the bitter and already far-reaching division that had been made decisive by the election of 1800.[92] Not only spoils and politics were charged, but extravagance in the "shameful profusion of public money."[93] It was inaccurately assumed that the new circuit system would cost the national government $137,000 annually, whereas the actual cost was less than $50,000.[94] More fundamental in the criticisms of the Republican opposition was their profound disagreement with the Federalist premise, to which reference has more than once been made, that expansion of federal judicial jurisdiction to the full extent of constitutional power was essential to foster nationalism and national power at the expense of decentralization buttressed by forces of localism and State power.

These and other issues were to be paraded prominently and vituperatively in the course of the debates on the repeal of the 1801 Act, which, once the Republicans were in power, was a foregone conclusion.[95] Yet the review of the history of the 1801 Act, the essence of which had long been desired in many quarters, has demonstrated conclusively that the Act was not introduced in consequence of Adams' defeat in 1800 and passed solely for the purpose of perpetuating Federalist policies in the judiciary. On the contrary, the debates on the bill in Congress reveal almost no Republican objection to the patronage it would provide the outgoing administration. The great outcry came

---

[90] 2 Stat. 103–108.

[91] Quoted in Warren, *Supreme Court*, I, 193.

[92] For a sampling of inflammatory charges in the Republican press, see Turner, "Federalist Policy," 20, note 91.

[93] These words were actually used by Representative Claiborne in the House on January 9, 1800, *Annals of Congress*, X, 900 (6th Cong., 1st sess.), but the accusation was constantly reiterated during the course of debates on repeal. See chapter 5 infra.

[94] *Annals of Congress*, XI, 27–30

(7th Cong., 1st sess.). The salary of each of the fifteen circuit judges in the first five circuits was $2,000, and that of the circuit judge for the Sixth Circuit was $1,500—a total of $31,500. If contingent expenses are estimated at half that amount, the total cost of the new system was well under $50,000.

[95] The correspondence of the period is replete with indications and assurances that repeal of the 1801 Act would be one of the first measures to be proposed by the new Administration, as in fact it was. See chapter 5 infra.

afterwards, when the Act had been passed, and Adams set about making new appointments with speed and determination during the remaining three weeks of his term of office. Before then even Jefferson appears not to have appreciated the opportunity it would give the federal courts to extend national power. On December 19, 1800, he wrote to Madison that he did not believe the bill would be pushed because the appointments thereunder "could not fall on those that create them."[96] Soon afterwards, however, he took alarm, and again wrote to Madison, but this time to tell him that he dreaded the Judiciary Bill "above all the measures meditated, because appointments in the nature of freehold render it difficult to undo what is done."[97]

Federalist leaders had hardly been insensitive to the potentialities that the Act would afford in the way of new judicial appointments. Thus, General Gunn had written to Hamilton on December 13, 1800, that if the opportunity of extending the influence of the judiciary were not seized, "the ground will be occupied by the enemy the very next Session of Congress, and, Sir, we shall see . . . scoundrels placed on the seat of Justice."[98] Governor Davie wrote to John Steele at about the same time that "a great deal will depend on the appointment of these Judges, they ought to be men of known weight of character, and men of active and popular, as well as professional talents; on their exertions will depend in a great measure the cause of Federalism in the Southern States."[99]

Unquestionably partisan politics were a factor in the appointments actually made to the judicial positions that the Act created; unquestionably, also, as Henry Adams says, "the Federalists felt bound to exclude Republicans from the bench, to prevent the overthrow of those legal principles in which, as they believed, national safety dwelt. Jefferson understood the challenge, and was obliged to accept or decline it."[100] However, because the appointments helped to fire the Republican assault on the judiciary, and because they have so often been the starting-point for attacking the 1801 Act on the grounds of haste and political jobbery, it is necessary to pause at this point to review the episode of the so-called midnight appointments—an episode intimately connected with the history of the Supreme Court.

---

[96] T. Jefferson to J. Madison, Dec. 19, 1800, in P. L. Ford, ed., *The Works of Thomas Jefferson* (New York, 1904–1905), IX, 159.

[97] T. Jefferson to J. Madison, Dec. 26, 1800, *ibid.*, IX, 161.

[98] J. Gunn to A. Hamilton, Dec. 13, 1800, Papers of Alexander Hamilton, Manuscripts Division, Library of Congress.

[99] John Steele Papers, Folder 20, Southern Historical Collection, Chapel Hill, N. C.

[100] Adams, *History of United States*, I, 275.

E. THE APPOINTMENT OF THE "MIDNIGHT JUDGES"

In the spring of 1800 President Adams had appointed John Marshall as Secretary of State, and he still held that position, at Adams' request, when he was nominated and later confirmed as Chief Justice. In that period the Secretary of State was charged with many duties relating to domestic affairs that today would seem entirely alien to the post. Those duties included responsibility for the preparation and authentication of all Presidential commissions, and, in addition, the Secretary issued instructions to, and corresponded with, United States marshals and attorneys.[101] Hence, letters relating to the judiciary, when not addressed directly to the President, came to Marshall, who was thus in the felicitous position of holding two of the three offices most intimately connected with the appointment of the new judges. From this fact, from the fact that as a member of the judiciary committee of the House he had helped to prepare the 1801 Bill,[102] and from the existence of a close personal relationship between Adams and Marshall, it may be inferred that the latter's advice was both sought and given in making the choices for the new judgeships, in which, as Chief Justice, he had a vital interest. Unfortunately, however, the precise extent of his influence cannot be gauged with any precision.

Adams regarded the task of making the appointments as one requiring his personal and careful attention, and the task can scarcely have been an easy one during the period of anger and humiliation that clouded the final weeks of his administration. It goes without saying that the test of the wisdom of his selections must be found in the calibre of the men ultimately appointed. A strong party man, Adams did not favor, personally or otherwise, the appointment of persons who entertained anti-Federalist principles, and failure to appoint "safe men" to the new positions would have been viewed as a complete breach of trust by those who stood for the principles of nationalism that he had so ardently espoused. In offering the Chief Justiceship to John Jay, Adams had referred to the need of "security . . . against the effects of visionary schemes or fluctuating theories."[103] Yet he was no believer in the sort of patronage that rewards mere efficient party work. He did not believe that "political services alone constituted a claim to office."[104] At the outset he announced the standards that would govern his selection of

---

[101] G. Hunt, *The Department of State of the United States* (New Haven, 1914), 128–29.

[102] *Annals of Congress*, X, 197 (6th Cong., 1st sess.).

[103] J. Adams to J. Jay, Dec. 19, 1800, in Johnston, *John Jay Papers*, IV, 284.

[104] G. Hunt, "Office-Seeking During the Administration of John Adams," *American Historical Review* II, 241 at 261 (1897).

judges: "I may have been too indifferent to the smiles of some men & to the frowns of others—but neither will influence my judgment I hope in determining nominations of judges—characters at all times sacred in my estimation."[105]

An exceedingly thorough and scholarly evaluation of Adams' final appointments has been made by Professor Kathryn Turner Preyer,[106] and, again, as with her account of the Judiciary Bill of 1801, little more need be said beyond summarizing her conclusions, which are well supported by unequivocal evidence. Even while the Judiciary Bill was still before Congress, requests and inquiries had begun to pour into the capital, and the stream became more swollen after the Bill became law, especially when it was learned that Adams would be glad to receive suggestions as to suitable candidates. Thus he wrote to Richard Stockton on January 27 that if the Judiciary Bill should pass, he would be glad to have advice "relative to appointments in other states as well as your own."[107]

Both before and after the Act became law, local as well as national figures wrote to Adams on behalf of prospective candidates, and even for themselves.[108] Others wrote to Marshall,[109] or asked friends to write on behalf of themselves or their associates.[110] Adams wrote that the selection of judges would cost him "much anxiety and dilligence [sic]" and that he could make no promises nor give any encouragement until the merits of all the candidates were weighed.[111] Yet, although all those selected were Federalists, it is clear that the problem did engage his close personal attention, particularly in the Second and Third Circuits,[112] where the Bar was eminently distinguished and where its members appeared with great frequency before the federal courts.[113] Although

---

[105] J. Adams to R. Stockton, Jan. 27, 1801, *John Adams Letter Book,* Adams Family Papers, Manuscripts Division, Library of Congress.

[106] Turner, "Midnight Judges."

[107] J. Adams to R. Stockton, Jan. 27, 1801, *John Adams Letter Book,* Manuscripts Division, Library of Congress.

[108] Numerous other letters concerning possible candidates were received by Adams at this time and are preserved in the Adams Papers at the Massachusetts Historical Society: Samuel Otis (Jan. 13), Richard Stockton (Jan. 17), John Bayard (Jan. 25), Charles Chauncey (Jan. 27), John Rodgers (Jan. 31), Harry Innes (Feb. 10), Samuel Chase (Feb. 13), Willis Alston (Feb. 14). For further evidence of Adams' wish to

receive suggestions for suitable appointments, see Turner, "Midnight Judges," 495, note 11.

[109] See, e.g., J. H. Morison, *Life of Hon. Jeremiah Smith, LL.D.* (Boston, 1845), 143–44.

[110] Extended references may be found in Turner, "Midnight Judges," 496–519.

[111] J. Adams to Dr. J. Rodgers, Feb. 6, 1801, in *John Adams Letter Book*, Manuscripts Division, Library of Congress.

[112] Turner, "Midnight Judges," 502–13.

[113] See chapter 5 infra. Apparently the appointment of John Sitgreaves to the Fifth Circuit was Adams' choice alone. Turner, "Midnight Judges," 514.

the political character of the appointments requires no documentation, most of them were deserving men of proven ability at the Bar or on the bench—for example, Jeremiah Smith of New Hampshire, Samuel Hitchcock of Vermont, John Lowell of Massachusetts, Benjamin Bourne of Rhode Island, Jared Ingersoll of Pennsylvania (declined), Philip Barton Key of Maryland, Charles Lee of Virginia (declined), and Joseph Clay of Georgia. Indeed, Professor Crosskey has characterized the new judges as an "extraordinarily able group of men," and he observed that without possible doubt they would "bear comparison with any equal number of judges ever chosen by any President, before or since."[114] Although it must be admitted that a few of the new judges, such as Richard Bassett of Delaware and William McClung of Kentucky, owed their appointments to importuning relatives, in general the selection followed local wishes or national recommendations.[115] Even those with less experience (such as Adams' nephew, William Cranch, and John Marshall's brother, James, who were appointed to the newly created District of Columbia court) were known to be competent.[116] Judged even from a political standpoint, as a whole, "the group of midnight judges reflected the relatively moderate political positions of the men who had selected them. They were not facsimiles of the fanaticism which had led the Federalists to prosecute the Whiskey Rebels . . . and to enforce the Sedition Act with such vigor."[117]

Adams has been accused not only of partisanship and nepotism but of violating at least the spirit of the Constitution in many of the appointments he made. Article I, Section 6, of the Constitution[118] limited his selection of the new circuit judges under the 1801 Act by precluding the appointment of any member of the House or Senate then serving in Congress, because the judgeships had been created during their terms of office. It is, nevertheless, averred that he "evaded" the Constitution by promoting several district judges to the new circuit judgeships and then filled the vacancies thus created by the appointment of senators and representatives.[119] One historian states that there were

---

114 W. W. Crosskey, *Politics and the Constitution in the History of the United States* (Chicago, 1953), II, 761.

115 See Turner, "Midnight Judges," 496–517.

116 See Beveridge, *John Marshall*, II, 560, note 2, and III, 346, note 7. As explained above, this court was created by an Act that became law on February 27, 1801, and was composed of three judges having the powers of circuit court judges. 2 Stat.

103–108. See text accompanying note 90 supra.

117 Turner, "Midnight Judges," 521–22.

118 That section provides: "No Senator or Representative shall, during the Time for which he was elected, be appointed to any civil office under the Authority of the United States, which shall have been created, or the Emoluments whereof shall have been encreased during such time. . . ."

119 Channing, *Students' History*, 260.

only two such appointments,[120] but in fact three senators and one representative were appointed to four of the six district judgeships made vacant by the promotion of district judges to the new circuit courts.[121] Of course, to the extent that there were new vacancies to fill, Adams was likely to consider only Federalists for the appointments; however, the care that he took to seek advice about all the new appointments extended to the vacated district judgeships, as well as to the circuit positions.[122] As Professor Max Farrand has said, "it would seem to be a wholly natural proceeding to promote some of the district judges to the higher positions that were opened, and it would depend solely upon the character of the men themselves, whether it were right that members of Congress should be appointed to the district judgeships thus vacated. . . ."[123]

Not all to whom Adams offered circuit judgeships accepted. For example, Theophilus Parsons of Massachusetts refused to permit himself to be considered on the ground that the salary minus expenses, "will not support . . . my family."[124] Richard Stockton of New Jersey declined Adams' offer, probably on the ground that he wished to run for governor of his State;[125] Jared Ingersoll of Pennsylvania wrote that the salary of a circuit judge "would not maintain my family."[126] Edward Tilghman, also of Pennsylvania, made it known that he would not accept;[127] and Charles Lee of Virginia was approved but declined. For all of those who declined, replacements were found before Adams left office, but two positions in the Fifth Circuit became vacant after March 4,[128] and to them Jefferson subsequently appointed Dominick Hall and Henry Potter.[129]

---

[120] McMaster, *History of the People*, II, 610.
[121] Senators Green, Paine, and Read were appointed respectively to the districts of Rhode Island, Vermont, and South Carolina. Representative Hill was named to the district judgeship of North Carolina.
[122] As to Adams' solicitude about qualified judges, see text accompanying note 111 supra.
[123] Farrand, "Judiciary Act of 1801," 686.
[124] T. Parson to H. G. Otis, Jan. 23, 1801, in S. E. Morison, *The Life and Letters of Harrison Gray Otis* (Boston, 1913), I, 213.
[125] W. R. Fee, "Richard Stockton," *Dictionary of American Biography* (New York, 1936), XVIII, 47.
[126] J. Ingersoll to J. Adams, Feb. 23, 1801, in *John Adams Letter Book*.

[127] See letter from Senator W. Bingham to W. Tilghman, Feb. 27, 1801, Gratz Collection, Box 32, Historical Society of Pennsylvania, Philadelphia.
[128] Thomas Bee did not receive his commission until after Jefferson had taken office. He returned it in order to continue in his position as district judge. T. Bee to J. Madison, Mar. 19, 1801, Madison Papers, XXII, Library of Congress. John Sitgreaves also declined the commission.
[129] Dominick Augustine Hall (South Carolina) was appointed Chief Judge, *vice* Thomas Bee who had declined, and Henry Potter (North Carolina) was appointed associate judge, *vice* John Sitgreaves who had also declined. *Journal of the Executive Proceedings of the Senate* (Washington, 1828), I, 401, 405. When Sitgreaves,

The final list of circuit judges nominated and approved during the Adams administration was as follows: *First Circuit*: Benjamin Bourne (Rhode Island), John Lowell (Massachusetts), Jeremiah Smith (New Hampshire); *Second Circuit*: Egbert Benson (New York), Samuel Hitchcock (Vermont), Oliver Wolcott (Connecticut); *Third Circuit*: Richard Bassett (Delaware), William Griffith (New Jersey), William Tilghman (Pennsylvania); *Fourth Circuit*: Philip Barton Key (Maryland), Charles Magill (Virginia), George Keith Taylor (Virginia); *Fifth Circuit*: Thomas Bee (South Carolina), Joseph Clay, Jr. (Georgia), John Sitgreaves (North Carolina); *Sixth Circuit*: William McClung (Kentucky).[130]

F. THE EFFECTS OF THE 1801 ACTS

The intemperate and misguided charges that the primary purpose of the 1801 Act was to afford an opportunity to pack the judiciary with Federalist judges, as well as to increase their numbers, have, one hopes, been answered by the preceding discussion. Moreover, it should be observed that emphasis on the "central" features of the Act—the elimination of circuit riding for the Supreme Court judges and the creation of new circuit courts—has tended to distract attention from other provisions of the legislation. Central they were, because in creating the new courts Congress evidently wished to make it more feasible for the Supreme Court to become an institution, regularly meeting at ascertained and predictable sessions in Washington, without being hampered by the travel conditions that attended the additional and diversionary functions of circuit riding. The implications of these features, as well as other provisions of the Act, make it plain that much more was expected at the time from the legislation, and this conclusion is further supported by its background—for example, in the correspondence of Adams, Sedgwick, Wolcott, and others already referred to. The "enlargement of the judiciary" was far from a mere enlargement

---

who had remained on the District Court of North Carolina, died in March 1802, Jefferson nominated Potter to that Court and Edward Harris (North Carolina) to Potter's place on the Circuit Court. Both were confirmed in April 1802. *Ibid.*, I, 418, 422, 423. The dates given in *Legislative History of the United States Court of Appeals . . .* (Committee on the Judiciary: U. S. Senate, 85th Cong., 2d sess., Washington, 1958) are at variance with the original Sen-

ate Journal and the entries are incomplete. Potter's name was suggested to Jefferson by Nathaniel Macon in a letter of April 20, 1801. He was subsequently characterized as a "uniformly sound Republican." N. Macon to T. Jefferson, Willis Grandy Briggs Papers, Southern Historical Collection, Chapel Hill, N. C.

[130] See note 129 supra for substitutions in the Fifth Circuit as a result of withdrawals of Thomas Bee and John Sitgreaves.

of numbers; indeed, as stated, only sixteen new judgeships were created. Nationalists envisaged that the federal court system should no longer be what it had been in the decade following 1789, with narrow scope and little prestige. To bring a coherent system of justice close to men's doors was one purpose, for many a litigant had traveled miles only to find a court could not convene because of the ill health of a judge or his inability to arrive in time; to expand federal jurisdiction through provisions lowering the requisite monetary amounts was another; to enhance the diminished prestige of a judiciary, appointed rather than elected, was a third; to dignify the courts through the abilities and reputations of the judges was a fourth. With respect to the latter, it should be recalled that nearly every judge appointed to the Supreme Court, by both Washington and Adams, had been both a leader of the Bar and a public figure in his own State. Moreover, the appointments that Adams made or attempted to make to the new circuit courts were, for the most part, distinguished lawyers who had often served with ability as district judges in their own communities, even though—as is well known—all of them were Federalists.

Consideration of the types of cases that would be drawn into the federal courts, as reconstituted under the 1801 Act, emphasizes the nationalist aspects of the legislation, which would inevitably have drawn or transferred litigation from the State to the federal courts. Whereas before 1801 a very substantial portion of the cases coming before the federal courts had their origins in maritime disputes (contracts, insurance, bills and notes, admiralty), after the Act it was quite clear that something approaching an avalanche of land disputes would now originate in or be transferred to the district and the new circuit courts. For example, the latter had primary jurisdiction to hear and determine intricate and difficult cases relating to land titles, many already *sub judice* and snarled in jurisdictional disputes arising from State and Territorial boundary problems. Likewise, it appears to have been no coincidence that the national Bankruptcy Act, which was passing through Congress at the same time, would likewise result in a large increase in federal court business.[131] How far, in practice, these changes would have materialized is difficult to assess. The new circuit courts did convene, and several cases came before them; but the surviving records are incomplete, and the new system was abolished by mid-1802, when the 1801 Act was repealed.

It was not long before thoughtful Republicans began to perceive these ramifications of the Act, which went far beyond the initial cries of "spoils" and "midnight judges," in its ineluctable incursions on

---

[131] See Turner, "Federalist Policy."

cherished States' rights. Some of these fundamental arguments were to surface in the debate on repeal that began almost as soon as the new administration took office.

A second Judiciary Act, which became law on February 27, 1801, provided for the establishment of a new court for the District of Columbia, having all the powers of the circuit courts and the national circuit judges, and for the appointment of three judges thereto.[132] As stated above, Adams immediately named his nephew, William Cranch, and James Marshall, brother of the Chief Justice, to this court. The chief judgeship he offered to the aging Thomas Johnson of Maryland, who had resigned from the Supreme Court in 1793, but he declined the new appointment after Jefferson took office[133] and thus left vacant another judicial position for the new President to fill.[134] That Act also provided for numerous appointments of clerks, marshals, attorneys, and justices of the peace. To these lesser offices, and very much at the last minute, were appointed supposedly "deserving" local members of the Federalist party. These appointments were swiftly approved by the Senate on March 2 and 3,[135] and the last commissions were hurriedly signed in the office of Secretary of State, John Marshall, and thereafter delivered before the President's term expired at midnight on March 3. These lesser appointments were, in effect, "midnight" appointments, and at least four commissions (including that of William Marbury, as justice of the peace) had not been delivered when Jefferson became President. It was this circumstance that gave rise to the celebrated case of *Marbury* v. *Madison*, in which Marbury sought to have the Supreme Court issue a writ of mandamus to compel the new Secretary of State, James Madison, to deliver his commission.[136]

---

[132] 2 Stat. 103–108. See text accompanying note 90 supra.

[133] Johnson's tardy rejection of the office "excessively mortified" the Chief Justice. John Marshall to James Marshall, Mar. 18, 1801, Marshall Transcripts and Photostats, Manuscripts Division, Library of Congress. See also E. S. Delaplaine, *The Life of Thomas Johnson* (New York, 1927), 507.

[134] Jefferson appointed William Kilty, a Republican, who was later to gratify the President by his decision in *Ex Parte Bollmann*. See chapter 8 infra.

[135] *Journal of the Executive Proceedings of the Senate* (Washington, 1828), I, 388–89.

[136] 1 Cranch 137 (1803). See chapter 6 infra.

CHAPTER V

Jefferson's Attack on the Federal Judiciary

F EW MEN who have assumed the high office of President of the United States have been so distrusted, disliked, hated, or feared by so many leading citizens of the country as was Thomas Jefferson in 1801. The Presidential election of 1800 was a close one, far closer than is often appreciated. Jefferson and Burr received an equal number of electoral votes, and the election remained deadlocked in the House of Representatives for several weeks. The stalemate was broken only by the last-minute switch by James A. Bayard of Delaware, who cast his vote for Jefferson in return for certain assurances held out by way of a "bargain" to some of the leading Federalists whereby Jefferson let it be known that he could be counted on not to disturb the established order, and more specifically, that he would adhere to three principal Federalist policies—public credit, the maintenance of the Navy, and the retention of subordinate officers of the government.[1]

In spite of widespread popular approval of Jefferson, John Adams also had significant support; he polled 65 electoral votes as opposed to Jefferson's 73. If New York, the swing State, had supported him, Adams would have had more electoral votes in 1800 than in 1796.[2] This heavy support was his notwithstanding certain disadvantages under which he labored, including the intrigues of Hamilton against him, his sponsorship of the Alien and Sedition Acts, the countervailing issues arising from the Virginia and Kentucky Resolutions, and the almost frenzied opposition of the Republican politicians and their newspapers.[3] Thus Jefferson's victory was indeed a narrow one.

---

[1] M. Davis, ed., *Memoirs of Aaron Burr* (New York, 1837), II, 130–32 (deposition of James A. Bayard).

[2] C. Beard, *Economic Origins of Jeffersonian Democracy* (New York, 1915), chapter 13.

[3] See chapter 2 supra.

V: *Jefferson's Attack on the Federal Judiciary*

It was inevitable, with the outcome so close, that party feuds should have continued to dominate the political scene even when the voting was over. The campaign that had preceded the election was fought not only on identifiable political issues but on the basis of strong personal and partisan feelings; it remains almost unparalleled in American history for the bitterness it engendered. The rancor it provoked was not abated by Jefferson's accession to office, despite the relief many felt over Burr's defeat. New England Federalists, represented by such men as Theodore Dwight of New Haven, could see in Jefferson only an atheist who espoused the radical Jacobinism that had spilled the blood of France and was bent on the total destruction of civilization.[4] Hamilton at one point was even prepared to accept Adams as President to save the country from the "fangs" of Jefferson,[5] while William Barry Grove, a leading North Carolina Federalist, viewed Jefferson as a cunning politician who employed "arts, & machiavellian policy to get at the head of American affairs."[6] Many high-minded Virginians honestly feared Jefferson almost as much as they opposed his political philosophy and theories of government; others, including George Washington and John Marshall, had experienced Jefferson's cunning and duplicity at first hand. In the famous letter to Mazzei, Jefferson had castigated Washington as an apostate who had gone over to the heresies of Federalism, one of the men "who were Samsons in the field & Solomons in the council, but who have had their heads shorn by the harlot of England."[7] As late as 1802, it is reported that Martha Washington still spoke of Jefferson "as one of the most detestable of mankind,"[8] and his election "as the greatest misfortune our country had ever experienced,"[9] for she was still outraged by the abuse that Jefferson had heaped upon her husband while he lived and upon his memory after

---

[4] See F. Van Der Linden, *The Turning Point: Jefferson's Battle for the Presidency* (Washington, 1962) passim, especially 296–317. For a more favorable view of Jefferson's role, see D. Malone, *Jefferson the President: First Term, 1801–1805* (Boston, 1970), 487–93.

[5] A. Hamilton to T. Sedgwick, May 4, 1800, in H. Syrett, ed., *The Papers of Alexander Hamilton* (New York, 1976), XXIV, 452–53 (hereafter cited as Syrett, *Hamilton Papers*).

[6] W. B. Grove to J. Hoag, Mar. 14, 1801, William Barry Grove Papers, Southern Historical Collection of the University of North Carolina, Chapel Hill.

[7] P. L. Ford, ed., *The Works of Thomas Jefferson* (New York, 1904–1905), VII, 72, 76 (hereafter cited as Ford, *Works of Jefferson*). The description, as it originally appeared in the New York *Minerva*, January 25, 1787, was of men "who were Solomons in council, and Sampsons in combat, but whose hair has been cut off by the whore England." *Ibid.*, 75. The differences are attributable to many translations of the original statement. The *Minerva* version was translated from the French, which in turn was translated from an Italian translation of the original letter.

[8] *Ibid.*

[9] *Ibid.*

his decease.[10] It is small wonder that John Marshall felt constrained to write Hamilton in January of 1801:

> To Mr. Jefferson . . . I have felt almost insuperable objections. His foreign prejudices seem to me totally to unfit him for the chief magistracy of a nation which cannot indulge those prejudices without sustaining debt & permanent injury. . . . By weakening the office of President he will increase his personal power. He will diminish his responsibility, [and] sap the fundamental principles of the government. . . .[11]

The anti-Federalists, known generally as Republicans, saw Jefferson in a far different light. To them he was a great leader—the apostle of equality, the enemy of monarchy and mercantile interests, the champion of agrarianism, and the protector of States' rights against the encroaching national government.[12] United by harmony of interests and disciplined by local leaders and caucuses, their strength was formidable in comparison with that of the Federalists, whose unity was by now wracked with factiousness and disagreements. The Republicans saw, but probably exaggerated, the dangers, if not the virulence, that could result from the defeated party. "[O]ur foes," wrote one of Jefferson's new cabinet officers, "are not conquered, though they crouch it is but to secure their prey. . . ."[13] In Connecticut, he went on to say, the torrents of abuse from the pulpits were incredible, and the Federalists "[design] to make themselves terrible in the opposition."[14] Another Republican in Connecticut at the same time wrote that "the malignity of the federalists here is wholly inconceivable to any . . . a corps most systematically organized. The Governor and Council, joined to the corporation of Yale College . . . make all the arrangements;"[15] while from their pulpits the clergy preached that the new administration had brought in "men of no *religion*, men *profligate in their morals*."[16]

Jefferson and his followers were especially outraged that the Federalists had managed to retain control of the federal judiciary. The Revolution of 1800 brought a Republican into power as head of the

---

[10] For specific comments on the extent of abuses heaped on Washington see J. McMaster, *A History of the People of the United States* (New York, 1885), II, 249–50, 289–91, 302–306.

[11] Syrett, *Hamilton Papers*, XXV, 290.

[12] See generally D. Malone, *Jefferson and the Ordeal of Liberty* (Boston, 1962), 312–25; C. Bowers, *Jefferson and Hamilton: The Struggle for Democracy in America* (Boston, 1925), 140–60.

[13] G. Granger to T. Jefferson, Apr. 15, 1801, printed in G. Hunt, "Office-Seeking During Jefferson's Administration," *The American Historical Review* III, 270, 273 (1898).

[14] *Ibid.*

[15] P. Edwards to T. Jefferson, May 12, 1801, in *ibid.*, 275.

[16] *Ibid.*, 276.

executive branch and gave the party a large margin in the House, accompanied by a somewhat smaller margin in the Senate, yet the courts remained largely unaffected by the "revolution." The judiciary, far from responding to the election, not only remained in Federalist hands but had been augmented and made more powerful by the Act of 1801 creating new circuit judgeships that President Adams had all but filled before he left office. These "midnight appointments" of judges to the district and circuit courts were accordingly a major reason for Jefferson's hostility, more particularly since they were accompanied by appointments of Federalists to the offices of United States attorneys and marshals, as discussed in the preceding chapter.

Jefferson and the other Republican leaders were fully cognizant of the problems they could face with a Federalist judiciary opposing attempts at reform by the new administration. The Presidency was now in the hands of one who had among his aims the destruction of the Federalists' accomplishments during their twelve-year monopoly of office: taxes must now be reduced, the Army disbanded, and the Navy beached. To these Republican goals, the views held by Federalists, including the judiciary, were wholly antithetical.

Among the specific Republican complaints against the Federalist judges was that they had taken it upon themselves to apply, without reference to national statutes or the Constitution, precedents drawn chiefly from the English common law. It was objected that the courts had thus become lawmakers and had assumed powers that they had never been given, expressly or otherwise. On the other hand, it had been the general position of the federal judges that the common law—as embodied in English decisions and usages—was as much a part of the federal jurisprudence as it was of the law of the several States. Jefferson's view of the adoption of English common law by American courts was expressed in a letter he wrote to John Randolph in 1799, nearly eighteen months before he took office. To him all the evils accomplished by the Federalists were inconsequential "in comparison with the audacious, bare-faced and sweeping pretension to a system of law for the US without the adoption of their legislature, and so infinitively beyond their power to adopt."[17] Hence, it was even more aggravating that the entire federal bench was in the hands of judges who were likely to continue to adhere to English precedents and who, as James Monroe wrote to Jefferson, would use their strategic offices "to promote reaction."[18] In the same letter Monroe went on to say, "You

---

[17] T. Jefferson to J. Randolph, Aug. 18, 1799, in Ford, *Works of Jefferson*, VII, 384.

[18] J. Monroe to T. Jefferson, Mar. 3, 1801, in S. M. Hamilton, ed., *Writings of James Monroe* (New York, 1898), III, 261, 263–64.

see that Adams has done everything in his power to embarrass yr. admn. In some of his appointments, too, he has nominated his enemies to strengthen his party."[19]

To Republicans, the attitude of the judiciary had been obnoxiously displayed in its rigorous enforcement of the Sedition Act and in the use that had been made of jury charges to instruct and "educate" the public in the nationalist principles for which Federalists stood.[20] Even more outrageous to the Republicans, and for reasons that were better founded, was the conduct of individual judges on the bench. Often rude, frequently partisan or intemperate, many of them had also taken the opportunity—especially in charges to grand juries—to lecture and preach on morality, religion, and politics. Not even the Supreme Court judges escaped censure for such conduct, even though occasionally they were praised for it.[21] Other objections included the participation by two Chief Justices in a mission sent to draft treaties which it would be the business of the Supreme Court to expound.[22] And even Congress had reacted sharply when the State of Georgia had been brought before that Court as a defendant.[23]

The stage was thus set for a confrontation between the new Republican administration and the firmly entrenched Federalist judiciary. No adequate presentation of the early history of the Supreme Court and the foundations of its power can be made without explaining why and to what extent it became embroiled in the fierce party strife that marked the Republican victory in the opening years of the new century. Reference has already been made in an earlier chapter to the strong political divisions that separated the country in 1800.[24] Those divisions, intensified by the opposing programs of the two party factions, became such as to split the nation apart almost as widely as at the time of ratification. Because the victors in the 1800 election found themselves still confronted by their political opponents in the judiciary, it was inevitable that the Supreme Court should be drawn into the controversy.

During the course of the first twelve years of the Supreme Court's existence, that body was not regarded as possessing particular importance, and it had decided few cases of major significance. The compara-

---

[19] Ibid., 264.

[20] See text accompanying notes 123–33 infra.

[21] See text accompanying note 125 infra.

[22] Especially the Jay Treaty, negotiated by John Jay while Chief Justice. See J. Marshall, Life of George Washington (Philadelphia, 1840), II, 365–66.

[23] The State of Georgia was brought before the Supreme Court in Chisholm v. Georgia, 2 Dall. 419 (1793), which led to the enactment of the Eleventh Amendment. See M. Field, "The Eleventh Amendment and Other Sovereign Immunity Doctrines: Part One," University of Pennsylvania Law Review CXXVI, 515 (1978).

[24] See chapter 2 supra.

tive unimportance in the public mind of the Court, and indeed of the entire federal judiciary, is attested by the frequent resignations and refusals of appointments under both Washington and Adams.[25] Two specific events, however, brought the Court into the vortex of politics: one was the Republican victory at the polls; the other, connected with it, was the enactment in the final weeks of the Adams administration of the Judiciary Act of 1801, which so greatly enlarged the powers of the national courts and at the same time made it possible for the outgoing President to appoint members of his own party to the newly created judgeships.

Personalities played a dominant role in the definition and ultimate resolution of the conflict between the judiciary and the other two branches of the national government. Among the principal protagonists of the opposing sides were President Jefferson and his cousin, Chief Justice John Marshall. The two men typified the gulf that separated Republicans from Federalists. In addition, personal enmity and mutual distrust had long characterized their relationship. Marshall's antipathy to Jefferson has been referred to. Jefferson, throughout his life, "regarded Marshall with a repugnance tinged by a shade of some deeper feeling, almost akin to fear."[26] "The judge's inveteracy," he wrote to Albert Gallatin in 1810, "is profound, and his mind of that gloomy malignity which will never let him forego the opportunity of satiating it on a victim."[27] Jefferson was even prepared to believe that Marshall's *Life of Washington* was written and intended to be published in time to influence the 1804 Presidential election.[28] Beyond these personal antagonisms were antipathies of principle discussed in an earlier chapter.

The frustration that the victorious Republicans felt against the judicial stronghold vented itself initially in their refusal to issue commissions to certain of the judges whom Adams had appointed.[29] Second, and more important, those feelings evidenced themselves in measures instituted to repeal the 1801 Act and thereby to abolish the positions to which the new judges had been appointed, which was accomplished by the Act of 1802. Third, they pressed for and obtained legislation which, in April 1802, recessed the Supreme Court for fourteen months.[30] Finally, it expanded into a full-dress onslaught on the judiciary through the use of the impeachment power.[31] Out of these efforts arose in

[25] A. Beveridge, *The Life of John Marshall* (Boston, 1919), II, 552–53.

[26] H. Adams, *History of the United States of America* (New York, 1889), I, 194.

[27] T. Jefferson to A. Gallatin, Sept. 27, 1810, in H. Adams, ed., *The Writings of Albert Gallatin* (Philadelphia, 1879), I, 492.

[28] Beveridge, *John Marshall*, II, 265–68.

[29] See Malone, *Jefferson*, 73.

[30] See *ibid.*, 131–34.

[31] See *ibid.*, 458–85.

differing form two of the burning constitutional issues of Jefferson's first term: the "legitimacy" of the powers of the federal courts and the independence of the judiciary. As Jefferson took the oath of office of the Presidency on March 4, 1801, the shadow of impending battle loomed large. Yet the struggle was not to begin immediately.

A. REPUBLICAN EFFORTS TOWARDS RECONCILIATION

The beginning of President Jefferson's administration seemed so auspicious that even some Federalists were lulled into a sense of security. The new President's First Inaugural Address was studiously restrained, temperate, and even philosophical in tone. Of New Englanders, who tended to be strong Federalist supporters, he wrote to General Knox: "[W]e will go on attending with the utmost solicitude to their interests, & doing them impartial justice, and I have no doubt they will in time do justice to us."[32] For all the objections to the evils that he perceived in commercial and manufacturing interests, and his view of the banks as invented for purposes of corruption, Jefferson was too astute a politician, too shrewd an observer of contemporary events, not to wish for the support of the interests he had so willingly denounced before he became President. He apparently concluded that the "reformed order of things" could not be achieved, nor the country governed, without the support, or at least the acquiescence, of those interests.

Jefferson's conciliatory language, couched in phrases that professed harmony and assured continuity rather than revolution, must have sounded strange and out of place to his supporters and his enemies alike, for the principles he announced were not radically different from those of President Washington. Those who knew Jefferson, however, could hardly have been unaware that at heart he had triumphed as a Virginia "republican" opposed to "monarchists"; that no change in his political views had occurred in the three years since he penned the strongly-worded draft of the Kentucky Resolutions; and that he still firmly believed that "freedom could be maintained only by preserving inviolate the right of every State to judge for itself what was, and what was not, lawful for a majority to decide."[33] Similarly, his antipathy to manufacturing and banking interests had not abated. He seems also to have concluded that New England's political importance was not great, and in any event he had formed a strong antipathy to-

---

[32] T. Jefferson to H. Knox, Mar. 27, 1801, Ford, *Works of Jefferson*, IX, 236, 237–38.

[33] Adams, *History of United States*, I, 206.

wards that sector of the country.[34] It is small wonder that Federalists began accusing Jefferson of duplicity and worse, when, at the very time of his soothing public assurances, his private correspondence ran in a totally opposite vein. Those letters show Jefferson's true conviction that the methods and intentions of the past were wrong and must be replaced and forgotten. He believed that his two predecessors "had involved the government in difficulties in order to destroy it, and to build up a monarchy on its ruins."[35] Indeed, it was nearly a quarter of a century before Jefferson appears to have expressed any doubt that the revolution of 1800 was as real a revolution in the principles of government as that of 1776 was in its form.[36] Until then, at least, he firmly believed that he was the founder of a new republic, modeled upon the State of Virginia; he also believed that the monarchical principle of centralization could be nullified by firmly assuring States' rights, and promoting agriculture "with commerce as its handmaid" in the simple, traditional, and popular type of southern society that was his ideal. The general government, he wrote to Gideon Granger in 1800, should "be reduced to foreign concerns only."[37] Much later Jefferson elaborated somewhat on this view, stating that the federal government should act principally in the capacity of "our foreign government, which department alone is taken from the Sovereignty of the separate States."[38]

Jefferson's philosophy of government is difficult to explain in its entirety. Even in his letters there are inconsistencies of attitude and expression, which frequently varied according to the subject and object of his correspondence, and which make it difficult to construct a rational, cohesive scheme or picture of his political philosophy. His admirers have nevertheless sought to do so, generally at the expense of considering the points of time at which he expressed himself, the people to whom he wrote, and the purposes of a particular letter. Moreover, inconsistencies, or elements that are not currently popular, are often disregarded. All too frequently Jefferson has been judged on the basis of his public utterances, which, as noted above, were often at variance with the feelings expressed in his private correspondence. In part, this divergence between publicly and privately expressed sentiments was a result of caution; but it was also a result of Jefferson's

---

[34] See, e.g., his letter to John Taylor of June 1, 1798, to the effect that New Englanders are marked "like the Jews, with such a perversity of character as to constitute, from that circumstance, the natural division of our parties." Quoted *ibid.*, 312.

[35] See *ibid.*, 208.

[36] See, e.g., T. Jefferson to S. Roane, Sept. 6, 1819, in Ford, *Works of Jefferson*, XII, 135–36.

[37] T. Jefferson to G. Granger, Aug. 13, 1800, *ibid.*, IX, 138, 140.

[38] T. Jefferson to R. Gannett, Feb. 14, 1824, *ibid.*, XII, 341–42.

character—secretive and frequently devious—and of his predisposition to employ the "third-party technique" by which his own views were imputed to others for particular purposes. For these reasons, to take a phrase that Harold Ickes used to describe President Franklin Roosevelt, it is "difficult to come to grips with him."

Probably the views Jefferson expressed after his retirement are generally more accurate indications of his real attitudes than those stated either publicly or privately in the heat of party conflict during his terms of office. Jefferson was possessed of an ingrained distrust of government, although he believed it to be a necessary evil.[39] Since he saw in all governments an inevitable tendency to curtail personal liberty, he was convinced that political power must come from the voters at large. This principle involved popular control of nearly every office in government, including not only the executive and legislative branches but the judiciary as well. "I know no safe depository of the ultimate powers of the society but the people themselves; and if we think them not enlightened enough to exercise their control with a wholesome discretion, the remedy is not to take it from them, but to inform their discretion by education."[40] Again, if the legislative and executive branches should err, elections would bring them to rights.[41] Yet the Constitution deprived the people of control over the judiciary, and Jefferson came early to believe and assert that this was a "reprobated system."[42]

In his later years, Jefferson spoke freely in broad philosophical terms of the great revolution of 1800 that restored the government to the people, yet when he was President he was as anxious as the Federalists to guard against the tyranny of majorities. His views, though republican, were hardly democratic. He believed that "an *elective despotism* was not the government we fought for,"[43] and his principal objection to the Virginia constitution was the extensive power vested thereunder in the legislature.[44] Although Jefferson spoke in general terms about universal manhood suffrage,[45] such a doctrine was academic in the face of the political realities in the South, probably the most tenacious of all parts of the country in clinging to property qualifications on the suffrage. His belief in popular control of government did not prevent him from agreeing that even the power of the national legislature was subject to certain limits. His adherence to the constitu-

[39] See chapter 2 supra.

[40] T. Jefferson to W. Jarvis, Sept. 28, 1820, Ford, *Works of Jefferson*, XII, 163.

[41] T. Jefferson to A. Thweat, Jan. 19, 1821, *ibid.*, XII, 196.

[42] T. Jefferson to S. Roane, Sept. 6, 1819, *ibid.*, XII, 136.

[43] T. Jefferson, "Notes on Virginia" (1782), *ibid.*, IV, 20.

[44] *Ibid.*, IV, 20–21.

[45] T. Jefferson to J. Moon, Aug. 14, 1800, *ibid.*, IX, 142.

tional doctrine of checks and balances was openly announced in his first Message to Congress,[46] and ironically, until his conflict with the judiciary as President, he had more than once avowed his belief in the power of the courts to declare legislation null and void.[47] Moreover, he favored a bill of rights because of "the legal check which it puts into the hands of the judiciary."[48] He even went so far as to state as a principle, and to act upon it, that the executive had the constitutional right to pronounce invalid an act of Congress.[49]

Even if there is evidence to support a conclusion that in practical effect "Jeffersonian Democracy" did not "involve any fundamental alterations in the national Constitution"[50] and that it "simply meant the possession of the government by the agrarian masses led by an aristocracy of slave-owning planters,"[51] it is important to remember that he regarded the election of 1800 as a real revolution, comparable except in lack of bloodshed to what had been accomplished in France a decade earlier.[52] There is also evidence that his political theories, tinctured as they were with fanaticism and at times malevolent hatred, might have driven him to more extreme measures had the exigencies of practicality not prevented such action. Once in office, however, Jefferson felt no such restraint with respect to the judiciary. If the revolution was to succeed and to be carried out in all its articles, all branches of the government had to change in response to the popular will.

A principal plank of the platform that had brought the Republicans into office was the promise of the restoration of States' rights. To curb the powers of the national government was a prime objective, and a serious threat to the accomplishment of this goal was posed by the system of national courts created under the Judiciary Act of 1789 and extended by the Act of 1801. Numerous Republican objections to the 1801 Act had been made during the debates on the bill in Congress.[53] Fears as to the increase in the power of the national courts, which could be used as an effective political engine, began to be voiced increasingly, and the new appointments that that Act, and the Act of February

---

[46] Thomas Jefferson Papers, Manuscripts Division, Library of Congress. A printed, but not wholly accurate, version of Jefferson's First Annual Message to Congress is printed in Ford, *Works of Jefferson*, IX, 321–42.

[47] Beard, *Jeffersonian Democracy*, 454–62.

[48] T. Jefferson to J. Madison, Mar. 15, 1789, in Ford, *Works of Jefferson*, V, 81.

[49] See, e.g., the Alien and Sedition Acts. Also see text accompanying notes 61–62 infra. See also the excised portion of Jefferson's First Annual Message to Congress, note 46 supra.

[50] Beard, *Jeffersonian Democracy*, 467.

[51] *Ibid.*

[52] Adams, *History of United States*, I, 191.

[53] See text accompanying notes 140–44 infra.

27 for the District of Columbia, made possible added fuel to the flames.[54] It was also feared that if the Supreme Court judges were no longer required to ride circuit they might well decide to reside in Washington, instead of in their respective circuits, and that that circumstance would further enlarge their political potential.[55] The following extract from Martin Van Buren's *Autobiography* is instructive:

> The appointment of so large a number of officers for life by an administration from which the People had already withdrawn their confidence, and the extension of the Judiciary so far beyond the wants of the public service, aided by the extraordinary excitement of the period, drew upon that Act and its authors the greatest odium.

> Mr. Jefferson and his associates in the Government saw, as they believed, in the bold measure of their retiring opponents the extent to which the latter counted upon the Judicial power as a political engine, and they saw in the Judiciary the only portion of our political system that was virtually irresponsible to the People. They knew that the possessors of such a power must in the sequal by the workings of the human heart and the irresistible law of human nature be hostile to the principles upon which the Government should be conducted and by which its Republican spirit could be alone upheld.[56]

The Republicans saw in the 1801 legislation a concerted effort to elevate the national judiciary at the expense of the State courts. Consequently, they wished to remodel the entire judicial system in order to check the flow of business to the Supreme Court and thereby counteract the growth of centralization and nationalism which the federal courts had helped to promote. Late in his life Jefferson deplored even more the incursions that the judiciary had made on States' rights. On August 19, 1821, he wrote to Nathaniel Macon,

> There are two measures which if not taken, we are undone. 1st to check these unconstitutional invastions of state rights by the federal judiciary. How? Not by impeachment in the first instance, but by a strong protestation of both houses of Congress that such and such doctrines, advanced by the supreme court, are contrary to the constitution: and if afterwards they relapse into the same heresies, impeach and set the whole adrift. For what was the government divided into three branches, but that each should watch over the others, and oppose their usurpations?[57]

---

[54] See Beveridge, *John Marshall*, III, 59 et seq.

[55] See note 141 infra.

[56] J. Fitzpatrick, ed., *The Auto-* biography of Martin Van Buren (Washington, 1920), I, 218–19.

[57] T. Jefferson to N. Macon, Aug. 19, 1821, Ford, *Works of Jefferson*, XII, 207.

V: *Jefferson's Attack on the Federal Judiciary*

A few months earlier, Jefferson had written to Judge Spencer Roane: "The great object of my fear is the federal judiciary. That body, like gravity, ever acting, with noiseless foot, and unalarming advance, gaining ground step by step, and holding what it gains, is ingulphing insidiously the special governments into the jaws of that which feeds them."[58] In the same vein, but more forcefully, he wrote to William T. Barry on July 2, 1822:

> We already see the power, installed for life, responsible to no authority (for impeachment is not even a scare-crow) advancing with a noiseless and steady pace to the great object of consolidation. the foundations are already deeply laid, by their decisions, for the annihilation of constitutional state-rights, and the removal of every check, every counterpoise to the ingulphing power of which themselves are to make a sovereign part. if ever this vast country is brought under a single government, it will be one of the most extensive corruption, indifferent, and incapable of a wholesome care over so wide a spread of surface.[59]

By this date, the Supreme Court had already upheld and extended Federalist principles of nationalism and centralization; and under Marshall's leadership it would continue much further in that direction. Nevertheless, within a matter of days after Jefferson's unctuous protests to Congress in 1801 about the need for saving the expenditures on the judges' salaries, he bitterly complained to John Dickinson about the Federalist complexion of the Bench, saying that the Federalists "have retired into the Judiciary as a strong-hold."[60]

That the Constitution deprived the people of control over the judiciary galled Jefferson throughout his life, but in 1801 that barrier appeared to him none too substantial. Constitutional amendment, removal from office, impeachment, new appointments, and court-packing were the obvious avenues to attain his goal; of these five the last four were the means to which he would in fact resort. By late 1802 he had fostered the enactment of legislation abolishing the positions of the new circuit judges and enlarging the Supreme Court again to six members; in 1804 he was deftly to engineer impeachment proceedings against the first of the Supreme Court judges; and in 1808 he could rejoice in the increase in the number of those judges from five to seven. Every vacancy that presented itself was filled not only by him but by Madison as well with "sound Republicans," yet to his dismay each turned out to have sound judicial qualities when elevated to the Bench—Johnson,

---

[58] T. Jefferson to S. Roane, Mar. 9, 1821, *ibid.*, XII, 201–202.

[59] T. Jefferson to W. Barry, July 2, 1822, Thomas Jefferson Papers, Manuscripts Division, Library of Congress.

[60] T. Jefferson to J. Dickinson, Dec. 19, 1801, quoted in Adams, *History of United States*, I, 257.

Duval, Livingston, and especially Story. That the way to his goal through constitutional amendment was not attempted is explicable in terms of the small Republican majority in the Senate and more particularly by Jefferson's unwillingness to risk his popularity by a proposal requiring the approval of two-thirds of the Senate and three-fourths of the States for success.[61] This same unwillingness was also reflected in his decision not to erase symbolically the Alien and Sedition Acts from the statute-book, in spite of the advice of John Randolph and others who were of the opinion that a sort of declaratory Act on the subject was needed.

Jefferson espoused the view that the arrangement provided by the Constitution made "all the departments co-equal and co-sovereign within themselves."[62] "[E]ach department," he wrote Spencer Roane in 1819, "is truly independent of the others, and has an equal right to decide for itself what is the meaning of the constitution in the cases submitted to its action."[63] He further stated that "[e]ach of the three departments has equally the right to decide for itself what is its duty under the constitution, without any regard to what the others may have decided for themselves under a similar question."[64] The constitution has erected no single tribunal "to dominate any one of the departments."[65] Hence, the doctrine of judicial supremacy, against which he inveighed for the rest of his life, was anathema to him. Yet in dealing with the executive's supposedly "co-equal" power, the legislature, Jefferson went on to cite the case of the Sedition Law. Although passed by the legislature duly elected by the people, it was "a law unauthorized by the constitution, and therefore null."[66] ("Null," we must suppose, in the opinion of the executive, for he speaks there and elsewhere of this Act as one he was entitled to disregard by use of pardons and *nolle prosequis*). Thus, the following letter from Attorney-General Levi Lincoln to A. J. Dallas on March 25, 1801:

> The President of the United States has judged it inexpedient, that any further prosecutions should be commenced or continued under the law, commonly called the sedition law, except that one which was commenced against William Duane, Editor of the Aurora, in pursuance of a resolution of the Senate of the United States of May last. You will therefore take the proper measures for staying and discharging all such as may be depending in the Circuit Court for the Eastern District of Pennsylvania, except that above mentioned, and except

---

[61] Adams, *History of United States*, II, 240.

[62] T. Jefferson to W. C. Jarvis, Sept. 28, 1820, Ford, *Works of Jefferson*, XII, 162.

[63] T. Jefferson to S. Roane, Sept. 6, 1819, *ibid.*, 135, 137.

[64] *Ibid.*, 139.

[65] *Ibid.*, 162.

[66] *Ibid.*, 138.

such others as may be under special circumstances, which you may think of so much importance as to be stated to government.[67]

Is this not an expression of a belief in the executive's right to override the legislature? Much later, in March 1814, Jefferson wrote to Gideon Granger in the same vein, stating that he considered the Sedition Act "a nullity whenever I met it in the course of my duties."[68] Thoughts as to the chaos into which such doctrines could lead orderly government seem not to have occurred to him, for they could lead to continued uncertainty as to the validity of an enacted law, with no settled institutional way of providing for final determination of the matter.

Having first dealt directly as he did with the Alien and Sedition Acts, Jefferson could then devote his energy to the impending conflict with the judiciary. Once again his personal, as contrasted with his public, position is revealed in his private correspondence. Even before Jefferson was elected he had begun to turn over in his mind the most effective way of dealing with the Federalist judiciary establishment. In September 1801 he wrote to Robert Livingston: "I join you in taking shame for the depravity of our judges. Who could have believed that a branch of government which was the last in England to [word faded] to the torrent of corruption, should have led the way here? . . . Impeachment is clear [but?] nothing is at present provided."[69] Clearly, Jefferson agreed with James Monroe's warning on the eve of his Inauguration:

> This party has retired into the judiciary, in a strong body where it lives on the treasury, & therefore cannot be starved out. While in possession of that ground it can check the popular current which runs against them, & seize the favorable occasion to promote reaction, wh. it does not despair of. . . .[70]

Monroe's words were echoed by Jefferson in a letter to Joel Barlow of Connecticut two weeks later: "[T]he principal of [the Federalists] have returned into the judiciary as a strong hold, the tenure of which renders it difficult to dislodge them."[71]

It is in the light of expressions such as the foregoing that Jefferson's attack on the independence of the judges, the scope of their

---

[67] L. Lincoln to A. Dallas, Mar. 25, 1801, Thomas Jefferson Papers, Manuscripts Division, Library of Congress.

[68] T. Jefferson to G. Granger, Mar. 9, 1814, *ibid.*

[69] T. Jefferson to R. Livingston, Sept. 1801, *ibid.*

[70] J. Monroe to T. Jefferson, Mar. 3, 1801, *ibid.*

[71] T. Jefferson to J. Barlow, Mar. 14, 1801, Jefferson Miscellaneous Manuscripts, New York Historical Society, New York City (reference courtesy of New York Historical Society).

authority, and of their position as ultimate arbiter must be viewed. His own views were not only at variance with the express provision of the Constitution that made judicial tenure not subject to popular control (save for "high crimes and misdemeanors" for which impeachments were designed),[72] but those views were hardly modified, even in later life, by any sense of urgency for recognizing such factors as the importance of expanding and extending the national government.

In keeping with the tenor of his Inaugural Address, little that transpired publicly during the opening weeks of Jefferson's administration gave much hint to the Federalists, or to the public generally, of his designs on the judges and the independence of the judiciary. As stated at the beginning of this Chapter, first impressions were generally favorable. Alexander Hamilton wrote James A. Bayard that he looked forward to "a temporizing rather than a violent system."[73] Even Marshall referred to the Inaugural Address as "in the general well judged & conciliatory. It is in direct terms giving the lie to the violent party declamation which has elected him, but it is strongly characteristic of the general cast of this political theory."[74] John Marshall, however, at the time of Jefferson's first inauguration, was convinced that Jefferson was not honest.[75]

As late as December 1801 John Quincy Adams observed that great tranquility prevailed throughout the country and that "the violence of party spirit has very much subsided."[76] Jefferson encouraged these sentiments, partly because at the outset he probably intended to accommodate his views to the spirit of the bargain with the Federalists that had assured him the election, and partly because he genuinely believed that all but the die-hard "monarchists" could be won over to the ideal of conciliation he had expressed in his Inaugural Address: "We are all Republicans: we are all Federalists."[77] A week after the Inauguration he wrote to T. N. Randolph that "appearances of reunion are very flattering, in all states South of New England."[78] On March 27, 1801 the new President acknowledged a letter of congratulations from

[72] U. S. *Constitution*, Art. II, Sec. 4.
[73] A. Hamilton to J. Bayard, Jan. 16, 1801, in H. C. Lodge, ed., *The Works of Alexander Hamilton* (New York, 1904), X, 412, 413.
[74] J. Marshall to C. Pinckney, Mar. 4, 1801, Library Society, Charleston, South Carolina.
[75] Adams, *History of United States*, I, 194.
[76] C. F. Adams, ed., *Memoirs of John Quincy Adams* (Philadelphia, 1874), I, 186.

[77] Quoted in Adams, *History of United States*, I, 200. Thus, his inaugural statement that all were Republicans, all Federalists may have meant no more than that New England Federalists were so weak that they need not be taken into account so that harmony within the government might be restored. *Ibid.*, 319, 321.
[78] T. Jefferson to T. N. Randolph, Mar. 12, 1801, Thomas Jefferson Papers, Manuscripts Division, Library of Congress.

Henry Knox by saying, "I was always satisfied that the great body of those called Federalists were real Republicans as well as Federalists."[79] Two weeks earlier he had written Joel Barlow that "the recovery bids fair to be complete, and to obliterate entirely the line of party division which had been so strongly drawn. Not that their late leaders have come over, or ever can come over, but they stand at present almost without followers."[80]

In general, Jefferson was circumspect in his public utterances during the beginning of his term. He was always anxious for popularity and flattered by the adulation that was heaped upon him. On March 12, 1801 Jefferson wrote to T. N. Randolph that "a few removals from office will be indispensable. They will be chiefly for real mal-conduct, & mostly in the offices connected with the administration of justice. I shall do as little in that way as possible. . . . the prostitution of justice by packing of juries cannot be passed over."[81] The Republican newspapers in general also took a conciliatory line and referred to the opportunity that "once more recurs for reconciliation and harmony."[82]

Yet to many Federalists Jefferson remained a man of ineradicable duplicity. John Marshall had little to say on his behalf and commented briefly to Hamilton that "the morals of the author of Mazzei cannot be pure."[83] Whatever his intentions during this early period, the relative calm was soon to end. The storm broke on January 6, 1802 when Senator John Breckenridge moved for the repeal of the 1801 Act.

B. PLANNING THE ATTACK ON THE
FEDERAL JUDICIARY

The more radical Republicans had soon made it impossible for Jefferson to adhere for long to his publicly announced policies. Shortly after the conciliatory Inaugural Address, Jefferson's administration began the process of demolishing the parts of the Federalist governmental structure most objectionable to his Republican followers. One of the first and most important targets was the federal judiciary.

Only a few straws in the wind foretold to the public the direction that matters were to take. The main sources of these early indications were certain of the Republican newspapers. The extent to which these announcements were deliberately instigated is difficult to ascertain. The

---

[79] T. Jefferson to H. Knox, Mar. 27, 1801, *ibid.*

[80] T. Jefferson to J. Barlow, Mar. 14, 1801, Jefferson Miscellaneous Manuscripts, New York Historical Society, N.Y.

[81] T. Jefferson to T. N. Randolph, Mar. 12, 1801, Thomas Jefferson Papers, Manuscripts Division, Library of Congress.

[82] *National Intelligencer*, Mar. 9, 1801.

[83] J. Marshall to A. Hamilton, Jan. 1, 1801, in J. C. Hamilton, ed., *Works of Alexander Hamilton* (New York, 1851), VI, 501–503.

Aurora had castigated the 1801 Act and the midnight appointments as early as February 4, 1801.[84] In late March the *National Intelligencer* leveled its editorial guns at the appointments under the 1801 Act, commenting that the new judges were "men of certain political *traits*" and adding that "any undue influence of their political opinions upon the exercise of their judicial functions"[85] should be combatted by the appointment of Republicans to all available posts in the judicial system. The new judges were protected for the time being by the principle of tenure during good behavior; but the other judicial appointments Jefferson regarded as null and void, and he started to plan their replacement. "The only shield for our Republication citizens against the federalism of the courts," he wrote to Archibald Stuart, "is to have the Attornies & Marshalls republicans."[86] The Adams appointments to those offices Jefferson considered "nullities," at least with respect to the vacancies occurring after it was known that Adams' term was at an end. The new judges he determined to get rid of by a repeal of the Act of 1801, a course that he had decided upon at least as early as April of that year. If the office were to be abolished, the judge would go with it, and this was in fact the result of the repealing Act of 1802. Referring to an objectionable Federalist appointee, Jefferson wrote, "The judge of course stands until the law shall be repealed, which we trust will be at the next Congress."[87] Other federal judges who held office in the district courts and the Supreme Court could not be disposed of in so summary a fashion. Death and resignation would, and did, afford the opportunity to replace them with "sound" party men, and the rest, if they proved intractable, were to be removed by impeachment.[88]

On April 25, 1801, Jefferson wrote to Monroe that he thought it "highly probable the law [would] be repealed at the next meeting of Congress."[89] Thus, contrary to Warren's statement that no decision as to the repeal of the Act was reached before December,[90] the correspondence of Republicans reveals, as stated above, that Jefferson had formulated the plan at least by the end of the preceding April.

Aside from newspaper references, there were few other public warnings of the impending storm. Jefferson made three appointments, without special comment, to fill vacancies in the new circuit courts— one to the chief judgeship of the Circuit Court for the District of

---

[84] *Aurora*, Feb. 4, 1801.

[85] *National Intelligencer*, March 1801.

[86] T. Jefferson to A. Stuart, Apr. 8, 1801, Ford, *Works of Jefferson*, IX, 247–48.

[87] *Ibid.*, 247.

[88] See chapter 7 infra.

[89] T. Jefferson to J. Monroe, Apr. 25, 1801, Thomas Jefferson Papers, Manuscripts Division, Library of Congress.

[90] C. Warren, *The Supreme Court in United States History* (Boston, 1922), I, 204.

Columbia, and two to the Fifth Circuit. Behind the scenes, however, pressures for dealing with the new judges continued. In August Jefferson told his Attorney-General that "The removal of excrescences from the judiciary is the universal demand."[91] Meanwhile, subordinates were busy collecting detailed statistics as to suits instituted and pending in the circuit courts for the purpose of showing a decline in federal court business. Jefferson's private correspondence continued to reflect growing animus, and in December he wrote John Dickinson concerning the strength of the Federalist judiciary. He complained that "[t]here the remains of federalism are to be preserved and fed from the Treasury; and from that battery all the works of republicanism are to be beaten down and destroyed."[92] He wrote Benjamin Rush that, although no political controversy had arisen, "lopping off the parasitical plant engrafted at the last session on the judiciary body, will probably produce some."[93]

Doubts as to whether the 1801 Act could properly be repealed were entertained in some Republican quarters, however. Among the other possibilities was one suggested by the prominent Republican leader and spokesman, Joseph H. Nicholson, in a letter to Wilson Cary Nicholas on December 25, 1801.[94] After asserting that he had no doubt that the legislative power extended to undoing what an earlier Congress had done, Nicholson went on to say that if the 1801 Act was not repealable, it would be possible to transfer back to the old judges the duties of the Adams appointees. The new judges would then have no duties and could be dismissed a little more circuitously—"they would die a lingering death instead of a sudden one."[95]

John Breckenridge, one of Jefferson's lieutenants in the Senate, was also at work during this time. Breckenridge had been receiving letters from his constituents in Kentucky urging repeal of the 1801 Act, but he turned to John Taylor of Caroline for the arguments to be used in favor of repeal. Taylor confessed he did not know how far the President "lean[ed] toward the revision,"[96] but he said that all his hopes on the question rested with Jefferson. Obviously, not all Republicans were fully informed. On December 22, 1801, Taylor apologized for delay in replying to the Senator's letter and proceeded to outline his views and to suggest how far it might be safe to proceed in the attack.[97]

---

[91] T. Jefferson to L. Lincoln, Aug. 26, 1801, in Ford, *Works of Jefferson*, IX, 289–91.

[92] T. Jefferson to J. Dickinson, Dec. 19, 1801, quoted in Adams, *History of United States*, I, 257.

[93] T. Jefferson to B. Rush, Dec. 20, 1801, in Ford, *Works of Jefferson*, IX, 345.

[94] J. H. Nicholson to W. C. Nicholas, Dec. 25, 1801, W. C. Nicholas Papers, II, Manuscripts Division, Library of Congress.

[95] *Ibid.*

[96] Breckenridge Family Papers, XXI, Manuscripts Division, Library of Congress.

[97] *Ibid.*

Essentially, he suggested that the power of Congress to create inferior courts also included the power to abolish them. The constitutional provision for the payment of salaries "during their continuance in office"[98] protected the judges only so long as the office existed; when the office ceased, so did the salary. The principle of tenure during good behavior for the judges, he argued, was to assure their honesty in the exercise of their office and not to sustain "useless or pernicious offices"[99] for the sake of judges. Moreover, the basis of the "good behavior" principle was English and had its origins in the wish to counteract the influence of the Crown over the judges, who, unlike American judges, were removable by joint vote of the House of Lords and the House of Commons. "Whether courts are erected by a regard to the administration of justice, or with the purpose of rewarding a meritorious faction, the legislature may certainly abolish them without infringing the constitution, whenever they are not required by the administration of justice, or the merit of the faction is exploded, and their claim to reward disallowed."[100]

Politically astute, as always, the President's final version of his Message to Congress of December 8, 1801, intimating the repeal, was couched in the mildest terms expressed with studied caution: "The judiciary system of the United States, and especially that power of it recently erected, will of course present itself to the contemplation of Congress. . . ."[101] Stronger language had been deleted,[102] so as to connect the proposal firmly with the Republican program of economy and reduction of national expenditures, the Message went on to say that in order that Congress might

> be able to judge of the proportion which the institution bears to the business it has to perform, I have caused to be procured from the several States, and now lay before Congress, an exact statement of all the causes decided since the first establishment of the courts, & of those which were depending when additional courts and judges were brought in to their aid.[103]

---

[98] U. S. *Constitution*, Art. III, Sec. 1.

[99] Breckenridge Family Papers, XXI, Manuscripts Division, Library of Congress.

[100] *Ibid.*

[101] Thomas Jefferson Papers, Manuscripts Division, Library of Congress. See note 46 supra.

[102] *Ibid.* The full text of the deleted passages, which were later made available to William Branch Giles for presentation in the congressional debates, may be found in Beveridge, *John Marshall*, III, Appendix A, 605.

[103] Continuation of the quotation in note 101 supra. The costs of the new court system had long since been estimated by Jefferson. In a letter to Monroe, Mar. 26, 1800, he stated that the judiciary bill then before the House "will add 80 to 100 thousand dollars a year to the expense of that department." Thomas Jefferson Papers, Manuscripts Division, Library of Congress.

These statistics could not have been collected overnight, as their detail indicates. They purported to show that in most of the circuit courts there had been no recent increase in the number of suits instituted—whether at common law, in chancery, admiralty, or criminal prosecutions—and that in many of them there had been a decline. The figures were also intended to show that only a comparatively small fraction of the suits instituted were still pending; therefore, there was no need at the appellate or circuit level for additional courts and judges to take care of new or accumulated business.

How accurate these statistics were cannot now be conclusively determined. They were so inaccurate for the District of Kentucky, however, that on January 14, 1802, District Judge Harry Innes felt called upon, with many apologies, to make his own count in the Clerk's office and transmit the result to Senator Breckenridge.[104] Innes' count, substantiated by an official statement sent to the Secretary of State, showed that in his district 870 suits, rather than the 670 reported by the President's study, had been instituted between 1790 and 1801.

More than two months later, on February 26, 1802, well after the Bill for repealing the 1801 Act had passed the Senate and only a few days before it passed the House, Jefferson sent a corrected statement to Congress.[105] An accompanying statement from Secretary of State Madison attempted to point out that "the aggregate is not materially varied. . . ."[106] Even assuming that the statistics were properly revised and corrected for all the circuit courts, they were presented too late to have any effect on the strictly party vote by which the 1802 Bill was passed. By then the line had been drawn in the debates in Congress on the basis of judicial independence rather than on the initial basis of economy and lack of need.

While the President was publicly crying economy as the basis for repeal of the 1801 Act, he also alluded to problems relating to "the inestimable institution of juries."[107] It was well known that in many States the courts, and more often the United States marshals, picked whom they pleased to serve on trial and grand juries. Since the marshals, like the judges, were Federalists to a man, they tended to select for jury service those who shared their own political views. Inevitably, an impartial jury trial could not be had in many cases having a political tinge, and in trials under the Sedition Act the accused had been at a distinct disadvantage. Hence there was some merit in Jefferson's resolu-

---

104 Breckenridge Family Papers, XXI, Manuscripts Division, Library of Congress.

105 *American State Papers. Documents, Legislative and Executive, of the Congress of the United States,* *Miscellaneous* (Washington, 1834), I, 319–24.

106 *Ibid.,* 319.

107 Ford, *Works of Jefferson,* IX, 321 et seq.

tion to appoint Republican marshals, "the doors of entrance into the courts . . . as a shield to the republican part of our fellow citizens. . . ."[108] In his December 1801 Message to Congress, however, Jefferson shrewdly limited his remarks with respect to juries: "Their impartial selection also being essential to their value, we ought further to consider whether that is sufficiently secured in those states where they are named by a marshal depending on Executive will, or designated by the court, or by officers dependant on them."[109]

Even earlier, and certainly by the fall of 1801, however, more than one Federalist had divined Jefferson's intentions with respect to the judiciary, despite the outward political calm that prevailed.[110] James Bayard wrote that "[t]he judicial system is the victim on which the hearts of the whole [Republican] party is set."[111] Theodore Sedgwick wrote Rufus King that there was nothing that Republicans "more anxiously wish[ed] than the destruction of the judicial arrangements made during the last session. . . ."[112] Joseph Hales remarked sarcastically that "[t]he independence of our judiciary is to be confirmed by being made wholly subservient to the will of the legislature & the caprice of Executive visions."[113] Well before December 1801, and certainly before the Breckenridge motion in January, it was becoming apparent that the attack on the judiciary was about to begin.

C. POPULAR SUPPORT FOR THE REPUBLICAN ASSAULT ON THE COURTS

The Republican attack on the judiciary was facilitated in large measure by long-standing popular antagonism to the judicial system as a whole. That antagonism was widespread. To some extent, that sentiment originated in the general opposition to government of any kind that was felt in many parts of the nation, especially inland. Community isolation and the independence of the frontier not only bred individualism of the strongest sort; it also meant that vast segments of the populace had little experience with local government, and even less with the national government. Tom Paine had publicized ideas about government as a necessary evil, and his maxims were still widely quoted and accepted with approval. To the frontiersmen, at least, it was "govern-

---

[108] T. Jefferson to W. Giles, Mar. 23, 1801, *ibid.*, VIII, 25.

[109] Note 46 supra.

[110] See chapter 7 infra.

[111] E. Donnan, ed., "Papers of James A. Bayard, 1795–1815," *Annual Report of the American His-* *torical Association for the Year 1913* (Washington, 1915), II, 1948.

[112] T. Sedgwick to R. King, Dec. 14, 1801, in C. King, ed., *The Life and Correspondence of Rufus King* (New York, 1897), IV, 36.

[113] J. Hales to R. King, Dec. 19, 1801, *ibid.*, 39.

ment" that enforced contracts and the payment of debts. Moreover, as Henry Adams states, the American Bar, with whom the judges were associated, at this time was a sort of aristocracy conservative to a degree that annoyed reformers of every class. Both aspects, that of a privileged caste, and the conservatism of lawyers, were thorns in the flesh of democrats.[114]

Thus, special grounds existed for popular opposition to the federal courts. In part, such sentiments were based on growing support for States' rights, which led to objections to the jurisdiction of the national courts as incursions upon the proper sphere of the State courts. The federal judiciary also meant nationalism and more government. A correspondent of John Breckenridge wrote:

> The federal Court did very little. Mr. Innes was taken sick. Shall this court continue, it will ruin this Country. . . . The Judges sit on the bench cock and hats on their heads Made everybody stand abt. I had rather the Indians would fall on us, than to have this federal Court.[115]

The grand jury furnished another source of popular dissatisfaction with the court system. In a letter dated December 27, 1801 Judge Harry Innes wrote Senator Breckenridge to summarize the state of the docket for the Sixth Circuit and commented that "there can be no necessity for a continuance of the Circuit System in the Western Country."[116] He went on to say that the grand jury was a "useless and expensive body,"[117] that in eleven years no such jury had ever made a presentment "of their own knowledge,"[118] and that the jury "is frequently composed of persons who live very remote—the mileage is in this case very buthersome."[119] More specifically, popular antagonism to the judiciary had its roots in late colonial experience at the hands of judges appointed by the Crown at a time when the legislatures were looked upon as the champions of the people and the chief organ of the omnipotent popular will.[120] In this connection it may be observed that judges were also subject to the suspicion of, and disrespect for, intellectuals—an antagonism not new in American life and much commented on at the time by foreign writers. This popular hostility was reflected in the actions of early State legislatures whose members did

---

[114] Adams, *History of United States,* II, 195.

[115] Breckenridge Family Papers, Manuscripts Division, Library of Congress (no identification of correspondent or shown date).

[116] H. Innes to J. Breckenridge, Dec. 27, 1801, *ibid.*

[117] *Ibid.*

[118] *Ibid.*

[119] *Ibid.*

[120] A. H. Chroust, "The Dilemma of the American Lawyer in the Post-Revolutionary Era," *Notre Dame Lawyer* XXXV, 48, 62–63 (1959).

not hesitate to interfere with the traditional functions of the State courts. A particularly illuminating letter, which merits extensive quotation, was written by John Coburn to John Breckenridge in January 1802. After commenting on the great satisfaction he had felt on reading the President's Message, he wrote:

> This is the precious moment to eradicate every remnant of aristocracy, with its complex train of taxes and offices. Let us return as soon as possible to a system of State governments, they are the true and proper guardians of our all. We can certainly so regulate them as to render any interference of the general government, almost unnecessary. Our State Courts are safe and proper tribunals for every species of controversy between man and man. And I see no reason why the Genl Government would not receive the same measure of justice from those Courts, as from Federal State Courts. This eternal clashing of Courts with concurrent jurisdiction is to me absurd and dangerous. If internal taxation ceases, it still renders Federal Courts less necessary. But the greatest evil arising from the Federal plan of Courts, is the awful appeal to the Supreme Federal Court. What can ever make it necessary to resort to this tribunal, in cases, less than of national concern. If local prejudices too much prevail at any time, Let a change of venue be had.[121]

To be noted here is not only the principle of States' rights and the dislike of nationalism fostered by the federal courts, but the connection between taxation and those courts, which were regarded as instruments of oppression for the collection of debts and taxes, especially in outlying districts of the country such as Kentucky.

Earlier, in the 1790s, however, other grounds of opposition had appeared. First, a number of cases involving political issues on which there were sharp differences of opinion began coming before the federal courts. Among these were prosecutions for violations of Washington's neutrality proclamation, the treaty of peace with Great Britain, and the Alien and Sedition Acts. In convicting persons for such violations, the courts turned to the precedents of the English criminal law, and those decisions were viewed by many as imposing the "monarchical" and unsuitable common law on the United States without the consent of Congress. No doubt it was an assumption of power from the standpoint that neither the Constitution nor existing statutes made such offenses indictable, but the doctrine of federal common law was enforced, with the exception of *United States* v. *Worrall*,[122] until 1812.

---

[121] J. Coburn to J. Breckenridge, Jan. 1802, Breckenridge Family Papers, Manuscripts Division, Library of Congress.

[122] 2 Dall. 384 (1798).

V: *Jefferson's Attack on the Federal Judiciary*

Thus the judges were accused of importing English law into their decisions solely because the Federalists tended to be pro-British. Partisans of the French cause, and anti-Federalists everywhere, viewed these decisions as subjecting the nation to a foreign yoke; yet in their criticism they overlooked the fact that most of the federal judges had been trained in English law and were accustomed to apply it.

Thus a number of delicate questions on which the two major political factions were sharply divided—notably the constitutionality of the Alien and Sedition Acts, common law jurisdiction of the federal courts, and neutrality—had come before the Supreme Court judges at least on circuit, and nearly all of their decisions had been contrary to the views of the anti-Federalists. A further instance arose in 1800 when the Supreme Court was faced with deciding the question whether a state of war existed between the United States and France. In general, the Federalists took the position that it did, and the anti-Federalists—as warm supporters of the French—maintained that it did not. In *Bas v. Tingy*[123] the Court held that a limited state of war existed, thereby substantially sustaining the Federalist position.

The judges in the circuit courts, as well as on the Supreme Court, were considered not only to have exceeded their duly constituted authority but to have acted as political instruments of the now defeated party. Hence the earlier decisions and actions of Federalist judges became weapons in the hands of the Republicans in the attack on their opponents. For example, popular hostility was vastly increased by prosecutions under the Sedition Act; these cases were regarded as further evidence that the courts were being used as a means of political persecution.[124] While the Federalists were in power the opinion developed that no one was safe who ventured to criticize officials of the federal government. Not only was the Sedition Act widely unpopular in many sections of the country, especially in Virginia, but the partisan character of judges who intended to vindicate Federalist principles and to suppress "Jacobinism" became especially obnoxious. The attitude of Judge Chase in this respect caused his name to become a byword as an American Jeffreys. In journeying south to hold the Circuit Court in Virginia, for example, he remarked that he intended to teach the Bar "to distinguish between the liberty and the licentiousness of the press."[125]

Another ground for widespread dislike of the Federalist judges

---

[123] 4 Dall. 37 (1800).

[124] Beveridge, *John Marshall*, II, 420–21, and sources cited in *ibid.*, note 4.

[125] Testimony of John Thomas Mason at the trial of Judge Chase, J. Gales and W. Seaton, comps., *The Debates and Proceedings of the Congress of the United States* (Washington, 1834–1856), XIV, 216 (8th Cong., 2d sess.) (hereafter cited as *Annals of Congress*). See chapter 7 infra.

involved the alleged politicizing of the judicial functions by means of the grand jury charges in the circuit courts. As earlier stated, nearly all the members of the Supreme Court, at one time or another, ventured to lecture on religion, morality, or political principles in their charges to grand juries when the judges were on circuit. A collection of hand-written charges by Judge Chase for the period 1802 to 1806 has sur-vived,[126] and in them he deals with the purposes of government, as well as such current issues as neutrality and defense. All these exhorta-tions were delivered and declaimed in the name of patriotism and sound Federalist principles. In localities that were predominantly Federalist, before juries picked because of their politics, these charges were well received. "The Hon. Judge Patterson [sic] . . . delivered a most elegant and appropriate charge. . . . Politics were set in their true light; by holding up the Jacobins [viz. the Republicans] as the dis-organization of our happy country. . . ."[127] Elsewhere, Republicans in particular viewed these charges as extreme partisan politics, illustrating that the courts were engines and weapons of the Federalists. Well before the 1800 election, Jefferson became particularly irate over the propaganda in such jury charges. On June 4, 1797, he complained to Peregrine Fitzhugh that "[t]he charges of the federal judges have for a considerable time been inviting the grand juries to become inquisitors on the freedom of speech, of writing & of principle of their fellow-citizens."[128] He then went on to say that the grand juries of the several States might think it incumbent on them "to enter protestations against this perversion of their institution from a legal to a political engine, & *even to present those concerned in it.*"[129] It was Judge Chase's charge to the grand jury in Baltimore that later gave Jefferson a welcome opportunity to trigger the impeachment proceedings against him.[130]

Another complaint against the courts was the means of selecting grand juries, frequently done, as stated above, by Federalist marshals who picked men of their own political affiliation and hence aided, in part, the success of prosecutions. On March 26, 1801, Jefferson wrote Mrs. Sarah Mease condemning officers who selected jurors "for prin-ciples which lead necessarily to condemnation. [They] might as well lead [their] culprits to the scaffold without the mockery of trial."[131] Three days later Jefferson wrote to Gideon Granger, "Persons who have perverted their offices to the oppression of their fellow citizens, as mar-

---

[126] In the Chase Manuscripts, Maryland Historical Society, Balti-more.

[127] *The Oracle of the Day*, May 24, 1800, reprinted in Warren, *Supreme Court*, I, 166, note 2.

[128] Ford, *Works of Jefferson*, VIII, 35.

[129] *Ibid.*

[130] See chapter 7 infra.

[131] T. Jefferson to S. Mease, Mar. 26, 1801, in Ford, *Works of Jeffer-son*, VIII, 34.

shals packing juries, attorneys grinding their legal victims . . . will probably find few advocates even among their quondam party."[132] Again, to T. N. Randolph he wrote that "the prostration of justice by packing of juries cannot be passed over."[133]

Among practices that served to make the Federalist judges unpopular in many localities were political speeches delivered in public. At the close of the eighteenth century such activities were not regarded in the same manner as they are today, but Republicans made much of them to illustrate their accusation that Federalist judges were little more than party tools. Judge Chase left the bench without a quorum in 1800 in order to campaign for Adams, and Judge Bushrod Washington likewise endeavored to obtain support for the Federalists in the same campaign.[134] A major factor, therefore, in the popular animosity towards the national courts was the conduct of the judiciary itself—particularly of the Supreme Court judges when on circuit, where their manners, language, and conduct aroused public fear and gave Jefferson and the Republicans generally an opportunity that the new administration actively sought.

Other factors also contributed to the widespread criticism of the federal courts, notably the very deficiencies in the system created by the Act of 1789, including some that the Act of 1801 was intended to remedy. Chief among these was the inability of judges to hold the circuit courts by reason of illness, weather, or conditions of travel. As observed earlier, such happenings meant delays and expenses to litigants who frequently had to journey two or three hundred miles only to find the court unable to convene. Disregarding the salutary measures provided by the Act, the anti-Federalists were able to add charges of incompetence and inefficiency to the arsenal of weapons assembled to attack the national court system.

In the spring of 1801 the first of a series of three specific episodes occurred that also helped to fan into flame the Republican fires of hatred of the judiciary and to fortify their conviction of the necessity of proceeding with the assault on the judiciary. Two of the Federalist judges of the new Circuit Court for the District of Columbia instructed the District Attorney to institute a common law libel prosecution against the *National Intelligencer*, the administration newspaper, for publishing an attack on the entire judiciary.[135] One of the judges was James M. Marshall, brother of the Chief Justice; the other was William Cranch, soon to become the unofficial reporter of the Supreme Court decisions.

---

[132] T. Jefferson to G. Granger, Mar. 29, 1801, *ibid.*, 44.

[133] T. Jefferson to T. N. Randolph, Feb. 19, 1801, *ibid.*, IX, 185.

[134] See chapter 7, note 60 infra.

[135] *National Intelligencer*, June 12, 1801. See Warren, *Supreme Court*, I, 195.

Although the grand jury returned a presentment, the Republican district attorney refused to take further steps, and in September the jury refused to indict. Although the matter was dropped, Jefferson was incensed, and the Republican press immediately exploited the incident and unhesitatingly characterized it as Federalist partisanship.

The second episode involved the validity of an executive order in connection with the case of the *Schooner Peggy*.[136] The ship in question was an armed French vessel captured in 1800 over which condemnation proceedings had been instituted in the federal district court in Connecticut. Pursuant to the French-American treaty, ratified at the end of the Adams administration, whereby vessels not yet condemned were to be returned to their owners, the President ordered the proceeds of the sale of the vessel to be returned to the French claimants. The clerk of the district court refused to comply, and instead he applied to the newly created circuit court for an order as to the disposition of the proceeds. The circuit court held that the Presidential order was invalid and directed that the proceeds be paid into the Treasury. Although the Supreme Court was to hold in December that Jefferson's construction of the French treaty was correct, and that the money should be paid to the French owners,[137] the President was greatly irked at the circuit court's decision, which he viewed as a political move on the part of the new Federalist judges appointed by Adams pursuant to the 1801 Act.

The third episode, also charged with political overtones, was the institution of the celebrated proceedings in *Marbury* v. *Madison*,[138] in which William Marbury and three others sought by original petition a rule to show cause why a writ of mandamus should not be issued to compel Jefferson's Secretary of State, James Madison, to deliver to them commissions as justices of the peace—commissions that had been duly signed by President Adams but withheld.

The foregoing discussion is not intended as a digression but as an effort to underscore problems that the extension of the national judiciary and the application of the 1789 Act in the hands of a Federalist Congress had created. The managers in charge of the 1802 legislation had more in mind than merely setting back the clock and ridding the judiciary of the Federalist judges. The attack on the Supreme Court was part of an identifiable policy on the part of Republicans to reduce and confine the power of the federal courts generally. James A. Bayard recognized this plan in a letter to Hamilton in April 1802:

---

[136] United States v. The Schooner Peggy, 1 Cranch 103 (1801).
[137] *Ibid.*, 107.

[138] 1 Cranch 137 (1803). See chapter 6 infra.

> You have seen the patchwork offered to us, as a new Judicial system. The whole is designed to cover one object, which the party consider it necessary to accomplish—the postponement of the next session of the Supreme Court to February following. They mean to give the repealing act its full effect, before the Judges of the Supreme Court are allowed to assemble.[139]

Executive and legislative power, thus combined with widespread popular antipathy towards the federal judiciary, gave the Republicans the opportunity to act.

D. REPEAL OF THE 1801 ACT

As earlier stated, the pretext of extravagance, that is, the increased cost in the federal budget for the sixteen new circuit judges, had been used by Jefferson in his December Message to Congress for urging reconsideration of the 1801 legislation. This was the theme first picked up by Senator Breckenridge, and then by others, in opening the Senate debate on the proposed repeal measure early in January 1802. Breckenridge argued that to increase the number of federal courts when suits therein were in fact declining was totally unnecessary, while Senator Stevens Mason of Virginia then pointed out that the Supreme Court judges, with only ten suits then on their docket, would have little to do to earn their salaries, and that for want of employment they might do mischief in areas in which they should not be engaged.[140] The other two principal arguments in the Senate, however, related first to the independence of the judiciary—specifically whether, as the Republicans contended, courts might be abolished or reorganized in a manner and for the purpose of dismissing judges; and second, whether the several departments of government were competent to act outside their allocated spheres of power—specifically, whether the courts had power to declare acts of the legislature unconstitutional. Senator Breckenridge restated the standard Republican philosophy on these issues with great effectiveness, reciting verbatim certain portions of strongly worded passages that Jefferson had earlier written but had cautiously decided to omit from his December Message to Congress. It seems obvious that he had made these passages available to Breckenridge for his presentation in the Senate.[141] Despite strong countervailing arguments by the

---

[139] Hamilton Papers, LXXXIII, fol. 13539, Manuscripts Division, Library of Congress.

[140] *Annals of Congress*, XI, 26, 63 (7th Cong., 1st sess.).

[141] For these deleted passages, see Beveridge, *John Marshall*, III, Appendix A, 605.

Federalists, the repeal bill passed the Senate on February 3, 1802, by a vote of 16-15 on almost strictly partisan lines.

In the House, two pleas for postponement of consideration of the repeal failed, and the line of arguments then followed much the same course as in the Senate, but with less restraint. Probably the most effective of the Republican arguments was that of William Branch Giles, another of Jefferson's strongest lieutenants in Congress. Giles dwelt upon the past iniquities of the Federalist judges and upon the entrenchment of rabid Federalism in the judiciary, where life offices gave judges protection; he also introduced into debate consideration of the "impropriety" of sending a "process leading to a mandamus, into the Executive cabinet."[142] John Randolph of Roanoke delivered a fiery and imperious speech,[143] again bringing *Marbury* v. *Madison* into the debate even though the case would not be decided until a full year later. An eloquent reply to Giles by James A. Bayard, Federalist leader in the House, was characterized by John Adams as "the most comprehensive masterly and compleat argument that has been published in either house. . . ."[144] The speech dealt with the background of the 1801 Act and the reasons for its enactment, but then moved back to the arguments pertaining to the supervisory power of courts over legislation—a question that had begun to receive increasing attention in Congress. As Beveridge says, "The pending case of Marbury *vs.* Madison was in the minds of all."[145] Forcible resistance was even hinted by Federalist opponents of repeal, yet debate ran on until a vote was taken on March 3—the 59 Republicans in favor, the 32 Federalists against.[146] The Repeal Act had now passed through both houses of Congress.

Reactions to the repeal tended to follow or to echo, in one form or another, sentiments that had been expressed in the course of the debate. The Republican press, and Republicans generally, rejoiced in the victory of the people and the triumph of democratic principles. Following the passage of the bill in the House, the *National Intelligencer* on March 5 exulted: "Judges created for political purposes, and for the worst of purposes under a republican government, for the purpose of opposing the National will, from this day cease to exist."[147] James Blair wrote Breckenridge from Frankfort, Kentucky, as early as the second of March, congratulating him on "the happy termination of your

---

[142] The full text of Giles' speech is printed in *Annals of Congress*, XI, 579–602 (7th Cong., 1st sess.).

[143] *Ibid.*, XI, 662 (7th Cong., 1st sess.).

[144] J. Adams to J. Bayard, Apr. 10, 1802, in Donnan, "Papers of James A. Bayard," 152.

[145] Beveridge, *John Marshall*, III, 90.

[146] *Annals of Congress*, XI, 982 (7th Cong., 1st sess.).

[147] Quoted in Warren, *Supreme Court*, I, 209, note 3.

labours. . . . nothing can equal the applause and credit you univerally [*sic*] receive throughout this State by the People."[148] Another of the Senator's correspondents, John Shore, praised the repeal as having caused "very general satisfaction to the people here, a few lawyers exceptant."[149]

An occasional Republican thought the party measures had gone too far. John Randolph, for instance, reported to Joseph Nicholson that the repeal was extremely popular in Virginia, except with a few Republicans who thought it unconstitutional.[150] James Bayard wrote to Richard Bassett on March 8 that

> Notwithstanding the Party adhered together they were much shaken. They openly cursed the measure, if it had been possible for them to recede, they would have joyfully relinquished the project. But they had gone too far, & were obliged to go through. I have no doubt it was the most ruinous step they could have taken and such are the accounts we have from the Southard.[151]

On the Federalist side, Roger Griswold wrote to John Rutledge from Washington on April 21 that

> [t]he changes which are operating, and already executed have evidently depressed the spirits of the ruling party, and although they do not relinquish many of the projects which they had undertaken yet it is apparent that they pursue them with less acrimony. . . . This change of determination has probably resulted from finding that the work of destruction is not so popular as was expected.[152]

The *Washington Federalist* lost no time in declaring that Jefferson had "gratified his malice towards the judges . . . and laid the foundation of infinite mischief."[153] It went on to urge not only that the judges disregard the law, but that they declare the Act null and void. The editorial concluded that it might be expected that the next step would undoubtedly be the repeal of the law establishing the Supreme Court as part of the system to be pursued.

---

[148] J. Blair to J. Breckenridge, Mar. 2, 1802, Breckenridge Family Papers, Manuscripts Division, Library of Congress.

[149] J. Shore to J. Breckenridge, Mar. 14, 1802, *ibid.*

[150] See G. Tucker, *Life of Thomas Jefferson* (Philadelphia, 1837), II, 114.

[151] J. Bayard to R. Bassett, Mar. 8, 1801, Bayard Family Papers, Manuscripts Division, Library of Congress.

[152] R. Griswold to J. Rutledge, Apr. 21, 1802, The John Rutledge Papers, Manuscripts Division, Library of Congress (originals in the Southern Historical Collection of the University of North Carolina, Chapel Hill).

[153] Quoted in Beveridge, *John Marshall*, III, 92–93. See especially *ibid.*, 93, note 1.

Senator Plumer's reactions, expressed a few days before the final vote, were typical of Federalist despair. "The Judiciary, that bulwark of our rights, is to be placed in a state of dependence; the tenure of the judges office . . . is to depend upon the whim & caprice of a theoretical President, & his servile minions."[154] Governor Davie wrote John Steele that, in the eyes of Congress, the Constitution was like "a loose pair of trousers, which any man with a little tugging may draw over his backside: indeed all Constitutions are useless, if the doctrines of Mr. Breckenridge are to be supported by the ruling party. . . ."[155] Charles Lee wrote Levin Powell at Middleburg on July 11:

> The judiciary is certainly gone as you express it. And this is not all. Mr. Jefferson is well calculated to pull down any political edifice and those will not be disappointed who have feared he would employ himself as industriously and indefatigably in taking to pieces stone by stone the national building as Washington employed himself in putting them together. Even the foundation will be razed in less than four years. I hear that Jefferson's administration grows more and more unpopular in New England; and only the public discontents will arrest him in the course of folly and malevolence: for every thing done or to be done is after his own heart.[156]

Hamilton wrote Charles Pinckney in March that the repeal was a "vital blow to the Constitution,"[157] and one of Rufus King's correspondents wrote that the "federal party is completely down. . . . The repeal of the judicial bill . . . has excited a very powerful sensation in the minds of the leading federalists throughout the union. . . ."[158] Pinckney in turn wrote Hamilton on May 5 that the repeal was to be expected from "Persons who have been always hostile to the Constitution . . . a work whose adoption they opposed, and whose execution they have constantly counteracted. But I do not imagine they will stop here, they will proceed in their mad & wicked career, and the Peoples' eyes will be opened."[159]

Even more lurid language was used by Harrison Gray Otis in a letter to Rutledge dated August 2: "What scenes of infamy, selfishness, corruption and folly are daily developed by the ruling party. The prosecutions of Diocletian, the proscriptions of Scylla [meaning Sulla?],

---

[154] W. Plumer to Upham, Mar. 1, 1802, William Plumer Papers, Letters 1781–1804, Manuscripts Division, Library of Congress.

[155] J. Davie to J. Steele, undated, John Steele Papers, Southern Historical Collection, Chapel Hill, N.C.

[156] C. Lee to L. Powell, July 11, 1802, *ibid.*

[157] A. Hamilton to C. Pinckney, Mar. 15, 1802 in Syrett, *Hamilton Papers*, XXV, 562.

[158] See Warren, *Supreme Court*, I, 213.

[159] C. Pinckney to A. Hamilton, May 5, 1802, in Syrett, *Hamilton Papers*, XXVI, 2.

and of Robespierre were more sanguinary but no more inveterate than those of the chief who now commands."[160] On April 27 another correspondent wrote Rutledge from Washington:

> The effect of the Judiciary repeal & the enormous Acts of the Party here, have had a wonderful effect to depreciate property here. a Gentleman in Phila. was about to purchase a Plantation of Govr. Lee, but the repeal of the Judiciary, & the talk of negroe Insurrection broke off the Bargain. Stoddert was about to make a sale of City Lots here, but the same Reason operated also & he has been much injured.[161]

Along with such expressions, there were also made, apparently for the first time, concrete suggestions and plans for the secession of the New England States. It was a sort of call to arms, which moved towards the policies later to be proclaimed at the Hartford Convention.[162]

Pessimistic as the Federalists were about the existing state of affairs, there was still more to come, for the Republicans were not yet finished with the judiciary.[163] In February Bayard had prophesied gloomily that the height of the tide of folly was yet unknown, that "there is reason to fear that it will not stop till all the monads of Government are broken down, & the country inundated with the disorders and mischiefs against which government alone can protect society."[164] His fears were not without some foundation.

Despite the opinion of some Republicans that the attack on the judiciary had gone too far, their political leaders proceeded to take a further step and reported a bill (passed by the Senate without debate on April 8, 1802) abolishing the June session of the Supreme Court and providing that it should convene only in February.[165] What was feared, of course, was that the repeal of the 1801 Act would be declared unconstitutional, as the *Washington Federalist* had urged the judges to do. On April 12, before the bill had passed the House, Bayard wrote to Hamilton:

> You have seen the patchwork offered to us as a new judicial system. The whole is designed to cover one object, which the party consider it necessary to accomplish—the postponement of the next session of the Supreme Court to Feby following. They mean to give to the repealing act its full effect, before the Judges of the Supreme Court are allowed to assemble. Have you thought of the steps which our

---

[160] H. Gray Otis to J. Rutledge, Aug. 2, 1802, The John Rutledge Papers, Manuscripts Division, Library of Congress (originals in Southern Historical Collection, Chapel Hill).

[161] [Illegible] to J. Rutledge, Apr. 27, 1802, *ibid.*

[162] Beveridge, *John Marshall*, III, 97–98.

[163] See chapter 7 infra.

[164] J. Bayard to Andrew [surname omitted], Feb. 9, 1802, Bayard Family Papers.

[165] *Annals of Congress*, XI, 257 (7th Cong., 1st sess.).

Party ought to pursue on this subject. There will be a meeting to concert an uniform plan of acting or acquiescing before Congress adjourns, to be recommended in the manner which shall be thought advisable.[166]

In the House, Bayard spoke more plainly in urging that the second and supplementary Act should not become effective until after the June 1802 session of the Court. "Are gentlemen afraid of the judges? Are they afraid that they will pronounce the repealing law void?"[167] Joseph Nicholson said he was unconcerned whether or not the law was declared void, and that the postponement did not arise from any design. "We have as good a right to suppose gentlemen on the other side are as anxious for a session in June, that this power may be exercised, as they have to suppose we wish to avoid it, to prevent the exercise."[168] In reply, Bayard openly charged, "It is to prevent that court from expressing their opinion upon the validity of the act lately passed . . . until the act has gone into full execution, and the excitement of the public mind abated."[169] There was another and equally important motive, that of postponing the Court's decision in *Marbury* v. *Madison*, which was also likely to be decided at the June term unless the Court were recessed.

Despite the denunciations of the Federalists and the laborious arguments of the party's press, the bill passed the House on April 23 and became law on April 29. The ire of the Federalists knew no bounds. Judge Chase wrote Marshall that he would fight the legislation "although my ruin should be the certain consequence."[170] Even some Republicans, including notably James Monroe, thought that the recessing of the Court was too extreme a measure, that it might be construed as unwillingness on the part of the sponsors of repeal to "meet the Court on the subject."[171]

E.   THE EFFECT OF THE REPEAL ACT ON THE JUDICIARY

Practical questions were raised by the two Judiciary Acts of 1802. The March Act restored the *status quo ante* 1801; that is, it repealed the Acts of February 13 and March 3, 1801, and as of the first of July 1802 restored the former judicial system as if those Acts had never

---

[166] Syrett, *Hamilton Papers*, XXV, 600.

[167] *Annals of Congress*, XI, 1229 (7th Cong., 1st sess.).

[168] *Ibid.*

[169] *Ibid.*, 1235.

[170] S. Chase to J. Marshall, Apr. 27, 1802. The full text of the letter is reprinted at note 182 infra.

[171] J. Monroe to T. Jefferson, Apr. 25, 1802 in S. M. Hamilton, *Writings of James Monroe*, III, 342.

been passed. In addition, the April 1802 Act had made new provisions with respect to the constitution of the circuits and the jurisdiction of the circuit courts.[172] A primary question was whether, so long as doubts existed as to the constitutionality of the Acts and before they had been passed upon, the Supreme Court judges should hold the circuit courts. Another question concerned the status of the deposed judges.

The first question is illumined by a series of letters exchanged by the judges themselves. On April 6, Marshall wrote to Judge Paterson from Richmond that he had undoubtedly seen the duties to be assigned the judges of the Supreme Court under the bill recently reported to the Senate.[173] He went on to say that, although those duties would be less burdensome than theretofore, or than he had expected,

> I confess I have some strong constitutional scruples. I cannot well perceive how the performance of circuit duties by the Judges of the supreme court can be supported. If the question was new I should be willing to act in this character without a consultation of the Judges; but I consider it as decided & that whatever my own scruples may be I am bound by the decision. I cannot however but regret the loss of the next June term. I could have wished the Judges had convened before they proceeded to execute the new system.[174]

Two weeks later it was plain that the bill would be passed, that the June session of the Supreme Court would not be held, and that the judges would apparently be required to ride circuit. Marshall wrote to Paterson, Cushing, and probably the other judges as well on April 19.[175] The letters to Paterson and Cushing have been preserved, and the former was the longer one. Marshall began by saying that it appeared proper that the judges should communicate their sentiments to one another so that they might act "understandingly and in the same manner."[176] He proceeded to express the seriousness with which he viewed the question:

> I hope I need not say that no man in existence respects more than I do those who passed the original law concerning the courts of the United States, & those who first acted under it. So highly do I respect

---

[172] 2 Stat. 89–100. See note 7 of chapter 4 supra.

[173] J. Marshall to W. Paterson, Apr. 6, 1802, Paterson Papers, 639–64, Bancroft Transcripts, New York Public Library, New York City.

[174] *Ibid.*

[175] J. Marshall to W. Paterson, Apr. 19, 1802, *ibid.*, J. Marshall to W. Cushing, Apr. 19, 1802, Paine Collection, Massachusetts Historical Society, Boston (reference courtesy of the Massachusetts Historical Society).

[176] J. Marshall to W. Paterson, Apr. 19, 1802, Paterson Papers, 643–47, Bancroft Transcripts, New York Public Library.

their opinions that I had not examined them & should have proceeded without a doubt on the subject, to perform the duties assigned to me if the late discussions had not unavoidably produced an investigation of the subject which from me it would not otherwise have received. The result of this investigation has been an opinion which I cannot conquer that the constitution requires distinct appointments & commissions for the Judges of the inferior courts from those of the supreme court. It is however my duty & my inclination in this as in all other cases to be bound by the opinion of the majority of the Judges & I should therefore have proceeded to execute the law so far as that task may be assigned to me, had I not supposed it possible that the Judges might be inclined to distinguish between the original case of being appointed to duties marked out before their appointments & of having the duties of administering justice in new courts imposed after their appointments. I do not myself state this because I am myself satisfied that the distinction ought to have weight, for I am not—but as there may be some thing in it I am inclined to write to the Judges requesting the favor of them to give me their opinions which opinions I will afterwards write to each Judge. My own conduct shall certainly be regulated by them.

This is a subject not to be lightly resolved on. The consequences of refusing to carry the law into effect may be very serious. For myself personally I disregard them, & so I am persuaded does every other Gentleman on the bench when put in competition with what he thinks his duty, but the conviction of duty ought to be very strong before the measure is resolved on. The law having been once executed will detract very much in the public estimation from the merit or opinion of the sincerity of a determination, not now to act under it.[177]

The letter to Judge Cushing was shorter, but in the same vein. In it Marshall asked Cushing's opinion as to whether he and the other members of the Court should undertake to hold the circuit courts under the legislation then before Congress, on the assumption that it would pass. "For myself," wrote Marshall, "I more than doubt the constitutionality of this measure & of performing circuit duty without a commission as a circuit Judge. But I shall hold myself bound by the opinions of my brothers."[178] In other words, under the 1801 Act, circuit commissions were expressly authorized for the new circuit judges, but neither of the two 1802 Acts had expressly authorized the Supreme Court judges to resume riding circuit: if they had such authority it must be under the March Act, which nullified the 1801 Acts and therefore, by implication, reauthorized the judges to ride circuit.

On May 3 Marshall again wrote to Judge Paterson, having in the

---

[177] *Ibid.*
[178] J. Marshall to W. Cushing, Apr. 19, 1802, Paine Collection, Massachusetts Historical Society.

meantime received a letter from Judge Washington, presumably in reply to the same kind of letter that he had written to Paterson and Cushing:

> Mr. Washington states it as his opinion that the question respecting the constitutional right of the Judges of the supreme court to sit as circuit Judges ought to be considered as settled and should not again be moved. I have no doubt myself but that policy dictates this decision to us all. Judges however are of all men those who have the least right to obey her dictates. I own I shall be privately gratified if such should be the *opinion of the majority* and I shall with much pleasure acquiesce in it; though, if the subject has never been discussed, I should feel greatly embarrassed about it myself.
>
> I have also received a letter from Judge Chase whose opinion is directly opposite to that of Judge Washington, but he expresses an earnest desire, which he has requested me to communicate to every member of the bench, that we should meet in Washington, for the purpose of determining on the course of conduct to be pursued, in August next, when he is directed to hold a sort of a demi session at that place.
>
> I shall communicate this wish to Judge Moore and will thank you to correspond with Judge Cushing on the subject, and let me know the result.
>
> If we determine certainly to proceed to do circuit duty, it will I presume be entirely unnecessary to meet in August. If we incline to the contrary opinion, and are undecided, we ought to meet and communicate verbally our difficulties to each other.
>
> After hearing from Judge Moore I will again write you.[179]

Judge Chase had written Marshall on April 24 and had sent a copy to Paterson on the same day.[180] In a covering letter to Paterson, Chase urged him to ask Marshall to convene a meeting of the Court.[181] In his letter to Marshall, Judge Chase reiterated his request that the Supreme Court judges convene in Washington in July or August to consider their response to the Repeal Act collectively, rather than through correspondence. In his lengthy and enlightening response to Marshall's letter, Chase enlarged upon his belief in the courts' power to declare null and void those Acts passed by Congress that violate the

---

[179] J. Marshall to W. Paterson, May 3, 1802, *ibid.*

[180] The text of this letter is reprinted in full at note 182 infra.

[181] S. Chase to W. Paterson, Apr. 24, 1802, Chase Manuscripts, New York Historical Society, New York City (reference by courtesy of the New York Historical Society).

Constitution. (Judge Chase believed that the lower federal courts, as well as the Supreme Court, had that power). Because he was convinced that the Repeal Act was unconstitutional, at least insofar as its purpose was to destroy the office of the judges of the circuit courts, he urged that the Supreme Court judges should not act as judges in the circuit courts: he argued that the offices were, in fact, full, and that by acting as circuit judges the Supreme Court judges would be instrumental in carrying into effect an unconstitutional law.[182]

---

[182] Judge Chase to Chief Justice Marshall, Apr. 24, 1802. The original is held by the New York Historical Society. A copy is available in the New York Public Library, New York City. The full text of the letter is reproduced below:

Baltimore 24th April 1802

My dear Sir

I am honoured with your letter of the 19th instant, from Alexandria. I have seen the Act repealing the Judiciary Law of the last session, and reviving the former System; and I have also a copy of the Bill dividing thirteen Districts into six Circuits, and assigning one to each of the Judges of the Supreme Court etc., as passed the Senate. I most anxiously wish that the Judges could meet me, at Washington, on the first Monday of August next, when I must be there to prepare the Cases for trial. I greatly prefer a personal conference to a communication by letter; and in that case I think it would be proper to lay the result before the President; as our predecessors did in a similar case.—I feel every desire to yield my opinion to my Brethren; but my conscience must be satisfied, although my ruin should be the certain consequence. My office is necessary for the support of a numerous family; but I cannot hesitate one moment between a performance of my duty, and the loss of office.— If my Brethren should differ from me in opinion, and I should only *doubt*, what conduct I shall pursue, I will readily submit my judgement to theirs; which I very highly respect.— Without any reserve I will give you my present thoughts; holding myself at perfect liberty to change them, on being convinced that they are erroneous.—

I suppose it will not be questioned, that the repealing Act is constitutional, and will reverse every part of the Law repealed, *except* the establishment of the Circuit Courts, described in the Law, and the appointments, commissions, and salaries, of the Judges who qualified, and acted, and are ready to act under the Law. It is a *great* doubt with me whether the Circuit Courts, established by the Law, can be *abolished*; but I have *no doubt*, that the Circuit Judges cannot, *directly*, or *indirectly*, be deprived of their *offices*, or Commissions, or Salaries, during their lives; unless only on impeachment for, and conviction of, high Crimes and Misdemeanors, as prescribed in the Constitution.— As the Act of Congress evidently intended to *remove* the Circuit Judges from their offices, and to take away their Salaries, I am of opinion, that it is *void*.— The distinction of taking the *office* from the *Judge*, and not the *Judge* from the *office*, I consider as puerile, and nonsensical.—

It appears to me that the Constitution of the United States (Art. 1 s.8, and Art. 3 s.2) makes it the *duty* of Congress to constitute, ordain, and *establish* Courts *inferior* to the Supreme Court; for the trial and decision of *all* cases, to which the Judicial power of the United States is extended by the Constitution (Art. 3 S 2 & 3); and of which the Supreme Court, by the Constitution, has not *original* Jurisdiction; for I much doubt, whether the Supreme Court can be vested, by Law, with *original* Jurisdiction, in any *other* Cases, than the very few enumerated in the Constitution. In *all other* Cases, to which the Judicial power of the United States extends, the Supreme Court is vested with an *appellate* Jurisdiction; and if it can have *original* Jurisdiction, in *other* cases, the citizen would be deprived of the benefit of a hearing in the *inferior* Tribunals; and obliged to resort, in the commencement of his Suit, to the Supreme Court.— If Congress *neglected* to *establish Inferior* Courts to decide *all* the Cases, to which the Judicial power of the United States extends, they disobey the plain injunctions of the Constitution, and by *such neglect of* duty, they deprive the *several States*, and our own Citizens, and also Foreigners, of their *Right* of suing in such Inferior Courts; but there is no remedy.— In the establishment of Courts inferior to the Supreme Court, the Congress are the *sole Judges* of the *time*, when such Courts shall be established; of the number of such Courts; of the number of Judges to be appointed to hold them; of the portion, or District of the United States over which such Courts shall have *Jurisdiction*; of the time and place, at which such Courts shall hold their sessions; and of the Cases (Civil and Criminal) of which they shall take Cognizance.— But whenever Congress constitute Inferior Courts, and Judges are appointed, commissioned, and qualified, I am of opinion that, immediately thereupon, eo instante, such Judges become *constitutional Judges*; and hold *their Offices, and Commissions* under the Constitution; and on the *three* terms prescribed therein, to wit; 1°. That they shall hold their *offices* during *their good behaviour*; 2°. That they shall be removed from office only in *one* way, namely, by impeachment for, and conviction of Treason, Bribery, or other High Crimes & Misdemeanors; 3°. That their salaries shall not be diminished (a fortiori, not taken away) during their continuance in office.—

It appears to me that the Office, Commission, and Salary (all three) of a *Judge*, under the *Constitution* of the *United* States, are to be of *equal* duration. The *tenure* of his office is for *life*, if he does not forfeit it; his Commission is to continue as long as his office, to wit, for life; and his Salary is to remain *undiminished*, as long as his office and Commission, that is, for *life*, unless forfeited. If Inferior Courts, once established, can be *abolished* by Congress (which I doubt) it will *not* necessarily follow, that the Judges of such Courts will cease to be Judges.— I admit that Congress may, in their discretion, increase the number of Judges in any of the Courts established; they may also lessen the number of Judges in such Courts, on the *death* of any of them; they may diminish, or enlarge the Jurisdiction of any of the Courts; they may enlarge or contract the extent of the Districts or Circuits; and they may require *additional Judicial Duties*, of any of the Judges, agreeably to the provisions of the Constitution: But still the Judges, and their Offices must remain independent of the Legislature. If Congress should require of the Judges *duties* that are *impracticable*; or if Congress should impose duties on them that are unreasonable, and for the manifest purpose of compelling them to resign their Offices; such Cases (if they should ever happen) will suggest their own Remedy.— It cannot be questioned that the Judges of the Inferior Courts were intended, by the Constitution, to be as independent as the Judges of the Supreme Court.— By the Constitution these Courts were invested with Jurisdiction (Civil & Criminal) of *all Cases*, in Law, and Equity arising under the Constitution, and Laws of the United States, except only in a very few Cases, of which the Supreme Court was invested with *original* jurisdiction; and therefore the independence of the Judges of the Inferior Courts is as essentially necessary to guard the Constitution,

173

and the Rights of the States, and the Rights of *private* Citizens, and the Rights also of *Foreigners*, as the independence of the Judges of the Supreme Court.

The Constitution of the United States is certainly a *limited* Constitution; because (in Art. 1. s 9) it expressly *prohibits* Congress from making certain *enumerated Laws*; and also from doing certain specified Acts, in many cases; and it is very evident that these restrictions on the *Legislative power* of Congress would be entirely nugatory, and merely waste paper, if there exists no power under the Constitution, to declare Acts made, contrary to these *express prohibitions*, null & void. It is equally clear that the *limitations* of the power of Congress can only be preserved by the Judicial power. There can be no other rational, peaceable and secure barrier against violations of the Constitution by the Legislature, or against encroachments by it, on the Executive, or on the Judiciary branches of our government. The House of Representatives, from their wealth and numbers, have *now* more influence than the Senate; and it will rapidly increase; while the power of the Senate must forever remain almost stationary. These two bodies united, will always controul the Executive alone; and even if supported by the Judiciary: The Judicial power is most feeble indeed; and if the Legislative and Executive unite, to impair or to destroy its Constitution Rights, they must be irresistible; unless the great body of the people take the alarm and give their aid. It is provided by the Constitution that the Constitution of the United States shall be the *Supreme* Law of the Land; and by the Oath of Office prescribed by the Statute (22 September 1789) all Judges engage to discharge, and perform all their duties, as Judges, *agreeably to the Constitution*. Further, all Judges, by the Constitution (Art. 6 s 6) are required to bind themselves, by oath, to *support* the Constitution

of the United States. This engagement, in my judgement, obliges every Judge (or other taker thereof) not to do any affirmative act to contravene, or render ineffectual, any of the provisions in the Constitution. It has been the uniform opinion (until very lately) that the Supreme Court possess the power, and that they are in *Duty* bound, to declare acts of Congress or of any of the States, contrary to the Constitution of the United States, *void*; and the Judges of the Supreme Court have *separately* given such opinion. If the Supreme Court possess this power, the Inferior Courts must also have the *same* power; and of course ought to be as independent of Congress as the Supreme Court: but the Judges of *both* Courts will not be independent of, but dependent on, the Legislature, if they are not entitled to hold their *Offices* during their *good behaviour*; or if they have not a fixed and certain provision for their support that cannot be diminished; or if they can be removed from office, (or which is the same thing) if their *offices* can be taken from them, by Congress.— The Constitution has established *good behaviour* as the *tenure* by which *all Federal Judges* shall hold their *Offices*; and it has prescribed the mode, by which only, any of them can be removed from office.— By these wise provisions it evidently follows that they cannot be removed *directly*, or *indirectly* by Congress; and that they cannot be removed in any other way than by impeachment; Every other mode is a mere subterfuge and evasion of the Constitution.— It appears to me, that the repealing Act, *so far*, as it contemplates to affect the appointment, commission, and office, or Salary of any of the Judges of the Circuit Courts, is contrary to the Constitution, and is therefore, *so far*, void. If the constitutionality of this Act could be brought before the Supreme Court, by action of assize of office, or by action to recover the Salary, I should decide (as at present advised) that the Act is void; and I would by the first action restore the Judge to his Office, and, by the latter, adjudge him his Salary; but by neither of these modes, nor by any other (as Mandamus & Quo Warranto) could remedy be obtained. This *defect* of remedy to obtain a *Right* (which Justice abhors) will induce every Judge of the Supreme Court to act with the greatest caution; and he must, in my judgement, decline to execute the office of a Circuit Judge, if he apprehends, that he shall, thereby, violate the Constitutional Rights of the Circuit Judges.—

But are the Judges of the Supreme Court bound in duty, to hold the Circuit Courts?— I sincerely wish it was not our duty (especially at this time) to decide this question; but I am glad that we are not in any manner interested in the determination. If the Circuits had been as remote from our several places of residence & as extensive, as heretofore, our ease and convenience might be said, by ignorant, or bad men, to have some influence; but by the system proposed, of holding only *one* Supreme Court in the year, and all of us (except Judge Washington) having a convenient District, no such suspicion can be entertained.—

I have *three* objections to the Judges of the Supreme Court holding the Circuit Courts. First. If the repealing law has not *abolished* the Circuit Courts, which it certainly has not done, but has established Circuit Courts in the repealing Act, and also in the Bill intended to be passed, *substantially the same* with the Circuit Courts in the Law repealed; and if the repealing Act has not destroyed the office of the Judges appointed, commissioned, and qualified under the Law repealed; it follows that the *offices* of these Judges are *now full*; and consequently no Judge of the Supreme Court (nor any Judge of any District Court) holding this opinion, can exercise the *office* of a Judge of such Courts, without violating the Constitution.— Sec-

ondly, If the repealing Act be void, *so far*, as it intends to destroy the *office* of the Judges under the Law repealed, and a Judge of the Supreme Court (or of a District Court) should hold the Circuit Court, I think he would, thereby, be *instrumental* to carry into effect an unconstitutional Law.— If he executes the office of Circuit Judge, I think he, thereby, decides that the repealing was constitutional. I conceive that he must, *before* he acts, decide, whether the repealing Act was constitutional, or not. If he thinks it unconstitutional, he cannot act under it. If one person exercises an office, to which another has *legal title*, he is a *wrong-doer*, and ought to be removed; and the injured person ought to be restored to his office. Shall a *Judge* be a *wrong-doer*? It has never been controverted that Congress can, by Law, require the Judges of the Supreme Court to perform *additional Judicial Duties in the Supreme Court*. I will admit, for the sake of argument only, that Congress may, by Law, require the Judges of the Supreme Court to hold the Circuit Courts; yet, if Judges have been commissioned and qualified as Judges of *such* Courts, and have not been removed according to the Constitution, I cannot agree, that in such Case, the Judges of the Supreme Court can be obliged, by Law, to act as Judges of the Circuit Courts; because they will thereby *disseize*, or *dispossess* the Circuit Judges of their *offices*.— If there were *no Judges* of the Circuit Courts; and if Judges in *one* Court could be required to be Judges in another *distinct* and *separate Court*, with different Jurisdictions; and if the Supreme Court can take Original Jurisdiction of such cases of which the Constitution gives them *appellate Jurisdiction*; yet, I cannot assent, that the Judges of the Supreme Court shall hold the Circuit Courts; because I conceive that they would, thereby, become the *instruments* to *execute an unconstitutional* Law; and would, *thereby*, assist to deprive the Circuit Judges of their offices. If *other* persons had been appointed, and should hold the Circuit Courts, the Judges of the Supreme Court would be bound in duty, to redress this wrong, if the case could be brought before them. It seems to me, that there is a great and manifest difference between the Judges of the Supreme Court acting as Judges of the Circuit Courts under the *former*, and under the *present* system.

I am inclined to believe, that a Judge of the *Supreme Court* cannot act as a Judge of a Circuit *Court without*, or *with* a commission. No one can deny that a Judge of the Circuit Court is an *officer* of the *United States*; and the Constitution (Art. 2 s 3) directs the President to *commission all the officers* of the United States. I apprehend *no one* can hold any office under the United States, without a Commission to hold such office.

But I think (as at present advised) that a Judge of the Supreme Court cannot accept, and act under a Commission, as *Judge* of a *Circuit Court*. The Constitution (Art. 3 s 1) vests the Judicial power of the United States in *one Supreme* Court, and in such inferior Courts as the Congress may, from time to time, ordain, and *establish*; and gives the Supreme Court (Art. 3 s 2) *original* Jurisdiction in causes of Ambassadors etc. etc.; & *appellate* Jurisdiction of the cases enumerated. It appears to me, that Congress cannot, by Law, give the Judges of the Supreme Court *original* Jurisdiction of the *same* Cases, of which it *expressly* gives them *appellate Jurisdiction*. If a case originates in the Circuit Court, and is tried there, the Judge of the Supreme Court may, alone, (or with the District Judge) hear & decide a *case*, of which the Constitution *expressly gives him appellate* Jurisdiction. The Constitution intended that the Judges of the *Supreme* Court should not have *original Jurisdiction*, but only in the few cases enumerated. The inference is just that, as the Consti-

tution only gave the Supreme Court *original* Jurisdiction in a few *specified* cases, it intended to *exclude* them from *original* Jurisdiction in *all* other Cases; and more especially as it gives them *appellate Jurisdiction* in *all cases* that should arise under the Constitution or Laws of the United States.— But the Judges have held Circuit Courts ever since the formation of the Federal Government, until the late Judiciary Law. The fact is so. I can truly say that I never considered the question. I acted as a Circuit Judge, because my predecessors had done so before me, without any enquiry into the subject. But I now see that my holding the Circuit Courts will certainly do an *injury* to the *Rights* of other Judges, and will assist to exclude them from their office. It is under this impression that I feel a very great reluctance to act as a Circuit Judge.— By the Constitution (Art. 2 s 2) all judges are to be nominated by the President to the Senate, and the President, with the advice and consent of the Senate, is to *appoint* them. If Congress, by Law, requires a Judge of the Supreme Court to hold a Circuit Court, does not Congress, thereby, substantially *nominate* and *appoint* a Judge of the Circuit Court?— All Judges are to act under an *oath* of office. Does the oath of office of a Judge of the Supreme Court extend to his duties as a Judge of a Circuit Court?— If not, he will act as a Judge of a Circuit Court, *without any oath.*—

Unless the sentiments of my Brethren should induce me to change my present opinion, I shall certainly decline to take the Circuit assigned me; which would be very convenient, and highly agreeable to me, if my objections can be removed.—

I think it is in the power of the Judges to meet at Washington in July, or August next; and I wish you would urge it. I am confident their opinions would have great weight with the District Judges. I shall be happy to receive copies of

V: *Jefferson's Attack on the Federal Judiciary*

As Marshall had requested, Judge Paterson wrote Cushing, who replied on May 29, referring to Marshall's letter. In that reply he said in effect that if the question were arising *de novo*, by which he presumably meant after the 1789 Act, "doubts would have arisen."[183] However, he went on to say, "as the case is—to be consistent, I think with you, we must abide by the old practice."[184] Meanwhile, Marshall had received the opinions of Chase and Washington and transmitted these to Paterson, who passed them on to Cushing in a letter of May 25.[185] In replying to Paterson, Cushing made it clear that Judge Washington also agreed with them as to resuming the old practice.[186] Judge Chase, however, believed that the members of the Court should meet in August to determine a course of conduct. With the majority in favor of riding circuit, "we must," wrote Cushing, "leave brother Chase to exercise his Singular Jurisdiction in August."[187] The Chief Justice bowed to the views of the majority. However, it was not until February 1803 that the Court again convened in Washington.

The second problem, that of the fate of the judges dismissed by the repealing Act, involved obvious difficulties. If the 1802 Act were constitutional, the remedies of the judges would seem to be limited to what Congress might be willing to do. While the Supreme Court judges were considering through their exchanges of letters whether they should hold the circuit courts, the dismissed circuit judges were likewise confused as to their proper course of action. Prior to the Repeal Act, at least some of the circuit courts authorized and organized under the 1801 Act had convened.[188] On May 22 Judge Tilghman wrote on behalf of the other judges of the Third Circuit to Judge Jeremiah Smith of the First Circuit to request a meeting on July 17 to discuss the validity of the repealing law.[189] Smith replied that he had been assured in confidence that measures would be taken to test the validity of the Act.[190] In August Judge Bourne of the First Circuit wrote Tilghman that only

---

the opinions of all my brethren. The burthen of deciding so momentous a question, and under the present circumstances of our Country, would be very great on all the Judges assembled: but an individual Judge, declining to take a Circuit, must sink under it.

With my best wishes for your health and happiness, and with the highest respect and esteem, I have the honour to be, dear Sir,

> Your affectionate
> and obedient Servant
> S. Chase

[183] W. Cushing to W. Paterson, May 29, 1802, Miscellaneous Manuscripts Cushing, New York Historical Society, New York City.

[184] *Ibid.*

[185] W. Paterson to W. Cushing, May 25, 1802, *ibid.*

[186] W. Cushing to W. Paterson, June 8, 1802, *ibid.*

[187] *Ibid.*

[188] Warren, *Supreme Court*, I, 195–203. See also *New England Palladium* (Boston) for Apr. 19, 1803.

[189] J. Morison, *Life of Jeremiah Smith* (Boston, 1845), 148–49.

[190] *Ibid.*, 149.

four circuit judges had attended the meeting.[191] He went on to say that since the Supreme Court judges had decided to hold the circuit courts, the judges of the latter "dismissed" under the 1802 Act were bound to submit. "But it was our opinion that altho precluded from holding courts, yet our commissions of Judges, & our right to receive the compensation fixed by law, remained in full force. . . . The prevailing idea, at the meeting, was that the Subject would be most properly brought forward, by a memorial to Congress at their next session."[192]

Individual but almost identical memorials of the judges were duly prepared, signed by eleven of the circuit judges, and presented to the Senate. The judges who submitted memorials included Richard Bassett, Egbert Benson, Benjamin Bourne, William Griffith, Samuel Hitchcock, Philip B. Key, C. Magill, Jeremiah Smith, G. K. Taylor, William Tilghman, and Oliver Wolcott. The memorials were referred to a committee, comprised of Senators Morris, Ross, and Dayton, which reported to the Senate on January 28, 1803, that the question whether or not the judges had been deprived of their offices under the 1802 Act depended on the construction of the laws and Constitution of the United States and was not properly cognizable by the Senate.[193] However, in view of the "high and serious import" of the question, the committee believed that "a speedy investigation and final decision is of great moment to the commonwealth." For this reason they presented, without recommendation, a resolution for the Senate's consideration:

"*Resolved*, That the President of the United States be requested to cause an information, in the nature of *quo warranto*, to be filed by the Attorney General against Richard Bassett, one of the said petitioners, for the purpose of deciding judicially on their claims."[194]

The text of the judges' memorial, which prompted the committee's resolution, was as follows:

To the honorable the Senate and House of Representives of the United States, in Congress assembled: The undersigned most respectfully submit the following representation and memorial:

By an act of Congress, passed on the 13th day of February, in the year of our Lord one thousand eight hundred and one, entitled 'An act to provide for the more convenient organization of the courts of the United States,' certain judicial offices were created and courts established, called circuit courts of the United States.

In virtue of appointments made under the constitution of the United States, the undersigned became vested with the offices so

---

[191] B. Bourne to W. Tilghman, Aug. 14, 1802, Samuel Gratz Collection, Pennsylvania Historical Society, Philadelphia.

[192] *Ibid.*
[193] *American State Papers: Miscellaneous* I, 340, Jan. 28, 1803.
[194] *Ibid.*

created, and received commissions authorizing them to hold the same, with the emoluments thereunto appertaining, during their good behavior.

During the last session, an act of Congress passed, by which the above-mentioned law was declared to be repealed; since which no law has been made for assigning to your memoralists the execution of any judicial functions, nor has any provision been made for the payment of their stipulated compensations.

Under these circumstances, and finding it expressly declared in the constitution of the United States, that "the judges, both of the supreme and inferior courts, shall hold their offices during good behavior, and shall, at stated times, receive for their services a compensation, which shall not be diminished during their continuance in office," the undersigned, after the most deliberate consideration, are compelled to represent it as their opinion, that the rights secured to them by the constitution, as members of the judicial department, have been impaired.

With this sincere conviction, and influenced by a sense of public duty, they most respectfully request of Congress to review the existing laws which respect the offices in question; and to define the duties to be performed by the undersigned, by such provisions as shall be consistent with the constitution, and the convenient administration of justice.

The right of the undersigned to their compensations they sincerely believe to be secured by the constitution, notwithstanding any modification of the judicial department, which, in the opinion of Congress, public convenience may recommend. This right, however, involving a personal interest, will cheerfully be submitted to judicial examination and decision, in such manner as the wisdom and impartiality of Congress may prescribe.

That judges shall not be deprived of their offices or compensations, without misbehavior, appears to the undersigned to be among the first and best established principles in the American constitutions; and in the various reforms they have undergone it has been preserved and guarded with increased solicitude.

On this basis the constitution of the United States has laid the foundation of the judicial department, and expressed its meaning in terms equally plain and peremptory.

This being the deliberate and solemn opinion of the undersigned, the duty of their stations requires that they should declare it to the Legislative body. They regret the necessity which compels them to make the representation; and they confide that it will be attributed to a conviction that they ought not voluntarily to surrender rights and authorities intrusted to their protection, not for their personal advantage, but for the benefit of the community.[195]

---

[195] *Ibid.*

The plea of the judges, however, fell on largely deaf ears. In the Senate the debate turned again to the question of the judiciary's power to pass on the enactments of another branch. Senator Jackson of Georgia raised the issue in a manner that would have cast Congress in a humiliating light had it chosen to request that the matter be submitted for judicial resolution: "Ought we go to the Courts and ask them whether we have done our duty or whether we have violated the Constitution?"[196] Ultimately, resolutions requesting submission of the questions raised by the abolition of the circuit judgeships by the Repeal Act to the judicial branch failed in both houses of Congress. The issue was finally to reach the Supreme Court by a different route, with an outcome that was undoubtedly not expected by the Court's foes.

F.   THE VALIDITY OF THE REPEAL ACT

Little more than a month after the Congress rejected attempts to secure a judicial opinion on the validity of the Repeal Act, the constitutionality of the Act came before the Supreme Court by a traditional route. In December 1801 one John Laird had obtained a judgment "in a court for the fourth circuit, in the eastern district of Virginia."[197] As Judge Paterson described the facts subsequently:

> On this judgment, an execution was issued, returnable to April term 1802, in the same court. In the term of December 1802, John Laird obtained judgment at a court for the fifth circuit, in the Virginia district, against Hugh Stuart and Charles Carter, upon their bond for the forthcoming and delivery of certain property therein mentioned, which had been levied upon by virtue of the above execution against the said Hugh Stuart.[198]

The court in which the earlier judgment had been awarded had, in the meanwhile, been abolished by the Repeal Act of 1802. The defendant therefore raised the constitutionality of the Repeal Act, but Marshall, hearing the case on circuit, rejected the sufficiency of his plea, and judgment was entered for the plaintiff. The case was then taken to the Supreme Court on writ of error as *Stuart* v. *Laird*. There Charles Lee, counsel for the plaintiff in error, focused attention on the importance of the question of the constitutionality of the Repeal Act and the subsequent Act affecting the federal judiciary for a determination of the merits of his client's case:

> If the acts of 8th March and 29th April, 1802, are constitutional, then it is admitted there is no error in the judgment; because,

---

[196] *Annals of Congress*, XI, 1260 (7th Cong., 1st sess.).

[197] Stuart v. Laird, 1 Cranch 298, 308 (1803).
[198] *Ibid.*

in that case, the courts ceased to exist, the judges were constitutionally removed, and the transfer from the one court to the other was legal. But if those acts are unconstitutional, then the court of the fourth circuit still exists, the judges were not removed, and the transfer of jurisdiction did not take place. The legislature did not intend to transfer causes from one *existing* court to another. If, then, the courts still exist, the causes not being intended to be removed from existing courts, were not removed.[199]

Lee proceeded to argue that the Repeal Act was unconstitutional, as well as to argue that the Supreme Court judges could not constitutionally be required to sit as circuit judges.

The Court's opinion, which was delivered by Judge Paterson, was a terse four-paragraph affirmance of the judgment below. Rejecting Lee's arguments that the Repeal Act was unconstitutional, Paterson held:

> Congress have constitutional authority to establish such inferior tribunals as they may think proper; and to transfer a cause from one such tribunal to another. In this last particular, there are no words in the constitution to prohibit or restrain the exercise of legislative power.
>
> The present is a case of this kind. It is nothing more than the removal of the suit brought by Stuart from the court of the fourth circuit to the court of the fifth circuit, which is authorized to proceed upon and carry it into full effect.[200]

The Court's earlier practice, Paterson stated, precluded a challenge to the judges' participation as circuit judges without distinct commissions. The opinion concluded with the admonition that "the question is at rest, and ought not now to be disturbed."[201] In the opinion of Warren, "No more striking example of the non-partisanship of the American Judiciary can be found than this decision by a Court composed wholly of Federalists, upholding, contrary to its personal and political views, a detested Republican measure; . . ."[202]

Chief Justice Marshall declined to participate in the decision because he had heard the case in the circuit court below. It is not without interest that only six days before *Stuart* v. *Laird* was decided he had delivered the opinion in the case of *Marbury* v. *Madison*.[203] Although the latter case did not involve the Repeal Act of 1802, it had nevertheless been a prominent issue in the people's minds as well as in the debates over the repeal.

---

[199] *Ibid.*, 302 (emphasis supplied).
[200] *Ibid.*, 308.
[201] *Ibid.*

[202] Warren, *Supreme Court*, I, 269–73.
[203] 1 Cranch 137 (1803); see chapter 6 infra.

CHAPTER VI

Marbury v. Madison

Marbury v. *Madison*[1] is widely regarded as a landmark decision of the United States Supreme Court in that it allegedly established the doctrine of judicial review of acts of Congress. Countless books and articles have examined aspects of the opinion and its implications, and recent writers in particular have concerned themselves with the supposed political motives of Chief Justice Marshall in choosing the course that he did in preparing the opinion, as well as with the question whether his formulation of judicial review comported with ideas prevailing at that time; more specifically, there has been a growing interest in prior State and federal precedents, in the intent of the Constitution's framers, in the debates at the ratifying conventions, and in the wording of the Constitution itself.[2] Although the work of these scholars and commentators deserves continuing thoughtful consideration and recognition, it seems useful for present purposes to examine *Marbury* v. *Madison* from a somewhat different vantage point, lest its basic significance be exaggerated.

Marbury was the first decision in which the Supreme Court declared void an act of Congress on the ground that it was contrary to the

---

[1] 1 Cranch 137 (1803).

[2] See, e.g., R. Berger, *Congress v. the Supreme Court* (Cambridge, Mass., 1969); A. M. Bickel, *The Least Dangerous Branch* (Indianapolis, 1962); W. W. Crosskey, *Politics and the Constitution in the History of the United States* (Chicago, 1953), II; C. G. Haines, *The American Doctrine of Judicial Supremacy*, 2d ed. (New York, 1959); L. W. Levy, ed., *Judicial Review and the Supreme Court: Selected Essays* (New York, 1967); C. Warren, *The Supreme Court in United States History* (Boston, 1922); S. H. Bice, "An Essay Review of Congress v. the Supreme Court," *Southern California Law Review* XLIV, 499 (1971); F. R. Strong, "Judicial Review: A Tri-Dimensional Concept of Administrative—Constitutional Law," *West Virginia Law Review* LXIX, 111 (1967); H. Wechsler, "Toward Neutral Principles of Constitutional Law," *Harvard Law Review* LXXIII, 1 (1959).

Constitution. The next case was the *Dred Scott* decision in 1857.[3] That fact alone raises such specific questions as: What did "judicial review" mean to the Court in 1803? What were the origins of John Marshall's conceptions of that doctrine, as it was then understood? Why did Marshall choose to incorporate in *Marbury* what is usually regarded as a lengthy "excursus" allegedly irrelevant to the issue directly before the Court? What was the contemporary political and judicial reaction to *Marbury*? Finally, what was the relevance of the decision to the course upon which Marshall had embarked as Chief Justice and to the development of the Supreme Court?

A. THE FACTUAL AND POLITICAL SETTINGS

The facts of *Marbury* v. *Madison* are generally familiar. Thomas Jefferson had been elected to succeed John Adams as President, effective on March 4, 1801. In the weeks preceding his departure from office, President Adams, with the acknowledged aid of the Federalists then in Congress, took certain steps earlier discussed to ensure continuing Federalist influence in the government.[4] Relevant to one of those steps was the act of February 27, 1801, which set up the basis of government for the District of Columbia. That act, *inter alia*, authorized the President to appoint a number of justices of the peace for five-year terms.[5] President Adams nominated forty-two such justices on March 2, and on March 3 all were confirmed by the Senate.[6] In accordance with usual procedure, the commissions were prepared at the office of the Secretary of State. At this point John Marshall held the office of Secretary of State concurrently with that of Chief Justice. The commissions were delivered to the President for signature and were then returned to the Secretary for affixing the formal seal, for recording, and for delivery to the appointees.[7]

It appears, however, that some of the commissions were never

---

[3] 19 Howard 393 (1857). It had previously been established in Vanhorne's Lessee v. Dorrance, 2 Dall. 303 (1795), that a federal court, in a case properly before it, could assess the validity of State legislation under State constitutions. Moreover, the federal Circuit Court for Pennsylvania had declared an act of Congress unconstitutional in Hayburn's Case (1792), an unreported decision discussed in M. Farrand, "The First Hayburn Case, 1792," *American Historical Review* XIII, 281 (1908).

After Marbury the Supreme Court also established that a State law could be invalidated if it conflicted with the federal Constitution. Fletcher v. Peck, 6 Cranch 87 (1810), discussed in chapter 10 infra.

[4] See chapter 4 supra.

[5] Act of Feb. 27, 1810, chapter 15, Sec. 11, 2 Stat. 103, 107.

[6] *Journal of the Executive Proceedings of the Senate of the United States of America* (Washington, 1828), I, 388, 390.

[7] K. Turner, "The Midnight Judges," *University of Pennsylvania Law Review* CIX, 494, 518–19 (1961).

delivered to the appointees. In his haste to finish up business before his term of office as Secretary expired, Marshall left the commissions at the Department of State.[8] Immediately after Jefferson was inaugurated, he directed his new Secretary of State, James Madison, to withhold seventeen of the forty-three commissions. Four of the seventeen men affected, including William Marbury, applied to the Supreme Court for a writ of mandamus to compel delivery of the commissions. The other thirteen took no action, perhaps because they regarded the positions as insufficiently important to make litigation worthwhile.[9]

It is useful to recall that the issues of the *Marbury* case were presented to the Court at a time of extreme political partisanship, and that for reasons earlier described the judiciary was close to the center of violent quarrels between Republicans and Federalists which had been erupting since at least 1798. It will also be recalled that a month before Jefferson's inauguration, John Marshall had been appointed Chief Justice, and the Judiciary Act of 1801 had been enacted into law.[10] In 1802, while the *Marbury* case was pending before the Court, Congress, by a strictly partisan vote, repealed the 1801 Act[11] and then passed a law postponing the next session of the Supreme Court for over a year, apparently out of fear that the Court would declare the repealing Act unconstitutional.[12] As a result, *Marbury* v. *Madison* did not reach the Supreme Court until 1803.

In light of the above, it is particularly important to emphasize what the Supreme Court did decide in *Marbury*, and why it decided the case as it did. Speaking for the Court, Marshall analyzed the three questions that he thought vital, though in an order different from that in which Charles Lee, counsel for petitioners, had presented them.[13] He concluded (1) that Marbury was lawfully entitled to his commission; (2) that Marbury did have a legal remedy, and that the situation was not one so political in nature that judicial relief could not be granted; but (3) that Section 13 of the Judiciary Act of 1789, which purportedly conferred on the Supreme Court the power to issue writs of mandamus, was unconstitutional as a basis of jurisdiction in this case, and hence the writ could not issue. The opinion proceeded to explain why the Court felt justified in rendering ineffectual a congressional act which it deemed inconsistent with the Constitution.

---

[8] I. S. Rhodes, "Marbury Versus Madison Revisited," *University of Cincinnati Law Review* XXXIII, 23, 33 (1964).

[9] A. J. Beveridge, *The Life of John Marshall* (Boston, 1919), III, 110.

[10] Act of Feb. 13, 1801, chapter 4, 2 Stat. 89. See chapter 4 supra.

[11] Act of March 8, 1802, chapter 8, Sec. 1, 2 Stat. 132.

[12] Beveridge, *John Marshall*, III, 94–97.

[13] 1 Cranch at 146, 154.

VI: *Marbury* v. *Madison*

Thus the actual *holding* of the case was merely that Marbury was not entitled to the remedy that he sought in the Supreme Court, because the law that authorized that relief did not comport with the mandate of the Constitution concerning the distribution of judicial power between the lower federal courts and the Supreme Court.[14] To attempt to explain why Marshall wrote the opinion in the way that he did—that is, by first establishing Marbury's right to his commission instead of confining the opinion to the Court's lack of jurisdiction—it is necessary to evaluate briefly the political situation in which the Court found itself, and then to examine critically Marshall's legal reasoning on each major point of the opinion.

From a political standpoint, Marshall's opinion has been considered as both expedient and tendentious, in that the ultimate refusal to grant Marbury's petition avoided a head-on collision with Jefferson, who had ordered that Marbury be denied his commission. A decision in favor of Marbury would have resulted in a direct confrontation between the power of the Presidency and the power of the Court. From the standpoint of the position of the judiciary, and of Marshall personally, this was a confrontation that would have been ill timed. In light both of the repeal of the 1801 Judiciary Act and of the postponement of the 1802 Supreme Court term by the Republicans in Congress, it was unlikely that Jefferson would quietly acquiesce in what he would have seen as an incursion upon his power by the Court, if efforts were made to enforce its decision.[15] The position of Marshall, and also of the Court, was precarious, and a decision in favor of Marbury would hardly have been welcomed. Moreover, the House of Representatives, at the beginning of the 1803 session, had impeached District Judge John Pickering, and already definite plans were afoot to impeach Judge Samuel Chase of the Supreme Court. There were open threats by the Republicans to impeach Marshall himself if he were to decide in favor of Marbury.[16]

In this political climate, it was perhaps particularly understandable

---

[14] *Ibid.*, 175–76.

[15] Andrew Jackson is reported to have shared Jefferson's attitude. Beveridge quotes Jackson as saying in response to John Marshall's majority opinion in The Cherokee Nation v. The State of Georgia, 5 Peters 1 (1831): "John Marshall has made his decision:—*now let him enforce it!*" Beveridge, *John Marshall*, IV, 551 (emphasis in original). To the same effect, see Warren, *Supreme Court*, I, 759.

[16] Beveridge, *John Marshall*, III, 111–12. Beveridge, among others, states that Marshall feared impeachment from more than a personal standpoint; Marshall did not want Spencer Roane, his probable successor, appointed, because of Roane's antinationalist bias. *Ibid.*, 113–14. See chapter 7 infra concerning the Pickering and Chase impeachments.

that Marshall should seize the opportunity to write an opinion that would avoid a political confrontation by turning to and relying upon the less controversial doctrine of judicial review.

B. THE BACKGROUND OF THE DOCTRINE OF JUDICIAL REVIEW

The principle of judicial review of legislative acts had been forming since at least the time of the Constitutional Convention. Forerunners of the principle undoubtedly can be found in colonial experience with enforcement of charters, in judicial nullification of legislation through interpretation,[17] and in political correction by the English Privy Council of acts emanating from an inferior level of government,[18] but the actual practice of judicial invalidation of acts of a coordinate branch of government did not arise until after the Revolution. Nothing in the federal Constitution expressly authorizes judicial review, although it has been effectively argued that the power was implied or properly interpolated in order to carry out the purposes of the framers.[19] Others have suggested that the review power was conferred under Article III, Section 2, whereby the judicial power of the federal courts "shall extend to all Cases, in Law and Equity, arising under this Constitution, . . ." and, further, that the Supreme Court "shall have appellate Jurisdiction, both as to Law and Fact, with such Exceptions, and under such Regulations as the Congress shall make."[20] In fact, two persons—Robert Yates of

---

[17] See S. E. Thorne, "Dr. Bonham's Case," *Law Quarterly Review* LIV, 543 (1938).

[18] See J. H. Smith, *Appeals to the Privy Council from the American Plantations* (New York, 1950), 523–653. Misapprehensions with respect to the nature of executive veto are referred to by J. C. Ranney, "The Bases of American Federalism," *William and Mary Quarterly* (3d Series), III, 8, note 24 (1946).

[19] E. S. Corwin, *The Doctrine of Judicial Review* (Princeton, 1914), 10–17; L. Hand, *The Bill of Rights* (Boston, 1958):
For centuries it has been an accepted canon in interpretation of documents to interpolate into the text such provisions, though not expressed, as are essential to prevent the defeat of the venture at hand; and this applies with especial force to the interpretation of con-

stitutions, which, since they are designed to cover a great multitude of necessarily unforeseen occasions, must be cast in general language, unless they are constantly amended. If so, it was altogether in keeping with established practice for the Supreme Court to assume an authority to keep the states, Congress, and the President within their prescribed powers. Otherwise the government could not proceed as planned; and indeed would almost certainly have foundered, as in fact it almost did over that very issue.

[20] *Ibid.*, 14–15. For a summary of various arguments about judicial review, see F. R. Strong, "Judicial Review: A Tri-Dimensional Concept of Administrative–Constitutional Law," *West Virginia Law Review* LXIX, 111, 118, note 23 (1967).

VI: *Marbury* v. *Madison*

New York and Luther Martin of Maryland—opposed the Constitution on the ground that the "arising under" clause would in fact confer review power.[21]

For contemporary views with respect to the judiciary's power to review the acts of coordinate branches of the government, the opinion of Alexander Hamilton in *The Federalist*, Number 78, is particularly important and relevant:

> [E]very act of a delegated authority, contrary to the tenor of the commission under which it is exercised, is void. No legislative act, therefore, contrary to the Constitution, can be valid. To deny this, would be to affirm, that the deputy is greater than his principal; that the servant is above his master; that the representatives of the people are superior to the people themselves; that men acting by virtue of powers, may do not only what their powers do not authorize, but what they forbid. . . .

> It is far more rational to suppose, that the courts were designed to be an intermediate body between the people and the legislature, in order, among other things, to keep the latter within the limits assigned to their authority. The interpretation of the laws is the proper and peculiar province of the courts. A constitution is, in fact, and must be regarded by the judges, as a fundamental law. It therefore belongs to them to ascertain its meaning, as well as the meaning of any particular act proceeding from the legislative body. If there should happen to be an irreconcilable variance between the two, that which has the superior obligation and validity ought, of course, to be preferred; or, in other words, the Constitution ought to be preferred to the statute, the intention of the people to the intention of their agents.[22]

Several other opinions are noteworthy. One is the statement of James Wilson, in the debates, that the section relating to cases arising under the Constitution would give the judges power to declare an act of Congress null and void.[23] Another is that of John Marshall, who declared at the Virginia Ratifying Convention that if Congress were

---

[21] Berger, *Congress v. the Supreme Court*, 201–202. See also E. S. Corwin, *Court over Constitution* (Gloucester, Mass., 1957), 231–62, for Yates' commentaries, written under the pen name "Brutus."

[22] *The Federalist* No. 78 (A. Hamilton) (New York, 1901), 101.

[23] "If a law should be made inconsistent with those powers vested by this instrument in Congress, the judges, as a consequence of their independence, and the particular powers of government being defined, will declare such law to be null and void; for the power of the Constitution predominates. Any thing, therefore, that shall be enacted by Congress contrary thereto, will not have the force of law." J. Elliot, *The Debates in the Several State Conventions on the Adoption of the Federal Constitution* (Philadelphia, 1836), II, 489.

to "make a law not warranted by any of the powers enumerated, it would be considered by the judges as an infringement of the Constitution which they are to guard. . . . They would declare it void. . . ."[24] Even the radical Patrick Henry thought that the judiciary was a barrier against legislative excesses; he stated at the Virginia Convention: "I take it as the highest encomium of this country, that the acts of the legislature, if unconstitutional, are liable to be opposed by the judiciary."[25] Raoul Berger, who has studied the debates of the ratifying conventions with considerable care, has concluded that not only was there no condemnation of judicial review, that no voice was raised in favor of legislative supremacy, but, on the contrary, that judicial review appears to have been regarded "as a necessary instrument of the new system [and] was taken for granted."[26]

Hamilton had gone even further in emphasizing that the judiciary must defend the Constitution against violations by the other departments, particularly the legislature, and must keep the latter within the assigned limits of its authority. He urged that this power did not "by any means suppose a superiority of the judicial to the legislative power" but that "where the will of the legislature, declared in its statutes, stands in opposition to that of the people, declared in the Constitution, the judges . . . ought to regulate their decisions by the fundamental laws, rather than by those which are not fundamental."[27] What Hamilton astutely perceived was the differentiation that had been taking place between authority and its exercise, between "law" and "politics"; he understood that the Constitution, while expressing the will of the people, embodied principles of immutable law, whereas the representatives of the people in the legislature were not the "people" but were only delegated persons having a limited and changing authority to act on behalf of the people.[28] It is the same differentiation that Marshall also perceived and that he referred to in *Marbury* when he stated: "The powers of the legislature are defined and limited; and that those limits may not be mistaken or forgotten, the constitution is written."[29] His point is elaborated below.

At least two important changes in political thought and governmental structure had been taking place in the latter part of the eighteenth century. First, the judiciary had begun to evolve as a more

---

[24] *Ibid.*, III, 553.
[25] *Ibid.*, III, 325.
[26] Berger, *Congress v. the Supreme Court*, 49. For a critique of Raoul Berger's analysis of both the "arising under" clause and the "exceptions" clause as they relate to the concept of judicial review, see S. H. Bice, "An Essay Review of Congress v. the Supreme Court," *Southern California Law Review* XLIV, 499 (1971).
[27] *The Federalist* No. 78, 102.
[28] G. S. Wood, *The Creation of the American Republic, 1776–1787* (Chapel Hill, 1969), 462.
[29] 1 Cranch at 176.

distinct entity and to separate itself from its supportive role to the executive, with the result that legal issues were tending to be separated from political issues and to be decided in what we would call a "legal" way, in accordance with more or less fixed norms or principles; other more controversial types of issues were being resolved by the executive and the legislature. This emerging distinction was not easy for many to grasp, since in the colonial period the courts—to some extent as hand-maidens of political power—had performed innumerable executive, administrative, and even legislative tasks. No doubt those earlier functions help to explain why judicial review, when it began to appear in the 1780s, seemed to be a political act that did not express, or was not responsive to, the will of the people. Even deeper-lying sentiments were present. The dread of royal power still lay heavily in the minds of those who had framed the Constitution, and it was to limit and check excessive exercise of power in the government that men had turned to popularly chosen legislative bodies. Yet it was not long before conservative opinion began to be alarmed by what were viewed as legislative excesses, reminiscent of magisterial decrees of the pre-Revolutionary period, because the legislatures were enacting laws to which the people at large had never given their full and unqualified assent.[30] Because the acts of legislatures could thus arguably be subject to scrutiny, a certain mistrust developed that had the effect of benefiting the judiciary. The reaction to early efforts to establish legislative supremacy, accompanied by legislative interference in judicial matters, had bred an increased respect for a judiciary that was, by constitutional definition, a separate department, one that had begun to act in accordance with what we, today, would describe as legal norms and principles. It is not surprising, therefore, that some people, with a growing fear of the new legislative power, began to believe that the continued existence of elective government in the United States depended upon having a vigilant judiciary. Thus an entirely new appreciation of its role began to emerge, and the idea surfaced that an independent rule of law was needed to curb the popular will. Ironically, as the late John Dickinson observed, the seventeenth-century doctrine of the supremacy of law—originally a device for checking the usurpations of English kings—was developed as an instrument for controlling the actions of popularly chosen officials and legislators.[31]

Against this background, it should not be startling that beginning in the 1780s courts began to hold unconstitutional legislative acts of a coordinate branch of government. Such cases arose, for example, in

---

[30] Wood, *American Republic*, 456.
[31] J. Dickinson, *Administrative Justice and the Supremacy of Law in* the United States (Cambridge, Mass., 1927), 95–99.

New York, New Hampshire, and Rhode Island.[32] It is also understandable that those decisions should have caused widespread dissatisfaction and opposition,[33] even among those who were anxious to restrain the domination of legislatures. Hence, it was not possible for judicial review to gain even limited acceptance until the new role of an independent judiciary, distinct from politics, was understood.

Insofar as the federal courts were concerned, Republicans as well as Federalists appear to have accepted the idea of judicial supremacy over acts of Congress; it had been Republicans, for example, who were eager to have the Supreme Court strike down as unconstitutional the Bank Act and the Alien and Sedition Acts.[34] In short, the idea of judicial review was hardly a new one when *Marbury* was decided. What was new was that the Supreme Court asserted that power, and that it did so for the first time in 1803.

It is relevant to note here that many of the early cases in which the federal courts purported to exercise review functions tended to be those in which the legislature had interfered with judicial functions, typically trial procedures.[35] On the other hand, cases in the State courts, though of less general significance than *Marbury*, nevertheless involved serious constitutional and political issues which strengthened the growing conviction that the judiciary had the power, in appropriate situations, to override the legislature.[36] Those cases are particularly important because they provide some guide to the first part of Marshall's opinion in *Marbury*, where he assumed the existence of the general principle of judicial review and proceeded to consider its scope from the standpoint of *executive* action.[37]

In Marshall's words, the executive had no lawful power to withhold Marbury's commission and could not "at his discretion sport away the vested rights of others." Surely, according to Marshall, the government of the United States would cease to be one of laws and not of men "if the laws furnish no remedy for the violation of a vested legal right."[38] The judiciary's powers of review could be set in motion where individual rights were violated or where specific duties were assigned by law, but not where the executive possessed a constitutional or legal discretion, as in situations where political matters were involved. In the

---

[32] Rutgers v. Waddington (1784) in J. B. Thayer, *Cases on Constitutional Law* (Cambridge, Mass., 1895), I, 63; J. Varnum, *The Case, Trevett against Weeden* (Providence, 1787); Crosskey, *Politics and the Constitution*, II, 968–71.

[33] See generally Crosskey, *Politics and the Constitution*, III, 938–75.

[34] Warren, *Supreme Court*, 266.

[35] See L. B. Boudin, *Government by Judiciary* (New York, 1932), I, 64–67; Crosskey, *Politics and the Constitution*, II, 971–73.

[36] Wood, *American Republic*, 457–63.

[37] 1 Cranch at 154–55. See discussion in chapter 8 infra.

[38] 1 Cranch at 166, 163.

latter areas, Marshall said, there exists no power to control the executive's discretion, and the acts of his officers "can never be examinable by the courts."[39] Thus the Constitution embodies rules of law which all must serve. It protects individual rights, and it also guarantees that one department of government shall not overstep its set bounds; these two principles are different, but the judiciary is bound to safeguard them both.[40] It follows that the courts have no power to encroach upon the powers of the executive or the legislature in areas where they are barred by force of the Constitution and accepted doctrines with respect to the separation of powers.

C. EXECUTIVE PRIVILEGE

The *Marbury* case involved even more important issues which, on reflection, are apparent in the petitioner's request for a mandamus. Not only had he been denied his commission by the duly delegated authority of the executive, that is, by the Secretary of State, but in the preliminary stages of the case the State Department's officers had taken the position (1) that they had no obligation to deliver it, and (2) that, by virtue of their status in the executive department, they were privileged to refuse to testify, when summoned, about any of the circumstances relating to the commission. This position, therefore, posed the much wider and more powerful threat that the executive might claim to be above the law, not only in the matter of defying a vested right, such as Marbury had to his commission, but in other matters to which executive privilege might be alleged to extend.[41] In other words, the actual facts in what might appear to be a relatively insignificant case brought into focus both the deep-seated fears and distrust of the new Republican administration and, more importantly, conceptions about the appropriate roles of the departments of government established by the Constitution.

Substance is given to what may appear a theoretical analysis, or one based even on expediency, by arguments of counsel in the early stages of the *Marbury* case. The Attorney-General, Levi Lincoln, who had been Acting Secretary of State at the time of the "transaction," was summoned. He stated, *inter alia*, that, while he respected the jurisdiction of the Supreme Court, he felt himself bound to maintain the rights of the executive; in particular, he stated that he did not believe he should answer questions as to any facts that came to his knowledge as the Acting Secretary.[42] Lincoln told the Court that "it was going a great way to say that every secretary of state should at all times be liable to be called upon to appear as a witness in a court of justice, and testify

---

[39] *Ibid.*, 166.
[40] See *ibid.*, 163–64.

[41] See *ibid.*, 144.
[42] *Ibid.*, 143.

to facts which came to his knowledge officially."[43] Charles Lee, counsel for Marbury, referring to the nature of the office of Secretary of State, observed that his duties were of two kinds and exercised in two distinct capacities: one was as a public ministerial officer of the United States, where his duty was to its citizens, and hence he was accountable to them; the other was as an agent of the President, where his duty was to him alone, and hence he was accountable only to him. As a public ministerial officer, totally independent of the President, he was as much bound to answer to facts that came officially to his knowledge as a marshal, a collector, or any other such officer.[44] However, in his capacity as agent of the President, and accountable only to him, the Secretary of State was bound to obey his orders, but he was not bound to answer to any facts that came officially to his knowledge in the discharge of *this* aspect of his duties, or to disclose anything that might tend to incriminate him.[45]

In this confrontation one can see not only the threat that the officers of the Department of State felt no obligation to deliver Marbury's duly signed commission, but also the elements of their claim that they were above the law and need not give testimony about any aspects of the transactions relating thereto. Marshall was astute to perceive, as he did again later in the trial of Aaron Burr,[46] that a direct confrontation or collision with the executive was unwise and should be avoided if possible. Accordingly, the Court offered the Attorney-General the opportunity to consider what answers he would give, but at the same time "had no doubt he ought to answer."[47] Lincoln was also assured that he would not be asked to disclose anything communicated to him in confidence, nor to state anything that would incriminate him. On the following day Lincoln again appeared and replied from his own knowledge to questions with respect to the nondelivery of certain of the commissions involved. He further stated that he did not believe that the particular undelivered commissions had ever been sent out.[48]

Of equal relevance to the issue of executive privilege, both in the *Marbury* case and later in the *Burr* case, is the fact that although James Madison was the nominal defendant in *Marbury*, he did not appear even as a witness. No effort seems to have been made to require his personal presence—a fact that again emphasizes Marshall's care to avoid a direct confrontation with the administration. It is also worthy of note that, although Attorney-General Lincoln was present for the interrogatories, and was permitted to make arguments concerning the

---

[43] *Ibid.*, 144.
[44] *Ibid.*
[45] *Ibid.*

[46] See chapter 8 infra.
[47] 1 Cranch at 144.
[48] *Ibid.*, 145.

scope of executive privilege,[49] Madison was not even represented by counsel in the case itself. Hence, the constitutional issue that the Court ultimately decided against Marbury, namely that Section 13 of the 1789 Judiciary Act was violative of the Constitution, was never raised in arguments.

D. THE FIRST PART OF
MARBURY v. *MADISON*

If one considers the entire antecedent political scene within which the judiciary had lived since 1789, and not merely the immediate pressures that the Court had begun to suffer and to fear with Jefferson's accession to power, it is possible to see that the first half of Marshall's opinion is not necessarily the reproof to the President and the Republicans it has conventionally been thought to be. Neither is it an "excursus" unnecessary to the opinion. To Marshall and his brethren then on the Court, this part of the opinion was probably the more important of the two portions. Carefully read, it can be seen not as a skewing round of the case in order to preach at Jefferson, but rather as a statesmanlike justification both of the decision that Marbury had acquired a vested right and of the extent of judicial power to protect individual rights. Indeed, it would seem acceptable to view this portion of the opinion as laying the ground for avoiding a constitutional issue as the basis for the decision. It is not until the second portion of the opinion, relating to the power of the Court to issue the mandamus, that the constitutionality of Section 13 of the Judiciary Act is reached. Meanwhile, in the first part, the opinion makes clear that there are political areas into which the Court may not intrude and where, as in foreign policy, the executive is accountable not to the judiciary but to the electorate. Hence, broadly speaking, matters involving political discretion are not reviewable by the courts; whereas, when the vested rights of individuals are at stake, it is proper that the judiciary intervene and provide a remedy for persons injured by unlawful or arbitrary exercise of legislative or executive power. Whether or not a right is "vested" is likewise to be decided by judicial authority.[50]

The line between the executive's "constitutional or legal discretion" and "individual rights" is not easy to draw, although Marshall found it "clear" insofar as Marbury's right was concerned. While individual rights can sometimes be involved in political decisions, those decisions are not reviewable under Marshall's logic, whether or not they involve individual rights. However, unless a line of some sort were to

---

[49] *Ibid.*, 143–46.   [50] *Ibid.*, 167.

be drawn, or such a distinction made and acted upon, either individual rights could be ignored and be at the mercy of political whim, or the judiciary could appear to the public as, and might even become, a super-agency of government, in a position constantly to override lawful and proper acts of the executive, the legislature, and their duly appointed officials. In this way, the courts could be seen as a threat to the authority of the people themselves, and many, including Jefferson, shared this view of the Federalist bench.

To draw such a line seemed vital to Marshall if the structure of the national government was to be preserved from any overreaching by one of the coordinate branches, and if the rights of individuals were to be safeguarded by a rule of law.[51] He felt obliged to explain how "political" rights comported with the rule of law, and he endeavored to do so by emphasizing that the original rights and the will of the people were incorporated into and had become embodied in the Constitution, which represented fundamental law. In theory, as in practice, the legislature—and the executive as well—could properly act in response to the voice of the electorate, but they were chosen representatives only, and must scrupulously adhere to the lines set by the Constitution as the most authoritative expression of the people's will. Thus, to the extent that political conflicts between interest groups were resolved by legislatures, with apparent wide support from the electorate, not only Marshall, but also other judges of the preceding decade,[52] seemed to be of the opinion that in practice they should not interfere, so long as there was no plain and unavoidable inconsistency with the Constitution. As James Bradley Thayer has expressed it, where purely political acts or acts of mere discretion were involved, "it mattered not that other departments were violating the constitution, the judiciary could not interfere; on the contrary, they must accept and enforce their acts."[53] Judicial review, on the other hand, involved no intrusion on the part of the courts, no exercise of political discretion, but rather the

---

[51] The concept of a "rule of law" derived from mediaeval ideals, especially of the thirteenth century. Emphasized by Lord Coke in his struggles with James I, it was elaborated by Blackstone and contemplates that wherever there is a vested legal right that is invaded, there is a legal remedy. See *ibid.*, 163, citing W. Blackstone, *Commentaries*, III, *23. For a discussion of Blackstone's influence on Marshall's jurisprudence, see D. R. Nolan, "Sir William Blackstone and the New American Republic: A Study of Intellectual Impact," *New*

York University Law Review LI, 731, 755–58 (1976). For a recent very able discussion of Marshall's views on the "rule of law" see W. E. Nelson, "The Eighteenth-Century Background of John Marshall's Constitutional Jurisprudence," *Michigan Law Review* LXXVI, 893 (1978).

[52] Wood, *American Republic*, 454–55.

[53] J. B. Thayer, "The Origin and Scope of the American Doctrine of Constitutional Law," *Harvard Law Review* VII, 129, 135 (1893).

comparison of a legislative act with the Constitution to ascertain if the two conflicted. Professor William E. Nelson has succinctly remarked that judicial review at this stage, and at the end of the eighteenth century, was believed "only to give the people—a single, cohesive, and indivisible body politic—protection against faithless legislators who betrayed the trust placed in them, and not to give judges authority to make law by resolving disputes between interest groups into which the people and their legislative representatives were divided."[54]

Marshall's attempt to draw some kind of line setting the limits of judicial review was particularly significant in light of the relief sought by Marbury—the issuance of a writ of mandamus. If mandamus were to be viewed, as Marbury contended, as an appropriate "appellate" writ for reviewing the actions of executive officers, then countless decisions—political in nature—could and would constantly come before the Supreme Court. The resulting burden may suggest Marshall's motive for examining, in the last part of his opinion, the propriety of the issuance of a mandamus by the Supreme Court. Thus, while *Marbury* defined the nature of judicial review of executive decisions, the review deemed appropriate to the Court and actually undertaken by it was a review of legislative actions as well: a comparison of the statutory provision in the 1789 Judiciary Act with the mandate of the Constitution.

From a doctrinal standpoint, a related matter should not be overlooked. Hate, grounded in genuine fear, inspired much of the real and serious differences between Federalists and Republicans in the opening years of the nineteenth century. Between Marshall and Jefferson, distrust was mutual and was exacerbated by personal animosity. Undoubtedly, those fears were, to some extent, groundless; but there can be little question, as already stated, that many middle-of-the-road Federalists, including the Supreme Court judges, genuinely feared that Jefferson would assert that, as the elected representative of the people, he was not accountable to the law but was above it. For this reason, among others, Marshall apparently chose not only to echo but to restate certain positions taken in the *Federalist Papers*, including those of Madison himself.

Jefferson's failure immediately to condemn the *Marbury* opinion should in no way be read as signifying his initial acceptance of its reasoning or to suggest an easing of the tensions between the President and the Chief Justice. It may well be that Jefferson remained silent about the opinion at the time it was rendered not only because he had "won" the case, insofar as the denial of Marbury's commission was

---

[54] W. E. Nelson, "Changing Conceptions of Judicial Review: The Evolution of Constitutional Theory in the States, 1790–1860," *University of Pennsylvania Law Review* CXX, 1166, 1172 (1972).

concerned, but also because he astutely perceived that raising a controversy over the decision could only harm his primary effort to strengthen the Republican party for the approaching election.[55] In discussing the Sedition Act, he later elaborated on his view of the *Marbury* opinion as threatening to "make the judiciary a despotic branch."[56] Perceiving that the "line" Marshall drew in *Marbury* could be pushed further and used against him as President, Jefferson did not hesitate, in the course of the treason trial of Aaron Burr, to write to the prosecuting district attorney in Richmond that *Marbury* should be "denied to be the law."[57]

Several other significant observations can be made concerning judicial review: it was not until 1857 that the Court again struck down an act of Congress;[58] contemporaneously with and following the decision of *Marbury*, a number of State legislatures denounced the doctrine of judicial review;[59] and, finally, political and social developments in the country during the ensuing decades of the nineteenth century wrought changes in the conception of judicial review, so that by the 1850s it was a doctrine available to perform other functions and achieve different ends than it had fifty years previously. Thus, during the first two or three decades of the nineteenth century, before this change came about, State courts were rarely called upon to resolve social conflicts among politically organized interest groups but left that resolution to the legislatures. Hence, judicial review, as it was viewed at the time *Marbury* was decided, and for the decades immediately thereafter, had a very limited scope. Even in his opinion in that case, Marshall went a long way towards helping us to understand why it was limited, namely, through drawing the general line by which he attempted to differentiate "law" from "politics" and by asserting that the former should not serve the latter.

E. THE SECOND PART OF *MARBURY*

Having dealt at length with the questions discussed above, and having determined that Marbury had a "legal title" to the office to which

---

[55] See Beveridge, *John Marshall*, III, 143–45.

[56] *Ibid.*, 144–45, quoting a letter from Jefferson to Abigail Adams, Sept. 11, 1804; also printed in L. J. Cappon, ed., *The Adams-Jefferson Letters* (Chapel Hill, 1959), I, 279.

[57] T. Jefferson to G. Hay, June 2, 1807, in P. L. Ford, ed., *The Works of Thomas Jefferson* (New York, 1904–1905), X, 396.

[58] Dred Scott v. Sandford, 19 Howard 393 (1857).

[59] See W. T. Utter, "Judicial Review in Early Ohio," *Mississippi Valley Historical Review* XIV, 3 (1927). In the last two decades of the eighteenth century hostility was also pronounced, and not all States had recognized judicial review on even a limited basis. Cf. Rhode Island discord resulting from Trevett v. Weeden, referred to by Nelson, "Judicial Review," 1172–73.

he had been appointed by President Adams and hence a right to his commission which Adams had signed,[60] Marshall then turned to a consideration of the nature of the writ for which Marbury had applied, and concluded that this was "a plain case for a mandamus."[61] The remaining question was whether it could lawfully issue from the Supreme Court. After reviewing such precedents as were available, Marshall observed that the doctrine advanced by the petitioner was "by no means a novel one."[62] He then pointed out that the 1789 Judiciary Act authorized the Court " 'to issue writs of mandamus, in cases warranted by the principles and usages of law, to any courts appointed, or persons holding office, under the authority of the United States.' "[63] Since Madison, as Secretary of State, was "precisely within the letter of description," Marshall continued, "if this court is *not* authorized to issue a writ of mandamus to such an officer, it must be because the law is unconstitutional, and therefore absolutely incapable of conferring the authority. . . ."[64] Under Article III of the Constitution, as quoted by Marshall, " 'the supreme court shall have original jurisdiction in all cases affecting ambassadors, other public ministers. . . . In all other cases, the supreme court shall have appellate jurisdiction.' "[65] That Article goes on to say, although Marshall does not quote it, ". . . both as to Law and Fact, with such Exceptions, and under such Regulations as the Congress shall make."[66]

In the course of his argument, Charles Lee advocated a broad view of appellate jurisdiction:

> The writ of mandamus is in the nature of an appeal as to fact as well as law. It is competent for congress to prescribe the forms of process by which the supreme court shall exercise its appellate jurisdiction, and they may well declare a mandamus to be one. But the power does not depend upon implication alone. It has been recognised by legislative provision as well as in judicial decisions in this court.[67]

He then quoted, in greater detail, part of the 1789 Judiciary Act referred to by Marshall, above, to the effect that the Supreme Court had power to issue writs of mandamus " 'in cases warranted by the principles and usages of law, to any courts appointed, or *persons holding office*, under the authority of the United States.' "[68] He then concluded that,

---

[60] 1 Cranch at 154–68.
[61] *Ibid.*, 173.
[62] *Ibid.*, 172.
[63] *Ibid.*, 173, quoting Act of Sept. 24, 1789, chapter 10, Sec. 13, 1 Stat. 73, 81.

[64] *Ibid.* (emphasis supplied).
[65] *Ibid.*, 174.
[66] United States *Constitution*, Art. III, Sec. 2.
[67] 1 Cranch at 148.
[68] *Ibid.* (emphasis in original).

alternatively, whatever the view taken of appellate jurisdiction, "Congress is not restrained from conferring *original* jurisdiction in other cases than those mentioned in the constitution."[69]

In his opinion, Marshall maintained here that the jurisdiction was not appellate but original. "To enable this court then to issue a mandamus, it must be shewn to be an exercise of appellate jurisdiction, or to be necessary to enable them to exercise appellate jurisdiction."[70] He continued, "It is the essential criterion of appellate jurisdiction, that it revises and corrects the proceedings in a cause already instituted, and does not create that cause."[71] Where there have been no such antecedent judicial proceedings, to issue a mandamus to an officer for the delivery of a paper "is in effect the same as to sustain an original action for that paper, and therefore seems not to belong to appellate, but to original jurisdiction."[72] Relentlessly, Marshall's reasoning moved on, as he stated that an act of Congress authorizing the Supreme Court to issue writs of mandamus to public officers did not appear to be warranted by the Constitution. Can a jurisdiction so conferred by the legislature be exercised? The people, he reasoned, had a right to, and did, establish for their future government certain basic principles. Those principles embodied in the Constitution are not only fundamental but designed to be permanent.[73] It follows that an act of the legislature repugnant to the Constitution is void. It is the duty of the judiciary in cases of conflict to determine what the law is; if there is a conflict between a legislative act and the Constitution, the latter must prevail, because "*courts, as well as other departments, are bound by that instrument.*"[74]

By italicizing the word "courts" in the last sentence of his opinion, Marshall undoubtedly intended to emphasize that the judiciary, as well as the executive and the legislature, was "under the law." His earlier reasoning, including the reference to a government of laws and not of men, which had been penned not long before by John Adams for the Massachusetts Constitution, seems to reinforce this interpretation of his thinking.

One of the crucial points in Marshall's reasoning, of course, is that relating to mandamus as an original as opposed to an appellate writ. Apart from his literal reading of Article III of the Constitution, it is more than plausible that Marshall believed that if that writ were to be allowed under the Supreme Court's original jurisdiction, he might have opened the floodgates to litigation relating to the kinds of political matters that he firmly believed the Court should avoid. Phrased differently, express recognition of this process of immediate review by

---

[69] *Ibid.* (emphasis supplied).
[70] *Ibid.*, 175.
[71] *Ibid.*

[72] *Ibid.*, 175–76.
[73] *Ibid.*, 176.
[74] *Ibid.*, 180 (emphasis in original).

mandamus would have deterred the Court from acting as the primarily legal institution he believed it should be.

The core of the problem to which these questions are addressed is necessarily to be found in the language of Section 13 of the Judiciary Act of 1789 already quoted.[75] The crucial sentence begins, "The Supreme Court shall also have appellate jurisdiction . . ." and then, after a semicolon, continues, "and shall have power to issue writs of prohibition . . . and writs of *mandamus*, in cases warranted by the principles and usages of law, to any courts appointed, or persons holding office, under the authority of the United States." Clearly, as Marshall recognized, the Secretary of State is a person holding an office under the authority of the United States, and that clause, taken by itself, would seem to authorize the Court to issue the mandamus—unless, as Marshall concluded, the law is unconstitutional because not authorized by Article III.[76]

Two other readings, however, are possible, and either of them would have avoided holding Section 13 unconstitutional: (1) that, as a matter of statutory construction, Section 13 was meant to provide mandamus as a procedure when and only when the Supreme Court had appellate or original jurisdiction on independent grounds; or (2) that in any event Article III forbids contraction, but not expansion, of original jurisdiction beyond the instances enumerated. The first of these —the statutory construction alternative—would have required dismissal of Marbury's claim; the second—the constitutional alternative—would have supported the mandamus. Either alternative would have avoided a decision that the act of Congress was unconstitutional. To what extent, if at all, Marshall or the other judges may have considered these further possibilities cannot be determined, especially since the constitutionality issue was not raised by Lee in the course of his argument, and neither Madison nor counsel on his behalf was present.

The statutory alternative requires closer analysis of Section 13. It should be observed that the first part of that section, as quoted above, first sets forth the circumstances in which the Supreme Court has original jurisdiction. It is in an ensuing but distinct sentence that the section states when the Court is to have *appellate* jurisdiction, and at the end of that sentence refers to the power to issue writs of mandamus. If the Section is read as a whole, the power to issue a mandamus could conceivably exist in situations where it had either original jurisdiction or appellate jurisdiction; it would therefore seem to have been intended to make the mandamus an appellate writ except where the Court had jurisdiction on independent grounds, as in cases between States or those involving ambassadors.

---

[75] See text at note 63 supra.   [76] 1 Cranch at 176.

Having assumed that Section 13 conferred jurisdiction by way of mandamus in original or appellate cases, Marshall next considered the constitutionality of the statute under Article III in the context of original jurisdiction where no independent ground existed. It is a curious fact that one of his brethren on the Court, William Paterson, had had a part in the enactment of the 1789 Act while he was serving in the Senate. That Act had been drafted by Oliver Ellsworth, one of the ablest lawyers of his day and subsequently Chief Justice. It had also had the support of several other distinguished lawyers who had helped to draft the Constitution. None of these men had ever imagined that an important section of the Act might be unconstitutional.[77] Nevertheless, despite the earlier express assumption (argued by Lee) that the law was constitutional and that the Court had previously acted on that assumption,[78] Marshall proceeded to announce in his opinion[79] the unconstitutionality of Section 13, and thus to declare void for the first time a vital provision of an act of Congress.

The construction of Article III of the Constitution urged by counsel, and which would have preserved the validity of Section 13, requires a closer analysis of that Article. The second paragraph of Article III provides:

> In all Cases affecting Ambassadors, other public Ministers and Consuls, and those in which a State shall be Party, the supreme Court shall have original Jurisdiction. In all the other Cases before mentioned, the supreme Court shall have appellate Jurisdiction, both as to Law and Fact, with such Exceptions, and under such Regulations as the Congress shall make.

Counsel had argued that the clause giving the Court original jurisdiction contained no negative or restrictive words so that the legislature had power "to assign original jurisdiction to that court in other cases than those specified."[80] Marshall's answer to that argument was a textual one, that if Congress could enlarge the scope of the Court's original jurisdiction, "[t]he subsequent part of the section is mere surplusage, is entirely without meaning. . . ."[81] The "subsequent part" states that in all other cases the Court shall have appellate jurisdiction with such exceptions as the Congress shall make. Thus, Marshall took the position that the specific grant of jurisdiction in the Constitution had "no operation at all" unless understood in an exclusive

---

[77] Beveridge, *John Marshall*, III, 128–29.
[78] I Cranch at 148–49. See United States v. Lawrence, 3 Dall. 42 (1795);

United States v. Peters, 3 Dall. 121 (1795).
[79] I Cranch at 176, 180.
[80] *Ibid.*, 174.
[81] *Ibid.*

sense.[82] He did not address himself to the apparent policy reasons for giving the Court original jurisdiction, one of which was to provide the highest forum for certain of the most sensitive types of litigants, a jurisdiction that arguably would not have been impaired by adding other classes of persons. Rather, Marshall's reasoning was formal and textual:

> If it had been intended to leave it in the discretion of the legislature to apportion the judicial power between the supreme and inferior courts according to the will of that body, it would certainly have been useless to have proceeded further than to have defined the judicial power, and the tribunals in which it should be vested. The subsequent part of the section is mere surplusage, is entirely without meaning, if such is to be the construction. If congress remains at liberty to give this court appellate jurisdiction, where the constitution has declared their jurisdiction shall be original; and original jurisdiction where the constitution has declared it shall be appellate; the distribution of jurisdiction, made in the constitution, is form without substance.[83]

What Marshall did, however, was to insist upon a literal construction of the text and to ignore the "exceptions" clause under which the Supreme Court had previously assumed that, although Congress could not contract the Court's original jurisdiction, it could *add* to it. Moreover, he appears not to have been concerned with the policy reason for original jurisdiction suggested above.

Beveridge refers to this decision, declaring unconstitutional Section 13 of the Ellsworth Judiciary Act, as courageous, statesmanlike, and foresighted, and he states that "for perfectly calculated audacity, [it] has few parallels in judicial history."[84] "Nothing," continues Beveridge, "but the emergency compelling the insistence, at this particular time, that the Supreme Court has such a power [i.e., of declaring an act of Congress unconstitutional], can fully and satisfactorily explain the action of Marshall in holding this section void."[85] "[B]y a coup as bold in design and as daring in execution as that by which the Constitution had been framed, John Marshall set up a landmark in American history. . . ."[86]

In its conventional interpretation, *Marbury* v. *Madison* did indeed come to be looked upon as a great landmark in American constitutional law, the source and precedent for judicial review of acts of Congress. Yet its significance goes much further. In a certain way, its subsequent

---

[82] *Ibid.*
[83] *Ibid.*

[84] Beveridge, *John Marshall*, III, 132.
[85] *Ibid.*, 133.
[86] *Ibid.*, 142.

history is comparable to that of Magna Carta, which became in the eyes of English parliamentarians of the seventeenth century (and of others even before) a palladium of constitutional liberties—even though it was, in fact, no more than a treaty between a weak king and an articulate group of hostile baronial feudal landowners. *Marbury* is important in other respects, particularly if one is prepared to read the decision as a whole rather than as a brief opinion (beginning on page 175 of the Cranch report) preceded by a lengthy preamble which so many have considered either as dictum or as an expansive "excursus" directed primarily at Jefferson. One can read the decision in light not only of pressing contemporary political problems but of Marshall's views of the conflicts in society. Elsewhere in his writings are traces, at least, of his concern for a reconciliation between transcendent popular will, as exhibited in the legislature, and immutable principles of law, as embodied in "a regular administration of justice."[87] As a "moderate" Federalist, and also a firm believer in the separation of the departments of government, he could perceive that a "safe anchorage ground" from the enthusiasms of "wild democracy" might be found in immutable principles, as well as in restraints upon the departments themselves.[88] It seems possible that a reason for Marshall's emphasis in the opinion on the functions of the separate departments of government, and for his demarcation of limits beyond which he thought it improper for the judiciary to trespass, was to extend a kind of olive branch to the coordinate executive department—an indication that the judiciary expected to cooperate, and not wage war—in his rationalization of the latter's duty to refrain from interjecting politics into the judicial branch.

Reference has already been made to the lines that Marshall felt it necessary to draw between the spheres occupied by the different departments of government, in this case the executive (in situations where it was not "above the law") and the judiciary (which though supreme in its own sphere could not trespass upon certain areas of executive power). His opinion in this respect is consistent with other decisions of this period, notably in the trial of Aaron Burr[89] and *Fletcher* v. *Peck*,[90] and also with decisions rendered by other federal judges, such as Judge Johnson in the South Carolina Circuit Court[91] and Judge Davis in the Massachusetts District Court.[92]

---

[87] J. Marshall, *The Life of George Washington* (London, 1807), V, 100–102.

[88] J. S. Adams, ed., *An Autobiographical Sketch by John Marshall at the Request of Joseph Story* (Ann Arbor, 1937), 9–10.

[89] See chapter 8 infra.

[90] 6 Cranch 87 (1810). See chapter 10 infra.

[91] Gilchrist v. Collector of Charleston, 10 F. Cas. 355 (C.C.D. S.C. 1808) (No. 5,420). See chapter 9 infra.

[92] United States v. The William, 28 F. Cas. 614 (D. Mass. 1808) (No. 16,700). See chapter 9 infra.

VI: *Marbury* v. *Madison*

From Marshall's analysis of the constitutional powers of the several departments of government, an integrated pattern emerges; indeed, he outlines it at the beginning of his opinion. To a substantial degree Marshall follows the presentation made by Charles Lee in the course of the latter's argument concerning, for example, the delineation of the rights of the departments vis-à-vis each other. Read as a whole, Marshall's decision is in fact an essay on American government, written, as earlier stated, at a time when the judiciary (and especially middle-of-the-road Federalists) were fearful and apprehensive that Jefferson, to say nothing of his officers, would assert that he was literally above the law because he had the mandate of the "people" behind him. Thus, in this respect, the opinion can be regarded as an intentional rebuke to Jefferson. From a broader standpoint, however, the decision should be viewed as a forceful declaration that in the framework of American government the executive is not above the law.

Marshall was not only a capable and careful lawyer; he was statesmanlike in his approach to the sensitive issues that *Marbury* raised. In his thinking—and this point is discernible not only in this opinion but in his other writings—it was the duty of the judiciary to keep from its door, or at least from that of the Supreme Court, various political matters that he did not regard as properly within its province. More specifically, Marshall did not wish to have the Court put in the position of granting a mandamus against Cabinet officers. To do so would be to invite a host of other applications, political in origin and nature, brought before that Court, and so, consequently, to blur or make impossible the distinction he believed it so important to make and to retain between political matters, which did not belong to the judiciary, and a rule of law that could and should be independent of politics and especially of executive control.

What should be borne in mind is that although a decision against Marbury on technical statutory grounds would have accomplished at least one of Marshall's general objectives, namely, discouraging the bringing of essentially political matters before the Court, it would not have served all his purposes. Although it would also have avoided a collision with Jefferson by his refusal to order Madison to deliver Marbury's commission, it would necessarily have narrowed the scope for asserting principles that Marshall and the rest of the Court wished to assert with respect to the protection of individual rights and the spheres within which the three departments of government could properly operate. Moreover, once he could reach out to the issue of judicial review, he was in a position to go forward and discuss (1) the respective weight of the Constitution, which defined where the Court's jurisdiction is original and where appellate, and of Congress, which has sought to alter it; and (2) whether, having found an act of Congress repugnant to the Constitution, the courts must nevertheless enforce the act.[93]

The answer to the question posed in the second issue is clearly in the negative, and we are again on familiar ground. "It is emphatically the province and duty of the judicial department to say what the law is. . . . If two laws conflict with each other, the courts must decide on the operation of each."[94] To close one's eyes to the Constitution while applying a law made by the legislature "would subvert the very foundation of all written constitutions."[95] "This [doctrine] is too extravagant to be maintained."[96] Then, following some examples of the applicability of the Constitution to situations that can come before the courts, Marshall concluded that "it is apparent, that the framers of the constitution contemplated that instrument, as a rule for the government of *courts*, as well as of the legislature."[97]

Finally, a decision on technical grounds only, that is by avoidance of the issue of constitutionality, would have weakened the force of the early part of the opinion—the part which is so often regarded as dictum but which, viewed in a large sense, is an issue that Marshall wished emphasized in the opinion, and which was, to the extent described, argued by counsel. To repeat what has already been said, it seemed vital both to protect the judiciary and to re-emphasize the supremacy of the rule of law in that difficult era when politics were threatening to engulf the judiciary. By referring to the separateness of the departments of government (for example, by noting that it would be inappropriate and "irksome" to attempt to "intrude into the cabinet, and to intermeddle with the prerogatives of the executive"[98]), Marshall was able to make two crucial points, which are explicitly stated in the decision: (1) "The province of the court is, solely, to decide on the rights of individuals . . ." and (2) "Questions, in their nature political, . . . can never be made in this court."[99]

While the foregoing statements are unquestionably overly generalized, they do attempt to draw some line between the powers of the executive and the nascent powers of the Supreme Court. The distinction is vital to an understanding of the business of the Court at this time and of the foundations of its power.

---

[93] 1 Cranch at 176–77.
[94] *Ibid.*, 177.
[95] *Ibid.*, 178.
[96] *Ibid.*, 179.

[97] *Ibid.*, 179–80 (emphasis in original).
[98] *Ibid.*, 169–70.
[99] *Ibid.*, 170.

CHAPTER VII

Impeachment

A. REPUBLICAN IMPEACHMENT OBJECTIVES

"The removal of the Judges, & the destruction of the independence of the judicial department, has been an object on which Mr. Jefferson has been long resolved. . . ."[1] So wrote Senator Plumer of New Hampshire on January 7, 1804. Two years earlier, on January 15, 1802, James Monroe had suggested to Breckenridge that "application of the principles of the English common law to our constitution" should be "good cause of impeachment."[2] Less than a month later, James A. Bayard wrote that "[t]he judicial system is the victim on which the hearts of the whole [Republican] Party are set. Until it is immolated, they consider that nothing is done." He then added tellingly, "It is contemplated to impeach Judge Chase. . . ."[3]

Thus it appears that the project of employing impeachment as a further means of destroying judicial independence and "reforming" the federal judiciary had been conceived almost at the opening of the new administration, well before the dramatic effort to impeach Judge Chase in 1805. Consequently, and in light of the repeal of the Judiciary Act of 1801, the attempt to impeach Chase had ramifications that went far beyond that particular case. Many leaders of the Republican party, including the President, had been incensed that the "revolution of

---

[1] E. S. Brown, ed., *William Plumer's Memorandum of Proceedings in the United States Senate, 1803–1807* (New York, 1923), 101.
[2] J. Monroe to J. Breckenridge, Jan. 15, 1802, Breckenridge Papers, XXI, Manuscripts Division, Library of Congress. For a printed reference, see

A. J. Beveridge, *The Life of John Marshall* (Boston, 1919), III, 59.
[3] E. Donnan, ed., "The Papers of James A. Bayard 1795–1815," *Annual Report of the American Historical Association for the Year 1913* (Washington, 1915), II, 148.

1800," which had given them control of the executive and legislative branches, was only two-thirds complete due to the immunity that the judiciary enjoyed from the popular will as exhibited at the polls. They saw in the Supreme Court, composed entirely of Federalists secure in their stronghold, not only a roadblock to schemes for change and reform but a body that was prepared, as the so-called excursus in *Marbury* v. *Madison* was soon to suggest, to challenge and override the will of the legislature and, no less important, that of the President. No careful observer of the political scene, in 1802 and 1803 particularly, could fail to perceive the new strength that the Court was beginning to exhibit, nor fail to understand that the Court, speaking now in unanimity through the single voice of John Marshall, might become a power of great magnitude.

Courts, in the late eighteenth century, were viewed as an arm of the administration. Harmony among the three branches was not only expected, but had existed to a substantial extent during the administrations of George Washington and John Adams. Indeed, one might suggest that despite the alleged independence of the three branches, disharmony was viewed far more as a political fact than as presenting constitutional or legal issues and problems. No method for reconciling differences among the branches of government had been worked out, or indeed envisaged, beyond the niceties of balance recognized and explained by Hamilton in the *Federalist Papers*.[4] Hence the election of 1800, which gave legislative and executive power to the Republicans but left the national judiciary in the hands of Federalists, created unforeseen problems. It is not unnatural that the Republicans should have been irked by this outcome, for it ran contrary to those political traditions with which they were familiar. Only the behavior of the judges in the years immediately preceding the Revolution of 1776 could provide an analogous situation, had the Republicans looked to it. But in 1801 men were far more concerned with the immediacies of what seemed to them a political anomaly. When one considers further that the factional strife of the late 1790s had pitted Republican against Federalist to the point that each group believed that the other was bent on total destruction of the Union—to the point of secession, if not bloodshed—it becomes possible to comprehend the rancor and hatred that men of both sides held for their opponents.

What Jefferson's own views on the judiciary were at the outset is not free from doubt. On several early occasions he criticized the use of impeachment. In 1788 he condemned the impeachment trial of Warren Hastings in England. Writing to William Rutledge he said, "I think

---

[4] *The Federalist* No. 78 (A. Hamilton) (New York, 1901).

you will find . . . that every solid argument is against the extraordinary court, & that every one in it's favor is specious only. It is a transfer from a judicature of learning & integrity to one, the greatness of which is both illiterate & unprincipled."[5] Jefferson also expressed grave doubts about the advisability of the use of the weapon of impeachment when, during his term as Vice-President, he presided over the impeachment trial of Senator William Blount of Tennessee.[6] On February 15, 1798, he wrote to James Madison as follows:

> I see nothing in the mode of proceeding by impeachment but the most formidable weapon for the purposes of a dominant faction that ever was contrived. . . . I know of no solid purpose of punishment which the courts of law are not equal to, and history shows, that in England, impeachment has been an engine more of passion than justice.[7]

He also made clear his understanding that, in order to be impeached, a man must be guilty of an indictable offense. In a letter to Henry Tazewell written on January 27 of the same year he stated:

> I devoted yesterday evening to the extracting passages from Law authors showing that in Law-language the term crime is in common use applied to *misdemeanors*, & that *impeachments*, even when for *misdemeanors* only are *criminal prosecutions*. These proofs were so numerous that my patience could go no further than two authors, Blackstone and Wooddeson.[8]

Many of Jefferson's letters on the subject of the removal of judges were cautious and often contradictory; they must be read from the standpoint of the recipient. He did not at first seem to have in mind wholesale removals on the sole ground of political affiliation, and he appears genuinely to have wished to conciliate the "honest part" of his opponents and further ensure his general popularity.[9] Removals, he wrote to John Randolph in March of 1801, would be chiefly "for real mal-conduct, and mostly in the offices connected with the administra-

---

[5] T. Jefferson to W. Rutledge, Feb. 2, 1788, in P. L. Ford, ed., *The Works of Thomas Jefferson* (New York, 1904–1905), V, 386 (hereafter cited as Ford, *Works of Jefferson*).

[6] See generally F. J. Turner, "Documents on the Blount Conspiracy, 1795–1797," *American Historical Review* X, 574 (1905).

[7] T. Jefferson to J. Madison, Feb. 15, 1798, in Ford, *Works of Jefferson*, VIII, 369–70.

[8] T. Jefferson to H. Tazewell, Jan. 27, 1798, in *ibid.*, VIII, 361.

[9] T. Jefferson to H. Gates, Mar. 8, 1801, in *ibid.*, IX, 205. See also O. Wolcott to G. Cabot, Aug. 28, 1802, in H. C. Lodge, *Life and Letters of George Cabot* (Boston, 1878), 325. ("It is the sole object of the administration to acquire popularity." *Ibid.*)

tion of justice."[10] Nevertheless, the Federalist-dominated judiciary had been a thorn in the flesh from the beginning, and it was from this situation, magnified by other considerations, that the decision to resort to impeachment as the most effective means of removing judges who entertained objectionable political views emerged.

Personal animosities must also be borne in mind. Jefferson had cherished the hope of appointing to the Chief Justiceship one of his close friends and confidants, Spencer Roane, a leading Virginia Republican. This hope, of course, had been frustrated by Ellsworth's resignation and by Adams' appointment of John Marshall. Moreover, Jefferson had long been an inveterate enemy of Marshall and had attacked both his conduct and his integrity in connection with the XYZ Mission. It has been said that Marshall was "as obnoxious to Jefferson as the bitterest New England Calvinist could have been; for he belonged to that class of conservative Virginians whose devotion to President Washington, and whose education in the common law, caused them to hold Jefferson and his theories in antipathy."[11] This personal animosity[12] that he bore towards the Chief Justice[13] was slowly fanned into a blaze by particular incidents, by pressures from fellow Republicans, and by his own belief that his expansive visions for the welfare of the people might be thwarted by the will of a man so wholly committed to a different philosophy of government.

Political expediency and accession to power helped to bring about a change in Jefferson's early views on the independence of the judiciary. Now, and throughout the remainder of his life, the idea that judges were irremovable become progressively more abhorrent to him. This conviction, born of resentment at the independence of the judiciary and of exasperation that Federalism was still a force in that branch of the government, he did not hesitate to express. Thus, on December 19, 1801, he wrote to John Dickinson that "by a fraudulent use of the constitution which has made judges irremoveable, they have multiplied useless judges merely to strengthen their phalanx."[14] Even as late as 1822 his thinking seems not to have changed greatly when he wrote to William T. Barry "[t]hat there should be public functionaries independant of the nation, whatever may be their demerit, is a solecism in a republic of the first order of absurdity and inconsistence."[15]

---

[10] T. Jefferson to J. Randolph, Mar. 12, 1801, Thomas Jefferson Papers, Manuscripts Division, Library of Congress.

[11] H. Adams, *History of the United States of America* (New York, 1889), I, 192.

[12] See chapter 5 supra.

[13] See text accompanying notes 26–27 in chapter 5 supra.

[14] T. Jefferson to J. Dickinson, Dec. 19, 1801, Thomas Jefferson Papers, Manuscripts Division, Library of Congress.

[15] T. Jefferson to W. Barry, July 2, 1822, *ibid.*

VII: *Impeachment*

It will be recalled that at the outset of his administration, Jefferson had refused to deliver commissions to a number of Federalist justices of the peace appointed by Adams in the closing days of his administration. Soon after, he was successful in obtaining the removal of sixteen Federalist judges through Congressional legislation that repealed the Judiciary Act of 1801, and the constitutionality of the repeal was upheld by the Court in *Stuart* v. *Laird*.[16] Those were but the first steps, and he was then prepared to go further, with the Supreme Court as his main object, and with Marshall as his particular target. Although he had written to Robert Livingston in September 1800 that "I join you in taking shame for the depravity of our judges" and "Impeachment is clear,"[17] in March of 1801 he was writing to Henry Knox that judges appointed for life were irremovable.[18] Nonetheless, impeachment was certainly being considered by the President and his lieutenants as a method of controlling and removing Federalist judges and for appointing sound Republicans in their stead.

Jefferson was by no means without support for the plan that had been taking shape in his mind. In the course of the debate on the 1802 Act, Robert Williams, an extreme Republican from North Carolina, noted that impeachments were possible under the Constitution.[19] The next year, on February 16, 1803, ardent Republican Caesar A. Rodney frankly stated to Joseph Nicholson that if the judges were to usurp unconstitutional powers, "I confidently trust that there will be wisdom & energy enough in the legislative & Executive branches . . . to arraign them for the abuse of their authority at the proper tribunal."[20] Radical members of the Republican party, notably Senator William Branch Giles, that "loud-mouthed bully"[21] of Virginia, whom some said "no man ever trusted without regret,"[22] firmly believed that members of the judiciary, like members of Congress, should be subject to the popular will in appointment and dismissal. In the course of the debates in the House on the repeal of the 1801 Act, when Giles was the majority leader in that body, he had flatly stated that the doctrine of the power of judges was a doctrine of irresponsibility and despotism and an "ex-

---

[16] 1 Cranch 299 (1803). See chapter 5 supra.

[17] T. Jefferson to R. Livingston, Sept. 2, 1800, Thomas Jefferson Papers, Manuscripts Division, Library of Congress.

[18] T. Jefferson to H. Knox, Mar. 27, 1801, in Ford, *Works of Jefferson*, IX, 237.

[19] J. Gales and W. Seaton, comps., *The Debates and Proceedings of the Congress of the United States* (Wash-

ington, 1834–56), XI, 531 (7th Cong., 1st sess.) (hereafter cited as *Annals of Congress*).

[20] C. Rodney to J. Nicholson, Feb. 16, 1803, Joseph H. Nicholson Papers, Manuscripts Division, Library of Congress.

[21] S. E. Morison, *The Oxford History of the United States 1783–1917* (Oxford, 1927), I, 233.

[22] H. Adams, *John Randolph* (Boston, 1898), 141.

press avowal, that the people were incompetent to govern themselves."[23] Popular sentiment, whipped up and played upon by Republican newspapers, likewise espoused the view that judges should be responsible to and subject to the control of the electorate, and that justice in a democracy should be popular justice and not committed to a body over whom the people had no control.

This was not novel doctrine. In the debates on the ratification of several State constitutions, the idea had been expressed more than once,[24] and the Constitution of Massachusetts, among others, expressly provided for the removal of judges on the address of the legislature.[25] Memories of the tyrannies of certain of the royal judges of the colonial period were not yet dead, and it was not forgotten that in the Revolutionary period many of the leading members of the Bar had been Tories. Antipathies to the technicalities of the common law as a British and therefore "monarchical" institution, which only "knaves" with legal training could understand, also played a part. Again, hostility to the judiciary had been fanned by that branch's role in enforcing the Alien and Sedition Acts.[26] Giles voiced his opinions in a letter to Jefferson on March 16, 1801: he felt that the President had been too mild in his Inauguration speech and stated that "[t]he judges have been the most unblushing violators of constitutional restrictions. . . ."[27] Three years later, as John Quincy Adams recounts, Giles espoused principles

> upon which not only Mr. Chase, but all the other Judges of the Supreme Court, excepting the one last appointed, must be impeached and removed. He treated with the utmost contempt the idea of an *independent* judiciary—said there was not a word about such an independence in the Constitution, and that their pretensions to it were nothing more nor less than an attempt to establish an aristocratic despotism in themselves.[28]

---

[23] *Annals of Congress*, XI, 596 (7th Cong., 1st sess.).

[24] See G. Winters, *Selection of Judges in New York and in Other States* (New York, 1955), 6; J. Gitterman, "The Council of Appointment in New York," *Political Science Quarterly* VII, 88 (1892).

[25] R. Berger, *Impeachment: The Constitutional Problems* (Cambridge, Mass., 1973), 145. See *The Boston Globe*, Aug. 2, 1978, 10. For a recent analysis of the historical and constitutional background of the impeachment Article of the Constitution, see "The Law of Presidential Impeachment" (Committee Report), *The Record of the Association of the Bar of the City of New York* XXIX, 159 (1974).

[26] Beveridge, *John Marshall*, III, 31–32, 43–48, 61–62.

[27] W. Giles to T. Jefferson, Mar. 16, 1801, Thomas Jefferson Papers, Manuscripts Division, Library of Congress. Also quoted in D. R. Anderson, *William Branch Giles* (Menasha, Wis., 1914), 77.

[28] C. F. Adams, ed., *Memoirs of John Quincy Adams* (Philadelphia, 1874), I, 322.

JOHN MARSHALL (B. 1755–D. 1835).
Federalist from Virginia. Chief Justice of the
U.S. Supreme Court (1801–1835).

JOHN ADAMS (B. 1735–D. 1826).
Vice President (1789–1797) and President (1797–1801) of the United States.
(Library of Congress)

THOMAS JEFFERSON (B. 1743–D. 1826).
Secretary of State (1790–1793), Vice President (1797–1801), and
President (1801–1809) of the United States.
(Library of Congress)

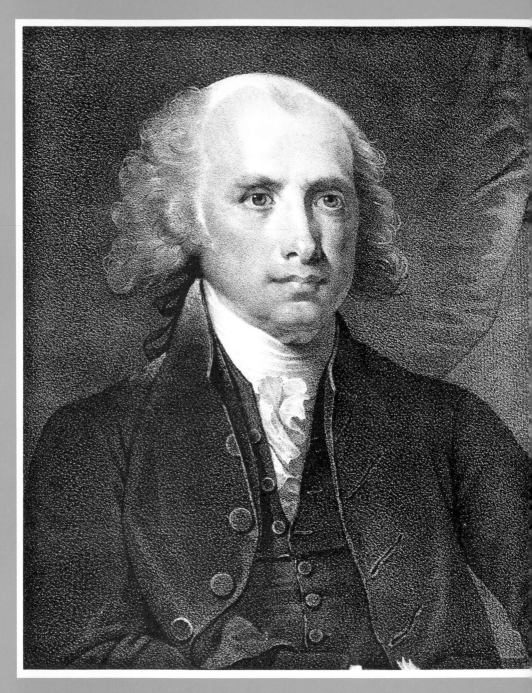

JAMES MADISON (B. 1751–D. 1836).
Member of Congress from Virginia (1790–1797),
Secretary of State (1801–1809), and
President of the United States (1809–1817).
(Library of Congress)

JAMES A. BAYARD (B. 1767–D. 1815).
Federalist member of Congress from Delaware (1797–1804) and
U.S. Senator (1805–1813).
(Library of Congress)

AARON BURR (B. 1756–D. 1836).
U.S. Senator from New York (1791–1797) and
Vice President of the United States (1801–1805).

LEVI LINCOLN (B. 1749–D. 1820).
Attorney-General of the United States (1801–1804).
(Library of Congress)

LUTHER MARTIN (B. 1748–D. 1826).
Lawyer; Attorney-General of the State of Maryland.
Defended Justice Samuel Chase in Senate impeachment trial (1804).
As Maryland Attorney-General represented the State in
McCulloch v. *Maryland* (1819).
(Library of Congress)

VII: *Impeachment*

Giles also stated to Senator Plumer that the Senate had authority to remove a judge, even if innocent, "if he was disagreeable in office, & a man better qualified ought to have it. And that a judge opposed to the administration & wrong headed, tho not corrupt should be removed."[29] Furthermore, patronage, and the wish to reward loyal Republicans, had quickly become a prevailing sentiment motivating appointments and removals from office. In an early letter to Jefferson, Giles wrote:

> a pretty general purgation of office, has been one of the benefits expected by the friends of the new order of things. . . . It can never be unpopular, to turn out a vicious man and put a virtuous one in his room; and I am persuaded from the prevalence of the vicious principles of the late administration, and the universal loyalty of its adherents in office, it would be hardly possible to err in exclusions. . . .[30]

He went on to recommend a neighbor of his as an appropriate replacement as marshal for the district of Virginia. Three years later he did not hesitate to exclaim: *"We want your offices* for the purpose of giving them to men who will fill them better."[31]

The impeachment program, therefore, had its beginnings partly in partisan politics and animosities and partly in the philosophy of government to which the Republicans had committed themselves. It also had a concrete basis in the impeachment provisions of the Constitution and in the antecedent English legal background, to which attention will later be directed.[32]

B. THE IMPEACHMENT OF PICKERING

Substance was given to the persistent rumors and Republican threats by the impeachment proceedings brought early in 1803 against John Pickering, Federal Judge for the District of New Hampshire. It was the first impeachment of a judicial officer under the federal Constitution and was apparently initiated principally to establish a precedent for more important impeachments that were expected to follow. For at least three years that aged and unfortunate man, once a leading citizen of his native State and the author of its Constitution, had been insane, and his malady had been aggravated, perhaps to relieve his

---

[29] W. Plumer, *Autobiography*, 142, Plumer Papers, Manuscripts Division, Library of Congress.

[30] W. Giles to T. Jefferson, supra note 27.

[31] C. F. Adams, *John Quincy Adams*, I, 322.

[32] See text accompanying notes 173–75 infra.

disturbed state of mind, by his having become an incurable drunkard.[33] His conduct on the bench had become so notorious and scandalous that it had been the subject of widespread complaint in New Hampshire and elsewhere, and there was general agreement on all sides that he was entirely incapable of performing his duties.[34] For a year, under the 1801 Act, Judge Jeremiah Smith had taken over his duties, but after that Act's repeal Pickering was reinstated, and there was no longer any obvious means for taking care of a situation in which a judge was unable to discharge his duties.[35] On December 12, 1802, Secretary Gallatin informed Senator Plumer that the Judge's disability had caused the government to lose several suits in which it was entitled to recover. Gallatin had not "yet laid the papers before the President," but "thought the Judge ought to be removed from office & intimated, that unless he resigned, measures would be taken to remove him."[36]

The choice of Pickering for the first judicial impeachment was an astute and strategic move. It could be defended on the ground of concern that the judiciary should be above reproach, and, with a district judge removed, it would be possible to hunt the real game. Hoping to avoid a showdown with the administration, and believing Judge Pickering's resignation to be impolitic, because his successor would be a Republican (probably the district attorney John Sherburne), Plumer inquired whether Judge Sewall, of the District Court of Maine, might be willing to act also for the District of New Hampshire during Pickering's disability.[37]

Within a few weeks, however, and probably much sooner, the matter was settled by the administration. By mid-January, Sherburne had collected depositions and forwarded them to Washington. On February 4, 1803, Jefferson sent the following Message, dated February 3, to the House:

> The inclosed letters and affidavits exhibiting matter of complaint against John Pickering District Judge of New Hampshire which is not within executive cognizance, I transmit them to the House of Representatives to whom the constitution has confided a power of instituting proceedings of redress, if they shall be of opinion that the case calls for them.[38]

---

[33] Beveridge, *John Marshall*, III, 165.

[34] *Annals of Congress*, XIII, 351–56 (8th Cong., 1st sess.).

[35] See 2 Stat. 97, Sec. 25; Beveridge, *John Marshall*, III, 165.

[36] W. Plumer to Judge J. Sheafe, Dec. 13, 1802, Letters 1781–1804, Plumer Papers, Manuscripts Division, Library of Congress.

[37] *Ibid*. It was rumored at the time that Pickering had agreed to resign if appointed Chief Justice of New Hampshire. See C. F. Adams, *John Quincy Adams*, I, 299.

[38] Thomas Jefferson Papers, Manuscripts Division, Library of Congress.

The accompanying papers, apparently consisting entirely of affidavits from Republican officeholders in Portsmouth, were intended to show that, because of his habitual intoxication, the Judge was unfit to perform his duties.

Under Article I, Section 2, of the Constitution, the power of impeachment was given to the House; Section 3 of the same Article assigned the trial of impeachments to the Senate. Under Article II, Section 4, civil officers were removable on impeachment for, and conviction of, treason, bribery, or "other high Crimes and Misdemeanors." The Message made plain the President's opinion that the conduct of Judge Pickering came within the scope of the impeachment power. Nearly a year later, on January 5, 1804, he told Senator Plumer, in response to the latter's inquiry whether Pickering's insanity was a cause for impeachment, that if the facts stated in the impeachment—viz., the denial of an appeal and his intoxication—were true, they were "sufficient cause of removal without further enquiry."[39] Despite his earlier personal opinions and doubts, the President was now evidently prepared, as in the Louisiana Purchase, to stretch the Constitution, and to use the means most readily at hand in order to accomplish his purpose of unseating the Federalist judges.

Yet Jefferson was impatient with the proceedings required in an impeachment—not, apparently, from constitutional scruples, but because of the time-consuming nature of the process. In January 1804, for example, he complained to Senator Plumer that it would take two years to try the Pickering impeachment and remarked: "This business of removing Judges by impeachment is a *bungling way*."[40] However, an amendment to the Constitution, which he had also considered, and which would have provided for the removal of judges by address of both houses of Congress,[41] appeared even more time-consuming to the impatient President, and such a course was beset with uncertainty at best. Accordingly, and since "the good work of *reform* cannot be delayed—The president & his Cabinet agree that impeachment conviction & removal from office is necessary."[42] However, although impeachment was the weapon to be used for continuing the assault on the judiciary, and although, as stated, a direct attack on Judge Chase and on the Supreme Court was apparently contemplated even before the

[39] W. Plumer, *Notes on Proceedings in United States Congress 1803–1804*, 282 (hereafter cited as Plumer, *Notes on Proceedings*), Manuscripts Division, Library of Congress. For a printed version, see Brown, *Plumer's Memorandum of Proceedings*, 100.

[40] Plumer, *Notes on Proceedings*, 283. For a printed version, see Brown,

Plumer's Memorandum of Proceedings, 101.

[41] Plumer, *Notes on Proceedings*, 286. For a printed version, see Brown, *Plumer's Memorandum of Proceedings*, 102.

[42] Brown, *Plumer's Memorandum of Proceedings*, 102.

1801 Act had been repealed,[43] the proceedings against Judge Pickering unquestionably strengthened the Republicans' hand. Not only did its successful outcome spur on the assault, but the fact that it was procured without proof of high crimes and misdemeanors in the narrow sense provided a most useful and persuasive precedent for the subsequent trial of Chase.

As pointed out, proceedings against Pickering were under consideration at least as early as the end of 1802, but it is possible that the administration might have stayed its hand against him for a time had it not been for the trial, conviction, and removal of a State judge in Pennsylvania. This was the impeachment of Alexander Addison, presiding judge of one of the county courts. While the repeal of the 1801 Act was still before Congress, the Pennsylvania House of Representatives sent to the State senate a series of articles charging Addison with high crimes and misdemeanors. Addison was an able lawyer, but a staunch Federalist, well known for his denunciation of Republican principles in his jury charges and for his strongly partisan speeches in political campaigns.[44] For other reasons, too, he was unpopular in democratic Pennsylvania. "His manner on the bench was imperious; he bullied counsel, browbeat witnesses,"[45] and, in the course of a trial that was to become a cause célèbre and assist in the founding of impeachment charges, he successfully prevented an associate judge from addressing the jury.[46] Addison's trial began in January 1803. He conducted his own defense, pleading for the independence of the judiciary and maintaining that there could be no impeachment except for an indictable offense.[47] However, the defense proved unavailing, and the Republican theory that a judge might be deposed for conduct or views of which the legislature disapproved was remorselessly applied. His conviction, particularly in view of the principle upon which it was obtained, was a most opportune event which obviously encouraged Jefferson to move ahead with the impeachment of Pickering, just as the subsequent conviction of Pickering encouraged the later proceedings against Chase. Addison was convicted on January 26, 1803, and on February 4, after word had reached Washington, Jefferson's Message about Pickering was sent to the House.[48]

---

[43] Donnan, "Papers of James A. Bayard," 148.

[44] Beveridge, *John Marshall*, III, 46, note 2.

[45] *Ibid.*, 46–47.

[46] *Ibid.*, 47. See R. Walters, Jr., *Alexander James Dallas* (Philadelphia, 1943), 126 (hereafter cited as Walters, *A. J. Dallas*).

[47] A. Addison, *Trial of Alexander Addison* (Lancaster, Pa., 1803), 101–43.

[48] The Pennsylvania removals from office—without express reference to impeachment—were praised in a letter from Jefferson to Duane a few months later on July 24. T. Jefferson to W. Duane, July 24, 1803, Thomas Jefferson Papers, Manuscripts Division, Library of Congress.

Parenthetically it should be noted that the Pennsylvania legislature, emboldened by its success, then proceeded to attempt impeachment of three of the four judges of the State Supreme Court in 1804. These judges were Federalists, but the fourth, Hugh A. Breckenridge, a Republican, asked the legislature to impeach him along with the others. The entire legal profession took alarm, and even A. J. Dallas, who had prosecuted Addison, refused to proceed and in fact led the defense.[49] Caesar Rodney, later to become Attorney-General of the United States, was summoned from Congress to lead the prosecution, but in the end the State senate found the judges not guilty by vote of 13–11.[50]

C.   EVENTS LEADING TO THE IMPEACHMENT OF CHASE

Although Pickering was impeached by the House in 1803, the trial itself did not open until early in 1804. Meanwhile, two occurrences in the spring of 1803 gave impetus to the renewed attack on the Court: one was the decision in *Marbury* v. *Madison*,[51] rendered on February 24; the other was a charge that Judge Chase delivered to the grand jury in Baltimore in early May.[52]

The political and constitutional significance of Marshall's decision in the *Marbury* case has been treated in the preceding chapter, but it should be recalled that the opinion, although representing a technical victory for the administration, went well beyond what was required by the decision. Although the full significance of the *Marbury* decision may have been lost on some contemporaries because, contrary to popular expectation, the precise holding was favorable to the Republicans in that it denied Marbury the remedy he sought, and although Republican animus was probably temporarily abated, the politically astute perceived the implications of the decision and did not hesitate to use it, when the time came, as a further justification for their attack on the Court. For example, a year and a half later, in December 1804, in the course of a conversation in Senator Adams' presence, Giles made it plain that Marshall's opinion was among the reasons for deciding to pursue the course of impeachment. If, said Giles,

the Judges of the Supreme Court should dare, AS THEY HAD DONE, to declare an act of Congress unconstitutional, or to send a mandamus

---

[49] Walters, *A. J. Dallas,* 129.
[50] See generally *Trial of the Pennsylvania Judges on Impeachment* (Philadelphia, 1805).
[51] I Cranch 137 (1803). See chapter 6 supra.

[52] See Chase notebook containing original jury charges, Chase Manuscripts, Maryland Historical Society (hereafter cited as Chase notebook).

to the Secretary of State, AS THEY HAD DONE, it was the undoubted right of the House of Representatives to impeach them, and
of the Senate to remove them, for giving such opinions, however
honest or sincere they may have been in entertaining them.[53]

The same idea was again voiced by Giles in debate a day or two later.
Writing to his friend Thomas W. Thompson, Senator Plumer reported
that it was Giles' view that

a judge might be removed from office altho he was not guilty of any
crime or misdemeanor; that mere error in judgment, or opposition in
opinion to the executive, is sufficient cause, and that the House may
lawful [sic] impeach and the Senate remove from office for either of
those causes. This is the language of the dominant party, & shows how
feeble a barrier paper constitutions are ag^t the encroachment of
power. . . .[54]

Giles was not alone in this view. Jefferson, too, was annoyed by
aspects of the *Marbury* opinion, probably not because of the assertion
of power to judge the validity of acts of Congress, but because the
exercise of the power could invalidate measures in which Republicans
were interested and because Marshall had pointedly lectured him on
the rights of appointees to office. Another of Marshall's opinions had
also, apparently, aroused the President's ire. This was *United States* v.
Fisher, decided early in 1805 and dealing with the question whether,
under the Bankruptcy Act of 1800, the United States was a preferred
creditor of an insolvent.[55] In the course of his decision, the Chief Justice
took the opportunity to assert the Hamiltonian doctrine of implied
powers and to express his disagreement with Jefferson's views in that
respect as set forth in the latter's celebrated opinion on the power of
Congress to charter a bank.[56]

Resentful though Jefferson was at the reproofs that had been
administered by Marshall, the opinion in *Marbury*, at least, was too
careful in its language, too guarded in its scope, to furnish an open
ground for impeachment of any one or all of the Supreme Court judges,
whatever might have been the wish of the Republican leaders. Nevertheless, that decision did help to furnish some ground for breaking the
uneasy truce that had prevailed for a short time and to revive the glow-

---

[53] C. F. Adams, *John Quincy
Adams*, I, 322.

[54] W. Plumer to T. Thompson, Dec.
23, 1804, Letters 1804–1807, Plumer
Papers, Manuscripts Division, Library
of Congress.

[55] 2 Cranch 358 (1805). It will be
recalled that Marshall had helped in
the drafting of that Act when he was
in Congress. See chapter 4 supra.

[56] See Beveridge, *John Marshall*, II,
71–74, and III, 163.

ing embers of hostility towards the judiciary that burned in the Republican camp. That the decision did not evoke greater hostility from the Republicans at the time may well have been the result of the fact that only six days later, in *Stuart* v. *Laird,* the Court declared constitutional the repeal of the Judiciary Act of 1801.

A far more effective weapon for pursuing the attack on the Court than the opinion in *Marbury* was placed in the hands of the Republicans by one of the judges themselves. This was the charge that Judge Chase delivered to a grand jury in Baltimore, on May 2, 1803, scarcely two months after the initiation of the impeachment proceedings against Pickering and the delivery of Marshall's opinion in the *Marbury* case. Chase could hardly have chosen a more inopportune time to give vent to his Federalist views than he did on that occasion. As Henry Adams says, if there was one judge in the United States who "should have known the peril in which the judiciary stood, it was Justice Samuel Chase of Maryland, who had done more than all the other judges to exasperate the democratic majority."[57] Twice his conduct on the bench had driven eminent counsel from his court, and he had outraged public sentiment as well as distinguished members of the Bar by his conduct in the course of the trials of John Fries and James Callender in 1800.[58] His manners, wrote Simeon Baldwin to Judge Lewis, were "far from conciliating—the prejudice is great against him. . . ."[59] His Federalist sympathies and his contempt for Republican principles were well known, and at least once he had deserted the bench to campaign for the party.[60] Prudence and caution were almost unknown to him, and, belonging as he did "to the old class of conservatives who thought that judges, clergymen, and all others in authority should guide and warn the people,"[61] he undertook to address the jury on the dangerous democratic tendencies of the administration and to criticize openly the dismissal of the sixteen new circuit judges through the Judiciary Act of

---

[57] H. Adams, *History of United States,* II, 147.

[58] For an account of the Callender trial, see J. P. Kennedy, *Memoirs of the Life of William Wirt* (Philadelphia, 1849), I, 80 et seq. An account of the Fries trial is in a letter from W. Lewis to A. Hamilton, Oct. 11, 1800, Hamilton Papers, LXXVIII, fol. 12757, Hamilton Papers, Manuscripts Division, Library of Congress.

[59] S. Baldwin to W. Lewis, Dec. 5, 1804, in S. E. Baldwin, *Life and Letters of Simeon Baldwin* (New Haven, 1919), 438.

[60] See J. Rutledge to A. Hamilton, July 17, 1800, in B. C. Steiner, *The Life and Correspondence of James McHenry* (Cleveland, 1907), 463, note 1. Separation of judicial from other functions was not customary at that period. Cf. Jay acting as Chief Justice and Ambassador to England in 1794 and Ellsworth serving as Chief Justice and Minister to France. Note also the political campaigning of Bushrod Washington. See G. Cabot to A. Hamilton, Nov. 29, 1800, in Lodge, *George Cabot,* 298–300.

[61] H. Adams, *History of United States,* II, 148.

1802[62]—an act that had already been upheld by the Court in *Stuart* v. *Laird*.[63]

Any doubts as to what Judge Chase in fact said are resolved by a manuscript collection of jury charges, in the Judge's handwriting, preserved in the Maryland Historical Society. The charge there recorded is substantially that appearing in the *Annals of Congress* and reprinted in part by Henry Adams.[64] The original, in Chase's own hand, contains the following:

> *Where* Law is *uncertain, partial* or *arbitrary*; *where* Justice is *not impartially* administered to all; where property is insecure, and the person is liable to insult & violence without redress, by Law; the people are *not free*; whatever may be their form of Government. . . . You know, Gentlemen, that our State, and national Institutions were framed to secure to every member of the Society *equal Liberty*, & *equal rights*, but the late alteration of the federal Judiciary, by the abolition of the office of the sixteen Circuit Judges, and the *recent* change in our State Constitution by establishing *universal suffrage*; and the further alteration that is contemplated in our State Judiciary, (if adopted,) will, in my Judgment, *take away all security for property*, and *personal Liberty*.—

> The independance of the National Judiciary is already shaken to its foundation; and the virtue of the people alone can restore it. The independance of the Judges of this State will be entirely destroyed, if the Bill for abolishing the two Supreme Courts, should be ratified by the next General assembly.—The change of the State Constitution, by allowing *universal* suffrage, will, in my opinion, *certainly*, & *rapidly* destroy all protection to property, and all security to personal Liberty; and our Republican Constitution will sink into a *Mobocracy*, the worst of all possible Governments. . . .[65]

> [T]he *modern* Doctrines, by our late *reformers*, that all men in a State of *Society* are entitled to enjoy *equal Liberty*, and *equal rights*, have brought this mighty mischief upon us: And I fear that it will rapidly progress, until peace & order, freedom and property, shall be destroyed.[66]

It would be difficult to imagine an harangue, even one calculatedly prepared for the purpose, that would more exasperate Jefferson than

---

[62] *Ibid.*, 148–49.
[63] 1 Cranch 299 (1803).
[64] *Annals of Congress*, XIII, 673–76 (8th Cong., 1st sess.). H. Adams, *History of United States*, II, 148–49.
[65] An undated, anonymous pamphlet in Box 2, Gabriel Duval Papers, Library of Congress, states that an immediate occasion for the change was provided by a recent change in the Maryland Constitution pertaining to universal suffrage.
[66] Chase notebook.

did this tirade when he learned of it. To dissent from the catechism of libertarianism was bad enough, but to do so in an official capacity and so openly through the medium of a jury charge was considered seditious and treasonable. Surely such freedom of speech did not belong to a government official.[67] Immediately Jefferson wrote to his lieutenant, Joseph Nicholson, who was already in charge of Pickering's impeachment:

> You must have heard of the extraordinary charge of Chase to the grand jury at Baltimore. ought this seditious & official attack on the principles of our constitution, and on the proceedings of a state, to go unpunished? and to whom so pointedly as yourself will the public look for the necessary measures? I ask these questions for your consideration. As [?] for myself, it is better that I should not interfere.[68]

This letter provides a notable example of Jefferson's penchant for, and skill in the use of, the "third-party technique." He had already become adept at acting through others in matters of politics, partly out of caution and partly to avoid responsibility should a suggested course of action not succeed. The fact that he wrote personally to Nicholson, then in charge of the Pickering impeachment, and stated that he deemed it unwise to interfere, seems to indicate that his objections to the charge were to be regarded as personal and not official, for in the Pickering case he had not hesitated to "interfere" to the extent of sending an official Message to the House.[69] Whatever may have been his doubts as to the effectiveness of impeachment proceedings, expressed later at the time of the Pickering trial and earlier during Blount's impeachment,[70] it is difficult to conceive what he meant by punishment unless it was impeachment. The desirability of a mere reprimand would have been less cautiously put forward; hence it seems clear that the letter was directly responsible for the initiation of the proceedings against Chase.

For once, the "hot-headed" Nicholson[71] was cautious, and he carefully weighed the pros and cons of proceeding to take the "neces-

---

[67] See the reluctant conclusion of L. W. Levy, *Legacy of Suppression* (Cambridge, Mass., 1960), 307, that "Jeffersonian principles respecting freedom of political expression depended upon whose ox was being gored. . . ."

[68] T. Jefferson to J. H. Nicholson, May 13, 1803, Thomas Jefferson Papers, Manuscripts Division, Library of Congress. For a printed version, see H.

Adams, *History of United States*, II, 150, or H. A. Washington, ed., *The Writings of Thomas Jefferson* (New York, 1857), IV, 486.

[69] H. Adams, *History of United States*, II, 150.

[70] See text accompanying note 7 supra.

[71] H. Adams, *History of United States*, II, 150.

sary meaures" suggested by the President. His doubts and uncertainties, together with those of Nathaniel Macon, another leading Republican, are vividly illustrated by several letters written to him by the latter during the course of the summer of 1803. The first letter, written from North Carolina, is dated July 26:

> But as to the impeachment of the Judge it certainly deserves my serious consideration. If it be an act which is impeachable and for which he ought to be impeached, it will undoubtedly be the constitutional duty of the next [House] of Representatives to impeach him; as to the effect, I have always believed the best way, to produce a good effect, is to do right; However, I will think of more on the subject and if we should both be again elected, we can talk it over at the next Congress; It seems to me, that he is certainly as guilty of a misdemeanor as the unfortunate New Hampshire Judge was, and if the mind has any thing to do with criminal acts, he is unquestionably more so, the one seemed to be the effect of misfortune and the other of mental depravity; But as to your being the mover for impeachment, if one should be proper I have not as yet, thought with the letter, which suggests its propriety; because it is not improbable, but the motives might be questioned as you both live in the same state, by those who were not personally acquainted with you, and I would not wish you to do a single act, where the least doubt could be entertained as to the purity of the motives where others could do the same act with as much propriety.[72]

Macon's caution on this last point was apparently in recognition of the fact that Nicholson, as a Marylander, would be a logical successor to Chase's place on the Bench if the impeachment succeeded. Indeed, it seems to have been widely accepted that this should take place.[73] Shortly thereafter, Macon wrote:

1. Ought a Judge to be impeached for a charge to a grand jury because it contains matter of which the grand jury have not cognizance?
2. Ought a Judge to be impeached for a charge to a grand jury, not legal but political?
3. Ought a judge to be impeached for delivering in his charge to the grand jury, political opinions which every man may fully enjoy and freely express?

---

[72] N. Macon to J. Nicholson, July 6, 1803, Joseph H. Nicholson Papers, II, 4156A–4156B, Manuscripts Division, Library of Congress. See also, E. M. Wilson, "The Congressional Career of Nathaniel Macon," *James Sprunt Historical Monographs No. 2*, 14 (1900).

[73] See W. E. Dodd, *The Life of Nathaniel Macon* (New York, 1908), 187–88.

4. Ought a Judge to be impeached for delivering his political opinions in a charge to the grand jury, and which any member of Congress might deliver to the House of which he is a member?

5. Ought a Judge to be impeached because he avows monarchical principles in his charge to a grand jury?

Is error of opinion to be dreaded when inquiry is free? Is the liberty of the press of any real value where the political charges of a Judge are dreaded? What effect have they produced (Judicial political charges) in the United States? If a Judge ought to be impeached for avowing monarchical principles to the Grand Jury in his charge, what ought to be done with those who appoint them who actually supported them in the field; I must stop or weary your with enquiries, perhaps was I more of the lawyer and less of the planter I might see that none of those questions touched the case. although the same principle is involved in the whole of them. it not does [*sic*] seem improper to examine each, because if either of them embrace the question it deserves the most serious consideration before a single step be taken— Change the scene, and suppose Chase had stretched as far on the other side, and had praised where no praise was deserving, would it be proper to impeach, because by such conduct he might lull the people to sleep while their interest was destroyed. I have said this much to hear your opinions on some of the points, nor can I quite [*sic*] without expressing to you my firm conviction that you, if any attempt be made to impeach, ought not to be the leader.[74]

Macon's caution did not mean that he was not anti-Chase or did not share the views of his fellow Republicans about the Judge. August 7 found him writing to John Steele as follows:

Have you seen Judge Chase' charge to the grand jury at Baltimore, if you have not, it is worth reading if only for its novelty; it has made some noise with us, indeed all are dissatisfied with it, such men as he, no matter to *what* party they may pretend to belong, are a real injury to the country, Their imprudence and ungovernable temper have no limits. They neither feel charity nor know moderation to those who may honestly differ with them in opinion, if in fact they have any opinion, more than others.[75]

At this point, it must be re-emphasized not only on behalf of Chase but also as a characteristic of the relationship of the judiciary to the

---

[74] N. Macon to J. Nicholson, July 6, 1803, Joseph H. Nicholson Papers, II, 1158A–1158B, Manuscripts Division, Library of Congress. For a printed version, see Dodd, *Nathaniel Macon*, 187.

[75] N. Macon to J. Steele, Aug. 7, 1803, in H. M. Wagstaff, ed., *The Papers of John Steele* (Raleigh, 1924), I, 403.

general government that the delivery of political speeches in the course of charges to grand juries was common, especially after the Revolution. Such jury charges were regarded as an appropriate means of popular education. They apparently had their origin in the practices of the English judges of assize who were accustomed to summarize under various heads abstracts of the crimes and offenses into which the jury was expected to inquire. To the extent that political crimes were cognizable, it was inevitable that politics should have entered into the charge. By the last decade of the eighteenth century in this country, when the strife between Federalist and Republican factions was becoming rampant, these preambles frequently became vehicles for harangues, in the course of which the presiding judge gave full vent to his personal party feelings. The manuscript collection of Judge Chase's jury charges above referred to contains, in addition to expectable references to common criminal offenses, statements as to the ends and purposes of civilized society, exhortations to patriotism, and discussions of equal rights, neutrality, and defense.[76] Other Supreme Court judges had freely indulged in the practice—Jay, Cushing, Wilson, Iredell, and Paterson.[77] For example, in May 1800 a Portsmouth, New Hampshire, newspaper reported that the circuit court had opened with Judge Paterson of the Supreme Court presiding:

> After the jury were empanelled the Judge delivered a most elegant and appropriate charge. The *Law* was laid down in a masterly manner: *Politics* were set in their true light by holding up the Jacobins as the disorganizers of our happy country, and the only instruments of introducing discontent and dissatisfaction among the well-meaning part of the Community. *Religion & Morality* were pleasingly inculcated and enforced as being necessary to good government, good order, and good laws; for "when the righteous are in authority, the people rejoice."[78]

Yet if these excursions into politics and political morality were edifying to the public and advanced the Federalist cause, they aroused and helped to consolidate the opposition, particularly since copies of the jury charges were frequently circulated through the press or other-

---

[76] See Chase notebook.

[77] See J. Goebel, Jr., *Antecedents and Beginnings to 1801. History of the Supreme Court of the United States*, ed., P. Freund (New York, 1971), 619–20; H. P. Johnston, ed., *The Correspondence and Public Papers of John Jay* (New York, 1890–93), III, 387, 478; G. J. McRee, ed., *Life and Correspondence of James* *Iredell* (New York, 1858), II, 347 et seq.; C. Warren, *The Supreme Court in United States History* (Boston, 1926), I, 58–60, 165–67 (hereafter cited as Warren, *Supreme Court*).

[78] W. H. Hackett, "The Circuit Court for the New Hampshire District One Hundred Years Ago," *The Green Bag*, II, 264 (1890).

wise.[79] Jefferson, somewhat earlier, had expressed the hope that judges who indulged in the practice should themselves be presented to grand juries.[80] In the course of the impeachment of Judge Addison who, as noted above, frequently indulged in political jury charges, Alexander Dallas characterized them as bold and pernicious:

> Even in the judicial history of England, where the spirit of party has sometimes raged with the most dreadful consequences, you will find it difficult to trace any instance to countenance the political declamations, the party invectives, which have of late become a sort of prelude to the commencement of every session of our courts of justice.[81]

Nevertheless, it should again be emphasized that before the Republicans came into power, and even for a short time afterwards, the judiciary was not expected to remove itself from political fields of action. Not only did Supreme Court and other judges often hold political as well as judicial offices (for example, Jay, Ellsworth, and Marshall), but they were active in political campaigns—Chase on behalf of Adams in 1800 and Bushrod Washington in support of C. C. Pinckney in the same year. In reciting a number of such instances and commenting that mere political activity previously had not been regarded as unfitting for a judge, Charles Warren states that the Republicans were nevertheless waiting for a favorable opportunity to carry out "the threats of impeachment which had been hanging over Chase for three years."[82] That opportunity came when, with excessive zeal, Chase delivered his 1803 jury charge, which was widely reported, assailed, and defended in newspapers throughout the country.[83]

D.   THE IMPEACHMENT OF CHASE

During the course of the summer of 1803, it was decided to entrust the management of the Chase impeachment to John Randolph, partly because it might be unseemly for a potential candidate for the Judge's office to take the lead, and partly because Randolph was regarded as more experienced in debate than any other man then in the House. The choice was a grave mistake. Randolph was no lawyer, and the very qualities that made him so brilliant, eloquent, and formidable on the floor of the House were fatal to him in legal argument. A master of vituperative invective, he was haughty and lacked balance; fretful and peevish because of bad health, he was also insolent and hot-headed.

---

[79] See McRee, *James Iredell*, II, 347.

[80] T. Jefferson to P. Fitzhugh, June 4, 1797, in Ford, *Works of Jefferson*, VIII, 302.

[81] G. M. Dallas, *Life and Writings of Alexander James Dallas* (Philadelphia, 1871), 82.

[82] Warren, *Supreme Court*, I, 276.

[83] *Ibid.*, 276–77.

In the view of one contemporary he was "impatient of obstacles, incapable of sustained labor or of methodical arrangement, illogical to excess, and egotistic to the verge of madness."[84] Henry Adams believes that Jefferson himself did not select Randolph to manage the proceedings because little personal sympathy existed between the two and because Randolph's intimates were no longer chiefly Virginians and owed no personal allegiance to the President.[85] The second of these reasons is not wholly convincing, since Jefferson's first choice was Randolph's friend Nicholson from Maryland. That he acquiesced, however, in the choice of Randolph must be presumed, and, as events were to prove, hardly a worse selection for the prosecution could have been made.

The impeachment matter was deftly and without advance notice brought before the House on January 5, 1804, by Randolph's alluding to the importance of preserving unpolluted the fountain of justice.[86] Referring to certain remarks made nearly a year before by Representative Smilie of Pennsylvania[87] with respect to the conduct of Judge Chase, Randolph said that the charge demanded attention, and after investigation he believed that it furnished grounds for an impeachment. No accusation was made, but he asked for the appointment of a committee of inquiry to report whether Chase had so acted in his judicial capacity as to require the interposition of the constitutional power of the House of Representatives.

Jefferson was told on the same day what had transpired, and he immediately inquired of his private secretary what part of Chase's conduct had been referred to as the grounds for impeachment. When told that it was the case of Cooper, he remarked to Senator Plumer:

> There are three cases to which I suppose the House would refer, Fries, Cooper, & Callender—But the conduct of Judge Chase was, perhaps the most extraordinary [sic] in the trial of Callender—He there refused to admit Col Taylor, late one of your senators, as a witness for Callender because he could not prove the whole of the case.[88]

Shortly afterwards, Plumer noted that Eppes, the President's son-in-law, expressed on the floor of the House the same ideas, "the very same that he mentioned to me in private conversation."[89] These epi-

---

[84] H. Adams, *History of United States*, II, 151.

[85] *Ibid.*

[86] *Annals of Congress*, XIII, 805–806 (8th Cong., 1st sess.).

[87] *Annals of Congress*, XI, 528–30 (7th Cong., 1st sess.).

[88] Plumer, *Notes on Proceedings*, 283. For a printed version, see Brown, *Plumer's Memorandum of Proceedings*, 100–101.

[89] Plumer, *Notes on Proceedings*, 287. For a printed version, see Brown, *Plumer's Memorandum of Proceedings*, 102.

sodes indicate how closely the President was in touch with, if not actually guiding, the course of the impeachment.

On January 6, 1804, as requested by Randolph, the House appointed a committee "to enquire into the judicial conduct of Samuel Chase" and to report whether he had so acted in his judicial capacity as to require impeachment by the House.[90] The debates following Randolph's resolution clearly demonstrate not only the partisan nature of the attack on Chase but the determination to prosecute it by every feasible means. It seems entirely clear that Randolph and several other Republican leaders were prepared to assume in advance that Chase was, and would be proved to be, guilty of whatever charges could subsequently be brought against him. Federalists who pressed for a disclosure of details justifying the House inquiry made no progress with suggestions as to the fairness or propriety of the procedure.[91] Even George W. Campbell, a Republican from Tennessee, thought the inquiry as proposed by Randolph would be novel and unprecedented and that approval of the resolution as it stood was equivalent to expressing an opinion as to the probable guilt of Chase.[92] Randolph stolidly maintained that only an official inquiry could determine the facts.[93] He found support from another Republican, Joseph Clay of Pennsylvania, who urged that, because the House was responsible for the morality of the judiciary, an inquiry could be instituted at the slightest suspicion of judicial misconduct.[94]

When objection was raised that the proposed inquiry was not supported by precedents, Randolph retorted that the youth of the country released the House from a responsibility to precedent. "How is it possible," he asked, "in a Government hardly in its teens . . . to find precedents?"[95] If precedents were needed, Representative Smilie stated, they could be found in English practice, and he urged for consideration the impeachment of the Earl of Strafford. Although he disavowed approval of those proceedings, he pointed out that no evidence had been required to commence an inquiry.[96] The youthful James Elliot, a Federalist from Vermont, blasted his colleague's choice of authority and termed the trial of the Earl of Strafford "[a] gloomy and terrible precedent . . . utterly unsusceptible of application to the principles of a Republican form of Government."[97]

Joseph Nicholson, who had been absent when Randolph offered his resolution, urged that the impeachment of Warren Hastings in England provided sound precedent. In that case, he contended, a mem-

---

[90] *Annals of Congress,* XIII, 850 (8th Cong., 1st sess.).

[91] *Ibid.,* 813–14 (8th Cong., 1st sess.).

[92] *Ibid.,* 817 (8th Cong., 1st sess.).

[93] *Ibid.,* 811 (8th Cong., 1st sess.).

[94] *Ibid.,* 809 (8th Cong., 1st sess.).

[95] *Ibid.,* 818 (8th Cong., 1st sess.).

[96] *Ibid.,* 822 (8th Cong., 1st sess.).

[97] *Ibid.,* 846 (8th Cong., 1st sess.).

225

ber of the House of Commons successfully moved for an impeachment inquiry without adducing proof to support his motion.[98] James Elliot answered that Hastings' impeachment had indeed been initiated by a single member of the House of Commons, but, insisted Elliot, that individual had exhibited specific charges of misconduct.[99] Elliot re-iterated the Republican Campbell's argument that the House was the grand inquest of the nation, but stated that its practice ought to be analogous to that of a grand jury in commencing its inquiries upon sub-stantial factual bases.[100]

As the argument progressed, an amendment was introduced to extend the inquiry into an examination of the conduct of Richard Peters, Federal District Judge in Pennsylvania.[101] As Judge Peters wrote, he was turned out "like a *bag-fox*, to amuse and weary the hounds, and divert them from the real *Chase*."[102] The amendment was favorably received by Republicans, since it made the inquiry of Chase seem less partisan; at the same time, Federalist members saw in it an opportunity to lessen the impact of the attack on Chase. On January 7 the amended motion was carried by a vote of 81–40.[103]

Many apparently voted for the motion to inquire into Chase's conduct because it asked for an inquiry only, and not impeachment, which would require specific charges, but Senator Plumer observed that these people did not understand that when the committee of in-quiry had gathered ex parte testimony and reported an impeachment, "they will be under a kind of necessity to impeach."[104] He added that the procedure was "similar to the French *denouncing* a victim & like them his condemnation will follow of course."[105] Subsequently, Judge Peters' name was dropped because it was found that he had not "so acted in his judiciary capacity as to require the interposition of the Constitutional powers of this House."[106] It is of interest and importance to note at this point that the House refused to impeach Judge Griffin, even though he had concurred in every decision made by Chase at the trial of James Callender.[107]

---

[98] *Ibid.*, 842–43 (8th Cong., 1st sess.).

[99] *Ibid.*, 846 (8th Cong., 1st sess.).

[100] *Ibid.*, 847 (8th Cong., 1st sess.).

[101] *Ibid.*, 821, 850, 873–74 (8th Cong., 1st sess.). See also Plumer, *Notes on Proceedings*, 284.

[102] R. Peters, "Extract of Letter from Richard Peters Esq. dated January 25, 1804," Pickering Papers, XXVII, 44, Massachusetts Historical Society, Boston (reference courtesy of the Massachusetts Historical Society).

[103] *Annals of Congress*, XIII, 875 (8th Cong., 1st sess.). See also Plumer, *Notes on Proceedings*, 284.

[104] Plumer, *Notes on Proceedings*, 287. For a printed version, see Brown, *Plumer's Memorandum of Proceedings*, 102.

[105] Brown, *Plumer's Memorandum of Proceedings*, 101.

[106] *Annals of Congress*, XIII, 1171, 1181 (8th Cong., 1st sess.).

[107] See generally *Annals of Congress*, XIII, 1171–81 (8th Cong., 1st sess.).

VII: *Impeachment*

If the Republicans were triumphant about the outcome, certainly few Federalists seriously doubted the conclusions that the committee of inquiry would reach. "The violence of Randolph and Co. against the judges," wrote Fisher Ames, "somewhat exceeds my estimate of the man and the party. . . ."[108] The expressions of the Reverend Manasseh Cutler, in a letter written on January 10, 1804, offer further typical Federalist sentiments:

> Never before have I seen the demon of Jacobinism display the cloven hoof with equal audacity. Never have I believed that the hottest, maddest Democrats would have openly and boldly avowed principles advanced in the course of these debates. But it appears evidently to be the prosecution of the system formed when the *Judiciary* was at first attacked—not merely to remove Federal Judges, which his Democratic Majesty in his work of destruction had not power to assail— but to prostrate, completely, the Judiciary branch of our government. What will you say to such principles as these? That a Judge is impeachable for an opinion, in a law point, if that opinion should be judged erroneous by the House of Representatives? That a judge ought in duty to favor the ruling political party? And that he is bound to be governed by the will of the people (so-called)? The next to be impeached, we are told, is to be Judge Bee, of North Carolina, but it is doubtful whether it will be brought forward this session. The utmost secrecy is preserved in the Cabinet—no one but those immediately concerned can tell us what is to be on the morrow. Democracy is progressing, if not with hasty strides, with unabated zeal. Will none of their destructive measures awaken the public mind? Will the people see with indifference their judges converted into mere automatons on the bench, or, what is infinitely worse, made the servile creatures of the Legislature?[109]

Senator Plumer, writing to his brother Daniel, remarked that "[t]he attempts to destroy by removals the Judges of our Courts of law is a bold measure. It is tending to encrease the power & influence of the President. It is a bold stroke that will, if successful, render personal liberty & the property of Individuals insecure."[110] Several days later, he commented to Jedidiah Morse on the administration's attitude towards the judiciary:

> But the attack on our Judges is the most serious & alarming measure yet attempted by the present administration. If this does not arouse

---

[108] F. Ames to T. Dwight, Jan. 25, 1804, in S. Ames, ed., *Works of Fisher Ames* (Boston, 1854), I, 337.

[109] W. P. and J. P. Cutler, *Life, Journals and Correspondence of Rev. Manasseh Cutler* (Cincinnati, 1888), II, 158.

[110] Senator W. Plumer to D. Plumer, Jan. 24, 1804, Letters 1804–1807, Plumer Papers, Manuscripts Division, Library of Congress.

N. England, & indeed the federalists throughout the U. States, I shall consider that we are given up to suffer severe chastisements of heaven. It is not difficult to see to what point the present rulers are aiming, & their success hitherto, emboldens them to pursue their object with increasing vigor. How far they may be permitted to go, cannot be foreseen. I pray that they may be stopped short of bloodshed.[111]

Luke Wheeler wrote to Chase from Norfolk, Virginia, and referred to the astonishment and regret that "the whole Federal Interest and every real Patriot of our Country" felt at "the daring attempt about to be made on the independence of the judiciary." He went on to say that Chase's friends had more than an ordinary interest "for the part which you are destined to act in this extraordinary Scene. Some of us who know your warmth of temper and wonted contempt of your foes, may have their solicitude increased on that score; But I trust & believe that you will preserve a coolness and dignity commensurate with this all important case."[112]

Meanwhile, the Republican leaders were collecting ex parte testimony against Chase in order further to vilify him and excite popular odium against him, so as to increase the certainty of conviction.[113] At the end of January Randolph requested that the House begin printing the evidence as soon as possible because of its increasing volume.[114] Many months before the articles of impeachment were presented to the House, they were published in pamphlet form and then also printed in the Republican organ in Washington.[115] The evidence apparently consisted in large part of the "private opinions & suspicions of lawyers, who considered themselves as brow beaten by the judge."[116] "Jocular conversation in private circles, expressions dropped while traveling in stages, at taverns and boarding-houses, have been brought to condemn him."[117] The evidence also included, however, detailed accounts of the trials of Fries and Callender. The committee of inquiry had lost no time in preparing interrogatories and obtaining depositions relating primarily to those trials. Most of these were answered within two weeks.[118] Counsel for the defendants in those two trials—George Hay

---

[111] W. Plumer to J. Morse, Feb. 3, 1804, *ibid.*

[112] L. Wheeler to S. Chase, Jan. 24, 1804, Chase Papers, Maryland Historical Society, Baltimore.

[113] W. Plumer to J. Sheafe, Feb. 22, 1804, Letters 1804–1807, Plumer Papers, Manuscripts Division, Library of Congress.

[114] *Annals of Congress,* XIII, 959 (8th Cong., 1st sess.).

[115] Beveridge, *John Marshall,* III, 171.

[116] J. Elliott to his Vermont constituents, Dec. 24, 1804, in Plumer, *Notes on Proceedings,* II, 214.

[117] M. Cutler to Dr. Torrey, Mar. 1, 1805, in Cutler and Cutler, *Rev. Manasseh Cutler,* II, 192.

[118] See *Report of the Committee Appointed on the Seventh of January Last to Enquire into the Official Conduct of Samuel Chase,* Rare Book Room, Library of Congress.

and Philip Nicholas in the former, William Lewis and Alexander J. Dallas in the latter—testified tediously as to the prejudice and improprieties of Chase on those occasions. Samuel H. Smith, publisher of the *National Intelligencer*, who was present when the Baltimore charge was delivered, produced a copy thereof. The committee also examined individuals concerning the scope of the Judge's charge and address to a grand jury at Wilmington, Delaware, in 1800. Inquiries were directed even to members of the Supreme Court, and Marshall and Washington testified that certain remarks concerning the Callender trial, made by Chase on a social occasion in the preceding winter, were not intended to be serious.[119] On March 9, the *National Intelligencer* and other newspapers began publishing the testimony, "contrary to every principle of law & justice, & the effect of this publication must have been . . . to condemn the Judge in the public mind before he could have time to prepare his defence."[120] Two days later, Plumer recorded that Chase was

> very obnoxious to the *powers that be*, & must be *denounced*, but articles will not be exhibited ag⁺ him this session. The accusers have collected a volume of ex parte evidence against him, printed & published it in pamphlets, & now it is publishing in the Court gazette to be diffused in every direction. This conduct is highly reprehensible; & if a party to a suit at law, pending the same, was to practise in this manner he would merit punishment.[121]

Many saw in the proceedings the unfolding of a design, soon to be frankly admitted by Giles, to impeach the entire Court,[122] and they began to perceive that the removal of Chase was only a step, though an exceedingly important one, in that direction. Judge Sheafe thought that the Republicans meant "only to overawe the Court, which I fear they will in some measure effect by what they have done and are doing."[123] Timothy Pickering was more blunt. They "are all Federalists," he wrote to a correspondent on February 11. "They stand in the way of the ruling power. . . . The judges, therefore, are, if possible, to be removed."[124] A month later, on March 14, he wrote that the mea-

---

[119] *Ibid.*, 68–69, 111, 112.

[120] J. Elliott to his Vermont constituents, Dec. 24, 1804, in Plumer, *Notes on Proceedings*, II, 213–16.

[121] W. Plumer to J. Smith, Mar. 11, 1804, Letters 1804–1807, Plumer Papers, Manuscripts Division, Library of Congress.

[122] C. F. Adams, *John Quincy Adams*, I, 322.

[123] Judge Sheafe to W. Plumer, Mar. 7, 1804, Letters 1804–1807, Plumer Papers, Manuscripts Division, Library of Congress.

[124] T. Pickering to T. Lyman, Feb. 11, 1804, in H. Adams, ed., *Documents Relating to New England Federalism 1800–1815* (Boston, 1877), 344.

sures "are made questions of *party*, and therefore at all events to be carried into effect according to the wishes of the prime mover," that is, Jefferson.[125] "They hate Marshal, Patterson &c worse than Chase," wrote Jeremiah Smith, "because they are men of better character. . . . Depend upon it they will be obnoxious as long as they retain either [their offices or good names]. If they will neither die or resign they give Mr J the trouble of correcting the *procedure*—There is no other way of reconciling the public to the designs of administration ag^t the Judges but by bringing the public to hate them."[126] Federalist newspapers expressed similar views and pointedly observed that Chase was marked only as the first victim and that others would follow.[127]

Aware of the immediate course ahead, Chase's friends and his brethren on the Court were active in taking steps to prepare for his defense. The strategy received careful attention. James Bayard, still a member of the House, wrote to R. G. Harper that the Judge should defend himself and that any aid he received should be in the course of preparing himself rather than in the trial.

> I think decidedly whether with a view to a personal or general effect the Judge ought to have no advocate but himself. His talents knowledge and firmness qualify him in an eminent degree to encounter the difficulties of the situation.
>
> If he appears singly against the host of managers his condition becomes at once distinguished and interesting. The great effect would be produced by seeing an Individual struggling against the efforts of the House of Representatives.
>
> In my own opinion the event of the impeachment is already determined. If the Judge is to fall it will be more honorable and useful to him and productive of a better effect upon the public mind to fall after having fought the battle singly than after having been defended by the arms of others.
>
> In the case of Lord Clive the same course was recommended by Mr. Dunning and afterwards followed by the best effect. Mr. Dunning prepared the speech, but it was delivered by Lord Clive.
>
> If it be determined to have Counsel they ought to be taken from Maryland and in a manner that shall not betray apprehension either of the weight of the charges which can be maintained or of superiority of those who are to advocate them. In my judgment however the best

---

[125] T. Pickering to T. Lyman, Mar. 14, 1804, in *ibid.*, 359.

[126] J. Smith to W. Plumer, Feb. 11, 1804, Letters 1804–1807, Plumer Papers, Manuscripts Division, Library of Congress.

[127] See text accompanying note 170 infra.

step that could be taken as soon as the impeachment is resolved upon would be to announce (indirectly) that the Judge, conscious of the falsehood or futility of the charges against him and reposing on the sense of his own integrity had determined singly to meet and oppose the host of his Persecutors.[128]

It seems evident that the committee of inquiry had before it, probably from the outset, a series of numbered charges, despite the fact that no charges against Chase had been made during the debate other than general references to his conduct in the trials of Fries and Callender. Judge Chase had procured a copy of these charges at least as early as January 13, when he sent a copy to Judge Paterson from Baltimore. It is unfortunate that no copy of the list is available, particularly because in the letter that accompanied it Chase referred to the list of charges by number, saying, "If the first and fourth Charges had any foundation in truth, I should be very uneasy."[129] Marshall also was disturbed by the same two charges.[130] If these charges were the same as those that later appeared in the committee's Report—and there is good reason to believe that they were—the first referred to the Judge's "arbitrary, oppressive and unjust" conduct in the trial of John Fries, and the fourth related to his exclusion of the testimony of Colonel Taylor in the trial of Callender.

The copy of the charges that the committee had before it was nevertheless helpful to Chase in assembling evidence for his defense. John Marshall, at his request, undertook to gather the recollections of persons who had attended the Callender trial, particularly with respect to Chase's alleged exclusion of Colonel Taylor's testimony, which it was anticipated would be a primary ground for impeachment proceedings. In a letter to Chase, dated January 23, 1804, he commented thereon and proceeded to express an opinion that is not only entirely uncharacteristic of Marshall but utterly inconsistent with his views on judicial independence. After stating that, even if Colonel Taylor's testimony were admissible, its exclusion constituted an extraordinary ground for impeachment, he went on to say:

According to the antient doctrine a jury finding a verdict against the law of the case was liable to an attaint: & the amount of the present

---

[128] J. Bayard to R. Harper, Jan. 30, 1804, in Donnan, "Papers of James A. Bayard," 160–61.

[129] S. Chase to W. Paterson, Jan. 13, 1804, Bancroft Transcripts, Paterson Papers, New York Public Library, New York City.

[130] J. Marshall to S. Chase, Jan. 23, 1804, Etting Manuscripts, Pennsylvania Historical Society, Philadelphia. For a facsimile, see Beveridge, *John Marshall*, III, 176–77.

doctrine seems to be that a Judge giving a legal opinion contrary to the opinion of the legislature is liable to impeachment.

As, for convenience & humanity the old doctrine of attaint has yielded to the silent, moderate but not less operative influence of new trials, I think the modern doctrine of impeachment should yield to an appellate jurisdiction in the legislature. A reversal of those legal opinions deemed unsound by the legislature would certainly better comport with the mildness of our character than a removal of the Judge who has rendered them unknowing of his fault. The other charges except the 1st & 4th which I suppose to be altogether unfounded, seem still less to furnish cause for impeachment. But the little finger of [blotted out] is heavier than the loins of [omitted].[131]

According to Beveridge, Marshall's extraordinary suggestion for review of Supreme Court decisions by the legislature was provoked by his serious alarm. "Had we not the evidence of Marshall's signature to a letter written in his well-known hand, it could not be credited that he ever entertained such sentiments. They were in direct contradiction to his reasoning in Marbury *vs.* Madison, utterly destructive of the Federalist philosophy of judicial control of legislation."[132]

Bushrod Washington was likewise apprehensive, but in a letter to Chase he managed to conceal his alarm more effectively than did his Chief. Washington suggested hopefully that Chase might turn the inquiry to his own purposes in vindicating his character and his actions. He added sympathetically, "I cannot but feel great distress that you should at your time of life & in your state of health be exposed to the trouble & expense which must attend it."[133]

Chase's friends at the Bar rallied to his defense as the work of the committee progressed. Robert G. Harper, ardent Federalist from Maryland and son-in-law of Charles Carroll, urged James A. Bayard and Alexander Hamilton to join him in serving as Chase's counsel without compensation. Harper told both men that the Judge specifically desired their services.[134] But, as noted above, Bayard replied that Chase would stand a better chance defending his own cause and that any help he received should not show.[135]

Joseph Hopkinson of Philadelphia eagerly offered his services. He told the Judge that the leading lawyers of his city considered the inquiry

---

[131] *Ibid.*
[132] Beveridge, *John Marshall,* III, 178.
[133] B. Washington to S. Chase, Jan. 24, 1804, Etting Papers (Jurists) #14, Pennsylvania Historical Society, Philadelphia.

[134] R. Harper to J. Bayard, Jan. 22, 1804, Etting Papers (Jurists) #13, and R. Harper to A. Hamilton, Jan. 22, 1804, Etting Papers (Jurists) #13, *ibid.*
[135] J. Bayard to R. Harper, Jan. 30, 1804, in Donnan, "Papers of James A. Bayard," 160–61.

"a gross and unprecedented violation of justice and the security of Courts." Hopkinson described the process of impeachment as a "mean and prostituted instrument of party malevolence and private hate. . . . Impeachment is the ready instrument of removal. . . ."[136]

Judge James Winchester referred to the power of impeachment as "the most terrible engine which faction can employ," and went on to say:

> I should not however be willing to abandon the principle "that impeachment will lie only for some *high* crime or misdemeanor"—not for acts simply evil because prohibited, but *mali in se* in their very nature.—this seems countenanced by the restriction on the power of the Senate to pass a Jud[t] by leaving the party liable to Indictment, trial & punishment at Law—and the inference is fair that unless the *act* is punish[bl] at Law without impeachment it is not a proper subject for impeachment—I say the *act* punish[bl] because from locality or other causes, acts highly criminal may not be triable. . . . If some such restraint is not allowed, what are the boundaries of this power . . . ?[137]

The foregoing reactions are presented in detail to emphasize the political aspect of the impeachment. Taken altogether, these sentiments —many of them expressed by lawyers—suggest that there was no precise legal content to the phrase "high crimes and misdemeanors" understood at the time. It was not a term of art; impeachment was seen as a political, rather than a judicial, problem, and in the early 1800s there were no rigid standards to separate "impeachable" offenses from those that were not. Alfred North Whitehead once aptly remarked of the framers of the Constitution that they "had an uncommonly clear grasp of the general ideas that they wanted . . . then left the working out of the details to later interpreters. . . ."[138]

Why the administration did not attempt to abolish the Supreme Court itself, as had been done in the case of the circuit courts, can only be conjectured. It seems likely that the repeal of the 1801 Act had aroused public opinion in Congress and elsewhere to a greater degree than had been anticipated. Certainly the Bar had become alarmed because the repeal had involved a frontal attack on the principles of judicial tenure. Impeachments that attacked only individuals could be expected to be more palatable, especially if the public mind were pre-

---

[136] J. Hopkinson to S. Chase, Jan. 20, 1804, Etting Papers (Jurists) #12, Pennsylvania Historical Society, Philadelphia.

[137] J. Winchester to S. Chase, Jan. 26, 1804, Chase Papers, Maryland Historical Society.

[138] L. Price, ed., *Dialogues of Alfred North Whitehead* (Boston, 1954), 203.

pared and incited in advance by partisan pamphlets and newspapers. Yet Jeremiah Smith, referring to the impeachment proceedings against Pickering and Chase, remarked:

> Why not repeal the law under which they were appointed? There is in my opinion no pretence for saying that there is any difference between Judges of the Sup & Inf courts. The constitutional doctrine of tenure attaches to both but if there is a difference certainly the District Judges stand on the same footing as the Circuit Judges.[139]

Randolph's resolution to impeach Chase was offered to the House on March 6, 1804.[140] On March 12, within an hour of the Senate's conviction of Pickering on impeachment charges, the committee's report, that Judge Chase "be impeached of high crimes and misdemeanors," was approved by the House sitting as a Committee of the Whole by a vote of 73–32. Judge Peters' exoneration was approved unanimously.[141] Randolph and Early were thereupon instructed to designate a committee to prepare the articles of impeachment, and the committee, consisting of Messrs. Randolph, Early, Nicholson, Clay, and Boyle, was appointed the next day.[142] On March 13 Randolph informed the Senate that the House had been ordered to impeach Chase and that it would, in due course, exhibit particular articles against him.[143]

E. THE TRIAL OF PICKERING

As earlier stated, the impeachment proceedings against Pickering were generally understood to be a prelude to the proceedings to be taken against Chase, and it is therefore important to go back over the events of the preceding ten days. Pickering had been ordered to appear for trial before the Senate, sitting as a "Court of Impeachments," on March 2, 1804. He was then given five weeks in which to assemble witnesses, prepare his defense and travel the twelve days to Washington in the middle of the winter. The first three articles charged that the Judge, in willful contravention of a federal statute, had failed to require the indemnity bond prescribed, had refused to hear the government's testimony, and had, with intent to injure the revenues of the United States, refused an appeal from his own arbitrary decree. The fourth article charged that he was a man of loose morals and intemperate

---

[139] J. Smith to W. Plumer, Jan. 28, 1804, Letters 1804–1807, Plumer Papers, Manuscripts Division, Library of Congress.

[140] *Annals of Congress*, XIII, 1093 (8th Cong., 1st sess.).

[141] *Ibid.*, 1180–81 (8th Cong., 1st sess.).

[142] *Ibid.*, 1182 (8th Cong., 1st sess.).

[143] *Ibid.*, 272 (8th Cong., 1st sess.).

habits and that he had attempted to perform his judicial duties in a state of complete intoxication. None of the articles referred to his insanity; all underscored willful intent for the purpose of providing a foundation for criminal misconduct on the bench. It has been stated that all virtually "proclaimed in writing that Pickering was to be sacrificed to political expediency."[144]

When Pickering's name was called, he did not appear. A petition submitted by the Judge's son was then heard. It asked for a postponement so that evidence might be collected and then presented to show that when the alleged crimes had been committed the Judge was insane, "his mind wholly deranged, and altogether incapable of transacting any kind of business which requires the exercise of judgment, or the faculties of reason; and, therefore, . . . incapable of corruption of judgment, no subject of impeachment, or amenable to any tribunal for his actions."[145] It was also alleged that the state of his health, his poverty, and his mental derangement were such that he was unable to attend the proceedings.[146]

The Republicans were confronted with a dilemma. If the proof of insanity were admitted and accepted, they must decide either that he could not be impeached—if he were mentally irresponsible for high crimes and misdemeanors—or that, even though insane, he might nonetheless be guilty under the Constitution of high crimes and misdemeanors. More importantly, from the standpoint of the objectives of his accusers, to decide that insanity might be pleaded by way of bar to impeachment could open the way to a similar defense by Judge Chase in the ensuing proceedings, a point expressly raised by Senator Jackson of Georgia.[147] In any event, it seems to have been generally felt that the acquittal of Pickering would be fatal to the case against Chase.

After a prolonged debate of three days, Robert G. Harper was permitted to testify as agent for Pickering's son. Harper was a brilliant, skillful, but pompous and insolent lawyer from Baltimore, and his appearance added to the political overtones of the case. His testimony was conclusive on the matter of insanity. The Republicans, however, took the position that insanity was no bar because impeachment did not necessarily imply criminality, and they accordingly ignored Harper's evidence. To the majority of the Senate, as the theory was to be articulated, an impeachment proceeding was an inquest of office in judicial form; the Senate was not a court of justice but part of the constitutional

---

[144] L. W. Turner, "The Impeachment of John Pickering," *American Historical Review* L, 485, 495 (1949).

[145] *Annals of Congress*, XIII, 328–29 (8th Cong., 1st sess.).

[146] *Ibid.*, 329–30 (8th Cong., 1st sess.). See also W. Plumer to —. Livermore, Mar 4, 1804, Letters 1804–1807, Plumer Papers, Manuscripts Division, Library of Congress.

[147] C. F. Adams, *John Quincy Adams*, I, 299.

machinery for making appointments and removals. Hence, instead of a vote on whether Pickering was guilty of high crimes and misdemeanors, it was moved that a vote be taken as to whether or not he was "guilty as charged." The Senate voted 19–7 in favor of the motion, and 20–6 that he should be removed from office. The voting was strictly along party lines, and the Republicans even refused to allow the report of the proceedings to be printed.[148]

From a political standpoint, the conviction of Pickering provided for the moment an impressive precedent. On the basis of ex parte evidence, an absent defendant who was unable either to plead or to defend himself was convicted by a partisan body of men intent upon a purge of the judiciary. That Chase's impeachment would follow that conviction seems nowhere to have been doubted.[149] From a legal standpoint, the importance of the conviction lay in the tacit adoption of the view that "misdemeanors" in the impeachment article of the Constitution did not necessarily imply criminality but extended to cases of misbehavior in which neither intent nor criminality was involved. It might have been interpreted to mean that any act or word that a political majority thought objectionable could be viewed as a misdemeanor and hence a basis for impeachment and removal. The subsequent undermining of this interpretation as a result of the failure to convict Chase deprived the Pickering case of value as a precedent, but it is nevertheless an important phase of the history of the Court. Also, as Henry Adams says, the proceedings were "[s]o confused, contradictory, and irregular" that Pickering's trial "was never considered a sound precedent."[150]

Although there were difficulties with the view, voiced by Giles, that a judge could be impeached for holding unpopular political views,[151] there were also objections to the view, voiced by the Federalists, that impeachment was only possible for indictable offenses.[152] Under the latter position, if some act short of a criminal misdemeanor were committed, or an act done that was not indictable because the accused was insane, and therefore lacked the necessary intent, the people were powerless to protect themselves. In the end, these difficulties could be overcome by interpreting the phrase tenure "during good behavior" to

---

148 *Ibid.*, I, 311. Senator Adams' eyewitness account of the trial will be found in *ibid.*, I, 302–304. See also W. Plumer to Dr. J. Park, Mar. 10, 1804, and W. Plumer to Judge J. Smith, Mar 11, 1804, in Letters 1804–1807, Plumer Papers, Manuscripts Division, Library of Congress.

149 Cutler and Cutler, *Rev. Manasseh Cutler*, II, 167–68.

150 H. Adams, *History of United States*, II, 158.

151 C. F. Adams, *John Quincy Adams*, I, 322.

152 This view was used by Chase's defense, Joseph Hopkinson and Luther Martin. See *Annals of Congress*, XIV, 354–94, 429–82 (8th Cong., 2d sess.).

require active execution of judicial office, and impeachable misdemeanors to include service while insane and failure to fulfill official duties.[153]

Needless to say, the Federalists were shocked by the conviction of an insane and friendless old man on the basis of ex parte evidence in proceedings in which there had been no real hearing and in which the accused had not even been represented by counsel. Just before the final question of conviction was put, Senator Plumer wrote to Jedidiah Morse:

> The idea of convicting a man of high crimes & misdemeanors, & inflicting punishment on him, when in a state of constant, confirmed insanity, incapable of discerning right from wrong, is certainly a novelty in judicial proceedings. I regret that it was reserved for the Senate of the United States to give the world such a precedent! . . . This decision will amount to a declaration, that whenever a majority of the House of Representatives accuse a judge, two thirds of the Senators present, may, if they please, under the *form of a trial* remove him from office. Conviction & removal will follow the accusation as certainly as it did in revolutionary France. The independence of our Judiciary is no more. We shall find that Paper constitutions are but feeble bulwarks ag⸀ the encroachments of the dominant party.[154]

Several days later he wrote to Thomas Thompson: "Impeachments are to be considered only as signals given by the House to the Senate to remove judges from office; & the question is, not whether the accused is guilty of crimes, but must he be removed?"[155] During the Senator's gloom, he wrote to Jeremiah Mason that it was

> the opinion of some gentlemen, who are not slaves to Virginia . . . That if a judge, circumstanced as he is, can be found guilty, the independence & security of the Judiciary is gone—That Chase, Peters, & other judges, who are to be impeached, will also be removed from office. . . . The judges of the Supreme Court must fall; they are

---

[153] C. F. Adams, *John Quincy Adams*, I, 310.

In March 1804 Adams wrote of the "principle assumed, though not yet openly avowed, that by the tenure of *good behaviour* is meant an active, continued, and unerring execution of office. So that insanity, sickness, any trivial error of conduct in a Judge, must be construed into misdemeanors, punishable by impeachment."

[154] W. Plumer to J. Morse, Mar. 10, 1804, Letters 1804–1807, Plumer

Papers, Manuscripts Division, Library of Congress. Despite extensive evidence of Pickering's reputation for intellectual ability and moral integrity in the years preceding his mental disintegration, he has suffered at the hands of modern historians. See L. W. Turner, *William Plumer of New Hampshire* (Chapel Hill, 1962), 123, note 50.

[155] W. Plumer to T. Thompson, Mar. 19, 1804, Letters 1804–1807, Plumer Papers, Manuscripts Division, Library of Congress.

denounced by the Executive, as well as the House. They must be removed; they are obnoxious unyielding men; & why should they remain to awe and embarrass administration? Men of more flexible nerves can be found to succeed them. Our affairs seem to approach an important crisis.[156]

In the aftermath of the Pickering trial political rewards were given to three of the New Hampshire witnesses against Pickering: the district attorney, John Sherburne, succeeded Pickering as district judge; John Steele, clerk of the Court, was appointed district attorney; and Shannon, the other star witness, succeeded him to the clerkship.[157] Steele refused the appointment and returned his commission on the ground that he was "unwillingly made a contributory instrument in creating vacancies,"[158] but Senator Plumer observed that the real reason for Steele's refusal was his disappointment that he had not been appointed district judge.[159]

F.   THE TRIAL OF CHASE

Republican strategy in the Chase trial followed the pattern set by that of Pickering. It was the aim of the Republicans to make impeachment an inquest into fitness for office rather than a criminal trial, so as to avoid what Senator Giles termed entanglement with the rules of courts. The Federalists, on the other hand, took the position expressed by Senator Plumer:

> There can be no principle of law better known, or that is more clearly founded in the reason & fitness of things, than That a Judge is never to be punished for error of judgment . . . the constitution authorizes the one house to impeach, & the other to try, civil officers *only* in case they have committed *high crimes & misdemeanors*.[160]

On March 26, 1804, the House committee reported seven articles of impeachment.[161] The first charged Chase with conducting himself "in a manner highly arbitrary, Oppressive, and unjust" in several particulars towards Fries. The second stated that, as a result of the "irregular conduct" set forth in the first, John Fries was condemned to death

---

[156] W. Plumer to J. Mason, Jan. 14, 1804, *Letters, 1781–1804, ibid.*
[157] Plumer, *Notes on Proceedings,* 274. For a printed version, see Brown, *Plumer's Memorandum of Proceedings,* 181.
[158] J. Steele to J. Madison, Apr. 24,

1804, Plumer, *Notes on Proceedings,* II, appendix 61.
[159] Brown, *Plumer's Memorandum of Proceedings,* 181.
[160] *Ibid.,* 232–33.
[161] *Annals of Congress,* XIII, 1237–40 (8th Cong., 1st sess.).

without having counsel "in manifest violation of law and justice." In the third article was the accusation that "Samuel Chase, with intent to oppress and procure the conviction of" James T. Callender in his sedition trial at Richmond in 1800 overruled the objection of John Bassett, a prospective juror, who wished to be excused from serving on the jury because he had made up his mind as to the criminality of the publication that was the basis for Callender's indictment. Article four charged the Judge with improperly rejecting the testimony at the Callender trial of Colonel John Taylor who appeared on behalf of the defendant. Article five contained very general charges of misconduct by Chase during the Callender trial, stating that his demeanor was characterized by "manifest injustice, partiality, and intemperance" in the use of rude and contemptuous expressions towards counsel and by repeated and vexatious interruptions. In the sixth article was the charge that Chase had stooped "to the level of an informer" by forcing a Delaware grand jury and district attorney in June 1800 to seek out an allegedly seditious printer after the jury had informed the Judge that they wished to be dismissed because of the lack of business to be investigated. That article also accused Chase of saying to the jury "that a highly seditious temper" existed in Delaware. The incident that had precipitated Jefferson's letter to Nicholson formed the basis of the seventh article. Chase in delivering his Baltimore jury charge was accused of uttering "an intemperate and inflammatory political harangue," intended to raise opposition and excite odium against the State of Maryland and the government of the United States.

These articles of impeachment, wrote John Quincy Adams to his father, "contained in themselves a virtual impeachment not only of Mr. Chase, but of all the judges of the Supreme Court from the first establishment of the national judiciary."[162] Without reference to the defense later mounted at the trial by Chase's counsel, both the nature of the articles and their ultimate object as a second major attack on the Court seem reasonably clear. The political hatred, grounded to a substantial extent on real fear that Republicans and Federalists felt towards each other, had again surfaced as an attack on institutions. The judicial process was being used, as it was again to be used in the Burr trial, for political ends. In the case of Chase, the impeachment was a further effort to break the power of the Federalists in the only area where they still had substantial power—a power that, if used even under a narrow construction of the Constitution, could defeat actions of the legislative and executive branches of the government. Chase's

---

[162] Adams to his father, Mar. 14, 1805, in W. C. Ford, ed., *Writings of* | *John Quincy Adams* (New York, 1913–17), III, 116.

enemies were confident that their case had been considerably strengthened by adding to the original articles the provision that additional
charges could be added at any later date.[163] It is particularly interesting
to note at this point the effort to expand the constitutional process of
impeachment to accomplish what to many—such as Senator Giles—
was a clearly political end, and to do it through whatever instruments
could be used for that purpose. It was not so much Chase's work on
the Supreme Court as his action in sedition cases, over which he presided on circuit, that aroused Republican wrath.

Judge Chase immediately wrote a circular letter, addressed to the
leading newspapers in the nation, in which he complained of the
"wanton venom and abuse" contained in the impeachment articles and
urged that they be presented against him in more precise form before
the adjournment of Congress. Leaping characteristically to the offensive, he demanded an immediate trial, assuring his Federalist readers
that this would surely repair his damaged reputation.[164] Chase's letter
was printed in a number of widely circulated newspapers, without respect to their political affiliations, but it provoked a quick retort from
the Republican press. The *National Intelligencer* asserted that it had
purposely withheld comment on the inquiry, but that it could resist no
longer from attacking the "boasted purity of a character that assumes
an unspotted reputation of forty years. . . ." The paper accused Chase
of distortions and untruths, and it characterized his letter as a "mass of
misrepresentation, seldom found in an anonymous essay."[165]

Congress adjourned before action was taken on the report of
Randolph's committee. Chase's friends immediately commenced to work
for what many feared was a hopeless cause. Edmund J. Lee wrote from
Virginia that he was gathering witnesses to testify in Chase's behalf, and
he added that he had been informed by John Bassett that his response to
questions during the Callender trial concerning his qualifications as a
juror had not been recorded accurately in the depositions collected by
the committee.[166] John Marshall assured his colleague that he was
making every effort to communicate with potential witnesses and to
collect favorable evidence. This information, he hoped, would be ready
by the opening of the next term of Court in February 1805.[167]

The Chief Justice's fears continued, however, to be reflected in
his correspondence. The articles were " 'sufficient to alarm the friends
of a pure, and, of course, an independent Judiciary, if, among those

---

[163] *Annals of Congress*, XIII, 1239–
40 (8th Cong., 1st sess.).
[164] *National Intelligencer*, Apr. 4,
1804.
[165] *Ibid.*

[166] E. Lee to S. Chase, Nov. 15,
1804, Etting Papers (Jurists) #17,
Pennsylvania Historical Society.
[167] J. Marshall to S. Chase, Jan. 23,
1804, Etting Manuscripts, *ibid.*

who rule our land there be any of that description,' " Marshall told his brother after Congress adjourned.[168]

The Republican press gloated over the anticipated success against Chase. " 'Whence and for what cause has originated this novel cry about the sanctity and impunity of Judges? It seems as if they had a charter from heaven to do as they pleased,' " railed the *Independent Chronicle*, " 'and it was sin against the elect to say, why do ye so? . . . Judge Chase has tried many a man, and doubtless acquitted some. It is his turn now to be tried, and this will be performed by at least as good and learned men as himself . . . namely the Senate of the United States.' "[169]

The Federalist newspapers now warned that Chase was only the first of the Supreme Court judges to be attacked: " 'Judge Chase was marked for the first victim. . . . All possible means have been used to embitter the public mind against him and to consign him to infamy and execration. . . . Behold this aged patriot, one of the pillars in our revolutionary struggle, rudely dragged by a Virginian stripling before the National tribunal.' "[170]

The theory behind the original articles of impeachment was not, however, the Giles view that had prevailed in the proceedings against Pickering. Summary proceedings would hardly suffice against so able and so widely known a man as Judge Chase. The charges, and the subsequent trial, make it entirely clear that Randolph now took the position that the Senate was a court and that there must be a formal trial in the course of which criminality would have to be proved. In this posture, the range of the attack appeared to be narrow, that is, against Chase rather than against the Supreme Court as a whole; but his conviction would at the very least serve as a stern warning to the other judges. Randolph's strategy, however, was deep. By the time the matter was again brought up in the House on December 3, 1804, two new articles had been quietly introduced, and two of the original articles had been combined, so that the total now numbered eight. A new fifth article charged that, contrary to the law of Virginia, where the case was tried, Chase had issued a capias against Callender, in accordance with federal practice on the basis of the 1789 Judiciary Act. No evil intent was alleged, as in the previously drawn articles, but the purpose was quite clearly to make error in law a ground for impeachment. The new sixth article went further and charged that Chase had ignored the mode of process usual in Virginia, with intent to oppress because Callender had been tried in the same term of court in which he had

---

[168] John Marshall to James M. Marshall, Apr. 1, 1804, in Beveridge, *John Marshall*, III, 176.

[169] Warren, *Supreme Court*, I, 279.
[170] *Ibid.*, 281, quoting from the *Connecticut Courant*.

been indicted. Since an early Supreme Court decision had held that the United States courts were not bound to follow the modes of process usual in the State courts,[171] conviction under this sixth article would have set a precedent for impeaching all the other judges whose practice was in accord with that decision. It seems clear that during the intervening months Randolph and his supporters had decided to broaden the charges by the insertion of the two new articles in order to turn the Chase proceedings into a precedent that would serve as a formidable political weapon for attacking the entire Court.[172]

Recent scholarship has given considerable attention to impeachment generally, and several writers have dealt expressly with the trial of Chase.[173] Even a summary of the various views expressed is not possible here, but certain of the views expressed merit both attention and comment. Efforts to reconstruct the English law of impeachment at the time of the framing of the Constitution are welcome, since the debates on the impeachment article reveal both familiarity and concern with English precedents. A review of those precedents permits certain general statements: first, that in England by the time of the American Revolution the standard of "high crimes and misdemeanors" had a limited meaning; second, that it included political crimes of a special nature; and third, that it was without roots in the ordinary criminal law and had no relation to whether an indictment might lie in the particular circumstances. These statements summarize a portion of Raoul Berger's reading,[174] based on thirteen impeachments from 1386 to 1695, as to what English impeachment was *not*, and it appears to be borne out in part by the proceedings at the Convention of 1787. It seems open to question, in the light of the Convention debates, whether the phrase in the Constitution was intended to have, in the form in which it finally appeared, a narrow and technical meaning.[175] It is therefore far more difficult to say what the framers expressly intended impeachment to be, especially in view of their wish to avoid certain pitfalls of exactitude and to concentrate on generalities at the expense of the specific and the technical.

A review of American colonial impeachments in the eighteenth century illustrates the political bias inherent in most impeachments— cases brought to trial not because the defendant had committed an indictable offense but because his actions had been politically unpopular.[176] In addition, many of the State constitutions after the Revolution contained impeachment provisions similar to English practice of the

---

[171] Berger, *Impeachment*, chapter 8.

[172] H. Adams, *John Randolph*, 138.

[173] See, e.g., Berger, *Impeachment*, 224–51.

[174] *Ibid.*, 67–69.

[175] *Ibid.*, 74, 86. See also *The Federalist* No. 79. (New York, 1901).

[176] Berger, *Impeachment*, 95.

time. The use of impeachment had tended to be against judges who could not be dismissed, denied office at the polls, or otherwise expelled.[177] In general, impeachments seem to have been "confined to political characters, or political crimes and misdemeanors, and to political punishments."[178] Although offenses that were considered grounds for impeachment might include those that were indictable, they were more likely, as Chief Justice Hughes later remarked, to be those involving serious political misbehavior.[179]

Against this background, the impeachment of Chase is understandable, and on its face the curious fact is that the Republican whips were unable to muster the required two-thirds vote in the Senate to convict him. It would be rash to say that under earlier English or American colonial standards he would have been convicted. But unquestionably the trial and conviction of Callender under the Sedition Act—which was an open wound in the Republicans' side—and the open criticism of the motives and policies of the government in his 1803 grand jury charge were "political" offenses as that term was understood by Republicans like Giles and Randolph. On the other hand, if "high crimes and misdemeanors" had in fact acquired a narrow and technical meaning, it is understandable, in light of the prosecution and defense at the trial, that even Republican Senators would not have wished to convict him.

Thus, the conduct of the trial, presided over by Vice-President Aaron Burr with extraordinary impartiality despite the favors that Jefferson had promised and secured for him (e.g., postponement of the indictment/murder charges in connection with the Hamilton duel), becomes important to note. Even though no clear-cut definition emerges of "high crimes and misdemeanors," the charges under the eight impeachment articles appear not to be indictable but indeed to melt away into the auras of political antipathies and personal vindictiveness. The trial itself has been vividly described more than once, and colorfully as well as effectively (though not without partiality) by Beveridge, so that a rehearsal of the pomp, circumstance, and fashionable attention given to it does not require repetition here.[180]

Probably among the most damaging of the impeachment articles against Chase were those relating to his conduct as circuit judge at the trial of Callender at Richmond under the Sedition Act, and, indeed, Raoul Berger's analysis of the impeachment focuses on four of those

---

[177] D. S. Alexander, *History and Procedure of the House of Representatives* (Boston, 1916), 331.

[178] J. D. Andrews, ed., *The Works of James Wilson* (Chicago, 1896), II, 46.

[179] C. E. Hughes, *The Supreme Court of the United States* (New York, 1928), 19.

[180] Beveridge, *John Marshall*, III, 179–222.

charges.[181] They alleged that Chase prejudged Callender's guilt, that he maliciously and illegally excluded testimony by a defense witness, that he refused to discharge a juror who, before trial, admitted that he had a predisposition to find the defendant guilty, and that he had been intolerably rude to defendant's attorneys—in short, that he had conducted himself in a manner "highly disgraceful to the character of a judge."[182] Despite the essentially political nature of the trial and the exonerating votes of the Republican-dominated Senate, Berger, among others, has concluded that on these charges alone Chase was guilty of high crimes and misdemeanors and that he should have been impeached. Chase's own defense and that of his attorneys took a technical line. Grave though the charges were, and serious enough, if believed, to have resulted in conviction, Chase—with respect to several of the charges—conceded the facts or sought to explain them away on the ground that his conduct, even if true, was excusable. Indeed, little time at the trial was spent on the facts, whereas a great deal was expended in attempting to show that Chase's conduct at the Callender trial was not unfair and at worst was indiscreet or grounded on unintentional mistakes of law insofar as Virginia procedure was involved. It is noteworthy that the statement of John Bassett that Chase behaved fairly and properly during the course of the Callender trial was not challenged.[183] Furthermore, George Hay, counsel for Callender, openly admitted that he hoped to turn that trial into a political statement of opposition to the Sedition Act[184] and that to that end he and other defense counsel baited Chase ceaselessly during the trial, interrupting him constantly and repeatedly asking him for postponement.[185]

The voting in the Senate was no across-the-board acquittal. To convict Chase required a two-thirds vote on any one of the impeachment articles, and when Burr read the totals there had not been the required constitutional majority of twenty-three votes on any one of them. Ironically, the Republicans were responsible for his acquittal, for, had they followed party lines and the wishes of Jefferson or Randolph, they could have mustered twenty-four votes. Six of them—possibly influenced by Madison—voted him innocent of all the charges. Even Senator Giles voted him not guilty on articles one, four, five, and six.

A variety of factors contributed to the failure of the impeachment attempt. There was a marked contrast between Randolph's management of the trial and the skillful handling of Chase's defense, and,

---

[181] Berger, *Impeachment*, 230–49.
[182] *Annals of Congress*, XIII, 1237–38 (8th Cong., 1st sess.).
[183] *Annals of Congress*, XIV, 224 (8th Cong., 2d sess.).

[184] *Ibid.*, 205 (8th Cong., 2d sess.).
[185] P. S. Clarkson and R. S. Jett, *Luther Martin of Maryland* (Baltimore, 1970), 216.

although Chase's circuit court behavior had been blameworthy, his excesses were to some extent counterbalanced by his record as a hero of the Revolution and by his unquestioned integrity on the Supreme Court. Furthermore, Republican anxieties had been allayed since the federal judiciary had not lived up to pretended fears and was fulfilling its duties responsibly. Broader political factors also contributed to the acquittal. Jefferson's visionary ideas and known hatred of Marshall were mitigating factors; the furor over the Sedition Act had subsided; the importance of an independent judiciary was being recognized; and Randolph had been alienating the Republicans as well as losing the support of Jefferson.

Neither the attempt at impeachment nor its failure was without effect. In the future, judges in general, and Chase in particular, were far more cautious in their grand jury charges.[186] Impeachment, having failed, was abandoned as a method of political attack, and Jefferson moved from the use of the third-party technique to direct attack, notably in his management of the treason trial of Aaron Burr. As that trial,[187] and also the controversies surrounding the Embargo,[188] were to show, the Court had not yet entirely succeeded in extricating itself from political turmoil. But in weathering the impeachment storm, the Court moved closer to its goal of being able to settle down to its judicial business as a recognized independent segment of the government.

---

[186] An examination of Chase's jury charges, note 52 supra, reveals the later moderation.

[187] See chapter 8 infra.
[188] See chapter 9 infra.

CHAPTER VIII

Habeas Corpus, Treason, and the Trial of Aaron Burr

JUSTIFICATIONS FOR including in this volume a chapter on the trial of Aaron Burr are obvious. Even though the indictment and trial took place in the federal Circuit Court at Richmond, and the case never reached the Supreme Court of the United States, the trial of Aaron Burr was intimately connected not only with the politics of the time but with the history of the Court. From a technical standpoint, the trial was an outgrowth and aftermath of *Ex parte Bollmann*,[1] a case the Supreme Court had decided on appeal, which involved many of the same constitutional problems and legal issues. Of the latter, among the most important for present purposes is the clear evidence of Marshall's efforts to define and separate the spheres of politics and of law, to secure more permanently the continued existence of the rule of law. The significance of the case, however, is much broader. Burr's trial raised issues of executive privilege and of the power of the judiciary to defeat assertions of that privilege; it provides further illustrations of the continuing personal clashes between Marshall and Jefferson; and, finally, it reveals another aspect of what Leonard Levy has termed "the darker side" of Thomas Jefferson and his political supporters.[2]

From another standpoint, the Burr trial provides illustrations of John Marshall's extraordinary legal talents at work on a case at the trial level, revealing not only the care and meticulousness of his scholarship and his keenly balanced judgment, but also his ability to reach out and formulate—on the basis of existing doctrine and accepted substantive and procedural rules—new and revised concepts in American law, notably that of treason. No one who has studied the full history of the Burr trial—and the existing documents and commentaries are

---

[1] 4 Cranch 75 (1807).
[2] L. Levy, *Jefferson and Civil Liber-* *ties: The Darker Side* (Cambridge, Mass., 1963).

voluminous—can leave it without reaching the conclusion that Marshall's capabilities as a lawyer were of the highest order. The trial evidences his intimate acquaintance with the English common law and statutes as well as with American constitutional law and precedents. The case likewise reaffirms the long-held conviction that Marshall was more than a great judicial statesman; he was an exceedingly able and perceptive judge of enormous understanding, competence, and learning, who set for himself the task of removing the judiciary from politics, so far as feasible, and of building a genuine "rule of law."

This chapter does not purport to recount the full history of the Burr case, nor even to deal with all its major aspects. Excellent commentaries have been written; many of them, but not all, have been published within the last two decades.[3] Beveridge, for example, regarded the Burr case as so important that he devoted nearly one-half of the third volume of his four-volume biography of John Marshall to the Burr "conspiracy," arraignment, and trial. It might further be noted that the printed record of the trial alone (without reference to related and extended debates reported in the *Annals of Congress*) amounts to some 400 pages.[4] Hence, it is no easy task concisely to place the Burr

---

[3] Among the standard studies are T. Abernethy, *The Burr Conspiracy* (New York, 1954); A. Beveridge, *The Life of John Marshall* (Boston, 1919), III, 274–545; D. Malone, *Jefferson and His Time: Jefferson the President, Second Term, 1805–09* (Boston, 1974), 215–370; Levy, *Jefferson and Civil Liberties*, 70–92; W. McCaleb, *The Aaron Burr Conspiracy*, 2d ed. (New York, 1936); W. McCaleb, *A New Light on Aaron Burr* (New York, 1963) (hereafter cited as McCaleb, *New Light on Burr*); F. Philbrick, *The Rise of the West: 1754–1830* (New York, 1965), 234–52; N. Schachner, *Aaron Burr, A Biography* (New York, 1937). McCaleb's writings have been consolidated into one volume published by Argosy-Antiquarian Ltd. (New York, 1966).

[4] See D. Robertson, *Reports of the Trials of Colonel Aaron Burr for Treason and for a Misdemeanor in the Circuit Court of the United States*, 2 vols. (Philadelphia, 1808) (hereafter cited as Robertson, *Burr Trial Reports*). Robertson's report, drawn from his shorthand notes of the trial proceedings, has been re-

printed by Da Capo Press (New York, 1969).

A copy of the trial proceedings was sent by Jefferson to Congress on Nov. 23, 1807. That copy is reproduced in J. Gales and W. Seaton, comps., *The Debates and Proceedings of the Congress of the United States* (Washington, 1834–56) (hereafter cited as *Annals of Congress*), XVII, 385–778 (10th Cong., 1st sess.). The Burr trial is also reported at some length (205 pages) in *Federal Cases*. The reporter segmented the proceedings into eleven cases (Nos. 14,692a–h, 14,693, 14,694a–b) "in order to render more accessible the various opinions delivered by the chief justice." United States v. Burr, 25 F. Cas. 2, n.1 (C.C.D. Va. 1807) (No. 14,692a). The reports are drawn from J. Coombs, *The Trial of Aaron Burr for High Treason* (Washington, 1864). An historical note on "Burr's Western Expedition in the Year 1806" is appended at 25 F. Cas. 15–25 (No. 14,692a), which is largely drawn from J. Parton, *The Life and Times of Aaron Burr* (New York, 1858).

trial within its political and legal setting, or to explain its significance as one of the greatest American criminal trials, and its relevance to the development of American law and of the Supreme Court as an American institution.

A. AARON BURR: AN EXPEDITION THAT FAILED

Aaron Burr was born of a distinguished family; his father had been the president of Princeton, and Jonathan Edwards was his maternal grandfather.[5] His services to his country during the Revolution—at Quebec, Monmouth, West Point, and elsewhere—were considered not only heroic but brilliant. After the War, Burr developed an extensive and distinguished law practice in New York, served in the United States Senate, and in 1801 missed being elected President of the United States instead of Jefferson "by the merest chance."[6] Personal antagonisms, particularly the persistent and venomous hostility of Alexander Hamilton, had resulted in numerous defeats for Burr in his attempts to secure public office in New York and elsewhere both before and after his term as Vice-President.[7] Although he had served with distinction as Vice-President under Jefferson, he made the political mistake of voting against the 1802 Judiciary Act in defiance of the Republican program.[8] Thereafter Burr progressively fell into disfavor with Republicans as well as with Federalists.[9] When he left office in March 1805, after fourteen years in politics, he was a ruined man, hopelessly in debt, his law practice gone, and his personal reputation close to destruction.[10] In New York he was under grand jury indictment for having challenged and killed Hamilton in their now famous duel. The New York coroner's inquest after the latter's death had found a verdict of willful murder,

---

[5] Beveridge, *John Marshall*, III, 276, note 1.

[6] *Ibid.*, 279. In the election of 1800, Republican electors failed to ensure the selection of Jefferson as President and Burr, his running-mate, as Vice-President when they cast an identical number of ballots for each man. Pursuant to Art. II, Sec. 1 of the Constitution, the election was decided by the House of Representatives. Each State was entitled to cast one vote, and on the thirty-fifth ballot Jefferson received the necessary majority of nine votes. Hamilton was instrumental in Jefferson's victory by persuading some of Burr's supporters to cast blank ballots. See J. Blum, B.

Catton, E. Morgan, A. Schlesinger, K. Stumpp, and C. Woodward, *The National Experience*, 2d ed. (New York, 1968), 164. The Twelfth Amendment, adopted in 1804, remedied the electoral college's procedures by directing the electors to "name in their ballots the person voted for as President, and in distinct ballots the person voted for as Vice-President. . . ."

[7] H. Adams, *History of the United States of America* (New York, 1891), II, 173–91; Beveridge, *John Marshall*, III, 277, note 1.

[8] Beveridge, *John Marshall*, 279.

[9] *Ibid.*

[10] *Ibid.*, 276.

and in New Jersey, where the duel was fought, Burr was named in a second indictment for murder.[11]

Available evidence points to the conclusion that it was at this time that Burr decided to seek his fortunes in the West. How clearly formed his plans were is not entirely certain, but he seems generally to have envisaged two distinct courses: first, if a war with Spain were to be declared—and to many, including the President,[12] that eventuality seemed reasonably certain at the time—he would help to lead an expedition into and conquer Mexico; second, if there were no war, he intended to settle the enormous Baron Bastrop land grant on the Washita River, west of the Mississippi, where he had arranged to make vast purchases.[13] In the course of a tour of the western States, in the spring and summer of 1805, Burr had been given a hero's welcome—notably in Tennessee by his fervent admirer Andrew Jackson, and likewise in New Orleans, by his former comrade-in-arms General James Wilkinson.[14] Wilkinson was commander of the American Army and Governor of the Territory of Louisiana; nevertheless, at the same time he was a pensioner of the Spanish government.[15] Wilkinson favored the Mexican expedition and other exploits,[16] but it was he who ultimately ruined Burr and provided the basis for the charges of conspiracy and treason brought against him.

The gist of the charges levied against Burr was that he had engaged in a treasonous conspiracy to revolutionize the West by force of arms. It is pertinent to note that "dismemberment of the Union" had been periodically under contemplation by the extreme Federalists of the New

---

[11] *Ibid.*, 285–86; McCaleb, *Burr Conspiracy*, 12. McCaleb states that these indictments were issued in spite of the fact that all of the rules required under the duelling code had been observed by Burr. In 1804, "duelling was an ordinary mode of settling personal differences." E. Channing, *A History of the United States* (New York, 1917), I, 296–97.

[12] The President adverted to the threat of a Spanish war in messages to Congress on Dec. 3, 1805, and Dec. 6, 1805. See *Annals of Congress*, XV, 11–16, 18–19 (9th Cong., 1st sess.).

[13] McCaleb has concluded that the possession of the Washita lands was of secondary importance to Burr's primary plan to lead a Mexican expedition, and that the land grant provided a tangible object to attract participants in his expedition and a legitimate cover for his real purposes. McCaleb, *Burr Conspiracy*, 76.

[14] *Ibid.*, 30–41.

[15] Beveridge, *John Marshall*, III, 283; McCaleb, *New Light on Burr*, 12. There is evidence that Wilkinson was enrolled as a pensioner of Spain from 1787 until 1807. See D. Clark, *Proofs of the Corruption of General James Wilkinson and of his Connexion with Aaron Burr* (Philadelphia, 1809), 11–12, 16, 18–24.

[16] McCaleb asserts that the "Burr Conspiracy" was "incubated" by Burr and Wilkinson, following the latter's design, in Washington during the winter of 1804-1805. McCaleb, *New Light on Burr*, 12. Philbrick takes a different view of those meetings. See note 21 infra.

England States,[17] and that the Spanish had long attempted to sow the seeds of disunion in the West.[18] It should be recalled that Jefferson himself had not been averse to the partitioning of the Republic should that prove desirable,[19] and he had expressed that sentiment in an 1803 letter to John C. Breckenridge in which he defended the Louisiana Purchase.[20]

The extent to which Wilkinson intended to betray his country to serve the interests of his Spanish employers is still a matter of controversy, but the furtherance of his personal interests was clearly his prime motivation.[21] Burr, on the other hand, appears to have had no real plans to dismember the Union, and it was probably obvious to him in 1805 that western sentiment did not support such a course of action.[22] In order to obtain money for his forthcoming Mexican expedition, however, Burr followed the example of the New England Federalists[23] and approached the British Minister, Anthony Merry, with a request for several frigates and smaller vessels and a loan of one hundred thousand pounds, allegedly for the purpose of "the revolutionizing of the Western States."[24] He plainly lied when he suggested that, like the Northeastern Federalists, the Westerners could be encouraged to separate and that many were anxious to have Burr lead them. He told the British that if their support was not forthcoming, the inhabitants of

---

[17] Beveridge, *John Marshall*, III, 282–84.

[18] Beveridge states that General Wilkinson was retained on the Spanish payroll in order to facilitate the Spanish acquisition of American western lands. *Ibid.*, 283.

[19] See chapter 1 supra.

[20] The future inhabitants of the Atlantic & Missipi States will be our sons. We leave them in distinct but bordering establishments. We think we see their happiness in their union, & we wish it. Events may prove it otherwise; and if they see their interest in separation, why should we take side with our Atlantic rather than our Missipi descendants? It is the elder and the younger son differing. God bless them both, & keep them in union, if it be for their good, but separate them, if it be better. T. Jefferson to J. Dickinson, Aug. 12, 1803, in P. L. Ford, ed., *The Works of Thomas Jefferson* (New York, 1904–1905) X, 28–30.

[21] See Wilkinson's trial testimony in *Annals of Congress*, XVII, 589–609, 616–22 (10th Cong., 1st sess.). Philbrick has concluded, unlike others, that there is no evidence that Wilkinson was a traitor. Philbrick, *Rise of the West*, 252, note 48.

[22] McCaleb paints the following portrait of the western views which Burr saw first-hand during his 1805 travels: "Everywhere was talk of war with Spain over the boundaries of Louisiana. The questions uppermost in the minds of Westerners were: 'When do we get at them? How far is it to Santa Fe? How far is it to the City of Mexico?'" McCaleb, *New Light on Burr*, 13. The West was a hotbed of nationalism, not disunion. *Ibid.*, 8–9.

[23] Beveridge states that five months before Burr commenced his intrigues with the British Minister, "Pickering, Griswold, and other New England Federalists had approached Anthony Merry with their plan to divide the Union." Beveridge, *John Marshall*, III, 288.

[24] *Ibid.*

Louisiana would doubtless turn to France.[25] Nevertheless, Burr's efforts to gain British funds failed.[26]

General Wilkinson and Colonel Burr had been close friends as well as fellow officers during the Revolutionary War. It is not surprising, therefore, that they should have resumed that friendly relationship later on when Wilkinson had been put in command of the armies. Moreover, as is now well known, they had long had a secret cipher between them for correspondence—and its use was soon to prove disastrous to Burr.[27] Among matters that they still had in common was the promotion of parallel, though perhaps largely independent, personal self-interests. Those interests crossed and coalesced insofar as the Southwest and Spanish territories were concerned, particularly if war with Spain were to break out. It seems probable that in the winter of 1804–1805 Wilkinson at the very least gave Burr reason to hope for a military or other appointment in an impending war with Spain, yet there does not appear to be any evidence of a wrongful compact between them.[28] Wilkinson had virtually promised Burr that there would be a war with Spain, thereby fueling Burr's plans for a glorious expedition against Mexico. Wilkinson's own interests would have tended towards leading such an expedition himself.[29]

During the early part of 1806 Burr was busy in the East with his projected expedition.[30] By August he had stirred the interest of a number of young men eager for adventure and had scheduled a rendezvous for November on the Ohio River. Land grants in the Washita tract, which were valuable for access to the New Orleans market and to local Indian trade,[31] were promised to many of the men recruited. As Burr headed westward for a second time, with war against Spain "on every tongue,"[32] his headquarters at Harman Blennerhassett's Island in western Virginia bustled with activity as provisions were gathered, boats built, and recruits prepared. Under Blennerhassett's direction, the Island was transformed into a supply-center for cornmeal, barrels of pork, and other foods needed for the expedition south.[33]

[25] The details of Burr's request are reported in a letter from A. Merry to Lord Harrowby, Mar. 29, 1805, in Adams, *History of United States*, II, 403; McCaleb, *Burr Conspiracy*, 25–28.

[26] H. Adams, *History of United States*, III, 229, 233.

[27] *Ibid.*, III, 219, 246.

[28] Philbrick, *Rise of the West*, 246–48.

[29] *Ibid.*, 247.

[30] McCaleb, *Burr Conspiracy*, 60–66.

[31] *Ibid.*, 76.

[32] *Ibid.*, 74.

[33] *Ibid.*, 73, 80. Burr's partner, Blennerhassett, was "a romantic Irish exile, . . . fascinated with a plan to conquer Mexico, to make Burr emperor, and himself a grand potentate of the court." S. Morison and H. Commager, *The Growth of the American Republic*, 4th ed. (New York, 1950), I, 399.

Meanwhile, the basis for later conspiracy charges was forming. Late in 1805 the Spanish occupied two outposts on American soil east of the Sabine River. After withdrawing under protest, they reoccupied them in March 1806. In March, and later in May of 1806, Secretary of War Dearborn ordered Wilkinson to leave his headquarters in St. Louis and drive off the Spanish.[34] Wilkinson's response was to do nothing, even though the second order was "specially authorized by the President of the United States."[35] At this point, with war virtually at hand, and only Wilkinson's inaction standing in the way of his expedition, Burr evidently sought to push Wilkinson into action, directly and through intermediaries such as his friend Senator Jonathan Dayton of New Jersey.[36] On July 29, 1806, Burr sent off his famous cipher letter to Wilkinson, written in the East just before he started west. It was this letter, later altered by Wilkinson, that became the chief evidence against Burr in his treason trial.[37] In that communication, after acknowledging a letter from Wilkinson, dated May 13, 1806, Burr outlined plans for a rendezvous on the Ohio River in November, and indicated that money and men would be available for their expedition. He stated that British and American naval forces were "ready to join,"[38] but he did not refer directly to Mexico, nor did he propose that a war with Spain be provoked. A Wilkinson letter to Burr written in May crossed this one; in effect it stated, "I am waiting for you."[39] Burr sent one copy of his July 29 letter overland in the care of one Samuel Swartwout, a youth of twenty-two, and the other by sea to New Orleans by Dr. Justus Erich Bollmann, who had become a warm supporter of Burr's western enterprise, and, incidentally, had been instrumental earlier in rescuing Lafayette from prison in Vienna.[40]

To cut through, without detailed description, the tangled web of rumors, allegations, self-serving declarations, and the tissues of lies that beset the path of Burr's ambitions is an almost hopeless task. Conflicting interests detailed in newspaper reports, letters, and conversations have been traced at length in the scholarly works cited herein. Nonetheless, even in the face of these complexities, the conclusion of Professor

---

[34] McCaleb, *New Light on Burr*, 20–26; Philbrick, *Rise of the West*, 241.

[35] McCaleb, *New Light on Burr*, 26.

[36] J. Dayton to J. Wilkinson, July 24, 1806, in *Annals of Congress*, XVII, 560 (10th Cong., 1st sess.).

[37] The letter is reproduced by Beveridge, *John Marshall*, III, 614–15; McCaleb, *Burr Conspiracy*, 68–69. McCaleb states that the letter was "altered and deciphered in various

ways by Wilkinson," *ibid.*, 68; Philbrick states only that it has been "somewhat variantly translated." Philbrick, *Rise of the West*, 248.

[38] Philbrick, *Rise of the West*, 249, believes that given the absurdities within the letter, it was intended as a joke.

[39] *Ibid.*, 248.

[40] Beveridge, *John Marshall*, III, 307, note 1; see McCaleb, *Burr Conspiracy*, 70.

Francis S. Philbrick seems sound: there was no conspiracy to commit treason, and no intent to do so either by levying war or dismembering the Union, on the part of Aaron Burr.[41] Historians have continued to employ the word "conspiracy" to describe Burr's actions in the West that led to his trial and ultimate acquittal, but it seems apparent that the term has been inappropriately used.[42]

As early as 1805 various persons had begun to weld together rumors about Burr's possible intentions with respect to provoking secession in the West.[43] Newspaper publication of such rumors alarmed many Westerners,[44] but apparently neither Jefferson nor his Cabinet gave credence to the lurid tales of Burr's alleged "treasonable" purposes periodically brought to their attention. This is borne out by Cabinet memoranda of October 22 and 25, 1806, in which favorable reports of Burr's activities were noted.[45] Others, notably Joseph Daveiss, United States Attorney for the District of Kentucky, had also been reporting word of a western conspiracy to Jefferson,[46] and early in November Daveiss succeeded in having Burr charged before a grand jury with violating the laws of the United States by planning to invade Mexico and plotting a secession of the West. Defended by the young Senator-elect, Henry Clay, and supported by the local populace, Burr was discharged.[47]

During the summer of 1806 the crafty Wilkinson was apparently aware of Burr's growing disfavor with Jefferson and others in the federal government. Wilkinson's own reputation had been damaged by his failure to obey orders during the course of events along the Sabine in the spring, and evidently he hoped to regain the administration's confidence by denouncing Burr. The July 29 cipher letter from Burr provided him with an opportunity, and two weeks after its receipt, on October 20, 1806, he wrote Jefferson that "a numerous and powerful association" of unknown origins planned to rendezvous in New Orleans and attack Vera Cruz.[48] To save himself from published accusations—including the charges that he was a pensioner of Spain and linked with

---

[41] Philbrick, *Rise of the West*, 248–51.

[42] *Ibid.*, 247.

[43] These speculations may have been fueled by letters written by Blennerhassett to an Ohio newspaper in which he called for separation of the western States. Beveridge, *John Marshall*, III, 311.

[44] Adams, *History of United States*, III, 275–76.

[45] *Ibid.*, 278–80, 281; Beveridge, *John Marshall*, III, 323.

[46] Beveridge, *John Marshall*, III, 315.

[47] *Ibid.*, 317–19; Adams, *History of United States*, III, 277–78. See United States v. Burr, 25 F. Cas. 1 (C.C.D. Ky. 1806) (No. 14,692) (district Judge refusing to issue a warrant himself for Burr's arrest on Daveiss' motion, but summoning a grand jury).

[48] McCaleb, *Burr Conspiracy*, 123; Beveridge, *John Marshall*, III, 320–21.

Burr in a Spanish conspiracy to sever the Union—Wilkinson wrote a second confidential letter to Jefferson on the twenty-first, denouncing the alleged plans of the unnamed conspirators and reporting pretended details of the enterprise in terms of its magnitude and consequences.[49] Unctuously, he went on to say that he was "uninformed of the prime mover and Ultimate Objects of this daring Enterprize [and] ignorant of the foundation on which it rests."[50] (It was this second letter that subsequently became the object of a subpoena *duces tecum* issued by John Marshall to the President.[51]) At this point, Jefferson took immediate action and issued his famous Proclamation of November 27, declaring that a conspiracy by American citizens to engage in a military expedition against Spain had been discovered, warning citizens engaged therein to withdraw, and directing the authorities to seize the conspirators' vessels, arms, and military stores.[52]

Although Burr had not been referred to by name in the Proclamation, and no more than a conspiracy unlawfully to attack the Spanish had been charged (that is, treason had not been alleged), it was not difficult—in the light of circulating newspaper stories linking Burr to a conspiracy to dismember the Union—to conclude that he was the object of the Proclamation, and that its issuance was directed against a far greater crime than incitement of a war already anticipated. These conclusions were given substance, at least in the Southwest, by irresponsible public accusations made against Burr by Wilkinson in November and December 1806 in which he declared to the people of New Orleans that the enemy, "at least 2000 strong," was en route, planned to sack their city, attack Mexico, and if successful, separate the West from the Union.[53] At this time, "Burr had not even started down the Mississippi with his nine boats manned by sixty young men."[54]

Other developments rapidly ensued. On January 16, 1807, John Randolph rose in the House to demand clarification of the November proclamation, and after a heated debate a resolution was passed requesting the President "to lay before this House . . . information" respecting the conspiracy.[55] Jefferson replied in a special message to the Senate and House on January 22, in which he named Burr, *"whose guilt is placed beyond question,"* as the "prime mover" in a conspiracy

---

[49] McCaleb, *Burr Conspiracy*, 125.

[50] J. Wilkinson to T. Jefferson, Oct. 21, 1806, in Beveridge, *John Marshall*, III, 322.

[51] See text accompanying notes 178–92 infra.

[52] "Proclamation Against Burr's Plot" in Ford, *Works of Jefferson*, X, 301–302.

[53] Beveridge, *John Marshall*, III, 331. See McCaleb, *Burr Conspiracy*, 170–81, for a full account of Wilkinson's actions.

[54] Beveridge, *John Marshall*, III, 331.

[55] *Annals of Congress*, XVI, 334–59 (9th Cong., 2d sess.).

to sever the Union and attack Mexico.[56] Needless to say, Burr's alleged guilt had not been established at this time by any lawful process. As John Adams remarked, "if his guilt is as clear as the Noon day Sun, the first Magistrate ought not to have pronounced it so before a Jury had tryed him."[57] Nevertheless, "[f]rom that moment, the popular mind was made up, and the popular voice demanded the life of Aaron Burr."[58]

As Jefferson was able to report in his message to Congress, the arrest of Samuel Swartwout and Dr. Bollmann had already taken place in December. Burr's messengers had been seized by Wilkinson, as commander of the Army, in New Orleans during a "reign of lawless violence that has no parallel in American history."[59] Both men were denied counsel and access to the courts and sent by warship to Baltimore for delivery into the hands of the President. In the case of Bollmann, a court order in response to his application in New Orleans for a writ of habeas corpus was defied by Wilkinson on the grounds of national security and because Bollmann was accused of treason against the United States.[60] At this point, Wilkinson forwarded to Jefferson his own version of the July 29 cipher letter from Burr, together with an account of his arrest of Bollmann and Swartwout.[61] Wilkinson's other lawless acts have been detailed elsewhere and require no repetition,[62] but it should be noted that while the General was parading his patriotism, he was still secretly serving Spain and receiving money from its envoys.[63]

Upon arrival in Baltimore, Bollmann and Swartwout were placed under military guard and taken to Washington for imprisonment. There they were held, pending decision on an application to William Cranch, Chief Judge of the Circuit Court of the District of Columbia, to issue a bench warrant against them on a charge of treason, and to hold them for trial.[64] The prisoners were represented by eminent counsel: Charles Lee, Robert Goodloe Harper, and Francis Scott Key. On January 27, after long arguments, the court divided on what had now become a political issue, for in the evidence presented by United States Attorney Jones was a copy of the message sent to Congress by Jefferson on January 22. Jones also stated he was acting "in obedience to instruc-

---

[56] *Ibid.*, 39–43 (emphasis supplied).
[57] J. Adams to B. Rush, Feb. 2, 1807, in Beveridge, *John Marshall*, III, 338, note 2.
[58] Beveridge, *John Marshall*, III, 342.
[59] *Ibid.*, 332.
[60] McCaleb, *Burr Conspiracy*, 183.
[61] *Annals of Congress*, XVI, 43 (9th Cong., 2d sess.); see Beveridge, *John Marshall*, III, 334.

[62] See J. Jacobs, *Tarnished Warrior* (New York, 1938), 234–36; R. Shreve, *The Finished Scoundrel* (Indianapolis, 1933), 171–85.
[63] See Beveridge, *John Marshall*, III, 332–36, 337.
[64] United States v. Bollmann, 24 F. Cas. 1189 (C.C.D.C. 1807) (No. 14,622).

tions received from the president of the United States, whose wish was that [Bollmann and Swartwout] should be surrendered to the civil authority."[65] Cranch, the lone Federalist appointee on the Court, was in favor of discharging the prisoners for want of probable cause,[66] but his two Republican colleagues, Fitzhugh and Duckett, ruled that they should be imprisoned without bail, and held for trial for treason by levying war.[67] Counsel for the prisoners then applied to the United States Supreme Court for a writ of habeas corpus, and on February 5 Chief Justice Marshall directed the jailer to show cause why the writ should not issue.[68]

Meanwhile, on January 23, Senator Giles of Virginia, well known as Jefferson's unofficial representative in the Senate,[69] secured the speedy passage of a bill to suspend the privilege of the habeas corpus writ.[70] A few days later, however, on January 26, the House, astounded by the Senate's actions, rejected the bill by a vote of 113–19.[71] Thus, the Supreme Court did not lose its jurisdiction to decide the case of Bollmann and Swartwout.

As one of about a dozen constitutional law cases that came before the Court in the period covered by this volume, the *Bollmann* case has great importance, especially in its pertinence to Marshall's efforts to de-politicize the judicial process, on which he had already taken a firm stand.[72] Further, the relevance of the *Bollmann* decision with respect to evidence of the conspiracy and the law of treason in the later trial of Burr himself is obvious. That relevance is enhanced by the fact that the decision in *Burr* was to be rendered by John Marshall himself, sitting on circuit. The *Bollmann* case has added significance in that the de-

---

[65] *Ibid.*, 1189.

[66] *Ibid.*, 1192–93 (Cranch, C. J., dissenting).

[67] *Ibid.*, 1193–94 (Duckett, J); 1194–96 (Fitzhugh, J.). John Quincy Adams reported to his father that the trial provoked such interest that the Senate was "scarcely able here to form a quorum . . . and the House . . . actually adjourned." J. Q. Adams to J. Adams, Jan. 30, 1807, in Beveridge, *John Marshall*, III, 346.

[68] *Ex parte Bollman*, 4 Cranch 75, 75 note * (1807).

[69] Beveridge, *John Marshall*, III, 346.

[70] In successive motions on the floor of the Senate that day, Giles had himself appointed to a committee along with John Quincy Adams and Samuel Smith of Maryland to consider suspension of the privilege,

reported a bill out of the committee, resolved that it should be passed as amended, and moved that the following message be delivered to the House: "The Senate have passed a bill suspending for three months the privilege of the writ of *habeas corpus*, in certain cases, which they think expedient to communicate to you in confidence, and to request your concurrence therein, as speedily as the emergency of the case shall, in your judgment, require." *Annals of Congress*, XVI, 44 (9th Cong., 2d sess.). Evidently only Senator Bayard of Delaware voted against the bill. J. Q. Adams to J. Adams, Jan. 27, 1807, in Beveridge, *John Marshall*, III, 347.

[71] See *Annals of Congress*, XVI, 402–25 (9th Cong., 2d sess.).

[72] See chapter 6 supra.

cision outlined below fired radical Republicans to the point of urging a constitutional amendment to remove criminal jurisdiction from the Supreme Court and even to impeach the entire Court.[73]

In an opinion issued on February 13, 1807, Marshall held that the Supreme Court was granted jurisdiction to issue writs of habeas corpus by Section 14 of the Judiciary Act of 1789: "[A] court possessing the power to bail prisoners not committed by itself, may award a *habeas corpus* for the exercise of that power."[74] To the objection that the writ ought not be granted when a lower court having the power to commit a prisoner and award bail had acted, Marshall answered that *United States* v. *Hamilton*[75] was precedent for the Supreme Court's jurisdiction to grant the writ in such a case.[76] Marshall then considered whether Congress' grant of jurisdiction to issue the writ in the present case was constitutional. If Bollmann and Swartwout had presented their applications for a writ to the Supreme Court in the first instance, he indicated that a case outside the original jurisdiction granted the Court by Article III, as in *Marbury* v. *Madison*,[77] would have been presented, and the congressional grant of jurisdiction would have been unconstitutional. However, Marshall found that the jurisdiction the Court was being asked to exercise in this case was clearly appellate. "It is the revision of a decision of an inferior court, by which a citizen has been committed to jail."[78] Justice Johnson, dissenting,[79] stated that Section 14 of the Judiciary Act vested only original power, which could be exercised by individual Supreme Court judges, but for the Court as a body to issue a writ of habeas corpus was outside the limitations of Article III, as construed in *Marbury*.[80] Contemporaneously with the proceedings in the Supreme Court, a motion by Representative Broom of Delaware, offered on February 7, to "make further provision for securing the privilege of the writ of habeas corpus," was the subject of considerable debate,[81] although it was eventually indefinitely postponed by a narrow margin of 60–58, on February 19.[82]

Following the Court's February 13 decision, Charles Lee moved that the prisoners be discharged or admitted to bail, because of technical deficiencies in the order of commitment, while Key contended

---

[73] Beveridge, *John Marshall*, III, 357.

[74] *Ex parte Bollmann*, 4 Cranch 75, 100 (1807).

[75] 1 Dall. 17 (1795).

[76] 4 Cranch at 100.

[77] 1 Cranch 137 (1803).

[78] 4 Cranch at 101.

[79] Judge Chase, who was prevented by ill health from attending, concurred with Johnson. Beveridge, *John*

Marshall, III, 349, note 1. Judges Washington and Livingston joined with Marshall. Judge Cushing was also absent. 4 Cranch at 93, note *.

[80] 4 Cranch at 103–107 (Johnson, J., dissenting).

[81] See *Annals of Congress*, XVI, 472, 502–54, 555–90 (9th Cong., 2d sess.).

[82] *Ibid.*, 590.

that the Court should examine whether there were grounds to hold the prisoners for a charge of treason.[83] On February 17 Marshall ruled that "it is unimportant whether the commitment be regular in form or not" and that the Supreme Court would examine the sufficiency of the evidence upon which the commitment was grounded, as "the court below ought to have done."[84] Four days of argument then commenced on the sufficiency of the evidence of treason, focusing on the affidavit of General Wilkinson. The prisoners' position was put forward by Luther Martin as well as by Key and Harper; the Government was represented by United States Attorney Jones, and Attorney-General Caesar Rodney.[85] Finally, Marshall delivered his opinion for a unanimous Court on February 21.

Marshall began by stating that the scope of the Court's inquiry was whether the accused should be discharged or held for trial, and if the latter, to determine the place of trial and the possibility of bail. They would be discharged, he said, only if " 'it manifestly appears that no such crime has been committed, or that the suspicion entertained of the prisoner was wholly groundless.' "[86] He noted that the specific charge brought against Bollmann and Swartwout was treason in levying war against the United States, and quoted the constitutional definition of treason in Article III, Section 3: "Treason against the United States shall consist only in levying war against them, or in adhering to their enemies, giving them aid and comfort."[87] He held that to support this charge of treason, war must have actually been levied, and distinguished the crime of conspiring to levy war, which would not constitute treason.[88] In the case of levying war, he said, it "must be brought into operation by the assemblage of men for a purpose treasonable in itself, or the fact of levying war cannot have been committed."[89] It was not necessary that a man actually appear in arms against his country, for "if a body of men be actually assembled for the purpose of effecting by force a treasonable purpose, all those who perform any part, however minute, or however remote from the scene of the action, and who are actually leagued in the general conspiracy, are to be considered as traitors."[90] This latter dictum, dealing with a matter not directly before the Court, was to be a source of embarrassment to Marshall in the *Burr* trial, for if evidence of levying war were proved against those on Blennerhassett's Island, it could be argued that Burr was at least an accessory.[91] It also raised a question, later to be resolved in *Burr*,

---

[83] 4 Cranch at 108–109 (C. Lee); *ibid.* at 111–14 (F. Key).
[84] *Ibid.*, 114.
[85] *Ibid.*, 114–24.
[86] *Ibid.*, 125 (quoting "a very learned and accurate commentator").

[87] *Ibid.*, 126.
[88] *Ibid.*
[89] *Ibid.*
[90] *Ibid.*
[91] See text accompanying notes 238–39 infra.

whether in treason "all are principals"—the English doctrine of constructive treason.[92]

To test the sufficiency of the evidence of "levying war" in *Bollmann*, Marshall proceeded to state that a mere "enlisting" of men is not an actual levying of war until they assemble, and that such an assembling is not necessarily an overt act of treason unless it is for the purpose of executing a treasonable design.[93] In examining the evidence the Court was faced with a difficulty regarding the admissibility of that portion of Wilkinson's affidavit that purported to be "as near the substance of the [July 29 cipher] letter from Colonel Burr to General Wilkinson as the latter could interpret it."[94] The Court divided two to two on whether a commitment for probable cause could be founded on such evidence, which could not be admitted at trial, and Marshall "deemed [it] necessary to look into the affidavit" to determine "whether, if admitted, it contains matter which would justify the commitment of the prisoners . . . on the charge of treason."[95] Marshall concluded that not one syllable of the letter "has a necessary or a natural reference to an enterprize against any territory of the United States,"[96] although he recognized that its vague wording suggested an expedition against Mexico which would constitute a high misdemeanor.[97] Although such an expedition would be an indictable offense, it was not the offense charged; nor was the offense committed within the District of Columbia, so the prisoners could not be tried there consistently with the Sixth Amendment. Marshall rejected the view that, because the prisoners were apprehended by military rather than civil authority, General Wilkinson might lawfully have them tried in whatever place he selected.[98] Emphasizing that the decision of the Court did not acquit Bollmann and Swartwout of the misdemeanor, but only required the prosecution to institute proceedings in the place where the offense was committed, the judges held that the prisoners must be discharged, because they had not committed the offense charged.[99]

Chief Justice Marshall's February 21 opinion in *Bollmann* is more noteworthy for his discussion on the meaning of "levying war" than for his assessment of the evidence of levying war before him. Nonetheless, the evidence requires a brief summary because of its later importance in the *Burr* case. There had been *acts*: a few men had gathered boats at Blennerhassett's Island on the Ohio River, in Wood County, Virginia, and they had sailed down the River. But the Court found no evidence

---

92 See text accompanying notes 226–37 infra; J. W. Hurst, *The Law of Treason in the United States* (Westport, Conn., 1971), 88–89.
93 4 Cranch at 127.
94 *Ibid.*, 130.

95 *Ibid.*, 131.
96 *Ibid.*, 132–33.
97 *Ibid.*, 131.
98 *Ibid.*, 136.
99 *Ibid.*, 136–37.

of *purposes* treasonable in themselves, let alone acts of aggression against the United States. The acts did not demonstrate the requisite intent for the offense charged. It followed, to those who were later to rely on *Bollmann* in the *Burr* case, that Burr's activities were not treasonable, and hence that those of his associates were not acts of accessories, or "principals," even under the common law doctrine that in treason all are principals.[100]

The famous dictum in *Bollmann*, referred to above, has occasionally led historians to say that John Marshall later reversed himself in *Burr* in order to spite Jefferson.[101] However, such a conclusion overlooks the careful way in which Marshall was attempting (aside from the unfortunate dictum) to define treason so that the rights of individuals would be secured by the rule of law, and not be at the mercy of the passions of men. He was concerned lest the definition of this crime be tailored in an ex post facto fashion to fit the actions of particular dissenting citizens.[102] Contrary to this concern, the dictum in *Bollmann* went too far, or was too general, in considering those only remotely involved in a conspiracy that developed into treason to be traitors as well. In *Burr*, John Marshall realized this inconsistency and framed a narrower and more precise definition of treason that did not coincide with the common law definition of "constructive treasons."

Among the points that Marshall was attempting to establish in *Bollmann* were the following: (1) to define treason as an act of levying war against the United States; (2) to make it clear that a military commander, specifically General Wilkinson, could not lawfully imprison men, under the pretense of public safety and martial law, and have

---

[100] See text accompanying notes 234–39 infra.

[101] See E. Corwin, *John Marshall and the Constitution* (New Haven, Conn., 1919), 108–109.

[102] Consider, for example, Marshall's articulation of this concern in *Bollmann*:

Crimes so atrocious as those which have for their object the subversion by violence of those laws and those institutions which have been ordained in order to secure the peace and happiness of society, are not to escape punishment because they have not ripened into treason. The wisdom of the legislature is competent to provide for the case; and the framers of our constitution, who not only defined and limited the crime, but with jealous circumspection attempted to protect their limitation by providing that no person should be convicted of it, unless on the testimony of two witnesses on the same overt act, or on confession in open court, *must have conceived it more safe that punishment in such cases should be ordained by general laws, formed upon deliberation, under the influence of no resentments, and without knowing on whom they were to operate, than that it should be inflicted under the influence of those passions which the occasion seldom fails to excite, and which a flexible definition of the crime, or a construction which would render it flexible, might bring into operation.*

4 Cranch at 126–27 (emphasis supplied).

them tried in whatever place he selected; and (3) to establish that those who committed acts short of treason could be punished pursuant to criminal sanctions of general applicability enacted by the legislature, "formed upon deliberation," but without particular "resentments" or "passions."[103]

The last point was probably, as Beveridge states, intended as a rebuke to Jefferson, for "[t]here can be no doubt that Marshall was referring to the recent attempt to deprive Bollmann and Swartwout of the protection of the courts by suspending the writ of habeas corpus."[104] All three points were designed to insure that the rule of law would supersede political opportunism disguised by a veil of supposed national security. Strict construction, and adherence to the law enunciated by the Constitution, required "that the crime of treason should not be extended by construction to doubtful cases; and that crimes not clearly within the constitutional definition, should receive such punishment as the legislature in its wisdom may provide."[105]

Congress had not been unaware of the dangers of the administration's attempt to suspend the writ of habeas corpus. The debates in the House over Representative Broom's resolution, mentioned earlier, "to make further provision for securing the writ of habeas corpus," reveal that Congress had not missed the threat to law and government posed by Wilkinson's actions in New Orleans and Jefferson's support of them. On February 17 Broom commenced the House debate concerning his resolution with references to Wilkinson's "violations of Constitutional privileges" including the Fourth, Fifth, and Sixth Amendments, and to his contempt for and willful disobedience of writs of habeas corpus. He said:

> The civil authority at New Orleans has been trampled under foot, and the commander of the army, in the plentitude of his power, avows his disobedience to laws and Constitution, and takes on himself all the responsibility of the violation of our Constitutional rights of personal liberty. . . . [O]ur citizens have been arrested without any warrant, and without any process of law whatever; deprived of their liberty; confined in military prisons, and transported, under military guards, two thousand miles from the place where the offence was committed.[106]

John Randolph of Virginia was not reluctant to pin the responsibility for Wilkinson's actions on Jefferson and his administration:

---

[103] See note 102 supra.
[104] Beveridge, *John Marshall*, III, 351.

[105] 4 Cranch at 127.
[106] *Annals of Congress*, XVI, 506 (9th Cong., 2d sess.).

Permit me to remind the House that if those who have been called into public life on account of their professed attachment to correct principles ever quit the grounds of trial by jury, the liberty of the press, and the subordination of the military to the civil authority, they must expect that their enemies will perceive the desertion and avail themselves of the advantage.[107]

Furthermore, he stated that, "In the Declaration of Independence, transportation for trial is alleged as one of the grievances imposed by the British Government on the colonies. Now, it is done under the Constitution, and under a republican Administration. . . ."[108] As for Wilkinson (and veiling his disdain for the President only thinly), Randolph stated that he did not like "this business of canonizing and sanctifying men before they are dead. . . . If a man breaks the Constitution, which they were all sworn to support, punish him. If the violator be Washington, Franklin, or Jefferson . . . punish him."[109]

Bollmann and Swartwout were but two of the smaller fish caught in Wilkinson's net. Three others—Peter Ogden, James Alexander, and General John Adair—had already been set free by court orders because there was no proof that they were "conspirators."[110] The same was now true of Bollmann and Swartwout. It was then that Senator Giles threatened to take steps to amend the Constitution so that the Supreme Court should have no jurisdiction in criminal cases, and the wrath of the Republicans was such that, according to John Quincy Adams, there were again threats to impeach every judge on the Court.[111]

While these events were taking place in New Orleans and Washington, Burr himself, with nine boats and sixty young adventurers, was slowly floating down the Ohio and Mississippi Rivers in apparent ig-

---

[107] *Ibid.*, 535.

[108] *Ibid.*, 538.

[109] *Ibid.*

[110] Ogden was arrested with Bollmann and Swartwout and released pursuant to a writ of habeas corpus after Wilkinson had sent the latter "conspirators" to Washington. See Jefferson's Jan. 22, 1807 Message to the Congress in *Annals of Congress*, XVI, 43 (9th Cong., 2d sess.); Beveridge, *John Marshall*, III, 333. According to Beveridge, Ogden was rearrested after his release with his friend James Alexander, who had sought the original writs of habeas corpus. Further writs to secure their release were ignored, and the local judge who issued them resigned from the bench in protest. That judge was seized by Wilkinson's soldiers but released pursuant to an order of the United States District Court. Beveridge, *John Marshall*, III, 334–35. Adair was a friend of Wilkinson's who possessed evidence of the General's participation in a conspiracy with the Spanish. He was seized and sent to Baltimore under military guard, but released there on a writ of habeas corpus. *Ibid.*, 335–36, 344. Alexander was also released in Baltimore after being sent there under military guard. *Ibid.*, 343.

[111] See text accompanying note 73 supra.

norance of these developments. In a document that Jefferson sent to Congress accompanying his January 22 message, it is revealed that Burr passed Fort Massoc, Tennessee, on December 31, 1806, "having nothing on board that would even suffer a conjecture, more than a man bound to market. . . ."[112] It was not until Burr reached the Territory of Mississippi that he learned that his expedition was considered by the authorities and the public alike to be criminal and treasonous.[113]

Pursuant to directions from the War Department, the acting governor of the Territory, Cowles Mead, had prorogued the legislature and called out the militia. Confronted by the civil authority on January 17 Burr promptly offered to surrender himself and to permit his boats to be searched, which was done. These events are recorded in a letter from Mead to the War Department, in which he appears to have been both embarrassed and apologetic to report that the capture of New Orleans was to be accomplished by less than one hundred men, many ignorant of Burr's plans, armed with a few rifles and hunting pieces.[114] Burr then voluntarily went into court and prepared to await trial in the United States Court of the Territory.[115] Bail in the amount of $5,000 was furnished for Burr's release, and the grand jury impaneled to investigate his "crimes" asserted, on the basis of the evidence, that they were "of the opinion that Aaron Burr has not been guilty of any crime or misdemeanor against the laws of the United States or of this Territory, or given any just alarm or inquietude."[116] They went on to present as "grievances" the sending of the militia against Burr and, in addition, Wilkinson's military outrages in New Orleans as "destructive of personal liberty."[117] After the jury had been dismissed, since there was no legal charge before the court, Burr asked to be discharged, but the Republican judge, Thomas Rodney (father of Caesar Rodney, who was soon to become Jefferson's Attorney-General), denied the request and ordered Burr to renew his bond or be jailed.[118]

At this point Wilkinson moved again. Having met determined opposition from the legislature of the Territory of New Orleans, which had expressed alarm at the "late privation" of citizens' rights and had adopted a resolution to Congress denouncing Wilkinson's "acts of high-

---

[112] Capt. Daniel Bissell to Gen. Andrew Jackson, Jan. 5, 1807, in *Annals of Congress*, XVI, 1017–18 (9th Cong., 2d sess.).

[113] McCaleb, *Burr Conspiracy*, 219–20.

[114] C. Mead to Department of War, Jan. 19, 1807, in *Annals of Congress*, XVI, 1019 (9th Cong., 2d sess.).

[115] *Ibid.*

[116] Quoted in Beveridge, *John Marshall*, III, 365; see McCaleb, *Burr Conspiracy*, 228.

[117] Beveridge, *John Marshall*, III, 365.

[118] *Ibid.*; McCaleb, *Burr Conspiracy*, 229.

handed military power,"[119] he sent officers in disguise to capture Burr[120] and apparently others to assassinate him.[121] Counseled by friends that he should go into hiding, Burr bade farewell to his companions and wrote to the Governor that he would again appear in court if he could be assured of fair legal proceedings. His bail was then declared forfeited and a reward offered for his capture.[122]

Burr attempted to head east but was soon overtaken and arrested by military authorities. He demanded to be taken before the civil courts for trial, but was kept within a military stockade and, after two weeks, sent north overland through the wilderness to Washington under military guard.[123] En route his escort was ordered by the Government to proceed instead to Richmond, which was the seat of the judicial circuit in which the alleged crimes had been committed.[124] Coincidentally,[125] Chief Justice Marshall, sitting as Circuit Judge, was to preside over Burr's trial in Richmond. Burr arrived on March 26, 1807, in a shabby homespun suit with a floppy white hat covering his face, and shortly thereafter Marshall wrote out and signed the writ that finally delivered Burr from the military to the civil authorities.[126]

---

[119] Beveridge, *John Marshall*, III, 364.

[120] See *Annals of Congress*, XVII, 528–29 (10th Cong., 1st sess.) (testimony of General Wilkinson).

[121] Beveridge, *John Marshall*, III, 365; McCaleb, *Burr Conspiracy*, 230.

[122] Beveridge, *John Marshall*, III, 366; McCaleb, *Burr Conspiracy*, 230–31.

[123] Beveridge, *John Marshall*, III, 368–70; McCaleb, *Burr Conspiracy*, 233.

[124] McCaleb, *Burr Conspiracy*, 238.

[125] Gore Vidal in his recent novel, *Burr* (New York, 1973), recites that Marshall told Luther Martin some years after the trial that the selection of Richmond for the site of the trial was part of a deliberate plan on the part of Jefferson "to destroy the Supreme Court" as well as Marshall himself. If Marshall favored Burr in any way during the proceedings it could provide a basis for the Chief Justice's impeachment. *Ibid.*, 353. Without speculating about the truth of Vidal's reconstruction of Marshall's views, it is certainly credible that the possibility of impeachment had already crossed Jefferson's mind. See chapter 7 supra. After Marshall re- fused to commit Burr on a charge of high treason on Apr. 1, 1807, United States v. Burr, 25 F. Cas. 2, 12–15 (C.C.D. Va. 1807) (No. 14,692a), see text accompanying notes 130–37 infra, Jefferson wrote to Senator Giles that "the nation will judge both the offender & judges for themselves. If a member of the Executive or Legislature does wrong, the day is never far distant when the people will remove him. They will see then & amend the error in our Constitution which makes any branch independent of the nation." T. Jefferson to W. Giles, Apr. 20, 1807 in Ford, *Works of Jefferson*, X, 387; McCaleb, *Burr Conspiracy*, 260. See Corwin, *Marshall and the Constitution*, 113. The constitutional amendment to which Jefferson referred in his letter to Giles was one offered by John Randolph after the acquittal of Justice Chase by the Senate in March 1805, which provided for the removal of judges on the President's motion to both houses of Congress. See *Annals of Congress*, XIV, 1213 (8th Cong., 2d sess.); Beveridge, *John Marshall*, III, 389.

[126] Beveridge, *John Marshall*, III, 370.

VIII: *Habeas Corpus, Treason, and Trial of Aaron Burr*

Aaron Burr's commitment for grand jury action and his subsequent trial were among the most dramatic events of the time, and they excited general public interest.[127] From an historical standpoint, it has been written that the potentialities of the Burr trial were "so portentous that . . . next to the Confederate War it posed the greatest threat of dismemberment which the American Union has ever faced."[128] Many authors have accorded the episode an importance in political history that far exceeds its undoubted legal significance. Perhaps, as Professor Philbrick suggests, they have been mesmerized by a belief in a "conspiracy," which has yet to be proved.[129] A necessarily brief account of the trial proceedings, highlighting aspects of legal import without ignoring political developments, follows.

The case at Richmond began with a motion by United States Attorney George Hay to commit Burr on two charges: one of treason in assembling an armed force to attack New Orleans; the other a high misdemeanor in commencing a military expedition against Spain.[130] The record of the *Bollmann* case in the Supreme Court was placed before Marshall,[131] and Hay "minutely examined" the evidence of treason in the case—chiefly that related to Burr—emphasizing the cipher letter to Wilkinson and the latter's affidavit.[132] Burr's counsel, John Wickham and Edmund Randolph, asserted that there was no evidence in the record that an overt act of treason had been committed, and, given the "trivial" evidence to support the misdemeanor charge, Burr should be released on bail.[133] Burr addressed the court on his own behalf to explain his alleged "flight," to protest against the illegal orders of autocratic military authorities that had sent him under guard, and without access to the courts, from Alabama to Richmond, and also to put on record his appearances before the grand juries in Kentucky and Mississippi and the favorable verdicts of those investigations.[134]

---

[127] It has been reported that hundreds of spectators were turned away from a local hotel in which the proceedings commenced with the result that the trial was removed to the Virginia House of Delegates. *Ibid.*, III, 372–73. See United States v. Burr, 25 F. Cas. 2, 11 (C.C.D. Va. 1807) (No. 14,692a). Among the lawyers involved in the case were many of the era's foremost attorneys. Burr's counsel included Edmund Randolph, former attorney-general and secretary of state, Charles Lee, Luther Martin, and local notables: John Wickham, Benjamin Botts, and John Baker. The prosecution was conducted principally by United States Attorney George Hay, assisted by Attorney-General Caesar Rodney, William Wirt, and Virginia's Lieut. Gov. Alexander McRae. McCaleb, *Burr Conspiracy*, 266–67.

[128] Abernethy, *Burr Conspiracy*, 274.

[129] See text accompanying notes 41–47 supra.

[130] United States v. Burr, 25 F. Cas. 2, 3–4, 11 (C.C.D. Va. 1807) (No. 14,692a).

[131] *Ibid.*, 4.

[132] *Ibid.*, 4–7, 11.

[133] *Ibid.*, 11.

[134] *Ibid.*, 11–12.

On April 1 Marshall delivered his opinion on the motion, which was written with great care, prudence, and legal exactitude. In it was a thinly veiled reference to the "hand of malignity," which must not be permitted to "grasp any individual against whom its hate may be directed, or whom it may capriciously seize, charge him with some secret crime, and put him on the proof of his innocence."[135] After reviewing the affidavits produced by the Government and noting the passage of months since the alleged assembling of troops to levy war took place, and the five-week interim following *Bollmann* in which the Government knew such evidence was needed, Marshall found no basis to support the allegation that Burr had assembled such an army.[136] Mere suspicion, he stated, "ought not to be continued, unless this want of proof can be . . . accounted for."[137] As for the statutory misdemeanor charge, Marshall found that Burr "would be put on his trial for carrying on a military expedition against a nation with whom the United States were at peace," and set bail at $10,000.[138] Throughout the opinion Marshall paid scrupulous attention to appropriate procedures, often reiterating the grounds for his reasoning, and bolstering those grounds with quotations from the *Bollmann* opinion, lest local prejudices be more inflamed than they were. He was also careful to note that the prosecution could seek an indictment from the grand jury for high treason, if it "be furnished with the necessary testimony."[139]

Jefferson's reactions to Marshall's course of action, both at this time and in the course of the trial, are revealed in his letters, particularly those to Senator Giles and Government counsel.[140] The letters make unpleasant reading for those who are offended by the assertion that Jefferson's personal antagonisms could or did become public policies. Further evidence of his growing animosity towards Burr, and also towards Federalists generally, appears not only in the writings of his detractors, such as Beveridge[141] and McCaleb[142] but also in the pages of more neutral and measured narrators.[143] It is sufficient here to suggest that there is much truth in the charge against the President that, with regard to the Burr case, his view of legal doctrine was obscured by what may be called his political purposes. The array of evidence against Jefferson, from the time that he declared Burr's guilt as "beyond question"[144] to his subsequent issuance of blank pardons and the col-

---

[135] *Ibid.*, 12.
[136] *Ibid.*, 15.
[137] *Ibid.*
[138] *Ibid.*
[139] *Ibid.*
[140] See, e.g., note 125 supra.
[141] See Beveridge, *John Marshall*, III, 384–469.

[142] See McCaleb, *New Light on Burr*, 96–122.
[143] See Abernethy, *Burr Conspiracy*, 233, 244–45, 249; Philbrick, *Rise of the West*, 244–45.
[144] See text accompanying note 56 supra.

lection of blatantly false affidavits,[145] as he contrived to make himself the guiding hand of the prosecution, almost astounds the mind. Little wonder that the work of a modern scholar such as Leonard Levy can be devoted to Jefferson's "darker side."[146]

On April 6 Senator Giles alerted Jefferson to the political dangers that could ensue if all measures were not taken to produce evidence to prove Burr a traitor, and he insisted that unless Wilkinson appeared in person as a witness, the "character of the administration" would be implicated.[147] It appears that Jefferson needed no such urging; indeed, Beveridge states that from the time the President received word of Marshall's decision to hold Burr only for a bailable misdemeanor, "the prosecution of his former associate became Jefferson's ruling thought and purpose."[148] Beveridge remarks further, and not without justification, "A personal antagonism, once formed, became with Thomas Jefferson a public policy."[149]

Marshall set Burr's appearance for trial at the next term of the circuit court, which was to commence on May 22, 1807.[150] In the interim, Jefferson almost literally took the prosecution into his own hands, prompting expressions of outrage from contemporaries such as Andrew Jackson, then present in Richmond, who denounced Thomas Jefferson "as a persecutor who sought the ruin of one he hated,"[151] and young Winfield Scott, who made similar accusations.[152] Meanwhile, Jefferson proclaimed to Giles that witnesses would be produced and evidence collected to "satisfy the world, if not the judges," of Burr's treason.[153] After decrying the "tricks of the judges to force trials before it is possible to collect the evidence,"[154] Jefferson stated that an "inquiry" had been commissioned to summon witnesses from all parts of the West by appealing to their patriotism, and enumerated the "overt

---

[145] See T. Jefferson to G. Hay, May 20, 1807, in Ford, *Works of Jefferson*, X, 394–401. All the letters written by Jefferson to United States Attorney Hay during the Burr trial (fourteen in all) are collected in *ibid.*, 394–409. They clearly reveal the close supervision by the President of the Burr prosecution.

[146] Levy, *Jefferson and Civil Liberties.*

[147] W. Giles to T. Jefferson, Apr. 6, 1807, in D. Anderson, *William Branch Giles: A Study in the Politics of Virginia and the Nation from 1790 to 1830* (Menasha, Wis., 1914), 110.

[148] Beveridge, *John Marshall*, III, 384; see Levy, *Jefferson and Civil Liberties*, 71–72.

[149] Beveridge, *John Marshall*, III, 384.

[150] United States v. Burr, 25 F. Cas. 2, 15 (C.C.D. Va. 1807) (No. 14,692a).

[151] Beveridge, *John Marshall*, III, 404.

[152] W. Scott, *Memoirs of Lieut.-General Scott* (New York, 1864), I, 13 ("It was President Jefferson who directed and animated the prosecution, and hence every Republican clamored for execution.")

[153] T. Jefferson to W. Giles, Apr. 20, 1807, in Ford, *Works of Jefferson*, X, 385.

[154] *Ibid.*, 383.

acts" that in his view established probable cause for Burr's commitment for treason. In preparation for the trial Jefferson also sent to Hay a signed statement that Bollmann had earlier given to the President in complete confidence on the latter's express word of honor that it should never be revealed, but that Jefferson now believed would be helpful to Hay in examining Bollmann.[155]

Burr's trial began on May 22, presided over by Chief Justice Marshall and District Judge Cyrus Griffin. Following the calling of the grand jurors, Burr personally challenged the composition of the panel. Although the grand jury was, for the most part, clearly hostile to Burr,[156] there were two in particular whom he wished removed— Senator Giles and W. C. Nicholas. Both voluntarily withdrew, after some argument and discussion,[157] and with two substitutes, one of whom was John Randolph, the grand jury was impaneled, and Marshall appointed Randolph as foreman.[158]

The Government's chief witness, General Wilkinson, had not yet arrived in Richmond, and court was adjourned until Hay was prepared to present testimony to the grand jury. Then, on May 25, Hay gave notice in open court that he intended to resubmit his earlier motion to commit Burr on a charge of treason.[159] Following Burr's motion that the grand jury withdraw, which was sustained, Hay formally made the motion, which was at once attacked by the defense as an interference with the grand jury's performance of its functions.[160] Hay replied that Burr, free on bail, might readily escape when he learned that Wilkinson had arrived in Virginia and was ready to appear against him in a trial for treason.[161] Burr's counsel complained of the harassment of their client, stating that a public examination of the evidence against Burr at this point would increase the prejudice against him in the public's mind, and prejudice the grand jury.[162] Burr himself entered the argument to point out that nearly six months earlier even the President had "declared that there was a crime," yet even now the prosecution was asking that he be imprisoned when there was no evidence to secure his indictment by the grand jury. Conceding the President's great legal talents, Burr stated that "he ought to know what [constitutes war]" and

[155] See ibid., 385; T. Jefferson to J. Bollmann, Jan. 25, 1807, in M. Davis, ed., Memoirs of Aaron Burr (New York, 1837), II, 388.

[156] As eventually constituted, the grand jury consisted of fourteen Republicans and two Federalists, including many of Jefferson's "most earnest personal friends." Beveridge, John Marshall, III, 413, notes 1–2.

[157] See United States v. Burr, 25

F. Cas. 55, 56–59 (C.C.D. Va. 1807) (No. 14,693); Robertson, Burr Trial Reports, I, 38–44.

[158] 25 F. Cas. at 59; Beveridge, John Marshall, III, 413.

[159] United States v. Burr, 25 F. Cas. 25, 25 (C.C.D. Va. 1807) (No. 14,692b).

[160] Ibid., 26.

[161] Ibid.

[162] Ibid.

he had proclaimed that civil war existed six months ago. "And yet, for six months they have been hunting for it, and cannot find one spot where it existed."[163]

Marshall delivered his written opinion on the committal motion on May 26. He first held that the court retained the power to commit Burr, and then considered whether there were any circumstances in this case that made commitment inappropriate. He stated that such factors as "the attention which should be bestowed on prosecutions, instituted by special order of the executive," "the peculiar inconveniences and hardships" of Burr's case, and the "improper effects" (prejudicial publicity) that the examination of witnesses in open court might now have, were either for the prosecutor's consideration in deciding whether or not to bring the motion, or for the judge to consider in weighing the testimony in support of it,[164] but that they "cannot deprive the attorney for the United States of the right to make his motion."[165] Marshall expressed particular concern for Burr's right to a trial free from "any attempt which may be made to prejudice the public judgment, and to try [him], not by the laws of his country and the testimony exhibited against him, but by public feelings, which may be and often are artificially excited against the innocent as well as the guilty," but held that the remedy for that concern "is not to be obtained by suppressing motions which either party may have a legal right to make."[166]

Hay was evidently taken aback, for he had expected that his motion would be denied and that Marshall's ruling could then be used to further excite popular prejudice.[167] Hay then changed his tactics and asked to have Burr's bail increased, which would avoid the alleged newspaper notoriety to which Marshall had referred by obviating the need for Burr's imprisonment. This request for additional bail was refused by Burr's counsel, so that Hay felt compelled, in spite of the considerations mentioned in Marshall's opinion, to examine witnesses in support of his motion to commit.[168] On May 28, after a few witnesses had been called and examined,[169] the wrangling about subjecting Burr to the custody of the court from day to day or increasing his bail resumed, and Marshall expressed his concern about the "very improper

---

[163] Robertson, *Burr Trial Reports,* I, 78.

[164] 25 F. Cas. at 27.

[165] *Ibid.*

[166] *Ibid.*

[167] Beveridge, *John Marshall,* III, 423.

[168] United States v. Burr, 25 F. Cas. 55, 60 (C.C.D. Va. 1807) (No. 14,693); Robertson, *Burr Trial Reports,* I, 81–82.

[169] Hay offered as evidence an affidavit of one witness who was not in attendance, which prompted objections from Burr's counsel and an opinion in which Marshall held that the affidavit was inadmissible because it appeared that it was not accompanied by a legally administered oath. See United States v. Burr, 25 F. Cas. 27 (C.C.D. Va. 1807) (No. 14,692c).

effects on the public mind" that this evidentiary hearing might have.[170] He expressed his wish "that the personal appearance of Colonel Burr could be secured without the necessity of proceeding in this inquiry."[171] At that point Burr voluntarily offered to furnish additional bail, thereby relieving the court of its embarrassment, provided that it was understood that his giving bail would have no effect on the question of probable cause.[172] Receiving such assurance, Burr found four sureties who gave bond for an additional $10,000.[173]

The way was now clear for the Government to present its case to the grand jury, but the prosecution refused to proceed pending Wilkinson's arrival, despite the fact that numerous Government witnesses were by now on hand. The court met and adjourned each day from May 29 to June 3, and the grand jury was twice adjourned, from June 3 to June 9 and from June 9 to June 11.[174] As the proceedings lagged, the President continued to send directions to Hay. Among them was an instruction to have *Marbury* v. *Madison* "brought before the public, & denounced as not law; & I think the present a fortunate [occasion for doing so], because it occupies such a place in the public attention."[175] Hay was authorized to state that Jefferson himself had determined that "the doctrines of that case were given extra-judicially & against law"; and that this was a consequence of the fact that those doctrines were announced in a case over which the Court had no jurisdiction.[176]

Only a few days before, in writing to his son-in-law, John W. Eppes, Jefferson insisted that Marshall's partiality towards Burr was evident from the early proceedings, and that they demonstrated "the original error of establishing a judiciary independent of the nation, and which, from the citadel of the law can turn it's guns on those they were meant to defend, & controul & fashion their proceedings to it's own will."[177]

Suddenly, on June 9, Burr dropped a bombshell onto the stalled proceedings. Personally addressing the court, he stated that Jefferson, in his January 22 Message to Congress, had referred to a letter dated October 21 and to other papers received from Wilkinson. These, Burr claimed, were now indispensable to his defense, as were certain widely published orders of the Government to the Army and Navy, issued as

---

[170] Robertson, *Burr Trial Reports*, I, 105.

[171] *Ibid.*

[172] *Ibid.*

[173] *Ibid.*, 106; See United States v. Burr, 25 F. Cas. 55, 61–62 (C.C.D. Va. 1807) (No. 14,693).

[174] 25 F. Cas. at 63.

[175] T. Jefferson to G. Hay, June 2, 1807, in Ford, *Works of Jefferson*, X, 397.

[176] *Ibid.*, 396–97.

[177] T. Jefferson to J. Eppes, May 28, 1807, *ibid.*, 412–13.

he descended the Mississippi, to destroy Burr's person and property.[178] The Secretary of the Navy had apparently refused to let Burr or his counsel inspect the latter orders, in accordance with a precedent set in the 1806 trial of William S. Smith and Samuel G. Ogden, in which three Cabinet members had refused to appear in court and had screened themselves behind the President's alleged instructions.[179] Hence, said Burr, unless Hay was prepared to produce the required documents, he felt it necessary for the court to issue a subpoena *duces tecum* to the President requiring him to produce them.[180] Marshall called for argument on Burr's motion to issue such a subpoena, but Hay stated that he would concede the court's power to grant it.[181] The following day Burr presented an affidavit in support of his motion, and there followed three days of debate which opened the celebrated controversy over "executive privilege" and which to this day has not been entirely resolved.[182]

---

[178] United States v. Burr, 25 F. Cas. 30, 30 (C.C.D. Va. 1807) (No. 14,692d).

[179] United States v. Smith, 27 F. Cas. 1192, 1194 (C.C.D. N.Y. 1806) (No. 16,342). See Beveridge, *John Marshall*, III, 436 note 1.

[180] 25 F. Cas. at 30.

[181] *Ibid.*, 31.

[182] In United States v. Nixon, 418 U.S. 683, 713 (1974), a unanimous Supreme Court held that when the executive asserts "privilege as to subpoenaed materials sought for use in a criminal trial . . . based only on the generalized interest in confidentiality, it cannot prevail over the fundamental demands of due process of law in the fair administration of criminal justice. The generalized assertion of privilege must yield to the demonstrated, specific need for evidence in a pending criminal trial." Chief Justice Burger's opinion quotes freely from Chief Justice Marshall's opinions on the privilege issue given during the Burr trial, both in its analysis of the competing interests of the judicial and executive branches when a claim of privilege is asserted, 418 U.S. at 707, 708, and in delineating the responsibilities of the district court in conducting an examination of "presumptively privileged" presidential documents, *ibid.*, at 713–15. Professor Freund has concluded that the opinion in United States v. Nixon "largely confirmed" the principles regarding executive privilege established in the Burr trial. P. Freund, "Foreword: On Presidential Privilege, The Supreme Court, 1973 Term," *Harvard Law Review* LXXXVIII, 13, 31 (1974).

It is of interest to note that subsequently, in Nixon v. Administrator of General Services, 433 U.S. 425 (1977), a divided Court held that former President Nixon's claim of executive privilege over his Presidential papers and tape recordings survived his tenure in office, *ibid.* at 449, but that the intrusion into Presidential confidentiality contemplated by the Presidential Recordings and Materials Preservation Act, Pub. L. No. 93–526, 88 Stat. 1695 (1974), 44 U.S.C. 2107 (Supp. V 1975), was mitigated by procedural safeguards adequate to protect privileged materials, so that the Act did not on its face violate executive privilege, 433 U.S. at 455. Mr. Justice Powell concurred in the opinion with respect to the executive privilege issue, emphasizing the fact that "the incumbent [President Ford], having made clear in the appropriate forum his opposition to the former President's claim, alone can speak for the Executive Branch." *Ibid.* at 502 (Powell, J., concurring) (footnote

The arguments that followed Burr's totally unexpected motion were heated, with the vitriolic invectives of Luther Martin countered by the brilliant eloquence of Hay's associate, William Wirt.[183] Despite Marshall's strong admonition to counsel that they "had acted improperly in the style and spirit of their remarks; that they had been to blame in endeavoring to excite the prejudices of the people," he was scarcely heeded.[184] Finally, on June 12, Marshall delivered his opinion: he had decided to grant Burr's motion and issue the subpoena, postponing any consideration of the privileged nature of the documents requested until the President should raise the issue on the subpoena's return.

The political and constitutional importance of Marshall's decision justifies a brief summary of his opinion and reasoning. He began by stating, "Upon immemorial usage . . . and . . . a sound construction of the constitution and law of the land, . . . any person charged with a crime in the courts of the United States has a right, before or after indictment, to the process of the court to compel the attendance of his witnesses."[185] Marshall then proceeded to the questions whether a subpoena *duces tecum* could be directed to the President, and whether it should be in this case. He noted first that Hay had not questioned the authority of the court to issue a subpoena *ad testificiandum* to the President, but nonetheless Marshall felt obliged to support that authority. He observed that the Constitution admitted of no exception to the right of an accused to the compulsory process of the court, and the law of evidence reserved an exception only for the king. Marshall then took the opportunity to note that presidents, unlike kings, were subject to impeachment and removal from office and, upon the expiration of their term, returned to "the mass of the people" from which they were

---

omitted). Chief Justice Burger dissented, finding that the Act, in requiring Government agents "to review and catalog thousands of papers and recordings that are undoubtedly privileged" will render "the Presidential privilege of one occupant of that office . . . a nullity." *Ibid.* at 518 (Burger, C.J., dissenting) (footnote omitted). Justice Rehnquist, also dissenting, specifically rejected Justice Powell's view in arguing that the principle of separation of powers "may not be signed away by the temporary incumbent of the office which it was designed to protect." *Ibid.* at 557 (Rehnquist, J., dissenting).

[183] Among Martin's arguments was one addressed to the actions of Jefferson: "The president has undertaken to prejudice my client by declaring, that 'of his guilt there can be no doubt.' He has assumed to himself the knowledge of the Supreme Being himself, and pretended to search the heart of my highly respected friend. He has proclaimed him a traitor in the face of that country, which has rewarded him. He has let slip the dogs of war, the hellhounds of persecution, to hunt down my friend." Robertson, *Burr Trial Reports*, I, 128.

[184] *Ibid.*, 147–48. A vivid account of the arguments is contained in Beveridge, *John Marshall*, III, 435–43.

[185] 25 F. Cas. at 33.

elected.[186] He concluded, therefore, that a President could be exempted from the requirements of the Constitution only "because his duties as chief magistrate demand his whole time for national objects."[187] That demand, he added, was not unremitting, "and if it should exist at the time when his attendance on a court is required, it would be shown on the return of the subpoena, and would rather constitute a reason for not obeying the process of the court than a reason against its being issued."[188]

As for the subpoena *duces tecum*, Marshall concluded, "The propriety of introducing any paper into a case, as testimony, must depend on the character of the paper, not on the character of the person who holds it."[189] With regard to the particular documents requested, Marshall reiterated that any grounds for non-disclosure, such as an assertion that they contained matters not relevant to the case, or whose disclosure would endanger the public safety, would have "due consideration on the return of the subpoena."[190] One passage of Marshall's opinion, which the prosecution felt criticized them unduly for hoping that Burr would be convicted,[191] illustrates his belief that the accused's ability to defend the charges against him outweighed any disrespect that might be felt by the chief executive in being forced to respond to a subpoena:

> It is not for the court to anticipate the event of the present prosecution. Should it terminate as is expected on the part of the United States, all those who are concerned in it should certainly regret that a paper which the accused believed to be essential to his defence, which may, for aught that now appears, be essential, had been withheld from him. I will not say, that this circumstance would, in any degree, tarnish the reputation of the government; but I will say, that it would justly tarnish the reputation of the court which had given its sanction to its being withheld. Might I be permitted to utter one sentiment, with respect to myself, it would be to deplore, most earnestly, the occasion which should compel me to look back on any part of my official conduct with so much self-reproach as I should feel, could I declare, on the information now possessed, that the accused is not entitled to the letter in question, if it should be really important to him.[192]

As it happened, on the day that Marshall delivered his opinion, Jefferson wrote to Hay concerning executive privilege and his intentions:

---

[186] *Ibid.*, 34.
[187] *Ibid.*
[188] *Ibid.*
[189] *Ibid.*

[190] *Ibid.*, 37.
[191] See Robertson, *Burr Trial Reports*, I, 189.
[192] 25 F. Cas. at 37.

"Reserving the necessary right of the President of the US to decide, independently of all other authority, what papers, coming to him as President, the public interests permit to be communicated, & to whom, I assure you of my readiness under that restriction, voluntarily to furnish on all occasions, whatever the purposes of justice may require."[193]

The clarity of Jefferson's legal reasoning with respect to the privilege issue, as it appears in this letter and several that followed, is worthy of emphasis. First, wrote Jefferson, though the point had not been argued by Hay, the Constitution could not intend that compliance with subpoenas in court proceedings should "leave the nation without an executive branch, whose agency . . . is understood to be so constantly necessary, that it is the sole branch which the constitution requires to be always in function."[194] Therefore, the Constitution could not intend that the executive "should be withdrawn from its station by any coordinate authority."[195] Second, and more important, although many papers in the President's possession were clearly public documents (e.g., land grants and patents), others, to permit the "advantageous conduct" of the nation's affairs, "should remain known to their executive functionary only. He, of course, from the nature of the case, must be the sole judge of which of them the public interests will permit publication."[196] This idea echoes certain views earlier expressed by Marshall himself in the opinion in *Marbury* v. *Madison.*[197] Notwithstanding his reservations, Jefferson promptly forwarded to Hay several of the requested documents, accompanied by a letter in which he "presumed" that papers previously sent, together with those forwarded that day,

---

[193] T. Jefferson to G. Hay, June 12, 1807, in Ford, *Works of Jefferson*, X, 398.

[194] T. Jefferson to G. Hay, June 17, 1807, in Ford, *ibid.*, 401.

[195] *Ibid.*

[196] *Ibid.*

[197] The intimate political relation, subsisting between the president of the United States and the heads of departments, necessarily renders any legal investigation of the acts of one of those high officers peculiarly irksome, as well as delicate; and excites some hesitation with respect to the propriety of entering into such investigation. . . .

It is scarcely necessary for the court to disclaim all pretensions to such a jurisdiction [which would intrude into the cabinet or intermeddle with the prerogatives of the executive]. An extravagance, so absurd and excessive, could not have been entertained for a moment. The province of the court is, solely, to decide on the rights of individuals, not to inquire how the executive, or executive officers, perform duties in which they have a discretion. Questions, in their nature political, or which are, by the constitution and laws, submitted to the executive, can never be made in this court. Marbury v. Madison, 1 Cranch 137, 169–70 (1803) (footnote omitted).

"will have substantially fulfilled the object of a subpoena from the District Court of Richmond, requiring that [the Secretaries of War and of the Navy] & myself should attend the Court in Richmond. . . ."[198]

Curiously, Marshall's decision and his opinion on the subpoena issue evoked little or no adverse criticism, even from Republicans.[199] Jefferson's expectedly angered response was directed not at Marshall but at Luther Martin, whom he characterized in a subsequent letter to Hay as an "unprincipled and impudent federal bull-dog" who would be "put down" by "evidence" Jefferson had received that "Luther Martin knew all about [Burr's] criminal enterprise." "Shall LM," he asked, "be summoned as a witness against Burr . . . [or] [s]hall we move to commit LM as *particeps criminis* with Burr?"[200]

Evidently a copy, but not the original, of Wilkinson's letter was turned over to the court, and Jefferson's production of documents sufficiently satisfied the subpoena so that further resolution of the executive issue was not required at this stage of the trial.[201] The issue was raised again during the subsequent trial—after Burr's acquittal on the charge of treason—with respect to another Wilkinson letter in Jefferson's possession.[202]

Professor Freund's recent article on executive privilege summarizes Marshall's opinions on the issue at each stage of the Burr trial,[203] and assesses the applicability of the principles Marshall then established to the issues raised in the Watergate tapes case.[204] He concludes:

> The Burr trials may be taken to have established four principles, all pertinent to and important for the tapes case: (1) There is no absolute privilege in a criminal case for communications to which the President is a party. (2) Upon a particularized claim of privilege by the President the court, giving due respect to the President's judgment, will weigh the claim against the materiality of the evidence and the need of the accused for its production. (3) For purposes of determining whether disclosure is required, the material sought may be ordered to be produced for in camera inspection by the court, with the participation of counsel and, it seems, the accused. (4) In lieu of such production, the court may direct that inferences shall be drawn favorable to the accused, or that the prosecution be dismissed.

* * *

---

[198] T. Jefferson to G. Hay, June 17, 1807, in Ford, *Works of Jefferson*, X, 400.

[199] See Beveridge, *John Marshall*, III, 450.

[200] T. Jefferson to G. Hay, June 19, 1807, in Ford, *Works of Jefferson*, X, 402–403.

[201] See Freund, "Foreword: On Presidential Privilege," 27.

[202] See text accompanying notes 278–80 infra.

[203] Freund, "Foreword: On Presidential Privilege," 23–30.

[204] See note 182 supra.

In the tapes case these principles were largely confirmed, and the mechanics of an in camera inspection were refined.[205]

The day after Marshall had rendered his opinion on the subpoena issue, the portly Wilkinson arrived in Richmond, dressed in full military regalia. He was "too much fatigued" to present himself immediately to the court, but two days later he strode into court "swelling like a turkey cock."[206] Duly sworn, the Government's witnesses were being called one by one to testify before the grand jury. When Wilkinson's turn came, he produced Burr's cipher letter of July 29, 1806, but was forced to admit not only that in the version sent to Jefferson he had erased the opening sentence "Yours, postmarked 13th of May, is received," but also that he had altered several other words and phrases.[207] These admissions were especially damaging to Wilkinson because they showed that although he had pretended to know nothing of Burr's "plot" until he had received the cipher letter, he had in fact written to Burr several months earlier about the western project. As foreman of the grand jury, John Randolph began to harp upon the inconsistencies in testimony and on the ciphered letter. He remarked that Wilkinson was "the only man I ever saw who was from the bark to the very core a villain."[208] Although Randolph demanded that Wilkinson be indicted immediately for misprision of treason, politics saved him and he escaped grand jury indictment by the narrow margin of a 7–9 vote,[209] although Randolph was later to state on the floor of the House that none of the grand jurors doubted Wilkinson's moral guilt.[210] As Randolph wrote, "Politics have usurped the place of law, and the scenes of 1798 [those attending the Alien and Sedition laws] are again revived."[211]

After having heard forty-eight prosecution witnesses,[212] the grand jury returned bills of indictment on June 24 for treason and misdemeanor against Burr and, in absentia, Harman Blennerhassett.[213] The treason charge, of course, would have to be supported by findings consistent with its definition in Article III, Section 3, of the Constitution: "Treason against the United States, shall consist only in levying War against them, or in adhering to their Enemies, giving them Aid and

---

[205] Freund, "Foreword: On Presidential Privilege," 30–31 (footnote omitted).

[206] Beveridge, John Marshall, III, 456.

[207] Ibid., 463–64.

[208] J. Randolph to J. Nicholson, June 25, 1807, in ibid., 464.

[209] McCaleb, Burr Conspiracy, 278.

[210] See Annals of Congress, XVII, 1397–98 (10th Cong., 1st sess.).

[211] J. Randolph to J. Nicholson, June 25, 1807, in Beveridge, John Marshall, III, 464, note 3.

[212] See J. Brady, The Trial of Aaron Burr (New York, 1913), 69–70.

[213] The bills of indictment against Burr are recorded at Annals of Congress, XVII, 388–89 (10th Cong., 1st sess.); Robertson, Burr Trial Reports, I, 306.

Comfort. No person shall be convicted of Treason unless on the Testimony of two Witnesses to the same overt Act, or on Confession in open Court." The misdemeanor indictment charged Burr with setting in motion an expedition against territory belonging to the King of Spain. It should be noted that there is some evidence that the grand jury may have indicted Burr on the charge of treason because of a misunderstanding about what constituted levying war against the United States, as earlier defined by Marshall in *Ex parte Bollmann*.[214] On August 8, 1807, Harman Blennerhassett recorded in his journal of the trial proceedings that

> two of the most respectable and influential of that body [the grand jury], since it has been discharged, have declared they mistook the meaning of Chief Justice Marshall's opinion as to what sort of acts amounted to treason in this country, in the case of Swartwout and Ogden [and Bollmann]; that it was under the influence of this mistake they concurred in finding such a bill against A. Burr, which otherwise would have probably been ignored.[215]

The calling of the witnesses before the grand jury gave rise to several lengthy arguments and motions that required resolution by the Chief Justice. One of these related to the testimony of Dr. Bollmann, who was pardoned by the President against his wishes in order to force him to testify;[216] another related to the scope of a witness' privilege against self-incrimination.[217] In addition, on June 17 Burr moved for an attachment against General Wilkinson "for the irregular examination of witnesses, practicing on their fears, forcing them to come to [Richmond], and transporting them from New Orleans to Norfolk."[218] On June 27 Marshall delivered an opinion in which he concluded that there was insufficient evidence to hold Wilkinson in contempt of court for obstructing the administration of justice.[219]

In the meantime, Marshall had committed Burr to prison for lack

---

[214] See text accompanying notes 87–105 supra.

[215] W. Safford, *The Blennerhassett Papers* (Cincinnati, 1864), 314.

[216] See United States v. Burr, 25 F. Cas. 55, 63–64 (C.C.D. Va. 1807) (No. 14,693) (Bollmann went to the grand jury with the questions of the effect of his pardon and the extent to which he could be compelled to testify against himself reserved for future resolution).

[217] See United States v. Burr, 25 F. Cas. 38 (C.C.D. Va. 1807) (No. 14,692e) (allowing Burr's secretary, one Willie, to refuse to testify with respect to a cipher letter in his handwriting, sent by Burr to Bollmann, if an answer "may disclose a fact which forms a necessary and essential link in the chain of testimony, which would be sufficient to convict him of any crime").

[218] United States v. Burr, 25 F. Cas. 55, 67 (C.C.D. Va. 1807) (No. 14,693).

[219] See United States v. Burr, 25 F. Cas. 41 (C.C.D. Va. 1807) (No. 14,692f).

of "any precedents where a court has bailed for treason, after the finding of a grand jury. . . ."[220] Burr pleaded not guilty to the charges against him on June 26, and trial was set for August 3, but two weeks more passed before the Government was prepared to proceed and the trial jury was selected.[221] There was considerable difficulty in finding a panel of jurors who had not already formed and expressed opinions adverse to Burr, and Marshall issued a lengthy opinion on juror qualifications during the voir dire process.[222] By Monday, August 17, however, twelve had been agreed upon and the treason trial began.

At this point, it is vital to understand that the indictment, drawn up and presented by Hay, specified that Burr's overt act of levying war took place on Blennerhassett's Island, and it is not anticipative of subsequent conclusions to be drawn to state here that, with all its resources and with the enormous amounts expended to secure affidavits and to bring in more than 140 witnesses, the prosecution was unable to prove the sort of notorious assemblage, in force, that was held necessary to constitute the overt act of "levying war" within the definition of treason. Indeed, Government counsel admitted that on the crucial dates named in the indictment, December 10 and 11, 1806, Burr had been in Kentucky.[223]

When the trial opened and the Government's examination of witnesses began, Burr's counsel insisted that the overt act be proved before collateral testimony on Burr's intentions was introduced.[224] On August 18 Marshall directed that the court would not interfere with the order in which the prosecution presented its testimony, since evidence of the intent with which a group of men assembled was relevant to a finding of an overt act of levying war, but he warned counsel that evidence of Burr's "general evil intention" would not be relevant to the charge in the indictment.[225]

Accordingly, the Government again proceeded to call its witnesses. After 7 of the 140 or so had been examined, Burr addressed the court, asking for a decision whether he, although absent from the place where the alleged overt act took place, "should be denominated a principal in the treason" if proof was made that he "counseled and advised the operations."[226] After several more witnesses had testified, Hay agreed that argument on Burr's motion to arrest testimony might proceed.[227] The arguments on this motion lasted for eight days and raised directly

---

[220] 25 F. Cas. at 70.
[221] See ibid., 74–87.
[222] United States v. Burr, 25 F. Cas. 49 (C.C.D. Va. 1807) (No. 14,692g).
[223] Beveridge, John Marshall, III, 491.
[224] United States v. Burr, 25 F. Cas. 52, 53 (C.C.D. Va. 1807) (No. 14,692h).
[225] Ibid., 53–54.
[226] United States v. Burr, 25 F. Cas. 55, 113 (C.C.D. Va. 1807) (No. 14,693).
[227] Ibid., 115.

the issue whether Burr might be convicted under the English doctrine of "constructive" treason, that is, whether he would be guilty as a principal if he were proven to be an accessory to treason.

Burr's counsel, Wickham, opened the argument and attempted to establish four points: that under the Constitution one must be present and personally participate in an overt act of war to be guilty of treason; that, if not, at least the indictment must specifically state that the acts of treason charged were accessorial and not personal in nature; that such accessorial acts of treason can only be proved after the principals have been found guilty; and, finally, that the evidence presented had not proved in any event that an overt act of war had taken place on Blennerhassett's Island.[228] With regard to the last point, he argued that "force and military array were essential ingredients" of levying war, and to the extent that *Ex parte Bollmann* suggested otherwise, it was obiter dictum.[229] Wirt[230] and Hay, arguing for the Government, both relied on Marshall's decision in *Bollmann*, and Hay in particular pointed out that the Supreme Court "has solemnly decided" that one need not be present at the place where a battle is fought to levy war.[231] When arguments on the motion were concluded, Marshall felt compelled to comment, "A degree of eloquence seldom displayed on any occasion has embellished a solidity of argument and a depth of research by which the court has been greatly aided in forming the opinion it is about to deliver."[232]

That opinion, delivered on August 31, has been referred to as a "state paper of first importance,"[233] and it is certainly one of the cornerstones of American substantive criminal law. In addition, the opinion exhibits Marshall's extensive knowledge of and familiarity with the common law, supported as it is by extensive discussion of English and American decisions and commentators, as well as by his concern for protecting individuals from unwarranted prosecutions.

First, Marshall examined the question whether, "conformably to the constitution [one] can be convicted of treason who was not present when the war was levied."[234] He described this constitutional issue as one "of infinite moment to the people of this country and to their government, and requires the most temperate and the most deliberate consideration."[235] He then examined the English doctrine of constructive

---

[228] *Ibid.*, 116–22.

[229] *Ibid.*, 122. See text accompanying notes 90–91 supra.

[230] 25 F. Cas. at 136. A portion of Wirt's argument, "which for nearly a hundred years was to be printed in American schoolbooks," Beveridge, *John Marshall*, III, 497, is reprinted in *ibid.*, III, 616–18.

[231] 25 F. Cas. at 138.

[232] *Ibid.*, 159. A summary of the arguments is contained in Beveridge, *John Marshall*, III, 491–504.

[233] Beveridge, *John Marshall*, III, 504.

[234] 25 F. Cas. at 159.

[235] *Ibid.*

treason, that all accessories to treason are guilty as principals, but very carefully concluded that a definitive answer to the question whether that doctrine was applicable in the United States need not be answered in this case. He emphasized, however, that the Constitution would allow a conviction for treason only if the actions for which one was indicted amounted to levying war, notwithstanding the form such an indictment would take in English practice.[236]

> All those who form the various and essential military parts of prosecuting the war, which must be assigned to different persons, may with correctness and accuracy be said to levy war . . . and to commit treason under the constitution. It will be observed that this opinion does not extend to the case of a person who performs no act in the prosecution of the war—who counsels and advises it—or who, being engaged in the conspiracy, fails to perform his part. Whether such persons may be implicated by the doctrine that whatever would make a man an accessory in felony makes him a principal in treason, or are excluded because that doctrine is inapplicable to the United States, the constitution having declared that treason shall consist only in levying war, and having made the proof of overt acts necessary to conviction, is a question of vast importance, which it would be proper for the Supreme Court to take a fit occasion to decide, *but which an inferior tribunal would not willingly determine unless the case before them should require it.*[237]

As for his dictum in *Ex parte Bollmann*, Marshall expressed his view that the opinion was still "perfectly correct," but hastened to add that the *Bollmann* dictum was not intended to embrace the English doctrine of constructive treason: "Some gentlemen have argued as if the Supreme Court had adopted the whole doctrine of the English books on the subject of accessories to treason. But certainly such is not the fact."[238] Under the language of the *Bollmann* decision, "Those only who form a part, and who are leagued in the conspiracy, are declared to be traitors. . . . They must 'perform a part,' which will furnish the overt act; and they must be 'leagued in conspiracy.' The person who comes within this description in the opinion of the court levies war."[239]

Marshall next proceeded to consider whether the prosecution had offered evidence of any overt act on the part of Burr that *could* amount to levying war, without regard to acts alleged in the indictment. Marshall reviewed the opinions of such men as Coke, Hale, and Blackstone on the meaning of treason by levying war in order to determine that meaning of the term most likely contemplated by the framers of the

---

[236] *Ibid.*, 160.
[237] *Ibid.*, 161 (emphasis supplied).

[238] *Ibid.*
[239] *Ibid.*

Constitution. He concluded from these authorities that the words "have not received a technical [meaning] different from their natural meaning, so far as respects the character of the assemblage of men which may constitute the fact. It must be a warlike assemblage, carrying the appearance of force, and in a situation to practice hostility."[240] He further concluded that opinions rendered by American judges had required even more to constitute levying war than had their English counterparts, that on the facts of the cases before them, the actual exercise of force had been required.[241] However, since the prosecution had argued that all these authorities had been supplanted by the law as set forth in *Bollmann*, Marshall returned to that decision, adding that it would "be expected that an opinion which is to overrule all former precedents, and to establish a principle never before recognized, should be expressed in plain and explicit terms."[242] He then affirmed that various statements in that opinion put forward by the prosecution did not contradict the view that "an assemblage of men which might be construed to amount to a levying of war must appear in force or in military form" and that in *Bollmann* the Court did not contemplate "a secret, unarmed meeting, although that meeting be of conspirators, and although it met with a treasonable intent, as an actual levying of war."[243] Marshall buttressed this conclusion with references to his opinion on the original motion to commit Burr for treason, and his charge to the grand jury.[244]

Turning from the considerations of the merits of the case as it stood independent of the pleadings (the constructive treason issue and the definition of levying war with respect to an assemblage of men) to arguments connected with the indictment, Marshall first considered whether the indictment, charging Burr with levying war on Blennerhassett's Island, and charging no other overt act, could be supported by proof that others had levied war at that place. This point raised the "constructive presence" doctrine which would have attributed to Burr the overt acts of his followers, despite his absence, because they were connected with him in a treasonable conspiracy. Marshall pointed out that the two counts of the indictment charged Burr with levying war on the Island, and with proceeding with a group of men down the river towards New Orleans, which they intended to seize by force. In fact, Burr was not on the Island, nor in the district of Virginia, at the times the indictment alleged the overt acts to have taken place, and that fact caused Marshall to consider whether the indictment had to specify the place and manner in which the overt acts were committed, or whether it was sufficient to charge Burr with levying war generally. He con-

---

240 *Ibid.*, 165.
241 *Ibid.*
242 *Ibid.*

243 *Ibid.*, 168.
244 *Ibid.*

cluded that the specification of the location of the acts was required to show the jurisdiction of the court, and to conform with the constitutional provision "that the offenders 'shall be tried in the state and district wherein the crime shall have been committed.' "[245] As for specificity about the circumstances of the acts of levying war, they were required to be charged "in common justice . . . to afford a reasonable certainty of the nature of the accusation and the circumstances which will be adduced against [the defendant]," buttressed by the constitutional provision "which says that in all criminal prosecutions the accused shall enjoy the right 'to be informed of the nature and cause of the accusation. . . .' "[246] It followed, therefore, that since specificity in the indictment was required, "the charges must be proved as laid."[247]

Marshall then turned to the question whether the terms of the indictment could be met through the application of the doctrine of constructive presence. Again, he reviewed the ideas expounded by commentators on the English law of treason, and he concluded that the cases discussed were not explained by the notion of "legal" as opposed to actual presence, but rather by the constructive treason doctrine.[248] In such circumstances, the indictment, said Marshall, "would state the truth of the case"[249]—that is, it would allege that the person in question was absent from the scene of the overt act, but seek to have him convicted on the basis that in treason all are principals. Marshall again noted that the constructive treason doctrine might not be compatible with the Constitution, but in any event, "it would be going very far to say that this defect, [the inability to convict one of constructive treason] if it be termed one, may be cured by an indictment stating the case untruly."[250]

Thus, having found the constructive presence rationale urged by the prosecution to be unsupported by the common law, Marshall proceeded to the issue whether Burr could be said to have been "legally present" at "the levying of war in Blennerhassett's Island."[251] Marshall conceded that had Burr "not arrived in the island, but . . . taken a position near enough to cooperate with those on the island . . . the question whether he was constructively present could be a question compounded of law and fact, which would be decided by the jury, with the aid of the court. . . ."[252] In Burr's case, however, Marshall found the evidence to be unequivocal that Burr was in no way constructively present at the Island, "aiding and assisting in the particular act which was there com-

[245] *Ibid.*, 170 (quoting United States *Constitution*, Art. III, Sec. 3).
[246] *Ibid.*, (quoting United States *Constitution*, Amend. VI).
[247] *Ibid.*

[248] *Ibid.*, 171–72.
[249] *Ibid.*, 171.
[250] *Ibid.*
[251] *Ibid.*, 172.
[252] *Ibid.*

mitted."[253] To the prosecution's argument that in cases of treason the theater of action should be extended so that one levying war in Kentucky may be deemed constructively present in Virginia, Marshall replied that the argument was "too extravagant to be in terms maintained,"[254] for it would allow one to be considered present at any overt act anywhere, to be tried in any State in which an overt act had been committed, and to be proved guilty of acts without having personally participated.

Marshall quickly dismissed the Government's contention that Burr's indictment did not, in fact, allege him to have been present, stating that this question was "decided by the indictment itself."[255] The Government also contended that Burr's indictment could have truly averred his presence on the Island by yet another variation of the "constructive presence" rationale—that he was present because he *caused* the assemblage to take place. Marshall recognized that there was some support for this theory in the writings of Lord Hale, but found Hale's "dicta" repugnant to principles put forward by Hale and all other commentators, namely, "that the indictment must give notice of the offence; that the accused is only bound to answer the particular charge which the indictment contains, and that the overt act laid is that particular charge."[256] Marshall went on to state that if the prosecution's argument on this point were accepted, "the fact that the accused procured the assemblage on Blennerhassett's Island must be proved . . . positively, by two witnesses, to charge him with that assembly."[257] The difficulties of proving such a typically secret transaction would lead one to infer, said Marshall, that "procuring treason" was not an overt act of levying war within the constitutional definition.[258] Moreover, to accept this doctrine "would seem to imply the decision that the United States . . . have a common law which creates and defines the punishment of crimes accessorial in their nature."[259] The explanation of this statement is that at common law one who procured treason would be an accessory before the fact. This, in turn, would imply that the constructive treason doctrine was consistent with the constitutional definition of treason, which Marshall once again refrained from deciding: "I will not pretend that I have not individually an opinion on these points; but it is one which I should give only in a case which absolutely required it, unless I could confer respecting it with the judges of the supreme court."[260]

---

[253] *Ibid.*
[254] *Ibid.*, 173.
[255] *Ibid.* The terms of the indictment, reproduced in *ibid.*, 87–89, did not admit the possibility of its being read in this fashion.

[256] *Ibid.*, 174.
[257] *Ibid.*, 176.
[258] *Ibid.*
[259] *Ibid.*
[260] *Ibid.*

Marshall administered the fatal blow to the prosecution's "procurement as presence" argument by holding that even if procurement of treason were an overt act within the constitutional definition, "no man can be convicted for the procurement under an indictment charging him with actually assembling. . . ."[261] Marshall also agreed with the contention of Burr's counsel that to convict the defendant of an accessorial act of treason, in any event, would require that the guilt of the principals be previously established by a court conviction.[262] To the prosecution's argument that Burr had waived his right to demand the prior conviction of a principal by pleading to his indictment, Marshall simply responded, once more, that Burr's indictment should have alleged an overt act of procuring treason if that was the crime for which he was to be tried, and a man "charged as having committed an act, cannot be construed to waive a right which he would have possessed had he been charged with having advised the act."[263]

Having thus settled the law of the case, Marshall concluded that the further testimony of prosecution witnesses in this case would be irrelevant, since that testimony was conceded to relate to "subsequent transactions at a different place and a different state" than that charged in Burr's indictment.[264] He did leave an opening for Hay to produce the testimony of "two witnesses that the meeting on Blennerhassett's Island was procured by the prisoner," which, if forthcoming, would require an opinion on the constructive treason issue which Marshall had reserved.[265] However, as Marshall had anticipated in his opinion, Hay informed the court the following day "that he had nothing to offer to the jury of evidence or argument."[266]

It is worth mention, in addition, that at the close of Marshall's opinion he responded to intimations in the arguments of the Government's counsel that a decision in Burr's favor could lead to the Chief Justice's impeachment:

> That this court dares not usurp power is most true. That this court dares not shrink from its duty is not less true. No man is desirous of placing himself in a disagreeable situation. No man is desirous of becoming the peculiar subject of calumny. No man might he let the bitter cup pass from him without self-reproach, would drain it to the bottom. But if he have no choice in the case, if there be no alternative presented to him but a dereliction of duty or the opprobrium of those who are denominated the world, he merits the contempt

---

261 *Ibid.*
262 *Ibid.*, 177–78.
263 *Ibid.*, 178.

264 *Ibid.*, 179.
265 *Ibid.*, 180.
266 *Ibid.*

as well as the indignation of his country who can hesitate which to embrace.[267]

The jury was then instructed to apply the law as announced in Marshall's opinion to the facts as proved, and find a verdict of guilty or not guilty. When the foreman, Colonel Edward Carrington, announced the verdict, there was an uproar in the court room: the jury found that Burr was "not proved to be guilty under this indictment by any evidence submitted to us. We therefore find him not guilty."[268] The form of this verdict was challenged by Burr's counsel, who protested that it was irregular and hence should be altered to read simply "not guilty."[269] Hay, on the other hand, thought that the verdict should be recorded as found. Following some discussion and after hearing the opinion of certain members of the jury, Marshall decided that the verdict should remain as found but that an entry of "Not Guilty" be recorded.[270]

Not only was United States Attorney Hay outraged by Marshall's opinion and the verdict that followed, but Jefferson was even more irate. The President instructed Hay to demand that Burr and the other "conspirators" be committed on a treason charge "in order that they should be tried in the place where it should appear that the crime had been committed."[271] A lengthy argument ensued, but Marshall set the motion aside because Burr and the others were still to be tried for a misdemeanor under the second count of the indictment.[272]

Jefferson's views were strongly expressed in a letter to Hay on September 4 in which he wrote that Marshall's motives had been "not only to clear Burr, but to prevent the evidence from ever going before the world. But this latter case must not take place."[273] Accordingly, he instructed Hay that "not a single witness be paid or permitted to depart until his testimony had been committed to writing. . . . These whole proceedings will be laid before Congress, that they may . . . provide the proper remedy."[274] Jefferson was equally adamant in his wish that the indictment for misdemeanor be pressed, less with the expectation that Burr would be convicted than that Marshall would convict himself

---

[267] *Ibid.*, 179.
[268] *Ibid.*, 180.
[269] *Ibid.*
[270] *Ibid.*, 181. Following the recording of the verdict, Marshall "politely thanked the jury for their patient attention during the whole course of this long trial, and then discharged them." *Ibid.* See Robertson, *Burr Trial Reports*, II, 446–47.

[271] United States v. Burr, 25 F. Cas. 187, 187 (C.C.D. Va. 1807) (No. 14,694).
[272] *Ibid.*
[273] T. Jefferson to G. Hay, Sept. 4, 1807, in Adams, *History of United States*, III, 470; Beveridge, *John Marshall*, III, 515.
[274] T. Jefferson to G. Hay, note 273 supra.

in the court of public opinion. In a subsequent letter he reported to the United States Attorney that Madison agreed that the misdemeanor trial should proceed, for even "[i]f defeated, it will heap coals of fire on the head of the Judge. . . ."[275]

Quotations from the foregoing letters are set out less to produce added evidence of the President's vindictiveness and his penchant for turning personal antagonism into judicial or political issues than to emphasize two points already referred to in earlier chapters: first, the recurrent use of public opinion and the press in court proceedings of the day, especially by the government;[276] second, to emphasize that the concept of an independent judiciary was a thorn in the flesh of eighteenth-century-minded persons, like Thomas Jefferson, who continued to insist that the "third branch" of the government should be responsible to and represent the people.[277] Marshall, on the other hand, despite constant efforts to thwart him for political reasons, was endeavoring to build a rule of law that stood apart and was distinct from the vagaries of changing politics and the expediencies of the moment. Marshall's many opinions on motions, as well as his final decisions in cases fraught with political overtones (such as *Marbury* and *Burr*), reveal the sensitivity to the political effects that his language and rulings could have. Nonetheless, his rulings are couched in language that was nearly always soundly grounded upon legal precedent and reasoning.

When his second trial, for the misdemeanor charge, began in the first week of September, Burr immediately requested that the letter demanded from the President in the earlier subpoena *duces tecum* now be produced along with the second letter sent privately by Wilkinson to Jefferson on November 21, 1806.[278] He further stated that the President was in contempt for withholding the first letter and that process should be issued against him.[279] Hay admitted that he had the November 21 letter, on which Burr's counsel was now focusing, but wished to withhold certain passages of it. A subpoena *duces tecum* was issued by Marshall against Hay, who then offered to submit the entire letter to the court for its inspection.[280]

Hay's offer was instigated by Jefferson's earlier instructions, apparently sent in mid-August, when it was feared that Marshall might

---

[275] T. Jefferson to G. Hay, Sept. 7, 1807, in Ford, *Works of Jefferson*, X, 408.

[276] See chapter 7 supra.

[277] See chapter 2 supra.

[278] United States v. Burr, 25 F. Cas. 187, 189–90 (C.C.D. Va. 1807) (No. 14,694); see text accompanying notes 178–98 supra. The November 21 letter evidently contained "scandalous charges by Wilkinson against other respectable officials" and would "provide a basis for impeaching [Wilkinson's] credibility." Freund, "Foreword: On Presidential Privilege," 24.

[279] 25 F. Cas. at 190.

[280] *Ibid.*

enforce the earlier subpoena. On one occasion, in "a mere draft of a letter to Hay, which may never have been sent, but which is of the utmost importance"[281] to an understanding of Jefferson's views, the President wrote of "a spirit of reconciliation & [a] desire to avoid conflicts of authority between the high branches of the govmt. which would discredit it equally at home & abroad."[282] He continued by saying that he trusted Marshall would have the "prudence or good sense" not to permit the trial to become a conflict between the executive and judiciary but expressed concern that the issuance of "any process which should involve any act of force to be committed on the persons of the Exve or heads of depmts" could result in "breaking up the government."[283] Whether the foregoing letter was actually sent is not important because it illustrates Jefferson's perceptive anticipation of the course that events might take if the executive and judiciary were to clash over the issue of executive privilege. More importantly, it reveals his sensitivity to the appropriate relationship among the chief branches of government, which, on this occasion, he was able to view, at least in principle, more objectively than when his personal emotions became involved.

As it happened, the constitutional crisis foreseen by Jefferson did not occur, for on September 9 Hay presented to the court an excised copy of Wilkinson's letter, accompanied by a certificate from the President, which evidently was satisfactory to Burr.[284] The issue had not been resolved, however, when Marshall was required to deliver another and important opinion on the scope of executive privilege in the context of a defense motion to continue Burr's trial until the Wilkinson letter was produced. In that opinion, delivered on September 4,[285] Marshall held that, under the circumstances, Burr should be entitled to see the entire letter to judge for himself its materiality to his defense.[286]

Professor Freund has succinctly summarized this opinion of Mar-

---

[281] Ford, *Works of Jefferson*, X, 406.

[282] *Ibid.*

[283] *Ibid.*, 407.

[284] 25 F. Cas. at 193. The certificate read in part:

On re-examination of a letter of Nov. 12, 1806, from Genl. Wilkinson to myself . . . I find in it some passages entirely confidential, given for my information in the discharge of my executive functions, and which my duties & the public interest forbid me to make public. I have therefore given above a correct copy of all those parts which I ought to permit to be made public. Those not communicated are in nowise material for the purposes of justice on the charges of treason or misdemeanor depending against Aaron Burr; they are on subjects irrelevant to any issues which can arise out of those charges, & could contribute nothing towards his acquittal or conviction. . . .

T. Jefferson to G. Hay, Sept. 7, 1807, in Ford, *Works of Jefferson*, X, 409.

Professor Freund has surmised that Burr's counsel did not further contest the issue because acquittal on the misdemeanor charge "was confidently expected." Freund, "Foreword: On Presidential Privilege," 29.

[285] 25 F. Cas. at 190–92.

[286] *Ibid.*, 192.

shall, emphasizing his search for a "middle way" in defining the scope of a criminal defendant's right to a subpoena when confronted by a claim of executive privilege:

> In an ordinary case an affidavit of materiality would suffice to order production. But the President may have sufficient reasons for withholding a document whose exposure would be of "manifest inconvenience." It would be "a very serious thing," however, to withhold from the accused "any information material to the defence." But "on objections being made by the president to the production of a paper, the court would not proceed further in the case without such an affidavit as would clearly show the paper to be essential to the justice of the case." On the weight to be given to the President's objection, "the court would unquestionably allow their full force to those reasons." If a reservation of certain portions of a paper were made by the President, "all proper respect" would be paid to it. . . .[287]

With respect to Burr's application, Marshall found no need to enter into a balancing of these competing interests because Jefferson had waived his objections to production by delegating to Hay the discretion and authority to make such objections.[288]

Following these preliminary motions, more than fifty witnesses were called against Burr on the misdemeanor charge, but the evidence, taken as a whole, seems clearly to have shown that Burr's objective was the settlement of the Washita lands, and that the Mexican adventure was conditioned entirely on the existence of a state of war with Spain.[289] On September 15, after Marshall had rendered two opinions on the admissibility of evidence relevant to the misdemeanor charge and had "excluded almost the whole of his testimony,"[290] Hay moved that a *nolle prosequi* be entered on the indictment and that the jury be discharged. Marshall ruled that the jury could not be discharged at this stage of the case without Burr's consent. The defendant insisted on a

---

[287] Freund, "Foreword: On Presidential Privilege," 29.

[288] 25 F. Cas. at 192.

[289] Beveridge, *John Marshall*, III, 523. The testimony of these witnesses is collected in *Annals of Congress*, XVII, 422–683 (10th Cong., 1st sess.). Most of it was heard after the judgment of Burr's acquittal was rendered on September 15, on the prosecution's motion to commit Burr and Blennerhassett to another district for trial on a charge of treason. See

United States v. Burr, 25 F. Cas. 201, 201–202 (C.C.D. Va. 1807) (No. 14,694a).

[290] United States v. Burr, 25 F. Cas. 187, 201 (C.C.D. Va. 1807) (No. 14,694). Those opinions are contained in *ibid.*, 193–99, 200–201. In brief, they excluded any evidence other than testimony relevant to Burr's alleged acts of "beginning and setting on foot" an expedition against Spanish territory on Blennerhassett's Island as charged in the indictment.

verdict, and within less than an hour the jury returned with a verdict of "not guilty."[291]

Hay's next move was a motion to commit Burr, Blennerhassett, and Israel Smith upon a charge of treason by levying war "at the mouth of the Cumberland River, in the state of Kentucky."[292] The defendants were angered and "disgusted" with Marshall's even entertaining argument, and for giving wide scope to the introduction of evidence on this motion.[293] Republican leaders were likewise irate over Burr's acquittal on the misdemeanor count.[294] Interestingly, Hay wrote to Jefferson on October 15 that he believed that "a correct and perspicuous legal history of this trial would be a valuable document in the hands of intelligent legislators," but that it might nevertheless cause harm in arousing ill feelings against the "judicial system and the law itself."[295]

On October 20, after having heard testimony on the motion to commit since September 16, Marshall rendered his final opinion in the *Burr* trial, in which he sustained that motion.[296] He committed Burr and Blennerhassett for "preparing and providing the means for a military expedition" against Spain, and intimated that if the prosecution was "of opinion that a crime of deeper dye has been committed," the defendants could be charged with treason.[297] As for Smith, Marshall found no evidence on which to commit him, but held that he could be prosecuted in another district "[i]f he has really offended against the laws."[298] Marshall observed, after the opinion had been delivered, that Blennerhassett could be tried only in the district of Ohio, and with Hay's agreement, both men were committed to that district.[299] The Government, however, failed to pursue the prosecution, and Jefferson then turned his attention to Marshall.[300]

There were many who thought that Marshall had acted with timidity in the end and had yielded to public pressure in committing Burr and Blennerhassett.[301] On the other hand, praiseworthy though his conduct of the trial as a whole had been, Jefferson was infuriated by its outcome. Almost immediately he set in motion a congressional investigation of the proceedings with his Annual Message to Congress, delivered on October 27. In that Message, Jefferson stated:

---

[291] *Ibid.*, 201.

[292] United States v. Burr, 25 F. Cas. 201, 201–202 (C.C.D. Va. 1807) (No. 14,694a).

[293] Beveridge, *John Marshall*, III, 524.

[294] *Ibid.*, 525–26.

[295] G. Hay to T. Jefferson, Oct. 15, 1807, in *ibid.*, 526.

[296] See 25 F. Cas. at 202–207.

[297] *Ibid.*, 207.

[298] *Ibid.*

[299] *Ibid.*

[300] Adams, *History of United States*, III, 470.

[301] See Stafford, *Blennerhassett Papers*, 301.

I shall think it my duty to lay before you the proceedings, and the evidence publicly exhibited on the arraignment of the principal offenders before the circuit court of Virginia. You will be enabled to judge whether the defect was in the testimony, in the law, or in the administration of the law, and whether it shall be found, the legislature alone can apply or originate the remedy. The framers of our Constitution certainly supposed they had guarded, as well their Government against destruction by treason, as their citizens against oppression, under pretence of it, and if these ends are not attained, it is of importance to inquire by what means more effectual they may be secured.[302]

Revealing even more derogatory criticisms of Marshall's handling of the case are words from the first draft of his Message, eventually omitted by the President, questioning "whether there is a radical defect in the administration of law," and referring to "the wonderful refractoriness" of the law of treason as construed in Burr's case, "induc[ing] an awful doubt whether we all live under the same law."[303] Moreover, in this draft he observed that "[t]he right of the jury too to decide law as well as fact seems nugotory without the evidence pertinent to their sense of the law."[304]

Republican newspapers, especially the *Aurora* and the *Richmond Enquirer*, took up the pursuit. Letters that appeared and were widely copied proclaimed that Marshall should be impeached because of his "degrading" conduct. He was accused of "exhibit[ing] a culpable partiality towards the accused,"[305] and linked with Burr as "morally guilty" and "traitors in heart and in fact."[306] In Baltimore, Marshall, along with Burr, Blennerhassett, and Luther Martin, was hanged in

---

[302] *Annals of Congress*, XVII, 18 (10th Cong., 1st sess.).

[303] Ford, *Works of Jefferson*, X, 524.

[304] *Ibid.* Further indications of Jefferson's indignation with respect to the Chief Justice's handling of the Burr trial are contained in several of his letters written during this period. To General Wilkinson he complained that "[t]he scenes which have been acted at Richmond are such as have never before been exhibited in any country where all regard to public character has not yet been thrown off. They are equivalent to a proclamation of impunity to every traitorous combination which may be formed to destroy the Union. . . . However, they will produce an amendment to the Constitution which, keeping the judges independent of the Executive, will not leave them so, of the nation." T. Jefferson to J. Wilkinson, Sept. 20, 1807, in Ford, *Works of Jefferson*, X, 499–500. To William Thomson, who was preparing a publication of the trial proceedings, Jefferson commented that "it now appears we have no law but the will of the judge. Never will chicanery have a more difficult task than has now been accomplished to warp the text of the law to the will of him who is to construe it." T. Jefferson to W. Thomson, Sept. 26, 1807, in *ibid.*, 501.

[305] *Enquirer*, Dec. 4, 1807, in Beveridge, *John Marshall*, III, 534.

[306] *Enquirer*, Dec. 12, 1807, in *ibid.*, 535.

effigy.[307] Congressional reaction to the Burr trial was also hostile. Senator Giles reported a bill calling for the punishment of treason on February 11, 1808, and took the opportunity to engage in an elaborate criticism of Marshall's opinions in *Burr*.[308] Earlier a special Senate committee had been appointed to inquire whether Senator John Smith of Ohio should be removed from his seat for conduct arising out of his association with Aaron Burr.[309] On December 31 John Quincy Adams delivered the committee's report, in which it was resolved that Smith "had been guilty of conduct incompatible with his duty and station as a Senator of the United States," and should therefore be expelled from the Senate.[310] In the report Adams had occasion to cast doubts upon the validity of Marshall's opinion defining treason in the *Burr* case, since the indictment of Smith for treason was the same as the charges filed against Burr.[311] Adams' resolution eventually failed on April 9, 1808, after extensive proceedings on the floor of the Senate, by the narrow margin of 19–10, two-thirds of the Senators present being required for expulsion.[312]

So great was the popular outcry, so unified was Jefferson's vast Republican following at this time (the House was now almost unanimously Republican, and the Senate clearly pro-Jefferson) that Marshall might well have been impeached and convicted had not other affairs distracted the administration's attention. The attack on the American frigate *Chesapeake* by a British warship took place on June 22, 1807— at the height of the Burr trial—but next to nothing had been done about it beyond demanding an apology until July 30. On that date the President finally called a special session of Congress to commence on October 26.[313] Hence, the attacks on Marshall gave way to and were finally submerged by the deteriorating situation abroad, as war with Great Britain loomed imminent. It may well be that, as Beveridge surmises, "the thunders of popular denunciation [against Marshall were] gradually swallowed up in the louder and ever-increasing reverberations that heralded approaching war with Great Britain."[314]

---

[307] *Ibid.*
[308] See *Annals of Congress*, XVII, 108–27 (10th Cong., 1st sess.).
[309] *Ibid.*, 39.
[310] *Ibid.*, 62.
[311] *Ibid.*, 61.
[312] *Ibid.*, 324. See *ibid.*, 186–324.

Ironically, Senator Giles, apparently convinced of Smith's innocence, cast the decisive vote in his favor.
[313] *Ibid.*, 9.
[314] Beveridge, *John Marshall*, III, 545. See Adams, *History of United States*, III, 471.

CHAPTER IX

Executive Power and the Judiciary:
The Embargo

THE BURR TRIAL and its immediate aftermath should not be considered the last of the series of direct confrontations between Chief Justice John Marshall and President Jefferson over the role of the courts and the rule of law, on the one hand, and politics and the appropriate functions of the departments of government, on the other. The same threads so markedly apparent in the early years of the Republican administration ran on through succeeding episodes confronting the nation, even though its attention was diverted elsewhere. The executive branch continued to pose a serious threat to the Supreme Court and to the national judiciary generally.

Although the Republicans held a majority in Congress well after the 1800 election, and despite the clear influence of Republican party views upon congressional legislation, the ultimate leadership in Congress generally came from the executive, whether personally from President Jefferson or from his immediate political lieutenants, whose roles have been described. It was Jefferson who ordered, guided, suggested, and manipulated sentiment to bring about results that he and his Republican associates wished to achieve. Directly at times, but more often indirectly or covertly, it was primarily Jefferson who sought to bring the Federalist judges into line with his own policies. Sometimes, as in the unsuccessful impeachment trial of Chase, he acted chiefly through others. At other times, as in the Burr trial and his subsequent efforts to have Marshall condemned in Congress for its outcome, the President's interference was direct and unequivocal. His compulsive intermeddling in judicial business again appeared in the course of the enforcement of the Embargo laws, with which this chapter is mainly concerned.

The increasingly grave foreign situation, which worsened as the Burr trial was moving towards a close,[1] became critical on June 22,

---

[1] See chapter 8 supra.

IX: *Executive Power and the Judiciary: The Embargo*

1807, when the British warship *Leopard* attacked the American frigate *Chesapeake*.[2] So serious had the situation become by the end of the year that it began to engage the full attention of the government. Despite the initial public clamor and Jefferson's July proclamation ordering British armed vessels from American waters,[3] Congress was not called to convene in special session until October, nearly four months after the incident. In view of the deteriorating situation in Europe, the lack of a more prompt and forceful response on the part of the administration is difficult to explain. England had announced a wholesale blockade of French ports in 1804. In the succeeding three years it had ordered seizure of neutral vessels trading with the enemy wherever they were found, and it had forbidden them to enter the harbors of long stretches of the European coasts.[4] France, in turn, by the Berlin Decree of 1806 had ordered a blockade of England and seizure of all ships that had entered its harbors.[5] British Orders in Council of 1807 had gone still further and had almost literally prohibited the oceans to all neutral vessels unless they were engaged in commerce with England or her colonies.[6] Napoleon's Milan decree followed shortly, directing that ships that submitted to the Orders in Council were to be seized in French ports or on the high seas.[7]

These actions on the part of the belligerents were open violations of international law, and from a practical standpoint they were so highly injurious to the commerce and shipping of the United States that its own ports were in effect blockaded. Moreover, impressment of American seamen—long a source of complaint—continued unabated. In April of 1806 Congress had vainly attempted to exclude certain British products and merchandise from American markets by enacting the Non-Importation Act,[8] but its principal effect was to encourage smuggling. Hence, little of much consequence had been done by the executive or by Congress until the latter was convened at the end of October 1807. The administration's response to British policies and to the demands of the war-hawks who sought armed retaliation was to

---

[2] For an illuminating and detailed account of the incident giving rise to the "Chesapeake Affair," see H. Adams, *History of the United States of America* (New York, 1890), IV, 1–27.

[3] T. Jefferson, "Chesapeake Proclamation," July 2, 1807, in P. L. Ford, ed., *The Works of Thomas Jefferson* (New York, 1904–1905), X, 434.

[4] *State Papers and Publick Documents of the United States* (Boston, 1817), VII, 99–100 et seq.

[5] *Ibid.*, V, 478–79.

[6] *Ibid.*, VI, 62–68.

[7] *Ibid.*, 470–71. For an official collection of acts, decrees, orders, and proclamations affecting commercial rights of neutral nations issued by Great Britain, France, and other belligerent powers from 1791 through 1803, see *ibid.*, VII, 86–171.

[8] An Act to prohibit the importation of certain goods, wares, and merchandise, chapter 29, 2 Stat. 379 (1806).

stifle American world trade and severely to restrict even coastal commerce. Summarizing his reaction to the diplomatic dilemma, Jefferson wrote to General John Armstrong, the American Minister to France, that "[d]uring the present paroxysm of Europe, we have thought it wisest to break off all intercourse with her."[9] From this decision came the first Embargo Act, which Jefferson obtained from Congress in December 1807.[10] It was followed by the supplementary Acts of January,[11] March,[12] and April in 1808,[13] each of which increased the stringency of the law and the penalties for violations.

Thus, it is not surprising that the attention of the executive and of Congress had been directed away from the judiciary, and from Marshall in particular.[14] Under the new legislation, the President was empowered to impose an unlimited ban on all exports, and, although the Embargo was accepted at first as a necessary evil, it soon began to bear with particular hardship upon those who depended on foreign commerce as well as on coastal and Mississippi River trade for their livelihoods. Anger followed close upon hardship, and in New England sentiment towards the administration rapidly became hostile to the point of serious discussion of rebellion and separation from the Union.

The period that began with the Embargo and continued approximately to the War of 1812 further illustrates the continuing collisions between the judiciary and the other branches of government, as well as the currents of hostility that ran against many of the Court's decisions. It also provides instances of the Court's efforts to extricate itself from politics and political divisiveness and to restrict itself to cases and issues that were primarily legal and bearing upon individual rights. These efforts were attempts to draw lines of demarcation between what the Court viewed as the appropriate functions of the separate departments of government. This reflected the Supreme Court's struggle to establish what has been referred to as a rule of law, to keep from it the intrusions of executive policies, and to prevent, insofar as possible, controversial

---

[9] T. Jefferson to J. Armstrong, May 2, 1808, in Ford, *Works of Jefferson*, IX, 194.

[10] An Act laying an Embargo on all ships and vessels in the ports and harbors of the United States, chapter 5, 2 Stat. 451 (1807).

[11] An Act supplementary to the act, intituled "An act laying an embargo on all ships and vessels in the ports and harbors of the United States," chapter 8, 2 Stat. 453 (1808).

[12] An Act in addition to the act,

intituled "An act supplementary to the act, intituled An act laying an embargo on all ships and vessels in the ports and harbors of the United States," chapter 33, 2 Stat. 473 (1808).

[13] An Act in addition to the act intituled "An act laying an embargo on all ships and vessels in the ports and harbors of the United States," and the several acts supplementary thereto, and for other purposes, chapter 66, 2 Stat. 499 (1808).

[14] See chapter 8 supra.

political issues from coming before it. Although Marshall has been accorded general acclaim for the successes of the Court in this direction, one must bear in mind that even when the Court spoke unanimously, there were other different and independent voices behind it.

A recurrent theme of hostility towards the national courts runs like a red thread through such episodes as the impeachment of Chase and the trial of Burr, and it was noticeable in certain of the cases that arose during the Embargo period. That thread was the theory adopted by Republican leaders in the House, and to some extent in the Senate, to the effect that the courts should act in harmony with Congress and the executive because the latter branches, as duly elected representatives of the people, stood for the popular will. Hence, those leaders could plausibly assert that Federalist judges in an otherwise Republican government were an anomaly; they could point to impeachment as a means to promote such harmony rather than merely to punish a crime or misdemeanor; moreover, they could argue that a judicial decision declaring void an act of Congress or of the executive should be grounds for removing the judge who opposed the government's policy.

The distrust and even fear of the national judiciary that had characterized the attitude of the Republicans since their advent to power in 1801 had by no means dissipated during the ensuing years. If they had won the battle to prevent judicial reform through the 1802 Repeal Act,[15] they had lost both in the impeachment of Judge Chase and in their efforts to have Aaron Burr convicted of treason.[16] In this period, Jefferson's anti-judiciary view and policies, as well as his personal dislike of and resentment against John Marshall, were hardly less strong; even in 1808 Philip Barton Key could write about "the storm that is gathering" around the judiciary.[17]

Despite the Court's efforts to draw what today may be seen as neutral "constitutional" lines between the proper spheres of action of the departments of governments, "politics" so dominated men's thinking—whether radical or conservative—that sharp and strong divisions of opinion persisted and grew. Mounting distrust not only of Jefferson but of Republican policies could be seen in growing sectional divisions. Federalists in New England were alarmed at what they perceived as a Jeffersonian campaign to discredit and undermine the judiciary. Southern Federalists gave voice to similar concerns. Many in the North con-

---

[15] See chapter 5 supra.
[16] See chapters 7–8 supra.
[17] P. Key to J. London, Esq., of Wilmington, North Carolina, Jan. 4, 1808, quoted in H. G. Connor, "The Granville Estate and North Carolina," *University of Pennsylvania Law Review* LXII, 671, 692 (1914).

sidered the annexation of Louisiana an unconstitutional act that posed a threat to their economic and political interests.[18]

Accordingly, the Embargo laws, enacted towards the end of the "four lean years,"[19] exacerbated these tensions. Their actual and potential effect on the commerce of the eastern seaboard was immediately obvious to the Federalists, and to others as well who envisaged the destruction of their prosperity at the instigation of Jefferson. Within a short time the Embargo laws gave rise to a number of important cases, and with them came a change and shift in Republican policy, made necessary by new events and circumstances that directed the administration's attention away from vindictiveness towards the federal courts and judges. By the same token, there was also a shift in the work, and hence also in the outlook, of the Supreme Court, which now attempted, through new cases coming before it, further to accommodate the disparate functions of the several branches of government in accordance with the mandates of the Constitution. Beginning at least as early as 1808, the promotion of nationalism became an aspect of the Court's effort to promote the rule of law, protecting the judiciary on the one hand and, on the other, acknowledging the force and validity of legislation where acts of Congress did not violate what the Court regarded as fixed principles protecting individual rights. Another characteristic of the Court's work in this period was its general unwillingness to "make" law in areas where, despite strong reasons of policy, Congress or the executive had not acted. Another feature also persisted, namely, the Court's desire to avoid, where possible, cases of a political nature and thus to minimize the potential for direct confrontations with administration policies. This point of view is equally identifiable in the lower federal courts, where such problems could also be acute.

Two decisions deserve particular attention in this regard before consideration of other cases that illustrate the problem of collisions between the executive and the judiciary. One such case, in which the Court was able to avoid direct confrontation with the administration, involved the English common law rule as to expatriation—"once a subject, always a subject"—which had been used repeatedly by the British to justify the seizure and impressment of "English" subjects from American vessels. This practice had been going on for almost a decade before the *Chesapeake* affair,[20] and had been consistently de-

---

[18] For a description of the political climate relative to these issues, see C. Warren, *The Supreme Court in United States History* (Boston, 1928), I, 320–24.

[19] 1805–1809. See S. E. Morison,

The Oxford History of the United States 1783–1917 (Oxford, 1927), I, 255–69.

[20] This practice received congressional attention as early as 1798. See J. Gales and W. Seaton, comps., *The*

nounced by the administration. In *M'Ilvaine* v. *Coxe's Lessee*,[21] decided in 1808, it was held that because one Coxe, by express provision of a New Jersey statute, was a citizen of that State, he was incapable of throwing off his allegiance thereto.[22] The Court decided the expatriation issue on that ground and was thus able to avoid expressing an opinion on the common law rule, which the administration had been opposing at the executive level, chiefly through the diplomatic avenues of the State Department. The Court had been animated by a desire to find a "legal" solution and to avoid any "political" confrontation. Regardless of the Court's motives, the decision pleased the administration, which looked to the result rather than the reasoning behind it.

In another series of cases, also decided in the 1808 Term, the Court was directly faced with the question whether or not to follow an English doctrine with regard to British captures of vessels at sea. The question arose in *Croudson* v. *Leonard*,[23] which involved an American vessel condemned by a British court for attempting to break a blockade. A majority of the Court, in an opinion by Judge Washington, held that the English rule as to the conclusiveness of the decisions of foreign prize courts must be followed.[24] Livingston and Chase dissented. Judge Washington saw no proper judicial concern with problems that might result from such an inflexible adherence: "[i]f the injustice of the belligerent powers, and of their courts [i.e., those of Britain and France], should render this rule oppressive to the citizens of neutral nations . . . let the *government* in its wisdom adopt the proper means to remedy the mischief."[25] In an explicit formulation of his view of the distinction between the spheres of law and politics, Judge Washington went on to say, "I hold the rules of law, when once firmly established, to be beyond the control of those who are merely to pronounce what the law is, and if from any circumstance it has become impolitic, in a national point of view, it is for the nation to annul or modify it."[26]

The significance of this case lies in the Court's unwillingness to denounce or disregard an English doctrine merely because it could harm American neutral interests. Rather, the Court took the position that the remedy lay elsewhere than in the judicial department, thereby again emphasizing the distinction between "legal" and "political" ques-

---

Debates and Proceedings of the Congress of the United States (Washington, 1834–1856) (hereafter cited as *Annals of Congress*), IX, 2546 (5th Cong., 2d sess.).

[21] 4 Cranch 209 (1808) (decision of the Court); 2 Cranch 280 (1805) (first argument).

[22] 4 Cranch at 215. For the Court's statement of the narrow basis for its decision, see 4 Cranch at 211.

[23] 4 Cranch 434 (1808).

[24] *Ibid.*, 442–43.

[25] *Ibid.*, 442 (emphasis supplied).

[26] *Ibid.*, 442–43.

tions, which had been discussed at length in the *Marbury* case. For obvious reasons, the decision was much resented by the administration,[27] which still clung to the older but obsolescent eighteenth-century idea that it was the duty of the judiciary to support policies of the legislature and of the executive. Leading Republicans therefore continued to resent and resist the independence of the judiciary, which was still composed largely of members of the Federalist party

Other opinions reflect changing conceptions of the judiciary as a separate department of government. In *Talbot* v. *Seeman*,[28] for example, Judge Chase stated that he was opposed to having counsel read certain instructions from the President in connection with the seizure of some French armed vessels, while Judge Paterson and John Marshall took the position that orders from the executive could not be binding on the judiciary.[29] Such distinctions were viewed as overly sophisticated by leading Republicans; the decisions they led to, however, were viewed as either correct or partisan, depending upon whether the result favored or impeded the administration's policies.

In the highly charged atmosphere engendered by the Embargo, when nearly every decision involving it was looked upon as a vote of confidence for, or as an insult to, the President, there arose two further cases of much wider notoriety and of greater legal and political importance than those just discussed. The first of these, *Gilchrist* v. *Collector of Charleston*,[30] was heard in May 1808 by Judge William Johnson of the Supreme Court, sitting on circuit in the District of South Carolina. The case involved the Act of April 25, 1808.[31] Section 11 of that Act had vested in collectors of customs the authority "to detain any vessel ostensibly bound with a cargo to some other port of the United States, whenever in their opinions the intention is to violate or evade any of the provisions of the acts laying an embargo, until the decision of the President of the United States be had thereupon."[32] Jefferson interpreted this authority very broadly, and on May 6 wrote to Secretary of the Treasury Gallatin that "it would be well to recommend to every collector to consider every shipment of provisions, lumber, flax-

---

[27] In a letter to Jefferson dated June 22, 1810, Madison referred to a Pennsylvania decision that held to the contrary on the same issue. Madison characterized it as a "masterly opinion," "a most *thorough*, investigation, and irrefragable disproof of the . . . doctrine . . . adopted by a decision of the Supreme Court of the U.S." G. Hunt, ed., *The Writings of James Madison* (New York, 1908), VIII, 104.

[28] 1 Cranch 1 (1801).

[29] See *ibid.* at 10 note (a).

[30] 10 F. Cas. 355 (C.C.D. S.C. 1808) (No. 5,420).

[31] See note 13 supra.

[32] 2 Stat. at 501.

seed, tar, cotton, tobacco, &c., enumerating the articles, as sufficiently suspicious for detention and reference here."[33]

The collectors' right of determination was thus apparently eliminated, and popular furor in the newspapers was intense.[34] Within less than three weeks, the validity of the President's order was brought to a test in *Gilchrist*. In accordance with the criteria announced in Jefferson's directive, a vessel belonging to Gilchrist and others, loaded with rice for Baltimore, had been detained in Charleston, despite the personal belief of the Collector there that the real destination of the ship was Baltimore and that the owners did not plan to break the Embargo. The Collector, facing possible discharge or other sanction if he disobeyed instructions, or a ruinous action for damages by the owners if he complied, willingly submitted to the jurisdiction of the court when Gilchrist applied for a mandamus to compel issuance of a clearance. For reasons that are not clear, the United States Attorney in Charleston did not oppose the motion.[35]

The complete lack of opposition to Gilchrist's motion no doubt explains the brevity of Judge Johnson's opinion, which disposed of the jurisdictional question in a single sentence: "It is not denied that if the petitioners be legally entitled to a clearance, this court may interpose its authority, by the writ of mandamus, to compel the collector to grant it."[36] The opinion proceeded to present a convincing argument to the effect that discretionary authority vested in collectors by act of Congress (which might have, but did not, vest that discretion in the President or any other appropriate officer) could not legally be altered by an instruction of higher executive officials. "[T]he act of congress," Johnson stated, "does not authorize the detention of this vessel."[37] Without the sanction of law, he wrote, "the collector is not justified by the instructions of the executive, in increasing restraints upon commerce. . . ."[38]

---

[33] T. Jefferson to A. Gallatin, May 6, 1808, in H. Adams, ed., *The Writings of Albert Gallatin* (Philadelphia, 1879), I, 386.

[34] See Warren, *Supreme Court*, I, 325, note 2.

[35] See "Judge Johnson's remarks on the publication of the attorney general's letter to the president, on the subject of the mandamus issued by the circuit court of South Carolina to the collector, in the case of The Resource," 10 F. Cas. at 359, 361.

[36] *Ibid.*, 356.

[37] *Ibid.*, 357.

[38] *Ibid.* The opinion also noted that the "instructions" from Secretary Gallatin, like the passage from Jefferson's letter quoted in text accompanying note 33 supra, were in reality more in the nature of advice or a recommendation than "orders" in any strict sense. See 10 F. Cas. at 356. The extent to which this fact influenced Judge Johnson's resolution of the case is unclear, although his brief opinion concludes with the observation that "from a temperate consideration of [the letter from Gallatin to the Charleston collector supposed by both parties to require detention] this case does not appear to come within the spirit and meaning of the instructions which it contains." *Ibid.*, 357.

"The officers of our government, from the highest to the lowest, are equally subjected to legal restraint; . . . all of them feel themselves equally incapable . . . to attempt an unsanctioned encroachment upon individual liberty."[39]

This was the decision; these were the words of the President's own appointee, a Republican judge admonishing a Republican President, and the *Gilchrist* case has often been acclaimed on this ground.[40] What appears to have escaped the attention of most lawyers and historians is that Johnson was making almost exactly the same distinctions between law and politics and between vested individual rights and the shifting policies of other government departments that Marshall had made earlier in *Marbury* v. *Madison*. No one on the Supreme Court at this time, except Marshall himself, was more articulate about this distinction than the recently appointed Johnson, who, although he was still in his thirties, did not hesitate to speak up for the independence of the judiciary, for individual rights, and particularly for the principle of the separateness of the departments of government. Until now, the administration had believed him to be a sound Republican.[41] On the Court, however, although he frequently differed with his brethren, his voice was heeded because of his clear judicial capacities and his independence of mind.

Jefferson was indignant at this block in the way of his Embargo policy, which he viewed as a personal attack. Relations between Johnson and the President became strained, as evidenced by Johnson's curious attempt to initiate correspondence with a letter concerning a horticultural matter in 1809.[42] Press reaction to Johnson's opinion was almost as strong as it had been to the decision of the *Burr* case.[43] Republican newspapers immediately assailed it as another example of judicial high-handedness; Federalists, on the other hand, praised the Judge and took delight in the fact that Jefferson's first Republican appointee to the Supreme Court had frustrated the President's own policy.

Johnson's opinion so disturbed Jefferson that he procured an opinion from his Attorney-General, Caesar A. Rodney, attacking Johnson's statement of the law, and sent it to all collectors and marshals.[44] Jefferson also distributed it to the press, and, upon reading the letter

---

[39] *Ibid.*, 356.

[40] See, e.g., D. Morgan, *Justice William Johnson: The First Dissenter* (Columbia, S.C., 1954), 65, 67; Warren, *Supreme Court*, I, 326–27.

[41] Morgan, *Justice William Johnson*, 49–51.

[42] *Ibid.*, 73–74.

[43] Warren, *Supreme Court*, I, 326–27.

[44] T. Jefferson to C. Pinckney, July 18, 1808, in A. A. Lipscomb, ed., *The Writings of Thomas Jefferson* (Washington, 1904), XII, 104 (hereafter cited as Lipscomb, *Writings of Jefferson*).

in a Charleston paper, Judge Johnson stated that "an act so unprecedented in the history of executive conduct could be intended for no other purpose than to secure the public opinion on the side of the executive and in opposition to the judiciary."[45] In the letter, dated July 15, 1808, Rodney attempted to deliver telling blows against Johnson's assumption of jurisdiction, including the arguments that a judge in the Circuit Court had no power to issue a mandamus under the Judiciary Act of 1789,[46] and that Johnson had sought to impose unlawful restraints upon the government in a case where "there was a controlling power in the chief magistrate of the United States."[47] He went on to say that there did not appear to be anything in the Constitution "which favours an indefinite extension of the jurisdiction of courts, over the ministerial officer within the executive department," and he objected particularly to the "interposition by a mandatory writ, taking the executive authority out of the hands of the president, and prescribing the course, which he and the agents of any department must pursue."[48] Rodney pointed out that even the Supreme Court, in *Marbury* v. *Madison*, had refused to issue a mandamus to the Secretary of State on the ground that it would be an exercise of original jurisdiction not authorized by the Constitution.[49] Ironically, because the statements were made by a Republican official, the Attorney-General remarked upon the separateness of the departments of government, which in his view "should dictate great circumspection to each, in the exercise of powers having any relation to the other."[50] In language reminiscent of the *Marbury* opinion, he pointed out that the courts are the source of legal redress for wrongs committed by ministerial officers, none of whom is above the law, but that there exists a material and obvious distinction between redressing a wrong committed by an executive officer and compelling him by a mandatory writ to follow a prescribed course of action.[51] Rodney's opinion then concluded with the assertion that to permit an executive function to be defeated in the name of judicial power could thwart a vital part of the Constitution.[52]

As might be expected, Rodney's views, as well as the impropriety of Jefferson's action in publishing them, aroused indignation and violent criticism in the Federalist press, and, from Republican papers, praise for a just rebuke to a member of the judiciary.[53] As for Judge Johnson,

---

[45] 10 F. Cas. at 359.
[46] "Letter from the attorney general to the president of the United States, relative to the proceedings of the circuit court of South Carolina in the case of The Resource," *ibid.* at 357.
[47] *Ibid.*, 358.

[48] *Ibid.*
[49] *Ibid.*, 357.
[50] *Ibid.*, 358.
[51] *Ibid.*, 358–59.
[52] *Ibid.*, 359.
[53] Warren, *Supreme Court*, I, 331–34.

it was from his own copy of the Charleston paper that he first learned of Rodney's opinion,[54] and he was so outraged when he learned that the opinion had been given to the newspapers that he published a reply in which he set forth an elaborate defense of his decision several times longer than the original opinion. In this reply he stated:

> The courts do not pretend to impose any restraint upon any officer of government, but what results from a just construction of the laws of the United States. Of these laws the courts are the constitutional expositors; and every department of government must submit to their exposition; for laws have no legal meaning but what is given them by the courts to whose exposition they are submitted. It is against the law, therefore, and not the courts, that the executive should urge the charge of usurpation and restraint: a restraint which may at times be productive of inconveniences, but which is certainly very consistent with the nature of our government: one which it is very possible the president may have deserved the plaudits of his country for having transcended, in ordering detentions not within the embargo acts, but which notwithstanding, it is the duty of our courts to encounter the odium of imposing.[55]

In conclusion, he stated:

> There never existed a stronger case for calling forth the powers of a court; and whatever censure the executive sanction may draw upon us, nothing can deprive us of the consciousness of having acted with firmness, impartiality and an honest intention to discharge our duty. . . . It may be possible to prove the court wrong in interposing its authority; but certainly establishing the point of their want of jurisdiction will not prove the legality of the instructions given to the collector. The argument is not that the executive have done right, but that the judiciary had no power to prevent their doing wrong.[56]

Rodney was not to be quelled by Johnson's reply, and he wrote to the President lamenting the state of his profession: "The judicial power, if permitted, will swallow all the rest. They will become omnipotent. . . . It is high time for the people to apply some remedy to the disease. You can scarcely elevate a man to a seat in a Court of Justice before he catches the leprosy of the Bench."[57]

Later in the year, a grand jury of the Circuit Court in Georgia took the extraordinary step of issuing a presentment against Johnson "for improper interference with the Executive."[58] His decision was

---

[54] *See* text accompanying note 45 supra.

[55] 10 F. Cas. at 364.

[56] *Ibid.*, 366.

[57] C. Rodney to T. Jefferson, Oct. 31, 1808, as reproduced in Warren, *Supreme Court*, I, 336.

[58] Warren, *Supreme Court*, I, 337.

characterized as an "attempt of the Judiciary to defeat the intentions and salutary measures of our government, by issuing a mandamus and compelling an officer of the revenue to violate those measures."[59] To this condemnation of his issuance of the mandamus, Judge Johnson firmly replied on December 15, 1808:

> It is very far from correct in fact that the Circuit Court had the least wish or idea of embarrassing the execution of the Embargo Laws. The single question before the Court was whether the law or the instructions of the Executive was to govern. If you are prepared, gentlemen, to waive the government of the laws and submit without repining to every errour or encroachment of the several Departments of government, avow it to your fellow citizens, and prevail on them to abolish the Constitution, or get into office a feeble and submissive Judiciary. For what cause are we now reproached? For interposing the authority of the laws in the protection of individual rights, of your rights and the rights of succeeding generations. If such is to be the reward of his discharge of a painful and invidious duty, so important to the security of those who censure us, small will be the inducement to discharge it with fidelity.[60]

Most customs collectors, on the basis of the opinion of Jefferson's Attorney-General, proceeded to ignore Judge Johnson's decision,[61] and some who did so were sued.[62] At the end of July, Gallatin wrote to Jefferson that if the Embargo were to continue, two principles should be adopted:

> [First,] that not a single vessel shall be permitted to move without the special permission of the Executive; [and second,] that the collectors be invested with the general power of seizing property any-

---

[59] *Ibid.*

[60] *Ibid.*, 337–38.

[61] Five years later, in M'Intyre v. Wood, 7 Cranch 504 (1813), the Supreme Court, in a brief opinion written by Judge Johnson, decided that "the power of the Circuit Courts to issue the writ of mandamus, is confined exclusively to those cases in which it may be necessary to the exercise of their jurisdiction." *Ibid.*, 505. Johnson's opinion concluded with an almost sheepish reference to *Gilchrist*:

> A case occurred some years since in the Circuit Court of South Carolina, the notoriety of which may apologize for making an observation upon it here. It was a manda-

mus to a collector to grant a clearance, and unquestionably could not have been issued but upon a supposition inconsistent with the decision in this case. But that mandamus was issued upon the voluntary submission of the collector and the district attorney, and in order to extricate themselves from an embarrassment resulting from conflicting duties. *Volenti non fit injuria.* *Ibid.*, 506. Despite this attempt at a distinction, the ultimate resolution of the issue upheld the position Rodney had taken earlier.

[62] See, e.g., A. Gallatin to T. Jefferson, Nov. 8, 1808, in Adams, *Albert Gallatin*, I, 427.

where. . . . I am sensible that such arbitrary powers are equally dangerous and odious. . . . Congress must either invest the Executive with the most arbitrary powers and sufficient force to carry the embargo into effect, *or give it up altogether.* And in this last case I must confess that, unless a change takes place . . . I see no alternative but war.[63]

As the year wore on, and as Congress was about to convene, Jefferson inquired of Gallatin whether it might not "be well to have a bill ready for Congress on the defects which experience has developed in the embargo laws? Mandamus. The discretion of the collector expressly subjected to instructions from hence."[64] Accordingly, Gallatin suggested to Senator William B. Giles that remedial legislation to aid in the stringent enforcement of the Embargo be introduced in Congress.[65] In the course of his explanation, one of the most interesting and extraordinary statements of the entire controversy was made. Writing both as Secretary of the Treasury and as chief enforcement officer of the President, Gallatin openly admitted that the President had no authority to give binding instructions to the collectors of customs, and that the Act of April 25, 1808, was badly worded and impracticable.[66] He further admitted that, aside from the jurisdictional problem, Judge Johnson's view of the law was correct, and that "the court, supposing they had jurisdiction, could not, from the manner in which the question was brought before them, have decided otherwise than they did. . . ."[67] For this as well as for other reasons, a change in the law, by means of the Enforcement Bill, referred to below, was introduced in the Senate in December 1808.[68] Curiously, Gallatin's letter was reported to the Senate and ordered to be printed.[69] However, no changes in the Judiciary Act, with respect to the mandamus issue, were advanced, despite a proposal on that subject in Gallatin's letter. Giles, while supporting the measure, could not forbear a gratuitous reproach of the judiciary generally, and he denounced the "disgrace" witnessed the previous year in Marshall's conduct of the *Burr* trial.[70]

The *Gilchrist* case did not gain lasting importance because a courageous judge was willing to stand up to an overzealous President intent on rigorous enforcement of the Embargo laws. Historically, the decision did not strikingly change the course of events. Its political im-

---

[63] A. Gallatin to T. Jefferson, July 29, 1808, in *ibid.,* 398–99 (emphasis supplied).
[64] T. Jefferson to A. Gallatin, Oct. 25, 1808, in *ibid.,* 420.
[65] A. Gallatin to W. Giles, Nov. 24, 1808, in *ibid.,* 428.
[66] *Ibid.,* 429.

[67] *Ibid.,* 434.
[68] *Annals of Congress,* XIX, 238 et seq. (10th Cong., 2d sess.). See text accompanying note 87 infra.
[69] *Ibid.,* 232–35.
[70] *Ibid.,* 274–75. See also the indignant reply of Senator Hillhouse of Connecticut, *ibid.,* 282–98.

portance, which was very considerable, derives less from the opposing interest groups involved—shipowners and merchants versus the administration's attitudes expressed in the Embargo policy—than from the collision that it brought about between the executive and judicial branches of the government and from the deep undercurrent of partisan politics it aroused. The decision took on crucial importance in the continuing efforts that were being made by the Supreme Court judges (in this case a Republican judge) to separate law from politics. Ironically, from the standpoint of the Republicans, judicial independence—so distrusted and denounced by the President since his accession to power —was soon to work in favor of the administration. Even before the new Enforcement Act became law, the validity of the Embargo Act had been fully upheld by a Federalist judge in a United States District Court in Massachusetts, as appears below. Yet party feeling ran so high that both Federalists and Republicans were slow in perceiving that the attitudes of the national courts did not stem from party affiliations or aberrations.

The unconstitutionality of the Embargo Act had been repeatedly charged in New England and elsewhere. Since the decision of *Gilchrist* in May of 1808, anti-Embargo sentiment had intensified and spread. This was especially true in Massachusetts, where Federalist policies were still favored and where economic welfare depended so heavily on shipping. There, anti-Embargo sentiment had reached such a pitch that open violations of the laws were commonplace, and on at least one occasion customs officials were prevented by a mob from carrying out their duties.[71] So flagrant were these violations that respectable opinion in the Commonwealth sought to sanction them by proclaiming that the Embargo laws were unconstitutional, and even Chief Justice Parsons had openly, publicly, and extrajudicially condemned them.[72]

Debate on the constitutionality of the Embargo reached its first real peak in *United States* v. *The William*,[73] heard by Judge Davis in October 1808.[74] The case itself was an action brought by the United States for the forfeiture of a vessel alleged to have broken the Embargo. Chief counsel for the defendants, and therefore arguing against the constitutionality of the Embargo, was Samuel Dexter, one of the leading members of the Massachusetts Bar at that time. Among those who argued in favor of the Embargo was Joseph Story, still a young attorney and three years away from his appointment to the Supreme Court.[75]

---

[71] A. Gallatin to T. Jefferson, Aug. 17, 1808, in Adams, *Albert Gallatin*, I, 406.

[72] Warren, *Supreme Court*, I, 341–42.

[73] 28 F. Cas. 614 (D. Mass. 1808) (No. 16,700).

[74] Warren, *Supreme Court*, I, 345.

[75] *Ibid.*, 344.

The highly respected Judge Davis was an ardent member of the Federalist party; he was a man who the commercial interests, at least, felt confident would be receptive to their positions and their arguments. He had served as United States Attorney under President Adams and had been appointed by the latter to the district judgeship in 1801.[76]

Since the evidence of the acts alleged against *The William*'s owners seemed clear, Dexter and his associates concentrated their defense efforts on trying to demonstrate that the Embargo laws were unconstitutional. Early in the course of the trial, and in order to dispose of that issue, Judge Davis wrote a strong opinion that rejected these contentions. To the chagrin of Federalists and to the surprised delight of Republicans, Davis upheld the right of Congress to enact the Embargo laws as an exercise of the commerce power and of the war power. Much of the opinion necessarily dealt with the issue of judicial review and with the power of the courts to declare acts of Congress invalid. Davis held that that power extended only to cases that involved repugnancy to express provisions or restrictions contained in the Constitution.[77] Thus, he limited judicial review to situations in which "the superior, commanding will of the people . . . would be clearly and peremptorily expressed."[78] Judge Davis' language is instructive, the more so since it is not clear that he was familiar with the *Marbury* decision:[79]

> To extend this censorial power further, and especially to extend it to the degree, contended for in the objections to the act now under consideration, would be found extremely difficult, if not impracticable, in execution. To determine where the legitimate exercise of discretion ends, and usurpation begins, would be a task most delicate and arduous. It would, in many instances, be extremely difficult to settle it, even in a single body. It would be much more so, if to be adjusted by two independent bodies, especially if those bodies, from the nature of their constitution, must proceed by different rules. Before a court can determine, whether a given act of congress, bearing relation to a power with which it is vested, be a legitimate exercise of that power, or transcend it, the degree of legislative discretion, admissible in the case, must first be determined. Legal discretion is limited. It is thus defined by Lord Coke, "Discretio est discernere, per legem, quid sit justum." Political discretion has a far wider range. It embraces, combines and considers, all circumstances, events and projects, foreign or domestick, that can affect the national interest. Legal discretion has not the means of ascertaining the grounds, on which political

---

[76] *Ibid.*, 343.
[77] 28 F. Cas. at 619. The decision should not have come as a surprise to members of the Bar because it is wholly consistent with Marbury v. Madison.
[78] *Ibid.*, 620.
[79] *Ibid.*, 617, note 1. But see reference note 82, infra.

discretion may have proceeded. It seems admitted, that necessity might justify the acts in question. But how shall legal discretion determine, that political discretion, surveying the vast concerns committed to its trust, and the movements of conflicting nations, has not perceived such necessity to exist? Considerations of this nature have induced a doubt of the competency, or constitutional authority of the court, to decide an act invalid, in a case of this description.[80]

At the time, the opinion seemed to be a great victory for Republican supporters of the Embargo, but its practical effect was considerably lessened by subsequent developments in the case. Dexter, apparently confident of the jurors' sympathy, continued to argue the issue of the Embargo's unconstitutionality, despite repeated admonitions from the bench. Finally, in a highly dramatic confrontation, Davis threatened to commit him for contempt; but Dexter replied that he could not, in good conscience, refrain from bringing up the constitutional question.[81] The judge did not carry out his threat, and Dexter continued to press the issue. Ultimately, a verdict for the defendants was returned.[82]

Evaluations of *The William* case by Charles Warren and Henry Adams stress the courage and impartiality of Judge Davis in making a decision that was detrimental to the interests of his political associates and that threatened to arouse the resentment of his own community.[83] Little attention has been drawn, however, to the fact that Davis' failure to commit Dexter, despite his flagrant disregard of repeated admonitions from the bench, revealed that the judge was significantly more considerate of local sentiment than these authors have suggested. Even though the jury was probably strongly inclined to find for the defendants, it seems possible that a different result might have been reached had Davis carried out his threat.

As case after case alleging violations of the Embargo came before the Massachusetts District Court, the juries refused to convict.[84] According to John Quincy Adams, over forty cases were tried in the course of seven or eight weeks by the District Court at the end of 1808, yet not a single conviction was obtained.[85] Other signs of anti-administration feeling were becoming apparent: for example, the number of

---

[80] *Ibid.*, 620.

[81] "Sigma" [Lucius Manlius Sargent], *Reminiscences of Samuel Dexter* (Boston, 1857), 60–61, excerpted by Warren, *Supreme Court*, I, 345, note 2.

[82] An especially interesting account of the case is given in C. P. Curtis, "A Strange Story about Marbury *versus* Madison in Salem, 1808," *Pro-*

ceedings of the Massachusetts Historical Society LXXI, 133 (1959).

[83] See H. Adams, *History of United States*, IV, 268–70; Warren, *Supreme Court*, I, 347–48.

[84] J. Q. Adams to E. Bacon, Dec. 21, 1808, in W. C. Ford, ed., *The Writings of John Quincy Adams* (New York, 1914), III, 277.

[85] J. Q. Adams to W. Giles, Jan. 16, 1809, in *ibid.*, 287.

Federalist electors of the President was forty-seven in 1808, compared with fourteen in 1804.[86] Probably the newspapers of the time best reflect the growing sentiment against the Embargo that eventually became its death knell.

Becoming more zealous and adamant, the administration sought and obtained, in January 1809, enactment of the so-called Enforcement Act,[87] which gave Jefferson sweeping powers over the movement of goods anywhere near American borders. This legislation, which attempted to close every hole in the Embargo through which a limited trade had been carried on, was greeted with violent hostility in New England. Coasting vessels were required to post prohibitively costly bonds, collectors were granted virtually despotic powers, and the right to plead distress or accident was almost eliminated. Even after the Enforcement Act of 1809, smuggling continued, the militia failed to act, and juries were obdurate in their refusals to convict, whatever might be the facts of the cases. States'-rights sentiment mounted, and the views that had prompted the Virginia and Kentucky Resolutions of 1798–1799,[88] so abhorrent to most other States at that time, rose again in New York and Connecticut. Public opinion began to proclaim the rights of States and to denounce the legislative acts regarded as unconstitutional.[89] Sentiment among New Englanders, at least, was growing in favor of separation from the Union, a sentiment that was to lead extreme Federalists to convene the Hartford Convention.[90]

Earlier, along the coast and elsewhere, efforts were made to close the dragnet and to enforce the Embargo through other forms of court action, but also without success. Smuggling from Canada to Vermont had reached such a point in May of 1808 that the President had proclaimed a state of insurrection. State troops and Army units had been called upon, but smuggling continued, and violence reached a peak with the murder of revenue officers and militiamen. Several of those accused were indicted for treason by order of Attorney-General Rodney, but, when they were brought to trial before the United States Circuit Court,[91] Judge Livingston joined in holding that the indictment could not be sustained: "[N]o single act in opposition to or in evasion of a law, however violent or flagrant when the object is private gain, can be construed into levying war against the United States."[92] This decision,

---

[86] H. Adams, *History of United States*, IV, 287.

[87] An Act to enforce and make more effectual an act intituled "An act laying an embargo on all ships and vessels in the ports and harbors of the United States," and the several acts supplementary thereto, chapter 5, 2 Stat. 506 (1809).

[88] See chapter 2 supra.

[89] Warren, *Supreme Court*, I, 358–60.

[90] *Ibid.*, 357–58.

[91] United States v. Hoxie, 26 F. Cas. 397 (C.C.D. Vt. 1808) (No. 15, 407).

[92] As quoted in Warren, *Supreme Court*, I, 352.

which effectively barred treason indictments as a means of Embargo enforcement, set in motion unsuccessful efforts by Republicans in Congress to obtain legislation expanding the law of treason or making "seditious acts" criminal.[93]

Another decision, *United States* v. *William Smith*, also impeded for a time the effectiveness and the intended operation of the Embargo. In that case, John Marshall held that a criminal indictment could not be supported for violation of one of the Embargo Acts because the statute provided for forfeitures and civil fines, which were therefore to be regarded as exclusive remedies in the absence of express provisions for criminal penalties.[94] Significantly, Marshall avoided going further into the vexing and controversial question of the federal common law of crimes, discussed in the next chapter, but he did state in the course of his opinion that the Court need not decide "whether an indictment can be supported in this Court on common law principles."[95] This legislative defect in all four Embargo Acts was cured by the Enforcement Act, with the result that thereafter criminal indictments were obtainable for Embargo violations.

A different type of "interference" on the part of the federal courts appeared in decisions hampering or neutralizing the effect of the so-called "stay-laws," which were enacted in certain southern States favorable to the administration's Embargo policy. These laws were intended to assist debtors whose businesses were harmed by the Embargo laws: in Virginia and Georgia, for example, they provided that the collections of judgments by execution were to be postponed until six months after the repeal of the Embargo Acts.[96] When a case involving the Virginia stay-law came before John Marshall, sitting in the federal Circuit Court, he held that this type of State law was not binding on the processes of the federal courts.[97] The result of this decision, which did not consider the constitutionality of the law as an impairment of the obligation of contract, was to provide those with access to the federal courts through diversity of citizenship an advantage over in-State plaintiffs. It therefore encouraged the latter group to assign judgments to citizens of other States, and in this way diminished the effectiveness of the Embargo.[98]

The foregoing decisions are illustrative less of judicial interference with administration policies that had been put into operation by the executive or by the Congress than of the independence of the federal courts, which were attempting to move "law" away from "politics" and thus play a new and different role. In fact, in some situations the courts

---

[93] *Ibid.*, 353.
[94] *Ibid.*, 355.
[95] *Ibid.*, 355–56.

[96] *Ibid.*, 353.
[97] *Ibid.*, 353–54.
[98] *Ibid.*, 354.

aided administration policy, not because they necessarily approved of that policy from a political point of view, but because the formulation and enforcement of the policy seemed proper under the kinds of distinctions and differentiations that Marshall had made in *Marbury*. Judge Davis' decision on the constitutionality of the Embargo reflects this point. Political decisions were properly within the province of the Congress and the executive when made pursuant to the fundamental law in the Constitution. Thus, in the case of *The William*, Judge Davis cautiously took the position that since some political judgment was involved in the restrictions imposed by the Embargo, the judiciary was not the appropriate branch to determine its validity.

So stringent had regulation become, so close was all seagoing commerce to coming to a standstill, that even Gallatin—who had drafted the Enforcement Act of 1809—declared a week before its enactment: "What I had foreseen has taken place. A majority will not adhere to the embargo much longer; and if war be not speedily determined on, submission will soon ensue."[99] The Embargo was staggering to its end, and Jefferson finally admitted his anxieties.[100] He had asked for and obtained power and more power, and, with the increase in the authority he acquired, he had become steadily more insistent that commerce, industry, and even agriculture yield to the great objective he had set for himself. As increased hostility became apparent among large, active, and powerful sectors of the country, it was plain that the Enforcement Act could not be carried out, that the goal could never be attained. Both houses of Congress soon voted to repeal the Embargo laws and to substitute a non-intercourse act prohibiting trade with England and France.[101] Three days before leaving office, the President signed an end to the Embargo.

At least as early as 1809, perceptive observers, whether Republican or Federalist, could see the bent of the national judiciary in the cases that arose from the Embargo Acts. Not only had those Acts been declared constitutional by a federal district judge, but constitutionality was clearly presumed in later cases that reached the Supreme Court. If there were decisions that seemed to hamper the effective administration of the Acts, there were others that, for different reasons, supported and furthered those laws. In short, any charge that the primarily Federalist bench was deliberately conspiring to embarrass or thwart the Republican administration is groundless. It is submitted that an im-

---

[99] A. Gallatin to J. Nicholson, Dec. 29, 1808, in Adams, *Albert Gallatin*, I, 449.

[100] See, e.g., T. Jefferson to Dr. G. Logan, Dec. 27, 1808, in Lips-comb, *Writings of Jefferson*, XII, 220.

[101] *Annals of Congress*, XIX, 353 et seq., 1303 et seq. (10th Cong., 2d sess.).

portant key to understanding the work of the federal judiciary in this area lies in the interpretation first presented in the chapter discussing the decision of *Marbury* v. *Madison*,[102] and subsequently enlarged upon here in the discussion of the decisions by Judge Johnson and Judge Davis.

---

[102] See chapter 6 supra.

CHAPTER X

States' Rights and the National Judiciary

W HILE THE continuing confrontations between President Jefferson and the Supreme Court were still at their peak, and even before the Chase impeachment and the Burr trial had exacerbated that relationship, there began to come before the Court a series of cases that produced a new and historically important conflict. This conflict was constitutional in nature. It arose out of the necessity of resolving a very different set of problems involved in the working relationship between the several State governments and the national government. They were problems that were to enlarge in scope and to tax the energies of the Court during most of the nineteenth century.

The nationalism that had resulted from the Revolution, the Conventions, and the acceptance of the Constitution was in many ways still fragile. Without referring again to the popular support that in some localities the Virginia and Kentucky Resolutions had received in their efforts to nullify the Alien and Sedition Acts, it is appropriate to re-emphasize the precarious position of the national judiciary at the time John Marshall assumed the office of Chief Justice. The Supreme Court's decision in *Chisholm* v. *Georgia*[1] in 1793, sustaining the right of a citizen of one State to bring an original suit in the Supreme Court against another State for breach of contract, had been nullified by the Eleventh Amendment to the Constitution. When the Federalists left office in 1801, with them went many of the forces that had generated the spirit of nationalism. From the new Republican majority came efforts to trim the Court's jurisdiction and its nascent powers, efforts that have been discussed in earlier chapters in connection with the repeal of the 1801 Judiciary Act, the impeachment of the judges, and

---

[1] 2 Dall. 419 (1793).

plans to move against Marshall after the Burr trial. Vacancies on the bench were sedulously filled by Republicans throughout this period. Nevertheless, despite efforts by Congress, by the States, and by the executive to diminish the growing potential of the judiciary in order to deter the growth of the kind of nationalism fostered by the Federalists, the Supreme Court became involved in a series of cases that seemed to lead inexorably in the direction of national supremacy. This process occurred less because the judges were nationalistically-minded than because of their growing awareness of the importance of establishing a recognized set of fixed principles, elsewhere termed the rule of law, that would be binding everywhere in the country. Indeed, the Court not only fostered that supremacy but at the same time, through its successes, actually increased its own importance and thereby further strengthened the foundations of its own power.

In discussing the problem of division of powers, as contrasted with separation of powers, in the federal government, there is a tendency to forget that the subordinate State governments had preceded the national government: the former were created out of practical necessity, not as part of a theoretical scheme embodied in a constitution. The basis for the controversies over the place of these working governments in a theoretical scheme arose from conditions existing at the time of the adoption of the federal Constitution, not in the situation created by its adoption. In other words, the States continued to press for powers they had exercised *before* the Constitution, rather than seeking in the first instance to obstruct possible powers engendered within and by the Constitution. In the early national period, arguments on behalf of the States could be made from a position of real strength; the new government was unsure of itself, and the States exercised a great deal more de facto power than they could after the 1820s. This fact is a reflection of the development and extension of the new federal government, but the conflict is nonetheless a persistent thread in the period with which this Volume is concerned. As the actual exercise of State power decreased, those who sought to look to and rely upon conditions prevailing in the era of the framing of the Constitution, but in a new and different frame of reference, often found themselves seriously thwarted. Ultimately the conflict was to lead to the battlefield, where much of the ideal of States, *qua* independent States, was permanently subjugated.

It is convenient to denominate the time period from the adoption of the Constitution until the Supreme Court's decision in *Cohens* v. *Virginia*[2] as distinct from the period thereafter and until the Civil War;

---

[2] 6 Wheat. 264 (1821).

if the first period may be referred to as the "move for power," the second may be termed the "move for independence." The former period is essentially one of change during which the country became more nationalistic, and less a mere conglomeration of States with dominant local loyalties. As a reflection of this change, and because the basic analysis of contemporaries changed only slowly, the arguments in support of States' rights tended to be emotional declarations of political belief.[3] Among the causes of the ascent of nationalism were changes in

---

[3] "Madison's Report on the Virginia Resolutions," in J. Elliot, ed., *The Debates in the Several State Conventions on the Adoption of the Federal Constitution, as Recommended by the General Convention at Philadelphia in 1787*, 2d ed. (Philadelphia, 1888), IV, 546 (hereafter cited as Elliot, *Debates*), principally a tract against the constitutionality of the Sedition Act of 1798, was generally taken to be expressive of the arguments justifying States' rights. These same arguments were invoked by the Virginia Supreme Court of Appeals in Hunter v. Martin, 18 Va. (3 Munford) 1 (1814), *rev'd sub nom.* Martin v. Hunter's Lessee, 1 Wheat. 304 (1816), refusing to abide by a Supreme Court reversal of a judgment of the State court on the ground that Supreme Court appellate jurisdiction of State court judgments is unconstitutional. Chief Justice Roane cites Madison's Report approvingly, 18 Va. at 31–32, and Judge Cabell's remarks are illustrative of the States' rights positions:

> The two governments, therefore, possessing, each, its portion of the divided sovereignty, although embracing the same territory, and operating on the same persons and frequently on the same subjects, are nevertheless separate from, and independent of, each other. From this position, believed to be incontrovertible, it necessarily results that each government must act by *its own* organs: from no other can it expect, command, or enforce obedience, even as to objects coming within the range of its powers.

Ibid., 8 (emphasis in original). On appeal, the Supreme Court reversed and held that it could order a State government to act in a way compatible with the national power on national questions. Later, in Cohens v. Virginia, 6 Wheat. 264 (1821), the Supreme Court, per Chief Justice Marshall, once again asserted this power in a way which laid the question to rest. He added:

> The American states, as well as the American people, have believed a close and firm union to be essential to their liberty and to their happiness. They have been taught by experience, that this union cannot exist, without a government for the whole; and they have been taught by the same experience, that this government would be a mere shadow, that must disappoint all their hopes, unless invested with large portions of that sovereignty which belongs to independent states. Under the influence of this opinion, and thus instructed by experience, the American people, in the conventions of their respective states, adopted the present constitution.

Ibid., 380–81. The idea that the Constitution was the result of a popular decision, not a compact between States, seemed to be firmly established. Nonetheless, the original argument was reiterated:

> It is not a question at this day, that all power emanates from the people, and that the Federal Constitution was formed by them. But this does not enable us to determine the quantum of power which they intended to delegate to it. I take it to be equally clear, that having in each State established independent sovereignties, before the formation of this government, that they did not intend to take from the soverign [*sic*] power of

the economy of the country brought about by the opening of the West, and the devastations wrought by the protective trade legislation involved in the Embargo, which led among other things to the decline of the aristocratic form of power inherent in the large landed estates predominant in the South. As one area of the country fell into a position of economic inferiority or superiority economically, vis-à-vis other sections, the nature of the political struggle necessarily altered. Another change during the period also had political importance: the men who had been responsible for the original constitutional plan of government began to die off. Others took up their arguments, but in different contexts, without the background and experience of framing the Constitution behind them. This, then, was the period during which the Supreme Court, groping through the political storms, established its power to control the States on many questions of national importance. It was a period of definition, and it is this process that underlies much of the subject matter of this chapter.

Americans of that time were particularly sensitive to the appearance or actuality of domination by others, especially by groups or factions. The States'-rights argument was in some measure, at least, an assertion by a minority party of their ability to rid themselves of the fetters imposed by a dominant majority.[4] The Supreme Court, not

---

these States more than was essentially necessary for the establishment of the federal government, and that it is not the duty of the judiciary of the States to attempt to enlarge or diminish the power which is given. Ansley v. Timmons, S.C.L. (1 McCord), 328, 331 (1825) (Colcock, J.). Thus the argument that the people made the Constitution, and surely intended it to be supreme, is avoided. In this particular case the South Carolina Court of Appeals went on to assert that each State had the right and the power to maintain its own militia, even to the point of conscripting aliens. Later, in response to the South Carolina Ordinance of Nullification against the protective tariff in 1832 President Jackson declared: "I consider then, the power to annul a law of the United States, assumed by one state, *incompatible with the existence of the Union, contradicted expressly by the letter of the Constitution, unauthorized by its spirit, inconsistent with every principle on which it was founded, and destructive of the great object for which it was formed*." Elliot, *Debates*, IV, 585 (emphasis in original). In opposition to the judicial and executive declarations of their country, the States' righters eventually went on to lead the country into war.

[4] See H. Agar, *The Price of Union* (Boston, 1950), 109–10:

States' rights are the support of a minority in resisting the will of a distant majority. There can be no federal government without states' rights, or with too much states' rights; and no one has ever been able to define what "too much" means. Only compromise, delay, inefficiency, the willingness of a minority not to obstruct beyond the limits of human patience, only such fruits of political experience can make a large federal system work. Nothing is more fatal to federalism than the insistence on logic and definition; for it is not logical to seek to divide power, and it is not possible to define with clarity

subject to immediate political control, but nevertheless available as a potential political weapon, was feared on both sides because it seemed to possess the power to destroy "legitimate" resistance by individual States, and under the color of States' rights that power was resisted. The Republicans, leaders of the political attack on the Supreme Court, found themselves in the ambivalent position of attempting to hold together the Union for their own purposes, and yet trying to obstruct the centralizing tendencies of the Supreme Court. Although they were the party in power, the Republicans were unable to do both; consequently, they failed to do either.

There are, then, two aspects to consider in evaluating the actions of the Supreme Court during the first decade of the nineteenth century: the constant political and legal attacks by those who represented localism, and the strong yet gradual trend, led by the Court, towards taking control of governmental powers away from the States and gathering it into the hands of the national government.

The cases considered below may seem disconnected, but there is a common or connecting link between them. The link is the theme of growing national supremacy, with a shift in issues to one of federal versus State power. In the first years of Marshall's term of office, few cases of this sort presented themselves, particularly while the Court was heavily embroiled in its struggle with the executive; but later they came to bulk very large in the business of the Court. Singled out for particular discussion in the earlier period are the backgrounds of eight decisions: *Huidekoper's Lessee* v. *Douglass*,[5] the *Olmstead* affair (*United States* v. *Peters*),[6] *Miller* v. *Nicholls*,[7] *United States* v. *Fisher*,[8] *Fletcher* v. *Peck*,[9] *United States* v. *Hudson and Goodwin*[10] and its sequel *United States* v. *Coolidge*,[11] and the earlier stages of the *Fairfax* case, which, styled as *Martin* v. *Hunter's Lessee*,[12] was finally decided in 1816.

---

the areas of division. The problems of federalism cannot be solved; but subtle, human, compromising, undogmatic, and boldly illogical parties can sometimes allay them. This passage is worth two observations. First, clearly the experience Agar looks for is lacking in this period of time; those who follow have more of this experience. Second, the attempt to force the rationalizations and theoretical observations of a bygone age into the justification of a desperate, uncompromising, dogmatic course of action almost did destroy a "large federal system."

[5] 3 Cranch 1 (1805).
[6] 5 Cranch 115 (1809).
[7] 4 Wheat. 311 (1819).
[8] 2 Cranch 358 (1805).
[9] 6 Cranch 87 (1810).
[10] 7 Cranch 32 (1812).
[11] 1 Wheat. 415 (1816).
[12] 1 Wheat. 304 (1816).

X: *States' Rights and the National Judiciary*

A. THE "PENNSYLVANIA REBELLION"

1. Huidekoper's Lessee v. Douglass

Two great questions confronted the Court in the early ninteenth century. The first was that of enforcing its decrees; the second was the extent of its jurisdiction. Of the two, probably the more important, and certainly first in time, was the enforcement question. In three early cases the Court found itself in direct conflict with the Commonwealth of Pennsylvania, and the circumstances that led to those confrontations are such that the conflict has sometimes been referred to as the "Pennsylvania Rebellion." The political significance of these cases is heightened by the fact that, since the election of 1800, Pennsylvania had become solidily Republican and, though independent on many issues, was inclined to be more than friendly towards the administration. Moreover, in national politics, its representatives in Congress were beginning, as early as Jefferson's second term, to hold the balance of power on a sustantial number of national issues.[13]

The first of the three cases involved in the "Pennsylvania Rebellion," *Huidekoper's Lessee v. Douglass,*[14] involved not only an important question of jurisdiction, but also, more particularly, the issue whether the Court could enforce its judgment against a State. The problem presented was the interpretation to be given to an act relating to the grant of certain lands in the western part of Pennsylvania. Those lands were viewed as a vast source of wealth, and the legislature had devised a method for selling them by warrants and patents.[15] Warrants were to be issued to purchasers who bought large quantities of land, entitling the purchasers (presumably speculators) to have a survey made and a patent issued, provided the patentee complied with certain settlement and residence requirements. Patents were to be issued to purchasers who actually settled the land and improved the tract once the purchase price for each entire 400-acre tract had been paid.[16]

When the Act establishing the system of warrants and patents was passed in 1792, an Indian war was being fought over the area to be sold, and settlement was at a virtual standstill. In order to prevent the war from interfering with sales, the Act contained the following proviso:

---

[13] H. Adams, *History of the United States of America* (New York, 1890), II, 194–204.

[14] 3 Cranch 1 (1805).

[15] An Act For the Sale of the Vacant Lands Within This Commonwealth, chapter MDCXIII, *Laws of the Commonwealth of Pennsylvania, 1700–1800* (Philadelphia, 1810), III, 70.

[16] S. Buck and E. Buck, *The Planting of Civilization in Western Pennsylvania* (Pittsburgh, 1939), chapter 10.

Provided always nevertheless, That if any such actual settler, or any grantee in any such original or succeeding warrant, shall, by force of arms of the enemies of the United States, be prevented from making such actual settlement, or be driven therefrom, and shall persist in his endeavors to make such actual settlement as aforesaid, then, in either case, he and his heirs shall be entitled to have and to hold the said lands, in the same manner as if the actual settlement had been made and continued.[17]

The interpretations of this proviso formed the basis for the bitter controversy that culminated in the Supreme Court's decision in 1805: some had argued that it dispensed with the requirement of settlement altogether; others asserted that settlement was merely postponed.

On August 21, 1793, the Holland Land Company invested $222,071 and purchased warrants for 499,660 acres of land in the region[18] "north and west of the rivers Ohio and Allegheny, and Conewango creek."[19] Apparently the Company's agent either ignored the settlement requirement or believed the proviso to be an excuse from that condition in light of existing hostilities with the Indians. Whatever his belief, the land purchase had been carried out.

The Indian hostilities were ended with the treaty of Greenville in 1796,[20] and immediately afterwards there was an influx of settlers into the area. Without regard to any rights the Company might have had by virtue of its warrants, settlers moved onto the land, made improvements, and then claimed rights under the 1792 Act. Had the interpretation that the proviso merely delayed the two-year settlement requirement been adopted and literally enforced, the Company would have been unable to maintain an ejectment action, and would have lost more than half its holdings. Governor Mifflin was not blind to this situation, however, and in his administration the Board of Property adopted the interpretation that the proviso dispensed with the requirement of settlement. Under that interpretation, most of the Company's patents were granted by 1799, through the presentation of "prevention certificates," sworn to before a justice of the peace, which recited that the Company had been prevented by enemies of the country from developing their tracts.

The interpretation adopted by Governor Mifflin's Board created bitterness among the settlers and other farmers; these sentiments, among

---

[17] An Act For the Sale of the Vacant Lands, Sec. IX, 73.

[18] P. Evans, *The Holland Land Company* (Buffalo, 1924), 33.

[19] An Act for the Sale of the Vacant Lands, Sec. II, 233.

[20] See *State Papers and Publick Documents of the United States* (Boston, 1817), II, 89; F. L. Paxon, *History of the American Frontier 1763–1893* (Boston, 1924), 77–78.

others, contributed to the overwhelming Republican political victory in 1799. Under the ensuing administration of Governor McKean, the Board of Property adopted a different interpretation of the proviso— that it merely postponed the settlement requirement. Further applications for patents by the Company were refused, and the Board hinted that it might consider the patents already granted to be void.[21] When the Company brought a mandamus suit against the chairman of the Board of Property, to show cause why the remaining patents should not be granted, the State Supreme Court decided that if the Company had not complied with the conditions of settlement, it was not entitled to its patents, and therefore discharged the petition.[22]

Although the interpretation adopted by the Board of Property under Governor McKean, and the decision of the State Supreme Court in the mandamus suit, might seem to have been fatal to the Holland Land Company, that proved not to be the case. While rigorously adhering to the interpretation that the proviso merely postponed the settlement requirement, the State courts almost invariably turned up circumstances, such as the wrongdoing of the defendant, that permitted them to give judgment for the grantees. This practice provoked the settlers to petition the Pennsylvania General Assembly to take action. A bill was introduced in the legislature to prescribe the conditions to be met by patent applicants (conditions that the Company would be unable to satisfy), but it was defeated.[23] A second bill, calling for judicial decision of the controversy by staging a trial with feigned issues, was enacted into law on April 2, 1802.[24]

The trial of that case took place at Sunbury, in the central part of the State. The Holland Land Company, on advice of counsel, refused to participate in the proceedings,[25] but the court nonetheless proceeded to hear the arguments in the case of *Attorney-General* v. *Grantees* on November 25, 1802.[26] On the following day, Judge Yeates delivered his charge to the jury. In essence his charge espoused the Republican interpretation of the proviso, namely, that it merely postponed the requirement of settlement. He qualified his charge, however, with the caveat that "every case must be governed by its own peculiar circumstances. Until the facts really existing, as to each tract of land, are

---

[21] Evans, *Holland Land Company*, 123–34.

[22] Commonwealth v. Coxe, 4 Dall. 170 (Pa. 1800).

[23] Evans, *Holland Land Company*, 133–36.

[24] An Act to Settle the Controversies Arising from Contending Claims to Land Within That Part of the Territory of This Commonwealth, North and West of the Rivers Ohio and Allegheny, and Conewango Creek, chapter MMCCLXXXVIII, 17 Pa. Stat. 133 (1802).

[25] Evans, *Holland Land Company*, 141.

[26] 4 Dall. 237 (Pa. 1802).

ascertained with accuracy, the legal conclusion cannot be drawn with any degree of correctness."[27] The jury returned a general verdict for the Attorney-General,[28] but because of the nature of the feigned issues, and the caveat, the decision was next to useless in the settling of disputes.

After the trial of the feigned issues at Sunbury, the Land Company appealed to the Pennsylvania legislature for relief, but none was forthcoming.[29] When this effort failed, the Company, as a non-resident, resorted to the federal circuit court in Philadelphia, as it was entitled to do under Section 11 of the Judiciary Act of 1789. Several ejectment actions were instituted in the summer of 1802 in the name of Huidekoper.[30] This appeal to the federal courts at once provoked an antagonistic response in the legislature, and a measure was passed providing for funds to employ counsel "to attend to the interests of the state" in the Land Company suits in federal courts.[31] After two postponements, two ejectment actions were tried in April 1804 at Philadelphia; but the two federal judges, Richard Peters and Bushrod Washington, could not agree on the proper interpretation of the proviso. Consequently, the results were inconclusive.[32] Under an Act of Congress of 1802, the warrantees were entitled to an appeal to the Supreme Court, and when a third ejectment action, against Douglass, was brought in the Circuit Court with the same inconclusive results, certification of the issues was requested by counsel for the Company, and the case was taken up on appeal.

Three questions were certified to the Supreme Court: 1) Does the proviso excuse a warrantee from performing the condition in Section 9? 2) If such a warrantee is prevented, but yet persists in his endeavors, what is the state of his title? 3) Is the Commonwealth the only agency that can take advantage of forfeiture for non-compliance with Section 9?[33] In February of 1805 the Supreme Court, speaking through John Marshall, handed down a unanimous opinion in favor of the warrantees. The opinion stated that the proviso should be construed *reddendo singulis*, that is, on the principle of referring each phrase to its appropriate subject, and therefore the fact of prevention for the dura-

---

[27] *Ibid.*, 244; see also Evans' discussion of the case, *Holland Land Company*, 141–42.

[28] 4 Dall. at 245.

[29] Evans, *Holland Land Company*, 142.

[30] *Ibid.*, 145.

[31] An Act for Ascertaining the Right of This State to Certain Lands Lying North and West of the Rivers Ohio and Allegheny, and Conewango Creek, chapter MMDXXI, 17 Pa. Stat. 872 (1804).

[32] See Huidekoper v. Burrus, 12 F. Cas. 840 (C.C.D. Pa. 1804) (No. 6,848); Huidekoper v. McClean, 12 F. Cas. 848 (C.C.D. Pa. 1804) (No. 6,852).

[33] Huidekoper's Lessee v. Douglass, 3 Cranch 1, 8–10 (1805).

tion of the two-year period excused the performance of the condition completely. Marshall also pointed out:

> This is a contract; and although a state is a party, it ought to be construed according to those well established principles which regulate contracts generally.
>
> The state is in the situation of a person who holds forth to the world the conditions on which he is willing to sell his property.
>
> If he should couch his propositions in such ambiguous terms that they might be understood differently, in consequence sales were to be made, and the purchase-money paid, he would come with an ill grace into court, to insist on a latent and obscure meaning, which should give him back his property, and permit him to retain the purchase-money.[34]

These words with respect to the contract of a State may appear remarkable, in light of the aftermath of *Chisholm* v. *Georgia*. Yet when one looks forward five years to the language of *Fletcher* v. *Peck*, discussed below, they accord with expressions in the latter case, even though in 1805, when *Huidekoper* was decided, the Court was under a barrage of political attacks from the Republicans.

A bill presented in the General Assembly in Pennsylvania, the purpose of which was to cause all of the lands in question to revert to the State so that the legislature could deal with them anew, was defeated in the House.[35] In 1807 the Pennsylvania legislature approved a Kentucky resolution proposing an amendment to the United States Constitution that would have deprived federal courts of diversity jurisdiction as well as of jurisdiction over suits between citizens of the same State claiming land under grants of different States.[36]

More important, the same legislature resolved to deny the authority of the federal courts to take jurisdiction of any suit brought under the Act of 1792 in which

> the interest and sovereignty of the State is deeply involved; for take away the right of an individual State, to dispose of her own soil, as she may think proper, or prevent her from enforcing the observance of her contracts, by her own courts, and subject her to the controul of the judicial authority of the United States, and such State remains no longer sovereign and independent.[37]

---

[34] *Ibid.*, 70–71.
[35] Evans, *Holland Land Company*, 155–56.
[36] See H. Ames, *The Proposed Amendments to the Constitution of* the United States (New York, 1896), 157–58.
[37] *Journal of the Senate of the Commonwealth of Pennsylvania* (Lancaster, Pa., 1808), XVII, 337 (Mar. 19, 1807).

On March 31 Governor McKean, inveterate Republican though he was, vetoed the resolution, objecting to such an intrusion by the State legislature into the federal judicial process. "[A] just sense of law and order, would seem to prescribe an acquiescence in that judgment," for the resolution was "extraordinary either as an instrument of advice or intimidation" and its consequences must be "abortive or . . . injurious."[38]

Other Republicans who did not share the Governor's view charged that the Court had "prostrated the sovereignty of Pennsylvania."[39] Some basis for resentment may be thought to have existed, since the Court seemingly had strained to read the proviso as excusing, rather than postponing, performance of the condition. In any event, the State courts continued to support their original interpretation of the law of 1792, while invariably finding circumstances that would warrant a decision in favor of the Company. In actuality, therefore, the decision of the United States Supreme Court did little to change matters in Pennsylvania, but it was nevertheless a judicial step in the whittling away of State powers.

2.   *The* Olmstead *Affair*

The so-called Pennsylvania Rebellion surfaced again in the famous *Olmstead* controversy. Three years after the decision in *Huidekoper*, the State again opposed the Supreme Court in an incident that had its beginning over twenty-five years earlier. On June 15, 1778, one Gideon Olmstead, a Connecticut mariner, was captured by the British. He was sent to Jamaica, where, with three other captured Americans, he was impressed and put on board the sloop *Active*. On September 6, while en route to New York, Olmstead and his fellow Americans seized control of the sloop, confined the loyal part of the crew belowdecks, and made for the New Jersey shore. On September 8, when within sight of Little Egg Harbor, New Jersey, they were overhauled and taken as a prize by the armed sloop *Convention*, fitted out by the Commonwealth of Pennsylvania. On September 14, 1778, a libel was brought in the Pennsylvania Court of Admiralty by Thomas Huston, master of the *Convention*. The master of the *Convention*'s consort, the privateer *Le Gerard*, filed suit as a second claimant, and Olmstead and his associates filed claims on the entire vessel, contending that the *Active* was their prize. On November 4 the jury gave a general verdict of one-quarter to Olmstead and associates, three-quarters to the other

---

[38] *Ibid.*, 437 (Mar. 31, 1807).
[39] C. Warren, *The Supreme Court*
in *United States History* (Boston, 1922), I, 370.

claimants.[40] When judgment was entered on November 5, an appeal was taken to the Court of Appeals, which had been given jurisdiction over appeals from State courts of admiralty by the Continental Congress. The Appeals Commission decided in December "that the judgement or sentence of the Court of Admiralty aforesaid be in all its parts revoked, reversed and annulled."[41] As a consequence, the Olmstead group was to receive the entire award.

George Ross, the judge of the Court of Admiralty, decided, however,

> that although the court of appeals have full authority to alter or set aside the decree of a judge of this court, yet that the finding of the jury in the cause does establish the facts in the cause without re-examination or appeal. And therefore the verdict of the jury still standing, and being in full force, this court cannot issue any process, or proceed in any manner whatsoever contradictory to the finding of the said jury.[42]

He accordingly ordered the marshal to sell the sloop and pay the proceeds into court. On January 4, 1779, the order was obeyed, but not without another bout with the Appeals Commissioners. On appeal by Olmstead, they ordered the marshal to hold the proceeds of the sale, but the latter paid the money into the Court of Admiralty in defiance of the order.

A report of this affair was submitted to a committee of the Congress on January 19, 1779, and that committee recommended that the Court of Appeals should have the power to examine questions of fact as well as questions of law, apparently lest juries possess the ultimate power of executing the law of the nation in all cases of capture.[43] The State was requested to appoint a committee to confer with a committee of the Congress to iron out the dispute. Nevertheless, on November 29, 1779, the legislature of the State passed a resolution empowering Judge Ross to pay over the money, which he accordingly did.

Pennsylvania's share, approximately 11,500 pounds in Pennsylvania currency, was paid to the treasurer of the State, David Rittenhouse, in the form of loan office certificates of the United States. Rittenhouse gave Judge Ross a bond of indemnity, in case the latter should be compelled later to pay the amount to Olmstead. The certifi-

---

[40] See United States v. Peters, 5 Cranch 115, 121 (1809).

[41] W. C. Ford, ed., *Journals of the Continental Congress* (Washington, 1904) XIII, 87 (Jan. 19, 1779) (hereafter cited as Ford, *Continental Congress Journals*).

[42] Quoted in United States v. Peters, 5 Cranch 115, 120.

[43] Ford, *Continental Congress Journals*, XV, 1222.

cates were then funded in the name of Rittenhouse and kept among his private papers.[44] Appended thereto was the following, in the hand of Rittenhouse:

> Note. The above certificates will be the property of the state of Pennsylvania, when the state releases me from the bond I gave in 1778, to indemnify George Ross, Esq. judge of the admiralty for paying the fifty original certificates into the state treasury as the state's share of the prize.[45]

Thus, the certificates remained among the personal holdings of David Rittenhouse, thereby putting him in the position of a "stakeholder."

In 1792 suit was brought in the Lancaster County Common Pleas Court to compel Judge Ross to pay the money awarded to Olmstead by the judgment of the United States Appeals Commissioners. Judgment was had by default, and Ross' executors brought suit in the Supreme Court of Pennsylvania on the bond of indemnity given by Rittenhouse to Ross.[46] The Supreme Court of Pennsylvania held that a common law court had no jurisdiction over a dispute in admiralty, and that the old United States Court of Appeals had no jurisdiction to overturn the facts as decided by a jury.

In 1795 the United States Supreme Court decided *Penhallow* v. *Doane's Administrator*,[47] affirming the decree of enforcement by the circuit court in New Hampshire, holding that the new federal district courts had jurisdiction to enforce the decrees of the old Court of Appeals. Apparently relying on this case, Olmstead, in 1802, again filed a libel in the federal district court for the District of Pennsylvania, with Judge Peters presiding. The State had anticipated just such a move and had passed an act requiring the treasurer to call upon the executrices of Rittenhouse, now deceased, and to give them a bond of indemnity in exchange for the certificates of "stock." They refused, however, on the advice of counsel.

The case of *Olmstead* v. *The Active*[48] appeared for trial in the federal district court before Judge Peters in December 1802. On January 14, 1803, Judge Peters decreed that the certificates be transferred and delivered, in execution of the judgment and decree of the old federal Court of Appeals. State reaction was prompt. Governor McKean sent a message to the General Assembly on January 31, 1803, in which he indignantly declared:

---

[44] United States v. Peters, 5 Cranch 115, 124 (1809).
[45] *Ibid.*
[46] Ross v. Rittenhouse, 1 Yeates 443 (Pa. 1795).

[47] 3 Dall. 54 (1795).
[48] 18 F. Cas 680 (C.C.D. Pa. 1803) (No. 10,503a).

By the ingenuity exercised in this business, an act of Congress, an act of the General Assembly of this state, and a verdict of a jury, are held for nought; by a strained construction, the Treasurer of the state is converted into a stakeholder, and a sentence given in favor of the libellants, without summons, notice to, or hearing of the commonwealth of Pennsylvania, the other only real party. . . .[49]

He went on to declare void the judgment of the District Judge:

The Commonwealth, not being made a party to the suit, cannot sustain an appeal to the Supreme Court of the United States; and resistance would be extremely disagreeable, though the whole process should be held as *coram non judice*, which must be the case, if it had been a party; . . . and as this decree has been passed during the session of the general assembly . . . , I have conceived it my duty to lay the affair before you, for advice and direction.[50]

The legislature's "advice and direction" was quickly forthcoming. In a lengthy bill, enacted into law on April 2, 1803, the General Assembly recited its version of the story, defied the decree of the federal District Court as an illegal usurpation of jurisdiction, and reiterated Pennsylvania's right to establish the courts of the State as the State saw fit:

Therefore it hath become necessary for the general assembly of Pennsylvania, as guardians of the rights and interests of this commonwealth, and to prevent any future infringements of the same, to declare: That the jurisdiction entertained by the court, or committee, of appeals over the decree of George Ross . . . was illegally usurped and exercised in contradiction to the just rights of Pennsylvania in that suit, and that the reversal of the decree of the said George Ross, in that suit, was null and void; that the jurisdiction entertained by Richard Peters, judge of the district court . . . was illegally usurped and exercised. . . .[51]

The legislature also directed the Attorney-General of the State to require payment from the executrices, and, failing that, to bring suit to obtain money; it further authorized and required the Governor to "protect the just rights of the state" in the property and persons of Rittenhouse's executrices "by any . . . means . . . necessary" and to protect the

[49] *Journal of the Senate of the Commonwealth of Pennsylvania*, XIII, 189 (Jan. 31, 1803).
[50] *Ibid.*, 189–90.
[51] An Act Relating to the Claim of This Commonwealth, Against Elizabeth Sergeant and Esther Waters, Surviving Executrices of David Rittenhouse, Esquire, deceased, chapter MMCCCXL, 17 Pa. Stat. 472 (1803).

325

executrices "from any process whatever, issued out of any federal court. . . ."[52]

Republican newspapers, especially the *Aurora*, applauded the challenge to the judiciary and castigated the federal courts for attempts to "legislate for the separate States, or set aside their legislative acts, or bring State independence under the control of jurisdiction. . . ."[53] Note should be taken of the date—April 1803—just after *Marbury* v. *Madison* had been decided, and scarcely a year after the 1802 Act had repealed the Judiciary Act of 1801.

Judge Peters, either because of an unstated fear of impeachment or the desirability, expressed below, of avoiding what seemed to be an impending conflict between the State and national governments, refused to issue compulsory process. There the matter rested for five years, until Olmstead petitioned the Supreme Court for a mandamus against Peters. The latter filed his return, in which he pointed out his reasons for withholding compulsory process:

> But from prudential, more than other motives, I deemed it best to avoid embroiling the government of the United States and that of Pennsylvania (if the latter government should choose so to do) on a question which has rested on my single opinion, so far as it is touched by my decree. . . . If this be not considered a legal cause, it must be deemed a candid acknowledgment that I do not invariably obey a rigorous dictate of duty, or follow an inflexibly strict construction of law.
>
> I entertained a hope that a legislature succeeding that by which the act before mentioned [of April 2, 1803] was passed, would, under a more temperate view of the subject, have repealed it; and enabled and directed the executive of the state, or some other authority, to put this case in a legal train of investigation. . . .[54]

During the February term of 1809 the case, styled *United States* v. *Peters*, was argued in the Supreme Court. On February 20 Marshall speaking for the Court declared:

> If the legislatures of the several states may, at will, annul the judgments of the courts of the United States, and destroy the rights acquired under those judgments, the constitution itself becomes a solemn mockery; and the nation is deprived of the means of enforcing its laws by the instrumentality of its own tribunals. So fatal a result must be deprecated by all; and the people of Pennsylvania, not less

---

[52] *Ibid.*, Sec. 2, at 479.
[53] Warren, *Supreme Court*, I, 375, quoting Aurora, Apr. 11, 1803.

[54] United States v. Peters, 5 Cranch 115, 117 (1809).

than the citizens of every other state, must feel a deep interest in resisting principles so destructive of the union, and in averting consequences so fatal to themselves.[55]

After referring to the Act requiring payment to the State, Marshall continued:

> If the ultimate right to determine the jurisdiction of the courts of the union is placed by the constitution in the several state legislatures, then this act concludes the subject; but if that power necessarily resides in the supreme judicial tribunal of the nation, then the jurisdiction of the district court of Pennsylvania, over the case in which that jurisdiction was exercised, ought to be most deliberately examined; and the act of Pennsylvania, with whatever respect it may be considered, cannot be permitted to prejudice the question.[56]

Having thus put to one side the effect of the resolutions of the State legislature, Marshall went on to examine whether the State was a party to the suit in the first place. He found that the decree of the old Court of Appeals had extinguished the State's right to the money, and that Rittenhouse held the money in his own right. True, he intended to turn it over to the State, but nonetheless the money was in his name, thus removing the suit from the ban of the Eleventh Amendment:

> Since, then, the state of Pennsylvania had neither possession of, nor right to, the property on which the sentence of the district court was pronounced, and since the suit was neither commenced nor prosecuted against that state, there remains no pretext for the allegation that the case is within that amendment of the constitution which has been cited; and, consequently, the state of Pennsylvania can possess no constitutional right to resist the legal process which may be directed in this cause.[57]

Although Pennsylvania had "no constitutional right to resist," resistance had already been approved under the Act of April 2, 1803. As soon as Governor Snyder, McKean's successor, was apprised of the situation, he sent a message to the Assembly on February 27, 1809, declaring:

> It now becomes my Duty . . . to protect the property and person of the said Executrixes, against such process. Painful as this Duty is, I am compelled, and am now making arrangements to call out a portion of the Militia for the service; that being the only means in the power of the Executive.

---

[55] *Ibid.*, 136.
[56] *Ibid.*

[57] *Ibid.*, 141.

As the execution of this Law may produce serious Difficulties, as it respects the relation of the State Government with that of the United States, I have thought proper to make this communication; on which the Legislature can act as, in their wisdom, they shall think expedient.[58]

Both houses of the legislature again took the position that the federal courts did not have the requisite jurisdiction to reverse the decree in the State Court of Admiralty. They reported:

[O]ught the State now to succomb [sic], and pave the way for future encroachments, lest she should be charged with resisting the authority of the General Government?

Will the Legislature tamely betray the trust confided to them, by sacrificing the rights of the State, after their predecessors had so long defended them?[59]

The report went on to maintain, contrary to Marshall's opinion in *Peters*, that the money had been in the possession of the State while it was in the possession of Rittenhouse. The committees then proposed Resolutions:

That, as a member of the Federal Union, the Legislature of Pennsylvania acknowledges the supremacy, and will cheerfully submit to the authority, of the General Government, as far as that authority is delegated by the Constitution of the United States. But, whilst they yield to this authority, when exercised within constitutional limits, they trust they will be not considered as acting hostile to the General Government, when, as Guardians of the State Rights, they cannot permit an infringement of those rights, by an unconstitutional exercise of power in the United States' Courts.

[I]t is to be lamented, that no provision is made, in the Constitution, for determining disputes between General and State Governments, by an impartial tribunal, when such cases occur.

[T]he Legislature is seriously impressed with the insecurity of the State Rights, if the Courts of United States are permitted to give unlimited extension to their power, in deciding on those Rights. . . .

That, should the independence of the States, as secured by the Constitution, be destroyed, the libertries [sic] of the People, in so extensive a Country, cannot long survive. To suffer the United States Courts to decide on State Rights, will, from a bias in favor of power,

---

[58] *Journal of the Senate of the Commonwealth of Pennsylvania*, XIX, 268–69 (Feb. 27, 1809).

[59] *Ibid.*, 301 (Mar. 6, 1809).

necessarily destroy the Federal Part of our Government: And, whenever the Government of the United States becomes consolidated, we may learn from the history of Nations, what will be the event.[60]

Thus, the Report continued, there was a choice of the lesser of two evils: resistance or submission to "arbitrary" will. The solution proposed was to "procure an amendment to the Constitution of the United States, that an impartial tribunal may be established, to determine disputes between the General and State Governments. . . ."[61] These resolutions were adopted on April 3, 1809,[62] and were handed to the senators and congressmen from Pennsylvania to introduce into Congress; the Governor was instructed to circulate the proposed amendment among the States, which he accordingly did, but with no success.[63]

Meanwhile, the "rebellion" proceeded rapidly. Pursuant to orders from Governor Snyder, Brigadier General Michael Bright arrived in Philadelphia with his troops. He discovered that Judge Peters would issue process against the executrices of Rittenhouse the following day and forthwith stationed his troops around their house. When the federal marshal attempted to serve the writ, he found his way blocked by the bayonets of Bright's militia. The State's recourse to such drastic measures was by no means popular, however. Apparently most of the militia were naturalized citizens, who now found themselves opposing the very government that they had sworn to uphold; in addition, the marshal had been very careful to take down the names of those involved, threatening them with trials for treason. Consequently, some units of the militia refused to serve at all; others disobeyed orders and would not stand guard duty. The marshal, who had not been idle, had summoned fully two thousand citizens of the city to serve on a *posse comitatus* to help serve the writ, but many of these apparently belonged to the same militia as that which had been ordered to resist the *posse*.

Almost immediately, General Bright was indicted by a federal grand jury for resisting the laws of the United States, and his arrest was ordered. Even the *Aurora*, hitherto one of the strongest opponents of the federal judiciary, now supported Judge Peters: "This issue is in fact come to This: whether the Constitution of the United States is to remain in force or to become a dead letter. . . . [T]he independence of the Judiciary, in its strict and constitutional sense, exists and demands

---

[60] *Ibid.*, 305–306.
[61] *Ibid.*, 307.
[62] *Ibid.*, 523–29.
[63] The proposed amendment was not supported by any other State, and at least ten States passed resolutions disapproving it. Ames, *Proposed Amendments to the Constitution*, 160, note 3. Newspaper reaction to the Pennsylvania situation is summarized in Warren, *Supreme Court*, I, 377–78.

to be supported and maintained. . . . The decree of the Court must be obeyed."[64]

By April 6, 1809, Governor Snyder showed signs of weakening, particularly as alarm had spread in the legislature. On that date, seeking a way of retreat, he requested the intervention of the President, and at the same time he transmitted the April 3 defiant resolutions to the legislature:

> While I deeply deplore the circumstance which has led to this correspondence, I am consoled with the pleasing idea, that the Chief Magistracy of the Union is confided to a man who merits, and who possesses so great a portion of the esteem and confidence of a vast majority of the citizens of the United States; who is so intimately acquainted with the principles of the Federal Constitution, and who is no less disposed to protect the sovereignty and independence of the several States, as guaranteed to them, than to defend the rights and legitimate powers of the General Government; who will justly discriminate between opposition to the Constitution and laws of the United States, and that of resisting the decree of a judge, founded, as it is conceived, in a usurpation of power and jurisdiction not delegated to him by either; and who is equally solicitous with myself, to preserve the Union of the States, and to adjust the present unhappy collision of the two Governments in such a manner as will be equally honorable to them both.[65]

President Madison, only recently installed in office, sent as absolute a refusal as courtesy would permit:

> Considering our respective relations to the subject of these communications, it would be unnecessary, if not improper, to enter into any examination of some of the questions connected with it. It is sufficient, in the actual posture of the case, to remark, that the Executive of the United States is not only unauthorized to prevent the execution of a decree sanctioned by the Supreme Court of the United States, but is expressly enjoined, by statute, to carry into effect any such decree where opposition may be made to it.
>
> It is a propitious circumstance, therefore, that whilst no legal discretion lies with the Executive of the United States to decline steps which might lead to a very painful issue, a provision has been made by legislative act transmitted by you, adequate to the removal of the present difficulty, and I feel great pleasure in assuring myself that

---

[64] As quoted in Warren, *Supreme Court*, I, 379.

[65] J. Gales and W. Seaton, comps., *The Debates and Proceedings of the* *Congress of the United States* (Washington, 1834–1856), XXI, 2267 (11th Cong., 1st and 2d. sess.) (hereafter cited as *Annals of Congress*).

the authority which it gives will be exercised in a spirit corresponding
with the patriotic character of the State over which you preside.[66]

Madison was referring to the provision in the Act passed by the Pennsylvania legislature on April 4 indemnifying the executrices and, in
effect, establishing a fund upon which the federal decree could operate.
Thus, Governor Snyder was faced with the prospect of being forced to
back down on his show of force.

Events moved swiftly in Philadelphia. General Bright was arrested
by federal officers, and released on bail on April 12, 1809; the State
officers gradually lost control over the situation as the people and the
militia became more and more disaffected; and the executrices themselves threatened to remove to Lancaster and submit to federal custody
there. On April 15, 1809, the federal marshal slipped into the Rittenhouse home and served the federal process on the executrices; a member of the family was deputized, and the executrices were placed under
arrest. An application for a writ of habeas corpus was promptly made to
the State Supreme Court on their behalf, but the application was refused
by Chief Justice Tilghman, and it became apparent that the State had
lost in this dispute. The legislature appropriated sufficient funds to
comply with the judgment, and papers were arranged accordingly. When
payment was officially acknowledged, the judgment was finally satisfied
on November 24, 1809. Meanwhile, in late April, President Madison
had written to Attorney-General Rodney that "the Olmstead affair
[had] passed off without the threatened collision of force . . . a blessing
compared with such a result."[67]

At almost the same time, General Bright and other officers of the
Pennsylvania militia were brought to trial in the federal district court,
charged with treason. They were convicted and sentenced to fine and
imprisonment by Judge Bushrod Washington, but were pardoned by
President Madison shortly thereafter.[68] Thus ended potentially the most
violent conflict between the States and the Supreme Court in the struggle
for supremacy.

3.   Miller v. Nicholls

At about the time that the *Olmstead* controversy reached the
Supreme Court, a third conflict that had been developing between
Pennsylvania and the federal government came to a head. The dispute

---

[66] *Ibid.*, 2269.
[67] J. Madison to C. Rodney, Apr. 22, 1809, Rodney Family Papers,
Manuscripts Division, Library of Congress.
[68] Warren, *Supreme Court*, I, 385–87.

arose over the applicability to the State of a creditors' priority statute enacted by Congress in 1797 in favor of the United States.

William Nicholls had been employed as a collector of license fees for Pennsylvania. After Nicholls left the employ of the State, the State Comptroller settled his account, and, in December of 1797, determined that Nicholls owed the State $7,894.69. According to the terms of the State statute under which the accounts of collectors of public revenue were settled, this determination created a lien on all of Nicholls' real property within the State "in the same manner as if judgment had been given in favor of the commonwealth against such person for such debt in the supreme court. . . ."[69]

Nicholls, however, had also been employed as a collector of federal revenues, and he was found to have a $29,271 deficit in his federal accounts. He retired from the service and on June 9, 1798, executed a mortgage on his real estate to one Henry Miller, supervisor of the revenues for the District of Pennsylvania, to the use of the United States. A federal statute provided that the United States should have first priority to the satisfaction of debts owed to it as a result of a settlement of the accounts of collectors of federal revenues who were insolvent or bankrupt.[70]

Miller brought a *scire facias* on the mortgage, which was continued in the State Supreme Court from September 1800 until March 6, 1802, when judgment was rendered in favor of the mortgagee.[71] A *levari facias* was issued in the September term of 1803, the property sold, and the proceeds, $14,530, paid into court.[72] Meanwhile, Nicholls had become legally bankrupt in May of 1802;[73] it is at least a possibility that this action was taken to facilitate the government's claim to a priority. Previously, Nicholls had filed an appeal from settlement of his State account to the Pennsylvania Supreme Court, but in September 1802, after his bankruptcy of 1802, his appeal was dismissed, and it was determined that Nicholls owed the State $9,987.15.[74] Apparently the proceeds of the sheriff's sale were retained in court pending the State's claim under the settlement, although Miller was legally entitled to the money. In March 1805 State Attorney-General McKean moved

---

[69] An Act to Give the Benefit of Trial to the Public Officers of This State and to Other Persons Who Shall be Proceeded Against in a Summary Manner by the Comptroller-General of This State, chapter MCXXXIII, Sec. 8, 11 Pa. Stat. 435 (1785).

[70] An Act to Provide More Effectually for the Settlement of Accounts Between the United States, and Re-

ceivers of Public Money, chapter 20, 1 Stat. 512 (1797).

[71] See United States v. Nicholls, 4 Yeates 251, 251–52 (Pa. 1805).

[72] *Ibid.*, 252; see also *Journal of the Senate of the Commonwealth of Pennsylvania*, XIX, 123 (Jan. 14, 1809).

[73] 4 Yeates at 252.

[74] *Ibid.*

to take the money due the State out of court; the next day Alexander Dallas, the United States Attorney, opposed the motion and interposed the claim of the United States to the entire sum.[75] The question of priority was argued before the Pennsylvania Supreme Court during the March term of 1805, and on September 13, 1805, the motion of the State Attorney-General was granted by the unanimous opinion of the Court.[76]

Before this time, in 1804, the United States Supreme Court, in *United States* v. *Fisher*,[77] had rejected the claim that the priority statute infringed the prerogative of the States. In reversing the circuit court decision of Judge Washington in that case, the Court had also held that the priority of the United States applied to all debts owed the United States in cases of insolvency, regardless of their origin. This claim of priority, asserted in an opinion written by Marshall, was the necessary consequence of the supremacy of the laws of the United States on all subjects to which the legislative power of Congress extends. In that case, however, the State did not have a prior lien, and on this ground it might have been distinguished. The Pennsylvania court, however, apparently had not had an opportunity to see the opinions of either the circuit court or the Supreme Court in that case.[78] All of the Pennsylvania judges expressed disbelief that Congress could have intended so serious a step in derogation of State sovereignty as to create in the United States a first lien when the State had an earlier claim:

> It would certainly require strong, clear, marked expressions, to satisfy a reasonable mind, that the constituted authorities of the union contemplated by any public law, the devesting of any pre-existing right or interest in a state. . . .
> . . . [C]ongress have the concurrent right of passing laws to protect the interest of the union, as to debts due to the government of the United States arising from the public revenue; but in so doing, they cannot detract from the uncontroulable power of individual states to raise their own revenue, nor infringe on, or derogate from the sovereignty of any independent state.[79]

After an abortive appeal to the Pennsylvania High Court of Errors and Appeals, a writ of error was taken to the Supreme Court.[80] By

---

[75] *Journal of the Senate of the Commonwealth of Pennsylvania*, XIX, 124.

[76] *Ibid.*, 125.

[77] 2 Cranch 358 (1805), *rev'ing* 25 F. Cas. 1087 (C.C.D. Pa. 1803) (No. 15103). See text at note 88, infra.

[78] See Judge Breckenridge's opinion suggesting that he had not seen Judge

Washington's opinion in Fisher at circuit or that of the same case on appeal to the United States Supreme Court. 4 Yeates at 259–60.

[79] *Ibid.*, 258–59.

[80] An Act Relating to the Lien of this Commonwealth on the Estate of William Nichols, Deceased, chapter MMMXXIV, 18 Pa. Stat. 927 (1809).

then, in 1808, the radical Republicans of western Pennsylvania had won the State election of that year, and States'-rights feelings were running high. The record was improperly certified, and the State was requested to rectify the deficiency,[81] but did so only after carefully deleting all reference to the federal statute.[82] The deletions were accomplished simply by scratching out with a pen, and not very thoroughly at that. What was eliminated apparently related to the competing liens, federal and State, and the question was narrowed simply to whether the State had a lien or not. It is worth noting that at the same time the Supreme Court issued a citation to the Governor and State Attorney-General, notifying the State to become a party, if it thought fit, and raise the issue of the right of the State to retain its lien.[83]

In response to this citation, the legislature, in a black mood and still aroused over the *Olmstead* controversy,[84] adopted a resolution on February 1, 1809:

> [I]t is inexpedient for this commonwealth to appear or become a part to the said suit, or in such manner to permit her right aforesaid, to be questioned, declaring at the same time a firm determination to support the constitution of the United States, and to submit to all lawful powers and authorities derived therefrom, but conceiving that this commonwealth has never surrendered to the general government a power to defeat or destroy her right to enforce the collection of her own revenues, without which power she could not exist as a sovereign state. . . .[85]

The resolution proceeded to require payment into the State treasury of the funds derived from the sheriff's sale, pending the decision on the writ of error. Dallas, who had been appointed by Jefferson, wrote to the United States Attorney-General Caesar A. Rodney that the legislature's conduct might be very mischievous, and that they had "prostrated the constitutional barrier between the Judicial and the Legislative Departments."[86] There the matter lay dormant until ten years later in 1819, when the Supreme Court finally dismissed the appeal after finding

---

[81] See Return to Writ of Error From the Supreme Court of the United States by A. J. Dallas, filed January 28, 1809, manuscript in the National Archives. Miller *ex. rel.* United States v. Nicholls, 4 Wheat. 311 (1819). (Copy attached to Nicholls memo by Dyer).

[82] *Ibid.*

[83] *Journal of the Senate of the Commonwealth of Pennsylvania*, XIX, 126.

[84] See text accompanying notes 40–68 supra.

[85] An Act Relating to the Lien of this Commonwealth on the Estate of William Nichols, 18 Pa. Stat. at 927.

[86] A. Dallas to C. Rodney, Feb. 6, 1809, Rodney Family Papers, Manuscripts Division, Library of Congress.

that no federal question was raised by the altered record and hence no jurisdiction under section 25 of the Judiciary Act.[87]

The justification for the detail with which the two preceding controversies have been presented, and for what in the *Nicholls* case may seem to be a digression, is to underscore the complexities of federal-State relations which stemmed, on the one hand, from situations and the posture of institutions in the late colonial period and, on the other, from the "radical," "conservative," and "moderate" political factions that had been developing since the 1790s. Although deference and even solicitude were paid to ideas about law and legal procedures at the State level, there was a constant intrusion of political ends and motives, so that not only was the growth of nationalism hampered at the expense of statism, but the expansion of a general rule of law itself was impeded. It should be recognized, therefore, that two of the general themes of this Volume are closely intertwined in the sense that the separation of law from politics at the national level—one of the most significant developments of this period—was but one of the major tasks of the Supreme Court; another task was to recognize and resolve the competing claims of the nation and of the States that comprised it.

4. United States v. Fisher

United States v. *Fisher*,[88] decided in 1805,[89] and already referred to in the *Nicholls* controversy discussed above, involved the constitutionality of a federal statute that gave the United States priority in cases of bankruptcy. Marshall, who rendered the opinion, decided in favor of the Government and, interestingly for the future, outlined the doctrine of implied powers[90] which he was later to develop in *McCulloch* v. *Maryland*. For present purposes, the importance of the *Fisher* case is illustrated by a statement made by the United States Attorney for Pennsylvania, Alexander J. Dallas, a Jefferson appointee. In the course of

---

[87] Miller v. Nicholls, 4 Wheat. 311 (1819).

[88] 2 Cranch 358 (1805).

[89] A. J. Beveridge, *The Life of John Marshall* (Boston, 1919), III, 162, states that the decision was rendered in the 1804 term. See, however, 2 Cranch at 370, where it is noted that Harper apologized for the necessity of closing his argument because he was acting as counsel in the Chase impeachment, which neces- sarily places the case in the February 1805 term.

[90] "In construing [the Necessary and Proper] clause it would be incorrect, and would produce endless difficulties, if the opinion should be maintained that no law was authorized which was not indispensably necessary to give effect to a specified power." 2 Cranch at 396. (Marshall, C. J.).

his argument he stated that "[t]he constitution is the supreme law of the land, and not only this court, but every court in the union is bound to decide the question of constitutionality"[91] when an act of Congress and the Constitution are in clear conflict with each other. Significantly, he added that the Court was not to decide that an act is unconstitutional *"on the ground of inconvenience, inexpediency or impolicy."*[92] Here there is a strong echo of Marshall's own words in *Marbury* v. *Madison*, in which he attempted to draw a line between the review of "legal" issues as opposed to those which were politically infected or clearly within the province of the legislative or executive departments.[93]

B. *FLETCHER* v. *PECK*

Shortly after the Pennsylvania controversies, the Supreme Court was again called upon to decide the constitutionality of a State law in *Fletcher* v. *Peck*,[94] decided in 1810. This case is generally accorded special prominence because of its relevance to the law of contracts, and it remains a leading case in the interpretation of the contract clause of the Constitution. Yet if one were to characterize the case by type, it would be more accurate to term it a "property" rather than a "contracts" decision. Also, the case has a far greater—and often unrecognized—importance in constitutional law because of the Court's further contribution to the effort to separate law from politics. In holding that the motives of a legislature cannot be inquired into once it has acted, the Court was giving clear notice that this kind of judicial inquiry into the actions of the legislative branch was not proper. Such questions belonged not to "law" but to "politics."

The background of the case is extensive, and the sources voluminous, but a brief summary must suffice.[95] By virtue of the early English grants from the Crown, the colonies had western boundaries extending far into the wilderness.[96] In 1763, however, those boundaries had been defined to extend to the middle of the Mississippi River.[97] Georgia had

---

[91] *Ibid.*, 384.

[92] *Ibid.* (emphasis supplied).

[93] Marbury v. Madison, 1 Cranch 137, 170 (1803).

[94] 6 Cranch 87 (1810).

[95] See generally Beveridge, *John Marshall*, III, 546–602; C. P. Magrath, *Yazoo: Law and Politics in the New Republic* (Providence, 1966); C. H. Haskins, "The Yazoo Land Companies," *Papers of the American Historical Association* V, 61 (1891).

[96] Because of uncertainties about the geography of the new world,

many of the early colonial grants provided that the colonies' boundaries should extend to "the South Seas." C.f. N. Shurtleff, ed., *Records of the Governor and Company of Massachusetts Bay* (Boston, 1853–54), I, 7.

[97] By the Treaty of Peace between Great Britain and Spain. See W. Stevens, *History of Georgia* (Philadelphia, 1859), II, 460–61. Stevens notes that the boundaries as established by this Treaty were those taken as the basis of settlement for the Treaty of Peace in 1783.

made some attempts to do something with the vast stretch of land that now comprises most of the present States of Alabama and Mississippi,[98] but those attempts were largely unavailing because of the unrest of the large and powerful Indian tribes inhabiting the region.[99] By 1789 the State's interest in disposing of the land had become such that an act was passed authorizing the sale of 25.5 million acres to several land companies.[100] When the speculators tendered practically worthless scrip by way of payment for the grant, the State refused to accept it.[101] The grantees then proceeded to bring a number of suits against Georgia to

---

[98] An Act for Opening the Land Office, 1 Dig. Ga. Laws 258 (1783). An Act to Repeal and Amend Some Part of an Act, Intitulated "An Act for Opening the Land Office," *ibid.*, 286 (1783). Because of the Indian troubles, little was done under the auspices of these Acts. It is significant to note that the boundaries of the disputed territory were laid out in some detail and did correspond fairly closely with the territory eventually ceded to the Union. See also "An Act for Laying Out a District of Land Situated on the River Mississippi, and Within the Limits of This State into a Country to be Called Bourbon." February 7, 1785, 1 Watkins 304, and "An Act to empower the delegates of this State in Congress assembled to sign and deliver a deed of cession to the United States, of certain western territory belonging to this State." February 1, 1788, 1 Watkins 370.

A number of points should be noted about these two Acts: first, the county was among the few areas to which the Indian title had been extinguished; it had been settled by British settlers from west Florida, and Spanish colonists from New Orleans, and was claimed by both. The inhabitants, however, were of a mood to be ruled by no one; the governments of the foreign countries had enough trouble controlling them, let alone the weak State of Georgia. Second, the later Act repealed the first. Between these two Acts an event of some importance occurred in the Beaufort Convention between Georgia and South Carolina to settle their boundary dispute; South Carolina recognized Georgia's claim, and ap-

peared to relinquish its own claim, when it turned around and ceded it to the United States. Now that the United States was involved in the dispute, Georgia, having Indian and Spanish troubles, no doubt thought it might make a bargain and get out. The result was this curious Act, offering to cede part of the area for $171,428 and 45/90, which the State claimed to have expended on the Indian troubles, for a guarantee to pay the costs of any necessary defenses, for a guarantee to maintain free use of the waterways, and finally for a guarantee of the territorial rights of the State. Congress rejected the cession, Appendix XXIX, Watkins 757, but if "the said State extend the bounds of her cession, and vary the terms thereof [reduce the price on account of the debt owed the United States], Congress may accept the same. . . ." So resolved July 15, 1788. If this cession had been made, then the whole Yazoo controversy would not have occurred as it did and the United States would have obtained a much better bargain than it did in 1802.

[99] To assess the amount of trouble that the Indians were causing, one need only scan the number of laws passed by the Georgia Assembly attempting to deal with this problem, not to mention the number of Indian treaties that were written and signed in this period. See also Stevens, *History of Georgia*, II, 410–56.

[100] "An Act for disposing of certain vacant lands or territory within this State." Dec. 21, 1789, 1 Watkins 387.

[101] See Haskins, "Yazoo Land Companies," 73–74.

compel performance of the contract. One of those suits was *Chisholm v. Georgia*.[102] The Supreme Court's decision in that case, that a State could be sued in a federal court, aroused a storm of indignation that soon culminated in the Eleventh Amendment.[103] The fear of federal domination was very much in evidence.

Late in 1794 enough members of the Georgia State legislature had been cajoled, bribed, threatened, or bullied by representatives of a new and seemingly more respectable group of speculators[104] (organized in four land companies) to vote in favor of a bill[105] that disposed of vast

---

[102] 2 Dall. 419 (1793). Virtually all of these suits were by members of the "South Carolina Yazoo Co.," which was the original company lobbying for the passage of the bill. It had not withdrawn its deposit and now its members brought suit on these deposits, serving the Governor and Attorney-General of the State. Other suits never reached the Court because of the Eleventh Amendment.

[103] See Ames, *Proposed Amendments to the Constitution*, 156–57; Hollingsworth v. Virginia, 3 Dall. 378 (1798). Although the amendment was not approved until 1798, it was soon held to bar suits against States, no matter when they arose.

[104] Among those involved were James Gunn, United States Senator from Georgia; Matthew McAllister, federal attorney for Georgia; Wade Hampton of South Carolina, later a member of Congress and a general in the War of 1812; Congressmen Robert Goodloe Harper and Thomas P. Carnes; Nathaniel Pendleton, a federal judge for Georgia; Robert Morris, the Philadelphia financier; and Supreme Court Judge James Wilson. Haskins, "Yazoo Land Companies," 83. See also G. G. Smith, *The Story of Georgia and the Georgia People, 1732 to 1860* (Macon, Ga., 1900), 173: "No men stood higher in Georgia than the men who composed these several companies and the members of the Legislature who made the sale. . . ."

[105] As has been pointed out, "[i]n all probability, the horrifying pictures of the utter corruption and depravity of the legislators voting for the Act of January 7, 1795, are greatly exaggerated. Stories of public corrup-

tion feed one upon another, and grow by leaps and bounds." H. Hagan, "Fletcher v. Peck," *Georgia Law Journal* XVI, 1, 10 (1927). Despite one writer's assertion that "for a hundred years with the masses in Georgia the one thing needed to render a public man odious was to say he was connected with the Yazoo fraud," Smith, *Georgia and the Georgia People*, 174–75, it appears that a number of men who supposedly were parties to the corruption later were elected or appointed to State office. Stevens, *History of Georgia*, II, 490. Furthermore, it does not appear that anyone was ever convicted for his participation in this scheme. It has, however, been suggested that the lack of criminal convictions was probably due to an absence of statutory provisions making bribery of legislators a crime. Hagan, "Fletcher v. Peck," 10, note 18. Moreover, the affidavits obtained by the legislature that repealed the sale seem strong evidence of fairly widespread bribery. See Document F included by the land commissioners in their report to Congress, Feb. 14, 1803, Document No. 74, *American State Papers. Documents, Legislative and Executive of the Congress of the United States in Relation to Public Lands* (Washington, 1834), I, 132, 144 (hereafter cited as *American State Papers: Public Lands*). The congressional commissioners also observe in the course of their report: "A comparison of the schedule annexed to the articles, and which is declared to be a part of the agreement, with the yeas and nays on the passage of the act authorizing the sale, shows that all the members, both in the Senate and in

JOHN RANDOLPH (B. 1773–D. 1833).
Member of Congress from Virginia (1800–1813, 1816–1817, 1820–1825).
Manager of impeachment trial of Justice Samuel Chase (1804).
(Library of Congress)

SPENCER ROANE (B. 1762–D. 1822).
Jurist and political writer from Virginia. States'-rights theorist.
(Colonial Studios, Richmond, Va., from portrait in Supreme Court anteroom, Commonwealth of Virginia, Richmond)

CAESAR AUGUSTUS RODNEY (B. 1772–D. 1824).
Member of Congress from Delaware (1803–1804). Manager of
impeachment trials of District Judge John Pickering and
Justice Samuel Chase (1804). Attorney-General of the
United States (1807–1811).
(Library of Congress)

JAMES WILKINSON (B. 1757–D. 1825).
Soldier, brigadier-general in U.S. Army.
Governor of the Louisiana Territory (1805–1806).
Chief witness in trial of Aaron Burr at Richmond (1807).
(Library of Congress)

SAMUEL CHASE (B. 1741–D. 1811).
Federalist from Maryland.
Associate Justice of the Supreme Court (1796–1811).
(Library of Congress)

BUSHROD WASHINGTON (B. 1762–D. 1829).
Federalist from Pennsylvania and Virginia.
Associate Justice of the Supreme Court (1798–1829).
(Library of Congress)

ALFRED MOORE (B. 1755–D. 1810).
Federalist from North Carolina.
Associate Justice of the Supreme Court (1799–1804).
(Library of Congress)

WILLIAM JOHNSON (B. 1771–D. 1834).
Associate Justice of the Supreme Court (1804–1834).
(Library of Congress)

unsettled lands purported to belong to the State and comprised of 35 million acres in what are now the States of Alabama and Mississippi. These fertile and potentially valuable lands were disposed of to the interested speculators at approximately 1½ ¢ per acre.[106] The enabling legislation, reluctantly approved by Governor George Mathews, became law in January 1795.[107] It appeared that, with one exception, every member of the legislature voting in favor of the sale owned shares in the purchasing land companies.[108]

Despite the corruption, Georgia received a much better deal than it would have, had the abortive 1789 transaction gone through. The State found itself in extreme financial straits. The treasury was empty, State troops were clamoring for their pay, and the State's population was sparse and poor. The vast unsettled western lands were the State's most obviously saleable assets.[109] The public reputation of the new investors was unblemished, and they paid nearly $500,000 in cash for the land. The speculators also came into a better deal than had their predecessors. Eli Whitney's recent invention of the cotton gin had suddenly rendered the arable portions of the land more valuable,[110] and, in a treaty with the United States, Spain renounced its claim to the territory.[111] Between 1795 and 1796 the land companies sold the land to investors and to other purchasers of every class, many of whom, innocent of the fraud, invested their life savings.[112]

---

the House, who voted in favor of the law, were, with one single exception, (Robert Watkins, whose name does not appear), interested in and parties to, the purchase." *Ibid.*, 134. A particularly vivid description of the enactment of the sale is given in Beveridge, *John Marshall*, III, 546–50.

[106] Haskins, "Yazoo Land Companies," 82.

[107] Document K, *American State Papers: Public Lands*, I, 152. After an earlier vote by Governor Mathews, the Act was amended to take care of some of his objections and then attached as a rider to a bill providing for the payment of State troops, which Governor Mathews signed. Despite the general anger directed at those legislators who passed the bill, no one has suggested that the governor was improperly influenced to sign. His action has been attributed to weakness rather than corruption. Haskins, "Yazoo Land Companies," 82, note 1.

[108] Haskins, "Yazoo Land Companies," 84.

[109] See Stevens, *History of Georgia*, II, 472–73.

[110] Whether this invention had any actual effect on the purchasers is questionable, although it may have made them willing to pay more money for the land. Beveridge considers it an event of great importance in their minds. Beveridge, *John Marshall*, III, 555–56. See also Magrath, *Yazoo*, 37. Hagan suggests that the increase in the value of the land due to the invention of the cotton gin lent added fury to the anguished cries of the Georgians protesting the sale. Hagan, "Fletcher v. Peck," 10–11.

[111] No. XXXIII, Appendix, 1 Watkins 760. Spain and England before her had claimed north to the mouth of the Yazoo River as part of their holdings of West Florida. See also Report of the Commissioners, *American State Papers: Public Lands*, I, 152.

[112] Haskins, "Yazoo Land Companies," 87–88.

While the rest of the country avidly bought up the western lands, the people of Georgia, animated by the thoroughgoing corruption of their legislature, mounted a campaign for rescission of the grant. Senator James Jackson, already a popular hero as a result of his service in the Revolution and in the Indian wars,[113] resigned from the Senate and returned home from Philadelphia to lead the public hue and cry for repeal,[114] although his Senate colleague from Georgia, James Gunn, had engineered the Georgia Act. Popular feeling swept anti-Yazoo candidates to victory in the legislative election of 1795, which was almost completely dominated by the controversy over the land sale. One of the first acts of the new legislature was to pass a bill, of which Jackson was perhaps the author, repealing the land grant. Feeling was so strong that the new assembly provided that the record of the corruption be placed in their journals lest it be too soon forgotten. In addition, the "usurped act,"[115] providing for the sale, was publicly and ceremoniously burned, the fire supplied from heaven (as legend has it) by means of a magnifying glass which concentrated the sun's rays into a flame.[116] The act was then expunged from all official State records.[117]

---

[113] For an adulatory contemporary biography of General Jackson, see T. Charlton, *The Life of Major General James Jackson, Part One* (Augusta, Ga., 1809).

[114] Although it has been asserted that Jackson did not express any dismay over the sale until it had already become unpopular, Beveridge, *John Marshall*, III, 560–61; Hagan, "Fletcher v. Peck," 10, his correspondence shows that he did not approve of the sale from the beginning. A. Jackson to J. Tatnall, Jan. 6, 1795 in Charlton, *Major General James Jackson*, 206–208. When the matter came up for discussion in the Senate in March 1795, however, the Senator apparently did not express his feelings. See Beveridge, *John Marshall*, III, 560 and note 3. Nevertheless, in the spring of that year he wrote letters attacking the sale in two Georgia newspapers and soon hurried home to put himself at the head of the insurgents. Smith, *Georgia and the Georgia People*, 174. It had even been asserted that the people might not have been so disturbed had it not been for Jackson. *Ibid.* This, however, seems improbable, since William H. Crawford, later United States Senator,

Minister to France, Secretary of the Treasury, and candidate for President, had presented a petition from the citizens of Columbia County to the Governor before the bill was signed requesting him to veto it. Beveridge, *John Marshall*, III, 551–52; Stevens, *History of Georgia*, II, 477–78.

[115] The term is that used by the rescinding Act, which, in a lengthy and argumentative preamble, declared that the previous legislature did not have the power to sell the western lands, at least in so large a block and under such liberal conditions, because such a sale was inconsistent with the sovereignty of the State and was not for the good of its people. The rescinding Act concluded that the legislature "did usurp a power" to pass the Act. *Digest of the Laws of Georgia* 577 (Watkins and Watkins, rev. ed. 1801).

[116] Beveridge suggests that Jackson held the glass, Beveridge, *John Marshall*, III, 565–66, but other writers do not concur in this. See *ibid.*, III, 566, note 1.

[117] See Haskins, "Yazoo Land Companies," 86. This extreme measure is but one example of the fervor of the

X: *States' Rights and the National Judiciary*

Meanwhile, however, few of the purchasers had been idle. Many of them had sold their lands, much of it to individuals but also to new companies hastily organized in other parts of the country, particularly in New England. In one sale dated the same day as the rescinding Act, the Georgia Mississippi Company sold 11 million acres at 10¢ an acre, in a complex transaction involving formation of the New England Mississippi Land Company "to serve as both vehicle and shield for subsequent sales."[118] The announcement of the rescinding Act aroused widespread consternation and gave rise to a vociferous controversy by pamphlet and newspaper over the propriety of the original act and of that rescinding it.[119]

The issue immediately appeared in Congress, in all probability because of President Washington's concern over relations with the powerful Indian tribes in the area.[120] The United States was the only body constitutionally entitled to deal with these Indians, and the government did not wish to disturb unnecessarily the leaders of a large

---

people of Georgia at the time. Smith declares, "Such was the extent of the angry feelings aroused by the [sale] act . . . that anything like a calm consideration of the matter was impossible then, and for fifty years afterward there was but one side of the case looked at. . . ." Smith, *Georgia and the Georgia People,* 169. Almost every county had made some sort of petition to the State government against the sale, including presentments by the grand juries of all but two counties. See Beveridge, *John Marshall,* III, 559–60; J. Harris, *Georgia, From the Invasion of De Soto to Recent Times* (New York, 1896), 131. State Senator Robert Thomas of Hancock County, who had voted for the sale, fled from the ire of his constituents to South Carolina, but was killed there apparently by one of the opponents of the sale. See A. Chappell, *Miscellanies of Georgia* (Atlanta, 1874), 119; Harris, *Georgia,* 130. Gunn was repeatedly burned in effigy, Beveridge, *John Marshall,* III, 559; Stevens, *History of Georgia,* 480. The Constitutional Convention, planned for 1795, met but was unable to do more than enact a few amendments before it broke up in the excitement. Stevens, *History of Georgia,* 498–99.

[118] G. Dunne, "Joseph Story: The Germinal Years," *Harvard Law Review* LXXV, 707, 712 (1962).

[119] Haskins, "Yazoo Land Companies," 88.

[120] *Annals of Congress,* IV, 1231 (3rd Cong., 2d sess.). Washington received copies of Georgia's Act of sale and immediately passed them on to Congress, expressing concern that sale of these lands would "deeply affect the peace and welfare of the United States." Much debate in later years centered on what he meant by this. Opponents of claims under this Act were sure Washington was exposing the corruption in Georgia's sale, see *Annals of Congress,* XIV, 1022–1108 (8th Cong., 2d. sess.), whereas others asserted that Washington's concern was over possible Indian conflicts. Washington made no mention of either irregularities of sale or Indians, but the first action taken by Congress was discussion of a resolution to forbid individual or State treaties with the Indians. *Annals of Congress,* IV, 1252 (3rd Cong., 2d. sess.). The subsequent resolve to obtain cession from Georgia admitted some confusion as to ownership, but made no mention of corruption attending the sale. *Ibid.,* IV, 1278–82.

force of trained warriors.[121] Likewise, the United States did not want the land companies to open any negotiations with the Indians, or to ignore their rights, as recognized by United States treaties.

Since 1788 the United States had wished to obtain title to these unsettled lands, and Georgia had been anxious to be rid of them and the attendant problems of management and Indian relations.[122] The United States took the initiative, and in 1798 Congress passed an act to appoint commissioners to arrange for cession.[123] Appointed by Jefferson were Secretary of State James Madison, Secretary of the Treasury Albert Gallatin, and Attorney-General Levi Lincoln.[124] Georgia's commissioners were James Jackson, Abraham Baldwin, and John Milledge.[125] After considerable deliberation, terms were agreed upon and presented to Congress for ratification. The essence of the agreement was that Georgia transfer to the federal government the western lands (and claims against them) in return for a payment of $1,250,000, but that one-tenth of the Yazoo lands could be reserved for satisfying claims made against the lands. In February 1803, pursuant to the agreement, the commissioners for the United States reported to Congress that, notwithstanding the fact that under all the circumstances the title of the Yazoo claimants could not be supported, various equitable considerations rendered a compromise appropriate. Accordingly, they proposed that 5 million acres of the former Georgia lands be allotted for satisfaction of all legitimate claims that resulted from the 1796 rescission Act, and that the claimants be permitted to elect compensation, in land or in money, not exceeding $5,000,000, which would be derived from sales of land in the Mississippi Territory. Congress, however, declined to do more than enact legislation three weeks later that set aside 5 million acres to settle claims "derived from any act or pretended act of the State of Georgia, which Congress may hereafter think fit to provide for."[126] A political solution to the problems of the Yazoo claims was merely deferred.

---

[121] See Beveridge, *John Marshall*, III, 553.

[122] On February 1, 1788, the Georgia legislature passed an Act empowering itself to cede certain western territories to the United States, but nothing was done. 1 Watkins 370. See also *Digest of the Laws of Georgia 1755–1800*, 370–71.

[123] *Annals of Congress*, VIII, 1318 (5th Cong., 2d sess.), finally approved April 7, 1798, *ibid.*, IX, 3719–21.

[124] See also no. 69, *American State Papers: Public Lands*, I, 13. *American State Papers: Public Lands*, no.

46, is the appointment by John Adams of three different persons to deal with cession. This was done December 31, 1799 and was possibly a futile attempt to bulwark Federalist appointments in the face of the forthcoming Republican administration.

[125] Haskins, "Yazoo Land Companies," 89.

[126] An Act Regulating the Grants of Land, and Providing for the Disposal of the Lands of the United States, South of the State of Tennessee, chapter XXVII, Sec. 8, 2 Stat. 229 (1803).

X: *States' Rights and the National Judiciary*

On its surface the task of settling the disputed claims appeared to be a complicated but minor matter. Georgia's furor over the 1795 Act was largely quieted by the rescinding Act of 1796, and although the issue festered for years, there was little more that could be done after the cession. Nevertheless, the basic problem of the disputed claims was far from settled, and the controversy continued for sixteen years on the floor of Congress, primarily as a consequence of the personal vendetta carried on by John Randolph of Roanoke against the northern purchasers, thereby dividing the Democratic-Republican party on sectional lines.

There was, however, another vital aspect of the "Yazoo Fraud," and that was the validity of the 1796 Act rescinding the 1795 Act. The efforts to force a judicial determination of the validity of the political settlement on the floor of Congress and the proceedings that culminated in *Fletcher* v. *Peck* afford another example of Marshall's attempt to separate law and politics. *Fletcher* marked one of the first stages in settling the law of public contract and has been termed "one of the earliest and strongest judicial assertions of the supremacy of Nationalism over Localism."[127] The case also involved an equally significant constitutional issue as to the power of the judiciary to inquire into the motives of the action of another branch of government—here, the legislature.

The numerous New England investors in particular were anxious to have a judicial determination of the validity of the titles which they had purchased.[128] By the Eleventh Amendment they were prevented from suing the State of Georgia, and the 1796 rescinding Act forbade the courts of that State from entertaining appropriate action there. Thus it came about in 1803 that one Robert Fletcher, of Amherst, New Hampshire, brought suit against John Peck, of Boston (who had dealt extensively in Georgia lands), in the United States Court for the District of Massachusetts. The suit was for recovery of money paid, because of breach of warranty of title with respect to 15,000 acres of land in the disputed territory, which was allegedly conveyed to Fletcher by Peck.

Several indicators point to the conclusion that the case was actually

---

[127] Beveridge, *John Marshall*, III, 556. This case has also been widely viewed as establishing the primacy of vested property rights among nineteenth-century constitutional values. See, e.g., Magrath, *Yazoo*, 102–103.

[128] Among the legal challenges to the 1796 rescission Act, at least two reached judgment before *Fletcher*. Bishop v. Nightingale, 1 Circuit Ct. Records, Chancery (C.C.D. Conn.

1802) (Federal Records Center, Boston), failed to produce a decision on this ultimate issue. Derby v. Black, *Columbian Sentinel*, Oct. 9, 1799 (Sup. Jud. Ct. Mass. 1799), decided in favor of the claimants, holding the rescission repugnant to the federal Constitution, but does not appear to have been influential in the development of the Yazoo controversy.

feigned.[129] First, although the suit was filed in 1803, it was continued "by consent" from term to term until October 1806; for this delay there was no apparent reason unless it may have been the speculators' hope of gaining relief through Congress, which had been active in the dispute. Second, the pleadings neatly set forth warranties in the conveyance covering almost every possible point of controversy as to the legitimacy of the title, including the question of Georgia's original title to the lands vis-à-vis the federal government, Spain, and the Indians. In addition, John Quincy Adams, who represented Peck before the Supreme Court, mentioned in his *Memoirs* that Judge Livingston had declared to him the reluctance of the Court to decide the case, because it "appeared manifestly made up for the purpose of getting the Court's judgment upon all the points."[130] Adams did not give his own view as to the *bona fides* of the suit, but he did quote a statement of Marshall from the Bench that unmistakably alludes to the collusive nature of the case.[131] Moreover, there is additional indication of the Supreme Court's reluctance to decide the case in Judge Johnson's separate opinion, in which he stated that he had been "very unwilling" to decide the case at all because of the "strong evidence, upon the face of it, of being a mere feigned case."[132] Nevertheless, he wrote, his confidence in the attorneys engaged by the parties "has induced me to abandon my scruples, in the belief that they would never consent to impose a mere feigned case upon this court."[133] Judge Johnson's remarks have been appropriately characterized as naïve, at the very least, in light of the fact that, respectable though counsel were, they had long been identified with Yazooists and were clearly interested in obtaining a decision from the Supreme Court.[134] Finally, the original copies of the pleadings, recently uncovered by the clerk of the United States District Court in Boston, increase the suspicion. For example, in Fletcher's declaration the allegations of the acreage and value of the land are in each instance altered from 1,000 acres and $250, respectively, to 15,000 acres and $3,000.[135] This

---

[129] This has been the suggestion of a number of commentators. See, e.g., Beveridge, *John Marshall*, III, 592; Chappell, *Miscellanies of Georgia*, 134–36; D. Loth, *Chief Justice: John Marshall and the Growth of the Republic* (New York, 1949), 261–64; Hagan, "Fletcher v. Peck," 23–24; Dunne, "Joseph Story," 746, 749. Magrath, *Yazoo*, 54, presents some of these arguments forcefully and with little apology for the "collusion."

[130] J. Q. Adams, *Memoirs* (Philadelphia, 1874), I, 546 (entry for Mar. 7, 1809).

[131] See text accompanying note 139 infra.

[132] 6 Cranch at 147.

[133] *Ibid.*, 148.

[134] Magrath, *Yazoo*, 81. John Quincy Adams had supported the claimants when he was in the Senate, and Joseph Story was in the pay of the New England Mississippi Land Company. *Ibid.*, 82.

[135] This information was provided through the courtesy of Professor Paul A. Freund of the Harvard Law School.

change brought the case not merely within the statutory jurisdictional minimum of $500 for the circuit court, but also within the $2,000 minimum for appeal to the Supreme Court. In the many handwritten pages of the declaration, with almost no other alterations, these changes stand out with exceptional clarity.

Collusive or feigned the suit may have been, and probably was, but it does not necessarily follow that it was collusive in an improper sense. "Arranged cases" of one kind of another, that is, suits brought to secure authoritative rulings from the Supreme Court, were not uncommon at the time.[136] Moreover, from a lawyer's point of view, an appropriate method of removing clouds on land titles often was, and still is, by way of a suit for breach of one or more of the covenants for title in a warranty deed, particularly when a real threat to seisin or quiet enjoyment is presented. Whether in such a situation the grantee sues his immediate grantor (whom he may or may not know personally), or a remote grantor in the chain of title, will depend on a number of factors. Finally, the names of counsel representing the parties—a point referred to above—are relevant to the importance of the suit and to its outcome. Fletcher had retained that great advocate Luther Martin to present his case; Peck was represented by Robert Goodloe Harper, a prominent Baltimore lawyer who had also been a land speculator, and by John Quincy Adams, who was subsequently replaced by Joseph Story. In any event, the fact remains that the issues presented by the case obviously seemed sufficiently important in all aspects for it to proceed to the stage of decision. It is, of course, the decision itself that is one of the most important aspects of the entire Yazoo controversy.

In 1806 a jury heard evidence relevant to Georgia's title to the lands, and returned a bulky statement of the facts as a special verdict, but left determination of the title question to the court. It was not until the October term of 1807 that the Circuit Court finally decided the case. Supreme Court Judge Cushing, sitting on circuit, decided in favor of the defendant Peck all questions raised by the pleadings and the jury verdict, thus upholding the transfer of title as against the claim of breach of warranty by the vendor.[137] Again, the progress of the case was slow, but Fletcher finally sued out a writ of error to the Supreme Court, and the case was argued there on March 1–4, 1809. Then, in spite of the elaborate preparation that the case had received, and with pleadings sufficient to bring into issue every point that the speculators wanted to

---

[136] See Warren, *Supreme Court*, I, 393, 395; Beveridge, *John Marshall*, IV, 282–83.

[137] The decision of the Circuit Court is unreported. The proceedings are discussed in Magrath, *Yazoo*, 53–56. Records of the case are found in Massachusetts Circuit Court Records, II, Federal Records Center, Boston.

have tried, the Court reversed for a defect in the pleadings.[138] This action is curious. The defect was minor; no one had seen fit to remark upon it previously. Furthermore, the Court permitted counsel to cure it immediately by amendment without returning the case to the Circuit Court. Perhaps the real reason for the reversal on this technicality was that recorded by Adams on March 11:

> With regard to the merits of the case, the Chief Justice added verbally, that, circumstanced as the Court are, only five judges attending [Chase and Cushing were absent because of illness], there were difficulties which would have prevented them from giving any opinion at this term had the pleadings been correct; and the Court the more readily forebore giving it, as from the complexion of the pleadings they could not but see that at the time when the convenants were made the parties had notice of the acts covenanted against; that this was not to be taken as part of the Court's opinion, but as a motive why they had thought proper not to give one at this term.[139]

With the pleadings amended, *Fletcher* v. *Peck* returned once again to the Supreme Court's calendar in the succeeding term. By then Adams had accepted an appointment as ambassador to Russia, and Joseph Story, still a young lawyer from Massachusetts,[140] joined Harper in arguing what was essentially the cause of the land companies. Martin's argument for the plaintiff was perfunctory, apparently because of his unusually excessive drinking at the time,[141] though possibly because of a prearranged agreement with the land company interests, as part of the general arrangement for a test case.[142] From the report of the decision it appears that Martin argued neither that the rescinding Act was effective nor that the corruption involved in the passage of the grant vitiated its effectiveness; his argument, as recorded by Cranch at least, was almost entirely technical. It centered on the invalidity of Georgia's title to the land and on the insufficiency of one of Peck's pleadings.[143]

The Chief Justice announced his opinion on March 16, 1810. On

---

[138] 6 Cranch at 125–27. Fletcher had pleaded that the legislature had no right to dispose of the land as it did. Peck's answer, to which Fletcher's demurrer was overruled by the Circuit Court, asserted that the *Governor* was "legally empowered to sell and convey" the territory. *Ibid.*, 93. Martin had picked up this disparity in his argument. *Ibid.*, 115.

[139] J. Q. Adams, *Memoirs*, I, 547 (entry for Mar. 11, 1809).

[140] For an account of this period of Story's life and his involvement with the Yazoo claimants, see Dunne, "Joseph Story." Only six years later Story was appointed to the Supreme Court.

[141] Beveridge, *John Marshall*, III, 586, note 1.

[142] See Magrath, *Yazoo*, 69.

[143] 6 Cranch at 115, 124–25.

all points the Court held in favor of the defendant Peck, and thus for the other investor-speculators in general. Why Marshall and the rest of the Court decided to proceed with this cause, despite the misgivings they had expressed earlier, is not clear.[144] It has been suggested that the Court's decision might have forestalled action by Virginia, which could have affected adversely Marshall's own speculations in the western part of that State, but there is nothing to indicate that Virginia ever contemplated any action similar to Georgia's rescinding Act or that Marshall ever thought Virginia had done so.[145] Nonetheless, the concurring opinion by Judge Johnson, which could easily have turned into a dissent, is both interesting and instructive. Reference has already been made to his qualms about the fictitious nature of the case, but he may well have been influenced to some extent by political pressures to help resolve Republican efforts to settle the Yazoo controversy and hence, ironically, to side with Marshall.[146] Although he strongly disagreed with certain aspects of Marshall's decision, his own concurring opinion has political overtones in that it enabled him to add his Republican endorsement in a manner that would not offend the Madison administration.[147]

Clearly, *Fletcher* v. *Peck* has great importance as the first major Supreme Court decision striking down a State statute. It is also a landmark decision in the law of contracts. Marshall emphasized that even though the original sales of the Georgia lands under the 1795 Act were infected with fraud, the subsequent purchasers were innocent; these purchasers, he said, must not suffer from any concealed defect arising from the conduct of those who had held the property, of which there had been no notice. The innocent purchaser "has paid his money for a title good at law, he is innocent, whatever may be the guilt of others, and equity will not subject him to the penalties attached to that guilt. All titles would be insecure, and the intercourse between man and man

---

[144] Beveridge nevertheless considers Marshall's resolve to decide the case as one of his greatest acts:

As in *Marbury* v. *Madison*, the supremacy of the National Judiciary had to be asserted or its inferiority conceded, so in *Fletcher* v. *Peck*, it was necessary that the Nation's highest court should plainly lay down the law of public contract, notify every State of its place in the American system, and announce the limitations which the National Constitution places upon each State.

Failure to do this would have been to sanction Georgia's rescinding act, to encourage other States to take similar action, and to render insecure and litigious numberless titles acquired innocently and in good faith, and multitudes of contracts entered into in the belief that they were binding. A weaker man than John Marshall, and one less wise and courageous, would have dismissed the appeal or decided the case on technical points.
Beveridge, *John Marshall*, III, 593.

[145] Loth, *Chief Justice*, 261.

[146] See Magrath, *Yazoo*, 82.

[147] *Ibid.*

would be very seriously obstructed, if this principle be overturned."[148] Marshall held that the Georgia land grant, accepted by a grantee, was a contract, and that "[w]hen . . . a law is in its nature a contract, when absolute rights have vested under that contract, a repeal of the law cannot devest those rights. . . ."[149] It should be noted, however, that others earlier had recognized the principle that *Fletcher* announced with respect to the constitutional aspect of impairment of contracts by a State, and hence that, at least to the Bar, the Supreme Court's holding was not quite the bold and courageous assertion that Beveridge ascribes to Marshall.[150]

The significance of the decision goes further: in declining to look behind the motives of the legislature in passing the 1795 Act, the Court firmly adhered to the principle of judicial self-restraint. Differently phrased, Marshall did the same kind of thing he had done in *Marbury*, and to a lesser extent in the Burr trial: the spheres of the government departments were distinct, and the idea was gaining currency that they were not to encroach on one another save where the Constitution defined division of function and power.[151] To have inquired into bribery charges would have invited numerous suits attacking State legislation before the Court, at a time when Marshall and others were attempting to dissociate law and the Court from politics, and from politically motivated cases. In addition to asserting the power of the federal courts to hold invalid a State act for conflict with the federal Constitution, Marshall prescribed an important and far-reaching limitation on the power of the judiciary insofar as the separation of powers was concerned.

Following Coke's death in the seventeenth century, a struggle of nearly a century ensued in England to secure the independence of the judiciary, and with it the idea that an abstract law, administered by technical legal specialists, should act as a check upon government. We inherited the successful establishment of these ideas,[152] and, ironically, in this country the idea of applying an abstract law as a restraint on governmental action had a much broader subsequent development than it did in England.[153] We inherited the idea that it was wrong for judges to be governmental officers, and, together with the idea of a law sovereign over laws emanating from mere government, came almost

---

[148] 6 Cranch at 133–34.

[149] *Ibid.*, 135.

[150] See Beveridge, *John Marshall*, III, 586.

[151] See chapter 6 and chapter 8 supra.

[152] See J. Story, *Commentaries on the Constitution of the United States*, 4th ed. (Boston, 1873), I, 375; W. Blackstone, *Commentaries*, I, *269.

[153] The political life of the colonists broke off from that of England towards the end of the seventeenth century, when in England the legal view of politics was strongest and questions of state were still approached from a legalistic angle. A. L. Lowell, *Government of England* (New York, 1908), II, 472, 481.

inexorably the proposition that courts have the power to overthrow governmental acts. "It is emphatically the province and duty of the judicial department to say what the law is."[154] As the late John Dickinson has remarked, in the hands of men such as Marshall and Story the doctrine of the supremacy of law—originally derived to check the usurpation of English kings—has been "turned into an instrument to control the action of popularly chosen officials and legislators. . . ."[155] In England, although theoretically parliament is bound by the law of the constitution, it is "in the last instance the supreme judge of that law."[156]

In the minds of those who framed our Constitution, the dread of royal power—both in the history of England under Tudor and Stuart kings, and in the period immediately preceding the American Revolution—influenced the division of powers among the new departments of government. Those few powers that remained in the English king, after the severance from them of the spheres of parliament and the judiciary, were assigned to the executive and its officials, and they were closely hemmed in by constitutional limitations. For these limitations and checks, in the period preceding the Federal Convention, men had depended on popular legislative bodies which were vested with very broad powers,[157] but thereafter conservative opinion turned back to the earlier view that an independent rule of law was needed to curb the popular will which was displacing that of ancient royal power. On the records of the time is a clear division of conviction as well as opinion between opposing schools of thought. One is represented by Jefferson, most succinctly perhaps in a letter to Edmund Randolph[158] to the effect that "[i]t is the will of the nation which makes the law obligatory. . . . law [is] law because it is the will of the nation. . . ." It was a principle that did not die easily, as evidenced, for example, by a statement of Chief Justice Waite: "For protection against abuses by legislatures, the people must resort to the polls, not to the courts."[159] The other school is represented by the position taken by Marshall, and later Story, who were speaking out for the doctrine of fundamental law as an instrument for controlling the actions of popularly chosen officials and legislators.[160]

---

[154] Marbury v. Madison, 1 Cranch 137, 177 (1803).

[155] J. Dickinson, *Administrative Justice and the Supremacy of Law* (Cambridge, Mass., 1927), 98. Similarly, Roscoe Pound referred to the judiciary as standing "between the public and what the public needs and desires." R. Pound, "Common Law and Legislation," *Harvard Law Review* XXI, 383, 403 (1908).

[156] Dickinson, *Administrative Justice*, 95.

[157] Story, *Commentaries*, I, 385.

[158] T. Jefferson to E. Randolph, Aug. 18, 1799, in P. L. Ford, ed., *The Works of Thomas Jefferson* (New York, 1904–1905), IX, 74.

[159] Munn v. Illinois, 94 U.S. 113, 134 (1876).

[160] See Dickinson, *Administrative Justice*, 98–99 and note 56.

Nevertheless, the contract clause—chiefly as a result of *Fletcher v. Peck*—became vital in American constitutional law during the nineteenth century. It has been observed that, during the ensuing eighty years, the contract clause was the justification for voiding State laws in some seventy-five decisions.[161] Marshall assumed, as did Johnson in his concurring opinion, that vested property rights had a special constitutional value, and from this assumption Marshall proceeded in two directions. One was to interpret the prohibition against impairing the obligation of contracts to include State as well as private contracts. On this point, available evidence from the Constitutional Convention and the State conventions[162] provides little support for the proposition that legislative grants were protected from impairment. The other direction in which Marshall moved, one for which he has been more severely criticized, was his extension of the meaning of "contract" to include not only an executory contract—that is, a promise to perform at a future date—but an executed contract, which in this case, he stated, included past legislative grants which could not be revoked by either party. His reasoning on this second point seems not to have been based, as is sometimes charged, upon a confusion between an executed "grant" and a "contract"[163] but on the broad meaning of the word contract, under which a grantor extinguishes his rights and therefore makes an implied promise by his grant not to undo what he has done: that is, the grantor may not act in derogation of the title he has transferred. Citing Blackstone, Marshall stated that an executed contract is no different than a grant. "It would be strange if a contract to convey was secured by the constitution, while an absolute conveyance remained unprotected."[164] Marshall's argument was not new, and indeed it seems clear that the core of his reasoning probably stems from a brief opinion by Hamilton in 1796, in which the latter stated, with respect to the contract clause, that "[e]very grant from one to another, whether the grantor be a state or an individual, is virtually a contract that the grantee shall hold and enjoy the thing granted against the grantor, and his representatives."[165]

It is said that there is little originality in Marshall's opinion;[166] that he drew on other sources for the conclusions he wished to reach. If so, this was not the only case in which he was indebted to the views of others that helped to strengthen his own position, particularly those of articulate Federalists such as Hamilton. In fact, in several respects

---

[161] B. Wright, *The Contract Clause of the Constitution* (Cambridge, Mass., 1938), 95.

[162] See generally *ibid*.

[163] See Beveridge, *John Marshall*, III, 590.

[164] 6 Cranch at 137.

[165] Quoted in Haskins, "Yazoo Land Companies," 99, note 4.

[166] Magrath, *Yazoo*, 82–83.

the indebtedness was not merely a coincidence of ideas.[167] To suggest such indebtedness, however, does not denigrate the importance of Marshall's decision.[168] The point is that Marshall said it and made it a part of his decision that Georgia's grant was a legal contract and that its repeal violated the contract clause. Marshall may also have owed to Hamilton the basis for the assertion that "the first principles of natural justice and social policy" had been violated by the repeal act, which had injured innocent purchasers.[169] However, the protection of bona fide purchasers was already acknowledged law in England.[170] This result was not perceived at the time, and has often been missed by historians, particularly since Republicans saw in the *Fletcher* decision a usurpation by the Court and condemned the judiciary for the contracts doctrine, which announced that a completed grant of lands under a legislative act was a "contract" within the meaning of the contract clause of the Constitution.[171]

Judge Johnson disagreed in his concurring opinion. Avoiding constitutional arguments, he relied on natural law, stating: "[T]he reason and the nature of things: a principle which will impose laws even on the deity,"[172] to support his position that when the Georgia legislature conveyed the property, it was irrevocably vested in each purchaser and that the legislature did not possess the power to revoke its own grants. He also disagreed that the contract clause of the Constitution precluded the attempted repeal of the grant because he did not view a grant as a contract, and he feared that Marshall's sweeping interpretation of impairment would unduly restrict legitimate State powers.[173] With considerable prescience, he drew a distinction between governmental rights of jurisdiction and rights of soil, by which he evidently meant to allow greater latitude to State governments to alter pre-existing arrangements by regulatory measures than by appropriating property. On the other hand, Johnson strongly supported Marshall in rejecting as "absurd" the contention that the judiciary could invalidate acts of legislators who were alleged to have been bribed or corrupted.[174]

After the Court's decision in favor of the claimants, Congress took still another four years to settle the disputed claims. Randolph continued to oppose any compromise of those claims which he had earlier

---

[167] *Ibid.*; see Warren, *Supreme Court*, I, 396–97.

[168] See Warren, *Supreme Court*, I, 392; Beveridge, *John Marshall*, III, 586.

[169] See Haskins, "Yazoo Land Companies," 99; Magrath, *Yazoo*, 83.

[170] J. N. Pomeroy, *A Treatise on Equity Jurisprudence as Administered in the United States of America*, 5th ed. (San Francisco, 1941), III, Sec. 735.

[171] See generally Beveridge, *John Marshall*, III, 595–600; Magrath, *Yazoo*, 86–87.

[172] 6 Cranch at 143 (opinion of Johnson, J.).

[173] *Ibid.*, 145.

[174] *Ibid.*, 144.

spoken of as "the plunder of the public property,"[175] and George A. Troup of Georgia took an equally strenuous stand in denouncing legalized fraud and corruption.[176] Their attempts eventually proved futile, and in January of 1814 a Senate committee reported a bill to effect the compromises presented ten years earlier by the commissioners. It soon passed by a vote of 24–8.[177] The bill then came before the House; after nearly a month, but with minimal debate, it passed on March 26 by a vote of 81–76.[178] The Senate concurred in certain amendments made by the House, and on March 31, 1814, the bill became law.[179] It was not until 1818 that the Treasury Department issued its final statement of the awards made. Most of the total, $4,282,151.12, went to persons living or having interests in New England, and the long compensation dispute was then finally settled.[180]

Fletcher v. *Peck* has legal significance beyond its disposition of federal constitutional questions. It came before the federal Circuit Court on the basis of the diversity of citizenship of the parties, and on appeal the Supreme Court was not limited, as in cases from State courts, to the federal questions; the Supreme Court was, and is, entitled to review all the issues that were properly before the federal trial court, including questions of general or State law. In *Fletcher* v. *Peck* one of these issues was the authority of Georgia to make the grant of lands under the Constitution of the State itself. It was in upholding this authority that Marshall made his majestic pronouncement on the presumption of validity of the acts of a legislature.

> The question, whether a law be void for its repugnancy to the constitution, is, at all times, a question of much delicacy, which ought seldom, if ever, to be decided in the affirmative, in a doubtful case. The court, when impelled by duty to render such a judgment, would be unworthy of its station, could it be unmindful of the solemn obligations which that station imposes. But it is not on slight implication and vague conjecture that the legislature is to be pronounced to have transcended its powers, and its acts to be considered as void.[181]

This profession of deference to the acts of the legislature has been reiterated countless times, in the context of Supreme Court review of

---

175 See Beveridge, *John Marshall*, III, 595–600.
176 *Ibid.*
177 *Annals of Congress*, XXVI, 612–13, 631, 636 (13th Cong., 2d. sess.).
178 *Ibid.*, 1697, 1771, 1836, 1855, 1873, 1890, 1892, 1925.

179 *Ibid.*, 689, 2817–22.
180 See *American State Papers. Documents, Legislative and Executive, of the Congress of the United States*, Class III, *Finance* (Washington, 1834), III, 281–83 (no. 537).
181 6 Cranch 128.

acts of Congress, even when a sentence of doom is placed on the law under review.

Thus the Supreme Court had a potential influence on the development of American law that extended beyond its authoritative rulings on the federal constitution and federal statutes. The Court could be a force, albeit not a mandatory one, towards the unification of the common law in the States, in the course of rendering decisions in diversity-of-citizenship cases. A preliminary survey of citations in early State reports to Supreme Court decisions in this period tends to suggest, except in New York and Pennsylvania, that the State judges did not recognize the growing power of the national judiciary merely by deferring to it by reason of its stature and eminence; rather, they tended to cite Supreme Court decisions as instances of what a "strong" or "good" court had concluded (either as *primus inter pares* or as part of a string of cases) in order to buttress their own decisions—much as a Massachusetts court might today cite a New York or Illinois decision. Nevertheless, an early Massachusetts case stands out so markedly as a justification for deferring to a divided opinion of the Supreme Court, that it merits reference and a short quotation. The case is *Baxter* v. *New England Marine Insurance Co.*,[182] which held that in an action on an insurance contract the judgment of a foreign court condemning the insured ship for breach of a blockade is conclusive evidence of such breach. In the course of the opinion, Judge Sedgwick stated:

> In the Supreme Court of the *United States*, in the case of *Groudson & Al.* vs. *Leonard*, it has been determined, by the opinion of four judges against two, that *the sentence of a foreign court of admiralty condemning a vessel for a breach of blockade is conclusive evidence of that fact, in an action on a policy of insurance.* If this decision is to be considered as an authority in the national courts, (and I think it will), it would be with extreme reluctance that I should feel myself bound to dissent from it, by prescribing a different rule for the administration of justice in the courts of the state. There seems to be a peculiar propriety in respecting the decisions of the supreme court of the *United States* upon this subject: because there is delegated to the national government an authority to regulate commerce: and because it is highly interesting to commerce, that the same rule of decision, in this respect, should pervade the whole country. It would indeed be inconvenient, embarrassing and disreputable, that in different actions, depending at the same time, in the national and state courts, brought on the same policy, and governed by the same facts, contrary judgments should be rendered; and this might be the case, if different rules of decision were adopted by them respectively.[183]

---

[182] 6 Mass. 277 (1810).   [183] *Ibid.*, 299–300.

C. *UNITED STATES* v. *HUDSON AND GOODWIN*

If, in a broad sense, one can accept a distinction between (1) those cases that were primarily political in nature and to which, therefore, "fixed principles" of law could not be applied by the Court were it to entertain such cases, and (2) cases that were susceptible of orderly resolution in accordance with "fixed principles" of law, and which the Court felt were its business to decide, the question still remains whether there was an intermediate area or third class in which the Court deliberately abstained from deciding a case even though strong policy considerations could justify non-abstention.

It is submitted that *Marbury* v. *Madison* and *Fletcher* v. *Peck* are illustrative of the distinction above suggested as to the first two classes of cases. The third class, if it can justifiably be identified as such, is illustrated by citations in which the Court was called upon to make decisions in areas where the legislature had passed no express laws but nevertheless might act because it was clearly within its province to do so. Absent a legislative act, should the Court intervene by judicial legislation?

For example, when all the stockholders of a corporation reside in a State other than the opposite party to a suit, is the corporation a "citizen" for purposes of the required diversity of citizenship, in order to sue or be sued in the federal courts? Or, similarly, can corporations sue or be sued in the federal courts when only some of their stockholders reside in States other than the residence of the adverse party?[184]

An important example involved the question whether the federal courts could take cognizance of common law crimes, that is, could a federal court hear an indictment for an offense that was a crime at common law but that was proscribed by no statute? A number of judges in the 1790s had answered that question in the affirmative. Judge Chase, however, in deciding *United States* v. *Worrall*[185] on circuit in 1798, had refused to entertain indictments at common law. With the exception of Judge Johnson, other Supreme Court judges when sitting on circuit, seem not to have followed Judge Chase.[186]

The issue finally came before the Supreme Court as a result of a series of criminal indictments under the common law. These were for libelous attacks against President Jefferson—a curious irony, if not anomaly, in light of the outraged position the Republicans had taken

---

[184] See Bank of the United States v. Deveaux, 5 Cranch 61 (1810). See Warren, *Supreme Court*, I, 433.

[185] 2 Dall. 384 (C.C.D. Pa. 1798).
[186] Warren, *Supreme Court*, I, 434–35.

earlier with respect to the Sedition Act. Jefferson had ordered nearly all these cases dismissed when he learned of them[187]—all, that is, but one that survived from Connecticut and reached the Supreme Court on an issue of jurisdiction.

That case was *United States* v. *Hudson and Goodwin*,[188] which was decided in 1812. At the time, both political parties, (though not the Bar) appear to have been of much the same opinion in their opposition to indictments in federal courts for common law crimes. Since the other cases had already been nol-prossed, neither Attorney-General William Pinkney nor counsel for the defendants was willing to argue the case. Hence the Court, in a brief opinion by Judge Johnson, replete with generalizations, decided this important question without careful rehearsal of the legal and especially the practical issues involved. Johnson stated that, in the consideration of the Court, the matter had long been "settled in public opinion. . . . [A]nd the general acquiescence of legal men shews the prevalence of opinion in favor of the negative of the proposition."[189] It was therefore held not to be within the implied power of the federal courts to exercise criminal jurisdiction in common law cases.

The decision in *Hudson* seems to have been acceptable from a political standpoint, particularly in limiting in this respect the powers of the federal judiciary. Yet the practical effect, as Judge Story was soon to point out,[190] was severely disadvantageous to the government, since Congress had defined by statute only a few federal crimes. Under existing wartime conditions, when merchants in the Northeast, at least, were particularly strong in their opposition to the 1812 War and anxious to take advantages of loopholes in the law to engage in illegal trade, congressional legislation was badly needed but was not forthcoming. Trading with the enemy had become even more prevalent by 1814, but even Attorney-General Richard Rush was opposed to common law indictments to suppress these actions.[191]

---

[187] T. Jefferson to T. Seymour, Feb. 11, 1807, and T. Jefferson to W. C. Nicholas, June 11, 1801, Jefferson Papers, Manuscripts Division, Library of Congress. Professor Horwitz identifies Jefferson's position against a federal common law of crimes as a reaction to indictments of American citizens for pro-French activity and more generally as an expression of fear that federal judges might employ common law powers to exceed the constitutional limits of the federal government. M. Horwitz, *The Trans-*

formation of American Law 1780–1800 (Cambridge, Mass., 1977), 10. Horwitz conceives of the attack on common law crimes as a more fundamental assault on the unitary notion of law prevailing in the eighteenth century. *Ibid.*, 9–16.

[188] 7 Cranch 32 (1812).

[189] *Ibid.*, 32.

[190] Warren, *Supreme Court*, I, 438.

[191] *Annals of Congress*, XXVII, 1821 et seq. (13th Cong., 2d. sess.); see Warren, *Supreme Court*, I, 439.

Nevertheless, it is not surprising that such an indictment was sought in a case in which the defendants had rescued by force a prize captured by an American privateer. No statute governed the situation as a crime, yet Judge Story, sitting on circuit, took the position that the act was a crime under admiralty law and therefore punishable in federal court even in the absence of statute. The circuit court was divided, so the case, *United States* v. *Coolidge*,[192] went up to the Supreme Court. Attorney-General Rush declined to argue, on the ground that the *Hudson* case was controlling; no counsel appeared on behalf of the defendants. Again, without argument, the case was decided by the Court, and again in favor of the defendants. Judge Johnson rendered the decision, and, while admitting to differences of opinion among the judges, who would have welcomed argument, he held that the earlier case of *Hudson* would not be reconsidered.

Whether the three cases—*Deveaux, Hudson,* and *Coolidge*—are viewed as examples of judicial self-restraint, or whether they are seen (as seems more probable from the standpoint of the second decade of the nineteenth century) as examples of the Court's unwillingness to intrude on what it viewed as the legislature's department, these cases fit into the mold outlined in *Marbury*, where Marshall distinguished between political matters subject to changing concepts, and doctrines and matters that are legal and guided by fixed principles. In situations where the legislature has acted, and has acted properly (as in the Embargo cases), the Court considered it its duty to enforce the will of Congress, whether or not the legislation was sponsored by Republicans, and whether or not the Court was dominated by Federalists. Where Congress had not acted (as in the Embargo cases prior to the Enforcement Act of January 1809, and in the federal crimes area) the Court declined to "legislate" or to announce as fixed principles conclusions that it apparently believed belonged to the legislative department of the government.

The Court could hardly have been unaware of the consequences of its failure to support the indictments in *Hudson* and in *Coolidge*. Indeed, it was Judge Story who clamored loudly, and more vociferously than most, for congressional action.[193] A bill to accomplish the necessary legislation was drafted by Story, and was revised by Marshall and Washington, in 1816; and then redrafted in 1818,[194] and much of the latter became law in the Crimes Act of 1825 to protect federal sovereignty.[195]

---

[192] 1 Wheat. 415 (1816), *rev'ing* 25 F. Cas. 619 (C.C.D. Mass. 1813) (No. 14,857).

[193] Story, *Commentaries*, I, 293, 298–300.

[194] *Ibid.*, I, 437.

[195] See Warren, *Supreme Court*, I, 441.

D. THE FAIRFAX CASE

In a further case, historically though not legally connected with others already discussed, the Court upheld and extended national supremacy when its jurisdiction came under attack from the States in the form of an assertion of the unconstitutionality of Section 25 of the 1789 Judiciary Act, granting the Supreme Court appellate review of State court judgments.[196] This was the case of *Martin* v. *Hunter's Lessee*,[197] and, though decided in 1816, its origins lie in the period covered by this Volume.[198] Moreover, its pertinence to the decisions discussed in the preceding sections of this chapter is apparent in what follows.

The case of *Fairfax's Devisee* v. *Hunter's Lessee*[199] had come be-

---

[196] An Act to establish the Judicial Courts of the United States, First Congress, First Session, chapter 20, Sec. 25, 1 Stat. 85 (1789). Section 25 of the Judiciary Act provided as follows:

And be it further enacted, That a final judgment or decree in any suit, in the highest court of law or equity of a State in which a decision in the suit could be had, where is drawn in question the validity of a treaty or statute of, or an authority exercised under the United States, and the decision is against their validity; or where is drawn in question the validity of a statute of, or an authority exercised under any State, on the ground of their being repugnant to the constitution, treaties or laws of the United States, and the decision is in favour of such their validity, or where is drawn in question the construction of any clause of the constitution, or of a treaty, or statute of, or commission held under the United States, and the decision is against the title, right, privilege or exemption specially set up or claimed by either party, under such clause of the said Constitution, treaty, statute or commission, may be re-examined and reversed or affirmed in the Supreme Court of the United States upon a writ of error, the citation being signed by the chief justice, or judge or chancellor of the court rendering or passing the judgment or decree complained of, or by a justice of the Supreme Court of the United States, in the same manner and under the same regulations, and the writ shall have the same effect, as if the judgment or decree complained of had been rendered or passed in a circuit court, and the proceeding upon the reversal shall also be the same, except that the Supreme Court, instead of remanding the cause for a final decision as before provided, may at their discretion, if the cause shall have been once remanded before, proceed to a final decision of the same, and award execution. But no other error shall be assigned or regarded as a ground of reversal in any such case as aforesaid, than such as appears on the face of the record, and immediately respects the before mentioned questions of validity or construction of the said constitution, treaties, statutes, commissions, or authorities in dispute.

[197] 1 Wheat. 304 (1816).

[198] See also Volume III of this History; W. Crosskey, *Politics and the Constitution in the History of the United States* (Chicago, 1953), II, 785–817; C. Warren, "Legislative and Judicial Attacks on the Supreme Court of the United States—A History of the Twenty-Fifth Section of the Judiciary Act," *American Law Review* XLVII, 6–12 (1913).

[199] 7 Cranch 603 (1813).

fore the Court in 1813. Although it was but one step in more than one hundred years of litigation concerning the validity of the title to the 300,000-acre Fairfax estate in northern Virginia, it was the harbinger of the decision in *Martin* v. *Hunter's Lessee*, which finally terminated that litigation.[200] The case dealt with the capacity of one Denny Martin, an alien who was the nephew of Thomas Lord Fairfax, a citizen of Virginia, to take land by Fairfax's devise. The decision in the case involved a number of important related problems, including the effect of Virginia's escheat laws and the construction of the 1783 Peace Treaty between the United States and Great Britain, as well as the Jay Treaty of 1794, insofar as they prohibited the confiscation of the land of aliens.

In 1789 the State of Virginia, acting under confiscatory legislation passed during the Revolutionary War, granted to one David Hunter a 788-acre tract of land in the area that had been devised to Martin at Fairfax's death in December 1781. Hunter brought an action of ejectment against Martin, but judgment was rendered in favor of the latter in the Virginia district court of Winchester in 1794, before the Jay Treaty had been approved.[201]

It is of considerable interest to note in passing that John Marshall had defended the Fairfax title in earlier litigation concerning its validity,[202] and in 1793 he and his brother James had organized a syndicate that purchased 160,000 acres of the Fairfax estate from Martin.[203] Despite the statement of Beveridge[204] that Marshall had no personal interest in the lands in controversy, it would appear that at the very least there was considerable interest on the part of the Marshall family in an outcome of the suit favorable to the defendant, Martin.[205] Thus, John Marshall eventually took no part in the decision rendered by the

---

[200] See Note, "Judge Spencer Roane of Virginia: Champion of States' Rights—Foe of John Marshall," *Harvard Law Review* LXVI, 1242, 1248–51 (1953).

[201] See Hunter v. Fairfax's Devisee, 15 Va. (1 Munford), 218, 222, 224 (1810).

[202] Hite v. Fairfax, 8 Va. (4 Call) 42 (1786). Beveridge, *John Marshall*, I, 191–96, describes Marshall's arguments in this case, in which "[his] name first appears in the reports of the cases decided by the Virginia Court of Appeals," with considerable detail. Those arguments are recorded in 4 Call at 69–81.

[203] See Beveridge, *John Marshall*,

II, 203–11; Note, "Judge Spencer Roane," 1249.

[204] Beveridge, *John Marshall*, IV, 150, note 2 ("John Marshall had no personal interest whatever in the land in controversy in the litigation"). Apparently the lands including the Hunter grant had been separately purchased by James M. Marshall. *Ibid.*, 150. But see G. Myers, *History of the Supreme Court of the United States* (Chicago, 1912), 235; Warren, "Legislative and Judicial Attacks on the Supreme Court," 8 and note 17.

[205] See Beveridge, *John Marshall*, IV, 147–51; Crosskey, *Politics and the Constitution*, II, 793–97; Note, "Judge Spencer Roane," 1249, note 59.

Supreme Court in *Fairfax,* nor in the later decision in *Martin* v. *Hunter's Lessee.*

On appeal from the district court, and after sixteen years had gone by, the Virginia Supreme Court of Appeals reversed the District Court decision and gave judgment in favor of Hunter.[206] Prosecution of the case had been halted in the period since 1796 when the Virginia legislature enacted an Act of Compromise. Pursuant to that Act, the Fairfax claimants relinquished any rights they might have in lands not specifically appropriated by Lord Fairfax ("the waste and unappropriated lands"), and in return the State of Virginia gave up its own claims to lands that Lord Fairfax had in fact appropriated to his own use.[207] Inasmuch as the Compromise had been worked out by John Marshall while he was a member of the Virginia legislature,[208] his personal interest in the outcome of the Fairfax litigation is even more apparent.

The panel of the Supreme Court of Appeals that heard Hunter's appeal from the District Court decision consisted of only two judges, President Judge William Fleming and Judge Spencer Roane, each of whom delivered an opinion in Hunter's favor.[209] Judge Roane[210] held that the anti-confiscation provisions of the 1783 peace treaty had no effect on the States' ordinary laws of alienage, and that, even if it did, the confiscation by Virginia of the lands in question took place in 1782, and thus the State's title to the land had been perfected prior to any operative effect of the treaty.[211] As for the 1796 Act of Compromise,

---

[206] Hunter v. Fairfax's Devisee, 15 Va. (1 Munford) 218 (1810). It is interesting to note that the case had been argued to the Supreme Court of Appeals in 1796, but was taken under advisement at that time and not reargued until 1809. *Ibid.,* 223.

[207] See Crosskey, *Politics and the Constitution,* II, 795–97; Note, "Judge Spencer Roane," 1248. Crosskey suggests that Hunter "lost interest" in his appeal for such a long period of time because he was afraid of an adverse decision being rendered by the Virginia high court until that court became dominated by Jeffersonians. Crosskey, *Politics and the Constitution,* II, 798.

[208] Beveridge, *John Marshall,* IV, 148–49; Crosskey, *Politics and the Constitution,* II, 795–96; Note, "Judge Spencer Roane," 1248.

[209] Judge St. George Tucker, the third member of the court, did not sit in the case, "being nearly related

to a person interested," 1 Munford at 223, apparently Hunter. Crosskey, *Politics and the Constitution,* II, 798. Tucker was later to represent Hunter in Martin v. Hunter's Lessee, after his resignation from the bench. See text accompanying note 228 infra.

[210] Judge Roane's career as a jurist, Jeffersonian political leader, theoretician of States' rights, and opponent of John Marshall, is analyzed in Note, "Judge Spencer Roane." It is interesting to recall that Jefferson, according to tradition, intended to appoint Roane Chief Justice of the United States Supreme Court, but Oliver Ellsworth's resignation shortly before Jefferson's inauguration gave John Adams the opportunity to appoint Marshall. *Ibid.,* 1242. See Kerr, "If Spencer Roane had been Appointed Chief Justice Instead of John Marshall," *American Bar Association Journal* XX, 167 (1934).

[211] 1 Munford at 231.

Roane stated that under its terms Denny Martin's purchasers (the Marshall syndicate) had agreed to relinquish their claims to the lands in question in exchange for Virginia's relinquishing claims to other lands. Because the appellees had already benefited from the Compromise in litigation with respect to other lands, Roane held, they could not now refuse to be bound by it with respect to the Hunter tract.[212] Judge Fleming, on the other hand, was of the opinion that various actions of the Virginia legislature prior to the Treaty of Peace with Great Britain were *not* sufficient to vest title to the Fairfax estate in the State.[213] Furthermore, since that treaty banned future confiscations of alien land, the Hunter grant of 1789 "was an exercise of power, without a right."[214] Nonetheless, Fleming held that Denny Martin's title was clearly extinguished by the Act of Compromise, since the lands in question were agreed by the parties to be among the "waste and unappropriated lands" of the Fairfax estate, which under the terms of the Act were relinquished by the Fairfax purchasers.[215] "[U]pon that ground, and upon that only,"[216] Fleming decided in favor of Hunter.

The Fairfax claimants, now represented by Philip Martin, heir at law and devisee of Denny Martin, who had died prior to the Virginia Supreme Court of Appeals decision, appealed to the United States Supreme Court. The Supreme Court issued a writ of error to the State court under Section 25 of the Judiciary Act, on the ground that the case "involv[ed] the construction of the treaties between Great Britain and the United States, the judgment of the Court of Appeals being against the right claimed under those treaties."[217] Judge Fleming "complied with the writ by certifying a transcript, 'improvidently,' as was afterwards decided by himself as well as the other Judges [of the Virginia court]."[218]

On March 15, 1813, Judge Story delivered the Supreme Court's opinion in *Fairfax's Devisee* v. *Hunter's Lessee*; Judge Johnson dissented, and Chief Justice Marshall and Judge Todd were absent.[219] Story held first that Denny Martin had a complete title in the lands devised to him by his uncle, which "could only be divested by an inquest

---

[212] *Ibid.*, 231–32.
[213] *Ibid.*, 234–35.
[214] *Ibid.*, 237.
[215] *Ibid.*, 237–38.
[216] *Ibid.*, 238. Beveridge has argued that, in fact, the lands in question were not intended to be included within the compromise, Beveridge, *John Marshall*, IV, 149; Crosskey has criticized the State court opinion for considering the Act of Compromise at all, since it was not included within "the agreed case" presented by the parties to the court and was therefore, under Virginia practice, beyond judicial notice. Crosskey, *Politics and the Constitution*, II, 786, 799.

[217] Fairfax's Devisee v. Hunter's Lessee, 7 Cranch 603, 603–604 (1813). See note 196 supra.
[218] Hunter v. Martin, 18 Va. (4 Munford) 1, 1 (1813).
[219] 7 Cranch at 618.

of office, perfected by an entry and seizure";[220] no grant by Virginia could be valid unless the State had fixed title in itself by such means. Story followed Fleming's reasoning in holding that Virginia's enactments prior to 1783 had not divested Martin's title, but he refrained from construing the anti-confiscation clause of the Peace Treaty with respect to later acts because the Jay Treaty of 1794 "completely protects and confirms the title of Denny [Martin], even admitting that the treaty of peace left him wholly unprovided for."[221] The Jay Treaty, Story held, confirmed Martin's title in him, his heirs and assigns, and protected him from any forfeiture on the ground of his alien status, since he was in complete possession and seisin of the land at the time the Treaty became law.[222] Story made no mention of the 1796 Act of Compromise; nor did Judge Johnson, whose dissent turned on his belief that the legislature of Virginia could validly dispense with the common law inquest of office in asserting its rights over alien property. Therefore, he viewed the grant to Hunter in 1789 as valid, so that Martin had no interest in the lands at the time of Jay's Treaty. As for the Peace Treaty of 1783, Johnson held it inapplicable to this case because it involved no "confiscation on account of the part taken by the devisee in the war of the revolution," within the terms of the anti-confiscation clause of that Treaty.[223]

At this point, the relationship of Story's opinion to those of Roane and Fleming in the Virginia Supreme Court of Appeals becomes more complicated and requires further analysis. In the first place, the decision of the Virginia court in favor of Hunter was based not on the opinion of Spencer Roane, as Story seems to have assumed, but on that of Judge Fleming, for the two judges divided on the issues of the validity of Martin's title and the effect of Virginia's grant to Hunter and the Peace Treaty of 1783 on that title. Therefore, with respect to those issues one could say that the resolution of the District Court in favor of Martin and the validity of the Treaty was affirmed by an equally divided court. Under the terms of Section 25 of the Judiciary Act, then, it is difficult to see how the Supreme Court had jurisdiction to entertain the appeal. The real ground of the decision in favor of Hunter, and *the only ground* common to both Roane's and Fleming's opinions, was the effect of the Act of Compromise on Martin's title. Yet this issue was not

---

[220] *Ibid.*, 622.
[221] *Ibid.*, 627.
[222] *Ibid.* The ninth article of the Jay Treaty provided "that British subjects who now hold lands in the territories of the United States . . . shall continue to hold them according to the nature and tenure of their re-

spective estates and titles therein; . . . and that neither they nor their heirs or assigns shall, so far as respects the said lands . . . be considered as aliens." *Ibid.*
[223] See *ibid.*, 628–32 (Johnson, J., dissenting).

addressed by Story in *Fairfax,* and his later explanation in *Martin* v. *Hunter's Lessee* of how the Supreme Court was able to take jurisdiction of the *Fairfax* case seems less than adequate, as will appear.

In any event, following Story's decision in *Fairfax,* a mandate from the Supreme Court was issued to the Supreme Court of Appeals of Virginia in a peremptory form commonly addressed to an "inferior" court, giving great offense, doubtless inadvertently, to the Virginia court: "You are hereby commanded that such proceedings be had in said cause, as according to right and justice, and the laws of the United States, and agreeably to said judgment and instructions of said Supreme Court ought to be had, the said writ of error notwithstanding."[224] The latter court requested oral argument on "[t]he question whether this mandate should be obeyed,"[225] and on December 16, 1815, the four judges of Virginia's highest court delivered seriatim opinions unanimously answering that question in the negative. The following opinion of the court was entered:

> The court is unanimously of opinion, that the appellate power of the Supreme Court of the United States, does not extend to this court, under a sound construction of the constitution of the United States; —that so much of the 25th section of the act of Congress, to establish the judicial courts of the United States, as extends the appellate jurisdiction of the Supreme Court to this court, is not in pursuance of the constitution of the United States; that the writ of error in this case was improvidently allowed under the authority of that act; that the proceedings thereon in the Supreme Court were *coram non judice* in relation to this court; and that obedience to its mandate be declined by this court.[226]

This opinion presented a direct confrontation to the Supreme Court's ability to review State court judgments, including those dealing with federal issues, under Article III of the Constitution. The Virginia court opinion was not, therefore, a narrowly based refutation of the Court's jurisdiction in *Fairfax,* which had been decided on State law grounds, even though Judges Roane and Fleming raised that contention in their separate opinions.[227]

---

[224] Hunter v. Martin, 18 Va. (4 Munford) 1, 3 (1815).

[225] *Ibid.,* 3.

[226] *Ibid.,* 58–59.

[227] Separate opinions were entered by Judges Cabell, *ibid.,* 3–16; Brooke, *ibid.,* 16–25; Roane, *ibid.,* 25–54; and Fleming, *ibid.,* 54–58. Both Judge Roane and Judge Fleming argued that in the case at hand, regardless of the constitutionality of Section 25, the writ of error was improperly issued because the validity of the Peace Treaty of 1783 had been *upheld* by the Virginia Court in Hunter v. Fairfax's Devisee and the case had been decided against Martin on the basis of the Act of Compromise of 1796. *Ibid.,* 46–50 (Roane, J.); *ibid.,* 57–58 (Fleming, J.).

X: *States' Rights and the National Judiciary*

On a second writ of error to the Supreme Court,[228] Hunter and the State of Virginia were represented by St. George Tucker, formerly a Judge of the Virginia Supreme Court of Appeals, and by Samuel Dexter of Massachusetts; their arguments are summarized elsewhere.[229] The Court's opinion in *Martin* v. *Hunter's Lessee* was delivered on March 20, 1816, with Judge Story once again speaking for the Court. Judge Johnson separately concurred, and Chief Justice Marshall and Judge Washington refrained from participating in the decision.

Judge Story's opinion in this case took the form of a lengthy treatise on the extent of the judicial power conferred by Article III of the Constitution, which included his famous dictum, since rejection by the Supreme Court, that "the whole judicial power of the United States should be, at all times, vested, either in an original or appellate form, in some courts created under its authority."[230] More to the point, Story held "that the appellate power of the United States does extend to cases pending in the State courts" and that Section 25 of the Judiciary Act "is supported by the letter and spirit of the constitution."[231] He based his conclusions on the language of Article III, buttressed by interpretations by State ratifying conventions, by the First Congress which enacted the Judiciary Act, and by earlier Supreme Court decisions under Section 25 which had been acquiesced in by State courts.[232]

As for the question whether the case presented to the Court was itself within Section 25, Story had no difficulty in determining that it was an appeal from a final judgment of the State court that denied the validity of a federal statute, namely Section 25.[233] Then, after demonstrating that the appeal in *Martin* v. *Hunter's Lessee* could not question the jurisdiction of the Court in the earlier case of *Fairfax's Devisee* v. *Hunter's Lessee*, Story nonetheless proceeded to examine the validity of the judgment in *Fairfax*, because of "motives of a public nature."[234] His examination of that issue resulted in his holding that the appellate

---

[228] Martin v. Hunter's Lessee, 1 Wheat. 304 (1816).

[229] See Volume III of this History; Warren, *Supreme Court*, I, 448–49.

[230] 1 Wheat. at 331. See Volume III of this History; Sheldon v. Sill, 8 Howard 440, 449 (1850) ("Congress may withhold from any court of its creation jurisdiction of any of the enumerated controversies"). For a further elaboration of Judge Story's views on this issue see P. Bator, P. Mishkin, D. Shapiro and H. Wechsler, *Hart and Wechsler's The Federal Courts and the Federal System*, 2d ed. (Mineola, N.Y., 1973), 313–15.

[231] 1 Wheat, at 351.

[232] *Ibid.*, 351–52. Even after the Supreme Court's opinion in Martin v. Hunter's Lessee, the power of that Court to review State court judgments was called into question by the Supreme Court of Massachusetts. See Wetherbee v. Johnson, 14 Mass. 412, 417 (1817) ("Whether the court of the United States, or the court of *Virginia*, are right on this important question, the present case does not call upon us to decide."); Warren, *Supreme Court*, I, 453 and note 1.

[233] 1 Wheat. at 353–54.

[234] *Ibid.*, 355.

jurisdiction of the Supreme Court extended to all cases in which a treaty's construction is called into question and the State court decision is against the title claimed to be within the treaty's protection. In other words, Story answered yes to his own rhetorical question, "If the court below should decide, that the title was bad, and therefore, not protected by the treaty, must not this court have a power to decide the title to be good, and therefore, protected by the treaty?"[235] With regard to the possibility that the original judgment of the Virginia court had been based on neither the invalidity of Martin's title nor a treaty but on the Act of Compromise, Story stated that since the Act was private in nature, it could not have been judicially noticed, and was therefore not among the facts before the State court.[236]

In light of the fact that the original decision of the highest court of Virginia in *Fairfax* had been based on the Act of Compromise, Story's justification of the Supreme Court's jurisdiction in that case seems less than adequate. Even if it was inappropriate, as has been suggested,[237] for the Virginia court to have gone outside the "agreed case" presented by the parties to reverse the District Court's affirmation of Martin's title, surely that issue, involving the scope of judicial notice available to the State judges, was a matter of State law. Story failed to explain why, "At all events, we are bound to consider, that the [Virginia] court did decide upon the facts actually before them."[238]

Finally, Judge Story avoided the question whether the Supreme Court could issue a writ of mandamus to the Virginia Supreme Court of Appeals to enforce its judgments by issuing the Court's mandate directly to the Virginia district court at Winchester.[239] Judge Johnson's lengthy concurring opinion was addressed principally to his view of the impropriety of the Court's ever resorting to the issuance of such compulsory process upon State courts to enforce its judgments.[240]

In spite of what may be viewed as shortcomings in Story's opinion in *Fairfax*, his fundamental holding in *Martin* v. *Hunter's Lessee* that the Supreme Court had appellate jurisdiction under Article III over

---

[235] *Ibid.*, 358. The question of the extent of Supreme Court authority to review State court determinations of State law issues, such as the existence of title, with respect to federal claims, has not always been answered in such a broadly affirmative fashion. See Bator et al. *Federal Courts*, 500–506.

[236] 1 Wheat. at 360. In contrast, Story justified basing his own decision in *Fairfax* on the Jay Treaty, which was also not part of the agreed case, by noting that treaties, as part of the supreme law of the land, must be subject to judicial notice, while private acts are not. *Ibid.*

[237] Crosskey, *Politics and the Constitution*, II, 799. On the jurisdictional issue in *Fairfax* generally, see D. Currie, *Federal Courts*, 2d ed. (St. Paul, 1975), 188–91; Warren, *Supreme Court*, I, 446. Cf. Murdock v. City of Memphis, 20 Wallace 590 (1875).

[238] 1 Wheat. at 360.

[239] *Ibid.*, 362.

[240] *Ibid.*, 362–82 (Johnson, J., concurring).

State court judgments involving federal questions has been a cornerstone of the American judicial system and of national supremacy. In the *Hudson* and *Coolidge* decisions, where Congress had enacted no applicable statutes, federal supremacy was weakened if not eroded. In contrast, in *Martin* v. *Hunter's Lessee* the Court dealt squarely with the constitutionality of an act that Congress *had* passed. In declaring it constitutional, at the expense of State sovereignty, Judge Story's opinion firmly strengthened not only the Supreme Court's own power but federal supremacy as well. In light of the flagrant violations of law that had been so conspicuous—and almost endemic—during the Embargo years and the War of 1812, and in light of the continued efforts of Republicans to discredit the judiciary and weaken the national courts, it is no exaggeration to state, as Warren has, that *Martin* v. *Hunter's Lessee* had a "vital effect upon the history of the United States [that] can hardly be overemphasized."[241] Indeed, this conclusion is strengthened, and a binding thread of continuity and strength revealed, when one reflects that the opinion was issued by Joseph Story, a Republican appointee, speaking for a Court consisting of five Republican judges, with the Federalist Chief Justice not even sitting.[242] Although Marshall did not participate in the case, its outcome can, in perspective, be viewed as a victory for his efforts to extricate the Court from partisan politics, and to establish a rule of law in the United States. The foundations of judicial power had been fixed firmly in place.

---

[241] Warren, *Supreme Court*, I, 450–51.

[242] Other than Judge Story, a Massachusetts Republican, the judges sitting for Martin v. Hunter's Lessee were William Johnson, Republican from South Carolina; Brockholst Livingston, Republican from New York; Thomas Todd, Republican from Kentucky; and Gabriel Duvall, Republican from Maryland. Story and Duvall were appointed by Madison; the others were Jefferson appointees. Warren counters any arguments that Story's opinion in Martin v. Hunter's Lessee was influenced by Marshall by demonstrating that Story held the views he expressed in that opinion long before he was confronted with the necessity of deciding it. *Ibid.*, 451–53.

PART TWO

By Herbert A. Johnson

Acknowledgments

AN ACKNOWLEDGMENTS SECTION for the second part of a book written over an extended period of time is bound to overlook one or more individuals or institutions that played a significant role in the book's preparation. Yet it is necessary at this time that public thanks be given to all who have been of help to me in my tasks of research and writing, including the following: Professor William E. Nelson of Yale Law School read an early draft of this part and made many valued suggestions for revision. Professor R. Randall Bridwell of the University of South Carolina Law School kindly read the chapters dealing with prize, admiralty, and maritime affairs with a critical eye, and his comments did much to improve their content. Dr. George M. Curtis III of the Papers of John Marshall staff at the Institute of Early American History and Culture provided critiques for the chapter on alien lands and sequestrations at an early stage of its development. George L. Haskins, author of Part I of this volume, has read several successive drafts of each chapter in Part II, and provided excellent suggestions for changes in presentation and style as well as many suggestions in the areas of historical interpretation and legal analysis. As usual my wife, Barbara, has read the materials with care to eliminate surplus verbiage and to correct errors in grammar and style that can detract from an author's personal sense of literacy. Finally our Editor-in-Chief, Professor Paul A. Freund, has taken care to read each chapter and provide me with the benefit of his familiarity with the Constitution and the history of the Supreme Court, thereby broadening my horizons and sharpening my analysis of critical issues.

The discussion in Part II draws heavily upon memoranda prepared directly by, or under the supervision of, Professor Haskins. Two of those memoranda proved to be of special importance for my particular use, namely those by John H. Mason, Esq., and David Glyn,

Esq., formerly students at the University of Pennsylvania Law School. Special studies were also conducted by Robert Knight and Paul R. Hensley, then graduate students at the College of William and Mary. At a final stage in the revision of the manuscript I was assisted by John Alex Moore, a graduate student in the Department of History at the University of South Carolina.

Statistical work on the Marshall Court has covered the period from 1968 through 1977. I am grateful to the Computer Center at the College of William and Mary, and particularly Robert Hanby and Roger Higgs, for their assistance in programming at a time when historical and non-quantitative materials were handled with much more difficulty than they are today. My work with the Marshall Court statistics resulted in two papers delivered at the Columbia University Seminar on Early American History in 1968 and the Southern Historical Association meeting in 1969. On those occasions I profited from the audience comments and particularly from suggestions by Professors James McClellan of Hampden-Sydney College and Eric L. McKitrick of Columbia University.

Preparation and proofreading of the manuscript have been facilitated through the typing skills of Estelle D. Brown, Genny Curtis, Janice Goings, Laura Long, and Belinda Sells. They have typed and retyped a series of chapter drafts and redrafts with patience and care, and I am most grateful to them.

Without additional funding and released time from my editorial duties on *The Papers of John Marshall* at Williamsburg, it would have been impossible to complete Part II. An American Council of Learned Societies fellowship, which I held from October 1974 to September 1975, permitted me to devote full-time effort to the research and writing. I also received additional support from the Permanent Committee of the Oliver Wendell Holmes Devise during that period, and also for the three-month period from January through March 1977, when the remaining chapters were being researched and partially written. From January to May 1976 and again from September 1977 to January 1978, I held an appointment as Lucy Hampton Bostick Visiting Research Professor at the Southern Studies Program of the University of South Carolina; a substantial portion of my time was devoted to the chapters on public lands and jurisdiction. While I have been at the University of South Carolina, Professors John G. Sproat, of the history department, and James B. Meriwether, of the Southern Studies Program, have arranged my teaching responsibilities in such a way that progress was accelerated on this volume, and Dean Richard E. Day has been similarly considerate in assigning instructional duties in the Law School. At the Institute of Early American History and Culture, where the bulk of the manuscript was prepared, I received like encouragement from Professor Thad Tate, Director of the Institute.

Acknowledgments

Librarians and institutional collections are essential to authors, and my debts are heavy to the staff at the Earl Gregg Swem Library of the College of William and Mary for their patient tolerance of my need for materials not generally available in the collections of a small library. Professor James Madison Whitehead, former Law Librarian at the Marshall-Wythe School of Law, was particularly helpful in giving me access to legal materials and acquiring additional printed materials for my use. I gained much from my research in the library of the Mariner's Museum, Newport News, Virginia, an excellent specialized collection relating to maritime history and law. More recently I have used the collections of the Thomas Cooper Library and Law Library of the University of South Carolina. To the directors and staffs of all of these libraries I express my sincere thanks and appreciation.

My family has provided me with continuing emotional support and encouragement to press on with a writing task that has demanded sacrifices in time and leisure from them. My wife, Barbara, has been particularly understanding and willing to undertake those parental duties that are normally shared, so that the full-time job of research and writing might be completed more speedily.

Herbert A. Johnson

Columbia, South Carolina
January 1979

371

CHAPTER I

Introduction: The Business of the Court

WHIRLWINDS OF POLITICAL and constitutional debate circled around the Supreme Court of the United States from 1801 to 1815, leaving the members of the Court with few illusions concerning the power of public opinion and political majorities to alter the course of constitutional development and the role of the Court itself as a bulwark of the rule of law and an instrument of constitutional decision. Pressures entirely outside their control bore down heavily upon the men at the vortex of the whirlwind, and it is not surprising that so many of the judicial activities of the Court were strongly conditioned by external circumstances. Unquestionably the Supreme Court was involved in struggle for its survival as a coequal branch of the federal government, and consequently its history as recounted above may be viewed as a protective and reflexive response to the political events of the day. Indeed the traditional historical interpretations of Supreme Court history from 1801 through 1815 have considered it a time of immense external preoccupations on the part of the justices—directed towards warding off the hostile thrusts at judicial power by Jeffersonian Republicans in the executive and legislative branches. It is not here asserted that this view is incorrect; that the challenge to Supreme Court authority and judicial power was clear and present in the minds of John Marshall and his colleagues is undeniable. Earlier chapters in this volume serve to affirm certain parts of this traditional view.[1] On the other hand, the "external" aspect of the Supreme Court's business—its political position, the defense of judicial independence in the Chase impeachment and the Burr case, and its work in the area of federal-State relations—should not be viewed as the only important aspect of its evolution from 1801 to 1815.

---

[1] For treatment of those external threats, see Part I.

Despite the political whirlwind that raised major philosophical and constitutional objections to the exercise of judicial power, the Supreme Court conducted its ordinary judicial business with a calm attention to its primary, though not its only, function—the objective and impartial resolution of disputes brought before its Bench by private litigants. This "non-constitutional" and "non-political" work of the Supreme Court seems for the most part to have escaped the attention of legal and constitutional historians. Yet to comprehend fully the achievements of the Court during the first fourteen years of John Marshall's Chief Justiceship, it is necessary that the work of the Court be considered as a whole, rather than simply as a group of major decisions that either triggered public comment or responded to public pressures and opinions.

The relationship between private litigation and adjudication in the Supreme Court and the political and constitutional significance of the Court and its pronouncements has been too long neglected. For the period under consideration this oversight has been particularly unfortunate, since it leaves the student of Supreme Court history with no clear explanation of how the essentially weak Court of the pre-Marshall era made such progress, both institutionally and intellectually, that it was able to embark upon the great era of constitutional adjudication that occurred in the climactic 1819 term.[2]

A closer look at all of the evidence leads one to the conclusion that the early Marshall Court did not accept a passive or defensive role. Rather, under the guidance of circumspect judges, it achieved remarkable growth. Cloaked from public view by the secrecy of the Court's conferences, and manifest only to those few who were willing to take the time to ponder its promulgated opinions, internal changes were being made in its administration and practice that would have a profound influence upon all future development of the Court. Indeed it is not exaggeration to suggest that the very foundations of the power and prestige attached to the present-day Supreme Court may be found in its internal evolution from 1801 to 1816.

Some institutions are born great, some achieve greatness, and

---

[2] There were of course external factors that influenced the Court's strong position in the 1819 term. Among them was the fact that this was the end of the "Era of Good Feelings" ushered in by the election of President James Monroe in 1816. See G. Dangerfield, *The Era of Good Feelings* (New York, 1952), especially 162–66. It is also significant that Chief Justice Marshall and the new President were boyhood friends who had remained free of personal animosity despite their political differences in the years from 1793 through 1801. L. Baker, *John Marshall: A Life in Law* (New York, 1974), 13, 89, 634–35; H. Ammon, *James Monroe: The Quest for National Identity* (New York, 1971), 3, 366–67, 467–68.

some have greatness thrust upon them; it was the good fortune of the early Marshall Court to draw upon all three sources as a basis for its phenomenal growth after 1801. Already endowed with sweeping constitutional powers in the fields of international law, admiralty and maritime law, and the adjustment of interstate controversies,[3] the Supreme Court in 1801 stood on the brink of a period in legal history when its decisions in these three fields were to become matters of great public concern.[4] The undeclared "Quasi-War" with France, and earlier prize cases involving the Haitian rebellion against French authority, left the Court with a backlog of admiralty matters on its docket. The exclusive authority of the federal judiciary in these areas was sanctioned not only by constitutional grant but also by long and willing acquiescence on the part of the States dating from 1781, if not earlier.[5]

Equally important was the fact that, as a relatively new judicial institution, the Court lacked fixed customs and usages concerning the assertion of its jurisdiction and its methods and techniques of reaching decisions and promulgating its opinions. In part this was the product of an unsettling turnover of personnel during the pre-Marshall years,[6] a situation that would be aggravated by the infrequent contacts between justices due to the burdens of circuit riding and the restriction of collegial sessions to but one per year. While the Constitution had established broad guidelines for Supreme Court jurisdiction and authority, the basic document for organization and practice was the Judiciary Act of 1789.[7] Although the 1789 Act had been modified in 1793[8] to reduce

---

[3] *U.S. Constitution*, Art. III.

[4] See the more detailed discussion in Part II, chapter 2, pp. 415–19, and the sources cited there.

[5] Federal authority to review State prize court decisions was asserted even before the Declaration of Independence and was specifically included in the Articles of Confederation, under which a regular appellate court was established to try prize appeals. H. Bourguignon, *The First Federal Court: The Federal Appellate Prize Court of the American Revolution, 1775–1787* (Philadelphia, 1977), 45, 77, 297–300, 309–10.

[6] Chief Justice Jay's service of six years was interrupted by his 1794–95 mission to Great Britain; his successor, John Rutledge, was denied confirmation and served for only one year; the third Chief Justice, Oliver Ellsworth, served for three years, concluding his service with a diplomatic mission to France. Among the Asso-

ciate Justices only William Cushing remained from the original group of four; John Rutledge resigned in 1791, John Blair resigned in 1796, and James Wilson died in office in 1798. Judge William Paterson, who remained on the Bench, had been appointed in 1793, and the other judge on the Bench in 1801, Samuel Chase, had been appointed in 1796. Associate Justice Thomas Johnson had served from 1790 to 1793, and Associate Justice James Iredell was on the Bench from 1790 to 1799. Newly arrived Justices Bushrod Washington (appointed in 1798) and Alfred Moore (appointed in 1799) remained in service in 1801. All in all, twelve men had constituted the Court since its inception thirteen years before and the leadership position of Chief Justice was shared by three of them.

[7] 1 Stat. 73–93 (Sept. 24, 1789).

[8] 1 Stat. 333–35 (Mar. 2, 1793).

the circuit duties of Supreme Court justices, the first major organizational change was the Act of February 13, 1801, which eliminated circuit duty altogether and created sixteen new circuit court judgeships.[9] Passed by the "lame duck" Federalist Congress, the Judiciary Act of 1801 stirred up the blaze of controversy discussed previously.[10] The 1801 Act was repealed during Thomas Jefferson's administration by the Act of March 8, 1802, and shortly thereafter Congress reorganized the judicial system by dividing the country into six circuits each with a circuit court composed of one justice and one district judge.[11] Though it allowed the circuit court to be held by a single judge, it required two annual sessions of the circuit court in each of seventeen districts. As new circuits were established in the West, new judges would become necessary.

These minor adjustments made in the overall establishment of judicial power by the Constitution and its statutory implementation in the Judiciary Act of 1789 should not obscure the fact that it was only in 1800 that the inadequacies of the original judicial system became patent. Popular sentiment coalesced with opinion at the Bar to secure the reforms embodied in the Judiciary Act of 1801, but the issue of midnight appointments made suspect the motivation underlying the legislation and generated powerful arguments for its repeal. While the genesis and repeal of the 1801 Judiciary Act has been discussed previously, it must be mentioned at this point as a contributing factor to the sense of instability and discontinuity that attached to the Supreme Court. After a decade of salutary neglect of judicial authority, Congress had begun to legislate in the area of court organization and jurisdiction. There was no indication that a continuous stream of statutes might not destabilize the Court's administration for several years thereafter.

Instability, uncertainty, and lack of authority firmly based upon custom and long usage—these three conditions provided at once the likelihood that the Court would be destroyed as an effective branch of government, or on the other hand, the possibility that the Court, revitalized by its being in the center of public attention, might choose for itself a new course leading to enhanced power and stature. Unbridled by a long and stultifying tradition of service within narrow parameters, the Supreme Court by virtue of the very lack of consensus concerning its place in law and constitutional government, had the opportunity to choose the role that it would undertake. That decision was made not

---

[9] An Act to provide for the more convenient organization of the Courts of the United States, Feb. 13, 1801, 2 Stat. 89–100.

[10] See discussion in Part I, chapter 4, pp. 107–109.

[11] 2 Stat. 132 (Mar. 8, 1802); 2 Stat. 156–67 (Apr. 29, 1802). The latter Act was amended by the Act of Mar. 3, 1803, 2 Stat. 244.

by one judge nor at any single time but rather piecemeal and by the entire Court as it pursued its normal business.

The pages and chapters following will be concerned with the business of the Supreme Court, the extent to which the function of the Court as an adjudicative tribunal increased its power and prestige, and the degree to which altered modes of doing business and deciding cases changed and enhanced the position of the Court in the federal government and in the federation of States. These are matters of considerable significance in the years from 1801 through 1815, and they form the basis for an explanation of how the relatively weak Supreme Court of the decade from 1789 through 1800 became the powerful instrument for nationalism and international probity that it would be in 1819 and so remain.

THE ALTERED NATURE OF SUPREME COURT BUSINESS

One of the fortuitous circumstances in the growth of Supreme Court power in our period was a shift in the nature of cases heard by the Court—away from the original-jurisdiction cases that had proved so disruptive in the pre-Marshall period, and towards the review of federal rather than State court decisions, under the appellate authority of the Supreme Court.

Fortunately for the Supreme Court, the politically explosive issue of State sovereignty that had only partially been laid to rest by *Chisholm* v. *Georgia* and the Eleventh Amendment to the Constitution[12] subsided during the first fourteen years of Chief Justice Marshall's tenure. Only the passage of time could soothe the impact of *Chisholm* upon the advocates of States' rights fearful for the residual sovereignty of the original States of the Union. The seriatim opinions of the judges in *Chisholm*, particularly the highly nationalistic statement by Chief Justice John Jay, predictably raised serious questions about the Supreme Court as a threat to the balanced federal Union cherished by the American people and particularly the followers of President Thomas Jefferson. Despite the existence of the Eleventh Amendment these apprehensions had not been quieted, and had the Marshall Court been faced with a series of confrontations between States' rights and national power, it is difficult to imagine its survival given the political realities of the day. Signifi-

---

[12] J. Goebel, *Antecedents and Beginnings to 1801, Volume I, History of the Supreme Court of the United States*, ed., P. Freund (New York, 1971), 726–41; C. Jacobs, *The Eleventh Amendment and Sovereign Immunity* (Westport, Conn., 1972), 41–74; D. Mathis, "Georgia Before the Supreme Court: The First Decade," *American Journal of Legal History* XII (1968), 112 at 115–19.

cantly the only major original-jurisdiction case, *Marbury* v. *Madison*,[13] involved not the sovereignty of the States but rather the authority and power of the executive branch of the federal government.

This diminished emphasis upon original jurisdiction should not be viewed as an abdication of the Supreme Court's role as an arbiter of disputes between the States or its work as a tribunal of international law; a substantial number of cases touched upon the nature of federalism and the proper place of the individual States in the Union that represented them in international affairs. The change in Supreme Court activity was not to be found in the nature of issues brought to the Court for adjudication but rather in the procedural mode by which those matters were presented. More extensive reliance upon appellate jurisdiction meant that delicate questions of Supreme Court authority to bring coercive sanctions to bear upon the States, so embarrassing to earlier Courts, were not raised in so pointed a fashion. Only at the end of our period, in the return of the mandate in *Fairfax* v. *Hunter's Lessee*,[14] did the clash of federal power with State recalcitrance arise again, and subsequently in *Martin* v. *Hunter's Lessee*[15] the Supreme Court soundly affirmed the duty of State courts to abide by Supreme Court mandates issued upon the conclusion of an appeal from State court decisions. Yet even the number of federal-question appeals— like *Fairfax* v. *Hunter's Lessee*—was extremely small. The number of appeals from State courts decreased from 8 percent of the docket in the first twelve years of the Court's existence to a mere 4.5 percent in the period 1801–15.[16] This occurred during a rise in the total number of cases from 87 in the earlier period to 378 in the following fourteen years.

Concurrent with this decreased involvement with litigation from State tribunals there was a rapidly increasing number of appellate cases drawn from the federal circuit courts in general. Over the fourteen-year period approximately 35 percent of the Supreme Court's appellate caseload was composed of matters on appeal from the Circuit Court for the District of Columbia, and an additional 60.5 percent originated in the other federal circuit courts.[17] Territorial expansion of the United States, increased litigation in federal tribunals based on diversity of citizenship, and the growing population and commercial importance of the District of Columbia combined to focus the attention of the Supreme Court upon the appellate supervision of the inferior federal courts. In

---

[13] 1 Cranch 137–80 (1803).
[14] 7 Cranch 603–32 (1813).
[15] 1 Wheat. 304–82 (1816).
[16] Goebel, *Antecedents*, 802. For the period 1801–15 the percentage is based upon a statistical analysis of 378 cases identifiable by docket and reported opinion, decided by the Marshall Court. Seventeen of those cases are appeals from the decisions of State courts. See Table 2 in the Appendix.
[17] See Table 2, Appendix.

addition the complex issues of federal land policy and real property law in the newly admitted States of Kentucky and Tennessee resulted in a growing number of appeals from those federal circuit courts to the Supreme Court after 1807.

The amount of admiralty business appealed from federal circuit courts remained consistent with the pattern established under Chief Justices Jay and Ellsworth. The absolute number of admiralty and marine insurance cases grew from 35, or 41 percent of the total caseload, in the earlier period, to 125, or 33.1 percent of the total caseload, in 1801 to 1815.[18] The significance of admiralty adjudications is enhanced by their connection with the enforcement of the Non-Intercourse and Embargo Acts. It is noteworthy too that this added emphasis upon admiralty and maritime business followed in the wake of an exceptionally productive period of admiralty law development in Great Britain.[19]

In moving away from the exercise of its original jurisdiction the Supreme Court abandoned what had been an unusual reliance upon the supremacy clause in the earliest years of its existence. For the most part the tribunal now concerned itself with the routine administration of justice within the system of federal courts; its future growth was to be based firmly upon the provisions of Article III, with a more occasional and desultory glance at the "linch pin of the Constitution" that carried not only the essence of effective federalism but also the specter of national unification.

This altered emphasis is remarkable not only for its suddenness but also for its fortuitousness. Clearly the ratification of the Eleventh Amendment had not eliminated all branches of original jurisdiction in the Supreme Court, although it had left many unresolved issues in its wake that required resolution before the original jurisdiction of the Court might again be discerned clearly. Neither might the judges, either individually or collectively, have prevented duly qualified litigants from bringing before the Court those original- or appellate-jurisdiction cases that involved the activities or the sovereignty of the States. Quite possibly the opinion of the Supreme Court in *Marbury* v. *Madison* served to discourage resort to original-jurisdiction litigation, and on the other hand, the Jeffersonian victory of 1801 may have effectively established the principle of State sovereignty as a practical matter so that invocation of original jurisdiction against the States was rejected out of hand.

---

[18] Goebel, *Antecedents*, 803; Table 5, Appendix.

[19] The initial reports of English admiralty cases appeared in 1801, edited by Sir George Hay and Sir James Marriott, and in 1810–12, edited by Christopher Robins, 165 English Reports, Full Reprint, *passim*. Both collections of cases, covering admiralty business from 1776–79 and 1798–1801, were frequently cited in the Supreme Court during the Marshall era. See discussion in Part II, chapter 2, pp. 448–49.

While it is patently impossible to explain this alteration in the Court's business, it is obvious that the lack of such politically dangerous cases did much to provide the Court with an opportunity to grow in more basic, but less obvious, channels. The statistical pattern seems to illustrate more persuasively the growing importance of the federal circuit courts in the appellate work of the Supreme Court, and the mode in which the creation of new federal districts had an important and palliative impact upon the activities of the high court. These were, therefore, years of change, not only in American society and territorial holdings but also in the public's view of the judiciary and the manner of conducting the Supreme Court's business; they were exciting times, even dangerous times, but this was also a period of great promise for astute judges who had both the intelligence and the fortitude to deal with their opportunities in a constructive fashion.

THE SUPREME COURT AND THE ROAD TO GREATNESS

The Supreme Court in the terms from 1801 to 1815 also worked, albeit unconsciously, towards greatness, and the labors were not solely those of its Chief Justice. For many generations historians have been content to explain the internal growth and rising esteem of the Supreme Court by making superficial reference to John Marshall's "influence" over his associate justices.[20] One may find ample evidence of Marshall's diligence in a statistical analysis of the business of the Court. From 1801 through 1815 he delivered 209, or 55 percent, of the opinions of the Court. Of the remainder, 27 percent were delivered by his colleagues and 18 percent were per curiam or seriatim opinions. For the shorter period from 1801 through 1810, Marshall's contribution is even more pronounced. During these nine terms of court, he delivered the opinion of the court in 65 percent of the cases decided; 26 percent were per curiam or seriatim opinions, and 9 percent were delivered by associate judges.[21] Undoubtedly the new Chief Justice was a man of considerable energy to take to himself the burden of composing such a

---

[20] A. Beveridge, *The Life of John Marshall*, 4 vols. (Boston, 1916–19), IV, 443; E. Corwin, *John Marshall and the Constitution* (New Haven, 1919), 115–16. But see D. Morgan, *Justice William Johnson: The First Dissenter* (Columbia, S. C., 1954), 288–91; D. Morgan, "The Origin of Supreme Court Dissent," *William and Mary Quarterly*, 3d Series, X (1953), 353–77; H. Johnson, "John Marshall,"

in L. Friedman and F. Israel, eds., *Justices of the United States Supreme Court, 1789–1969*, I (New York, 1969), 300–303. One of the most thoughtful and extensive considerations of the question of judicial unanimity is D. Roper, "Judicial Unanimity and the Marshall Court," *American Journal of Legal History* IX (1965), 118–34.

[21] See Table 1, Appendix.

large proportion of the Court's opinions, and indeed, it has been suggested that he did so in order to enable himself to make subtle alterations in the legal views of his colleagues.[22] The professionalism and intellectual independence of the other judges makes this latter explanation highly unlikely, yet the dominance of Marshall in the work of the Court and the inception of the Court's use of the majority opinion deserve further examination and an attempt at explanation.

The judges on the Supreme Court at the time of John Marshall's appointment were, for the most part, men who were past their prime and more honored for their past service to the Republic than renowned for their intellect or their political sensitivity. The thorough discussion of their personal and professional characteristics, set forth above,[23] precludes the need to consider them individually, but some attempt must be made to evaluate their collegial weight in juxtaposition to their new Chief Justice. Judges Cushing, Paterson, and Chase labored under the disabilities of age; the first two were fragile in health and perhaps suffering from a diminution of their early intellectual powers; the last, grown acerbic and intemperate, used his wit in ways that were damaging to the Court and highly partisan. Judge Alfred Moore, despite a promising career at the Bar before his appointment to the Court, had not made any significant mark on the work of the tribunal in his first year and would not do so before he resigned for reasons of ill health at the end of the 1804 term. So it was that among the sitting judges only Marshall's fellow Virginian, Bushrod Washington, might be considered an equal to the Chief Justice in physical vigor and soundness of mind. After 1801 it was Judge Washington's destiny to be eclipsed by Chief Justice Marshall, not because he lost intellectual power or the strength of his convictions, but rather because the two shared a common political and judicial philosophy. Indeed there exist letters between Marshall and Washington that indicate the Chief Justice's high opinion of the professional knowledge of his fellow Virginian, particularly in fields where Washington's duties on the circuit court had given him an encyclopedic grasp of admiralty and maritime law.[24] Undoubtedly the loss of the full correspondence between the two men has obscured the degree to which John Marshall relied upon Bushrod Washington as a partner and companion in his great work on the Supreme Court.

Given this situation it is not difficult to accept the theory of Marshall's domination of his colleagues on the Court from 1801 to

---

[22] W. Crosskey, *Politics and the Constitution in the History of the United States,* 2 vols. (Chicago, 1953), II, 1080.

[23] See Part I, chapter 3, pp. 85–103.

[24] See J. Marshall to B. Washington, May 25, 1813, Swem Library, College of William and Mary, Williamsburg, Va.

1805, when Thomas Jefferson's first appointee, William Johnson, joined the Bench. His 1822 report of the 1805 situation to Thomas Jefferson, correct although biased with hindsight and partisanship, does not seem implausible: "Cushing was incompetent, Chase could not be got to think or write—Paterson was a slow man and willingly declined the Trouble, and the other two [Marshall and Washington] . . . are commonly estimated as one Judge."[25] Yet even after Marshall's elderly Federalist associates involuntarily vacated their places by dying in office, their Jeffersonian Republican successors ostensibly continued to permit the preeminence of the great Chief Justice in the delivery of opinions. As a practical matter, it is obvious that the largest number of constitutional decisions delivered by the Chief Justice were to come well after Federalist political influence in the Supreme Court had been neutralized. After 1810 it is true that the delivery of opinions was shared more evenly with the associate judges, but John Marshall continued to deliver more majority opinions than any of his associates, including the voluble Joseph Story.[26]

Judge William Johnson's appointment to the Supreme Court, and the arrival of other Republican appointees after 1805, interjected a new partisan variable into the composition and activities of the Court. Before one attempts to assess the dynamics of Supreme Court decision-making after 1805, it is helpful to consider the administrative alterations that had occurred in the mode of conducting the Court's business between 1801 and 1805. While resort to a thorough statistical analysis is unnecessary, a modest effort in that direction demonstrates factors that have previously escaped scholarly attention.

AN ANALYSIS OF MARSHALL COURT OPINIONS, 1801–15

The opinions of the Marshall Court differ from those delivered in the first decade of the Court's existence in two fundamental characteristics: (1) the seriatim opinion, modeled upon the English practice and used almost to excess in the Jay Court, was utilized only seven times in the period from 1801 through 1815, and (2) "opinions of the Court" were made the primary vehicle for announcing the determinations of the Supreme Court. These developments created an aura of unanimity concerning the Court's actions, and they also relieved the elderly associate judges of the burden of preparing reasoned opinions on points of law argued at the Bar and discussed in conference. The new system of

---

[25] Quoted from the Jefferson papers in the Library of Congress in Morgan, *William Johnson*, 182.

[26] See Table 1, Appendix.

opinion delivery gave anonymity to individual judges under the cloak of a collegiate decision, and it also required a consolidation of their collective reasoning into one coherent statement of the law acceptable to each one of them. Ultimately the "opinions of the Court" were to be much more persuasive with the legal community and the nation at large because minor differences between the justices of the Court were adjusted internally.[27]

Within the practices of the Court under former Chief Justice Oliver Ellsworth there had developed a limited trend towards the "opinion of the Court" through the use of brief per curiam opinions delivered by the Chief Justice.[28] Like the later majority opinions, these per curiam statements also provided unitary statements of the Court's reasoning, to be announced not as an individual judge's position but rather as the collegiate view of the entire Court. Unlike the later "opinions of the Court," however, they were never utilized in matters of complexity or of major substantive concern.

In making the transition from seriatim and per curiam opinions to a modified practice in which the Court spoke through a collective opinion, the judges may well have elected to retain certain of the past practice in regard to the per curiam opinion of the Ellsworth Court. In part this may have been the vestigial influence of the per curiam as the ancestral form of the "opinion of the Court," or perhaps it may have been a factor in gaining acceptance of the new form of majority opinion, not only by the Bar and public, but even among the judges themselves. The preeminence of Chief Justice Ellsworth in delivering per curiam opinions clearly was also true of John Marshall's significant role in delivering majority opinions for the Court during the first decade and a half of his Chief Justiceship.

Historians have long been perplexed by the seeming deference shown to Chief Justice Marshall, even by colleagues who were senior in age, or who owed their judicial positions to appointment by Republican Presidents. The reports of the Court's opinions contain some tantalizing evidence concerning opinion writing and delivery practices, but far from definitive answers. For example, the 1803 case of *Stuart* v. *Laird*, on appeal from John Marshall's decision in the Virginia Circuit Court of the United States, contains reporter William Cranch's statement explaining why Judge William Paterson, third in seniority after Marshall and Judge Cushing, delivered the opinion: "March 2d. The Chief Justice, having tried the cause in the court below, declined giving an opinion. Paterson, J. (Judge Cushing being absent on account of ill health) delivered the opinion of the court."[29] Clearly the depar-

---

[27] Morgan, *William Johnson*, 45–47.
[28] *Ibid.*, 46.

[29] 1 Cranch 308 (1803).

ture from the usual procedure—that the opinion should have been delivered by the Chief Justice or the senior associate judge—troubled the reporter. Since apparently the irregularity would have drawn the notice of readers of the reports, it may be surmised that delivery of the opinion of the Court was understood to be reserved to the Chief Justice or the senior associate judge present on the Bench and participating in the decision.

Somewhat later Judge Cushing was presiding when *M'Ilvaine* v. *Coxe's Lessee*,[30] long debated in Court conference, was ready for announcement. This was a complicated case involving the alienage of a New Jersey landowner who had remained loyal to the British Crown during the American Revolution, and the issue of the alien ownership of real property in New Jersey. While the opinion might well have had serious consequences for John Marshall's private investments in the Fairfax manor lands in Virginia, he himself was absent from Court and therefore his disqualification for interest was not relevant. Cushing as the presiding justice delivered the opinion, a lengthy and erudite statement that seems well beyond his capacities at that time, and perhaps beyond his professional ability even at a younger age.

The reporter's comment in *Stuart* v. *Laird* and the quality of the opinion in *M'Ilvaine* v. *Coxe's Lessee* lead one to question the commonly accepted assumption that *delivery* of a majority opinion implied *authorship* of the opinion. They also suggest that as a routine matter, the delivery of opinions of the Court was not rotated among justices, or a shared labor, but that as a matter of form and protocol, the Chief Justice or the presiding judge delivered the opinion on behalf of his colleagues who were junior in rank.

Additional evidence concerning opinion assignment and delivery may be found in Chief Justice Marshall's opinion in *M'Ferran* v. *Taylor and Massie*,[31] which involved the rights of a purchaser under an inaccurate contract for the sale of land. When the seller agreed to sell such lands on Hington's fork, in Kentucky, as the purchaser should select, the seller was not aware that he did not own any land fitting that description. The Kentucky Federal District Court, exercising circuit court powers, ordered the defendant-seller to permit the purchaser to select such tracts from among the seller's lands as should satisfy the contract, and that damages be paid if the land so selected was not equal in value to that at Hington's fork. When the Supreme Court affirmed this district court decree, John Marshall concurred in the "general principles laid down." However he indicated that he

---

[30] 2 Cranch 280–336 (1805); 4 Cranch 209 at 211 (1808). The case is discussed further in Part II, chapter 4, pp. 497–502, 507–508.

[31] 3 Cranch 270–82 (1806).

did not, in consequence of the particular circumstances of this case, concur in the opinion which has been delivered. I will briefly state those circumstances.

In his bill, the plaintiff does not allege, that he was, in any degree, induced to make the contract, by supposing the land . . . to lie on *Hington's fork*. This representation, then, was an accidental circumstance which has not, in the slightest degree, influenced his conduct. . . . The person claiming damages in such a case should, I think, be left to his remedy at law. I should, therefore, have been disposed to affirm the decree of the district court. I am, however, perfectly content with that which I have been directed to deliver.[32]

Following this statement by the Chief Justice the reporter inserted a footnote indicating that four judges were present, presumably at the time the opinion was delivered. The minutes of the Supreme Court show that the same four judges, Marshall, Paterson, Washington, and Johnson, were present for argument of the case on February 12, 1806, and for the delivery of the opinion on February 14.[33] Since four judges constituted a majority of all Supreme Court judges then commissioned and sitting, Marshall's concurrence was essential to a final disposition of the case.

The *M'Ferran* opinion thus demonstrates once again reporter William Cranch's preoccupation with the membership of the Court present on decision date, and his wish to explain seeming irregularities in the delivery of Court opinions. In this particular instance the Chief Justice indicated that while he delivered the opinion, there were certain aspects where his personal opinion differed from that of the Court. Indeed, his concluding statement, that he had been "directed to deliver" the opinion, suggests that the Court as a group had arrived at its common judgment and he was merely performing his duty as presiding officer in accordance with established custom and practice.

Seniority and precedence meant much to men of John Marshall's generation, and although he himself might be inclined to ignore such niceties insofar as they concerned him personally, he would have been acutely aware of their consequence to others. A man so long in political life and so recently immersed in the protocol of diplomatic affairs could scarcely be insensitive to the demands of public etiquette. Conveniently, it was precisely this deference to dignity of office that might well be used to obtain acquiescence from those of his associates who outranked him in age and service to the Republic, if not in professional knowledge and energy. While no evidence survives to prove Marshall's assertion of the right of the senior judge to delivery of majority opinions,

[32] *Ibid.*, 282.
[33] Minutes of the Supreme Court, Feb. 12 and 14, 1806, RG 267, National Archives, Washington, D.C.

there is enough circumstantial evidence to suggest that this was the practice and custom that developed during the first years of his Chief Justiceship.

Unfortunately the documentary evidence concerning the Supreme Court provides little evidence to cast light on the role of each individual judge in the preparation of opinions of the Court. The few manuscript opinions that do survive from the period 1801 through 1815 are obviously final drafts, for they bear no marks of verbal corrections or insertions by other judges. For the most part the manuscript opinions of the Supreme Court prior to 1833 were thrown out by those who reported or printed the official edition of the Supreme Court reports, and thus they are lost forever. While a painstaking analysis of the style, word choice, and legal reasoning of the printed opinions might yield some evidence of mixed authorship, it would be a most arduous task that would likely add little to our knowledge of the internal operations of John Marshall's court. Yet the future historian of the Supreme Court must exercise great caution before accepting the presently unsupported anachronistic assumption that, because later practice of the Supreme Court established that the judge delivering the opinion was the principal author of the opinion, such a tradition was applicable prior to 1815.

The statistical analysis that has been made does not provide any definitive answer in regard to the role of seniority in the delivery of Court opinions. It does tend, however, to verify the suggestions set forth above, and to provide a firmer basis for evaluating those hypotheses. If all of the judges on the Supreme Court Bench from 1801 to 1815 are ranked with the Chief Justice first, followed by his associates according to their dates of commission, it is possible by reference to the minutes of the Court to determine who was presiding when any given case was announced to the Bar and a majority opinion was delivered. There are instances of disqualification of certain judges, either for personal or professional interest, or for not having been present at argument; these eliminate the judge involved from availability to deliver the opinion on behalf of the Court. In addition, the circuit assignments of the Chief Justice and other judges must be considered as a possible ground for disqualification, although as a practical matter this was not an invariable basis for disqualification. Despite these variables, it is possible to test the validity of the hypothesis concerning seniority and delivery of majority opinions. Chief Justice Marshall's robust health and attention to his duties prior to 1810 insured that he was almost always the senior justice present during the sessions of the Supreme Court; however, when Marshall was either absent from the Bench or disqualified for some reason, the majority opinion was almost invariably delivered by the senior associate judge. During the period 1801 through 1805 *all majority opinions conform to the seniority principle*; from

1806 to 1808 only one majority opinion per term varies from the rule; and in 1809 and 1810 only four majority opinions in each term failed to conform to this principle. Thereafter the 1812 term was marked by the late arrival of the Chief Justice in Washington, and by 1814 and 1815 as many majority opinions conform to the seniority rule as depart from it.

Whether the seniority rule began to play a less prominent role after 1810 or whether, as Donald Morgan has viewed the situation, John Marshall exerted less influence over the deliberations of the Court, it is noteworthy that the decline in the Chief Justice's preeminence in majority opinion delivery coincides with the first rupture in the ostensible unanimity of the Marshall Court and a sharp outbreak of dissenting opinions.[34]

While dissent among the judges of the Supreme Court was not totally suppressed before 1810, it tended to be well dispersed through a variety of cases and generally of little significance for the advancement of the Court's business. After 1810, however, the judges differed strongly over the territorial scope of municipal trade laws, a matter of immediate concern in extending comity to admiralty decrees condemning vessels on the high seas for failure to obey the internal navigation laws of foreign nations and colonies, and ultimately for actions under the Non-Intercourse and Embargo Acts brought against American merchants.[35] In these cases Marshall and his Federalist colleagues tended to favor a limited applicability of the American and foreign maritime jurisdiction, thereby restricting admiralty power to coastal waters except in matters of prize under international laws of war. Their Jeffersonian colleagues urged a broad and sweeping authority of nations to enforce their trade laws on the high seas. This clash produced a remarkable number of dissents, including two by Chief Justice Marshall in *Hudson and Smith* v. *Guestier* and *The Venus*.[36] Ironically, while admiralty and maritime business was the backbone of Supreme Court jurisdiction in these intermediate years, it was to prove the Achilles heel of the Court's unanimity, and the maritime litigation of the years prior to and during the War of 1812 may well have ended the Chief Justice's preeminence in opinion delivery and wrecked forever the reliance upon seniority in this matter.

---

[34] The "seniority rule" has been tested for the entire period of Marshall's Chief Justiceship, with these results. H. Johnson, "A Statistical Analysis of Marshall Court Opinions" (Paper delivered at the Southern Historical Association Annual Meeting, Washington, D. C., October 30, 1969), 14–16, and Plate V, 47.

[35] *Ibid.*, 17, and Plate VI, 48. See also P. Jackson, *Dissent in the Supreme Court: A Chronology* (Norman, Okla., 1969), 22–33.

[36] 6 Cranch 281 at 285 (1810); 8 Cranch 253 at 288–317 (1814).

Appellate cases reached the Supreme Court from a variety of inferior federal courts, the most prominent being the Circuit Court for the District of Columbia, which provided 32.5 percent of the total cases decided by the Court. Matters on appeal from other federal circuits seem to be roughly proportional to the population of the respective States, but there is a noticeable increase in appellate business from the Massachusetts and Rhode Island circuits in 1814 and 1815 due primarily to the prize and maritime litigation in New England. A similar increase is also obvious in the appeals heard from the Maryland circuit court. The Supreme Court judges who served on circuit in these three States, namely Story and Washington, became exceptionally active in developing the law in this field, and were joined by Judge William Johnson, circuit judge for South Carolina, and Judge Brockholst Livingston, circuit judge for New York.[37]

Throughout these years Chief Justice Marshall continued to make particularly heavy contributions to the law of negotiable instruments and the law merchant generally,[38] as well as to set forth the rules of law concerning the jurisdiction and powers of State and federal courts and matters of procedure.[39] During his years of law practice the Chief Justice had developed particular familiarity with mercantile litigation, and matters of jurisdiction and procedure were traditionally reserved for the Chief Justice.[40] Stemming from a use of the per curiam opinion in the Ellsworth Court for this purpose, the Chief Justice of the United States until the early years of the twentieth century was customarily expected to predominate in this area. The Chief Justice was also extremely active in cases involving business enterprise.[41] Defining the American law of corporations and partnerships and setting forth the legal rules for the conduct of business, Marshall's contributions in this field were certainly not limited to his opinion as to the applicability of the contract clause of the Constitution in *Fletcher* v. *Peck*.

Although the Court as presided over by Chief Justice Marshall was certainly not solely the product of his legal genius, it is clear that he was the individual most responsible for the alteration in internal arrangements that provided a period of general unanimity after the exceptionally divisive time of the Jay Court. The tendency towards

---

[37] See Table 2, Appendix.

[38] See Tables 6 and 7, Appendix.

[39] See Table 10, Appendix.

[40] For Marshall's practice in the mercantile and commercial law field see C. Cullen and H. Johnson, *The Papers of John Marshall*, II (Chapel Hill, 1977), 19–20, 30 note 3, 94–95. As to the Chief Justice delivering opinions in areas of jurisdiction and procedure, this was apparently part of the tradition of the Bar in the early part of the twentieth century. We are grateful to Frederick Bernays Wiener, formerly of the District of Columbia Bar and now a resident of Phoenix, Arizona, for sharing this tradition with us; it confirms the statistical findings made independently.

[41] See Table 8, Appendix.

collegiality in opinion writing, although sharply curtailed by 1810, was a formative influence in the subsequent history of the Court, as was the effort to avoid public dissent so obvious in Marshall's own writings and in the actions of the Court under his leadership.

THE RISING TIDE OF REPUBLICAN JUDICIAL APPOINTMENTS

Although Adams' policy of appointing relatively young men to the Supreme Court assured a Federalist voice in that tribunal's deliberations for several decades, it was apparent that the judges remaining from the group of President Washington's appointees would soon either retire because of illness or die in office. The tenacity of the old judges, however, resulted in their remaining in office and postponing the appointment of a Supreme Court judge by President Jefferson until March 1804, when Judge Alfred Moore resigned because of ill health. Seeking a candidate from the South, the President selected thirty-two-year-old Judge William Johnson of the South Carolina Constitutional Court as his first nominee to the Supreme Court Bench.[42] A prominent lawyer and eminent political leader of the Republican cause in South Carolina, Johnson had served with competence and ability in his State's highest appellate court; despite his youth he brought to the Supreme Court Bench, upon his confirmation by the Senate, a gifted and well-trained intelligence. A graduate of Princeton, Johnson was trained by clerkship in the Charleston law office of Charles Cotesworth Pinckney. Service in the State legislature, for a period as speaker of the House of Representatives, had made Johnson a competent politician, but beyond those political and professional achievements, he was actively involved in the establishment and governance of the newly established South Carolina College, presiding over the school's board of trustees from 1802 until his appointment to the United States Supreme Court.[43]

Aside from his competence and the energy and diligence of youth that Johnson brought to the Supreme Court, he was also recognized as a loyal and effective partisan of Jeffersonian Republicanism. His biographer, Donald G. Morgan, informs us that among the several South Carolina candidates of outstanding political and professional credentials, Johnson stood forth as the most steadfast in his adherence to the Republican cause.[44] The appointment files of the Jefferson administration contain a memorandum that provides a good understanding of the factors governing Johnson's appointment. The President and his advisers were clearly seeking a firm party man, one who would "possess

---

[42] On the appointment see Morgan, *William Johnson*, 49–52.

[43] *Ibid.*, 17–40.
[44] *Ibid.*, 50.

the confidence of the republicans." However an overzealous adherence to revolutionary ideologies learned abroad might disqualify a man for being a "Jacobin"; the document stresses respectability as a necessary quality in the appointee. William Johnson is succinctly described as "[a] state judge. An excellent lawyer, prompt, eloquent, of irreproachable character, republican connections, and of good nerves in his political principles. About 35 years old. Was speaker some years."[45] Judge Johnson, as the first Jeffersonian appointee, was carefully selected on grounds that combined ability, probity, and party loyalty. Obviously it was anticipated that William Johnson would have both the intellectual strength and the partisan devotion to President Jefferson that would be necessary to assure a strong Republican voice in the deliberations of the Supreme Court.

Next to be appointed to the Supreme Court was Associate Justice Henry Brockholst Livingston, the renegade brother-in-law of former Chief Justice John Jay and son of the late governor of New Jersey, William Livingston.[46] Like his fellow Jeffersonian appointee, Brockholst Livingston was a graduate of Princeton, where he was a classmate of James Madison, Jefferson's Secretary of State. After service as a staff officer in the Revolution and an unhappy tour of diplomatic duty in Spain as personal secretary to John Jay, Livingston returned to New York in 1783 to study law with Peter Yates of Albany. Thereafter he was active in State politics while building a successful law practice in New York City. His conversion to anti-Federalism has been dated either to the New York gubernatorial election of 1792 (lost by Jay on a technicality) or to his opposition to the Jay Treaty in 1795. Whatever may be correct, it is likely that personal animosity to Jay and friendship for Madison drew Livingston into Republican ranks. Appointed to the New York Supreme Court in 1802, Livingston had proved himself a vigorously independent judge, frequently concurring separately or dissenting from per curiam opinions announced by the Court. In four years on the bench he wrote 149 opinions that were reported and published. Having been passed over in 1804 because of President Jefferson's wish to appoint a judge residing in the South, Livingston was an obvious choice when Judge William Paterson of New Jersey died in 1806. He took his seat on the Supreme Court Bench at the February 1807 term of court.

Like Judge Johnson, Brockholst Livingston was a formidable lawyer and strong thinker who had served with distinction in the New

---

[45] Characters of the lawyers in South Carolina, Feb. 17, 1804, Appointment Files, RG 59, National Archives, Washington, D.C.

[46] G. Dunne, "Brockholst Livingston," in Friedman and Israel, eds., *Justices of the Supreme Court*, I, 387–97.

I: *Introduction: The Business of the Court*

York State courts before his elevation to the Supreme Court of the United States. As subsequent chapters show, his participation in the work of the Court is not adequately represented by the relatively small number of opinions authored by him. He differed from his colleagues in their conference discussions and at times his concurrences and dissents found their way into the public eye in the Court reports. In 1808 Joseph Story found Livingston to be "a very able and independent judge. He evidently thinks with great solidity and seizes on the strong points of argument." When Livingston died in 1823 both the Chief Justice and Judge Story mourned him as a valued associate who would not be easily replaced in the work of the Court.[47]

The creation of a western circuit of the federal courts and Congressional authorization for the appointment of a sixth judge to serve that circuit resulted in Thomas Jefferson's appointment of Thomas Todd, then chief justice of the Kentucky Court of Appeals.[48] A Virginian by birth, Todd moved to Kentucky shortly after the Revolution and was admitted to the Virginia Bar in 1788. He built an active and lucrative practice specializing in real property law and the litigation of contested Kentucky land titles; thereafter he served as chief clerk of the federal district court and the Kentucky legislature, and then was appointed a judge of the Kentucky Court of Appeals in 1801, rising in the same year to his position as chief justice.

Taking his seat on the United States Supreme Court in the March 1808 term, Todd contributed to but fourteen of the opinions of the high court in the period 1808 to 1826. The arduous nature of his circuit duties, coupled with ill health, caused him to miss several of the Washington meetings of the Court, but even with due allowance for those circumstances, his impact upon the deliberations of the Supreme Court seems to have been minimal. While a State court judge he had demonstrated antipathy to the adjudication of Kentucky disputes by federal judges, but once upon the Supreme Court of the United States he silently acquiesced in Marshall's major constitutional decisions, even in the area of local land titles. Admittedly his economic views were conservative, and in most matters he favored a strong national union, yet the lack of strongly voiced dissent must have surprised his contemporaries as much as it perplexes historians and biographers.

The last two appointees to the Supreme Court before 1816 were

---

[47] R. Cushman, "Henry Brockholst Livingston," in *Dictionary of American Biography* VI, 312–13; Baker, *John Marshall*, 703; J. Story to J. Marshall, June 22, 1823, Marshall Papers, College of William and Mary Library, Williamsburg, Va.

[48] F. Israel, "Thomas Todd," in Friedman and Israel, *Justices of the United States Supreme Court*, I, 407–11; E. O'Rear, "Justice Thomas Todd," *Register of the Kentucky State Historical Society* XXXVIII (1940), 112–19.

Gabriel Duvall of Maryland and Joseph Story of Massachusetts.[49] Duvall was a man of solid professional competence and ability who left a modest mark upon the jurisprudence of the early Marshall Court; Story was a firebrand of energy and intellectual brilliance who made an immediate and dynamic impact upon the Court and its mode of conducting business. Both were nominated on November 15, 1811, and confirmed two days later, Duvall to replace his deceased countryman from Maryland, Samuel Chase, and Story to take the seat of Judge William Cushing, who had died almost a year earlier. By virtue of Duvall's seniority in age, he would outrank Story in precedence on the Court.

Descended from an old and distinguished family, Duvall had seen legislative service in the Maryland House of Delegates, and for two terms as a member of the federal House of Representatives. Appointed chief justice of the Maryland General Court in 1796, he continued in that position until Thomas Jefferson appointed him comptroller of the Treasury in 1802. During the period from 1812 through the end of the 1815 term Judge Duvall delivered opinions in only four cases, but in his dissent in *Mima Queen* v. *Hepburn*,[50] a case involving a slave's petition for freedom, he demonstrated not only a firm grasp of Maryland law on the subject but also a willingness to differ publicly with the position taken by Chief Justice Marshall. Later Judge Duvall was to file a statement of dissent in *Dartmouth College* v. *Woodward*;[51] his failure to submit a dissenting opinion to the printer may well cloak substantial differences from both the majority opinion by Chief Justice Marshall and the more sweeping concurring opinion of Judge Story.

Duvall's appointment-twin, Joseph Story, joined the Supreme Court shortly after his thirty-second birthday. Trained at Harvard College and in the law offices of Samuel Sewell and Samuel Putnam, Story had already published a treatise on civil litigation and pleadings (1805) and served as counsel for the Massachusetts investors appealing to the Supreme Court in the Yazoo land fraud case, *Fletcher* v. *Peck*.[52] While serving in the federal House of Representatives he had been equivocal in his support of the Embargo, thereby losing the support of his anti-Embargo constituents even as he was held in disfavor by President Jefferson. Opposing Story's nomination to the Supreme Court by President Madison, Jefferson felt that the Massachusetts lawyer was "a

---

[49] I. Dilliard, "Gabriel Duvall," in Friedman and Israel, *Justices of The United States Supreme Court*, I, 419–28; G. Dunne, *Justice Joseph Story and the Rise of the Supreme Court* (New York, 1970), 17–95. On Story's appointment see M. Dowd, "Justice Joseph Story and the Politics of Appointment," *American Journal of Legal History* IX (1964), 265–85.

[50] 7 Cranch 290, at 298–99 (1813).
[51] 4 Wheat. 518, at 713 (1819).
[52] See Part II, chapter 1, note 46.

Tory." The characterization, although hostile, was not inaccurate. Story's strong nationalism, his tendency to give great weight to property rights and business interests, and his later advocacy of an expanded admiralty jurisdiction and the re-establishment of a federal common law of crimes, show a distinctly non-Jeffersonian approach to constitutional matters. In prize cases Justice Story brought to the Supreme Court the new philosophy of Cornelius van Bynkershoek, which rested upon the abdication of most of the rules of war as then applied by the civilized nations of the world, and substituted force and substantially unbridled national sovereignty.[53]

Consistent in his legal and political philosophy, Story did not hesitate to express his disagreement with the majority in *United States v. Hudson and Goodwin*, which struck down the concept of a federal common law of crimes.[54] Thereafter he worked diligently to obtain statutory recognition of a federal common law of crime.[55] In 1814 he wrote the majority opinion in *Fairfax's Devisee* v. *Hunter's Lessee*,[56] applying the supremacy of federal international agreements to avoid State action contrary to treaty provisions; and in 1816 he vindicated the jurisdiction and supremacy of the United States Supreme Court over State tribunals in regard to federal-question appeals (*Martin* v. *Hunter's Lessee*).[57]

Joseph Story combined a rigid independence in political and constitutional questions with a virtuoso knowledge of the law both ancient and modern. Fearless in his advocacy of unpopular judicial positions, he was also marked as a man not to be eclipsed by any other intellect. Among all of the appointees of Jefferson and Madison, this Massachusetts banker and lawyer was best qualified to present partisan opposition to Marshall on the Supreme Court. Yet, ironically, not only did Story's economic and political philosophy coincide with that of the Chief Justice, but it appears that in a number of ways Story was more conservative, more property-oriented, and more nationalistic than the Federalist Chief Justice. In the case of Judge Story the "influence" of the Chief Justice was not responsible for converting an ardent Jeffer-

---

[53] See Judge Story's dissents in Brown v. U.S., 8 Cranch 110 at 130–35 (1814); The Nereide, 9 Cranch 388 at 436–38, 448–49.

[54] 7 Cranch 32–34 (1812); Dunne, *Story*, 86, 90–91. The case is further discussed in Part II, chapter 8, pp. 639–45.

[55] Dunne, *Story*, 146–47, 240.

[56] 7 Cranch 618–28 (1813). See Part II, chapter 4, pp. 516–17.

[57] 1 Wheat. 304 at 323–62 (1816);

the point is discussed briefly in Part II, chapter 8, p. 624. Ironically, Virginia Justice Spencer Roane, who was instrumental in defying the mandate in Fairfax v. Hunter, was himself responsible for the growth of judicial review in Virginia. J. Radabaugh, "Spencer Roane and the Genesis of Virginia Judicial Review," *American Journal of Legal History* VI (1962), 63–70.

sonian Republican to a neo-Federalist; quite the contrary, Marshall very likely played a moderating influence upon his younger colleague, drawing him closer to the Jeffersonian mean than Story would have preferred.

When one examines the conduct of all of the Jeffersonian-Republican appointees, there is little basis for supposing a pervasive and all-encompassing "influence" by Chief Justice Marshall. Indeed, if Republican judges became neo-Federalists, that seems to have been a natural development from their past experiences and commitments. Brockholst Livingston, despite his espousal of the Republican party after being wounded in the internecine battles of New York partisan politics, was nonetheless an aristocratic landholder with strong connections to the landed gentry of New York and New Jersey. Duvall's antecedents likewise placed him among the well-to-do classes of society, and while Todd had commenced his life with a modest endowment, like Marshall he had built a good fortune from the tangled legal gnarl of land title disputes in Kentucky. In short, if Chief Justice Marshall exerted any compelling persuasive influence over his Jeffersonian-Republican colleagues, that pressure seems only to have been in the direction of reinforcing strong proclivities that they already had in favor of business enterprise, the security of property rights, and the expanded power of the federal government in its areas of legitimate concern.[58]

Yet the movement towards accommodation among judges of the Supreme Court cannot be considered solely a matter of Republican associates joining the Chief Justice in his Federalism. It is quite clear that John Marshall was not a doctrinaire Federalist of the old "High Federalist" variety; his loyalties ran to President Washington and President Adams, and not to Alexander Hamilton or the New England High Federalist leaders. Age and past political stands marked the Chief Justice as a "transitional figure," anxious to work for essential goals within a new political environment that required strong and vigorous party politics. His was a most moderate form of the old Federalist creed, free from entanglement with the excesses of the Alien and Sedition Acts, and skeptical of the value of prosecutions at the criminal Bar for political advocacy.[59] As a Virginian he was on friendly terms

---

[58] The coalescence of Jeffersonian and Federalist principles and programs has been reaffirmed in a recent political study. R. Ellis, *The Jeffersonian Crisis: Courts and Politics in the Young Republic* (New York, 1971), 237–38. See also Roper, "Judicial Unanimity," *American Journal of Legal History* IX (1965), as to basic social and economic agreement among both Republican and Federalist members of Marshall's Court.

[59] David Hackett Fischer characterizes Marshall as a "transitional figure" and not a "young Federalist." *The Revolution of American Conservatism* (New York, 1965), 380–82. Based on Marshall's position on the peace mission to France in 1800 and his opposition to the Sedition Act,

with most of President Jefferson's most intimate advisers, having known them at the Richmond Bar or having been raised with them in Virginia society and politics. Knowledge of Republicans gave him a better perspective and greater faith in their integrity, if not in their politics.[60]

THE CESSATION OF JUDICIAL POLITICS
AND THE RULE OF LAW

We have seen that there was a traditionally close connection between political authority and judicial power in the colonial period of American history.[61] In a perceptive essay, historian John D. Cushing has demonstrated that in Massachusetts the circuit-riding colonial judges were the recipients of public remonstrances against acts of government, most being entirely beyond their control or responsibility.[62] Conversely the same judges were not reluctant to include within their grand jury charges a series of statements concerning moral philosophy or even a disquisition on some timely political topic. Faced with an approaching revolution against the Crown, Massachusetts justices pleaded for patience and the retention of the status quo. With the establishment of an independent State government, grand jury charges continued to be used to advance political purposes. Judges continued to receive petitions and remonstrances from the public, and they in turn were not above proselytizing such political causes as the ratification of the constitution of 1780. It may be argued that the Massachusetts practice in this regard was not typical, yet there is evidence of political use of judicial authority in other American colonies and in the early national period. The Virginia dispute over the Northern Neck proprietary of Lord Fairfax was long embroiled in provincial and imperial politics, although it was a legal issue best left to the resolution of the courts and the Privy Council.[63] The major settlement was by a 1796 Act of the General

---

William N. Chambers denominates him a "moderate spokesman" of the Federalist party, and notes the opposition by High Federalists to Marshall's appointment as Secretary of State. *Political Parties in a New Nation: The American Experience, 1776–1809* (New York, 1963), 136, 142–43, 150. See also Baker, *John Marshall*, 308–10, 345–47, 359. Robert K. Faulkner points out that while Marshall supported the constitutionality of the Sedition Act, he considered it inexpedient and contrary to prevailing American public opinion. *The Jurisprudence of John Marshall* (Princeton, 1968), 171–72.

[60] Baker, *John Marshall*, 359.
[61] See discussion in Part I, chapter 7, pp. 206, 224–25.
[62] "The Judiciary and Public Opinion in Revolutionary Massachusetts," in G. Billias, ed., *Law and Authority in Colonial America* (Barre, Mass., 1965), 168–86.
[63] Cullen and Johnson, eds., *Marshall Papers*, I, 150–53; II, 140–49. See also J. Treon, *Martin v. Hunter's Lessee: A Case History* (Ph.D. diss., University of Virginia, 1970). Fairfax v. Hunter and Martin are discussed in Part II, chapter 4, pp. 513–18; chapter 5, pp. 554–57; chapter 7, pp. 597–98.

Assembly, but litigation continued in both Virginia and federal courts until 1816. One might suggest that judicial activity was in many respects merely the continuation of political controversy by other methods.

With the establishment of government under the federal Constitution and the evolution of a party system after 1795, the tendency towards political aims in the conduct of federal judicial business became even more pronounced. The Virginia dispute over debts owed by citizen planters to their former British mercantile suppliers was deeply tainted by hatred for British customs and bitter remembrance of wartime atrocities in the Old Dominion. John Marshall's legal defense of Virginia debtors doubtless provided the key to political popularity that saw him elected to the General Assembly and ultimately to the federal Congress in a predominantly Republican electoral district.[64] Political issues were frequently resolved in the courts, and it is not surprising that Federalist leaders sought to apply criminal sanctions to stem the tide of rising opposition strength. Unaware of the pitfalls inherent in using old mechanisms to combat new conditions of partisan politics, Federalist judges assumed that they might continue to cross the borderline between private law and popular politics with impunity.[65] As we have seen, the judges on the Supreme Court Bench in 1801, with the exception of Washington and Moore, had been raised to the Bar in the colonial period, and most had served as judges under the royal government or the Revolutionary State governments. Their conception of the place of judges in politics and in the profession was dangerously out of step with the realities of American public opinion and Republican political thought in the 1790s.

Similar insensitivity to changed circumstances clouded Republican perceptions of the Supreme Court, bringing on what may seem, in retrospect, to be an intemperate and malicious attack upon the Court and its personnel. As we have seen previously, impeachment and legislative alteration of the organization, jurisdiction, and administration of the Court, were steps designed to bring the judges to heel. It was anticipated that they would become loyal servitors of Republican policies and constitutional views, even as in bygone days they had supported the

---

[64] Baker, *John Marshall*, 157–63; in discussing Marshall's congressional campaign Baker does not give weight to the British debt cases in Marshall's practice. *Ibid.*, 303–14. See Cullen and Johnson, eds., *Marshall Papers*, II, 248–49.

[65] Concerning the activities of Justice Chase in the trial of cases under the Sedition Act see J. Smith, *Freedom's Fetters: The Alien and Sedi-*tion Laws and American Civil Liberties (Ithaca, 1956), 184–87, 326, 342–44. After Jefferson's election Chase continued to comment on political themes in his charges to grand juries. Beveridge, *Life of John Marshall*, III, 169–70; C. Bowers, *Jefferson in Power: The Death Struggle of the Federalists* (Cambridge, Mass., 1936), 268–74; Corwin, *Marshall*, 70–71.

positions of the Federalist party. When the Republican party assumed legislative and executive control it was faced with the possibility that a Federalist Supreme Court might paralyze the government for partisan political purposes. Neither the limitations, nor the extent, of judicial power had been tested during Federalist hegemony, and it ill suits the objective historian to discount the magnitude of the threat perceived by President Jefferson and his followers. As it was staffed on March 4, 1801, the Supreme Court loomed as the major stumbling block to the entire Republican legislative program.

After 1801 there occurred the assault upon judicial independence detailed previously; and simultaneously, or as a consequence of that attack, there was a marked alteration in judicial style on one hand and a judicially created distinction between law and politics on the other hand. Certainly by 1810 it was clear from the decisions of the Supreme Court that except to the degree that Republican legislation disregarded the legal rights of individual citizens, it would bind the Supreme Court in matters of policy and on political questions.

The change in judicial style is best demonstrated by a brief reference to the previously discussed impeachment trial of Samuel Chase. During the course of that proceeding Chief Justice Marshall had been subpoenaed to testify as to Chase's treatment of counsel appearing before him in the Circuit Court for Virginia. Contemporary reports characterized the Chief Justice's behavior on the stand as highly agitated and modest to the point of submissiveness.[66] Quite possibly this demeanor was the product of apprehension for the future of the Supreme Court should Chase be convicted of the impeachment by the Senate; and indeed contemporaries stated that in the event of a successful impeachment of Judge Chase,[67] Marshall's name soon would appear on a House-sponsored impeachment charge. However, on second glance, it seems more likely that Marshall himself found little to praise in his colleague's treatment of counsel or his conduct of trials under the Sedition Acts or in regard to the Fries rebellion in Pennsylvania. In temperament, Marshall was compassionate and gentlemanly; one finds it difficult to imagine his abusing a lawyer from the Bench. Indeed, at least once in Marshall's career as Chief Justice, he served as intermediary for Judge Joseph Story, who inadvertently offended a sensitive lawyer by characterizing the attorney's arguments as "subtle."[68] So

---

[66] Bowers, *Jefferson in Power*, 284–86; Beveridge, *Life of John Marshall*, III, 192–96.

[67] Beveridge, *Life of John Marshall*, III, 155–62, 176–79.

[68] L. Tazewell to J. Marshall, Jan. 18, 1827; Marshall to Tazewell, Jan. 19, 1827; Tazewell to Marshall, Jan. 20, 1827, Collection of Littleton Wickham, Richmond, Va.; Marshall to Tazewell, Jan. 20, 1827, Collection of Thomas B. Marshall, Westchester, Pa. (Photocopies in files of The Papers of John Marshall, College of William and Mary, Williamsburg, Va.).

concerned was Marshall for the feelings of counsel before the Supreme Court that even this teapot tempest seemed worthy of his attention.

Much more than matters of judicial style and decorum or the personality of the Chief Justice called for reform of the old mixture of law and politics in Court activities. In retrospect it is easy to see that the very essence of sound republican government required more than a nominal separation of powers between the federal courts and the political arms of the federal state. John Jay had recognized this early in his career as the first Chief Justice when he refused to provide an advisory office opinion at the request of President George Washington.[69] Subsequently, the judges had declined to serve as itinerant administrators of the Revolutionary War pension system.[70] These initial and tentative steps towards asserting a distinction between judicial and political power should not be overemphasized, for it is quite clear that while a single party dominated all branches of the government the likelihood of serious conflict was small. The rise of a two-party system made it necessary that the role of the judiciary be redefined, freed of the straitjacket of colonial practices, and made adaptable to the new environment of political party conflict. Either the Supreme Court would become an adjunct of the legislative power, subject to removal upon each change in control of Congress, or it would become an independent tribunal limited to the consideration of matters of law and those constitutional constructions required within the federal system or for the protection of the fundamental rights of American citizens.

Traditionally *Marbury* v. *Madison* has been viewed as the activist beginning of John Marshall's establishment of the Supreme Court as the instrument of judicial review of federal legislation. While that interpretation may be substantially correct, it is equally true that *Marbury* was the foundation upon which the Court announced a rule of law that would bind not only litigants but the Court itself in the enunciation and explication of the federal Constitution. In *Marbury* the Court denied itself an original jurisdiction in the area of the prerogative writ of mandamus. Standing alone *Marbury* might suggest a deft use of self-denial of original jurisdiction for the purpose of endowing the Supreme Court with the power of judicial review. Yet such an interpretation must give us pause. The Court demonstrated in less prominently noted cases that it was reluctant to extend its jurisdiction beyond the bound-

---

[69] T. Jefferson to Justices of the Supreme Court, July 18, 1793; Justices of the Supreme Court to G. Washington, July 20, 1793, in H. Johnston, ed., *Correspondence and Public Papers of* *John Jay*, 4 vols. (New York, 1890), III, 486–88.

[70] Hayburn's Case, 2 Dall. 409–10 (S. Ct. U.S. 1792).

aries prescribed by the statutes of Congress. For example in *Peisch* v. *Ware*,[71] the Court upheld the decision of a Delaware State court in an arbitration fixing a salvage award. Under the federal Constitution admiralty and maritime jurisdiction was given to the federal courts, but the Judiciary Act of 1789 contained a "saving clause" reserving to the States that maritime jurisdiction theretofore exercised by them as a common law remedy. Although the constitutional question was not raised in *Peisch*, it is clear that had the Court been grasping for enhancement of its powers, it would have been reluctant to give countenance to the validity of the State salvage award, and inclined to find either the State statute contrary to the Judiciary Act, or the Judiciary Act contrary to the Constitution. As we shall see later,[72] the decisions of the Court in areas of its own, and other federal court, jurisdiction tend in these years to be restrictive rather than expansive.[73] As John Marshall commented in *Bank of the United States* v. *Deveaux*, "The duties of this court, to exercise jurisdiction where it is conferred, and not to usurp it where it is not conferred, are of equal obligation."[74] Self-restraint and extreme caution in asserting jurisdiction characterized the Supreme Court from 1801 to 1815, and the same might be said of its opinions in the fields of substantive law.

In exploring the Supreme Court's work in substantive law we must be careful not to be trapped into drawing a sharp dividing line between public constitutional law and the more mundane concerns of private law. Indeed one of the historiographical problems in studying law in the early Republic has been the lack of serious scholarly attention to the impact of constitutional change upon private law and practice. Turning to *Marbury* we may find the beginnings of the Supreme Court's development of a rule of law that would distinguish matters of fundamental private right which had to be protected under any free, republican form of government, and those matters that although they impinged upon the use of private property, nevertheless were firmly within the ambit of executive or legislative prerogative, and thus beyond judicial scrutiny. Discussing the availability of mandamus against an executive officer, Chief Justice Marshall observed that the Secretary of State acted in two capacities. As the agent of the President and the

---

[71] 4 Cranch 347–66 (1808).

[72] See Part II, chapter 8.

[73] In considering its own original and appellate jurisdiction the Supreme Court sought positive grants of judicial power, first from the Constitution and secondly from congressional statutes. In Kempe's Lessee v. Kennedy, 5 Cranch 173 at 185 (1809), Chief Justice Marshall wrote that "the courts of the United States are all of limited jurisdiction, and their proceedings are erroneous, if the jurisdiction be not shown upon them."

[74] 5 Cranch 62 at 87 (1809).

executor of public policy, he would not be subject to mandamus; but as the keeper of the Great Seal and recorder of deeds and patents, he was a mere ministerial officer, and subject to such a court order to perform his official duties.[75] It was in keeping with American institutions that ministerial functions might be subjected to judicial direction when citizens were unconstitutionally wronged by the officer's recalcitrance or when in situations like the Burr case, the constitutional right to a fair trial required executive responsiveness to a *subpoena duces tecum*. This Marshall explicitly upheld in his opinion. What he left without undue emphasis was the obvious countervailing proposition— that as an executor of public policy the Secretary of State was beyond the reach of judicial power.

One case is inadequate to draw even a vague boundary line between politics and law, thereby identifying those situations where the judiciary may properly interpose its authority between the citizen and the political branches of government. We must look beyond the familiar words of *Marbury* for greater precision. The international law case *Schooner Exchange* v. *McFaddon*[76] provides a nice juxtaposition of law against politics. The *Exchange* was an American vessel that had been taken as prize by a French privateer and re-outfitted for war against Britain and her allies. She sailed as a French warship under the command of an officer of Emperor Napoleon's Navy. While in Philadelphia under the distress of weather, she was libeled by her original owner, who challenged the validity of her condemnation and demanded the return of his property. On behalf of the claimant it was urged that no relief from this injustice would be available outside the United States. Within the jurisdiction of the United States the government's authority was plenary, and therefore competent to adjudicate property rights in the vessel. While Marshall chose to ignore Alexander Dallas' countering argument for the United States (that admitting the claim would amount to a judicial declaration of war against France),[77] he doubtless felt the persuasive weight of that reasoning. He based his opinion upon the proposition that a seizure of a public armed vessel of another sovereign was contrary to international law and custom. To do so without previous notice would violate the national faith.[78] Presumably some action by Congress or the President would be necessary in Marshall's opinion before federal courts might authorize this form of retribution. As a result the original American owner was denied recovery.

---

[75] Marshall's opinion in 1 Cranch 137, 158, closely follows the argument of Charles Lee, counsel for Marbury, at 139–40, 149–50. On these points it is helpful to refer to Part I, chapter 6, pp. 191–92.

[76] 7 Cranch 116–47 (1812).

[77] *Ibid.*, 126.

[78] *Ibid.*, 137.

I: *Introduction: The Business of the Court*

Following the lead of the political branches of government in matters of international relations was a recurrent theme in this period. The most extreme case is *William* v. *Armroyd*,[79] an attempt to reclaim property in an American vessel seized by the French under Napoleon's 1807 Milan Decree. This decree had been declared subversive of neutral rights and international law, by means of a congressional resolution. After conceding the gross injustice of the French condemnation, and pointing to errors that were apparent on the face of the decree, Chief Justice Marshall nevertheless upheld the validity of the French prize award. Although the United States Congress had acted to condemn the Milan Decree,

> [u]nquestionably the legislature which was competent to [pass the resolution] was also competent to . . . give it effect by the employment of such means as its own wisdom would suggest. Had one of these been, that all sentences pronounced under [the Milan Decree] should be considered as void, and incapable of changing the property they professed to condemn, this Court could not have hesitated to recognize the title of the original owner in this case.[80]

Legal interests, as in the *Schooner Exchange*, were sacrificed, but within a jurisprudential framework fashioned in part from the doctrine of separation of powers, and in part from the distinction between law and politics.

Now clearly these are matters of international law, where even high courts are inclined to follow in the wake of the political authorities, and to observe public policy set down by legislatures acting in the name of the people. They are helpful to delineate the distinction between public policy matters and private law concerns, but more probative evidence must be found elsewhere. To do this it is revealing to consider five cases involving legislative power in the domestic sphere, and legal rights affected by the exercise of that power.

Three of these cases involve inchoate liens upon private property in favor of the federal government, which operate to render titles uncertain and to impair bona fide purchases for value. The first, *United States* v. *Fisher*, involved a priority in bankruptcy accorded the United States by the short-lived bankruptcy act of 1800.[81] The bankrupt had endorsed a bill of exchange to the United States, which claimed its priority over all other creditors of his estate. Against the government, the bankrupt's trustee argued that this statutory preference was limited

---

[79] 7 Cranch 423–34 (1813).
[80] *Ibid.*, 433–34.
[81] 2 Cranch 358–405 (1804); the case has been discussed briefly in Part I, chapter 10, p. 333, and in Part II, chapter 6, pp. 585–86.

to debts owed to the United States by revenue collectors and their agents, and that, in any event, the bankruptcy act in giving the preference acted as an impairment of the obligation of contract. As we know, the contract clause of the Federal Constitution inhibits *State* laws impairing the rights of contract, but not federal laws; on the other hand, there were even at this time principles of vested rights and equity that might be brought to bear upon the peculiar circumstances of this case. In particular, it was urged that other creditors of the bankrupt could not know of an unrecorded transfer to the United States and could not fairly be subjected to this priority in bankruptcy. While Judge Bushrod Washington's dissent was a powerful statement of these objections, the Supreme Court in a majority opinion by Chief Justice Marshall declined to consider political considerations that it presumed to have been considered by the legislature when it voted upon the bankruptcy act. Concentrating on the issue of statutory construction, Marshall's opinion draws a sharp distinction between statutes that merely regulate and those that depart from the system of laws and infringe "rights" and "fundamental principles." His point deserves special quotation:

> Where rights are infringed, where fundamental principles are overthrown, where the general system of the laws is departed from the legislative intention must be expressed with irresistible clearness to induce a court of justice to suppose a design to effect such objects. But where only a political regulation is made, which is inconvenient, if the intention of the legislature be expressed in terms which . . . leave no doubt . . . it would be going a great way to say that a constrained interpretation must be put upon them, to avoid an inconvenience which ought to have been contemplated in the legislature when the act was passed, . . .[82]

In interpreting statutes the Court would assume that ambiguities should be resolved in favor of legislative continuance of the "general system of the laws" unless a clear contrary intent was manifested. Statutes that overthrew "fundamental principles" or those that infringed rights might be upheld if the intent to do so was clearly expressed. Since no constitutional question was presented in *Fisher*, the Chief Justice did not proceed to the conclusion basic to a law-politics distinction—that when a right infringed by statute was so fundamental as to be guaranteed by the Constitution, the statute would be unconstitutional.

While it blurs the connection between legislative intent and constitutional limitations on legislative power, Marshall's position in *United States* v. *Fisher* nevertheless suggests that there is a distinction between legislative action that overthrows certain "fundamental principles" and

---

[82] *Ibid.*, 390.

legislative acts that are merely "political regulation." In 1804 we do not yet find the Supreme Court equating those "fundamental principles" with tangible rights of citizens, such as the constitutional guarantees to vested rights in private property, but the statement of the distinction is an important preliminary to that later stage of constitutionalism.

If *United States* v. *Fisher* represents a hard case for decision between private rights and public regulation, the twin cases of *The Mars* and *United States* v. *1960 Bags of Coffee* (representing the cargo of *The Mars*) raise the point in an even more vexing situation. On her outward journey *The Mars* had breached the provisions of the Non-Intercourse Act of June 28, 1809, and thereby incurred immediate forfeiture to the United States. However, she was neither apprehended nor condemned, but proceeded on her voyage, in the course of which she was sold to a bona fide purchaser for value. As we shall later see,[83] the Supreme Court upheld the forfeiture, reasoning that since title vested in the United States when *The Mars* left port, no ownership rights could be transferred to the innocent purchaser. From this majority opinion Judge Story dissented, claiming that such secret forfeitures would have a deleterious effect upon commerce within the United States and abroad.

Taken in the aggregate, it seems clear that *United States* v. *Fisher* in 1804 and *The Mars* and *United States* v. *1960 Bags of Coffee* in 1814[84] demonstrate a willingness upon the part of the Supreme Court to subordinate private property interests to congressional statutes designed to advance a specifically identified public policy or regulation. At the same time, in the dissenting opinions in those cases, and even in the text of the majority opinions, there are statements that would indicate some outer limits to those regulations that Congress may make.

The Yazoo land fraud case, *Fletcher* v. *Peck*,[85] is the leading case in this period for the limitation of legislative discretion. An apparently contrived action upon a covenant of title, *Fletcher*, it will be recalled, was designed to test the ownership of land speculators whose predecessors in title had helped to bribe the Georgia legislature and had secured a large patent including most of the rich farmlands now in the States of Mississippi and Alabama. When the reformed legislature, elected in the wake of the scandal, repealed the land grant, the speculators took the matter to a variety of courts, and it eventually reached the Supreme Court for decision in 1810. Chief Justice Marshall in his

---

[83] See Part II, chapter 6, pp. 571–72.
[84] United States v. Brigantine Mars, 8 Cranch 417–18 (1814); United States v. 1960 Bags of Coffee, 8 Cranch 398–416 (1814).

[85] 6 Cranch 87–148 (1810). See discussion in Part I, chapter 10, pp. 337–53.

majority opinion upheld the power of the Georgia legislature to make the grant, but denied its power to repeal the statute granting the land. "When . . . a law is in its nature a contract, when absolute rights have vested under that contract; a repeal of the law cannot devest those rights; . . ."[86] Certain "great principles of justice, whose authority is universally acknowledged," prevented such a revocation of the land grants. Marshall refused to endorse the hazardous constitutional principle that "a legislature may, by its own act, devest the vested estate of any man whatever, for reasons which shall, by itself, be deemed sufficient."[87] The Constitution of the United States had been adopted as a shield to protect the people "and their property from the effects of those sudden passions to which men are exposed."[88]

In *Terrett* v. *Taylor*,[89] the case involving glebe lands of the Episcopal parish at Alexandria, Virginia, the problem of vested property rights was again debated in the Supreme Court. In the wake of the American Revolution the Commonwealth of Virginia had at first granted corporate charters to former Anglican parishes; in 1786 this incorporation was revoked by legislative act and somewhat later the parish glebe lands were by statute transferred from the parishes to the county overseers of the poor. For the Supreme Court, Judge Joseph Story held the transfer of the glebe lands "utterly inconsistent with a great and fundamental principle of republican government, the right of citizens to the free enjoyment of their property legally acquired."[90] The revocation violated the fundamental laws of every free government, the spirit and letter of the federal Constitution and the case law in every respectable judicial tribunal.[91]

Both *Fletcher* v. *Peck* and *Terrett* v. *Taylor* involve State legislation found to be violative of the contract clause and the doctrine of vested property rights. As has been seen, the opinions of the Court do not provide guidance concerning the manner in which *federal* legislation would be judged, although we do find indications of some vague limits upon the exercise of federal legislative power. In matters of international relations and in the setting of domestic regulatory legislation, the Supreme Court was willing to accept policy guidelines established by Congress. The Court sought a constitutional or legislative foundation for its own jurisdiction and for the powers of the inferior federal courts. This tacit recognition of the authority of Congress over

---

[86] 6 Cranch 135.

[87] *Ibid.*, 134. However, in line with the previously discussed view of political regulations by the legislature, Marshall asserted that the motives of the Georgia legislature could not be inquired into by the judiciary.

[88] *Ibid.*, 137–38.

[89] 9 Cranch 43–55 (1815). See the discussion in Part II, chapter 6, pp. 580–81.

[90] 9 Cranch 50–51.

[91] *Ibid.*, 52.

a wide spectrum of political matters was entirely in accord with Jeffersonian views of legislative supremacy. Yet at the same time the early Marshall Court began to assert the supremacy of the federal government over the States and the limitations that the federal Constitution imposed upon State legislative activity. Thus the federal system itself provided a vehicle for the expansion of the principle of constitutional limits upon government, without provoking a clash between the judiciary and Congress in regard to legislative omnipotence at the federal level.

The distinction between politics and law is inherently imprecise and was certainly so in the years between 1801 and 1815. Nevertheless the cases we have considered indicate that the Supreme Court judges tended to view their function as one of balancing those two conflicting values in American constitutional government. While fundamental private rights were for the most part shielded from State legislation, the dissents in *United States* v. *Fisher* and *United States* v. *1960 Bags of Coffee* indicate that there was strong debate on the question of the limitations upon congressional powers of legislation. The fact that the Supreme Court did not strike down the harsh legislation represented by those cases is perhaps the strongest evidence that a distinction was being observed between political action and private law. When the two conflicted, the Supreme Court strained to uphold the constitutionality and soundness of federal legislation, and it was only the most extreme exercises of legislative power that provoked its invalidation of State legislation. Abridgement of private property interests would be permitted to go to extreme levels, but there was a limit beyond which the fundamental principles of republican and free government would be threatened. In *Fletcher* v. *Peck* and *Terrett* v. *Taylor* the Supreme Court judged that the threshold had been passed and declared that as a matter of law the State statutes involved violated the federal Constitution.

It would be excessive to assert that this distinction between politics and law was the only foundation upon which the early Marshall Court built its institutional strength. Obviously the change in judicial personnel, the addition of federal territories (including the very important District of Columbia), and the rising importance of the federal circuit courts all were significant factors and cannot be ignored. Yet these cases and several others tend to support the proposition that the distinction was present in the minds of the judges and influential in their decisions. In restricting the work of the Supreme Court to matters of law, the judges limited the likelihood of controversy with the political branches of the federal government. By all standards of Anglo-American history and common law practice the retreat into private law and constitutional guarantees of fundamental rights was strategically wise. It insured that the Supreme Court had a firm power base upon which to enunciate its occasional pronouncements of constitutional limitations upon legislative power. To paraphrase John Marshall in *McCulloch* v. *Maryland,* the Supreme Court was of limited jurisdiction and of competence restricted to matters of private right, but within that limited sphere it was supreme in federal matters.[92]

CONCLUSION

The Supreme Court from 1801 to 1815 experienced a number of changes—in its mode of conducting its business, in the nature of its judges (in terms of age, ability, and political affiliations), and in its view of its role in the system of American government. To deny that external pressures influenced these developments would be foolish, but to consider these matters as being entirely a product of political attack and public obloquy is to miss important aspects of the institutional growth of the Court. In a sense the Court under Marshall had accepted a sharply diminished role in politics, but in so limiting its activities it had secured a better control of law, the jurisdiction to which it had undoubted entitlement. Removing itself from partisan politics, it entrenched itself as the constitutional guardian of individual rights against the excesses and vagaries of popular government in a disturbingly new egalitarian age. In beating a strategic retreat before the armies of Jeffersonian legislators, the judges arrived at a delineation of judicial power such that even their detractors were forced to concede the validity of their pretensions, and Republican judges found incumbent Federalist judges to be of one mind with them. Upon this consensus was built the foundations of the Supreme Court of the United States as we know it today.

---

[92] While diversity-of-citizenship cases do not technically fit into the supremacy concept, as that jurisdiction was administered prior to the Civil War it was guided by the view that demanded that strangers in a State forum must not be dealt with unfairly. Hence any local customs that biased the trial of a diversity case were invalidated by supervening federal or international customs. R. Bridwell and R. Whitten, *The Constitution and the Common Law* (Lexington, Mass., 1977), 61–68.

CHAPTER II

Illegal Trade and Prize Cases

T HE EARLY YEARS of the Marshall Court were dominated by the influx of appeals from prosecutions for illegal trade and by prize cases arising during the War of 1812. Such a preponderance of business in these areas, amounting to at least 32 percent of all cases, gave the jurisprudence of the Court an international flavor, and provided it with an opportunity to exercise jurisdiction in fields traditionally beyond State concerns. On the other hand the Supreme Court's opinions in these areas placed it in constant danger of conflict with the President and Congress, and required a careful delineation of the role of the Court, not only in regard to the constitutional separation of powers but also in connection with its position as the highest court of the law of nations in the United States.

The opinions in the field of illegal trade provide evidence of the diligence of the Supreme Court judges in assisting with the enforcement of the various Non-Intercourse Acts and the Embargo. Excluded from that section of this chapter but included within the subsequent section on prize jurisdiction are cases dealing with illegal trade in time of war. Marine insurance cases revolving around the principles of prize law or the prohibitions on trade have been touched upon as necessary in this chapter, but full discussion of the subject of marine insurance has been deferred to the following chapter. In addition, the consideration of the principles of military salvage has been deferred to the section on civil salvage in the next chapter. This arrangement should provide the most succinct introduction to the field, although it admittedly ignores certain categorizations long accepted in the legal profession. As an example, marine insurance has long been considered a topic of common law cognizance, despite its infusion of principles into and from admiralty and prize law. Its inclusion in close proximity to admiralty and prize cases casts greater light upon the evolution of all of these fields of law and permits easy cross-reference by the reader.

ILLEGAL TRADE IN PEACE
AND "QUASI-WAR"

The use of commercial sanctions for economic, political, and diplomatic advantage was a well established custom in late-eighteenth-century America. Equally well entrenched was a national penchant for smuggling. And the alteration of the American provinces from royal colonies to independent States did not diminish the force of either tradition. Indeed, within a few years after the end of the War for Independence American leaders who had opposed the economic impact of the English Navigation Acts, or who had railed against English suppression of illegal trade, were themselves responsible for the reestablishment of a mercantile system for the American States and the enforcement of trade regulations by sanctions against smuggling.[1] Conversely, those merchants whose inclinations ran in the direction of dangerous, but profitable, trade on the outskirts of the law resumed their smuggling activities. In a sense the presence of illegal trade cases on the docket of the Marshall Court may be considered merely the continuum of an old tradition into the nineteenth century.

Improvising upon this hallowed tradition of trade regulation for commercial and diplomatic advantage, the United States government during the Napoleonic Wars began to use non-importation as a method of dealing with depredations upon her commerce by the leading maritime powers. As a lever to secure respect for American neutral rights, trade sanctions proved to be less effective than anticipated, resulting in eventual American involvement in an undeclared "Quasi-War" against the newly established Republic of France.

Unlike the American Revolution the "Quasi-War" with France from 1797 to 1800 was a limited state of belligerence that lacked the international status of a declared war.[2] American naval action was predicated not upon the international rules of war but rather upon statutory authorizations from Congress that permitted the President to utilize public armed vessels and privateers to curtail the depredations committed upon American commerce by French privateers.[3] At the outset the lack of a United States Navy coupled with increased American trade in the West Indies served to encourage French privateers to

---

[1] See M. Peterson, "Thomas Jefferson and Commercial Policy, 1783–1793," *William and Mary Quarterly*, 3rd Series, XXII (1965), 584 et. seq., for an analysis of Jefferson's thought on free trade and mercantilist regulation.

[2] A. DeConde, *The Quasi-War: The Politics and Diplomacy of the Undeclared War with France 1797–1801* (New York, 1966), 89–90.

[3] *Ibid.*, 74–108.

prey on American neutral shipping. With the failure of the XYZ Mission to France in 1798 the Adams administration took steps to protect American shipping against French privateers through an accelerated program of naval construction, and by the enactment of a series of statutes passed to implement a policy of defensive warfare.[4] Initially the Act of May 28, 1798, authorized the President to direct the commanders of naval vessels to seize and bring into port for condemnation those French ships found off the coast of the United States committing depredations on American commerce.[5] This Act was supplemented and enlarged by the Act of June 28, 1798, which provided a detailed system for the distribution of prize awards that would encourage the capture of ships more powerful in armament and size than the capturing vessel.[6] The Act for the Government of the Navy, passed on March 2, 1799, in addition to establishing rules of discipline for the naval service, made express provision for prize distributions and bounty money to officers and crew of public armed vessels of the United States.[7]

While a substantial number of prize cases were tried in the federal circuit courts,[8] the matters that reached the Supreme Court of the United States involved the attempts of naval officers to enforce the Non-Intercourse statutes enacted by Congress to prohibit American trade with the French Republic. The first of these three statutes interdicted vessels owned, hired, or employed, wholly or in part, by American residents, from trading directly or indirectly with territories belonging to the French Republic; it also provided for the cessation of trade between French possessions and the United States by means of French vessels. On seizure and condemnation of American vessels found in violation of the Act, one-half of the proceeds would become the property of the United States with the balance being awarded to the informer who would prosecute. French vessels trading in contravention of the Non-Intercourse statute were to be held and detained by the collector of customs until such time as they departed the United States without unloading their cargoes.[9]

The second Non-Intercourse statute, enacted on February 9, 1799,

---

[4] *Ibid.*

[5] An Act More Effectually to Protect the Commerce and Coasts of the United States, May 28, 1798, 1 Stat. 561.

[6] An Act in Addition to the Act More Effectually to Protect the Commerce and Coasts of the United States, June 28, 1798, 1 Stat. 574–75.

[7] An Act for the Government of the Navy of the United States, March 2, 1799, 1 Stat. 709–17, particularly sec. 6, at pp. 715–16.

[8] A total of ninety-five prizes were taken, resulting in seventy condemnations valued in excess of $700,000. G. Allen, *Our Naval War with France* (Boston, 1909), 222.

[9] An Act to Suspend the Commercial Intercourse Between the United States and France, and the Dependencies Thereof, June 13, 1798, 1 Stat. 565–66.

continued the same restrictions upon American trading vessels traveling to French possessions and French ships arriving in the United States. However, it went beyond the terms of the 1798 Act by permitting the President to instruct commanders of public armed vessels that they might stop any ship or vessel of the United States on the high seas to determine whether it was trading in violation of the Non-Intercourse Act. This represented an extension of an American municipal regulation to the high seas, but of course the application of naval power was expressly limited to ships owned by citizens or residents of the United States. Vessels so stopped and suspected of violating the statute were to be sent to the nearest port in the United States, and if found guilty were to be subject to the same forfeiture provisions as those applicable to vessels arrested in American ports or coastal waters.[10]

Last among the Non-Intercourse Acts of the "Quasi-War" period was the statute passed on February 27, 1800. The provisions concerning American vessels involved in prohibited trade were retained in substantially the same form as in the earlier acts, except that voyages from French territories as well as those *to* French possessions were interdicted. In addition, cargoes arriving in the United States from France in French bottoms were subjected to forfeiture rather than mere denial of entry.[11] The expanding scope of the Non-Intercourse Acts, paralleling a similar trend in the statutes authorizing reprisals on French armed vessels, provided ample latitude for the application of growing American naval power. Yet throughout the "Quasi-War" naval action was directed not against French commerce per se but rather towards reprisal against French armed vessels and the enforcement of commercial sanctions. As a result of this emphasis, the French armed vessels taken as prize were summarily handled in the lower federal courts, while issues concerning violation of the Non-Intercourse Acts were sufficiently complicated that appeal to the Supreme Court of the United States was necessary in four instances.

Since sanctions of the Non-Intercourse Acts were imposed solely against vessels owned by citizens or residents of the United States, the issue of citizenship and nationality was paramount on the adjudication of these appeals before the Supreme Court.

Two of the four Non-Intercourse cases involved one Jared Shattuck, a native-born American who in about 1790 had taken up residence in St. Thomas, a Danish possession in the West Indies. Subsequently

---

[10] An Act Further to Suspend the Commercial Intercourse Between the United States and France and the Dependencies Thereof, Feb. 9, 1799, 1 Stat. 613–16.

[11] An Act Further to Suspend the Commercial Intercourse Between the United States and France, and the Dependencies Thereof, Feb. 27, 1800, 2 Stat. 7–11.

naturalized as a Danish subject,[12] Shattuck purchased two American bottoms, the *Jane*, subsequently known as the *Charming Betsey*, and the *Mercator*. The recent American registry of the ships, coupled with their owner's nativity, resulted in their seizure by two warships of the United States Navy under the provisions of the 1800 Non-Intercourse Act. First among those cases was *Murray* v. *The Charming Betsey*, considered by the Supreme Court in 1804 on appeal from decrees in the District and Circuit Court of the United States for Pennsylvania that restored the vessel and cargo, the Circuit Court awarding damages equally between the parties.[13] Bound to Guadeloupe from St. Thomas she was seized by a French privateer, and two days later captured by the libelant, captain of the American frigate *Constellation*. On behalf of the claimant it was argued that the *Constellation* had no right to take an unarmed vessel from the possession of the French, and that since the *Charming Betsey* was a neutral vessel and not an American ship, she was not subject to the provisions of the Non-Intercourse Act, which was a mere municipal regulation.[14] Consequently they asserted that Captain Murray's seizure had been unlawful and he should bear the damage arising from his wrongful act and prosecution. In reply counsel for the Navy captain contended that he had the right to take an unarmed neutral vessel out of the possession of the French, since this was an incident growing out of the state of war between the two nations. The Non-Intercourse Act, they contended, was not a municipal regulation, but rather a war measure arising out of the hostilities between the United States and France.

Without directly deciding the character of the third Non-Intercourse Act in international law, Chief Justice Marshall for the Court observed that it should be construed so that, whenever possible, it would not conflict with the law of nations as applied in the United States. Upon examining the terms of the statute he failed to find any prohibition against the sale of American commercial vessels to neutrals.[15]

---

[12] Shattuck's citizenship and status under the Non-Intercourse Acts was subjected to considerable discussion by counsel in Murray v. Charming Betsey, 2 Cranch 64–126 (1804); Maley v. Shattuck, 3 Cranch 458–92 (1806); and the opinions contributed to the establishment of rules of commercial domicile, discussed in Part II, chapter 4, p. 522.

[13] 2 Cranch 64–124 (1804). The decree in the District Court is printed at 64–71 and the Circuit Court decree, affirming in part and reversing in part, is excerpted at 71.

[14] The case was argued at the 1803 term on behalf of claimants, who were represented by Luther Martin, Philip Barton Key and Jeremiah Mason. *Ibid.*, 70–75. On reargument in 1804 claimant was represented by Philip Barton Key, *ibid.*, 91–109, and Luther Martin, *ibid.*, 112–15. Libellant did not appear in 1803, but when the case was reheard in 1804 he appeared with Alexander J. Dallas as his counsel, *ibid.*, 75–91.

[15] *Ibid.*, 119. In Sands v. Knox a federal collector of the revenue appealed to the Supreme Court from a

At the same time Jared Shattuck, although native born, had taken such positive steps to place himself out of allegiance to the United States that he could not be considered under the protection of the United States, and therefore he was not within the group of citizens and residents falling under the injunction of the statute.[16] Finding but slight basis in the ship's papers for the seizure by Captain Murray, the Chief Justice was nevertheless reluctant to award damages against him, since he had acted in good faith, upon correct motives and from a sense of duty.[17] Thus the *Charming Betsey* was restored to her owner, but the damages remained divided between the libelant and the claimant, as established in the circuit court.[18]

Jared Shattuck's second involvement in litigation before the Supreme Court began when his schooner the *Mercator* was stopped by the United States armed schooner *Experiment* and seized for violation of the same Non-Intercourse Act.[19] Suspecting her of illegal trade and of being an American vessel, Lieutenant William Maley as commander of the *Experiment* sent the *Mercator* to his squadron commander; en route she was captured by a British privateer and subsequently condemned as prize in a Jamaica vice admiralty court. At the time she was condemned there was a state of peace between the United States, Great Britain, and Denmark.

Shattuck filed his libel in the United States District Court for Pennsylvania, asking that Maley file a libel against him and that damages be assessed against the naval officer for the loss he had sustained by Maley's unlawful seizure.[20] The libel was denied by the district court, but upon reversal by the circuit court, a rehearing was had and damages were awarded against Maley. From the affirmance of this decree

---

tort judgment imposed for his wrongful enforcement of the 1798 Non-Intercourse Act against a vessel sold bona fide to a foreign owner. Chief Justice Marshall observed that if the bona fides of the sale were not in issue the argument need progress no further, for The Charming Betsey had established that the statute did not apply to American vessels sold to foreigners before the enactment of the prohibition against the French trade. 3 Cranch 499, at 503 (1806).

[16] *Ibid.*, 116, 120. In a subsequent prosecution based upon a violation of sec. 5 of the Embargo Act of Jan. 9, 1808, the Supreme Court in a per curiam opinion upheld the condemnation of a vessel as a foreign vessel

since she had been captured and condemned and her new owner, although an American, had obtained a Danish burgher's brief. On these facts the ship, although originally American, was held properly condemned as a foreign bottom. Schooner Good Catharine v. United States, 7 Cranch 349 (1813).

[17] *Ibid.*, 122–24.

[18] Decree. *Ibid.*, 125–26.

[19] Maley v. Shattuck, 3 Cranch 458–92 (1806).

[20] The libel is at *ibid.*, 458–60; Maley's protestation in reply is at *ibid.*, 466; Shattuck's replication is in *ibid.*, 466–71, partially verbatim and partially paraphrased.

by the Circuit Court for Pennsylvania Maley appealed to the Supreme Court.[21]

Chief Justice Marshall, in his opinion for the Court, stated that there was not adequate basis for the American officer's seizure of the vessel for violation of the Non-Intercourse Act, although he had ample reason to suspect her of such a transgression and to subject her to search. Consequently Lieutenant Maley was liable for the damages and loss of the vessel sustained through the illegal seizure and her subsequent capture by the British privateer.[22] On the other hand, the mere fact that she was condemned by a British vice admiralty court was not in itself conclusive evidence that the *Mercator* was a French vessel.[23] Maley had seized her not as a suspected American bottom but rather as a French merchantman suspected of illegal trade with the United States prohibited by the Non-Intercourse Act. Shattuck's failure to take a timely appeal from the Jamaica vice admiralty decree was held not to release Maley from the payment of compensation for his wrongful seizure, but it did exonerate him from the claim that he should reimburse Shattuck for the costs of his belated and ineffectual appeal in the British courts.[24]

Two years before the opinion in *Maley* v. *Shattuck* was delivered the Supreme Court, speaking through Chief Justice Marshall, had established the potential liability of American naval officers who seized vessels for violation of the Non-Intercourse Acts without probable cause. In *Little* v. *Barreme*[25] the Danish brigantine *Flying Fish* had been taken by two American frigates as she was entering the harbor at Hispaniola. Libeled for violating the 1799 Non-Intercourse Act as an American bottom, she was restored to her owner, a native of Prussia who resided in St. Thomas. It appeared that her master spoke English fluently, that the supercargo was a Frenchman, and in the course of pursuit by the American warship, her logbook and papers had been thrown overboard. On the basis of these facts the District Court of

---

[21] Although the prominent Philadelphia admiralty lawyer, Peter S. DuPonceau, represented Shattuck in the district court and circuit court, the appeal was defended in the Supreme Court by Robert Goodloe Harper, Philip Barton Key and Luther Martin. John Breckenridge, the Attorney-General, prosecuted the appeal for the Navy lieutenant. *Ibid.*, 477–87.

[22] The Charming Betsey precedent was held to govern this case. See *ibid.*, 488–91.

[23] The British decree was held entitled to the evidentiary weight it would have in England, that is, that it was evidence of the facts upon which it was based. Condemnation did not, standing alone, prove that the *Mercator* was a French vessel, for she might have been declared forfeit as a neutral upon the basis of unneutral behavior. *Ibid.*, 488.

[24] *Ibid.*, 491, 492.

[25] 2 Cranch 170–79 (1804).

Massachusetts held that no damages would be awarded to the claimant upon the restoration of the vessel, presumably because of the suspicious and unneutral behavior of the master and crew of the *Flying Fish*.[26] The circuit court reversed, holding that damages should be awarded against the American naval officer since he knew of the neutral character of the *Flying Fish* when he ordered her into Boston.[27] The Supreme Court, by Chief Justice Marshall, confirmed the circuit court, noting that the 1799 Act applied only to cargoes bound for French ports and not cargoes coming from French ports. Consequently the seizure would have been unlawful even if the *Flying Fish* had proved to be an American vessel.[28] A subsequent alteration in the text of the Non-Intercourse Act in 1800 included return voyages as well as outbound voyages within the trading prohibitions on American vessels.[29] *Little* v. *Barreme* introduced a high standard of care to be applied in judging cases involving American warship commanders who made seizures under the Non-Intercourse acts.

Chief Justice Marshall's opinion in *Little* v. *Barreme* would also become a landmark case in the continuing constitutional debate over the emergency powers of the President. By limiting the authority of naval officers to the precise terms of the Non-Intercourse statute he conceded that congressional action delimited the discretion of the President in dealing with an emergency or crisis that threatened national security. In other words, if Congress does not act, the President possesses a power that is limited only by the nature and magnitude of the situation; on the other hand, if statutory procedures are enacted by Congress for dealing with the situation, they control executive initiative. The case was cited in Judge Tom Clark's concurring opinion in *Youngstown Sheet & Tube Company* v. *Sawyer* as controlling precedent.[30]

The net result of these Supreme Court opinions was to confirm the provisions of the 1800 Non-Intercourse Act that strictly limited its application to territorial waters and vessels of American registry. Seizures were to be made only for specific violations of the precise terms of the statute; the statute in turn would be construed in such a way as to insure its conformity to the rules of international law concerning neutral trade. While this strict interpretation was too long delayed in application to have been a hindrance to the conduct of the "Quasi-War" with France, it was a reaffirmation of traditional American views concerning the rights of neutrals. More important for the period we are studying, it will be seen to form the basis for future jurisprudence in the field

---

26 Judge John Lowell's opinion, *ibid.*, 172–75.

27 Decree, *ibid.*, 175–76.

28 *Ibid.*, 176, 178–79.

29 Compare, sec. 1, 1 Stat. 613–14 (1799), with sec. 1, 2 Stat. 7–8 (1800).

30 343 U.S. 579, at 660–62 (1952).

of illegal trade, which tends to limit the extraterritorial applicability of Non-Intercourse and Embargo statutes and to treat them as being predominantly municipal in character.

THE EMBARGO IN THE SUPREME COURT

Cessation of hostilities with the French Republic in December 1800 permitted a six-year respite in the use of the Non-Intercourse weapon, but by April 18, 1806, the depredations by British warships had reached such a point that a new Non-Importation Act was passed by Congress. Ostensibly designed to prohibit the entry of British goods into the United States, the statute omitted from the list of prohibited goods many of the major commodities carried in the British-American trade. In addition, the diplomatic leverage of the Act was further decreased by the long period of time before its effective date, November 15, 1806. Even after November 1806 the ongoing negotiations between the British ministry and American diplomats in London resulted in a suspension of the provisions of the law throughout most of 1807. As a consequence no prosecutions for violation of the 1806 law reached the Supreme Court of the United States.[31]

After President Jefferson refused to send the treaty of 1806 with Great Britain to the Senate for ratification, diplomatic relations with Britain deteriorated rapidly. In January 1807 new British orders-in-council reaffirmed the practice of impressment of seamen and made clear the way for increased seizure of neutral American property; in retaliation, the President permitted the Non-Importation Act to become effective on July 1, 1807. When in September 1807 the Berlin Decree of November 21, 1806, was put into effect by the French, thereby blockading the British Isles and subjecting American vessels trading there to seizure and condemnation, additional measures were called for to maintain peace.[32]

President Jefferson turned to his thirty-year-old plan for a commercial embargo and on December 18, 1807, requested Congress to

---

[31] An Act to prohibit the importation of certain goods, wares and merchandise, Apr. 18, 1806, 2 Stat. 379–81. See B. Perkins, *Prologue to War: England and the United States 1805–1812* (Berkeley, 1961), 109–39, characterizing the Non-Importation Act of 1806 as "worse than useless" for diplomatic purposes. *Ibid.*, 113.

[32] Perkins, *Prologue to War*, 148–50. For a detailed description of the British orders-in-council see W. Jennings, *The American Embargo, 1807–1809* (Iowa City, 1931), 23–30. Jennings indicates that the effect of these orders was to subject American shipping to the same restrictions as English vessels. British policy encouraged trade with the British West Indies under certain restrictions but prohibited American trade with the French West Indies. *Ibid.*, 30–32. French retaliatory action included blockading British ports. Caught in the middle the U.S. lost 917 vessels to British warships during the years 1805–10 and 513 to the French. *Ibid.*, 37.

pass a statute completely interdicting oceanic commerce to or from the ports of the United States.[33] Four days later the statutory foundation for the Embargo was signed into law, commencing the President's "peaceable coercion"[34] of his fellow citizens. While the Embargo Act, supplemented and greatly modified by subsequent legislation, did succeed in keeping a respectable portion of American shipping off the oceans, it did not bring sufficient economic pressure to bear on either Britain or France and failed to make them desist from their depredations on American commerce.[35] On the other hand, the execution of the Embargo laws provided the most strenuous test to date of the administrative capacity of the federal government. Drawing upon the substantial bureaucracy that had been established by his Federalist predecessors in the Treasury Department and Customs Service, President Jefferson employed a veritable army of inspectors and collectors in enforcing the Embargo.[36] Those cases that reached the Supreme Court evidence their diligence, as well as their dependence upon the

[33] L. Sears, *Jefferson and the Embargo* (Durham, N.C., 1927), 59–63. Sears notes that the statute's imperfections resulted in immediate calls for amendments and that Jefferson rapidly became chief apologist for the measure which had been passed in precipitous haste by Congress. *Ibid.* See also Jennings, *American Embargo* 39–41, who notes the ineffectiveness of the first two Embargo Acts. *Ibid.*, 47.

[34] L. White, *The Jeffersonians: A Study in Administrative History, 1801–1829* (New York, 1951), 423–52, subtitles his chapter on the Embargo "An Experiment in Peaceful Coercion," based upon Henry Adams' comment in *History of the United States of America*, IV (New York, 1890), 176.

[35] While France was only marginally vulnerable to American economic sanctions, Napoleon gradually came to recognize the danger of starvation that trade restrictions imposed on his West Indian colonies. Vacillating between respect and praise for American neutrality and contempt for feeble American attempts to protect neutral rights, he felt no inclination to make exertions to win American support. Sears, *Jefferson and the Embargo*, 302–17. As to Britain, the American Embargo resulted in severe hardship in the laboring classes and manufac-

turers engaged in the textile industry; it inflated prices, particularly of foodstuffs, and deprived Britain of nearly one–third of her export market. On the other hand these economic imbalances were inadequate to move the ministry to repeal the orders–in–council. *Ibid.*, 276, 279, 288, 298; Jennings, *American Embargo*, 70–84, is in substantial agreement with these assessments. The political leaders believed that the Embargo was hurting the United States more than Britain and they also took steps to open West Indian ports to American trade, thereby encouraging illegal trade for foodstuffs essential to the survival of those colonies. Sears, *Jefferson and the Embargo*, 259–60, 281.

[36] For the organization of the Treasury Department see L. White, *The Federalists: A Study in Administrative History, 1789–1801* (New York, 1948), 116–23; White, *The Jeffersonians*, 137–40. The mainstay for enforcement of the Embargo was the local collector; for a description of the duties of this office generally, see White, *The Federalists*, 303–308, and White, *The Jeffersonians*, 148–61, especially 156–57. In northern States many collectors resigned rather than aid in enforcing the Embargo and of those who remained, several were discharged for collusion with smugglers. Jennings, *American Embargo*, 116–17.

II: *Illegal Trade and Prize Cases*

President and his Secretary of the Treasury, Albert Gallatin, for direction and advice. The Supreme Court cases also indicate the legislature's difficulty of anticipating every possible mode of evading or avoiding the prohibitions in the Embargo laws. American merchants, having inherited the smuggling propensities of their colonial forebears, were ingenious in taking advantage of technical weaknesses in the statutes as well as entering into collusive schemes for circumventing those provisions.[37] As a consequence these Embargo cases form the basis for the development of a respectable body of case law in the fields of criminal law, constitutional law, and statutory construction, as well as the foundation of the American law of illegal trade in time of peace.

The initial Embargo Act of December 22, 1807, prohibited American vessels from leaving port on foreign voyages, excepting only ships under the immediate direction of the President. A system of bonds was instituted to insure that coastal vessels departing one port of the United States for another American port would pursue their voyages as certified.[38] Shortly afterward this brief statutory prohibition was strengthened by the so-called supplementary act,[39] which continued the bonding requirements and in addition established bonding systems for fishing and whaling vessels.[40] Sanctions were provided for departing an American port without a clearance or permit, for trading with a foreign port contrary to the provisions of the Embargo Act or the supplementary act, or for trading with or trans-shipping from another vessel any articles, whether of foreign or domestic manufacture or origin.[41] In an effort to control exportations from the United States in foreign bottoms, the supplementary act prohibited under heavy penalties the lading of any specie or goods in a foreign vessel other than provisions and sea stores necessary for her voyage.[42]

Far more comprehensive in its scope and detailed in its enforcement provisions was the Embargo Act passed on March 12, 1808.[43]

---

[37] For evidence from both British and American official sources see Jennings, *American Embargo*, 117–22. In U.S. v. Tyler, 7 Cranch 285 (1812), a Vermont resident was held properly fined for loading nineteen barrels of potash into carriages for transportation to Canada contrary to the Embargo Act of Jan. 9, 1809.

[38] An Act laying an Embargo on all ships and vessels in the ports and harbors of the United States, Dec. 22, 1807, 2 Stat. 451–53.

[39] An Act supplementary to the Act intituled, "An Act laying an embargo on all ships and vessels in the ports and harbors of the United States," Jan. 9, 1808, 2 Stat. 453–54. See Jennings, *American Embargo*, 46–47, for a convenient summary of the provisions of this Act.

[40] Sec. 2, 2 Stat. 453.

[41] Sec. 3, 2 Stat. 453–54.

[42] Sec. 5, 2 Stat. 454.

[43] An Act in addition to the Act intituled, "An Act supplementary to the Act, intituled An Act laying an embargo on all ships and vessels in the ports and harbors of the United States," Mar. 12, 1808, 2 Stat. 473–75. For legislative history and a summary see Jennings, *American Embargo*, 47–50.

Again this statute modified but did not repeal either the original Embargo Act of December 22, 1807, or the supplementary act of January 8, 1808. Most significantly the new statute embodied in its provisions an interdiction of overland trade with foreign possessions, thereby reviving a provision of the 1806 Non-Importation Act that had not been included in the first two Embargo statutes.[44] The applicability of the Embargo Acts to foreign vessels leaving American ports was clarified, and for the first time non-American ships were required to obtain clearances and post bonds when they engaged in the American coastal trade.[45] Administration of the coastal voyage clearance was tightened by the requirement that owners and masters were required to certify the unlading of their goods in an American port within a period of from four to six months after departure, depending upon the location of that port of destination.[46]

Two exceptions to the terms of the earlier Embargo Acts were authorized by the March 1808 statute. Small vessels engaged in river and lake navigation on waters not touching international boundaries might be permitted to trade without posting bonds in certain cases, and by posting bonds in reduced amounts in other circumstances. Discretion was to be vested in the Secretary of the Treasury to determine the advisability of these exceptions. In addition, American merchants who had held goods in foreign ports as of December 22, 1807, might, upon application to the President, receive permission to send a ship in ballast to recover those goods and bring them to the United States.[47]

Slightly more than a month after the passage of this March 1808 Act, the statutory basis for the Embargo was again implemented by congressional action.[48] The Act of April 25, 1808, limited the duration of coasting voyages still further, and required the personal approval of the President before coastal voyages might be authorized to terminate in an American port adjacent to foreign territory.[49] It also eliminated all foreign bottoms from the coasting trade, and introduced special measures concerning trade on the Mississippi River.[50] Undoubtedly the most helpful addition was that which authorized collectors to seize and detain vessels concerning which they had reason to believe that a voyage in violation of the Embargo Acts was intended. This was the first authorization to permit the collectors to detain a vessel "whenever

---

[44] Compare sec. 4, 2 Stat. 474 (1808), with sec. 3, 4, at 2 Stat. 379 (1806).

[45] Sec. 1, 2 Stat. 473–74 (1808).

[46] Sec. 3, ibid., 474.

[47] Sec. 2, 7, ibid., 474, 475.

[48] An Act in addition to the Act intituled, "An Act laying an embargo on all ships and vessels in the ports and harbors of the United States," and the Several Acts supplementary thereto, and for other purposes, Apr. 25, 1808, 2 Stat. 499–502; Jennings, American Embargo, 50–53.

[49] Sec. 1, 6, 2 Stat. 499, 500.

[50] Sec. 9, 4, ibid., 500, 501.

in their opinions" there was an intention to violate the Embargo.[51] The Enforcement Act of January 9, 1809, required fifteen sections to restate, construe, and further clarify the provisions of all of the preceding Embargo Acts.[52] Although it did not purport to be a codification, nor did it expressly repeal the pre-existing Acts, for all intents and purposes it may be taken to have accomplished that purpose.

While a detailed consideration of the specific provisions of the Embargo Acts is not necessary to this study, it is helpful that they be distinguished from the 1806 Non-Importation Act on the basis of the enforcement procedures involved. The Embargo Acts authorized two distinct modes of prosecution. One, based upon the common law action of debt for breach of the conditions in an Embargo bond, resulted in cases reaching the Supreme Court of the United States on writ of error. The other, commenced as a libel in admiralty against vessel, goods, or both, proceeded to a forfeiture or restoration to be followed by an appeal in admiralty to the Supreme Court. The Non-Importation Act relied exclusively upon the admiralty proceeding for forfeiture.

The Embargo statutes, in providing two modes of procedure, also permitted courts to assert jurisdiction in two forms. Jurisdiction *in rem* might be obtained preliminary to a libel for the statutory forfeiture; on the other hand, if the vessel or goods were not available for seizure, it was possible for the prosecutor to arrest an owner and proceed *in personam* on the basis of a condition violated in the Embargo bond. According to the opinion of the Supreme Court in *U.S.* v. *The Brig Eliza*,[53] a collector might seize a vessel upon her return from a foreign voyage and proceed for forfeiture, rather than being compelled to recover against her owner or master for the amount of the Embargo bond. Thus vessels in violation of the Embargo were subject to seizure on their inbound as well as their outbound voyages.

The eleven Embargo cases that reached the Supreme Court of the United States on appeal during the period from 1810 to 1815[54] re-

---

[51] Sec. 11, *ibid.*, 501, permitted detention until the instructions of the President could be obtained concerning the vessel.

[52] An Act to enforce and make more effectual an Act intituled, "An Act laying an embargo on all ships and vessels in the ports and harbors of the United States," and the several Acts supplementary thereto, Jan. 9, 1809, 2 Stat. 506–11. While this statute may for certain purposes be considered the culmination of all prior Embargo legislation, its short period of effectiveness under the Embargo,

from its passage to Mar. 1, 1809, limits its significance to this discussion. For further discussion of the last Embargo Act see Jennings, *American Embargo*, 53–58. Jennings notes the increasing severity of the legislation and its growing complexity. *Ibid.*, 58–59.

[53] 7 Cranch 113–15 (1812), with opinion by Chief Justice Marshall.

[54] Sloop Active v. United States, 7 Cranch 100–107 (1812); Crowell v. M'Fadon, 8 Cranch 94–98 (1814); Brig James Wells v. United States, 7 Cranch 22–26 (1812); Schooner

solved a number of ambiguities in the statutes, but perhaps more important in retrospect is their value as indications of the degree of executive discretion and prosecutive flexibility that the Supreme Court was willing to tolerate when private property interests were subject to forfeiture. Indeed the factual background of those cases gives an insight into the difficulty of obtaining compliance with the terms of the statutes and the ingenuity of merchants and ship captains in circumventing the letter as well as the spirit of the Embargo. At the very earliest stage of the Embargo it had become obvious from decisions in the circuit courts that the partisan loyalties of the judges were not to play a significant role in these cases. Republican Judge William Johnson earned the enmity of President Jefferson by his decision on circuit in South Carolina.[55] In the Gilchrist case he held that the collector at Charleston should be guided solely by the terms of the Embargo Acts and not limited in his discretion by the instructions issued by the President to the collectors.[56] Consequently a mandamus was awarded to the Charleston merchant who wished to ship cotton to Baltimore directing the collector to issue a clearance upon the posting of an Embargo bond. While the circuit court opinion was attacked in the public press and defended by Judge Johnson in the same medium, it was never appealed to the Supreme Court despite the jurisdictional issues left unresolved.[57] Subsequently the use of mandamus in situations similar to *Gilchrist* was

---

Juliana v. United States, 6 Cranch 327–28 (1810); Otis v. Bacon, 7 Cranch 589–96 (1813); Otis v. Watkins, 9 Cranch 339–58 (1815); Schooner Paulina's Cargo v. United States, 7 Cranch 55–68 (1812); Brig Short Staple's Cargo v. United States, 9 Cranch 55–64 (1815); Speake v. United States, 9 Cranch 28–39 (1815); United States v. Brig Eliza, 7 Cranch 113–15 (1812); United States v. Gordon, 7 Cranch 287–88 (1813); United States v. Hall & Worth, 6 Cranch 171–76 (1810). Three of these cases, Otis v. Bacon, Crowell v. M'Fadon and Otis v. Watkins, were appeals from prosecutions of customs collectors in the Massachusetts State courts, and the remainder were appeals from federal circuit courts. Three of the cases arose from actions to collect Embargo bond penalties: Speake v. United States, United States v. Gordon, and United States v. Hall & Worth; eight were libels for condemnation from which appeals were taken.

[55] See discussion in Part I, chapter 9, pp. 298–302.

[56] Gilchrist v. Collector of Charleston, 10 Fed. Cas. 355–66 (1808), involved Presidential instructions that vessels carrying certain commodities were to be detained, thereby establishing a uniform rule of detention in those cases. By way of contrast the Act of Apr. 25, 1808, vested discretion in the collectors subject to review by the President. See the Act, 2 Stat. 501. Subsequently in Crowell v. M'Fadon and Otis v. Watkins, 9 Cranch 339–56 (1815), the Supreme Court was to affirm the broad discretionary powers of the collectors under the statutory grant.

[57] For a discussion of the newspaper accounts see C. Warren, *A History of the Supreme Court*, I (Boston, 1937), 328–29. Subsequently the decision in Gilchrist invalidating Presidential instructions to collectors was reversed by the Act of Jan. 9, 1809, sec. 10, 2 Stat. 509–10, which specifically provided for Presidential instructions and general rules to guide the collectors.

held to be outside the jurisdiction of the circuit courts under the Judiciary Act of 1789 and the Constitution.[58]

Not long after Judge Johnson's demonstration of independence in the Gilchrist case, the litigation concerning the brigantine *William* in Massachusetts federal district court provided additional evidence that the judiciary divided on legal rather than political grounds.[59] New England had long been the locus of heated opposition to the Embargo; its journalistic attacks on the federal administration, coupled with certificates of necessity freely issued by a Republican governor of Massachusetts, created a situation in which illegal trade was condoned by the authorities and protected by public opinion.[60] Despite these circumstances, it fell to District Judge John Davis, a strong Federalist appointed by John Adams, to rule favorably upon the constitutionality of the Embargo Acts.[61] While the jury failed to convict the accused in spite of clear evidence of his guilt and the judge's ruling upholding the constitutionality of the Embargo, the case nevertheless provided the Republican administration with a strong precedent to support their legislative mandate against constitutional attack.

These demonstrations of political neutrality and strictly legal resolution of issues raised by the Embargo statutes were perpetuated in the opinions of the Supreme Court. The hostility of juries to the enforcement of the Embargo laws, and not the position of the federal judiciary, was the fulcrum around which smugglers worked their acquittals. However, it did fall to the Supreme Court to construe the terms of the various Embargo Acts in appeals from both State and federal courts concerning the condemnations. It is readily apparent that poor legislative draftsmanship was responsible for the inadequacies of the first Embargo Act, and that the overlay of subsequent legislation was at best remedial and piecemeal.

---

[58] M'Intire v. Wood, 7 Cranch 504–505 (1813), with opinion by Judge Johnson.

[59] See discussion in Part I, chapter 9, pp. 305–307.

[60] Sears, *Jefferson and the Embargo*, 143–96. For Massachusetts trade under liberal licensing policies of her Governor James Sullivan see *ibid.*, 188–89, 175–77.

[61] According to John Quincy Adams constitutional attacks upon the Embargo centered around the legal position espoused by Chief Justice Theophilus Parsons of Massachusetts. See H. Adams, *Documents Relating to New England Federalism, 1800–1815* (Boston, 1877), 58, 223; H. von Holst, *The Constitutional and Political History of the United States* (Chicago, 1877), 203; W. Story, ed., *The Life and Letters of Joseph Story*, 2 vols. (Boston, 1851), I, 185. In Gibbons v. Ogden, 9 Wheat. 1–239 (1824), the Supreme Court expressly upheld federal authority to impose an Embargo upon commerce. The opinion in United States v. Brigantine William is printed in J. Thayer, ed., *Cases on Constitutional Law*, 2 vols. (Cambridge, 1895), II, 1786–94; and in *Hall's American Law Journal*, II, 255. See also Warren, *History*, I, 342–47; Adams, *History of the United States*, IV, 266; Jennings, *American Embargo*, 65–67.

The original Embargo Act and all subsequent legislation on the subject attempted to regulate traffic so as to prevent foreign shipments of goods under the guise of coastal trade. The statutes specifically recognized, however, that deviations might be necessitated by the "dangers of the seas,"[62] and that what began as legitimate coastal voyages might result in compulsory arrival at a foreign port. This exception to the Embargo laws was considered in two Supreme Court opinions, *United States* v. *Hall & Worth* and *The Brig James Wells* v. *United States.*[63] In the first case the ship, bound for Nantucket and purportedly redirected to Charleston, landed in Puerto Rico, where her goods were seized by the Spanish authorities and sold; in the second a vessel en route from Connecticut to St. Mary's, Georgia, landed at St. Bartholomews under compulsion of weather, and when the authorities prohibited the reloading of her cargo, the supercargo ordered it sold. The Supreme Court opinions in both cases assigned a rigorous burden of proof to the owner of the vessel, requiring him to prove his efforts to remain within the coastal restrictions of his Embargo bond, as well as the compulsion of weather or imminent danger of sinking that frustrated those endeavors. In the *James Wells* case Judge Washington held that the claimants had not sustained this heavy burden, and hence they must forfeit the ship under the terms of the Embargo statute. The claimants in *United States* v. *Hall & Worth* were fortunate enough to have their factual proof accepted by the trial jury, binding upon the Supreme Court in its review of the case by writ of error. However, for the government it was argued that the dangers of the sea did not include losses or transactions that might occur as a result of a vessel "weathering" over in a prohibited port. This restrictive view of the exceptions to the statute was rejected in Chief Justice Marshall's opinion, the Court holding that when the dangers of the seas placed a vessel within the control of a foreign power, and thus prevented her owners from complying with the Embargo bond, the exception would apply.[64] Subsequently the exception for distress was limited by statute to conditions not caused by the negligence of the master or crew, and in the case of captures, the seizure was required to be hostile and not collusive.

An equal or even higher degree of proof was required in regard to exceptions claimed upon the basis of the seizure of a vessel by a warship or privateer, and its subsequent condemnation and sale in a

---

[62] 2 Stat. 453 (1807).

[63] United States v. Hall & Worth, 6 Cranch 171–76 (1810); Brig James Wells v. United States, 7 Cranch 22–26 (1812).

[64] 6 Cranch 176. In Durosseau v. United States, 6 Cranch 321–23, the Court held that the destruction of the goods was not critical, but rather the impossibility which prevented her owner from unloading them in accordance with the provisions of his Embargo bond. See sec. 7, Act of Jan. 9, 1809, 2 Stat. 506 at 508–509.

foreign port. In the leading case of *Brig Short Staple and Cargo* v. *United States*,[65] Chief Justice Marshall noted that "the interest which coasting vessels had in fictitious or concerted captures undoubtedly subjects all captures to a rigid scrutiny and exposes them to much suspicion."[66] However, where the testimony was full and complete, as it presumably was found to be in this case, and where it explained and and accounted for every circumstance in a reasonable manner, the Court was forced to accept the evidence as indicative of a real capture that would amount to justification under the terms of the Embargo statutes. From this opinion Judge Story, who had decided the case in the circuit court below, and one unidentified judge, dissented.[67] Even in the absence of the more precise 1809 standards for "dangers of the seas" exceptions, the Supreme Court had held that the factual situation in each deviation had to be sustained by precise proof, and the burden of proof in all cases was placed upon the claimant. This allocation of the burden of proof made prosecutions under the Embargo law an easier matter for the government, and at the same time indicated that the Supreme Court considered the Embargo laws less in the nature of criminal statutes and more as regulations of trade.[68]

While judicial construction defined the nature of permissible exceptions to the bonding requirements, the ambiguities in the statutes also called for Supreme Court statements concerning the applicability of the statutes to particular situations. For example in the *Short Staple* case just discussed, Chief Justice Marshall held that although the express terms of the Embargo Acts of December 22, 1807, and January 9, 1808, applied only to coasting vessels and fishing ships, the prohibition against foreign trade nevertheless also applied to registered oceangoing vessels. That ruling, however, was not commented upon in the opinion, and is obvious only upon reading the arguments of counsel for the owners.[69] Marshall thus skirted this issue arising out of the ambiguities of the statute, but evidenced a willingness to construe the statute broadly in light of the congressional intention to restrict all foreign trade.

On the other hand, when the terms of the Embargo Acts were precise the Supreme Court did not scruple to disallow a condemnation based upon a broad construction of the statute. This occurred in *The Sloop Active* v. *United States*,[70] where a cod-fishing vessel was seized in New London harbor with goods loaded in her hold without the knowledge or inspection of the local revenue officer, as required by the

---

65 9 Cranch 55–64 (1815).

66 *Ibid.*, 64.

67 *Ibid.*, 64, based on his opinion in the Circuit Court.

68 Of course the Court had rejected retrospective application of the 1809 Act in United States v. Hall & Worth, 6 Cranch 171 at 174.

69 9 Cranch 55, at 57–58, 59.

70 7 Cranch 100–107 (1812).

Embargo Act of April 25, 1808. She had not cleared the harbor, and counsel successfully argued that at the time of her seizure no statute prohibited the *intention* to export goods to a foreign port, and in any event, the offense did not occur until a vessel actually cleared the port.

For the Court, Chief Justice Marshall held that clearance from the port was a necessary precondition to the offense under section 3 of the supplementary act of January 9, 1808.[71] Since the *Active* was still within the limits of the port she was not subject to forfeiture under the Embargo statutes, regardless of what might be proved of the guilty intentions of her owners or master. On the other hand, the *Active* was a cod-fishing vessel, according to her registry, and her use to carry commodities found within her hold was a violation of the provisions of section 32 of the act for enrolling and licensing ships or vessels to be used in the coasting or shipping trade, passed on February 18, 1793.[72] That section prohibited the use of a vessel in any other trade than that for which she had been licensed under penalty of forfeiture of the ship, her tackle, furniture, and cargo. He rejected the contention that the Enrollment Act was merely a measure to protect revenue, hence not applicable to ships carrying domestic goods not subject to customs. While the statute in its entirety might be directed towards such a goal, Marshall held that the provisions of section 32 were not so limited. Consequently the *Active* as well as the cargo belonging to her owners and captain were forfeited under the Enrollment Act. That portion of the cargo owned by third parties was ordered restored, and the sentence of the circuit court was reversed in this regard, but affirmed in all others.

In its next term the Supreme Court was called upon to determine when a ship arrived in a port designated in her Embargo bond as the American destination. In *Otis* v. *Bacon*[73] the ship had arrived at Yarmouth, a harbor within the Barnstable customs district in Massachusetts, but she had not yet come to anchor in Barnstable proper. Seized for violation of the Embargo, her cargo was subsequently carried away by unknown persons and sold in the West Indies without the complicity of its owners. Bacon, the owner of the vessel and cargo, brought an action in trover in the Massachusetts State courts against the collector, who defended by pleading official action under section 11 of the Embargo Act of April 25, 1808.[74] On appeal to the Supreme Court of the United States from a judgment of the Supreme Judicial Court of Massachusetts rejecting the collector's reliance upon the statute, the Court by Judge Bushrod Washington held that a collector's duty under the statute was

---

[71] 2 Stat. 453–54, (1808); the Chief Justice's opinion is in 7 Cranch 105–107 (1812).

[72] 1 Stat. 305 at 316 (1793).
[73] 7 Cranch 589–96 (1813).
[74] 2 Stat. 499 at 501.

to detain an outbound vessel that he had reason to believe was to be carried out of the country in violation of the Embargo. That authority did not extend to goods that had arrived at the port of destination specified in the clearance issued to the carrying vessel. It was sufficient for this purpose that she be in the port of destination—that is, the port district specified—and the arrival there was adequate to place her beyond the reach of a legal seizure by the collector.[75]

Otis v. *Bacon* can be conformed with difficulty with the holding in *Crowell* v. *M'Fadon*,[76] another appeal from a trover award to a shipowner wronged by the United States collector for the Barnstable district. The cases may be distinguished in that in *Otis* the detention was justified upon the basis of section 11 of the Act of April 25, 1808, while in *Crowell* the collector relied upon both section 11 and section 6.[77] The decision of the Supreme Court in *Otis* v. *Bacon* might be considered binding only in regard to departures of vessels in United States ports other than those described in section 6 as being adjacent to foreign territory. The schooner *Union* in the Crowell case was carrying cargo consigned to Passamaquoddy in Maine before the collector at the port of origin had learned the terms of the act of April 25, 1808; subsequently the destination was changed to Machias. Strong headwinds forced her into Hyannis, in the Barnstable district, where she was seized and detained for the President's decision. President Jefferson affirmed the collector's action in detaining the vessel, and the collector thereafter offered to restore the cargo to the owner or his appointed agent. The Massachusetts courts held that the detention and unlading of the vessel were illegal and assessed damages against the collector. On appeal to the Supreme Court under section 25 of the Judiciary Act of 1789, the Court in a terse opinion by Judge Duvall held the detention justifiable. Under Duvall's *Crowell* opinion collectors might seize a vessel when it entered their district and they were of the opinion that it was in the course of violating the Embargo statutes. The detention being legal, and the unlading having been done with the owner's consent, no cause of action for damages might be maintained.[78]

Without a more explicit statement of Judge Duvall's analysis, we are left to speculate concerning the effect of *Crowell* v. *M'Fadon* upon

---

[75] Cranch 593–96 (1813).
[76] 8 Cranch 94–98 (1814).
[77] Sec. 6, 2 Stat. 499, 500.
[78] 8 Cranch 94–98 (1814). The Crowell case may be distinguished from Otis v. Bacon in two other minor particulars. First, in Crowell the cargo was handled with care after seizure and hence did not find itself on the way to the West Indies. Second, in Crowell the original shipment to Passamaquoddy, a port immediately adjacent to Canada, was a ground of suspicion even though under existing law it did not violate the Embargo.

the precedent of *Otis* v. *Bacon*. Clearly he saw no conflict between the two cases since he did mention *Otis* v. *Brown* and it was not cited in argument by counsel, who argued instead the need to place a requirement of reasonableness on the exercise of the collector's discretion, or to require probable cause for the detention. An examination of the two sections involved in these cases does little to dispel the mystery concerning their divergent resolutions. Section 6 is in its express terms no broader than section 11, and seems to follow a similar pattern of restricting departures and not arrivals. In addition section 11 appears to be the broader section, since it contains a general authorization for collectors to detain "whenever in their opinions the intention is to violate . . . the provisions of the acts laying an embargo."

The official report of *Crowell* v. *M'Fadon* indicates that Judges Washington and Livingston were absent on the decision date, and that Joseph Story disqualified himself because of past professional connection with the litigation. Both Washington and Livingston had been absent during part of the argument of the case, but were on the Bench on the decision date of February 28, 1814. They therefore temporarily absented themselves to avoid being counted with the Court in the decision of the matter. As a result a total of four judges were present when the decision in *Crowell* v. *M'Fadon* was announced—Marshall, Johnson, Todd, and Duvall. Had they not all agreed in Duvall's opinion a rehearing would have been required. This may perhaps explain the laconic and delphic nature of the majority opinion. Fortunately, the repeal of the Embargo years earlier precluded the need to clarify the discrepancies between the Crowell case and the Bacon case. However, the Duvall opinion in *Crowell* may be taken as an unfortunate grant of discretion to federal officers in administering laws, for Duvall stated the following weak standard to limit their actions: "The law places a confidence in the opinion of the officer, and he is bound to act according to his opinion; and when he honestly exercises it, as he must do in the execution of his duty, he cannot be punished for it."[79] In 1815 the Supreme Court in an opinion delivered by Judge Livingston reaffirmed the broad discretionary power in collectors, based upon its previous decision in *Crowell* v. *M'Fadon*.[80] With Judge Todd absent and Chief Justice Marshall filing what may be considered a dissenting opinion, the Court held that a collector was not liable merely for having formed an incorrect opinion, or for having made it without reasonable care and diligence. Chief Justice Marshall, after conceding that the statutory language did not require "reasonable care in ascertaining the facts," nevertheless argued that it was clearly implied that such care should be

---

[79] *Ibid.*, 98.

[80] Otis v. Watkins, 9 Cranch 339–58 (1815).

utilized by the collector, and that he should take similar care to insure the accuracy of the facts transmitted to the President.[81]

While the *Active* case, supplemented by *Otis* v. *Bacon* and *Crowell* v. *M'Fadon*, established the requirement that a vessel actually leave port before she could be condemned under the Embargo statutes, a matter of jurisdiction was raised by those holdings and partially resolved by *United States* v. *The Brig Eliza*.[82] There it was contended upon appeal that once the ship was out of the jurisdiction of the United States she was no longer subject to seizure and forfeiture; only a prosecution under the Embargo bond was available to the government.

Had this argument been accepted as the law of the case, and if the requirements of *Otis* v. *Bacon* had been vigorously applied—namely that actually leaving the port limits was required to constitute an offense —the enforcement of the Embargo acts would have been exceedingly difficult. Ships would have had to be intercepted between the time they left the port boundaries and the moment they passed from territorial waters into the high seas.

Although the Supreme Court sent the case back for further proof, Chief Justice Marshall observed in his short opinion that the judges were agreed that the *Eliza* was subject to forfeiture even after her return from the foreign voyage. In addition they construed the statutory sections to mean that the offense had not been completed until the ship arrived in a foreign port.[83] Although Marshall did not pursue the matter to its logical conclusion it is clear that the Court was of the opinion that the definition of the offense as one of departing the United States and entering a foreign port, coupled with the alternative penalties of forfeiture or fine, indicated an intention on the part of Congress to make the vessel subject to seizure and forfeiture at any point on her homeward voyage or upon her arrival in an American port. Furthermore, the Supreme Court was willing to accept the statutory authority of the United States over American vessels and cargoes wherever they might be seized for violation of the Embargo laws. The situation was to be distinguished from *Rose* v. *Himely* and *Hudson* v. *Guestier*, for in those cases a foreign admiralty court had attempted to exercise maritime jurisdiction over American vessels on the high seas.[84] While the United States might assert broad jurisdiction over the ships of American

---

[81] *Ibid.*, 356–58. From this we might conclude that Chief Justice Marshall adhered to Judge Washington's holding in Otis v. Bacon and also felt that the discretion of the collectors should be restrained by a standard of reasonable care in reporting the facts for the President's decision.

[82] United States v. Brig Eliza, 7 Cranch 113–15 (1812), construing the statutes at 2 Stat. 453–54 and 2 Stat. 474.

[83] 7 Cranch 115.

[84] See Part II, chapter 5, pp. 534–42.

registry and ownership, Congress had not mandated similar, and perhaps irregular, authority over foreign ships seized beyond American territorial waters. That principle, embedded in the Non-Intercourse Acts, was also firmly engrafted in the Embargo legislation.

Construed in this fashion, with the Supreme Court exercising a pragmatic judgment concerning enforcement difficulties that had been experienced by the executive branch of government, the Embargo laws of 1807 and 1808 became an effective instrument of national policy. Departing port limits without obtaining the necessary clearances or, even before a departure, having loaded a vessel secretly, was punishable under section 1 of the Act of December 22, 1807, section 3 of the Act of April 25, 1808, or in the case of coasting voyages, section 6 of the Act of April 25, 1808.[85] Once out of port limits, such ships were subject to seizure for violation of these sections, and this vulnerability continued in territorial waters and while they were on the high seas. Whenever an American vessel arrived in a foreign port, absent the defense of justification discussed above, she was subject to the penalties imposed by section 3 of the Act of January 8, 1808 (which also prohibited trading with vessels for foreign goods on the high seas), and section 4 of the Act of March 12, 1808.[86] These general prohibitions against foreign trade were in turn strengthened by a series of procedural requirements designed to give the port collectors the authority to oversee the lading of ships and to exercise broad discretion in the issuance of clearances;[87] failure to comply with these regulations subjected vessels, cargoes, or both to a variety of fines and in some instances forfeiture.

While the prohibition of foreign trade was the congressional intention, a majority of the provisions of the Embargo Acts involved strict control of coasting trade, fishing vessels, and traffic on the rivers and bays of the United States. Although most cases decided by the Supreme Court involved some aspect of foreign trade, it is quite clear from the evolution of the statutes that enforcement of the Embargo required that

---

[85] 2 Stat. 451–52 (1807); 2 Stat. 500 (1808).

[86] 2 Stat. 453–54, 474.

[87] Supervision of lading was authorized by sec. 2 of the Act of Jan. 9, 1809, 2 Stat. 506–507; cargo manifests were required under sec. 1, 4 of the Act of Apr. 25, 1808, ibid., 499; a report of sales of fish by fishing vessels was required by sec. 5 of the Act of Mar. 12, 1808, ibid., 475. Collectors were also authorized to seize unusual quantities of goods be-lieved by them about to be exported from ports adjacent to foreign territories by sec. 12 of the Act of Apr. 25, 1808, ibid., 501. Authority to search American vessels in territorial waters and on the high seas and foreign vessels in territorial waters was granted by sec. 7 of the Act of Apr. 25, 1808, ibid., 501; and the use of naval or military forces to enforce the Embargo was permitted by sec. 11 of the Act of Jan. 9, 1809, ibid., 510.

collectors be authorized to exercise close supervision of all trade, both maritime and overland, that might result in illegal trade with a foreign nation if permitted to continue without regulation.

Trans-shipment of cargo from a river craft to a seagoing vessel was subjected to the Supreme Court's scrutiny in the case of *The Schooner Paulina's Cargo* v. *U.S.*[88] The ship had been seized by the collector of Newport, Rhode Island, based upon his belief that she had violated the provisions of section 2 of the Act of April 25, 1808, which required lading under the supervision of the collector, and section 3 of the Act of January 8, 1808, which prohibited trans-shipment of goods of foreign or domestic manufacture.[89] There was a conflict in testimony whether the *Paulina* had been loaded at night or day, but it was undisputed that she did not have the collector's approval or supervision in doing so. Writing for the Court, Chief Justice Marshall noted that the stated intention of Congress in enacting the Embargo was to prohibit foreign trade; to prevent evasions of the law, certain transactions not in themselves amounting to a breach of the Embargo, but which might lead to it, had been prohibited. Congressional meaning was to be sought as a rule of guidance, but the Supreme Court nevertheless should insure by its holdings that acts which were a mere exercise of ownership over goods should not be improperly construed by implication to fall within the scope of the statute. "It is the province of the legislature to declare, in explicit terms, how far the citizen shall be restrained in the exercise of that power over property which ownership gives; and it is the province of the court to apply the rule of the case thus explicitly described, not to some other case which judges may conjecture to be equally dangerous."[90] Turning to section 3 of the Act of January 9, 1808, the Chief Justice noted it was under the trans-shipment provision that the *Paulina* was libeled. However, it was apparent that the Congress did not intend to prohibit a person from loading cargo into a vessel of any description, for the coasting trade was still legal, and there was no direct prohibition against lading a vessel with any articles whatsoever. A construction of the statutory section led him to believe that it was, by its introductory words, made subject to the limitation that the Acts prohibited were related to the regulatory and prohibitory provisions of the Embargo laws, as stated in the earlier statute and elsewhere in other sections of the same statute. This construction was supported by the fact that in many ports of the United States oceangoing vessels had to be loaded from lighters or rivercraft, or unloaded by the same method. Clearly the legislature did not intend to enact forfeiture in all such

---

[88] 7 Cranch 52–68 (1812).

[89] 2 Stat. 499–500 (1808); 2 Stat. 453–54.

[90] 7 Cranch 52 at 61.

cases. Finally the phrasing of the third section of the Act of January 9, 1808, would indicate that the trans-shipment prohibited was one that involved foreign voyages only.

The *Paulina* case marks the outer limit of executive discretion under the Embargo laws. While the Supreme Court was willing to permit broad authority, and even extraordinary official discretion, where the direct regulation of trade was authorized by Congress, it demurred when an ancillary regulation, only indirectly involved with trade, trespassed upon the rights of private property. Chief Justice Marshall's opinion makes it plain that the terms of the statute must be read in relation to its overall purpose; political decisions and valid congressional action might impose an Embargo and enforce it with the concurrence of the Supreme Court, yet acts of ownership inoffensive in themselves might be punished only if a connection could be shown to the prohibitions of the Embargo statutes. To Marshall's opinion there is appended the note that four judges concurred in his opinion, and that the other judges concurred in the result.[91] Among the concurring judges was William Johnson, whose brief statement of non-concurrence in the reasoning of the opinion indicates his belief that if intent to engage in foreign trade had been proved in the case of this trans-shipment, it would have fallen within the statutory language.

A fundamental part of the enforcement procedures for the Embargo involved prosecutions to collect the penalties in Embargo bonds. For the most part the detailed and highly specific provisions concerning bonding need not concern us, for variations in bonding requirements and their applicability to specific types of ships and particular shipping activities were not raised before the Supreme Court. The Court was, however, called upon to consider the possibility that undue influence in obtaining the execution of an Embargo bond might void that instrument, leaving the government without a remedy except in those cases where forfeiture was a concurrent penalty. The first of these cases, *U.S.* v. *Gordon*, arose on writ of error from the Circuit Court of Virginia, where the Chief Justice had ruled that a bond taken for three times the value of the ship and cargo, rather than for double that amount as required by the Act of December 22, 1807, and the supplementary act of January 9, 1808, was void as a matter of law. In the Supreme Court *U.S.* v. *Gordon* was denied a hearing on the basis of the procedural holding that a writ of error to the Supreme Court would not lie in a civil cause that had already been appealed to the circuit court by a writ of error.[92] The Chief Justice's ruling of the Circuit Court for Vir-

---

91 *Ibid.*, 68.
92 United States v. Gordon and Shepherd, 1 Brock, Rep. 190–95 (Cir.

Ct. Va. 1811); 7 Cranch 287–88 (1813).

ginia stood as the case law upon the subject until the 1815 term, when the full court heard argument in the case of *Speake* v. *U.S.*[93] That litigation involved an Embargo bond taken after the clearance had been issued and the vessel left her port; it was for more than double the value of the ship and cargo, and it had been subsequently altered without the consent of one of the original signatories. In the Circuit Court for the District of Columbia, where the suit was brought, the validity of the bond was upheld and the defendant appealed to the Supreme Court.

Judge Story wrote the majority opinion for the Court. He held that absent fraud, coercion, or circumvention the bond would be valid since it was taken voluntarily. The value of the vessel and goods being uncertain, the collector and owners by entering into a bond had adopted their prior agreement as to the value to be secured. Were the law otherwise, parties might avoid their obligations under the sealed instrument by proof that there was a slight error in the amount of the bond, or that there had been some innocent mistake that resulted in a penal amount too high or too low to secure the United States as required by law. Story's opinion then proceeded to demonstrate that subsequent alterations would not avoid the bond, nor would the fact that the bond was issued *nunc pro tunc* and related back to the time before the vessel's departure from port. On the balance the facts in *Speake* v. *U.S.* as reflected by parole evidence tended to show that no damage had been caused to any party by the alterations, nor had any impropriety resulted from the belated execution of the Embargo bond. There did appear to be an element of voluntary consent in the fixation of the penal amount. The equities of the case thus buttressed Judge Story's practical argument that certainty of enforcement was necessary in the case of such bonds and that oral testimony should not be permitted, save in exceptional cases, to vary the terms of the written instrument.

From Story's opinion in *Speake* v. *U.S.* Judge Livingston dissented, believing that any alteration in such an instrument should be accompanied by a new delivery and a memorandum in writing concerning the change. Chief Justice Marshall appended a brief note of dissent, adhering to his view in *U.S.* v. *Gordon* in the Virginia Circuit Court; however, he did not assert that as a matter of law the penal amount of the bond in *Speake* v. *U.S.* did violate the statute by specifying treble rather than double damages. As a practical matter it is not at all clear that *Speake* v. *U.S.* may be taken as a reversal of the position taken earlier in *U.S.* v. *Gordon*, and certainly both might have continued to be ruling case law, the later case rendering legal those bonds whose

---

[93] 9 Cranch 28–39 (1815).

penalties varied but slightly from the statutory formula, while the earlier annulled bonds entered into in an atmosphere of fraud or coercion which resulted in a penalty for treble damages.

Judge Story's opinion in *Speake* v. *U.S.* evidences once more the remarkable tendency of the Supreme Court to take into consideration the practicalities of Embargo enforcement. Story decided that the time set forth in the statute for taking the bond was merely directive to the collector, and the clearance might issue upon the collector receiving assurances of a subsequent execution of the bond *nunc pro tunc*. Similarly the alteration of the bond to remove the name of one surety and insert another, according to a prearranged plan between the parties and the collector, was quite acceptable in law, even though the actual substitution of the new surety was not made a matter of notice to the other obligors. Minor variations in evaluation of the ship and cargo should not be permitted to void otherwise valid Embargo bonds, for such defenses would result in endless litigation by parties wishing to avoid their undertakings on technicalities.

While President Jefferson may have been displeased with the initial handling of the Gilchrist case by Judge Johnson, it would appear that the Supreme Court, far from frustrating his executive activities in this field, actually played a constructive role in upholding the enforcement of the laws. Of course no case involving the Embargo statutes reached the Supreme Court until its 1810 term, well after the trade Embargo had been lifted and the United States had embarked upon another period of non-intercourse against the leading maritime powers. All the decisions were announced at a time when the opinions of the Court could no longer hamper the execution of the Embargo itself, but only provide redress to individuals prosecuted for their supposed delinquencies several years before. This factor undoubtedly insulated the Supreme Court from both public pressure and executive retribution. Yet the opinions evidence a clear understanding of the difficulties of the collectors in executing these laws, and provided a jurisprudential basis upon which the Republicans could claim retroactively a constitutional justification for the Embargo and most of their interpretations of the implementing statutes.

DRIFTING TOWARDS WAR

The nominal repeal of the Embargo Acts by the Non-Intercourse Act of March 1, 1809,[94] did not eliminate the Embargo from American

[94] Sec. 12, An Act to interdict the commercial intercourse between the United States and Great Britain and France and their dependencies, and for other purposes, Mar. 1, 1809, 2 Stat. 528 at 531; Jennings, *American Embargo*, 160–61.

law, for its sanctions continued to apply to commerce with Britain and France or their possessions. In addition the Non-Intercourse Act utilized bonding procedures derived from the Embargo statutes and a similar system of multiple damages in lieu of forfeiture. The substantial body of case law concerning the Embargo insured that any new regulatory scheme would find a rich body of law and custom pertaining to peacetime illegal trade. As a consequence there can be no sharp legal distinction between the period of the Embargo Acts and the subsequent time of non-intercourse with Britain and France and non-importation of goods from those nations. On the other hand, the rapid disintegration of the diplomatic situation, coupled with President Madison's futile attempts to avoid commercial difficulties and cool national enmities, marks this as a distinct period in the history of illegal trade.

Although the March 1809 Non-Intercourse Act derived its title from the attempt to deny American harbors and territorial waters to warships and merchant vessels of Great Britain and the French Republic, it also contained non-importation provisions directed against the introduction of goods of British or French origin into the United States. In their salient features the sections of the 1809 Act paralleled the sections of the 1806 Non-Importation Act which was repealed by the 1809 statute. The non-importation clause in the latter Act covered all British and French commodities, in contrast to the 1806 provision which prohibited only British goods and products listed in the statute.[95] The 1809 Act also provided for the simultaneous continuation of the Embargo as those statutes pertained to Britain and France, and it also permitted the President to suspend the provisions of the Act "in case either France or Great Britain shall so revoke or modify her edicts, as that they shall cease to violate the neutral commerce of the United States. . . ."[96] Certain of the clearance and control provisions of the Embargo laws were also maintained by the March 1809 Non-Intercourse Act to insure the continued interdiction of illegal trade under the guise of coastal or river commerce. These regulatory provisions were deleted from the new Non-Intercourse statute enacted on June 28, 1809, leaving only the bonding requirement for ships departing on oceanic voyages as a vestige of the administrative apparatus created for the Embargo.[97]

When the June 28, 1809, Non-Intercourse Act came up for re-

---

[95] The 1806 Act was repealed by sec. 17 of the 1809 Act, 2 Stat. 532. Compare sec. 4 of the 1809 Act, *ibid.*, 529, with sec. 1 of the 1806 Act, 2 Stat. 379.

[96] Sec. 11, 2 Stat. 530.

[97] Sec. 13 of the Jan. 9, 1809 Act required that a certificate of landing be provided within a "reasonable time"; this requirement was deleted from sec. 3 of the June 1809 Act. Sec. 15 of the Jan. 9 Act required bonds from river boats; the provision is not included in the June 28 Act. 2 Stat. 531, 532, 550–51.

newal in the 1810 session of Congress, the legislators interdicted assistance to British and French warships, but did not re-enact the non-importation clauses of the 1809 Act.[98] On the other hand, the 1810 statute provided that if Britain and France on or before the third of March 1811 failed to revoke or modify her edicts against American commerce, the President might declare that fact by proclamation. Three months after such a proclamation the non-importation provisions of the 1809 statute would be "revived and have full force and effect" upon the commerce of the nation refusing or neglecting to modify her edicts.[99]

Receipt of the ambiguous Cadore letter in late 1810, announcing French intentions to cease depredations upon American commerce under certain conditions, caused President Madison to proclaim that the French had complied with the Non-Intercourse Act.[100] Consequently the last Non-Intercourse Act, passed on March 2, 1811, limited the non-intercourse scheme to British commerce.[101] A year later a ninety-day embargo applicable to all foreign trade resulted in a virtual suspension of the 1811 Non-Intercourse law, but before its expiration date the United States had declared war on Great Britain, and the attention of the courts was drawn to the enforcement of sanctions under international law against illegal trade in wartime.

As instruments of international diplomacy the Non-Intercourse laws had been of dubious value, but once the legislature utilized statutory penalties that might be suspended or re-imposed by Presidential proclamation, a number of legal difficulties were bound to arise for resolution by the Supreme Court. One involved the adequacy of notice of a change in the law during a voyage. In *The Brig Penobscot* v. *U.S.*[102] the Court held that a ship bound for an American port was responsible for making inquiries at intermediate ports, as well as of vessels she met, concerning the legality of importations. The burden of obtaining actual notice of the state of the law rested upon the captain and owner of the

---

[98] An Act concerning the commercial intercourse between the United States and Great Britain and France, and their dependencies, and for other purposes, May 1, 1810, 2 Stat. 605–606.

[99] Sec. 4, 2 Stat. 606 (1810).

[100] Perkins, *Prologue to War*, 246–56, contains a detailed discussion of the ambiguities involved in the Cadore letter and argues persuasively that President Madison was aware of the pitfalls involved in accepting it as a basis for repeal of the Non-Intercourse Act as far as France was concerned. Perkins also shows that French attitudes and actions were quite opposed

to a favorable interpretation of Cadore's conditional offer.

[101] An Act supplementary to the Act intituled, "An Act concerning the commercial intercourse between the United States and Great Britain and France and their dependencies, and for other purposes," Mar. 2, 1811, 2 Stat. 651–52, also known as the Eppes bill, prohibited American imports from Britain, but not exports to Britain; it firmly committed the United States to a policy of demanding repeal of the British orders-in-council. Perkins, *Prologue to War*, 256–57.

[102] 7 Cranch 356–58 (1813).

importing vessel. Constitutional questions were also presented by the suspension or re-imposition of the Non-Intercourse laws by legislatively authorized executive action. While full consideration of this delegation-of-power issue must be postponed, it is appropriate to note here that in *Brig Aurora* v. *U.S.* the Supreme Court held that the legislature acted within allowable limits of its discretion.[103]

The formative impact of the Embargo on the law of peacetime trade regulations is shown by the nine cases[104] brought to the Supreme Court on appeal from prosecutions for violation of the Non-Intercourse Acts of 1809, 1810, and 1811. In *U.S.* v. *The Cargo of the Fanny* a vessel loaded with British goods arriving after the effective date of the Non-Intercourse Acts, but in the time between the repeal of the British orders-in-council and the American declaration of war in 1812, was driven ashore by bad weather and delayed in American waters by a threatened mutiny of her crew.[105] While it is not clear from Judge Johnson's opinion that the claimants were required to bear the burden of proving their entitlement to exemption from the law on ground of necessity, the detailed consideration of the justifying facts would lead one to surmise that the strict standards of proof set forth in the Embargo cases continued to be the rule of decision.[106]

Similarly the Embargo Act prosecutions provided guidance in construing the Non-Intercourse Acts. While libels under the 1809, 1810, and 1811 Non-Intercourse Acts were required to set forth the offense with specificity, some flexibility was permitted in the amount of proof required from the government. In *Schooner Hoppet and Cargo* v. *U.S.*[107] Chief Justice Marshall applied the common law rule that required a declaration in a criminal action to plead the acts constituting the offense, not merely the statute violated, as a basis for the action. Although he conceded that all of the "technical niceties" of criminal procedure at common law should not be transplanted into admiralty

---

[103] Cargo of the Brig Aurora v. United States, 7 Cranch 382–89 (1813).

[104] Schooner Anne v. United States, 7 Cranch 570–72 (1813); Cargo of Brig Aurora v. United States, 7 Cranch 382–89 (1813); Schooner Hoppet v. United States, 7 Cranch 389–95 (1813); Schooner Jane v. United States, 7 Cranch 363–66 (1813); Brig Penobscot v. United States, 7 Cranch 356–58 (1813); Ship Richmond v. United States, 9 Cranch 102–104 (1815); United States v. Cargo of The Fanny, 9 Cranch 181–83 (1815); United States v.

Brigantine Mars, 8 Cranch 417–18 (1814); United States v. 1960 Bags of Coffee, 8 Cranch 398–416 (1814).

[105] 9 Cranch 181–83 (1815).

[106] See Brig James Wells v. United States, 7 Cranch 22–26 (1812), and United States v. Hall & Worth, 6 Cranch 171–76 (1810). In Brig Struggle v. United States the Court held that in seeking exemption from the Non-Intercourse Act of June 28, 1809, the party seeking shelter would have to make out the *vis major* and leave no doubt of his innocence. 9 Cranch 71–76 (1815).

[107] 7 Cranch 389–95 (1813).

courts, nevertheless he felt that the common law rule concerning declarations was "so essential to justice and fair proceeding" that it should apply in "every court where justice is the object."[108] He observed that this degree of certainty in delineating the offense charged was "demanded by the free genius of our institutions in all prosecutions for offenses against the laws. . . ."[109] On the other hand, where the information was well drawn and the proof adduced by the government was strongly against the defendant but not absolutely conclusive of the identity of the vessel involved, the Supreme Court affirmed the decree of the circuit court in favor of the government.[110]

In *Ship Richmond* v. *U.S.*[111] the Supreme Court, speaking through Chief Justice Marshall, construed the Non-Intercourse Act of June 28, 1809, as prohibiting a departure in ballast, although that had not been specifically forbidden under the legislation. According to Marshall, the bonding requirements of the law, coupled with a view to the meaning and intent of the statute, made a departure in ballast punishable. Somewhat earlier the Supreme Court was required to construe the forfeiture provision of the Non-Intercourse Act (sections 4 and 5 of the Act of March 1, 1809),[112] and the majority held that forfeiture of goods attached immediately upon completion of the offense, thereby divesting any and all subsequent bona fide purchasers of title paramount to that of the government.[113] Judge Story, who had held to the contrary below, was joined by two of his colleagues in asserting that seizure and condemnation was necessary to perfect the government's title to forfeited goods, and that while once these procedures were accomplished the government's title by the doctrine of relation might date back to the time the offense was completed, the completion of the offense itself did not so transfer title as to defeat the claims of bona fide purchasers.[114]

While Supreme Court cases involving the post-Embargo Non-Intercourse statutes were not as large in number or as significant as the Embargo cases, they nevertheless provided the Court with additional opportunities to set forth rules of law concerning the regulation

---

[108] *Ibid.*, 394.

[109] *Ibid.*, 393. See also Schooner Anne v. United States, 7 Cranch 570–72 (1813), requiring precision in drawing libels.

[110] Schooner Jane v. United States, 7 Cranch 363–66 (1813).

[111] 9 Cranch 102–104 (1815).

[112] 2 Stat. 529 (1809).

[113] United States v. 1960 Bags of Coffee, 8 Cranch 398–416 (1814).

[114] Story's carefully reasoned opinion is in *ibid.*, 405–16; it contrasts sharply with the terse majority opinion of Judge Johnson asserting that "severe" laws are rendered necessary to enable the executive to carry into effect the measures of policy adopted by the legislature. *Ibid.*, 405. The precedent in United States v. 1960 Bags of Coffee was followed in United States v. Brigantine Mars, 8 Cranch 417–18 (1814). The constitutional ramifications of these cases have been discussed in Part II, chapter 1, pp. 405–406.

of foreign trade in time of peace. Since the Embargo Acts continued in effect during the Non-Intercourse period from 1809 to 1812, it is not surprising that there should be a continuity in the basic approach to problems of enforcement. During the latter period the prosecutions centered on the specific provisions of the 1809, 1810, and 1811 Non-Intercourse Acts, leaving the Supreme Court but little opportunity to cite precedents created under the earlier Non-Intercourse and Embargo statutes. On the other hand, the interrelationship between the Embargo Acts and the subsequent Non-Intercourse legislation is readily apparent when the cases are examined for adjudications of similar points of law and for continuing practices and usages in the courts.

PRIZE CASES IN THE WAR OF 1812

American prize jurisdiction evolved during the Revolution, based upon the need to establish regular procedures for the condemnation of enemy vessels seized by American warships and privateers on the high seas. Economic warfare in the eighteenth century was based upon armed capture of the enemy's commercial vessels, and international law recognized the right of the capturing crew to participate in the proceeds realized upon judicial sale of the forfeited vessel and cargo. Prize jurisdiction involved the judicial procedures and substantive rules established for the determination of the hostile character of the captured vessel and the termination of enemy owners' rights in the ship, her cargo, or both. In accordance with international law the owner, his agent, or the master of the ship might appear in the prize court as a claimant, to present evidence that the vessel or her cargo was not in fact enemy property, but rather the property of a neutral, or friendly, individual or firm.

Naval warfare, and hence the capture of vessels as prize, was not the exclusive domain of the public armed vessels of the warring nations. Ships built, manned, and operated by the nations in their sovereign capacities accounted for only a small proportion of the prizes taken in eighteenth- and nineteenth-century wars. Privateers, outfitted by citizens or subjects of the warring states, and commissioned by special letters of marque and reprisal to capture enemy vessels, were by far the largest number of litigants in the prize courts. Prize warfare was thus more in the nature of a business opportunity to benefit from the existence of war with foreign nations than it was a patriotic activity unalloyed with pecuniary motives. The exercise of prize jurisdiction was a necessary mode of controlling the possible excesses to which privateers might be led in their quest for legalized plunder. At the same time the compliance of prize courts with rules of international law was of utmost importance to the nation, lest undue harshness in condemnations or the disregard of the rights of neutral or friendly nationals cause diplomatic rifts with allies and neutrals.

For these reasons the separate American States were, early in the American Revolution, put under supervision by the Continental Congress in the exercise of their prize jurisdiction. As Professors Goebel and Bourguignon[115] have shown, the national authority was first exercised through a committee on prizes and captures, appointed by the Congress; this committee was replaced in 1781 by the Federal Court of Appeals in Cases of Prize and Capture, the predecessor of the Supreme Court of the United States in this field. It is apparent, both from the historical background of the Supreme Court's prize jurisdiction and from its position as the highest tribunal of international law in the United States, that prize cases were an area where broad and general authority might be claimed by the Supreme Court. Quite clearly the judges on the Court from 1812 to 1815 were engaged in searching foreign precedents for a sound body of substantive law upon which to predicate their prize awards. This was a particularly opportune time for the enunciation of an American law of prize, since the peculiar circumstances of the inception of the war raised significant and difficult issues for *de novo* resolution by the Supreme Court.

An extraordinary progression of events, both foreign and domestic, led to the congressional declaration of war with Great Britain on June 18, 1812.[116] Belatedly the Madison administration resorted to a general embargo on April 4, 1812, intended to cut off American grain supplies to British armies in the Iberian peninsula. However, advance notice of its enactment sent American merchantmen scurrying out of port in unprecedented numbers, thereby frustrating the intention of the Act and making American vessels not only subject to British capture when war was declared, but also leaving them to the mercy of the United States privateers upon their return with cargoes that violated the provisions of the Non-Intercourse Acts and were tainted with illegality as British goods being imported in time of war.[117] To confuse further the commercial consequences of the declaration of war, Britain had earlier repealed those orders-in-council considered by Americans to transgress neutral rights.[118] Immediately American merchants resident in London who had been holding cargoes for shipment to the United States, as well as British merchants anxious to resume trade

---

[115] J. Goebel, *Antecedents and Beginnings to 1801, Volume I, History of the Supreme Court of the United States*, ed., P. Freund (New York, 1971), 147–95; H. Bourguignon, *The First Federal Court: The Federal Appellate Prize Court of the American Revolution, 1775–1787* (Philadelphia, 1977).

[116] Perkins, *Prologue to War*, 373–417.

[117] *Ibid.*, 386.

[118] The struggle for repeal is traced in detail in *ibid.*, 300–41.

with America, dispatched their vessels in anticipation that repeal of the orders-in-council would result in immediate suspension of the Non-Intercourse laws. As a consequence of these two situations the United States entered the War of 1812 in such a circumstance that the normal rules of prize law had to be modified to extend a modicum of justice to the commercial victims of a muddled foreign policy on the part of both belligerents.

As a step towards adjusting the inevitable conflict between the Non-Intercourse Act of 1809 and the reprisal rights vested in privateers by virtue of their commissions, the Supreme Court determined that the municipal regulation of the Non-Intercourse law was superseded and merged into the belligerent rights that arose as a consequence of the declaration of war.[119] However, while Congress declared war, the law of nations and constitutional custom conferred upon the President, as commander-in-chief of the Army and Navy, certain powers and duties that were not dependent upon congressional grant but rather were annexed to, and made a part of, the executive duty to deal with the condition of belligerence.[120] The prize cases thus represent the commencement of the Court's statement of the breadth of the war powers of the American President, and at the same time they demonstrate the function of the Court as an expounder of the rules of international law in the United States.

With the repeal of the British orders-in-council a large number of British and American vessels left British ports bound for the United States. Vessels and cargoes belonging to British subjects found on the high seas when war was declared were subject to seizure and condemnation by the operation of international prize law; a similar situation arose as to property that a prize court might hold to be in the ownership of an American merchant domiciled in Great Britain, and hence subject to being characterized as British goods.[121] However, by Presidential instruction of August 28, 1812,[122] privateers were ordered to desist from disturbing American property on the high seas returning to the United States as a result of the alleged repeal of the British orders-in-

---

[119] In The Sally, 8 Cranch 382–83 (1814), claims were presented by the captor privateer and the United States, the former based upon the letter of marque and reprisal issued by the President, the latter upon the Non-Intercourse Acts. Judge Story for the Court held that "the municipal forfeiture under the non–intercourse law was absorbed in the more general operations of the law of war." *Ibid.*, 384.

[120] The Thomas Gibbons, 8 Cranch 421–31 (1814). See also H. Wheaton, *A Digest of the Law of Maritime Captures and Prizes* (New York, 1815), 49.

[121] The right of capture arose immediately upon declaration of war and no notice to the enemy was required. Wheaton, *Digest*, 16.

[122] The instructions are summarized in 8 Cranch 421 at 422.

council. A subsequent statute[123] confirmed the Presidential instructions in this regard and fixed September 15, 1812, as the date upon which it was to be presumed in law that notice of the declaration of war was received in England. Consequently after that date it was assumed that the property had been sent to America with knowledge of the state of war between the two nations and thus could not be protected either by the instructions or by the statute. In point of fact the actual news of the American declaration of war had arrived in England well before September 15, but in passing upon prize cases raising this discrepancy of dates the Supreme Court held that it was bound to accept September 15 as the terminating date for this exception to the rules of war.[124]

The license to expatriate goods as a result of the repeal of the British orders-in-council was construed to apply only to goods and vessels in Britain at the time of declaration of war. Property in Canada was not included, nor was a round-trip voyage from the United States to Canada or England included within the permitted trade.[125] However, if property dispatched in reliance upon the repeal of the orders-in-council were delayed en route, it might still claim exemption from condemnation upon the basis of the license. For example, goods shipped from England before the September 15 date, but which were delayed in Ireland by bad weather and the need for ship repairs, might still claim exemption from condemnation as prize when they reached the United States in the summer of 1813.[126] This limited license to permit American goods and vessels to enter the United States without fear of seizure as prize of war was therefore restricted in purpose as well as in time, and it applied only to property impressed with an American character.

American character did not necessarily attach to the property of all American citizens regardless of their residence. Those American merchants who had established a commercial domicile in Britain were considered to adhere to the enemy and impress their goods with a British character unless it could be proved that they were in the course of departing from Britain when the seizure of their goods was made.[127]

---

[123] 2 Stat. 789–90 (1813).

[124] The Thomas Gibbons, 8 Cranch 421, 429 (1814), presented this situation, but Judge Story held that until Sept. 15, 1812, a shipment might be made in reliance that the repeal of the orders-in-council might induce Congress to revoke the declaration of war.

[125] The Rapid, 8 Cranch 155–68 (1814), in which Judge Johnson stated for the Court that the right of removal of goods did not authorize an American-based merchant to make a round trip to Nova Scotia after

notice of the declaration of war. The rule was followed in The Sally, 8 Cranch 382–83 (1814).

[126] The Mary, 9 Cranch 126–51 (1815); but a departure eleven months after the declaration of war was held not timely in The St. Lawrence, 9 Cranch 120–22 (1815).

[127] The leading case, The Venus, 8 Cranch 253–317 (1814), was followed in The Frances (Thompson, Claimant), 8 Cranch 335–48 (1814), and The Frances (Gillespie's Claim), 8 Cranch 363–71 (1814). American prize law

II: *Illegal Trade and Prize Cases*

A mere intention to remove to the United States was not sufficient, but an actual setting about to terminate one's fiscal affairs and to leave the enemy nation was required. The right of removal of goods was limited in time, and could not be exercised by shipment in the company of hostile goods. The Supreme Court required that the evidence of removal show a clear and unambiguous indication of an intent to remove; the majority held that such an indication should be proved by evidence arising prior to the seizure.[128] On this point Chief Justice Marshall dissented, noting that under the circumstances "justice requires that subsequent testimony shall be admitted to prove a pre-existing fact."[129] Measures of removal timely undertaken after receipt of notice of the war should be admitted as evidence to prove that property shipped before such notice belonged not to an enemy, but to a friend. As a substantive matter Marshall rejected the presumption that American merchants resident in an enemy nation automatically become enemies of the United States; that general rule of attributing commercial domicile should not apply against an American citizen, but rather the Court should presume an intention to return home when notice of war is received.[130]

Chief Justice Marshall's differences from his associates in *The Venus* went far deeper than mere disagreement over presumptions of

---

considered the property of all merchants residing in a belligerent state to be subject to seizure and condemnation, according to Wheaton, *Digest*, 101. Only if an individual were sojourning in the enemy state for a very short time might he claim exemption from reprisals. Wheaton observed that ". . . time is the grand ingredient in constituting domicile," although it might not be decisive in all cases. *Ibid.*, 102–09.

[128] The Venus, 8 Cranch 253, 279–80 (1814), in which Judge Washington adopted the British rule which required the merchant to assume the burden of proof concerning his residence in a hostile country and his intention to remove. "If anything short of actual removal be admitted to work a change in the national character acquired by residence, it seems perfectly reasonable that the evidence of a bona fide intention to remove should be such as to leave no doubt of its sincerity. Mere declarations of such an intention ought never to be relied upon, when contradicted, or at the least rendered doubtful, by a continu-

ance of that residence which impressed the character." *Ibid.*, 281. This case and rule is discussed in Wheaton, *Digest*, 110–17, 124–25, and the English rule is given as, in addition, recognizing termination of business as evidence of intent to return home. *Ibid.*, 146.

[129] 8 Cranch 253 at 288–89. "The evidence of this intention [to remove] will rarely, if ever, be given in peace. It must therefore, be furnished, if at all, after the war shall be known to him; and that knowledge may be preceded by the capture of his goods . . . justice requires that subsequent testimony shall be received to prove a pre-existing fact. Measures taken for removal immediately after a war, may prove a previous intention to remove in the event of war . . ." *Ibid.*, 289.

[130] *Ibid.*, 292–93. The passage on presumption of intention to return is at *ibid.*, 295. Wheaton seems to have adopted Marshall's presumption in law that a merchant domiciled in a nation hostile to his native land would intend to return home. *Digest*, 124–25.

intention to return. Rather they indicate a thread of discord that was sharply to divide the Supreme Court in its prize decisions. A majority of the judges seem to have accepted the views of Judge Story, who felt that precedents from the English High Court of Admiralty should apply in prize matters. Those decisions and opinions, as Marshall was quick to demonstrate in his dissents, were neither responsive to the rights of neutrals nor in accord with the view of international law taken by nations with less naval strength than Great Britain.

> I respect Sir William Scott, as I do every truly great man; and I respect his decisions; nor should I depart from them on light grounds; but it is impossible to consider them attentively without perceiving that his mind leans strongly in favor of the captors.[131]

Marshall proceeded to indicate a British national bias that might have influenced Scott's jurisprudence, but whatever the causative factors in his opinions, Marshall felt it proper to examine the principles underlying them, and not to graft them into American law in situations where injustice might result.[132] As a former Secretary of State the Chief Justice had received ample exposure to the British tendency to disregard neutral rights of American merchants and seamen;[133] that in turn had reinforced his adherence to principles of American diplomacy developed during and after the Revolution that rejected British prize law and the Royal Navy's haughty pretensions upon the high seas. Practical experience fused with personal predilection to form Marshall's resistance to the ready reception of English prize law into American jurisprudence.

In a certain sense Marshall's colleagues on the Supreme Court were more than justified in applying the vigorous sanctions of English prize law against American merchants resident in Great Britain. The long period of Embargo and Non-Intercourse had created a circumstance in which legal trade between the United States and British territory was impossible. As a consequence American commercial activity in the British Isles and Empire was highly suspect, and a certain rough form of justice might be said to have been exacted upon those who had profited from illegal trade in past years. However, in situations where non-commercial goods were in the course of being removed from Britain, the Court seems to have granted considerable leeway in the

---

[131] 8 Cranch 299. Sir William Scott (1754–1836) was a former history teacher at Oxford who was admitted to Doctor's Commons in 1779 and appointed judge of the High Court of Admiralty in 1798. A member of the House of Commons from 1801–21, he was created Baron Stowell of Stowell Park in 1821.

[132] *Ibid.*

[133] B. Perkins, *The First Rapprochement: England and the United States 1795–1805* (Berkeley, 1955), 68–69, 154; A. Beveridge, *The Life of John Marshall*, II (Boston, 1916), 504–14.

date of shipment. Speaking for the entire Court in *The Mary*, the Chief Justice treated goods as being legally removed from the enemy's country and exempt from prize jurisdiction even though they had not departed the British Isles until the spring of 1813.[134] The shipment represented an investment of funds obtained from a legacy, and thus no possibility of illegal trade was involved. Although in *The Rapid*[135] there had been a journey to Nova Scotia to withdraw goods, and the two cases were distinguished on that basis, the Court in *The Mary* noted the additional distinction that *trading* had been involved in the Nova Scotian removal, but not in the voyage of *The Mary*. While the differentiation of commercial traders from incidental shippers was perhaps too distinctly made on the basis of these two cases, it nevertheless seems plausible that the pre-existing situation concerning illegal trade had a bearing upon the opinions of the various judges in the prize litigation before them.

The addiction of American merchants to illegal trade was again demonstrated by their ready acceptance of British licenses issued during the course of the War of 1812, designed to protect ships and cargoes on the high seas from becoming prize to British men-of-war and privateers. Three such cases reached the Supreme Court, two for trading to the Iberian peninsula, and one for carrying provisions to the West Indies. In all cases it was argued by the claimants that the British papers were obtained only to deceive the enemy, and that the actual intent of the voyage was to trade with neutrals. In *The Julia* the Court held that sailing on a voyage under the license of the enemy was a furtherance of his views and interests, and as such was an illegal act that standing alone subjected both ship and cargo to forfeiture as prize.[136] Adopting the opinion in the Circuit Court for the Massachusetts District condemning the *Julia* and her cargo, the Supreme Court noted that any contact with the enemy in time of war, even as little as the acquisition of the license, was prohibited to American citizens. Judge Story took notice of the active trade in British licenses being carried on in the United States during the war:

> The license is issued by the agents of the British government, and, I must presume, under its authority. It is sold (as is stated) in the market; and if it be a valuable acquisition, the price must be proportionate. . . . If such licenses be a legitimate article of sale, will they not enable the British government to raise a revenue from our citizens, and thereby add to their resources of war?[137]

---

[134] 9 Cranch 126–51 (1815).
[135] 8 Cranch 155–68 (1814).
[136] 8 Cranch 181–203 (1814), opinion by Judge Story, the Circuit Judge who wrote the opinion in the Massachusetts Circuit Court.
[137] *Ibid.*, 195, 196.

That very purchase of a license was also good cause to condemn the cargo of an owner who claimed lack of knowledge of the shipowner's British license. For, the Court observed in *The Hiram*,[138] would it not most probably be a subject of reimbursement to the shipowner by the proprietor of the cargo? Acceptance of the British license *ipso facto* made the ship and cargo illegal, leaving the Court without need to proceed to the consideration of whether the actual intent of the voyage, or the route of a completed voyage, might be accepted either in mitigation or exoneration. A vessel captured upon her return from a British licensed outward voyage might therefore be condemned, irrespective of her trading acts, as if she had been seized while outward bound.[139]

In *The Nereide*[140] the Supreme Court was presented with a question of hostile character acquired by neutral goods by virtue of their shipment aboard an armed British merchantman. One Manuel Pinto, a citizen of Buenos Aires temporarily resident in London, shipped his goods upon a British armed merchant ship that he had chartered for the voyage. Her master was to obey Pinto's directions concerning the disposition of the cargo, but the ship was under his command during the course of the voyage and the shipowner was to remain responsible for her crew and maintenance. By prearrangement she sailed with a British convoy for South America, and after becoming separated from her escorts, she was taken prize by an American privateer and brought into New York for condemnation. After the district court decreed the forfeiture of the cargo, Pinto appealed to the circuit court, which affirmed the sentence pro forma, from which sentence an appeal was taken to the Supreme Court.

Writing for the majority of a divided court, John Marshall reversed the lower courts and restored the cargo to Pinto on the basis of its being neutral property. Judge Johnson wrote a concurring opinion directed towards examining the consequences of a neutral merchant shipping his property on an armed belligerent vessel. In effect Johnson found no express provision in international law prohibiting such a shipment; on that basis he held the property of Pinto to be neutral and thus entitled to restoration. Judge Story, in a dissenting opinion for himself and an unidentified judge, reasoned that no writer had contended that a neutral merchant might ship property on an armed belligerent vessel without risk of capture. Consequently, Pinto's association with an armed British convoy placed him within the protection of the enemy. Furthermore, the lading of Pinto's goods on an armed belligerent ship created an identity of interest that in and of itself de-

---

[138] 8 Cranch 444–51 (1814), opinion by Judge Washington.
[139] The Julia, 8 Cranch 181, at 202–203.

[140] 9 Cranch 388–455 (1815), opinion by Chief Justice Marshall.

feated neutrality. The shipment under these terms made it possible that an act of the master, such as violation of a blockade or destruction of ship's papers, would subject the neutral cargo to condemnation. The resistance of the ship to capture was therefore also the resistance of the cargo. Concluded Story, "The whole enterprise was radically tainted with a hostile leaven."[141]

John Marshall and the majority took quite a different view of the same facts. They pointed out that the armed neutrality and subsequent treaty stipulations had been designed to provide relief to neutral trade during wartime. These arrangements enlarged the scope of neutral trade, and in the United States it had never been accepted that enemy ships tainted neutral goods they carried with the belligerent character of the vessel. Pinto had had no hand in the arming of the *Nereide*, for her arming and equipment was left to the owner. Neither could resistance to capture be attributed to Pinto, for the sole management of the vessel remained with the captain under the terms of the charter party. It was the law of nations that the property of a friend was the property of a friend wherever found, and there was nothing unlawful in a neutral shipping goods on the armed merchant vessel of a belligerent.

Undoubtedly the lack of unanimity among the justices concerning *The Nereide* reflects a sharper conflict of opinion in the conferences of the Court on the matter of the armed neutrality and its impact, if any, upon American prize law. While Judge Johnson construed the writers on international law as broadly as possible in sustaining neutral rights, Story demanded a high standard of specificity from the treatise writers. Unless a specific neutral right was expressly recognized in the treatises, it could not be construed to be in effect as a matter of international law. Similarly the Court must have debated at some length the contradictory arguments of counsel concerning the "free ships make free goods" provision of the 1795 treaty between Spain and the United States. On behalf of the captors it was urged that the inclusion of that clause in the treaty was a basis to imply the converse—that hostile ships made hostile goods. Furthermore, the municipal ordinances of Spain tended to show the latter proposition to be Spain's public policy, and the rule of reciprocity required that such an interpretation be applied by the Supreme Court against Spanish subjects. As indicated above, Chief Justice Marshall and the majority rejected the argument based upon the treaty; Marshall also stated that reciprocity in this situation would be a measure of retaliation against Spain, and such an election on the part of the government of the United States did not properly lie with the judicial branch but rather with a legislative prerogative vested in Congress. For the Supreme Court to venture into the

---

[141] *Ibid.*, 436, at 454.

matter would force them to "tread the devious and intricate path of politics."[142] Even in a matter so much involved with judicial business as the award of military salvage, the Congress had, by specific act, provided that the principle of reciprocity should govern the determinations of American admiralty courts.[143] That being the case the Court should not presume to invoke the rule of reciprocity in prize cases without legislative authorization.

The practice of shipping British goods under neutral cover resulted in some limitations on the protection of neutral rights in the Supreme Court. In *The Cargo of the Ship Hazard* v. *Campbell*[144] a Russian ship was seized off Amelia Island and carried into St. Mary's, Georgia, for condemnation. Her papers clearly indicated that the Swedish ownership of the goods was a cover under which the true owner expected to import British goods into the United States or the West Indies. Neutral ownership was thus being utilized to protect the goods from seizure by American privateers. After rejecting the assertion that the evidence showed the seizure to have been made in Spanish waters,[145] Judge Livingston for the Court held that the property was correctly condemned in the courts below, and that even if additional evidence had been permitted, it could not contradict the clear documentary proof of the British character of the cargo.

In this case the counsel for the claimants had argued that since both the United States and Russia had adopted the principles of the armed neutrality, the principle that free ships make free goods should, as between those two nations, be considered the law of nations. Consequently the cargo was protected by shipment under the Russian flag even though it was of a belligerent character. The captors argued that only a treaty between Russia and the United States containing these provisions would make them effective between the two nations; no law of nations could be recognized as applicable between them that was not equally binding upon all other nations. Significantly Judge Livingston, in delivering the Court's opinion in this case, did not touch upon the contentions involving the armed neutrality. We must assume that the rule that "free ships make free goods" was applicable only in those cases where an American treaty with the neutral nation made express provision for such a concession. Claims of neutrality based upon the principles of the armed neutrality might be entertained only if a specific treaty provision were applicable. The armed neutrality, as far as Ameri-

---

[142] *Ibid.*, 422–23; the quoted material is on 423.

[143] See discussion in Part II, chapter 3, p. 485.

[144] 9 Cranch 205–209 (1815), opinion by Judge Livingston.

[145] Capture in the territorial waters of a neutral state was illegal and divested a prize court of jurisdiction and required restitution to the owner. Wheaton, *Digest*, 54–55.

can prize law was concerned, formed an exception to, rather than a part of, the law of nations.

Subsequently an identical trade pattern raised the issue of payment of freight to a neutral shipowner from the proceeds of a prize award covering British cargo.[146] The charter party of the neutral vessel provided that she was to receive no freight on the voyage from England to Amelia Island, but upon her return the freight was to be payable on the homeward-bound cargo at a stipulated rate. Chief Justice Marshall for the Court noted that prior adjudications had settled the belligerent character of the cargo, and that the only question concerned the award of freight, if any, to the owner of the neutral carrying vessel. While there was no case of capture in which freight had been awarded on one cargo for freight accrued on another, it would be unjust to treat the outbound voyage as totally separated from the homeward voyage, thereby awarding the neutral carrier no recompense for his efforts.[147] Had the charter party provided for freight to Amelia Island it would be awarded to the shipowner without any question. On the other hand, the dependence of the computation of freight on the outbound voyage upon the freight stipulated on the cargo carried back to England left the Court without any factual basis upon which to compute freight. Consequently a quantum meruit award would have to be the basis of freight payment, and the lower courts correctly applied that rule in this case.

The Supreme Court's concern for neutral rights in the case of the *Societe* becomes more readily apparent when the charter party freight terms are examined in detail. By that agreement the *Societe* was to take on a return cargo of cotton or other goods at Amelia Island, or failing in that effort, she was to sail to the United States and there receive her cargo for the return to London. In effect, by stipulating to accept freight on the basis of the value of the return cargo, the neutral shipowner was taking his freight upon a contingency, and therefore might be considered to that degree a joint venturer in the voyage. Clearly the agreement looked towards a possible act of illegal trade with the United States, and was most advantageous to the owner of the enemy cargo. As the Chief Justice observed, the captors had not raised on appeal the question of whether any freight whatsoever was payable, leaving the issue to be decided only between the neutral shipowner and the proprietor

---

[146] Ship Societe, 9 Cranch 209–12 (1815), opinion by Chief Justice Marshall.

[147] In the 1814 term the Supreme Court had held that no lien upon enemy property would be recognized as an offset against the captors unless the lien were one recognized in international law independent of any contract between the consignee and consignor. The Frances (Irvin's Claim), 8 Cranch 418–20, opinion by Judge Washington.

447

of the condemned cargo. Yet the allowance of a freight award to stand in this case was clearly contrary to American wartime public policy, and encouraged illegal trade upon the high seas. There would seem to have been ample basis for a decree reversing the circuit court and ordering the prize to be condemned without deduction of freight to the captors.

In *Thirty Hogsheads of Sugar* v. *Boyle*[148] produce of the Danish island of Santa Cruz under British military occupation had been seized by an American privateer while en route to London. The goods were owned by one Adrian Benjamin Bentzon, a Danish subject and former Danish official of the island, who had departed subsequent to the British occupation. By the terms of capitulation the private property of Danish subjects on the island was secured to them. In argument counsel had urged that Bentzon's removal from Santa Cruz and his subsequent return to Denmark resulted in a continuation of his Danish commercial character and hence his neutral status despite the British occupation; on the other side it was claimed that whatever the proprietor's commercial character might be, the produce of lands in the military possession of the enemy was to be considered belligerent goods and subject to seizure and condemnation as prize. For the Court Chief Justice Marshall observed that British prize law in such cases should be applied—"that the proprietor has incorporated himself with the permanent interests of the nation as a holder of the soil, and is to be taken as a part of that country, in that particular transaction, independent of his own personal residence and occupation."[149] He observed that historically American prize law during the colonial period had been British prize law, and that upon the separation it continued to form the body of American prize law as far as it was adapted to American circumstances and had not been specifically altered by subsequent American action.[150]

In his observations on British admiralty precedents in the sugar case the Chief Justice established a standard for ascertaining ruling case law from the American colonial period that was deceptively simple. A precedent "established on ancient principles" in the British courts was to be accepted as received law in American prize matters, "unless it be very unreasonable, or be founded upon principles rejected by other nations."[151] Such law was to be considered international law and custom as enunciated by British courts. Unfortunately the division between "ancient principles" and modern British law was not as precise as one might wish. For example, Chief Justice Marshall noted that the

---

[148] 9 Cranch 191–99 (1815), opinion by Chief Justice Marshall.
[149] *Ibid.*, 197, quoting Sir William Scott.

[150] *Ibid.*, 198.
[151] *Ibid.*

very precedent applied in this case was one not reported until 1783— well after the independence of the United States had become assured. However, the principle, as distinguished from its publication, had (in his view) been established by past practice, since nothing in the opinion gave evidence that the rule was a novel one in English prize law.

As a practical matter English admiralty decisions were not reported during most of the American colonial period, and the bulk of the prize cases available for the use of John Marshall and his colleagues dated from the period of the first Napoleonic War from 1794 to 1800.[152] These opinions by Sir William Scott were to have an enormous influence upon the evolution of American prize and admiralty law, and citations to the early-nineteenth-century English cases ornament nearly all of the maritime cases decided by the Supreme Court. In effect the loose gauge by which Marshall determined their precedent value permitted their acceptance or rejection at the discretion of the Supreme Court. For all intents and purposes the Chief Justice had left it to the Supreme Court to establish on pragmatic lines those situations in which British prize law would govern, and a similar rule would seem to have been applied to all other maritime matters.[153]

The character of goods claimed as prize not infrequently depended upon the terms of shipment and the mode and time of transferring title. While a thorough analysis of these cases is inappropriate at this point,[154] it should be noted that as a general rule the transfer of title to a merchant resident in the United States had to be complete and irrevocable before the cargo would be considered to have an American character. If an American-based consignee had an option, exercisable upon the arrival of the goods in the United States, either to take title as a joint venturer with the shipper or to sell them as an agent for the consignor's account a capture *in transitu* would result in condemnation in an American prize court.[155] When goods remained subject to the account and risk of the shipper they retained his national character even though the transaction may have been financed by an advance from the American consignee.[156] While a maritime lien might arise in such circumstances under American municipal law, it was not part of

---

[152] See Part II, chapter 1, p. 379, note 19.

[153] In Croudson v. Leonard, 4 Cranch 438 (1808), Judge Washington stated that he did not consider himself bound by British decisions delivered after the American Revolution, but he read them as evidence of what the law had been prior to that date. As to the influence of international customs and usages applied by American federal courts in com-

mercial and maritime matters, see R. Bridwell and R. Whitten, *The Constitution and The Common Law* (Lexington, Mass., 1977), 51–55.

[154] They will be considered subsequently in Part II, chapter 3.

[155] The Frances (Gillespie's Claim), 8 Cranch 363–71 (1814); The Venus, 8 Cranch 253–317 (1814).

[156] The Frances (Irvin's Claim), 8 Cranch 418–20 (1814).

the law of nations and consequently not subject to consideration by the prize court; all of the cargo would be condemned as British goods if the consignor were British-based. Pragmatic reasons fortified theoretical ones; if collateral financial arrangements were controlling it would be too easy for enemy shippers to collude with neutrals. On the other hand, a shipment to an American consignee, directed to an American agent of the shipper because of doubts concerning the location of the consignee and his continuance in business, was held sufficient to transfer title to the American firm when the merchandise was laded on the captured vessel. But merchandise delivered for shipment to an agent with directions to deliver to the consignee if certain conditions were met was not adequate to constitute a change in title to the American consignee.[157]

To the foregoing case law in the Supreme Court it must be added that the character of the goods attached at the instant of shipment from England, and that no change of national character would be recognized while the goods were in transit.[158] For this reason the Court looked closely at the circumstances surrounding the shipment in attaching national character to seized goods. Commonly accepted principles of the mercantile law of sales were relied on to determine title when the vessel departed on her voyage, and it seems clear that the Supreme Court showed a genuine respect for the principles of sales law in judging these matters. At the same time liens and equitable claims unique to American municipal law but unknown to the law of nations were, in accordance with English admiralty usage, not considered sufficient in a prize court to attribute American character to goods. In this respect such potential encumbrances were treated by American prize courts much as bottomry bonds on vessels seized and condemned as prize of war.[159]

Certain deviations in voyages would also result in the assignment of a belligerent character to American vessels or goods. An example was the ship *Alexander*, which was on a voyage from Naples to the United States with an intermediate stop at Gibraltar, all under a British license issued before she had notice of the American declaration of war.[160] When her captain heard of war while still in European waters,

---

[157] The Merrimack, 8 Cranch 317–34 (1814), opinion by Judge Story.

[158] See Wheaton, *Digest*, 85. Grotius indicates that the law of sales, in regard to delivery, was not certain. A transfer of title might take place without delivery of the goods, but that must have been within the intention of the parties. However if the parties contracted to transfer title but possession remained with the seller, both the loss or the gain in the commodity inured to the benefit of the seller. H. Grotius, *The Law of War and Peace*, ed., F. Kelsey (Washington, 1925), 352–53.

[159] See discussion in Part II, chapter 3, note 126.

[160] The Alexander, 8 Cranch 169–80 (1814), opinion by Chief Justice Marshall.

he changed his destination and sailed to England, where he discharged his cargo and took on a new cargo to sail for the United States on May 9, 1813. Captured by an American privateer, the *Alexander* was condemned in the lower courts, and on appeal the Supreme Court affirmed, noting that with full knowledge of the war she had altered her course and sailed for England. At the time she was under no necessity to do so. Observed Chief Justice Marshall for the Court, "If such an act could be justified, it were vain to prohibit trade with the enemy."[161] Counsel for the claimants urged the right of removal of property from England, but Marshall rejected such a contention, observing that the precedent in *The Rapid*[162] precluded such a construction of the right of removal. Subsequently a similar case involving trade between the United States and St. Petersburg, with a stop in England after notice of the war, was also held to taint the vessel with a belligerent character and subject her to condemnation as prize even though she returned home in ballast.[163] A deviation made under compelling necessity after receipt of notice of the declaration of war might, however, under certain circumstances be held excused, and hence not a fit basis for condemnation of vessel or cargo.[164]

Noting that privateers' commissions fixed a low-water-mark limit to seizures off the coast of the United States and nations at war with the United States, and a three-league limit to seizures off the coasts of nations at peace with the United States,[165] the Supreme Court permitted the maximum possible use of privateers in American waters. While the majority of the Court followed Chief Justice Marshall in holding that timber floating in a non-navigable tidal inlet was not subject to prize jurisdiction,[166] Judge Story and one other dissenting justice asserted that any seizure by naval force, either on land or sea, subjected enemy property to the jurisdiction of prize courts.[167] This difference between the justices came to public attention in the opinion of *Brown* v. *U.S.*;

---

[161] *Ibid.*, 179.

[162] 8 Cranch 155 (1814); see discussion in Part II, chapter 2, note 136.

[163] The Joseph, 8 Cranch 451–56 (1814), opinion by Judge Washington; The Grotius, 8 Cranch 456–62 (1814), opinion by Judge Washington.

[164] The Mary, 9 Cranch 126–51 (1815), opinion by Chief Justice Marshall.

[165] The Joseph, 8 Cranch 451, 455, (1814). It was necessary that the capture be made by a duly commissioned privateer, but once that was done even the mere presence of one captor as prize master insured the prize court's jurisdiction. The Alex-

ander, 8 Cranch 169–80 (1814); Wheaton, *Digest*, 52–53.

[166] Brown v. United States, 8 Cranch 110–54 (1814).

[167] As to Judge Story's future propensity for extending admiralty jurisdiction, see C. Swisher, *The Taney Period, 1836–1864, Volume V, History of the Supreme Court of the United States*, ed., P. Freund (New York, 1974), 425. It should be noted that the *in rem* aspect of prize jurisdiction was recognized in passing by a dictum in The Brig Ann, 9 Cranch 291 (1815), and in The Mary, 9 Cranch 144 (1815).

it involved much more debate over the constitutional status of enemy property and the war powers of the President than it did over issues of prize law. However it demonstrates the caution with which most members of the Court approached the problem of territorial expansion of prize court jurisdiction. As such it parallels the Court's continuing division concerning the extent to which foreign prize decrees were to be considered binding under the law of nations, a matter of international conflict of laws to be discussed in chapter 3.

Despite the evolution of a remarkably rich body of material on American prize law, it would be overreaching to claim that the Supreme Court during this period had done more than merely to establish broad guidelines for the future development of the substantive and adjective law of prize. Undoubtedly English precedents had a pervasive influence upon the deliberations of the Court, and the individual justices varied in their view of reception of those rules into American jurisprudence. At the same time the conflict over the extent and nature of prize jurisdiction was part and parcel of the larger debate within the Court over the place of admiralty jurisdiction and its extent within the American federal system. By the end of the period it was possible for Henry Wheaton to prepare his *Digest of the Laws of Maritime Captures and Prize* (New York, 1815), which included an extensive treatment of American prize cases. The publication of that work demonstrated to the world that while American prize law might be similar in most major respects to English precedents, there were a sufficient number of differences to justify a treatise directed to the American legal community. The War of 1812 resulted in an outpouring of national zeal that produced the national anthem and numerous other symbols of Americanism, and while its contributions to the American law of prize may be limited, it can nevertheless be said that the prize cases considered by the Supreme Court during these years established a foundation upon which future prize jurisprudence would be developed.

In a more general sense the prize cases and the illegal trade cases that preceded them give us a better understanding of the Supreme Court's growing tendency to distinguish between law, and the private property rights that were subject to confiscation only by judicial action, and public policy, which formed an overarching national purpose against which claims of private privilege must be measured and balanced. Faced with grave national crises of diplomatic and military policy, the Supreme Court evidenced a willingness to permit Congress and the President to act forcefully in the pursuit of the general welfare and security of the United States. At the same time it made it patently clear that the constitutional limitations imposed by the American republican form of government required that the implementation of public policy should not disregard the rights and privileges of American citizens. The judiciary alone stood between the individual citizen and the excessive zeal of majority rule.

Appeals from lower federal court prize decrees added a new dimension to the work and thought of the Supreme Court. They required that the judges define the place of international law and custom in the American federal system. While this had been done in an imperfect way during the War for Independence, the supremacy of the central government was challenged and the work of the Federal Court of Appeals in Cases of Prize and Capture was shadowed by State resistance to its mandates. Hence it was Marshall's Court that had the first opportunity to act as the acknowledged supreme court of prize law in the United States. The existence of this unchallenged position as the supreme court of international law was the product of circumstances brought into existence by the ratification of the federal Constitution some twenty-five years before. But the manner in which the Court seized the opportunity to broaden its horizons and enrich American law with foreign precedents is a tribute to the abilities and acumen of its judges. When appropriate the prize law of the foreign states was absorbed into the international law of the United States. This enhanced the strength and vigor of federal jurisprudence in the field, and provided the judges with an experience in adjudicating cases that were not governed by binding precedents but that had to be considered in the light of their overall conformity with the orderly administration of the law of nations and their impact upon essential principles of American law and custom. The prize cases led the judges to examine the law of nations, the varieties of municipal law touching upon that law, and the principles of natural law and justice that formed the conceptual basis of all human legal systems.[168] Their sheer number and their pecuniary importance made them central to the work of the Court from 1812 to 1815; but their greatest impact was upon the minds of the judges who gave judgment in them.

---

[168] It has been argued that in the exercise of diversity jurisdiction the Supreme Court was governed by rules of private international law and international conflict of laws rules, thus insuring that federal purposes were served while preserving local State initiative in adopting local laws and customs not in conflict with federal requirements. Bridwell and Whitten, *The Constitution and the Common Law,* 51–68. Quite possibly the impulse stemmed from prize and admiralty cases of this period. It is also likely that the Court's experience with prize cases sharpened its conceptual tools of analysis. Can we ignore the fact that a mere four years after the end of the War of 1812 the judges began to lay down the broad concepts of American federalism and limited government contained in M'Culloch v. Maryland and Dartmouth College v. Woodward?

CHAPTER III

Marine Insurance and Instance Cases

THE ACTIVITIES of the Supreme Court in the fields of marine insurance and instance[1] cases in admiralty cannot be overlooked if the full contribution of the early Marshall Court to maritime law is to be properly evaluated. Although illegal trade cases and prize causes comprise the largest number of maritime cases in the period through 1815, the principles developed in litigation on policies of marine insurance were applied to those controversies, just as prize court rules were the constant concern of judges who attempted to construe the terms of insurance policies or the facts leading to, or exonerating, the insurer's liability. Similarly, instance cases drew upon both marine insurance and the prize and illegal trade cases when necessary, and by the very nature of American admiralty practice, some cases consisted of both prize and instance court matters presented simultaneously to the district and circuit courts of the United States sitting in maritime matters.

MARINE INSURANCE

The development of the law of marine insurance may have served as the nexus between modern rules of casualty insurance and the law of business contracts, as well as a substantial source of subsidiary case law in the fields of illegal trade regulation and prize jurisdiction. Indeed the assignment of marine insurance cases to the English common law courts in Tudor times did not deprive the subject of its maritime flavor nor of the strong influence of civil law traditions in its customs and usages. By the time the Marshall Court heard argument in its first

---

[1] The English convention has been adopted in the use of this term, namely, that all admiralty and marine jurisdiction not included within prize jurisdiction is instance court jurisdiction.

marine insurance case there had been a long history of litigation in the field, not only in Great Britain but also in the American colonies and States.[2] Because of the preeminence of English precedent and the relative lack of diplomatic and general policy considerations influencing most marine insurance adjudications, there was little if any American resistance to the wholesale adoption of English marine insurance. The standard English texts of Samuel Marshall and Sir James Allan Park were not only cited extensively in oral argument and in the opinions of the Supreme Court but they both had been issued in American editions before 1805, making English marine insurance law readily available and extremely persuasive as the Supreme Court established the foundations for American jurisprudence in the field.[3]

Although the rise of marine insurance litigation after 1801 can easily be attributed to the commercial situation created by the Napoleonic Wars and an increasing number of seizures for illegal trade and non-neutral behavior, the marked increase in appeals to the Supreme Court of the United States would seem predicated upon some other factors. All of the marine insurance cases heard by the Court from 1801 to 1815 were on appeal from the lower federal courts, indicating the establishment of federal jurisdiction based on diversity of citizenship and maritime jurisdiction. With the growth of the American marine insurance industry across State lines, it was probably inevitable that federal courts would become preeminent in the settlement of litigation in the field, yet it is remarkable that the earlier decisions of the Supreme Court contribute so little to marine insurance law, while many of the Marshall Court's opinions before 1815 are still cited in the field.

In its adjudication of marine insurance cases the Court was well aware of the heavy influence of commercial custom and usage that would prescribe caution in the construction of policies, and require a due respect for the accretion of tradition and formalism in business procedures. As Chief Justice Marshall remarked:

The contract of insurance is certainly very loosely drawn, and a settled construction, different from the natural import of the words,

---

[2] G. Gilmore and C. Black, Jr., *The Law of Admiralty*, 2nd ed. (Brooklyn, 1975), 54–55; J. Goebel, Jr., ed., *The Law Practice of Alexander Hamilton*, 2 vols. to date (New York, 1964–), II, 391–444; A. Browne, *An Historical View of the Law of Maritime Commerce* (Edinburgh: 1841), 13–15; F. Wiswall, Jr., *The Development of Admiralty Jurisdiction and Practice since 1800* (Cambridge, 1970), 1–11.

[3] Samuel Marshall's *A Treatise on the Law of Insurance* first appeared in a London edition in 1802; the first American edition was published at Boston in January 1805. Sir James Allan Park's *A System of the Law of Marine Insurances* was first published in London in 1787 and was in its fourth edition by 1800. The third American edition was published in Boston in 1800.

is given, by the commercial world, to many of its stipulations, which construction has been sanctioned by the decisions of courts.[4]

Somewhat later, in accepting English doctrine concerning the description of an insured voyage, he suggested that "it is dangerous to change a settled construction on policies of insurance," and John Quincy Adams, in argument before the Court, noted that "Lord Mansfield has observed that the merchants seldom introduce a written clause into a policy, but it ends in a lawsuit,"[5] thereby stressing the preference for existing forms of doing business and the improbability of judicial deviation from the rigid procedures developed over three hundred years of business and litigation. Obviously, this was an area of the law where change originated in commercial and underwriting practices, and even then at a slow and very deliberate pace.

As the prize cases discussed in the last chapter amply demonstrate, the Anglo-French wars from 1794 to 1815 were a period of high risk and uncertainty for marine insurance companies. Not only was privateer activity extensive, but the traditional rules of war were constantly being altered by both belligerents. As a result, there was pressure to change the forms of policies and reconsider limitations of risks, thereby providing adequate coverage for merchants at a premium adjusted to compensate for the additional risks. An example of this tendency was the insertion of a clause requiring "proof of neutrality in the United States only" into certain marine insurance policies written in 1795 and thereafter.[6] This practice resulted from the general acceptance of the English precedent in marine insurance matters, adopted by the Supreme Court in *Croudson* v. *Leonard*,[7] which treated the decree of a foreign prize court as conclusive on the issues of neutrality raised in subsequent actions on policies of marine insurance. The new clause was a contractual agreement between the insured and the underwriter, providing that such a foreign prize decree would not be binding in an action upon

---

[4] Maryland Insurance Co. v. Woods, 6 Cranch 45 (1810).

[5] Dickey v. Baltimore Insurance Co., 7 Cranch 331 (1812); Adams' argument is in Head and Amory v. Providence Insurance Co., 2 Cranch 146 (1804). William Murray, first Earl of Mansfield (1705–93), served as Chief Justice of the King's Bench from 1756 until his death.

[6] See discussion in Goebel, *Hamilton Law Practice*, II, 412–13.

[7] 4 Cranch 434–43 (1808). While it was common to read depositions of evidence read in the condemnation proceeding, the Supreme Court required that only the prize libel and the sentence be introduced as evidence of condemnation, Marine Insurance Co. of Alexandria v. Hodgson, 6 Cranch 206–21, at 220 (1810). The English rule was in conflict with the contemporary practice of French courts, which did not recognize the conclusiveness of foreign prize decrees pertaining to French subjects. See S. Marshall, *A Treatise on the Law of Insurance*, 1st Am. ed. (Boston, 1805), 288–97.

the policy, but that the insured might introduce proof of neutrality in any marine insurance case instituted in an American court. On the basis of this development, it was possible for insureds to collect from American insurance companies on policies warranting their goods and conduct neutral, even though the decree condemning the ship or goods held the property or conduct to be non-neutral. In *Maryland Insurance Co.* v. *Woods* the Supreme Court not only passed upon the legality of the new clause but it also held that its application was broad enough to encompass not only the neutral character of the condemned property but also the neutrality of the insured's conduct.[8]

Traditionally a policy of insurance contained a complete, although perhaps unduly formalized and abbreviated, description of the risks underwritten by the insurer. This was a statement of the property interests insured—the vessel, cargo, or freight for the voyage, or in some cases a combination of these. Next, the policy terms described the voyage by specifying terminal points and stipulating permissible delays and ancillary voyages to be covered. Insured losses might be limited either by the insured's warranties in the policy or by express exceptions to the policy coverage; it was also possible to restrict losses in certain commodity classes by listing cargo as a memorandum article, which precluded recovery except in the event of certain catastrophic losses of that cargo or the entire vessel and its cargo.[9]

Policy Exceptions—Deviation and Non-Inception

In containing precise descriptions of the route of the voyage, American hull insurance policies closely followed British underwriting practice.[10] The insured vessel was required to sail between the terminal points, and failure to do so would result in the discharge of the insurer from liability, either on the basis of non-inception of the contemplated voyage, or the less onerous ground of deviation from the route set forth in the policy. Non-inception, or alteration at the commencement of the

---

[8] 6 Cranch 29, at 45 (1810). It is unclear whether, absent a warranty of neutrality, non-neutral actions that resulted in a loss would be covered by the terms of the policy and the "proof only" provision. Clearly an act such as breach of blockade was illegal and the issuance of policies of indemnity for losses incurred through such acts would encourage blockade running. Goods not warranted neutral might be insured even though belligerent. But if actions were not warranted neutral, might they be insured if hostile?

[9] In regard to use of warranties see Gilmore and Black, *Admiralty*, 67–68; on memorandum articles see *ibid.*, 79–81; on total loss see *ibid.*, 83–85.

[10] "Every voyage insured must have a *terminus a quo* and a *terminus ad quem* . . ." and "the voyage insured must be truly and accurately described in the policy . . . ," comments Marshall, *Insurance*, 161, 227.

trip, resulted in a breach of the terms of the policy and immediately voided its coverage. Deviation, on the other hand, occurred after the insured voyage had begun, and the underwriter's liability under the policy did not terminate until such time as the insured vessel actually started on the variant course.[11] After that point the shipowner became his own insurer, and responsible for the acts of the master of the vessel.[12]

Warfare in the West Indies resulted in frequent naval blockades to the detriment of American merchantmen, who were tempted to deviate from their insured voyage paths. For example, when the ship *William and Mary* sailed for Laguira and "at and from" Laguira to a neighboring port, she carried hull insurance for that particular voyage.[13] Arriving at Laguira she found unfavorable markets for trading, and proceeded to neighboring Amsterdam in Curaçao. Nearing Amsterdam she sighted a warship of the British blockading squadron, and when she approached to make inquiry she was seized and later condemned for violating the blockade. At trial in the circuit court, the insurance company offered evidence to prove that the *William and Mary* had set sail for the distant islands of St. Thomas or Puerto Rico, with an intention to stop at Amsterdam if the British blockade had been lifted. The tender of this evidence was refused by the circuit court, which also refused to charge the jury concerning the legal effect of a deviation upon departure from

---

[11] Gilmore and Black, *Admiralty*, 66–67, touch upon the point. See also Marshall, *Insurance*, 392–413; J. Park, *A System of the Law of Marine Insurances*, 2nd ed. (London, 1790), 294–317. While non-inception and deviation are distinguishable, they arise from the same foundation. "The true reason why a deviation discharges the insurer," comments Marshall, *Insurance*, 401, "is not the increase of the risk; but that the party contracting has, without necessity, substituted another voyage for that which was insured . . ."

[12] As the *seriatim* opinions in Marine Insurance Company v. Tucker, 3 Cranch 357–98 (1806), indicate, a policy could not be vitiated for non-inception if the insured vessel carried goods bound for the terminal point specified in the policy. An agreement made to stop at an additional destination might only be considered as evidence of an intention to deviate and coverage under the policy would attach until the point of division between the two ports was reached and the vessel started on her way to the

non-insured destination. Judge Washington observed in his opinion, "The rule . . . which I consider to be firmly established . . . is that, if the ship sail from the port mentioned in the policy, with an intention to go to the port, or ports, also described therein, a determination to call at an intermediate port, either with a view to land cargo, for orders, or the like, is not such a change of the voyage as to prevent the policy from attaching, but is merely a case of deviation, if the intention be carried into execution, or be persisted in after the vessel has arrived at the dividing point." *Ibid.*, 391.

[13] Maryland Insurance Co. v. Woods, 6 Cranch 29–51 (1810). On the legal significance of insurance "at and from" a given place see Dickey v. Baltimore Insurance Co., 7 Cranch 327 at 329–31 (1813). See also Marshall, *Insurance*, 173, 259, 260, that insurance at and from a port covers risks from the time of her first arrival in port and continues as long as the ship remains there awaiting the voyage insured; insurance at and from an island permits coasting voyages.

Laguira for St. Thomas or Puerto Rico. As a result the Supreme Court sent the case back for retrial. It is obvious that the underwriter's liability continued until the British seizure off Amsterdam, unless it was there vitiated by non-neutral acts in breaking blockade. On the other hand, if the stop at Amsterdam (by terms of the policy and custom of trade a neighboring port to Laguira) was merely an intermediate call in pursuit of the voyage to the more distant islands, then a deviation commenced at Laguira, and from that point onward insurance coverage would terminate.

Policy Exceptions—Demurrage and Prolongation of Voyage

Although deviations normally involved departures from the voyage as specified in the policy, excessive delays in port, or the master's decision to extend the time at sea, might have a similar effect on the underwriter's liability. For example, a ship on a trading voyage from Baltimore to Barcelona delayed a coastal trading voyage permitted under the policy because of an unjustified fear of the Algerine pirates. After six months in port at Barcelona she sailed on an uneventful voyage along the Mediterranean coast of Spain, and then departed for America. While on her return transatlantic voyage she was captured by a British warship and condemned under a British order-in-council that had been issued while she lay in Barcelona harbor.[14] For the Supreme Court, Marshall held that an idle waste of time after completion of business in port was a deviation that discharged the underwriter. As far as the fear of capture was concerned, "the danger . . . must be obvious and immediate in reference to the situation of the ship at the particular time."[15]

The detention of a ship at sea for the purpose of rendering aid to another vessel discovered foundering and in distress might also be considered a deviation that would discharge the insurance company. This principle of insurance law was mentioned in argument of the salvage case of *Mason* v. *The Blaireau*, discussed below,[16] and counsel agreed that this was a correct statement of the accepted law. However, Chief Justice Marshall objected and pointed out that such a discharge of the underwriter would discourage sea captains from giving aid to vessels in peril.[17] The issue does not seem to have been raised for adjudication by the Supreme Court during our period, but would seem to present

---

[14] Oliver v. Maryland Insurance Co., 7 Cranch 487–96 (1813).

[15] *Ibid.*, 493.

[16] 2 Cranch 240–71 (1804). See Part II, chapter 3, notes 66–75.

[17] The argument is in 2 Cranch 257, 258, and Marshall's comment is in the reporter's note 1 to the argument on 257.

some fine points of usage of the maritime nations of the world and the public policy considerations and humanitarian purposes of the law of salvage.

Policy Exceptions—Changed Nature of the Voyage

An action that changed the nature of the voyage, as distinguished from its routing, might also void insurance coverage, even though the alteration in circumstances might not have increased the risk to the underwriter. This is shown by the memorable case of *Maryland Insurance Company* v. *LeRoy*,[18] in which a vessel insured for a voyage to and along the African coast exercised her license to stop and pick up water and "stock." However, in the policy the term "stock" was used in juxtaposition with the more specific identification of hogs, goats, and chickens, whereas the animals loaded on board were jackasses. The circuit court below charged the jury that if the underwriter's risk were substantially increased because of the loading of jackasses, his liability under the policy was canceled. On this ground of error the Supreme Court reversed, holding that this was not merely a misrepresentation in the making of the contract, but rather a departure from its terms. It was therefore of no significance whether the risk was increased or not, for any departure from the terms of the policy discharges the insurer. While "stock" might in some circumstances be a broad generic term, in this particular policy it was restricted to small animals by their designation in express terms. Although Judge Johnson in his opinion for the Court indicated a reluctance to add to the number of causes that would void a policy of insurance, he felt that justice required the insured to provide a good description of those risks. For that reason the contract as incorporated in the policy "must be substantially adhered to."[19]

Policy Exceptions—Mode of Trial

Questions of deviations and delays were mixed matters of law and fact that were appropriately left to the determinations of juries under the directions of the court. In addition to the factual issues to be considered by the juries, the Supreme Court made it clear that matters of trade usage might also be considered by the jury in evaluating the legal consequences of delays in port.[20] The existence of an ancient and established usage was also knowledge that might be charged to the

---

[18] 7 Cranch 26–31 (1812).
[19] *Ibid.*, 31.

[20] Oliver v. Maryland Insurance Co., 7 Cranch 487 at 491 (1813).

parties entering into a contract for marine insurance,[21] and the specific terms of the contract should be read in such a way as to accord with such a custom or usage. Evidence of trade usages thus served to mitigate the strict applications of doctrine of deviation and delay and at the same time they affected the interpretations of the expressed intentions of parties in marine insurance matters.

Insurance Coverage

Underwriting custom and usage had done much to define specific kinds of insurable property and the specific phraseology of policies assuring that property to the insured parties. However, the Supreme Court passed upon a number of appeals dealing with these matters, applying trade custom and standard rules of construction to the policies under litigation. In *Gracie* v. *Marine Insurance Company of Baltimore*[22] the Supreme Court held a policy to be a cargo, rather than a hull insurance policy. The case involved a policy on goods carried safely to Leghorn and deposited in quarantine at the lazaretto, an area some distance from the city where cargoes and passengers were landed to safeguard the inhabitants from tropical diseases. The cargo so deposited was subsequently seized and confiscated by invading French troops. Chief Justice Marshall pointed out that hull insurance ceases when the vessel reaches the port of destination and is moored safely there for twenty-four hours. On the other hand, in cargo insurance policies, the kind considered in this case, the extent of the coverage was determined by the intention of the parties.[23] Since it was established custom of the trade to Leghorn that unlading at the lazaretto was considered equivalent to a landing at Leghorn, and the parties had not stipulated otherwise, the cargo underwriter was not liable for loss through French military action at the lazaretto.

The responsibilities of a cargo insurance underwriter were more

---

[21] Use of the lazaretto in Leghorn, Gracie v. Marine Insurance Co. of Baltimore, 8 Cranch 83 (1814). As Samuel Marshall noted, "Every underwriter is assumed to be fully conversant in the usual course of the trade in which he becomes an insurer." *Insurance*, 182.

[22] 8 Cranch 75–84 (1814).

[23] The English rule on hull insurance was not as clear as the Chief Justice indicated, but it was usual underwriting practice to include twenty-four hours after arrival within the insurance coverage. That was done by express provision in the typical English hull insurance policy. See Marshall, *Insurance*, 172, 173. On the other hand Marshall, *ibid.*, 162, indicates a rule of marine insurance law to be that insurance attached to goods from the time of lading on board until they were safely landed at their destination, or if unlading was delayed, until a reasonable time after arrival. The lazaretto situation, resolved by resort to customs and usages of the trade, seems in accord with English rules. See *ibid.*, 164–69.

clearly defined in *Caze and Richard* v. *Baltimore Insurance Company*.[24]
An American ship en route from Bordeaux to New York during the
War of 1812 was seized by a British warship and condemned with her
cargo in Halifax. As the result of a reversal of the sentence, the proceeds
from the sale of the cargo were awarded to the insurance company to
which the cargo owner had already abandoned his interests. Thereupon
the shipowner claimed freight from the cargo underwriter. The Supreme
Court, in an opinion by Judge Story, held that no freight was due. There
was no obligation on the part of the insurer of the cargo to pay freight
since restitution at the hands of the prize court did not constitute his
voluntary acceptance of the shipment at Halifax. Although a lien for
freight would attach had the voyage been completed and the cargo delivered, such a lien was not impressed upon the goods at the time of
the seizure and could not arise as a consequence of any subsequent
event.

In regard to hull insurance the Court had drawn a precise line
between insurance of the vessel *for* the voyage and the insurance of the
vessel *and* the voyage, indicating that in the latter case not only the
value of the vessel was insured, but also the profits from the voyage.[25]
The underwriters of a policy on the vessel alone, that is *for* the voyage,
were held not liable if the profitability of the voyage had been destroyed
by the partial or total loss of the cargo; their only responsibility was
to indemnify the shipowner for the loss of the vessel. In such circumstances the shipowner might not abandon the vessel to the hull insurance
underwriter, for she was still capable of performing the voyage.

Freight insurance, as distinguished from hull, voyage, or cargo
insurance, was involved in *King* v. *Delaware Insurance Company*.[26]
This case arose from the abandonment of a voyage because of the false
rumor that the port of destination was blockaded. Speaking for the
Court, Chief Justice Marshall rejected the shipowner's contention that
mere rumor of a British blockade of the port of destination would be
sufficient basis for abandoning the voyage. When one thousand miles
from the American coast, the vessel whose freight was insured was met

---

[24] 7 Cranch 358–63 (1813).

[25] Alexander v. Baltimore Marine
Insurance Co., 4 Cranch 370–82
(1808). As Chief Justice Marshall
observed, "The underwriters insure
against the loss or damage to the
vessel, not against the loss or any
damage to the cargo. They insure her
ability to perform her voyage, not
that she shall perform it." *Ibid.*, 374.
There was a clear distinction between
insurance of the ship *for* the voyage

and the ship *and* the voyage. *Ibid.*,
377.

[26] Freight, in marine law, is the
carriage fee payable to the shipowner
upon the delivery of cargo; freight
insurance secures this amount to him
in the event the voyage is abandoned
because of necessity. Cargo insurance
protects the owner of goods shipped
on the vessel against their loss. King
v. Delaware Insurance Co., 6 Cranch
71–82 (1810).

by a British warship and informed that the Isle of France, a French colony, was blockaded. As a matter of fact, there was no actual blockade at the time the notice was given nor at any time before the ship's return to Philadelphia, where abandonment was made to the underwriter. Subsequent to her arrival in Philadelphia, the enactment of the American Embargo held her in port and prevented resumption of the voyage to the Isle of France. While the jury had held that the British warning was responsible for breaking up the voyage, Marshall considered that fact, in and of itself, not sufficient to sustain recovery as a matter of law. The disruption of the voyage and resultant loss of freight would have to be the direct result of one or more of the perils insured against in the policy, or recovery would have to be denied. In this instance there was no physical restraint by the warship, and the British orders-in-council in force at that time did not prohibit trade between the United States and French colonies. The master of the ship was free to proceed on his course and as a matter of international law and British admiralty instructions, he was entitled to do so. This abandonment had been caused by the American captain's fear of an illegal seizure and condemnation, and that remote possibility was an inadequate basis for abandonment and a claim of liability on the part of the insurance company.

Misrepresentations and Concealments

Because the marine insurer's liability was firmly based upon his contractual undertaking in the policy, it was not uncommon for defenses of misrepresentation and concealment to be raised in defense against policy claims. Except in the case of a fraudulent misrepresentation by the insured, which would void the contract in all cases, the Supreme Court applied the rule that only misrepresentations and concealments that were material to the risk were valid defenses by the insurer.[27] Thus an owner's misstatement of the value of the vessel did not release the insurer from liability on the contract.[28] Similarly, a stipulation that the vessel was seaworthy would void a policy only if it could be shown that at the time of sailing an unseaworthy condition existed which later aborted the voyage.[29] Evidence of her unsafe condition at some later date was not in itself adequate basis for invalidating the policy.

---

[27] This continues to be the modern rule. Gilmore and Black, *Admiralty*, 62. An extensive discussion of misrepresentations and concealments is in Marshall, *Insurance*, 335–53.

[28] Hodgson v. Marine Insurance Co. of Alexandria, 5 Cranch 100–15 (1809).

[29] Marine Insurance Co. of Alex-

andria v. Willson, 3 Cranch 187–92 (1805). The decision in this case, as well as its presentation to the Supreme Court, seems to be an unusual deviation from English insurance law, which created a presumption of unseaworthiness at the inception of the voyage unless circumstances were sufficiently explained by the insured

Non-disclosure of facts, absent fraud on the part of the insured, would not void a marine insurance policy unless the facts were material to the risk. Indeed the burden rested upon the insurer to so request information and draft his contracts of insurance, that the insured parties were neither damaged nor misled by his actions. Where a policy contained no warranty of neutrality, thereby allowing coverage of both neutral and belligerent insureds and property, the failure to disclose belligerent status was deemed not to increase the risk as a matter of law.[30] Where a policy was drawn in such broad terms that it covered any and all persons owning the vessel, it was not necessary to the validity of the policy that the names of all owners be supplied to the insurance company or be included in the policy. On the other hand, if individuals not named were excluded from coverage, and the insurance company, knowing that the applicants were operating under the misapprehension that express statement of a party's name was not required, did not correct the mistake, then the coverage might be enlarged in spite of the terms of the policy.[31]

Usages and customs of the insurance trade might also determine what circumstances might safely be concealed from the insurer. For example, the fact that vessels trading to the Spanish colonies of South America always carried duplicate sets of papers, thereby tacitly complying with the imperial ban on foreign trade to that region, might be a usage of which knowledge was charged to the underwriter.[32] The party seeking insurance was not required to acquaint the insurer with this usage; just as in *Gracie* v. *Marine Insurance Company of Balti-*

---

or the master of the vessel. See Marshall, *Insurance*, 363–73. The presumption does not seem to have been relied upon in argument before the Court and was not raised in the Court's deliberations.

[30] On the effect of the omission of the warranty of neutrality, see Hodgson v. Marine Insurance Co. of Alexandria, 5 Cranch 109 (1809). Maryland Insurance Co. v. Ruden's Administrator, 6 Cranch 339 (1810), held that the materiality of the misrepresentation or concealment to the risk was a mixed matter of law and fact to be left to the determination of the jury.

[31] Hodgson v. Marine Insurance Co., 5 Cranch 100, at 109 (1809). The Supreme Court stated the general rule to be that persons not mentioned in the policy were denied recovery, except where the underwriter, know-

ing of their mistaken assumption that they were insured, permitted them to proceed in ignorance of their exclusion from coverage. See also Graves and Barnewell v. Boston Marine Insurance Co., 2 Cranch 419–44 (1804), setting forth the general doctrine.

[32] Livingston and Gilchrist v. Maryland Insurance Co., 6 Cranch 274–81 (1810), and the same case on subsequent appeal, 7 Cranch 506–48 (1813). The continental writers differed on whether illegal trade, known previously to the underwriter, might void the policy. In England, on the other hand, a parliamentary statute mentioned the trade with the American colonies of Spain and Portugal and specifically authorized insurance contracts that would be valid despite the illegality of such trade in Spanish and Portuguese law. Marshall, *Insurance*, 51–55.

more,[33] the company was held to be knowledgeable concerning the usages at Leghorn in regard to quarantine of goods in the lazaretto of that port. Usages of trade were matters upon which the underwriter was put on inquiry, and in the absence of diligence by the insurer to obtain information concerning the customary trade practices, a concealment or omission would not void the policy. In a certain sense the usage as a matter of law was part and parcel of the risk the underwriter assumed when he issued a policy for the region affected by the use; consequently it was already part of the risk, and his failure to recognize the increase of the risk through the customary practice of trade did not void the policy. Of course the insurer's ignorance might result in his demanding a much lower premium, but that in itself would have nothing to do with the validity of the policy.

Warranties

The insertion of warranties into marine insurance policies was an established practice in international trade by 1801, and the early Marshall Court dealt with the matter through consultation of existing English precedents. The most extensively litigated warranty was that of neutrality, which excepted from insurance coverage any goods not of neutral character,[34] as well as losses incurred by acts of a non-neutral nature.[35] Neutrality as such was defined by the national character of the owner of the goods, and similar rules applied in marine insurance cases and prize cases. Nearly all attempts to recover on insurance policies for seizures by belligerents involved construction of one or both of these aspects of the warranty of neutrality. Similar in operation and

---

[33] 8 Cranch 75; see discussion in Part II, chapter 3, note 9. See also Marshall, *Insurance*, 286, et. seq.

[34] Under circumstances of necessity where carriage of belligerent goods was required of the vessel, the Court might hold that the warranty of neutrality was not broken and permit recovery on the policy. In Hallet v. Jenks, 3 Cranch 210–19 (1805), a merchant ship driven into Cape Francois was plundered of her cargo by French officials and repaid in produce of the island for the portion she retained but was forced to leave there. Prevented from carrying specie from the island, she loaded French goods with which she was captured by a British frigate and condemned for violating the American Non-Intercourse

Act of 1798. Chief Justice Marshall held that the Non-Intercourse Act excepted from its terms landings due to distress from bad weather. Even in time of actual war, he held, such an act of illegal trade would be justified by necessity.

[35] Non-neutral acts that would render a neutral vessel lawfully subject to capture and condemnation included armed resistance to visitation and search, an attempt to breach a blockade, sailing without proper documents or violation of terms in specific treaties. Marshall, *Insurance*, 300, 301. Other acts such as destruction of ship's papers or carrying duplicate sets of papers showing two national characters might also constitute a non-neutral act.

importance was the exclusion from policy coverage of losses due to the insured's engaging in acts of illegal trade, contrary to the municipal regulations of the condemning sovereign. For most purposes this exclusion may be treated as identical to the warranty against neutrality.[36]

From 1801 to 1815 the commercial situation caused a substantial growth of American federal case law concerning these two warranties, and added much to the accepted American definition of neutrality and illegal trade. As stated, it was the Napoleonic Wars that caused the development of a new policy clause, permitting collateral attack upon the prize decrees of foreign courts when the issue of neutrality was raised in marine insurance actions.

Blockades and the Warranty of Neutrality

Perhaps the most detailed discussion of the international law of blockade in this period is to be found not in texts but in marine insurance cases. An attempt by a neutral vessel to enter a blockaded port was considered a belligerent act that would subject the ship to seizure and condemnation by the blockading power.[37] Because of this rule of international law, recognized by the United States as well as by Britain and France, underwriters excepted blockaded ports from destinations that might otherwise be covered in the policy. Since blockades were never sufficiently stable to identify such by name in the policies, the provision was phrased in general terms so that attempted entry into all ports that were in fact blockaded at the time of entry would be prohibited on the pain of sacrificing policy coverage. The result was achieved either by an exception to the coverage of the policy, as in *Yeaton* v. *Fry*,[38] or by reliance upon the judicial construction of the warranty of neutrality, which protected the underwriter against nonneutral acts (which included breach of blockade) by the insured's vessel.[39]

Under established international law, when "normal" conditions of war existed, a captain of neutral merchant vessel was expected to make due inquiry at intermediate ports concerning the existence of an actual blockade at his port or ports of destination, and a capture re-

---

[36] Such an exclusion was involved in Church v. Hubbart, 2 Cranch 187–239 (1804), where the Court held it an aspect of illegal trade to hover off the coast of Brazil, even though no actual landing or trade took place before seizure by the Portuguese authorities.

[37] On breach of blockade and pen-alties, see H. Wheaton, *A Digest of the Law of Marine Captures and Prizes* (New York, 1815), 190–209.

[38] 5 Cranch 335–43 (1809).

[39] Fitzsimmons v. Newport Insurance Co., 4 Cranch 185–202 (1808); followed in Maryland Insurance Co. v. Woods, 6 Cranch 29–51 (1810).

sulting from failure to exercise due care and caution in this matter might result in a loss not indemnified by the insurance underwriter. On the other hand, merely sailing for a port without knowledge of its subjection to an actual blockade would not void the policy during the course of the voyage.[40] Sailing for a blockaded port with knowledge of the blockade might, under a line of English prize court precedents, be treated as a constructive attempt to enter, and hence subject the vessel to seizure for breach of blockade.[41] The American rule in this regard seems to have been that *an attempt to enter* the port, as distinguished from *an intention to do so*, would be the only basis for condemnation for non-neutral acts, and hence the sole basis for denying recovery under policies of marine insurance.

This divergence between English and American prize precedents in regard to breach of blockade resulted in uncertainties that had been resolved by the 1794 Jay Treaty provision that required a blockading squadron to "warn off" approaching merchant ships of the other contracting party, and to seize the neutral vessel for breach of blockade only if it made an attempt to enter after being duly warned of the blockade.[42] Under the Jay Treaty the Supreme Court held that merchantmen who might normally be required to make due inquiry at intermediate ports were released from this obligation. They might safely proceed to their destination, there to make inquiry of any British blockading squadron stationed there, relying upon the treaty guarantee of a warning before seizure for breach of blockade. Naturally the procedures stipulated in the Jay Treaty pertained only to the behavior of the two signatories, leaving the international law of blockade intact with regard to other belligerents and neutrals.

It is important to view the Jay Treaty provisions in the light of the standard policy clause stipulating "proof only in the United States" in regard to neutrality. Its effect was to provide the insured with an opportunity to attack collaterally a prize decree rendered in non-American courts, and to recover the insurance proceeds despite an outstanding foreign prize decree based upon a finding of non-neutral behavior. The rise of that clause in insurance practice in 1795[43] may well have been influenced by the blockade provisions of the treaty, for if a vessel were seized for breach of blockade and condemned on that

---

[40] Yeaton v. Fry, 5 Cranch 335 (1809); Fitzsimmons v. Newport Insurance Co., 4 Cranch 185–202, at 198 (1808).

[41] Fitzsimmons v. Newport Insurance Co., 4 Cranch 199–200.

[42] H. Miller, ed., *Treaties and Other International Acts of the United States*

of America, II (Washington, 1931), 259.

[43] The date is based on Professor Julius Goebel's discussion of the New York marine insurance business. Goebel, *Hamilton Law Practice*, II, 412, notes 100, 101, 102.

basis, the foreign prize sentence would be conclusive in the American marine insurance action, and the insured might not be permitted to submit proof concerning the failure of the British squadron to comply with the terms of the treaty. The case of *Fitzsimmons* v. *Newport Insurance Company*[44] is illustrative of the operation of the warning-off system, and the manner in which there might be recovery in certain cases. The ship *John* on a voyage from Charleston to Cádiz was stopped by a ship of the squadron blockading that part of the Spanish port on July 16, 1800; she had left for Spain without knowledge of the existence of the blockade. When the shipowner sued his underwriter by alleging unlawful seizure by the British, the Supreme Court reviewed the circumstances of the seizure in light of the Jay Treaty and upheld the right of the insured to recover. Although the captain of the *John* had been properly warned off, the admiral of the squadron had not thereafter released the merchant vessel from detention. It was true that the merchant captain asserted his intention to pursue his directed voyage to Cádiz, but mere intention to enter the blockaded port was held not adequate as a basis for condemnation under the treaty. The merchantman would have to be released from British control and, after being at liberty to proceed elsewhere, then attempt to enter the blockaded port, before the seizure would be lawful. In the case presented she was never free to proceed after being warned off, and as a result the British action was illegal, and as such might form the basis for recovery against the underwriter. The rule in *Fitzsimmons* and the Jay Treaty, coupled with the "proof only in the United States" clause, gave American merchantmen greater protection, not only against British blockading squadrons but also against the uncertainties concerning their duty to make inquiry and the legal effect of sailing with knowledge of blockade.

Even with the existence of the Anglo-American treaty clause concerning blockades, commercial activities were nevertheless daunted by the possibility of uncompensated losses to cargo owners and freighters. One such instance involved the ship *Cordelia*, which arrived off Surabaya in the Dutch East Indies, and there was twice warned off by a blockading British squadron.[45] Reluctant to breach the blockade, but without any suitable alternative port, she returned to the United States with her cargo intact. Having lost the profits of the voyage, the owners of the cargo abandoned[46] it to their underwriter, claiming indemnity under the clause assuring them against loss due to "unlawful arrests, restraints and detainments of all kings, princes and people . . ." They

---

[44] 4 Cranch 186, 200–201 (1808).
[45] M'Call v. Marine Insurance Co., 8 Cranch 59–66 (1814), with opinion by Judge Story. See also King v. Delaware Insurance Co., 6 Cranch 71–82 (1810).
[46] Abandonment is defined and discussed at pp. 470–71, below.

argued that this customary clause related to *unlawful arrests*, but that restraints and detainments by the plain meaning of the clause need not be unlawful to be covered by the policy. This contention the Supreme Court rejected, requiring that the plaintiff allege and prove illegal acts by the blockading squadron. In the case as presented, there was no such unlawful activity, for it was accepted international law that blockading squadrons might temporarily detain vessels and such a detention would not be sufficient interference to permit the insured to recover on his policy. Hence the Supreme Court again followed international law as then understood and accepted.

Cargo Insurance—General Average and Memorandum Articles

Although warranties were undoubtedly the most widely used technique for limiting an underwriter's liability, it was also possible to use the method of enumerating "memorandum articles," in order to eliminate or sharply restrict recovery for commodities that were highly perishable by nature or likely to suffer damage in the ordinary course of a sea voyage. Articles of a cargo contained in such a memorandum list would not form the basis for compensation except in the case of a total loss of the ship, or in a situation where substantial amounts of cargo had to be sacrificed to save the vessel and the remainder (termed a "general average" situation).[47] In the case of certain types of memorandum articles the insurance company might specify that its liability be limited to a fixed percentage of the value of the cargo unless there were a total loss or general average situation.[48]

---

[47] For a good discussion of memorandum articles and the general and particular average, see Gilmore and Black, *Admiralty*, 79–83. See also Marshall, *Insurance*, 138–55, who suggests that the use of the memorandum began in 1749. *Ibid.*, 139.

[48] In Biays v. Chesapeake Insurance Co., 7 Cranch 415–20 (1813), the Supreme Court dealt with the loss sustained when hides were accidentally dropped into salt water while being unladed at their port of destination. Since they were included as memorandum articles and were not totally destroyed, recovery was denied.

Somewhat more complicated was the case of Marcardier v. Chesapeake Insurance Co., 8 Cranch 39–50 (1814), where the vessel carrying the insured cargo, including memorandum arti-

cles, was damaged at sea and reached port with the cargo in a deteriorating condition. The evidence tendered by the insured showed clearly that the voyage could not have been pursued with any possibility of profit, and on that basis the venture had been abandoned to the underwriters. Justice Story in his opinion for the Court cited the rule that if the saved cargo was less in value than the freight, there was a clear case of total loss. Earlier, in Rhinelander v. Insurance Co. of Pennsylvania, 4 Cranch 29–46 (1807), Chief Justice Marshall for the Court had held that whether capture of a neutral ship by a belligerent was a total loss was to depend upon "general principles, on analogy and on a reasonable construction of the contract between the parties." *Ibid.*, 42.

Abandonment

Abandonment is the method by which an insured notifies his underwriter of the loss and assigns to the insurer all of his rights and interests in the property in return for his recovery of the amount insured under the policy. Since the practice was well established and recognized in international law by 1801, few questions concerning abandonment were presented *de novo* to the Supreme Court, which frequently decided the case on the basis of English precedent or the corresponding case law of one or more of the American State courts.

When a loss occurred, the insured or his duly authorized agent or broker was permitted a reasonable time during which to decide to abandon to the underwriter; what was reasonable was a mixed issue of law and fact that was left to the determination of the jury.[49] A vessel captured at sea might be abandoned by her owner at the time of capture or at any time before the prize court entered its decree of acquittal restoring the property to the owner. Should some time elapse between the entry of a restitution decree and the actual return of the ship to her owner's control, no valid abandonment might be made during that period, for the right of property vested in the former owner with the entry of the decree.[50] Once the abandonment was made, the state of the loss at the time of abandonment fixed the rights of the parties to the policy.[51]

Subsequent to abandonment the insured party or his agents might

---

Whether circumstances justified abandonment as a total loss was a matter for jury determination. Marine Insurance Co. v. Tucker, 3 Cranch 357–98 (1806).

Judge Story's Marcardier opinion examined the conflicting foreign precedents concerning the quantum of damage to the cargo as a whole that would justify abandonment as a technical total loss. Although English decisions were silent on the point, a French treatise and the case law in leading commercial States of the United States indicated that the destruction of more than one-half of the value of the cargo would result in a total loss. 8 Cranch 39, at 47–48. That rule was applied in Marcardier, but Justice Story was faced with the additional problem of how to deal with memorandum articles in arriving at the one-half loss ratio. He held that

memorandum articles would have to be included in the total value of the cargo for the purposes of the computation, but that in calculating the amount of cargo damaged memorandum articles might not be included. *Ibid.*, 49. Thus the non-memorandum article damage would have to be so great that it compensated for the damage to memorandum articles excluded from the computation.

[49] Chesapeake Insurance Co. v. Stark, 6 Cranch 268–73 (1810); Maryland Insurance Co. v. Ruden's Administrator, 6 Cranch 338 (1810).

[50] Marshall v. Delaware Insurance Co., 4 Cranch 202–208 (1808), citing Rhinelander v. Insurance Co. of Pennsylvania, 4 Cranch 29–46 (1807), and Chesapeake Insurance Co. v. Stark, 6 Cranch 268 (1810).

[51] Rhinelander v. Insurance Co. of Pennsylvania, 4 Cranch 29 (1807).

take steps to protect the interests of the underwriter under what was in John Marshall's day termed the "labor and travel" clause.[52] This policy provision bound the underwriter to reimburse the captain or other agent of the owner for the expenses he incurred in protecting the vessel or goods from loss, or to recover them if seized or detained. In *Biays* v. *Chesapeake Insurance Company* and *Gracie* v. *Marine Insurance Company of Baltimore*, the Supreme Court held that such expenses might be charged against the underwriter only if ancillary to a valid claim against the insurer under the terms of the policy.[53] In other words the "labor and travel" clause, now called the "sue and labor" stipulation, was appurtenant to, and dependent upon, the principal claim for its vitality.

Cancellation

Nearly every policy that came under litigation had had its coverage terminated by an abandonment growing out of a loss alleged to be within the coverage of the policy. It was possible, however, to cancel a policy by an agreement between the parties, provided the methods prescribed in the policy and the underwriter's corporate charter were closely adhered to. One of the earliest marine insurance cases to come before Chief Justice Marshall involved the manner in which a marine insurance policy might be canceled.[54] Examining the correspondence between the insured and his underwriter, Marshall found that there had been no more than a mere negotiation in regard to the terms for cancellation, and that the policy was still in force at the time the loss occurred. Had the insured wished to cancel coverage immediately, he might have done so by surrendering the policy to the insurance company, thereby terminating its coverage. None of the letters written by the insurance company could be legally binding, for its articles of incorporation provided that only an instrument in writing, duly signed and sealed with the corporate seal, might have such an effect. An instrument canceling an insurance contract would have to be executed with the same formalities as the policy itself. As a result of this close reading of the corporate charter concerning rights of cancellations, there could be no cancellation by a mere exchange of correspondence.

---

[52] Current parlance denominates this the "sue and labor" clause. Gilmore and Black, *Admiralty*, 85–86.

[53] 7 Cranch 415 (1813); 8 Cranch 75 (1814).

[54] The case of Head and Amory v. Providence Insurance Co., 2 Cranch 127–70 (1804), represents one of the rare situations in which a cancellation was in progress when the loss occurred.

Construction of Marine Policies

Strict construction, as we have seen in regard to concealments, had a much broader application in other directions than in the area of cancellation of policies. The Supreme Court early indicated its acceptance at face value of the amount specified in a valued policy as the worth of the vessel or goods insured. Thus the underwriter was estopped from challenging the value stipulated (unless intentionally misrepresented or concealed) even if it were far greater than the actual value of the property insured.[55] Should a policy commence with the traditional Lloyd's of London formula—a routine acknowledgment of the receipt of the premium—the company would be estopped to deny receipt of the premium even if, in fact, it had not been paid prior to loss. If there had been a mistake in the names of the parties insured, or an omission of a name, the terms of the written agreement would normally govern those entitled to recover. However, if the underwriter knew of the insured's erroneous assumptions and permitted the mistake to continue to the insured's detriment, he might then be held liable to persons not mentioned in the policy.[56] Again, when losses occurred the terms of each of the valued policies would govern, even though by virtue of successively acquired policies stipulating varying rates of currency exchange, the insured might recover more than the value of the insured property.[57]

Conclusion

As Chief Justice Marshall commented in *Yeaton* v. *Fry*:

> Policies of insurance are generally the most formal instruments which are brought into courts of justice; and there are no other instruments

---

[55] Hodgson v. Marine Insurance Co., 5 Cranch 100 (1809), and the same case on a subsequent appeal, 6 Cranch 206 (1810). These cases also held that if a valued policy (that is, a policy expressing the insured's interest as a given amount, rather than the property rights he held in a given vessel, cargo or freightage) were fixed in an action at law, it would be binding in a subsequent suit in equity. This Supreme Court opinion would seem to be contrary to the English rules which prohibited recovery of more than the true value, regardless of the number of policies obtained or whether they were valued policies or open policies. In England recovery on one policy when others covered the vessel in excess of its value would result in contribution to the underwriter compelled to pay the entire loss. Marshall, *Insurance*, 111, 115–17.

[56] *Ibid.*

[57] Pleasants v. Maryland Insurance Co., 8 Cranch 55–59 (1814).

which are more liberally construed, in order to effect the real intentions of the parties, if that intention can be clearly ascertained.[58]

On the other hand, companies engaged in the business of marine insurance underwriting were expected to perform their undertakings with great circumspection, in regard not only to the formalities of executing and canceling policies but also in light of broad knowledge attributed to them of the trade usages of shippers and seamen throughout the world. In these earliest decisions on marine insurance matters there is a definite indication that the Supreme Court intended to and did uphold high standards for marine insurance underwriters, and to allow recoveries in any instances that justice or equity would permit.

In a more general sense the marine insurance precedents established by the Court in this period provided a legal framework for the encouragement of American commercial activity, as well as a sound reception of traditional foreign rules of insurance liability that enhanced the reputation and competitive position of American insurance underwriters. While no specific decision cites the overall commercial orientation of the federal Constitution, it is apparent that the Supreme Court was guided in its decisions by an overarching purpose of encouraging trade both among the States and with foreign nations.

More specifically the work of the Court in this period of both international and civil war was directed towards the clarification of principles of marine insurance law that pertained to the warranties of neutrality and prohibitions or exceptions concerning illegal trade. The circumstances surrounding the "proof only in America" clause demonstrate the insurance industry's adaptation of its practices to the changing conditions of international prize law, and the Supreme Court's ready acceptance of this contractual provision shows not only judicial flexibility, but also adherence to the "constitutional purpose" of encouraging commercial activity in the United States and abroad.

INSTANCE CASES

Salvage

Salvage opinions of the Supreme Court during the years from 1801 to 1815 were the basis upon which American rules of salvage were to be expounded, established for the most part upon rules of

---

[58] 5 Cranch 335, at 342 (1810). Marshall also noted that since insurance policies were drafted by insurance companies, they should be construed strictly against the insurer. *Ibid.*, 341.

international practice as adopted by the English High Court of Admiralty. During this period the ordinary cases involving the salvage of derelicts and wrecks, denominated "civil salvage" cases, were supplemented by "military salvage" cases, which arose as incidental issues in the condemnation of enemy vessels as prizes of war.[59] All told, the five salvage cases that were before the Supreme Court during this period contribute far more than their small number would indicate in terms of American precedents and procedural clarifications.

Salvage is the reward provided in international maritime law to those who render assistance by saving life and property from the perils of the sea. Traditionally the property saved, or salved to be more precise, was brought before an admiralty tribunal to fix the amount of salvage payable before the vessel and goods, or the proceeds from their sale, might be released to the owners. Since salvage created a maritime lien against the vessel and goods saved, the admiralty court exercised *in rem* jurisdiction concerning the property brought before it for adjudication. The master and crew of the vessel that had engaged in the rescue operation were entitled to participate in salvage to the extent that their risk and labor entitled them to a proportion. The owner of the saving vessel also was entitled to salvage, and presumably a demise charterer, who leased the vessel and controlled her use, would also be qualified to part of a salvage award. On the other hand, the owner of cargo carried on a ship entitled to salvage, even though that cargo had incurred a risk, would not be allowed to participate in the award.[60] Salvage rules were unique to maritime law, for as Chief Justice Marshall observed in 1804:

> If the property of an individual on land be exposed to the greatest peril, and be saved by the voluntary exertions of any persons what ever . . . no remuneration in the shape of salvage is allowed. The act is highly meritorious, and the service is as great as if rendered at sea. Yet the claim for salvage could not, perhaps, be supported. It is certainly not made. . . . Let precisely the same service, and at precisely the same hazard, be rendered at sea, and a very ample reward will be bestowed in the courts of justice.
>
> The allowance of a very ample compensation for those services *at sea* is intended as an inducement to render them, which it is for the

---

[59] Three deal with recaptures: Talbot v. Seeman, 1 Cranch 1–43 (1801); The Adventure, 8 Cranch 221–29 (1814); and The Adeline, 9 Cranch 244–86 (1815). Two deal with salvage from derelicts or wrecks: Mason v. The Blaireau, 2 Cranch 240–71 (1804); Peisch v. Ware, 4 Cranch 247–366 (1808).

[60] See Gilmore and Black, *Admiralty*, 566–70.

public interests, and for the general interest of humanity, to hold forth to those who navigate the ocean.[61]

The individual seaman's right to participate in a salvage award depended upon the extent and meritorious character of his service, and it might be foreclosed if he subsequently embezzled a part of the goods saved. This is shown in the case of *Mason* v. *The Ship Blaireau*, where sailors who risked their lives in navigating a derelict vessel were held to be entitled to 50-percent greater salvage money than their companions who sailed in the relative safety and comfort of the salving ship.[62]

Civil Salvage

In civil salvage cases the salvage award was subject to the determination of the admiralty court before which the saved vessel or goods were libeled.[63] As a separate and independent American law of salvage evolved, the amount awarded to a salving ship and crew depended upon the labor expended and the skill displayed by the rescuers, as well as upon the value of the property saved and the danger threatening it. The lower courts also took into consideration the risk incurred by the salvors in rendering assistance to the vessel in peril. Such adjudication was subject to review and amendment upon appeal to a higher court, and the statutory aberration in American admiralty practice between 1801 and 1803, which required appeals in admiralty to be taken by writ of error, did not prevent the Supreme Court from a *de novo* consideration of the amount of salvage awarded.[64] As a general principle

---

[61] Mason v. The Blaireau, 2 Cranch 240, at 267 (1804). This reflection was undoubtedly a reaction to admiralty law and its variations from common law. By his own admission Marshall was not well acquainted with admiralty law in the course of his practice. See C. Cullen and H. Johnson, eds., *The Papers of John Marshall*, II (Chapel Hill, 1977), 301–302.

[62] 2 Cranch 240, at 242–47, 271. In the same case the Court held that the master of a salving ship who attempted to embezzle diamonds from the saved cargo thereby forfeited his claim to salvage. *Ibid.*, 259–61, citing the laws of Oleron. See also Gilmore and Black, *Admiralty*, 554–58. Of course, if a vessel were under an obligation to render aid, as in the case of a maritime collision, her crew could not recover salvage; nor could the crew of the ship saved recover unless, as in Mason v. The Blaireau, a seaman abandoned by his captain and fellows on the imperiled vessel and rescued by the salving ship subsequently rendered services to aid in her preservation.

[63] Peisch v. Ware, 4 Cranch 365 (1808), and Mason v. The Blaireau, 2 Cranch 267, 268 (1804). For the mode of computing a salvage award see Gilmore and Black, *Admiralty*, 559–66.

[64] Sec. 33, An Act to Provide for the More Convenient Organization of the Courts of the United States, Feb. 13, 1801, 2 Stat. 89, at 98, 99.

of international maritime law the total amount of salvage was not to exceed one-third of the value of the vessel and its cargo,[65] but for reasons that are not clear, the Supreme Court preferred to base its assessment of salvage maximums upon the "rule of reciprocity" used by the English High Court of Admiralty. According to this latter rule, a saved vessel was subject to the awards customary in the courts of her own nation or in the courts of the nation of the saving vessel. In other words, the rule of reciprocity represented an attempt to provide a universal law of salvage that would award the same amount regardless of the admiralty court that might fortuitously take cognizance of the libel. An example of the Court's use of the rule of reciprocity may be found in *Mason* v. *The Ship Blaireau,*[66] where a French vessel had been the victim of a collision and was abandoned by her captain and crew before she was discovered by her rescuer, an English vessel. In his opinion Chief Justice Marshall observed that French courts would permit the award of not more than one-third of the value of the vessel and cargo in such a situation.[67] That award, under the rule of reciprocity, would be applied in an English admiralty court had the vessel been libeled in the saving vessel's home port, and consequently became the proportion allowable in the federal courts of the United States.[68]

The salvage cases demonstrate a certain awkwardness of the Supreme Court in dealing with *in rem* jurisdiction of admiralty courts. For example, in *Mason* v. *The Blaireau,* Marshall dealt with the jurisdiction of American courts over salvage in a French vessel saved by a British ship. Ignoring the fact that the saved ship was before the tribunal for execution of a maritime lien in an *in rem* proceeding, the Chief Justice treated the problem as one of balancing the conveniences. Since it was most favorable to public convenience for United States courts to assume jurisdiction, and since the parties had assented to the jurisdiction of the court below, jurisdiction, he held, was properly taken of the case.[69] This and the previously discussed use of the rule of reciprocity in salvage cases indicates the Court's imperfect sense of the international character

---

[65] This proportion had been applied and approved by the Supreme Court in M'Donough v. Dannery, 3 Dall. 188–97, at 191 (1796). See Gilmore and Black, *Admiralty,* 563–66 for current practice.

[66] 2 Cranch 267–68 (1804).

[67] *Ibid.,* 268.

[68] The rule of reciprocity insured a modicum of uniformity in salvage awards, but at the same time it did not bind English courts as a matter of precedent; it seems to have continued in American practice to be used in this flexible manner. Gilmore and Black, *Admiralty,* 533, and note 4, 533. By 1828 Marshall stated in *dictum* that admiralty jurisdiction was not a creation of the Constitution or federal statutes, but rather was as old as navigation itself. D.W. Robertson, *Admiralty and Federalism* (Mineola, New York, 1970), 138, citing American Insurance Co. v. Canter, 1 Pet. 516, 7 L. Ed. 242 (1828).

[69] 2 Cranch 264 (1804).

of the substantive law of salvage and its uncertainty concerning the nature of *in rem* admiralty jurisdiction.[70]

Subsequently the Supreme Court demonstrated a sounder grasp of admiralty jurisdiction in the unusual cases of *Jennings* v. *Carson* and *The Adventure*.[71] The first cause arose from a condemnation by a New Jersey State admiralty court during the American Revolution, which was reversed on appeal to the Federal Court of Appeals in Cases of Prize and Capture, but the vessel in question was never restored to the owner. Years later, the owner filed a libel in the Federal District Court of Pennsylvania, claiming reimbursement for damages from the owner of the American privateer. Writing for the Supreme Court, Marshall indicated that prize courts exercised their jurisdiction not by virtue of a statutory mandate but rather as courts of international law. They proceeded *in rem*, and the vessel or goods were at all times subject to the order of the court and in its custody. Consequently, damages for failure to restore the vessel and cargo in accordance with the mandate of the Federal Court of Appeals could not be demanded from the captor, since he did not have custody of the goods taken as prize and could not deliver them without express order of the New Jersey State court of admiralty.[72] A clearer statement of the lack of *in personam* jurisdiction in prize cases would be difficult to find.

The Adventure[73] involved the crew of an American vessel captured and burned by a French privateer. Shortly thereafter the French privateer captured a British ship and presented her to the American crew, who then sailed it to Norfolk. The British master and crew filed a claim against the ship, which was libeled for salvage by the American seamen, and claimed by the government as forfeited property under the Non-Importation Act. The Supreme Court, in an opinion delivered by Judge Johnson, held that the exercise of jurisdiction in this case, and the award of salvage money, was within the power of the circuit court sitting in admiralty. The court might award salvage to the American crew, and enter appropriate orders to preserve the vessel until such time as it should either be confiscated as British property or restored to its owner at the termination of hostilities. In other words, *in rem* jurisdiction permitted the award of salvage and the discharge of the related maritime lien against the British vessel, even though the United States jurisdiction was based entirely upon the physical custody of the

---

[70] Of course Judge Story was not yet on the Bench and Judge Washington, despite experience in the Third Circuit which included Pennsylvania, was, like John Marshall, hampered by a lack of admiralty practice before his appointment.

[71] 4 Cranch 2–29 (1807); 8 Cranch 221–29 (1814).

[72] 4 Cranch 28–29.

[73] 8 Cranch 221–29 (1814); also discussed in Part II, chapter 3, notes 77–80.

ship. Difficulties in establishing the nature of *in rem* admiralty jurisdiction were resolved over the course of time by reference to international law and practice. While the confusing statements of the Supreme Court may have led to some temporary uncertainty in the law, they failed to cause any significant comment at the time or since.

Surprisingly, a much more important salvage case, in admiralty law and in its constitutional implications, has also received but little notice. This is the litigation in *Peisch* v. *Ware*, which presented to the Court the knotty problem of the relationship between the revenue laws and salvage activities in American coastal waters. The American ship *Favourite* anchored in Delaware Bay broke her moorings, and was abandoned upon a shoal when her entire crew went for assistance. Thomas Rodney, inspector of customs for Lewes, Delaware, spotted the derelict and gathered a salvage party, which succeeded in emptying the *Favourite* of her cargo, despite the return of her crew. The collector of the revenue proved to be a more formidable opponent when he demanded that the cargo, consisting of wines, brandies, and cordials, be taken from Rodney's warehouse for customs assessment at Wilmington. After the salvors obtained a writ of replevin from the Delaware courts to prevent this removal, the collector seized the goods as having been imported contrary to the revenue laws. Writing on behalf of the Court, Chief Justice Marshall examined the applicable revenue law in detail, and found that Congress intended it to apply to regular importations only, and not to cases where goods were brought in by salvors to save them from destruction. "To suppose them applicable to salvage goods, would be to suppose that the legislature designed to prohibit salvage entirely, or to forfeit the cargoes of all vessels which might have been wrecked on the coast."[74] Consequently, the forfeiture provisions of the customs laws did not pertain to the legitimate actions of the salvors in rescuing the property and bringing it to safety on land.

Although *Peisch* v. *Ware* did not produce dissenting or concurring opinions, there is evidence in Marshall's opinion that the judges were divided over the question of the validity of an arbitration proceeding undertaken in accordance with the provisions of a 1786 Delaware statute concerning salvage.[75] Counsel for the owner Peisch argued that he had entered into arbitration under the mistaken assumption that he was required to do so, but that in fact the Delaware statute had been repealed by the ratification of the Constitution and the assignment of original admiralty jurisdiction to the federal courts, as well as by the

---

[74] 4 Cranch 347 at 361 (1808).
[75] The Delaware statute is the Act of Feb. 2, 1786, 2 Del. Laws. 831;

Marshall's statement is at 4 Cranch 366 (1808).

enactment of the Judiciary Act of 1789. They also contended that in the *The Blaireau* the salvage award had been only one-third of the value of the vessel and goods, and that had been a case of great risk to the salvors. In reply, counsel for the salvors asserted that while the federal courts had been vested with admiralty jurisdiction, which included incidents such as salvage, that jurisdiction was "not exclusive cognizance." The Delaware statute was similar to a British act giving power to the wardens of the Cinque Ports to decide the question of salvage, and if the parties submitted to the jurisdiction and consented to the award, they should abide by the award. The case thus raised the issue of the extent of admiralty jurisdiction that might be considered to have been left to the various States under the "saving clause" of section 9 of the Judiciary Act of 1789.[76]

On this point of State-federal jurisdiction the Supreme Court Judges divided. Unfortunately their separate opinions on the matter are not identifiable from Marshall's unitary statement for the entire Court. However, Marshall's opinion does reflect the fact that two judges believed the award was entered into fairly and without fraud to either party, and for that reason it should not be disturbed, although the parties *might* have been mistaken as to the obligation created by the Delaware statute. Two justices did not think the award obligatory, but since it was the opinion of intelligent men upon the spot, and affirmed by the sentences of the United States district and circuit courts, they were not inclined to re-open the question. Three judges were of the opinion that the arbitral award was of no validity and ought to have no influence; in addition they believed that the salvage was too large and presumably should be reduced by the Supreme Court to the usual one-third maximum.

Absent any clarifying statement from the three groups of judges, we are left to speculate upon the Court's general view of the exclusive or concurrent nature of the federal judiciary's power in maritime matters. In a technical sense the Judiciary Act of 1789, in reserving certain maritime matters to the States, might be considered to have been in conflict with the express constitutional provision that "all cases of admiralty and maritime jurisdiction" should be vested in the federal courts. Yet in this case, to have declared a portion of the Judiciary Act

---

[76] The Judiciary Act provides that, "the district courts shall have . . . exclusive original cognizance of all civil causes of admiralty and maritime jurisdiction, . . . saving to suitors, in all cases, the right of a common law remedy, where the common law is competent to give it; . . ." 1 Stat. 73, at 77. See the arguments at 4 Cranch 349–57 (1808); see also Robertson, *Admiralty and Federalism*, 18–27, 123–26; Gilmore and Black, *Admiralty*, 20–21.

unconstitutional by a method analogous to that followed in *Marbury* v. *Madison* would have resulted in an *extension* rather than a *contraction* of federal jurisdiction.

A similar trade regulation/salvage case, *The Adventure*, provided the Supreme Court with the opportunity to advance the diplomatic policy of neutrality by its salvage award.[77] The crew of an American vessel, the *Three Friends*, had been taken aboard their French captor's vessel when their own ship was burned at sea. Shortly thereafter a British vessel was captured by the French privateer, and the ship was presented to the Americans, who sailed it to Norfolk, where they libeled it for salvage and the customs officials demanded the ship's forfeiture for violation of the Non-Intercourse Acts.[78] For the Supreme Court Judge William Johnson delivered an opinion upholding the validity of the French captain's gift to the American crew, indicating that they took possession under the grant from a French captor and hence would have been subject to British recapture at any point prior to their arrival at Norfolk.[79] However, the crew of the *Three Friends* had acted with complete propriety so far as the duties of neutrals were concerned, since they not only saved the vessel for her British owners but also brought her and the remaining cargo into an American admiralty court for disposition upon their arrival home. Normally, the vessel and cargo would be the subject of a restoration to her owner upon payment of salvage, Judge Johnson observed, but since war had been declared upon Britain after the arrival of the ship at Norfolk, his share would be held subject to the future order of the circuit court. On the other hand, the crew of the *Three Friends* were entitled to an amount of salvage to be measured by the peril incurred, labor sustained, or value decreed, all to be fixed by the court having cognizance of the libel. The maximum allowable, according to Judge Johnson, was one-half of the value of the property salved; but that, he noted, was awarded in extraordinary cases or when very small amounts were subject to salvage.

Turning to the claim that the landing of the ship had constituted a violation of the Non-Intercourse laws, and resulted in a forfeiture that had priority over the salvage claim, Judge Johnson held that Congress had no wish to prohibit salvage when it enacted the Non-Intercourse statutes. Clearly the ship was to be disposed of as property cast upon the shores of the United States in a casual manner, and hence not subject to forfeiture. He observed, "The case has no one feature of an illegal importation, and cannot possibly have imputed to it the violation of law."[80]

---

[77] 8 Cranch 221–29 (1814).
[78] *Ibid.*, 221–22.

[79] *Ibid.*, 226–29.
[80] *Ibid.*, 227.

III: *Marine Insurance and Instance Cases*

Military Salvage

Although civil salvage jurisprudence was firmly based upon international maritime custom and the rule of reciprocity, the award of salvage in vessels recaptured from an enemy was fully regulated by federal statutes. Unlike civil salvage, military salvage was based upon a public policy designed to reward those ships of war that recovered vessels and cargoes from the enemy that would, if left in enemy hands, aid in his war efforts. Military salvage was designed to encourage masters and seamen to recover American and allied vessels from the peril of condemnation before an enemy admiralty court, and as such might more properly be considered a part of the law of prize rather than the law of salvage. However, since the judicial practice then seems to have been to consider civil and military salvage as parallel branches of admiralty law, it is appropriate to consider military salvage cases in conjunction with the civil salvage litigation.

The congressional declaration of belligerency between France and the United States in 1798 formed the basis for Presidential instructions to the masters of armed vessels of the United States to seize, take, and bring into port those French vessels found hovering off the American coast to commit depredations upon American commerce.[81] As a corollary to this power, the statute also permitted American commanders to retake any ship of American citizens that might have been previously captured by such a hovering French ship. Absent any construction of the term "armed vessels," it would seem clear that the authorization extended to both public vessels and privateers. At the same time this statute embraced only a limited concept of commercial warfare. It was directed against French vessels found "hovering" off the American coast, and also limited to those that hovered for the purpose of committing depredations on American commerce. Similarly in regard to military salvage, the recaptor was authorized to seize only those vessels that belonged to American citizens, and only if they had been previously captured by the hovering vessel. It is not clear what rules would apply in the adjudication of salvage in non-American vessels captured off the American coast by a French ship. Similarly, congressional intent is unclear in the case of American vessels captured on the high seas by one French vessel but brought into American coastal waters by a vessel subsequently captured and condemned as a "hovering vessel."

Perhaps these patent ambiguities in the Act of May 28, 1798, were responsible for the passage of a more comprehensive statute one month

---

[81] An Act More Effectually to Protect the Commerce and Coasts of the United States, May 28, 1798, 1 Stat. 561 (1798).

later.[82] This Act formed the basis for military salvage decrees to privateers during the major portion of the "Quasi-War" with France; it also served as the basic legislation concerning recaptures by public armed vessels until it was superseded by the Act for the Government of the Navy passed on March 2, 1799. The June 28, 1798, statute provided guidelines for the award of salvage in the case of recaptured vessels that were unarmed, and that at the time of their capture by the French were owned by, or chartered by, a citizen or resident of the United States.[83] Such merchantmen were to be restored to their owners, subject to the payment of salvage to the amount of one-eighth of their value to the master and crew of the American warship making the capture. For the recapture of armed vessels the salvage provisions were so generous as to amount to bounties rather than a true form of salvage. Crews of American warships that captured French privateers and public ships of war of superior or equal force to their vessel were to share the entire value of the recaptured vessel; if the French armed vessel were of lesser force, the crews were allowed a moiety of the proceeds and the balance went to the United States. These salvage awards were of course applicable to recaptures by warships of the United States Navy; privateer recaptures continued to be governed by the rules of civil salvage previously described.

The 1799 Act for the Government of the Navy established a salvage rate for all ships or goods retaken from the enemy by the warships of the United States.[84] If the property had been in the enemy's possession for less than twenty-four hours, salvage was payable at the rate of one-eighth. Should the time of enemy possession exceed twenty-four hours, but not forty-eight hours, the rate of salvage was fixed at one-fifth; if more than forty-eight hours and less than ninety-six hours, one-third of the value was fixed as salvage. Any property held by the enemy more than ninety-six hours was to be restored on the payment of one-half of its value in salvage.[85]

One of the first cases heard by the Supreme Court after John Marshall became Chief Justice was that involving the ship *Amelia*, recaptured on September 15, 1799, while on a voyage from Calcutta to her home port of Hamburgh in Prussia.[86] First captured by a French privateer, she was recaptured by the United States frigate *Constitution* and brought to New York, where she was libeled for salvage, the captors having discovered papers identifying her as a neutral bottom

---

[82] An Act in Addition to the Act More Effectually to Protect the Commerce and Coasts of the United States, June 28, 1798, 1 Stat. 574–75 (1798).
[83] *Ibid.*
[84] Sec. 7, Act for the Government of the Navy for the United States, March 2, 1799, 1 Stat. 709, at 716.
[85] *Ibid.*
[86] Talbot v. Seeman, 1 Cranch 1–45 (1801).

illegally seized by the French.[87] At the time of the capture there was a state of belligerency between France and the United States, declared by Congress, but not an actual declaration of war. In accordance with the Government of the Navy Act of March 2, 1799, the district court awarded one-half the value of the vessel and her cargo to the officers and men of the *Constitution*. On appeal the circuit court reversed, reasoning that the *Amelia* was a neutral ship, and hence she was in no danger of condemnation by a French admiralty court.[88]

The appeal of the *Amelia* case raised the problem of how to deal with arbitrary French alterations in the traditional law of prize. Although a neutral vessel was in no danger of condemnation in a captor's prize courts under normal conditions, French decrees of 1798 made the *Amelia*'s condemnation possible.[89] Was the Court to assume the continuance of international practice in French admiralty courts or should it go behind the record in the case and assume that the vessel was in danger of condemnation by virtue of the new French rules? Speaking through the Chief Justice, the Court circumvented the technical prohibition against receiving new evidence upon a writ of error. Observing that the public laws of nations that are matters of international concern are of such notoriety that an admiralty court may properly take judicial notice of those laws, Marshall asserted that in this instance there was no reason to compel the parties to prove this aspect of foreign law as factual matter.[90]

Proceeding to consider the merits of the case, Marshall held that since the *Amelia* was an armed vessel sailing under French colors, her seizure was entirely legal in spite of her neutral ownership. It was true

---

[87] The facts are set forth in the libel and claim, *ibid.*, 1–3. At the time of the capture there was a state of belligerency between France and the United States based upon resolution of Congress, but there had been no actual declaration of war.

[88] The district court decree is discussed in *ibid.*, 3; the circuit court decree is set forth verbatim in *ibid.*, 3–4; the appeal on writ of error to the Supreme Court was upon an agreed statement of facts annexed to the record. This statement is printed in *ibid.*, 5.

[89] The French consular decree of Jan. 18, 1798, subjecting neutral vessels and cargoes to forfeiture was the subject of the colloquy between counsel. *Ibid.*, 11–15. The French decree had been originally brought to public attention on May 4, 1798, when

President John Adams released the XYZ dispatches to Congress in accordance with its request. In those dispatches the commissioners to France, including John Marshall, informed the government of additional French activity in violation of neutral rights.

[90] Hence the French decrees were not barred as factual evidence since they were matters of which the Court might take judicial notice. *Ibid.*, 37–39. The danger to the *Amelia*, and hence the entitlement to salvage, was dependent upon the operation of the French decree of Jan. 18, 1798, upon neutral bottoms, hence the text of the decree had to be before the court either on formal proof or as a matter of which the Court could take judicial notice.

that under ordinary circumstances a captured neutral vessel would not be subjected to salvage liens of a recaptor, but that rule depended upon her safety from condemnation in the admiralty courts of her captor. In the case of the *Amelia* the decrees of the French government and the nature of the *Amelia*'s cargo rendered probable her condemnation in France. The principle involved, according to Marshall, was that the right to salvage depended upon the recaptor's rendering a benefit to the owner. Ordinarily the capture of a neutral vessel by a belligerent from the hands of its enemy would not be such a benefit. However, in the light of the French decrees, the *Constitution* had saved the *Amelia* from a condemnation in a French admiralty court, and salvage was therefore payable.[91] The Supreme Court, though, reduced the assessment of salvage from one-half the value of the ship and goods to one-sixth of their value.[92]

Prior to the termination of the "Quasi-War" the newly constituted French government under the leadership of Napoleon Bonaparte revoked the decree of January 18, 1798, and restored the rights of neutrals as normally recognized in international law.[93] This action resulted in a reversal of the Supreme Court's position in regard to the recapture of neutral vessels. As Chief Justice Marshall had observed in *Talbot* v. *Seeman*:

> Whenever the danger resulting to captured neutrals from the laws of France should cease, then according to the principles laid down in this decree, the liability of recaptured neutrals to the payment of salvage would in conformity with general law and usage of nations, cease also.[94]

---

[91] *Ibid.*, 37–43. See the discussion in Wheaton, *Digest*, 239–40.

[92] In doing so it held that the terms of the Act of March 2, 1799, relied upon in awarding a moiety for salvage, applied only when the recaptured vessel was taken from the enemy both of the United States and of the nation of her owners. Since technically Hamburgh was not the enemy of France nor of the United States, the statutory salvage rate did not apply. The one-sixth awarded, although not so identified, would appear to have been based upon judicial discretion in assessment of salvage. *Ibid.*, 43–45. Subsequently An Act Providing Salvage in Cases of Recapture, Mar. 3, 1800, 2 Stat. 16–18, established a rate of one-sixth for the salvage to be awarded to privateers on the recapture of an unarmed vessel from the enemy and its restoration to its American owner. The same rate applied to vessels the property of the United States recaptured by privateers from the enemy. However, in these cases public vessels such as the frigate *Constitution* were to be awarded salvage in the amounts of one-eighth and one-twelfth respectively. This statute, of course, did not form a part of the law of the case in Talbot v. Seeman since the recapture occurred before the date of the statute.

[93] See L. Sears, *Jefferson and the Embargo* (Durham, N.C., 1927), 303.

[94] 1 Cranch 44 (1801).

III: *Marine Insurance and Instance Cases*

Talbot v. *Seeman* therefore was a recognition, for the purpose of cases falling within the scope of the French decree of January 18, 1798, of a situation in which earlier French disregard of international law jeopardized neutral rights and therefore justified the award of salvage to recaptors. In *Murray* v. *The Charming Betsey* the Chief Justice was presented with a salvage claim that arose subsequent to the French repeal of the decree of January 18, 1798, and upon the basis of that revocation, held that no salvage was payable for the recapture of a neutral vessel.[95]

Comprehensive statutory regulation of military salvage awards was obtained by the enactment of the statute of March 3, 1800, which applied to both American public warships and privateers commissioned by the President.[96] It provided that recaptors of vessels not outfitted as warships or privateers, or any lawful recaptors of goods, were entitled to one-eighth as salvage if the recapturing vessel were a public vessel, and one-sixth if a privateer. However, if the recaptured vessel had been equipped and had set forth as a warship or privateer, either before or subsequent to her capture, the salvage amount was fixed at one-half of her true value. An exception to this general rule applied to public vessels of the United States that had been recaptured from the enemy. In those instances a salvage award of one-sixth of the true value was payable to privateers, and one-twelfth to American warships, the award to be paid out of the United States Treasury.

In the case of recaptures of property belonging to individuals resident in, or subject to the jurisdiction of, a friendly nation, the recaptor was to be entitled to an award of military salvage equal in amount to the salvage that would be awarded in the courts of the owners' nation to recaptors of property belonging to citizens or residents of the United States. If such an amount was not established or was unknown, then the salvage allowable would be computed as if the recaptured property was that of a citizen or resident of the United States. This provision of the statute was subject to amendment by treaty between the United States and foreign powers, and also was to be suspended in the case of friendly nations where an American citizen or resident would not be entitled to restoration of his property upon payment of military salvage.

The 1800 Act also provided that military salvage in the case of recaptures should be payable only if the vessels or goods should not

---

[95] 2 Cranch 64 at 96, 121–24 (1804). The denial of salvage was also based upon the limitation of the Talbot v. Seeman precedent to the recapture of armed vessels capable of doing damage to American commerce.

[96] An Act Providing for Salvage in Cases of Recapture, Mar. 3, 1800, 2 Stat. 16–18 (1800).

have been "condemned as prize by competent authority before the recapture thereof." Passing of title as a result of the decree of an enemy prize court was therefore recognized as the point beyond which the property in a vessel or cargo could not be reclaimed by the original owner. Thereafter the original owner would be compelled to seek redress from his insurer, if any, and an American warship or privateer that captured the vessel or cargo would take no title under the rules of military salvage, but rather under the principles of prize law applicable to enemy property.

With the declaration of war upon Great Britain in 1812, Congress enacted a comprehensive statute covering the issuance of letters of marque that regulated the activities of privateers during the war, but left public warships subject to the provisions of the 1800 Act so far as military salvage was concerned.[97] The fifth section of the 1812 law provided that, in the case of recaptured property of American citizens or residents of the United States, the property would be restored upon agreement as to the salvage amount between the recaptors and the owner, or by decree of a court of competent jurisdiction, according to the nature of the case and agreeable to provisions previously established by law.[98] The 1812 Act was construed to incorporate the 1800 Salvage Act provisions concerning the rate of military salvage in *The Schooner Adeline and Cargo*.[99] When the American vessel was captured by a British warship in 1814 she carried a mixed American and French cargo, as well as letters of marque from the President of the United States. On her way to Gibraltar for condemnation she was recaptured by the American privateer *Expedition* and carried to New York City for adjudication. The district court condemned the French property as good prize, relying upon the French ordinance of 1779 that transferred property in captured goods twenty-four hours after capture and without further condemnation proceedings; the British rule of reciprocity would presumably have treated such goods as forfeit twenty-four hours after the seizure of the *Adeline* in the Bay of Biscay. On the other hand, the district court awarded the American-owned cargo to its original owners on the payment of one-sixth of its value in salvage to the recaptors. The vessel, by consent of the parties, was restored to her owners on the payment of one-half her value in salvage. On a *pro forma* affirmance by the circuit court, both parties appealed to the Supreme Court.[100]

---

[97] An Act Concerning Letters of Marque, Prizes and Prize Goods, June 26, 1812, 2 Stat. 759–64 (1812).

[98] *Ibid.*, 760.

[99] Schooner Adeline and Cargo, 9 Cranch 244–86, at 265 (1815).

[100] *Ibid.*, 244–45. Unfortunately the district court's decree is not printed, but its rationale is apparent from the argument of counsel as well as Judge Story's opinion. *Ibid.*, 270–74, 288.

III: *Marine Insurance and Instance Cases*

Speaking for the Supreme Court, Judge Joseph Story found that the Act of March 3, 1800, controlled the rate of salvage to be awarded in the case of American property in the *Adeline* and a portion of her cargo. He rejected the libelants' claim that they were entitled to one-half of the value of the cargo as military salvage, pointing to the express terms of the statute that limited salvage in regard to cargo to one-sixth in all cases, making immaterial the circumstance that the carrying vessel was armed. On the other hand, the award of one-half of the value of the armed vessel as military salvage was upheld under the terms of the 1800 Salvage Act.[101]

Judge Story also accepted the opinion of the district court concerning the forfeiture of cargo belonging to French nationals, based upon the French ordinance of 1779 and the British rule of reciprocity referred to above. Within the group of individuals affected by the operation of these rules he included all parties domiciled in France, whether French, Americans, or other nationals. In all of these cases, Story decided that their rights were governed by the law of France concerning recaptures. Although Story did not specifically refer to counsel's argument on the point, he was undoubtedly influenced by the argument of counsel Thomas Addis Emmet in his reference to the case in the Federal Court of Appeals in Cases of Prize and Captures, *Miller v. Ship Resolution*. Emmet referred to the Supreme Court of the United States as the "successor" to this prize court, and argued that therefore the Supreme Court must have judicial knowledge of the 1781 adjudication.[102]

In dealing with a formal objection of the claimant owners to the form of the libel against the *Adeline*, Story was compelled to answer the question whether a claim for military salvage must be set forth distinctly in a libel for prize.[103] He held that since liberal rules of amendment were applicable, the procedural irregularity was not fatal in any case. However, it was also true that military salvage decrees were of necessity incidental to prize court practice. Recaptures, he stated emphatically, were cases of prize, and the title to the goods depended in most instances upon future adjudication. That being the case, it would be impossible for a libelant to decide whether he should proceed in prize or for military salvage. As a result, the court would take legitimate jurisdiction of the property as prize, and having this

---

[101] *Ibid.*, 287.

[102] Compare *ibid.*, 288 with Miller v. Ship Resolution, 2 Dall. 4 (Fed. Ct. of Appeals in Cases of Prize and Capture, 1781). Under the Congressional ordinance governing the Miller case, a twenty-four-hour capture by an American ship vested title in the owner, master and crew. Thus the United States adopted the French ordinance of 1779 as a rule of decision during the American Revolution.

[103] 9 Cranch 284–87.

broad authority, would exercise dispositive power over all of the incidents of that jurisdiction, including military salvage.[104]

The opinions in matters of civil and military salvage, although few in number, covered a wide subject area and did much to form an American jurisprudence in this field of maritime law. There is an indication of growing awareness on the part of the Supreme Court of the nature and applicability of the law of nations in the field of salvage awards, and an increasing catholicity in the positions taken by each of the Supreme Court judges. While British admiralty cases played an important role at the commencement of our period, their persuasive influence was somewhat undermined by the diplomatic crises with Great Britain leading to the War of 1812 as well as by the availability of materials on the maritime law of salvage of Continental nations. This in turn led to an enlargement and enrichment of what had been a limited and relatively provincial area of American jurisprudence.

Charter Parties

The lease of a vessel for a particular voyage or for a specified period of time, termed a "charter party" in law merchant and admiralty parlance, had assumed much of its present-day complexity by the beginning of the nineteenth century and the law in the field seems to have been reasonably well settled. Consequently the work of the Supreme Court in this field was limited to the application of international maritime custom and usage in the construction of charter party contracts. Two cases dealing with charter parties, *Hooe and Co. v. Groverman*[105] and *Marcardier v. Chesapeake Insurance Company*,[106] came before the Court in the years from 1801 to 1815. Both raised the distinction between a demise charter and a voyage charter. A "demise charter," involving the transfer of possession and control of the vessel as well as a lease of her carrying capacity, in effect made the charterer the owner of the vessel for the time being, much as the lease of real property conferred many of the indicia of ownership upon the lessee. By way of contrast the "voyage charter" provided for the charterer's use of the carrying capacity of all or part of the vessel, while the general owner retained control of her navigation and maintenance.[107]

Hooe and Co. v. Groverman involved the general owner's claim for demurrage, or compensation for delay in the voyage resulting from the fault of the charterer. His vessel, the brigantine *Nancy*, was chartered

---

[104] Some reservations were expressed whether civil salvage, as distinct from military salvage, would not have to form the basis of a separate libel. Undoubtedly this would be the case in English admiralty where instance business was quite distinct from prize business.

[105] 1 Cranch 214–38 (1803).

[106] 8 Cranch 39–50 (1814).

[107] Gilmore and Black, *Admiralty*, 193–97.

by Hooe and Co. for the voyage from Alexandria to Havre de Grace in France. The owner had warranted her to be in good seaworthy condition and covenanted that she would be properly manned during the course of the voyage. When she departed the United States in June 1798 she was provided with provisional articles to supplement the terms of the charter party.[108] These articles instructed her captain to await instructions while standing off Falmouth, England, and to proceed to Havre de Grace or one of the enumerated alternate ports, depending upon the instructions of the American consul at Falmouth. When the *Nancy* reached Falmouth no instructions had been relayed by Hooe and Co., and her continuous hovering off the coast placed her in danger of seizure under the British "hovering act."[109] Upon the direction of the American consul she was ordered into Falmouth to await further instructions, but before arrival she was libeled by the British customs authorities as a vessel carrying French goods and held three months before her subsequent release.

Speaking for the Court, Marshall set forth the specific terms of the charter party, and indicated that the operative words were those by which Groverman, the general owner, rented the *tonnage* of the *Nancy* to Hooe and Co. In addition, Groverman had agreed to deliver the cargo to a specific firm at Havre de Grace, and Marshall noted that the control of the vessel during the voyage was to remain with his captain. Groverman had also agreed to keep the vessel well appareled and well manned, indicating that maintenance of the ship and employment of master and crew remained Groverman's responsibility. On the basis of these facts, Marshall held that the agreement was in the nature of a voyage charter, and that the terms of the provisional articles only served to reinforce this construction of the document.[110]

The Chief Justice then proceeded to analyze the nature of the American consul's agency, conceding at the outset that he acted as agent for Hooe and Co. (the charterer) and not for Groverman (the general owner). However, the consul's authority as delineated by the provisional articles was merely to convey Hooe and Co.'s instructions concerning the final port of destination in Europe, and not to order the *Nancy* into Falmouth. Bringing her to port was therefore the action of Groverman's captain, and not a compliance with instructions from Hooe and Co. or their authorized agent.[111] As additional support for

---

[108] The charter party and provisional articles are summarized in 1 Cranch 215–18 (1803).

[109] 5 Geo. I, chapter 11 (1718) and 3 Geo. III, chapter 22 (1762).

[110] 1 Cranch 236–38 (1803).

[111] *Ibid.*, 233, 235–36, 238. This was a strict construction of the agency conferred upon the American consul by the provisional articles and held the master of the vessel to an extremely close adherence to the terms of the provisional articles.

the decision Marshall indicated that the captain had acted prudently in not "hovering" off the British coast in violation of the trade laws of Britain. Because the delay of the voyage was directly attributable to that decision to land in Britain, the claim for demurrage was disallowed.

While Marshall had looked to the four corners of the charter party in *Hooe and Co.* v. *Groverman* in construing the contract, Judge Story was less cautious and more orthodox in dealing with a similar case in 1814. His opinion in *Marcardier* v. *Chesapeake Insurance Company*[112] more accurately reflected the standard view that the nature of a charter party is determined solely by which party possesses the "exclusive possession, command and navigation of the ship during the voyage."[113] The case involved an ill-starred voyage of the brig *Betsey*, chartered to carry goods from New York to Nantes in 1806. Stress of weather and other accidents had forced her into Antigua in the West Indies for repairs; while those necessary repairs were being completed her cargo, which had been partially damaged in the course of the voyage, was abandoned to the insurers as a total loss. The plaintiff, owner of the cargo that was the subject of the charter, charged that the master, who was also the general owner, had acted fraudulently in regard to him as the owner for the voyage, and therefore was guilty of barratry, a breach of duty to the vessel owner. Since a master of a vessel could not be guilty of barratry when he was himself the owner of the vessel, the construction of the contract as a demise charter was essential to the insured's claim based upon barratry. While the detailed discussion of the status of memorandum articles in settlement of marine insurance claims forms a major portion of this opinion,[114] Judge Story's distinction between a voyage charter and a demise charter, based on control of the vessel, has become a classic statement of that principle in American law. After ruling that the *Betsey* was under a voyage charter, he logically concluded that her captain could not commit barratry since he was both general owner and owner for the voyage. In *Marcardier* Judge Story cited the precedent of *Hooe and Co.* v. *Groverman* as well as the leading English decision of *Vallejo* v. *Wheeler*;[115] yet the enunciation of the clearest distinction between the two types of contract is contained in Story's opinion in *Marcardier*.

Hooe and Co. v. *Groverman* and *Marcardier* v. *Chesapeake Insurance Co.* provide a firm basis for the distinction between voyage charters and demise charters in American maritime law.

---

[112] 8 Cranch 39–50 (1814).
[113] See discussion in *ibid.*, 49–50.
[114] See discussion in Part II, chapter 3, note 48.

[115] I Cowper's Reports 143–56; 98 Eng. Rep. 1012–19 (K.B., 1774).

Bottomry Bonds

Financing repairs and other necessary disbursements while away from a vessel's home port was accomplished through the use of bottomry bonds in the late eighteenth and early nineteenth centuries. Bottomry loans arose from an emergency requirement to obtain credit when unanticipated expenses or repairs interrupted the voyage. The creditor under the bond acquired a maritime lien against the vessel predicated upon the successful completion of the voyage that gave birth to the bottomry bond.[116] If the encumbered vessel should sink during the course of the voyage the claim was discharged, and, as the Supreme Court held in *Blaine* v. *Ship Charles Carter*, if the lien was not foreclosed at the end of the voyage, the holder of the bottomry bond forfeited any priority based upon the date of the bond or the nature of the underlying consideration.[117] Consequently common law executions issued against the vessel subsequent to her arrival in her home port and served prior to her departure on a second voyage created a lien that would be superior to that under the bottomry bond.[118]

In the case of a bottomry bond, possession of the vessel remained in the hands of the obligor, and no manifestation of the maritime lien was apparent to subsequent creditors of the owner. The lien itself, unlike a mortgage in that it did not create a vested interest in the vessel, could only be realized upon when the obligee proceeded against the vessel in a court of admiralty.[119] The Blaine case also involved a subsequent bottomry bond issued by the owner of the ship *Charles Carter* while she was in the port of his residence. Judge Chase pointed out that such an owner might easily have executed a mortgage to obtain funds, and that no preference or priority over other security interests and creditors would be recognized merely because the parties had selected a bottomry bond as a security instrument.[120]

Blaine v. *Ship Charles Carter* serves to illustrate the temporary nature of the priority of a bottomry bond. Not only did it attach exclusively during the voyage for which credit was extended, but it also was predicated upon the impossibility of entering into a more formal type of security because of distance from her owner's port. Bottomry depended upon the emergency nature of the situation confronting the master and crew, requiring that they pledge the vessel as collateral so that she might complete her voyage. When this necessity disappeared

---

[116] Gilmore and Black, *Admiralty*, 632–33, 689–90.

[117] *Ibid.*, 518; 4 Cranch 328–33 (1808).

[118] 4 Cranch 328, at 332 (1808).

[119] Gilmore and Black, *Admiralty*, 25, note 85, 624–27, 632–33.

[120] 4 Cranch 332 (1808).

by completion of the voyage the preferred position of the holder of a bottomry bond also vanished.

Seven years later the Supreme Court heard a prize case concerning the brig *Mary*,[121] which had departed from Ireland at such a time that constructive notice of war between the United States and Britain might be inferred. However, in the course of trial below, and on the basis of additional proofs adduced in the Supreme Court, the Court reversed the decree of the circuit court condemning the *Mary* and held that she was an American vessel. Chief Justice Marshall, for the Court, stated in passing that there was no reason why the holders of a bottomry bond should file a claim based upon her American character, for "the interest of the bottomry bond could not have been asserted." Unfortunately, the reasoning supporting Marshall's dictum is not stated. Very likely it depended upon two considerations. First, the holder of a bottomry bond acquired no vested interest in the vessel until such time as his maritime lien under the bond was foreclosed. Since she had been seized and carried into port as prize, the priority of his security interest would be lost in the event of condemnation just as if the ship had been lost at sea. On the other hand, if upon trial she was restored to her owners and successfully completed the voyage, the holder of the bottomry bond might then proceed to enforce his maritime lien against the vessel. Second, the nationality of the holder of the bottomry bond would not enter into the determinations of the prize court adjudicating title to the vessel. Prize jurisdiction was not concerned with the enforcement of maritime liens in the English High Court of Admiralty, and a similar distinction prevented American prize courts from executing maritime liens (other than claims for military salvage) as a part of the process of adjudication.[122]

---

[121] 9 Cranch 126–51 (1815).

[122] The Federal Maritime Liens Act of 1910, 36 Stat. 604–605, eliminated the distinction between ship mortgages and bottomry bonds, creating in their place a statutory form of maritime lien in favor of suppliers of repairs, materials, or other necessaries. It is codified, in slightly altered form, in the current 46 U.S.C. sec. 971–75.

CHAPTER IV

The Articulation of American Nationality

W HEN CHIEF JUSTICE John Marshall presided over his first term of the Supreme Court of the United States few areas of the law were in a more chaotic state than the rules concerning citizenship in the United States and the various States of the federal Union. Yet no issue was more significant in American diplomacy, for the judicial articulation of American nationality and its perquisites was essential before the United States might assume its position in a world of nations still largely a community of monarchial states contemptuous towards the weak federal republic seeking its identity.

As John Adams' secretary of state, Marshall had been plagued by the British doctrine of perpetual allegiance, based in part on legal precedent, but even more strongly predicated upon British national self-interest served by the impressment of naturalized American seamen into the dwindling ranks of the Royal Navy. Concurrent with increasing Anglo-American animosity over impressment were international tensions over the efforts of American States to prevent the collection of debts owed by Americans to British merchants prior to the outbreak of the American Revolution. Finally, the British diplomats and attorneys for British private interests in the United States attempted to secure or regain title in American real property declared confiscated or escheated to the States during the Revolution. The independence of the United States had permitted the plea of alienage to be raised as a bar against actions to establish title brought by British subjects. Each of these major diplomatic impasses—impressment, British debt collection, and loss of American lands through alienage—was dependent upon litigation in the courts of the two contending nations, and in the United States public interest in the adjudications was kindled by the glowing resentment that had persisted undiminished since the last British soldier had left the territory of the thirteen colonies in 1784.

493

Like the substantive law of treason, the American law of citizenship was a product of ancient English practice adapted to comport with the novel circumstances of the new nation. The United States was republican and not monarchial in its executive branches of government, just as its sovereignty was exercised and shared in a federal rather than a unitary system of government. Citizenship in such a nation would, of necessity, lack the attributes of loyalty to the person of a crowned ruler; at the same time its focus would be diffused from allegiance to a single sovereign power to duties owed to both the federal government and one of its constituent State governments. Finally, English views of citizenship were closely tied to the feudal system from which the concepts of fealty and allegiance developed. Allegiance in medieval England was a personal bond between lord and vassal which ultimately tied all landholding freemen, through intermediaries or by direct relationship, to the king as paramount overlord. While vestiges of feudal land tenures existed in a few of the independent American States, they disappeared rapidly after the Revolution, leaving most land in allodial tenure. Allegiance was no longer intimately connected with personal feudal relationships, and there was a need to disassociate the concept of citizenship from rules of property law. Paramount among these problems was that of alien succession to real property in the American States. While the political background of the anti-alien landholding laws was clearly an effort to restrict foreign property holding in the new republic, it is obvious that the legal justification for the practice was ancient English law insuring the right of the king, as feudal lord, to limit succession to loyal subjects whose military obligations would be discharged promptly.

Removal of a crowned head from the political system of a common law jurisdiction created major conceptual problems in the development of a new view of individual obligations to the State. It demanded that the Supreme Court, with aid from State courts, move away from English monarchial precedents while still preserving the traditional Anglo-American relationship of subject and the State. In terms of the classic balance between rights and duties, the subject born under the protection of a king owed allegiance to that monarch and his legitimate successors. Protection demanded the rendition of allegiance on the one hand and obedience on the other. The welfare of the State depended upon the loyalty of its populace, and consequently no State would permit its people to transfer their allegiance or their persons to another sovereignty. Implicit in the mercantilist view of national power was a State's insistence upon continued loyalty and service from its populace and its outright rejection of a subject's rights of emigration or expatriation. English law through the instrumentality of *Calvin's Case* and various glosses upon the holding of that landmark decision created a system of perpetual allegiance that was an effective legal weapon against naturalized American seamen. On the other hand, total American rejection of the theory of perpetual allegiance was not to be lightly undertaken, for the loyalty of citizens to the new republic and its component States was just as vital to national defense and the general welfare as had been perpetual allegiance of the subjects of James I.

Faced with these currents and crosscurrents of high policy, the Supreme Court moved slowly towards a resolution of the nature of citizenship in the United States, and gradually began to delineate the jurisprudential consequences of citizenship and alienage. While English precedents were debated at great length, both in oral argument and in the opinions of the justices, it is clear that the intention was to create from the ashes of colonial subjectship a new phoenix of republican citizenship that would retain some of the public advantages of the older system of allegiance but repudiate those theories of British law that subordinated the individual by a form of perpetual allegiance that indelibly bound him to the sovereign of his birth.

As Professor James H. Kettner has argued persuasively,[1] the tendency in American law was to move from national status based upon nativity and the feudal rules of fealty and *legiance* towards a type of "volitional allegiance" that permitted transfer of loyalty from one sovereign to another by expatriation and naturalization. While this concept of "volitional allegiance" is an analytical tool, it overlooks the fact that American law has never completely embraced a rule of free transference of allegiance from one sovereign to another, nor has it recognized individuality to the extent that a free act of the will alone may either obtain citizenship or renounce it. Infants born in the United States are, under the Constitution, citizens of the nation and so remain until, as adults, they take such actions as may divest themselves of that status. Until recent times women might be naturalized or expatriated against their wishes if they married an alien or were married to an American who renounced his allegiance. Resident aliens have been forced into support of the United States through the doctrine of "temporary allegiance." The persistence of complicated rules concerning national status may be attributed to a fundamental desire to retain some of the state-oriented values of the English system of perpetual allegiance, while giving substantial legal defense to the Lockean doctrine that governments rest upon the consent of the governed. This intellectual struggle between the ideals of the American Revolution and the practical values of stability and order inherent in English perpetual allegiance has produced an uneven and imperfectly stated jurisprudence in our own day, and it is readily apparent that the early Marshall Court, while it did

---

[1] J. Kettner, *The Development of*   *American Citizenship, 1608–1870* (Chapel Hill, 1978), 173–209.

much to bring order to the subject, did not succeed in creating a firm basis upon which future generations might build with confidence.

Cases involving the issue of nationality before the Supreme Court in our period may be grouped into three major categories for purposes of discussion:

1. Those involving the property rights of British subjects and loyalists, seized by the States under wartime confiscation or forfeiture statutes, and mentioned in the peace treaty of 1783 and the Jay Treaty of 1794.
2. Those resulting from the descent of American lands to British subjects whose status was drawn into issue by statutes prohibiting alien land ownership.
3. Those arising under claims of national commercial character in prize cases or in avoidance of the penalties of the Non-Intercourse and Embargo Acts.

Of lesser magnitude, but nevertheless of significance in domestic constitutional litigation, were cases presenting issues created by the cession of the District of Columbia to the federal government, the relationship between State and federal naturalization decrees, and the consequences of naturalization for the wife and minor children of naturalized citizens.

Confiscations and forfeitures imposed by the States against British subjects and loyalist Americans took a variety of forms, but each seizure was based upon the war powers of the State and the right of a belligerent in international law to take the property of alien enemies. The Supreme Court recognized forfeitures based upon legislative fiat in *Smith* v. *Maryland*, but where the State legislation provided merely that real property *might* be seized from alien enemies, it required that a public act known as an inquest of office be held to vest title in the sovereign State.[2] Hence what one State might authorize by statute, another might be required to achieve through a judicial proceeding. The mode of forfeiture was therefore determined by State law and practice, and likewise the election to treat an individual as a citizen of the newly created State was governed by the legislation and public acts of the State making the election.

In *M'Ilvaine* v. *Coxe's Lessee*[3] the State of New Jersey, having seized a loyalist's lands and declared him a traitor, was held to have treated him as a citizen, and thus he might not for purposes of taking title to land be considered an alien to New Jersey. While the right of seizing alien enemy property and the impact of the Anglo-American

---

[2] Smith v. Maryland, 6 Cranch 286–307 (1810); inquest of office was required in regard to the Virginia confiscations, Fairfax's Devisee v. Hunter, 7 Cranch 603–32 (1813).
[3] 4 Cranch 209–15 (1808).

treaties of 1783 and 1794 more properly belong in our subsequent discussion of international law decisions of the Supreme Court, it is clear that Revolutionary War confiscations and forfeitures provide one of the leading sources of jurisprudence concerning the status of loyalists and British subjects. For that reason they drew judicial attention to the nature of citizenship and alienage, just as the value of the land involved brought the litigation to national attention. In terms of Supreme Court personalities and the dynamics of business before the Court the confiscation cases are particularly interesting because Chief Justice Marshall, deeply involved in the purchase of the Fairfax manors of Leeds and South Branch and a longtime attorney for the Fairfax interests, consistently disqualified himself from participation in the decision of these matters.[4] Furthermore, the flow of Revolutionary War forfeiture cases reached the chambers of the Supreme Court at the same time American diplomats were confronting the British over the issue of maritime impressments.[5] Small wonder that the brightest minds at the Supreme Court bar were recruited to litigate these cases, producing arguments of historical learning and legal logic that are unparalleled in the history of the Court.

The vagaries of William Cranch's reporting obscure the close relationship between the cases of *M'Ilvaine* v. *Coxe's Lessee* and *Lambert's Lessee* v. *Paine*.[6] Both involved succession to lands, either by devise or descent, but in the Lambert case a construction of the decedent's will was required before the issue of alienage was raised. *M'Ilvaine* was argued from February 15 to February 18, 1805, and judgment was reserved; the following day counsel began oral presentations in *Lambert's Lessee* v. *Paine*, which, after interruption, concluded on February 26 and 27. On March 1, 1805, the Supreme Court in a group of seriatim opinions affirmed the lower court's judgment in the Lambert case based upon its construction of the devise and thereby avoiding the issue of alienage.

---

[4] A. Beveridge, *The Life of John Marshall*, 4 vols. (New York, 1916–19), IV, 145, 153–54, 161–64; L. Baker, *John Marshall: A Life in the Law* (New York, 1974), 574–75. For Marshall's work as counsel for the Fairfax interests see H. Johnson and C. Cullen, eds., *The Papers of John Marshall*, I (Chapel Hill, 1974), 150–64.

[5] B. Perkins, *Prologue to War, England and the United States, 1805–1812* (Berkeley, 1961), 82–96.

[6] Judge Cranch was not unduly particular in the placement of his reports of cases in the proper year. As a consequence a number of cases argued and decided in the preceding term of the Supreme Court might appear with those argued and decided a year later. Similarly a case from a later year might be published in the volume for an earlier year if there were room for an additional opinion in that volume. Because of these variations the minute books of the Supreme Court are the only reliable evidence of the dates of argument or decision and those dates are used throughout this book. Lambert's Lessee v. Paine is reported in 3 Cranch 97–139 (1805); the argument in M'Ilvaine v. Coxe's Lessee is reported in 2 Cranch 280–336 (1804).

M'Ilvaine v. *Coxe's Lessee* remained dormant on the Court's docket until February 3, 1808, when re-argument began. After the conclusion of argument on February 5 the Supreme Court again took the matter under advisement, and its opinion, issued on February 23, 1808, finally reached the subject of alienage.[7]

New Jersey real property owned by Rebecca Coxe until her death in 1802 formed the subject of this litigation. Daniel Coxe, who would have been her heir-at-law before the Revolution, claimed title by inheritance and conveyed his interests to the lessor of the plaintiff. Defendant Rebecca Coxe M'Ilvaine was one of the grandchildren of the decedent's brother, William Coxe, who predeceased Rebecca Coxe in 1801. If Daniel Coxe were barred by alienage, the property would then have descended to the heirs of William Coxe. At issue then was the status of Daniel Coxe, who was born in the royal province of New Jersey, but removed to Philadelphia after the British occupation in 1777 and never thereafter resided within the territory of the independent State of New Jersey. A member of the royal governor's council in New Jersey and a colonel of the provincial militia, Coxe occupied a civil office under the Crown in Philadelphia and later in New York City. After the peace treaty and before the death of Rebecca Coxe he had held lands in England as a trustee, described himself in documents as "of Great Britain," and held a pension from the king in recognition of his loyalty and services rendered during the American Revolution.

The independent State of New Jersey had not failed to take notice of these activities on behalf of the British. By a general act of October 4, 1776, the legislature declared that all persons then living in New Jersey owed allegiance to the new government. Turning to Coxe individually it held an inquisition concerning him on August 1, 1778, and having found that he served as a police magistrate for the British "against the form of his allegiance to the state of New Jersey" declared his real and personal property forfeited and vested in the State. In February 1779 his estate was sold in accordance with this judgment. Sometime in 1778 or 1779 the State of Pennsylvania attained Coxe for treason, but he was pardoned of that offense by the Pennsylvania governor in 1802.

The United States Circuit Court for New Jersey gave judgment for the plaintiff below, thereby recognizing Daniel Coxe's status as a citizen and his capacity to hold title to New Jersey real property. In opening argument for appellants, William Tilghman of Pennsylvania[8]

---

[7] Minutes of the Supreme Court, I, RG 267, National Archives, Washington.

[8] Tilghman's argument is in 2 Cranch 280–92.

noted that the novel issue raised by the case was whether a native of New Jersey, born there under the colonial government, but who fled to areas occupied by British forces at an early stage of the war and subsequently adhered to the British cause, might nevertheless be capable of taking New Jersey land by descent in 1802. The issue according to Tilghman was whether Coxe had expatriated himself and whether that barred him from holding title. Tilghman strongly defended the right of expatriation, observing that "[o]f all people the Americans are the last who ought to call in question the right of expatriation. They have derived infinite advantage from its exercise by others who have left Europe and settled here. It is denied by the constitution of no state, nor of the United States."[9] On the contrary, expatriation was sanctioned by the constitutions of many States and by a statute passed by the Virginia General Assembly. British practice in the colonial period recognized expatriation through the enactment of naturalization laws, and the State of New Jersey's naturalization act, by demanding oath of abjuration, also gave tacit recognition to the right of expatriation. In light of these considerations, Tilghman contended that there could be no question that Coxe had expatriated himself. His treatment by the British authorities confirmed this, as did his own actions while in England.

The constitution of the State of New Jersey in Tilghman's opinion clearly based protection and allegiance in a reciprocal relationship, whereby allegiance was no longer considered to be perpetual as it had been in *Calvin's Case*. As a result, although New Jersey had adopted the common law, it did not thereby absorb the doctrine of the *antenati* from *Calvin's Case*. That would not only be inconsistent with the new political situation but it would read into New Jersey law principles enunciated in an English case that had been decided when "the ideas of the royal prerogative were extravagant and absurd." The binding precedent of *Calvin's Case* was weakened by the passage of time, the events of the Glorious Revolution of 1688, and the imperial rupture of the American Revolution.

> The Principal of natural allegiance does not apply to this country, No *antenatus* ever owed natural allegiance to the United States. There can be but one natural allegiance, and that was due to the King of Great Britain. American *antenati*, therefore, may hold lands in England, because they were born under the allegiance of the King of England; but English *antenati* cannot hold lands in America, because they were not born under the allegiance of the United States.[10]

---

[9] *Ibid.*, 286.

[10] *Ibid.*, 291. On the English law concerning *antenati* see Kettner, *Development*, 16–48. He also indicates that residents of territories lost in wars might, under certain circumstances, be held to be aliens. *Ibid.*, 50–51.

Either as an alien or as an expatriated citizen, Coxe was incapable of taking title to New Jersey lands by descent.

In answer to Tilghman, William Rawle argued that Coxe was not an alien, for as a resident when New Jersey became independent he was a citizen and entitled to inherit lands.[11] He could not be deprived of that right except as punishment for crimes, which was not the case, and even though he had made an effort to expatriate himself, he could not succeed in doing so without the consent of the State of New Jersey. "If allegiance be considered as a contract, which requires the consent of both parties to make, it cannot be dissolved but by consent of both."[12] Quite the contrary, the historical evidence is that the declaration of independence was a political act by the majority, which bound the minority as citizens, and consequently many of them, like Daniel Coxe, were punished for behavior deemed disloyal or traitorous. When New Jersey acceded to the Declaration of Independence she did so as a society, and "every inhabitant continued a member of the society. Every inhabitant, therefore, continued to retain his property, whether real or personal."[13] By its legislative act on October 4, 1776, the State declared Coxe, as an inhabitant of its territory, to be a citizen of New Jersey, and the criminal sanctions applied against him in 1778 were based upon his failure to abide by this allegiance.

Richard Stockton took up the appellee's argument from Rawle,[14] directing his attention to the doctrine of the *antenati*, and recalling that when the English king controlled provinces of France during the recurring wars between the two kingdoms, Frenchmen born under the protection of the English king were not considered aliens in England after English military occupation ceased.[15] The right of an *antenatus* to inherit was, according to Stockton, founded in justice, for a right once vested ought never to be divested except upon conviction of a crime. St. George Tucker in his edition of Blackstone's *Commentaries* not only considered *Calvin's Case* to be American law, but also specifically accepted the doctrine of the *antenati*.[16] Nothing in the rule in *Calvin's Case* limited the right of emigration; indeed it encouraged the exercise of that freedom, leaving the native-born subject secure in the certainty that he might always return home to the land of his birth as a fully accepted subject of his sovereign. Referring to an "empire . . . rent asunder by a revolution" and the need that the innocent should not suffer by virtue of the territory in which they found themselves,

---

[11] Rawle's argument is in 2 Cranch 292–308 (1804).

[12] *Ibid.*, 292.

[13] *Ibid.*, 294. Rawle found support for his argument in the Constitution of New Jersey and the New Jersey Statutes. *Ibid.*, 294–95.

[14] *Ibid.*, 307–21.

[15] *Ibid.*, 310.

[16] Stockton's reference to Tucker's edition of Blackstone is in *ibid.*, 311.

Stockton moved on to consider the possibility, horrifying though it was to him, that the American Union one day might be dissolved.[17] What then, he asked, would be the security of the citizen who held lands in a State other than his residence? Clearly the right of the *antenati* would protect him, since at the time of his birth both he and the people of the territory in which he became an alien owed a common allegiance to the same sovereign federal republic.

The only alternative to acceptance of the doctrine of the *antenati*, according to Stockton, was to treat those resident in the territory of the newly independent State as subject to the government on the ground of tacit consent predicated upon their remaining in residence, or on the foundation of the decision of the majority which binds all members of the society. "Hence as birth at the common law denotes the subject, so residence at the time of the revolution will draw with it the same consequences."[18] That principle was applied in New Jersey by its statutory declaration that residents as of October 4, 1776, were citizens and bound by allegiance to the newly independent State. Daniel Coxe had been proclaimed within the allegiance owed to New Jersey and punished for his failure to serve his State; New Jersey was thereafter estopped to say that he was an alien.

Could Coxe, having decided to absent himself from New Jersey and join the British, expatriate himself from his allegiance to his State? Stockton maintained that this was not possible without the consent of the State of New Jersey. Once residing within the independent State and having been proclaimed a citizen, he cannot unilaterally break the tie that bound him to New Jersey. Expatriation was unknown at common law and the common law had been received under the New Jersey constitution. Coxe therefore enjoyed a dual citizenship, or double allegiance, "a matter which happens here every day in the case of the naturalized Englishmen." This argument embraces simultaneously the theory that expatriation, if it takes place at all, must do so by mutual consent of subject and sovereign, and that dual citizenship was acceptable in American law.[19]

Ingersoll of Pennsylvania replied to Rawle and Stockton[20] by distinguishing *M'Ilvaine* v. *Coxe's Lessee* from *Calvin's Case*: "[T]his is a new case in the history of nations, to which the little case of Calvin, the Scotchman, bears no proportion."[21] The Revolution's impact and intent was the very opposite of that set forth by opposing counsel— the authority of the mother country was utterly rejected, and the inhabitants were left in such a state of nature that each might choose to

---

[17] *Ibid.*, 312.
[18] *Ibid.*
[19] *Ibid.*, 316–19.
[20] His argument is printed in *ibid.*, 321–36, and concludes the presentations at this term of Court.
[21] *Ibid.*, 322.

remain a British subject or become a citizen of his newly independent native State. That time of election continued until governments were fully organized, after which time continued residence was an implied consent to share the destinies of the new United States. In New Jersey the period normally would have ended on October 4, 1776, but a subsequent statute permitting freemen to return to their allegiance by August 1, 1777, extended the period of election at least to that date. Even if the right of election had passed by the time Coxe left New Jersey for Philadelphia, then Ingersoll argued that the right of expatriation still remained. Citing St. George Tucker's edition of Blackstone and James Wilson's lectures on the Law,[22] he found the right of emigration to be synonymous with the right of expatriation, and contended that this was a principle "as ancient as the society of man." The British rule of perpetual allegiance was contrary to divine law, the law of nature, the law of nations, and the constitution of New Jersey. Ingersoll concluded with an attack on the contention, tentatively advanced by St. George Tucker, that the peace treaty of 1783 and the Jay Treaty recognized the doctrine of the *antenatus* in American law; quite the contrary, he asserted, their only effect was to insure that lands not actually divested from their British or loyalist owners would be secured to them. The expatriation of Daniel Coxe, he concluded, induced the forfeiture of alienage as to the lands in question, casting the descent upon the defendant, Rebecca Coxe M'Ilvaine.

Counsel ranged broadly in their argument of *M'Ilvaine* v. *Coxe's Lessee*, at times concentrating upon nice points of statutory language and details in phraseology of treaty clauses; at other times they swept broadly into the writings of international jurists, the philosophy of John Locke, and even the example of expatriation provided by the story of Moses in the Bible. Basic to the case were extremely difficult questions concerning the nature of the State governments at the inception of the Revolution, and the foundation in natural and international law for citizenship in those bodies politic. Having been called upon to decide matters so fundamental to the legitimacy of American republican government, the Supreme Court hesitated, took the case under advisement, and prepared to hear oral argument in *Lambert's Lessee* v. *Paine* on the following day, February 19.

Lambert's Lessee v. *Paine*[23] involved the construction of two

---

[22] See R. McCloskey, ed., *The Works of James Wilson*, 2 vols. (Cambridge, 1967), I, 243–45, for the discussion cited by Ingersoll. Wilson was a strong advocate for the consensual basis of political societies. *Ibid.*, 227–46.

[23] 3 Cranch 97–139 (1805). As indicated in Part II, chapter 3, note 6, the case was argued and the opinion delivered in 1804, but it was not reported until 1805.

writings testamentary executed in 1782 and 1786 by George Harmer of Virginia. The first established an elaborate system of trustees to hold for the benefit of relatives of the testator resident in, and subjects of, Great Britain. The second instrument, without mentioning the first, devised the real estate in question to one George Gilmer, and provided in addition that Gilmer was to disburse the testator's personal estate to certain British relatives. Since the 1786 instrument neither revoked nor referred to the 1782 document, it was unclear whether it was a codicil to the earlier will, or an attempt to revoke it and substitute a new testamentary disposition. In the period prior to George Gilmer's death in November 1793 none of the testator's relatives achieved American citizenship and thus qualified to hold title to the Virginia realty. As a result the issue was whether the devise in the 1786 instrument was for Gilmer's life only, with a reversion to the testator's heirs who were unable to take title, or a fee simple estate to Gilmer whose heirs or devisees would take it at his death. To clarify the matter of title to the real property the Virginia General Assembly after the death of Gilmer passed a statute declaring that since it had been supposed that Gilmer's lands escheated to the Commonwealth, the lands were released by the Commonwealth to children and heirs of Gilmer and title was vested in them. The Circuit Court for Virginia, with Chief Justice Marshall on the bench, gave judgment for Gilmer's heirs, based upon a special verdict of the jury setting forth the above facts and the matter concerning the alienage of Harmer's British relatives.

Counsel for both parties anticipated that the appeal might involve both alienage and the construction of the testamentary writings. As a result a substantial part of their research and persuasive talents was devoted to briefing and arguing the legal status of citizens and aliens in the light of English and American precedents. For this reason *Lambert's Lessee* v. *Paine* is an important source of law concerning American nationality, even though its holding is strictly limited to the fields of real property and construction of wills.

John Minor of Richmond began his argument[24] for the British heirs of the testator by claiming that the 1786 instrument was but a partial revocation of the 1782 will, and consequently the residuary clause of the 1782 instrument governed the disposition of the realty after the death of Gilmer, the life tenant. In the alternative, he claimed that the Virginia statute transferring trusts into possession made John Lambert's interest a legal estate, and that property right, having been in existence and not taken by the Commonwealth of Virginia through an inquest of office found, was protected by the 1794 Treaty with

---

[24] *Ibid.*, 100–109.

Great Britain.[25] Dividing his argument as to alienage, Minor contended (1) that John Lambert was not an alien to Virginia and the United States, and (2) if he were an alien, his property interest vested by operation of the statute of uses was not taken by the proper process and hence continued to exist at the time of ratification of the Jay Treaty. Thus it was entitled to protection under the terms of that international agreement. Both assertions recurred in future argument on alien land-holding, and the contributions of Minor to future developments cannot be overstated.

In his argument that John Lambert was not an alien in Virginia, Minor quoted *Calvin's Case* that "an alien is a subject that is born out of the ligeance of the king, and under the ligeance of another." Lambert was born in 1750, at which time Virginia and Britain were ruled by the same king, hence he could not be an alien in Virginia and barred from inheriting realty unless his right to inherit had been forfeited by the conviction of a crime that worked corruption of the blood.[26] "The separation of the colonies from England could not, in law or reason, deprive him of this right."[27] He proceeded to demonstrate from *Calvin's Case* that, as an ancillary matter, the judges had declared that subjects of James I born in Scotland prior to his accession to the English throne could not claim the right to inherit lands in England; having been born before the conjoining of the two kingdoms by James' succession, they were aliens in England. This perpetual allegiance based upon the sovereignty of the land of one's birth, and which could not be varied by subsequent events, gave rise, Minor explained, to what American lawyers were to term the doctrine of the *antenati*. Accordingly, British

---

[25] The Virginia system of confiscation of alien lands and the requirement for an inquest of office found was considered and the inquest requirement was upheld by the Supreme Court in the later decision of Fairfax's Lessee v. Hunter, 7 Cranch 603–32 (1813).

The two Anglo-American treaties forbade first, future confiscations by the States after the execution of the 1783 Peace Treaty and second, divesting of property rights of British or American owners in the signatory countries by virtue of alienage. H. Miller, ed., *Treaties and Other International Acts of the United States of America* (Washington, 1931), II, 253–54. The phraseology was such that a complete divestment of title would have to take place prior to the effective dates of one or the other of the treaties. Hence the federal construction of State confiscation procedures was fundamental to the determination of these "federal question" cases.

[26] Citing Blackstone, *Commentaries*, I, 371.

[27] 3 Cranch 105 (1805). The argument is an interesting one, pitting the sovereignty of newly independent States against property interests. Viewed retrospectively from Chief Justice Marshall's decision and opinion in Dartmouth College v. Woodward, involving continuing obligations of an American State under a royal charter, Minor's argument and emphasis upon property rights cannot be dismissed lightly, although it was unproductive of a decision on those points in Lambert's Lessee.

subjects and loyalists born either in Britain or her dominions, or in the American colonies prior to the American Revolution, were not aliens in the American States, although individuals born in Britain or the Empire after the division of sovereignty were clearly aliens. Conversely, citizens of the American States born before the Revolution were entitled to inherit lands in Britain and the dominions since they were *antenati* and hence not barred by alienage. Minor pointed out that the English had in fact permitted Americans to inherit lands in England on this basis, claiming that a "liberal policy" should induce American courts to accept the *antenati* doctrine in this and other cases.

Turning to the Jay Treaty, Minor pleaded for a view that "treaties ought to be liberally expounded so as to meet the full intention of the contracting parties." The clause concerning possession of estates secured not only those in actual possession, but those that might have become vested except for the question of alienage.[28] Hence Lambert should recover because the treaty removed the bar to his recovery, and if he was an alien previous to the Treaty, he nevertheless took the land by devise and since Virginia had not proceeded against him by office found, he had title against all the world except the Commonwealth. That title might be extinguished only by office found or by his death, at which time the sovereign would take the freehold by operation of the rule of law that an alien could have no heirs.

Philip Barton Key of Maryland countered with the persuasive argument[29] that George Gilmer took a fee simple under the 1786 will or codicil. This was predicated upon English case law which held that where a testator who held a fee simple in land devised "all of my estate" to an individual, that person took a fee simple in the realty. Hence, Key argued, George Gilmer became absolute owner of the property in question and upon his death, his fee simple title passed to his heirs-at-law. On the other hand if it be considered that Gilmer took only a life estate under the devise, the testator's heirs lost the real property when it descended to them on Gilmer's death and before any of them had become American citizens. Key specifically denied the applicability of the English doctrine of *antenati* to American law:

> The English doctrine is, that a man can never expatriate himself, and hence they have allowed our citizens, born before the revolution to inherit to [*sic*] British subjects. But, by the revolution of 1776, and the declaration of independence, new relations took place. A new sovereignty was created, to which British subjects, not in this country at that time, never owed allegiance and, therefore, they can have no inheritable blood as to lands in this country.[30]

---

[28] 3 Cranch 108 (1805).   [29] 3 Cranch 109–15 (1805).   [30] *Ibid.*, 114.

Plaintiff's lessor had no rights because Virginia did not bring an inquest of office as to the lands; Key again asserted that Lambert's title was contingent upon the prior failure of title in John Harmer, testator's brother. While the chronological relationship between the date of death of John Harmer and George Gilmer (the purported life tenant) is not clear from the report of the case, Key argued that upon the death of the alien John Harmer, title would vest in the Commonwealth even without office found. The actual sequence of deaths did not matter, for if Gilmer held a life estate, then Harmer had a reversion, which on his death as an alien, would vest in the Commonwealth of Virginia. In either event, Lambert as a subsequently mentioned devisee or beneficiary under the 1782 will could not take title and thereby claim benefit of the 1794 Treaty.[31]

The oral arguments in *Lambert's Lessee* assume particular importance when compared to the subsequently announced opinions of the Supreme Court in *M'Ilvaine* v. *Coxe's Lessee* and *Dawson's Lessee* v. *Godfrey*.[32] In particular Philip Barton Key's view of the legal consequences of American independence can be considered a precursor of Judge Johnson's majority opinion in *Dawson*.[33] At the same time Judge Johnson refrained from entering into the consideration of the rights of property and inheritance so ably defended by John Minor in *Lambert's Lessee*. Had the construction problem not intervened in *Lambert's Lessee*, it is likely that the issue of property rights might have been met more directly in that case, but the passage of years permitted the Supreme Court to exercise the prerogative of overlooking Minor's conservative defense of the property rights secured by birth to the *antenati*. Indeed, in the light of the Supreme Court's other holdings in the cases based on vested property rights, it is surprising that the circumstances of the *antenati* did not elicit greater compassion. Since property rights were vested in subjects of the British crown prior to the Revolution, and the individual had not been convicted of a felony punishable by forfeiture or of treason against the United States, the sequestration, confiscation, or escheat of property on the ground of alienage was contrary to principles that the Court applied generally to all other cases.

In arguing *M'Ilvaine* Richard Stockton had touched upon the delicate subject of perpetual allegiance and the dual citizenship of British subjects who had been naturalized in the United States. Public concern over the problem of impressment was far deeper in its philosophical roots than the reports of the daily newspapers. There was a

---

[31] The impact of Key's construction of the wills must have been obvious for John T. Mason's reply was almost totally devoted to that point; on re-argument the discussion of construction was predominant.

[32] 4 Cranch 321–24 (1808).

[33] Compare 3 Cranch 115 with Johnson's opinion, 4 Cranch 322–23.

fundamental and profound divergence between Federalist and Republican attitudes concerning the nature of citizenship and allegiance. As a general rule Federalists tended to deny the existence of a right of expatriation, or at least the exercise of that right without the consent of the governing State. This position against voluntary expatriation was a stand in favor of strong government and the rights of society. It was in stark contrast to the rights of the individual as a free agent that inhered in Revolutionary rhetoric and had become the bedrock of the Jeffersonian political order.[34] In the years between the first arguments in *M'Ilvaine* and *Lambert* and the decision of *M'Ilvaine* in 1808 the impressment issue grew as a cause of Anglo-American tension, the Republican administrations began to use national and State law enforcement authority in uncharacteristic and inconsistent ways, but the basic divergence of philosophical attitudes concerning the rights of individual citizens in republican societies persisted unabated.

The opinion in *M'Ilvaine* v. *Coxe's Lessee*, delivered by Judge Cushing on February 23, 1808, addressed itself to the question of expatriation and the manner in which that right might be exercised.[35] Cushing pointedly avoided the issue of the alienage of *antenati* subjects of Great Britain who had never resided in New Jersey, for in a technical sense that did not apply to Coxe, who was a loyalist. He also eliminated the question of when, if ever, Daniel Coxe possessed a privilege to elect allegiance to his native State or adherence to the British crown. For Cushing and his concurring associates, the case turned upon one point—that New Jersey undeniably had asserted its sovereignty over Daniel Coxe by the act of October 4, 1776, and thereafter it took such legislative and judicial action as it deemed proper to compel return to his due allegiance to New Jersey. Coxe's property was forfeited because of his offenses against the State of New Jersey, and not through escheat because of alienage. His conviction of treason did not work against his status, for that would be unjust, but rather it was for the purpose of punishing him by confiscating his lands. Coxe's alienage depended upon the laws of New Jersey, and that State had consistently treated him as a citizen amenable to penal sanctions for failure to render allegiance. The peace treaty of 1783 did not in any way alter that situation, but rather accepted State determinations as the basis for citizenship or alienage. Both before and after the rati-

---

[34] I. Tsiang, *The Question of Expatriation in America Prior to 1907* (Baltimore, 1942), 43. Judge John Tyler of Virginia excepted to the right of expatriation by observing that "the moment a citizen is called on for his support, there is a *lien* (*obligation*) upon him, and he is bound to yield to the call of his country." L. Tyler, *The Letters and Times of the Tylers* (Richmond, 1884), I, 202. See also Beveridge, *Life of John Marshall*, IV, 4.

[35] 4 Cranch 209–15 (1808).

fication of the peace treaty Coxe possessed the right to inherit lands in New Jersey, and hence the lessor of the plaintiff was entitled to recover.

In thus affirming the judgment of the court below, the Supreme Court recognized a limited right of expatriation, one that might be exercised under conditions specified by State law and with the consent, either express or implied, of the sovereign authority of the State. While allegiance was not declared perpetual, it nevertheless was not to be easily discarded even by expatriate acts that demonstrated quite clearly a determination to select a new sovereign. Although *M'Ilvaine* did not resolve the question of the *antenati* and thus embrace a substantial portion of the doctrine of perpetual allegiance, it was despite this fact a strong affirmation of the right of the sovereign, even in a revolutionary situation, to establish guidelines for the expatriation process. Arguments of counsel concerning the natural rights of man to choose his allegiance and to transfer it freely were dismissed without mention in the opinion.

Twenty-two days after Cushing delivered the opinion in *M'Ilvaine*, Judge Johnson addressed himself to the doctrine of the *antenati*, raised by the appeal in *Dawson's Lessee* v. *Godfrey*,[36] an ejectment action for lands then situated in the District of Columbia. The case had not been argued at bar, but counsel relied upon the arguments in *Lambert's Lessee* v. *Paine* and *M'Ilvaine*. The Dawson case presented the single issue of alienage of a British subject, never resident in the American colonies or States, who by right of inheritance was entitled to the land unless barred by alienage. Maryland law applied to the portion of the District of Columbia involved in the case, and Maryland statutes prohibited alien landholding. The single question was whether Mrs. Dawson, as a British subject born before 1776, was an alien in Maryland and hence in the District of Columbia.

As Judge Johnson indicated, the doctrine of the *antenati* did not proceed directly from the resolution of *Calvin's Case*, for there the individual claiming rights to inherit English land was born *after* (*postnatus*) the devolution of the two crowns upon one sovereign, and not before (*antenatus*) the separation of two kingdoms. It was the dicta in *Calvin's Case* rather than the holding that gave rise to the doctrine of the *antenati*. The argument on behalf of Mrs. Dawson was therefore based upon "a supposed analogy . . . and the reasoning of the judges in *Calvin's Case*." Counsel in *M'Ilvaine* and *Lambert's Lessee* had argued at length that the relationship of English residents and the residents of the American colonies before 1776 was identical to that of Scotsmen and Englishmen after the union of the crowns in 1603. They enjoyed a

---

[36] 4 Cranch 321–24 (1808).

community of allegiance at birth, and the right to inherit depended not upon the state of allegiance when descent was cast, but rather the community of allegiance existing at the time of birth. Johnson observed:

> The latter proposition presents the weak point of their argument for the community of allegiance at the time of birth and at the time of descent both existed in *Calvin's Case*. And if the court in their . . . expressed opinions . . . go the length contended for by the counsel, they must be considered as mere *obiter* opinions . . . We have no doubt that the correct doctrine of the English law is, that the right to inherit depends upon the existing state of allegiance at the time of descent cast.[37]

Inheritance, noted Johnson, was not a natural and perfect right but rather a privilege that had its basis in the laws of society and the exercise of territorial jurisdiction.[38] To be entitled to inherit in Maryland (and hence in the District of Columbia) a right must be made out under the laws of that State. No right of alien inheritance can be found there, nor is there any exception at common law that would give the right of inheritance in the absence of an obligation of allegiance existing either in fact or in the supposition of the law.

The relatively short majority opinion in *Dawson's Lessee* resulted in the elimination of the doctrine of the *antenati* from American law.[39] Yet its impact cannot be so delimited, for the rationale and implications of the opinion are much broader than its holding, just as its reasoning and historical understanding may be subject to serious challenge. Judge Johnson's assertion to the contrary notwithstanding, it cannot be said that English law held that the right to inherit depended upon the state of allegiance at the time of descent cast. On the contrary, the rule had been, and continued to be after *Calvin's Case*, that one born in the protection of the English king might not thereafter be held an alien, even though he resided under the protection of a foreign sovereign at the time of descent cast. While the opinion in *Dawson* would seem to enunciate an American rule to be that the right to inherit depends on

---

[37] *Ibid.*, 322–23.

[38] This is a nice point of legal philosophy concerning the nature of property. Does it exist as a mere creature of the law subject to divestiture by legislative or judicial act? Traditionally property in Anglo-American law was held by a more secure tenure, although no absolute right to property in land had been recognized. Does a right to inherit property, subject as it is to the possibility of defeat by devise or death prior to the owner, partake of the attributes of property, and thus have some degree of isolation from public regulation or legislation on a retroactive basis?

[39] In Fairfax's Lessee v. Hunter, Justice Story unequivocally stated that Dawson's Lessee had settled all former doubts and that "it is now settled" that the rule of the *antenati* did not apply in the United States. 7 Cranch 603, at 620 (1813).

the laws of the territorial sovereign at the time of descent, and the status of the heir at that time, this principle was announced not as a *departure* from the English rule of perpetual allegiance but rather as a natural consequence of English common law on the subject. Judge Johnson's speculations concerning the mode of pleading alienage do not really grapple with the fundamental issue—did the American Revolution destroy the birthright of English subjects to inherit lands in the former dominions of their sovereign? Did not the revolting American States succeed to the sovereignty of the British monarch, and if that were the case, might not it be argued with equal strength that the continuing subjects of the English king who did not reside in America and had not participated in the Revolution were still in a status of non-alienage in regard to their former fellow subjects in America? Answering those questions in a direct manner might raise complicated juridical problems concerning the deprivation of rights acquired at birth, the right of legislatures retroactively to alter systems of inheritance, and the method and nature of the transfer of sovereignty from the Crown to the separate States and the United States.

Dawson must be considered but a partial and tentative step towards a new definition of citizenship. Upholding the *M'Ilvaine* precedent that State action determined who owed allegiance and thus was a citizen, *Dawson* repudiated the *antenati* gloss upon *Calvin's Case*, at least as far as it involved a Britisher's right to inherit American lands. According to Justice Johnson's opinion, the Revolution had produced a new sovereign power to which no British subject always resident in England ever owed allegiance. Yet there can be no doubt that such inheritance would have been valid before 1776, and the only State action that could have bearing upon its continuance after that date was the declaration of the State's independence. Would that, coupled with a judicial finding of alienage, be sufficient to alter rights or at least legal expectations of inheritance within the affected territory? Apparently it was the Court's opinion that it would, by operation of the State laws and Constitution. Yet changes of sovereignty in times of war, or even by treaties of cession, did not necessarily alter the municipal law of the territory involved, and those rules were well known in early America to be part of the common law of England.[40]

The Court's opinion in *Dawson* provided great discretion to State legislatures in altering systems of inheritance subsequent to

---

[40] Lands conquered by the British crown were considered to retain their municipal laws until English law was declared in effect. See J. Smith, *Appeals to the Privy Council from the American Plantations* (New York, 1950), 470–73, discussing Blankard v. Galdy, Holt 341; 2 Salkeld 411; 4 Modern 222; Comberbach 228 (K.B., 1688); and Dutton v. Howell, Shower 24 (House of Lords, 1693).

the birth of the would-be heir. While it is true that no living man has an heir, it is also apparent that individual subjects or citizens have familial ties recognized by municipal law and that those relationships at the time of an individual's death become operative to determine heirship. Inheritance is as much a matter of consanguinity as it is a product of municipal law, and the failure of the Supreme Court to deal with the property issue should not be permitted to obscure its significance. Indeed, the generally accepted modern American rule that statutes altering the rules of descent and distribution are not to be given retroactive effect but that they are effective only in regard to the estates of decedents dying after the date of enactment may serve to demonstrate the widespread acceptance of the *Dawson* opinion. The date of death, rather than the date of birth of the heir, fixes the constitutional limit of effective alteration. Such a rule, in the final analysis, is the only sound basis for effective legislative action in the field of inheritance.

Once the rule of the *antenati* had been eliminated from American law in the Dawson case, the question arose concerning the method by which British-owned lands might legally be confiscated by or escheated to the State governments during the course of the Revolution. Since the 1794 Treaty specified that lands then possessed by British subjects in the American States might not be subject to confiscation,[41] it was essential that the Supreme Court determine what lands had been validly confiscated during the war and what lands, as a consequence of improper or incomplete procedures, still remained in the possession of their original owners. In *Smith* v. *Maryland*,[42] an appeal from the Court of Appeals of Maryland, the real property was alleged to have been confiscated in accordance with a statute of 1780, which declared all British property within Maryland to be in the ownership and possession of the commissioners appointed under that act to take title. The Maryland precedent of *Norwood's Lessee* v. *Owings* held that as a result of the legislation all title to these lands was in the State, and that as of November 19, 1794 (the effective date of the Jay Treaty), no British subject could own land in Maryland.[43] Counsel for the British owners contended that the Maryland act applied only in those cases where there was actual possession of the property and it had been used or disposed of by State action. "The right to confiscate goods of an enemy is merely the belligerent right of capture. If the property be not taken during the war it can never be seized afterwards," contended Samuel

---

[41]Miller, ed., *Treaties*, II, 253–54.

[42] 6 Cranch 286–307 (1810).

[43] The appeal of this case to the Supreme Court did not reach the substantive issues but was decided instead upon the holding that only parties claiming directly under a treaty might have a federal-question appeal to the Supreme Court. Owings v. Norwood's Lessee, 5 Cranch 344–50 (1809).

Johnston for his clients.[44] On behalf of the State of Maryland, Robert Goodloe Harper and Richard Ridgeley argued that the statute did not authorize confiscation—it declared that British property *was* confiscated *eo instanti* upon passage of the act and no further steps were necessary.[45] That had been the holding in *Norwood's Lessee*, and "the laws of Maryland are to be construed by this court as they are construed in Maryland."[46] Because Maryland case law on the subject placed the instant case outside the scope of the 1794 Treaty, there was no federal question that would permit the Supreme Court to exercise jurisdiction. To this jurisdictional issue Harper devoted his argument. The result of the Maryland legislation was that at the time of the 1783 Peace Treaty there was no British property in Maryland, all having been vested in the State by the statute. No office found, entry, or seizure was necessary to perfect the State's title. "The question of the construction of the acts of Maryland is not open to this court."[47] In reply, Samuel Jones argued[48] that the confiscation was only in contemplation of the law, and that by the law of England, familiar to the negotiators of the 1783 Peace Treaty. Even the king, in the exercise of the high prerogative of the Crown, did not take title until an actual seizure had been made.

For the Supreme Court, Associate Justice Washington held at the outset that a question arising under the treaties of 1783 and 1794 was raised by the plaintiff in the court below, and the issue was whether the actions of Maryland constituted a "future confiscation" prohibited by the peace treaty. The construction of the laws of the State of Maryland was but a step in determining the federal question concerning the construction and meaning of the treaty. If the Maryland acts of confiscation left something to be done necessary to the perfection of the State's title, and that had not been accomplished when the peace treaty was signed, then the Supreme Court might, upon so finding, proceed to take jurisdiction of the cause as one arising under a treaty provision.[49] Proceeding to an examination of the Maryland statutes, Washington ob-

---

[44] 6 Cranch 293 (1810); Johnson's argument is in *ibid.*, 290–301. The later case of Brown v. United States, discussed in Part II, chapter 2, note 164, involved the question of alien enemy property rights. Marshall contended for the Court that timber floating in an inlet was on land and that while it might be confiscated, an actual seizure was required. There was a distinction between property on land and property of the enemy captured on the high seas. The exercise of discretion in regard to enemy property was to be directed by legislative policy rather than judicial decree, 6 Cranch 110, at 128–29. Story dissented, arguing that the property was maritime and hence subject to prize jurisdiction and that Congress, by its declaration of war and prize acts, had conferred authority on the President to declare such property forfeit without further proceedings. *Ibid.*, 129–54.

[45] 6 Cranch 301–302 (1810).

[46] The statement was made by Harper's co-counsel, Ridgeley. *Ibid.*, 301.

[47] Harper, *ibid.*, 302.

[48] *Ibid.*, 302–303.

[49] *Ibid.*, 304–305.

served the care with which they had been drawn to preclude reference to common law procedures: "[I]t would seem difficult to draught a law more completely operative to devest the whole estate of the former owner and to vest it in the state."[50] No further act by the commissioners was required to perfect title, and no seizure was necessary.

Contrary to the Maryland law, the Virginia acts of 1779 providing for escheats and forfeitures from British subjects prescribed procedures for inquests of office in the case of escheats.[51] Upon the death of Lord Fairfax in 1781 his rights in the Northern Neck proprietary descended to his British heir-at-law, and presumably subject to the provisions of the 1779 statutes. However, no inquest of office found was held prior to the peace treaty of 1783 or the Jay Treaty of 1794. Upon that basis Charles Lee and Samuel Jones argued for the British heir, Denny Martin Fairfax,[52] that while the title that descended to him might have been defeasible by an inquest of office found, since such procedure was never instituted before the execution of the Jay Treaty he held good title protected by the treaty provision. "It is one of the principles of the common law, upon which the security of private property from the grasp of power depends, that the crown can take only by matter of record," they asserted, citing Blackstone's *Commentaries*.[53] The peace treaty of 1783 found title in Denny Fairfax, and by its terms it released the forfeiture, and no subsequent act by the Virginia legislature could alter his title.

Robert Goodloe Harper in rebutting these arguments[54] contended that the Fairfax title was not that of an ordinary landowner—the proprietary grant contained a delegation of the power of the sovereign as to the lands in the Northern Neck, and as far as the waste lands in this litigation were concerned, to the extent they were not granted by Fairfax they passed "with other rights of sovereignty to the Commonwealth of Virginia, at the time of the revolution." In addition, Harper argued that in the case of an alien enemy there was no need for an inquest of office found. That procedure was applicable in the case of an alien friend. The title of the Commonwealth of Virginia was complete at the time of Lord Fairfax's death, for at that instant it vested in

---

[50] *Ibid.*, 306.
[51] Fairfax's Devisee v. Hunter, 7 Cranch 603–32 (1813).
[52] *Ibid.*, 612–15. The case was long in litigation, having been instituted by Marshall while he was in private practice in Virginia and first on the Supreme Court docket in 1795, at which time Marshall traveled to Philadelphia to argue the matter, only to have it marked off the docket. Technically

the case involved waste lands, rather than the manor lands purchased by Marshall and his associates, but the 1794 settlement with the Commonwealth of Virginia released State rights to manor lands in exchange for the release of Fairfax claims to the waste lands. Cullen and Johnson, *Marshall Papers*, II, 147–48.
[53] 7 Cranch 613.
[54] *Ibid.*, 615–17.

513

an alien and escheated. An inquest of office found in such a situation does not convey title to the sovereign; it merely recognizes the status of alien ownership and establishes proof of the sovereign's title. Consequently at the time the peace treaty was executed there was no title in Denny Fairfax, for the Commonwealth had succeeded to his title by virtue of alienage. Assuming that such was not the case, then upon the death of Denny Fairfax in 1800, since an alien could have no heirs, his title escheated to the Commonwealth. The provisions of the peace treaty did not restore titles escheated by alienage, but only those confiscated for acts committed during the war.

Counsel's arguments at the Supreme Court bar mirrored the differences in judicial reasoning that had divided the Virginia Court of Appeals in its consideration of *Hunter* v. *Fairfax's Lessee* in 1809.[55] Reversing the Winchester District Court's decision upholding the Fairfax title, the Virginia high court held that the Commonwealth's title to the land was good and that possession should be given to David Hunter, who had received a land grant in 1789. However, Judge Spencer Roane based his April 23, 1810, opinion upon the reasoning that the Virginia act of 1785, vesting title to the vacant Northern Neck lands in the Commonwealth, was valid as a natural consequence of the sequestration act of 1779. Citing a long line of unreported manuscript opinions of the Court of Appeals, Roane asserted that "the treaty of peace has nothing to do with the laws of alienage of the several states"[56] and that if the treaty were to have such an effect, it would have to be construed as creating new rights in aliens which had been destroyed by State action. That, he observed, was contrary to the expressed intent of the treaty, which was not to create new rights, but rather to protect those rights that already existed at the time the peace treaty was concluded.[57]

Judge William Fleming disagreed with Roane on this point. While he felt that the Virginia General Assembly might take title to alien lands by legislative act, Fleming insisted that

> the mode ought to be explicit, and clearly understood by all persons interested, and not by implication, that such and such acts of the Legislature, by strained construction, amount to an office found, to deprive any person, whether citizen or alien, of their [*sic*] justly acquired rights.[58]

Reviewing the Virginia statutes, Fleming pointed out that in 1782, and continuing to October 1783 when it mentioned the 1783 Peace Treaty

---

[55] I Munford (15 Va.) 218–38 (1810).
[56] *Ibid.*, 226.
[57] *Ibid.*
[58] I Munford (15 Va.) 234.

in a statutory provision, the legislature had been "quite undetermined" concerning the status of the Northern Neck. Since that situation persisted when the peace treaty was signed, the Commonwealth had not then acquired title, and it certainly could not do so by legislation subsequent to the date of the treaty.[59]

Judge Fleming fully accepted the arguments in favor of the Fairfax title. He concurred in the reversal of the Winchester District Court, not on the ground that Hunter's title was good under the Commonwealth but on the basis of his construction of the 1796 compromise between the Commonwealth of Virginia and the purchasers of the Fairfax manor lands. On the basis of the compromise Judge Fleming felt that the Commonwealth's title to the waste and vacant lands in the Northern Neck was secure;[60] hence he was willing to validate Hunter's title *nunc pro tunc* as of 1789, the date of his grant. In that compromise the syndicate composed of John Marshall, James Markham Marshall, and Rawleigh Colston, acting both as purchasers of the manor lands and as authorized agents for Denny Martin Fairfax, agreed to release all of Fairfax's claim to waste lands in the Northern Neck, in return for Virginia's recognition of the title of the syndicate to the manor lands conveyed to it by Martin after the purported seizures by the Commonwealth in 1782 and 1785. Under the agreement, which was ratified by a statute, "the title of Lord Fairfax, and of those who claim under him, was, by the act of compromise, clearly extinguished."[61] He concluded, "And, upon that ground, and upon that ground only, I am of opinion that the law is for the appellant."[62]

The long and involved history of Fairfax lands litigation before the Virginia courts has been treated elsewhere and need not unduly detain us at this point. It is necessary to note, however, that the original ejectment action that formed the basis for the 1813 opinion in *Fairfax's Devisee* v. *Hunter* was tried in the Virginia State courts in September 1793, and originally argued before the Court of Appeals on May 3, 1796. Thus the record before the court did not contain the 1796 compromise or its statutory implementation, nor did it refer to the provisions of the 1794 Jay Treaty. Judge Fleming went outside the record, and took judicial notice of these intervening circumstances, which in his opinion had a determinative impact upon the law of the case.

From the history of *Hunter* v. *Fairfax's Devisee* we must also note the continuing personal, professional, and financial interest of Chief Justice Marshall in the judicial recognition of Lord Fairfax's title to the Northern Neck lands. As early as 1786 he had appeared as counsel in *Hite* v. *Fairfax,* and his 1793 participation in the purchase of the manor lands supplemented his professional involvement with a direct pecuniary

---

[59] *Ibid.,* 234–35.   [60] *Ibid.,* 237–38.   [61] *Ibid.,* 238.   [62] *Ibid.*

interest in the litigation.[63] As a consequence the Chief Justice did not take part in the consideration of *Fairfax* v. *Hunter*, and the preparation of the opinion fell to Judge Joseph Story.

Writing the opinion of the Court, Story found that Lord Fairfax held good title to the waste lands at the time of his death, and noted with satisfaction that such a decision was in accord with the opinion of the Virginia Court of Appeals in three previously decided cases.[64] Upon Fairfax's death the title passed to Denny Martin Fairfax, then an alien enemy, who under the rules of common law might take lands, but who held them for the benefit of the State. The alien might convey the lands subject to certain limitations, and he might rent them or sue for their recovery, and such rights continued until the lands were actually seized by the sovereign. Story found contradictions in the English authorities concerning alien enemies taking by descent, but the general rule extrapolated from the precedents was discovered to be that the use of office found was to give public manifestation of the king's exercise of sovereignty, and to fix title, based upon the fact that such a seizure was "penal" towards the party dispossessed. As Justice Story noted, no seizure had been made during the war, and hence the forfeiture could not be "*ratione guerrae.*"[65]

Had it so desired, Virginia might by statute have dispensed with the procedure of inquest of office, but on grounds of public policy such a construction should be found only after the submission of persuasive evidence. In the case of Virginia, she had been careful to preserve the "useful and important restraint upon public proceedings" inherent in the procedure, for the inquest of office found

> prevents individuals from being harassed by numerous suits introduced by litigious grantees. It enables the owner to contest the question of alienage directly by a traverse of the office. It affords an opportunity for the public to know the nature, the value, and the extent of its acquisitions pro defectu haeredis; and above all it operates as a salutary suppression of that *corrupt influence which the avarice of speculation might otherwise urge upon the legislature.* [Emphasis added][66]

No act of the Virginia legislature divested his title by express terms, although there was reason to believe that the Commonwealth supposed

---

[63] Johnson and Cullen, *Marshall Papers*, I, 153–64; II, 140–49.

[64] Picket v. Dowdell, 2 Washington 106–15 (1795), in which Marshall had successfully argued for the appellants; Johnson v. Buffington, 2 Washington 116–21 (1795), and Curry v. Burns, 2 Washington 121–26 (1795).

Story's reference to these cases is in 7 Cranch 619 (1813).

[65] As noted in Part II, chapter 4, note 44, Judge Story would apply a different rule in regard to maritime alien enemy property.

[66] 7 Cranch 624.

itself in possession of the vacant and waste lands of the proprietary. Such a mistake ought not to be pressed to the injury of third parties. The title of Hunter, derived from a Commonwealth grant, could not be more extensive than that of the Commonwealth itself—that it was a title inchoate and imperfect that might be consummated by an entry under an inquest of office or a judgment at law in favor of the grantee.

Pointedly Judge Story noted that the Court did not pass upon the question of whether the 1783 Peace Treaty provision against future confiscations referred to escheats for alienage as well as forfeitures for acts during the war. The title of Denny Fairfax was secured to him by the 1794 Treaty, even if the peace treaty left him unprovided for. It was once in the power of Virginia to divest the title of Denny Fairfax (either before the 1783 Treaty, or even perhaps before the 1794 Treaty), but having failed to do so before the Jay Treaty became the supreme law of the land, Virginia might no longer hold an inquest of office to vest title completely in itself or its grantees.

From Judge Story's majority opinion, Judge William Johnson dissented,[67] claiming that whatever title might have remained in the devisee of Lord Fairfax was extinguished by the Commonwealth's grant to Hunter. No need existed for an inquest of office found in the case of an alien taking by descent, and since the Court had previously sanctioned legislative power to take lands without office found, in the case of *Smith* v. *Maryland*, it would be proper to uphold Virginia legislation concerning Lord Fairfax's estates on the same ground. Johnson agreed with his colleagues that when a case was appealed under article 25 of the Judiciary Act of 1789, it was essential that the Supreme Court make its own inquiry into the title of the parties litigant and that examination, of necessity, should precede consideration of how far a federal law or treaty applied to the case.

Smith v. *Maryland* and *Fairfax's Devisee* v. *Hunter* indicate the continuing Supreme Court tradition of giving considerable weight to State law concerning the status of persons and the attributes of citizenship. At the same time the Fairfax case represents a strengthening of federal supremacy, based upon the precedent of *Smith*, permitting inquiry into the correctness of State court adjudications that intimately involved rights arising under federal treaties.[68] Citizenship, as a status

---

[67] Opinion in *ibid.*, 628–32.

[68] The issue of an independent federal question was squarely raised by the Virginia Court of Appeals' refusal to comply with the Supreme Court mandate in Fairfax v. Hunter, based upon its contention that jurisdiction did not exist under Sec. 25 of the Judiciary Act of 1789. A subsequent writ of error brought the case of Martin v. Hunter's Lessee before the Supreme Court in 1816 and Judge Story's opinion carefully examined the constitutional and statutory basis for Supreme Court jurisdiction. He pointed out that a decision against a *title* set up by a party claiming the protection of a federal statute or

in international law as well as a subject of domestic concern, had been a matter of adjudication before the Supreme Court in regard to the prize cases of the War of 1812 as well as prosecutions for illegal trade before the war. As a result the Supreme Court's cognizance of the international aspects of the problem, and its acceptance of its constitutional role as the tribunal of international law in the United States, pressed the justices into a broader basis for jurisdiction than they might otherwise have deemed acceptable. The substantive questions of citizenship, naturalization, and expatriation after the controversial 1813 decision in *Fairfax* were to become increasingly matters of national regulation and practice.

Although the substantive law of naturalization began to assume a national uniformity during our period, it nevertheless remained a matter of concurrent jurisdiction between the States and the federal government in its administrative and procedural aspects. In *Campbell v. Gordon*[69] the Supreme Court, in a majority opinion by Judge Washington, held that a State court naturalization decree that failed to recite the applicant's qualifications for citizenship might not be attacked collaterally. For purposes of determining the naturalized citizen's status, the certificate of naturalization was presumptive evidence that the court was satisfied concerning the applicant's good character. This decision was reached despite the fact that the applicable federal naturalization statute, that of January 29, 1795, required that the court's findings be recorded. Upon that basis, counsel for the appellant had argued that a deposition by the clerk concerning the Virginia court's proceedings was not adequate proof under the federal requirement.[70] Judge Washington's opinion indicates the Supreme Court's inclination to dispense with procedural formalities and attendant objections, and to assert the finality of naturalization decrees in State courts.

---

treaty was the basis for jurisdiction under the Judiciary Act's Sec. 25. Story concluded, "From the very necessity of the case, there must be a preliminary inquiry into the existence and structure of the title, before the court can construe the treaty in reference to that title." 1 Wheat. 304, at 358. In his concurring opinion Judge Johnson considered this a question upon which he could give his opinion with confidence. He stated ". . . whether we consider the letter of the statute, or the spirit, intent or meaning, of the constitution and of the legislature . . . it is equally clear that the title is the primary object to which the attention of the court is called in every such case." *Ibid.*, 369.

[69] 6 Cranch 176–83 (1810). Campbell v. Gordon is the only case concerning derivative naturalization in our period and involves judicial construction of the 1795, 1802, and 1805 Naturalization Acts.

[70] A similar disposition in a per curiam opinion in Starke v. Chesapeake Insurance Co., 7 Cranch 420–23 (1813), would indicate the binding precedent of the Campbell case. In Starke a flawed certificate of naturalization from Maryland was accepted as proof of nationality to permit recovery on a policy of marine insurance.

IV: *The Articulation of American Nationality*

The parallel development of federal dominance in the substantive law of naturalization and ready acceptance of State naturalization orders in substantial accordance with federal laws was probably a result of American colonial experience with naturalization. Until the Parliamentary statute of 1740 standardized the rules and procedures for naturalization in the colonies, each colony applied its own law to the denization and naturalization of aliens. As a result the problem of naturalization in one colony unrecognized in others created serious problems in imperial relationships. After 1740 the colonial naturalization laws were in part continued in effect, resulting in some conflict and eventually giving rise to the provision in the Declaration of Independence condemning the British for refusing colonial self-determination as an alternative to the 1740 statute.[71] With the ratification of the Constitution and the enactment of naturalization statutes by Congress, the uniform national system had become predominant but at the same time certain flexibility in administration was permitted by judicial construction to accommodate varying State practices in the field. The end result was a uniform law, as required by the Constitution, but one that was loosely administered by various State tribunals. Federal interests and policy dictated that naturalization decrees receive immediate comity throughout the federal Union, and for that reason defects that might render other orders voidable were not permitted to weaken the conclusive effect of State naturalization decrees.

While the Supreme Court in our period was not presented with a case raising the issue of federal versus State citizenship, and whether birth or naturalization in one State brought equal standing in all others, it is at least clear from the foregoing discussion that the process of naturalization conferred federal citizenship as well as citizenship in the State of naturalization. Acquisition of status as an American citizen was thus formalized by the federal naturalization laws, and in an international sense this was adequate; for the more complex and politically sensitive question of the citizenship of persons within the States and the transferability of that citizenship between States, American constitutional law would be content to bide its time until the Civil War and the postwar amendments to the Constitution.

To the problem of citizenship among the various States, the Marshall Court made certain contributions during our period. For example, it held that a Maryland insolvency act ceased to apply to a

---

[71] For an excellent discussion of naturalization and denization in the American colonies see Kettner, *Development*, 65–105, 114–26. The 1740 parliamentary statute delegated to colonial courts the authority to naturalize persons who thereafter would be considered subjects throughout the empire. *Ibid.*, 127, 128.

resident of Maryland after the territory in which he resided[72] was ceded to the federal government to form the District of Columbia. Counsel for the former Maryland citizen argued that until Congress passed legislation concerning the district, Maryland law continued to prevail—including the private Maryland act authorizing him to declare insolvency. The Supreme Court, in an opinion by Chief Justice Marshall, disagreed. Unless the would-be insolvent was a citizen of Maryland at the time the deed to his trustees was executed, he could not take advantage of the State law. While this case may be taken as an early manifestation of Marshall's antipathy to insolvency legislation, it nevertheless shows a preference for limiting State legislation to territorial boundaries. Citizenship in one State might not be claimed while continued residence in ceded territory controverted that status.

Of course the legislation in *Reily* v. *Lamar* was a private bill permitting a Maryland resident and citizen to declare insolvency. For that reason it should be, and was by the Court, distinguished from a public act of Maryland applicable in the District of Columbia until such time as the Congress made other provisions for the government of the District. The special privileges conferred upon Reily by the Maryland legislature were contingent upon his remaining subject to their sovereignty, and the cession of the District of Columbia before his insolvency deed was executed in accordance with the law invalidated the insolvency as to his creditors.

The Reily case was decided in 1804, well before the Supreme Court had embarked upon its more extensive discussions of the right of expatriation. Yet the *Reily* insolvency would seem to reinforce the later tendency to hold expatriation to be a matter for the mutual consent by both the expatriate and the sovereign State. In the case of the cession of the District of Columbia, Reily, by remaining in the territory granted to the federal government, might be viewed as consenting to a transfer of allegiance to the new sovereign; at the same time the State of Maryland in making the cession surrendered to the federal government all jurisdiction over Reily and his fellow citizens in the future district. Allegiance viewed in the light of *Reily* v. *Lamar* was not perpetual, but it did have characteristics that derived from the ancient English doctrine. Maryland's cession was not subject to challenge by the inhabitants of the territory about to become the District of Columbia; their allegiance to Maryland, and hence the protection of Maryland's

---

[72] Reily v. Lamar, Beall and Smith, 2 Cranch 344–57 (1804). The problem of insolvency laws and their applicability when the insolvent altered his place of residence was an old one. The rule in the colonial period was that the insolvency proceedings in one colony did not affect a creditor's rights in other jurisdictions. See H. Johnson, "John Jay: Colonial Lawyer" (Ph.D. diss., Columbia University, 1965), 179–81.

laws, might be maintained only by physical removal from the ceded territory. A sovereign State's cession of territory and the allegiance of the inhabitants took effect unless and until those affected by the transfer repudiated it.

In addition to the citizenship questions raised by the cession of the District of Columbia, the Supreme Court was faced with the first of a line of cases challenging its diversity jurisdiction upon the basis of the "citizenship" of a domestic corporation. In *Bank of the U.S.* v. *Deveaux*[73] a Georgia statute imposed a tax upon the Georgia branch of the bank, and upon the refusal of the bank officials to pay the assessment, cash belonging to the bank had been seized. The bank brought action in the federal court, averring that its president, directors, and company were citizens of Pennsylvania. The Georgia officials pleaded in bar that the court did not have jurisdiction. Being a body corporate and politic, the bank, they contended, could neither sue nor be sued in the diversity-of-citizenship jurisdiction of the federal courts, for it was not a "citizen" within the terms of the Judiciary Act.[74] (At this time the federal courts did not have, under the statutes, general federal-question jurisdiction.) To this plea the bank demurred, and on the joinder in demurrer judgment was given for the defendants. From that judgment an appeal was taken to the Supreme Court, where Chief Justice Marshall wrote the majority opinion.

Marshall established first that the bank could sue as an entity by virtue of its act of incorporation (under the District of Columbia law). He then addressed the "much more difficult" question—whether it could sue in a federal court on the basis of diversity of citizenship. The general understanding previously appeared to be that it was possible for corporations to litigate in federal courts, and while no specific decision had been made on the point, a number of previous cases implicitly supported that position. Under English law it was not uncommon that corporations might be treated as "inhabitants" of cities for certain purposes, and in *Mayor of London* v. *Wood*[75] the judges had held that the courts might look beyond the corporation to seek the identity of the individuals composing it. Upon that basis the federal courts might, while considering a challenge to their jurisdiction, look through the corporation to the identity of the individual corporate members. Here the controversy was "substantially . . . between citizens of one state suing by a corporate name, and those of another state."[76] Counsel for the Georgia

---

[73] 5 Cranch 61–92 (1809).
[74] The jurisdictional statute is Sec. 11, Act of Sept. 24, 1789, 1 Stat. 78, 79.
[75] 12 Modern 669–89, 88 Eng. Rep. 1592–1603 (Exch. Ch., 1702).

[76] 5 Cranch 91 (1809). Marshall's opinion proceeds upon the basis of efficacy and loose constitutional construction. "A constitution, from its nature, deals in generals, not in details. Its framers cannot perceive mi-

officials[77] in the instant case had employed a "course of acute, metaphysical and abstruse reasoning,"[78] Marshall observed, in raising this hitherto unknown objection to federal diversity jurisdiction.

It is not unreasonable to suspect that whatever flexibility the justices were willing to permit in the areas of citizenship, expatriation, and naturalization may have originated in their familiarity with the appreciation of the more easily applied principles of international law concerning mercantile activities. The cases of *Murray* v. *Charming Betsey* and *Maley* v. *Shattuck*[79] provided the example of a native-born American citizen who had established a commercial domicile in St. Thomas, Danish Virgin Islands, and had taken steps to naturalize himself in that jurisdiction. As Chief Justice Marshall noted in the Murray case,[80] there was no reason to consider the question of expatriation, for it was clear that one might without formal expatriation nevertheless acquire a commercial domicile that would exempt him from the operation of a statute such as the Non-Intercourse Act of 1798. That conclusion was repeated in the Maley case, reaffirming commercial domicile as an alternative to expatriation in international adjudications.

Prize cases in the War of 1812 further reinforced the concept of commercial domicile and cast some additional light upon the judicial conception of American citizenship. As we have seen, American merchants resident in England when war was declared were permitted a period of time in which to terminate their business and return home; thereafter they would be treated as having a British character and be subject to seizure by American warships and privateers.[81] The concurring and dissenting opinion of Chief Justice Marshall in *The Venus*[82] demonstrates more clearly than the opinions of his colleagues the considerations that shaped the Court's determination in that case. While he agreed with Associate Justice Washington, writing for the majority, that the goods were of a hostile character, he refused to admit the conclusion that American merchants resident abroad immediately became enemies of their nation. The general rule for the attribution of

---

nute distinctions which arise in the progress of the nation, and therefore confine it to the establishment of broad and general principles." *Ibid.*, 87. The underlying reason for federal tribunals was to make impartial justice available in certain actions, among them cases between citizens of differing States. Hence actions by corporations falling within that category are within the spirit of the constitutional mandate. *Ibid.*

[77] Philip Barton Key and Robert Goodloe Harper argued on behalf of the Georgia officials; they were opposed by Horace Binney.

[78] 5 Cranch 88. Marshall conceded that this type of reasoning had been "ably employed," but nevertheless rejected the argument.

[79] 2 Cranch 64–124 (1804); 3 Cranch 458–92 (1806). The cases are discussed at length in Part II, chapter 2, pp. 410–13.

[80] 2 Cranch 120.

[81] See discussion in Part II, chapter 2, pp. 438–41.

[82] 8 Cranch 288–317.

commercial domicile need not be applied when the nation of residence became the enemy of the merchant's country. On the contrary, a presumption of intention to return home would arise under those circumstances. Furthermore, presumptions of continued allegiance and loyalty should apply to both native-born and naturalized citizens of the United States, for according to Marshall, *The Venus* presented the situation where

> [t]he claimants are natives of that country with which we are at war, who have been naturalized in the United States. It is impossible to deny that many of the strongest arguments urged to prove the probability that war must determine the native American citizen to abandon the country of the enemy and return home, are inapplicable, or apply but feebly, to citizens of this description. Yet I think it is not for the United States, in such a case as this, to discriminate between them.[83]

While Washington's majority opinion had noted arguments of counsel contrary to Marshall's position, no judgment was reached upon the consequences of a naturalized American citizen having acquired commercial residence in the land of his birth which subsequently became a belligerent to the United States.[84] That point had been raised dramatically by the attorney for the captors:

> [T]he national character of these parties . . . does not depend upon domicile. They were originally native subjects of Great Britain; and, after being naturalized in this country, they returned to England, and resumed their native allegiance, in violation of their oath of allegiance. By this conduct we contend that they lost the character of American citizens . . .[85]

He quoted Sir William Scott, to the effect that native character easily reverts, and it requires fewer circumstances to constitute domicile in such cases than to impress nationality upon a person native to another country.[86] Expatriation was not to be contested, for any man had a right to assume a new national allegiance—but to be valid his naturalization must not be undertaken with a view towards an eventual return to his native land. In reply Richard Stockton pointed to the continuing American contacts of the claimants, and to the rule of English naturalization law that naturalized subjects gain the same rights and privileges as a native.[87] They had neither forfeited nor abandoned their character

---

[83] *Ibid.*, 316–17.
[84] *Ibid.*, 277.
[85] *Ibid.*, 256.
[86] From the opinion in La Virginie, 5 C. Robinson 98–100, 165 Eng. Rep. 711–12 (Admiralty, 1804).
[87] 8 Cranch 262–63.

as American citizens, "nor could he throw off his adopted allegiance if he would. If found in arms against us he would be punished as a traitor."[88]

Absent a consideration of the problem in the majority opinion, we must consider Marshall's dissent persuasive evidence of Supreme Court disagreement over the indelible mark of naturalization in the United States. Stockton's argument afforded the naturalized citizen the same status as a native-born citizen, and in addition, he viewed citizenship so acquired as being either perpetual, or at the least indissoluble without the consent of the United States. Allegiance in Stockton's view, and presumably also to John Marshall, was very close to perpetual allegiance even though acquired through the processes of expatriation and naturalization. This substantial disagreement, both at the Bar and on the Bench, concerning the nature of American citizenship and the indelible nature of naturalization, shows the impact of the prize cases upon the development of an American law of citizenship. Based upon the rules of domicile in international law, and particularly the governing principles concerning commercial residence, the majority of the Supreme Court by 1814 had begun to view citizenship status in a manner not unlike the accepted view of domicile. An individual's intentions as evidenced by his acts determined not only his domicile, but also his nationality. Consequently naturalization was but a formality that might be sterile or meaningful, depending entirely upon the applicant's future behavior. On the other hand, Marshall seems to have viewed naturalization as the legal equivalent to birth within the United States or residence in one of the rebelling States when royal authority was overthrown and independent governments were established. Logically his view was inconsistent with both expatriation and naturalization, but it did have the virtue of demanding allegiance in all situations from all citizens, no matter how citizenship status was acquired.

At first glance Marshall's position appears to be a rudimentary form of perpetual allegiance, whereby American citizens became permanent members of the body politic, either at birth or at naturalization. Termination of their status as citizens might take place only with the consent of the United States government. The flow of immigrants into the United States and their subsequent elevation to citizenship status would be encouraged, but should they attempt to revert to their original loyalty they might not do so without public consent. Citizenship in the American Union would thus become a one-way street. Yet deeper reflection permits a more accurate analysis. As a man born in allegiance to George II, John Marshall was not unaware that his allegiance to the United States, and that of all Americans born before 1776, was predi-

---

[88] *Ibid.*, 263.

cated upon consent, in the Lockean sense. But at the same time, allegiance might not be withdrawn at the whim of the individual citizen, for national ends were to be achieved only through a loyal and devoted citizenry. Although consent of the people through the action of the majority had formed the States and the federal Union, such a consent mutually effectuated might not be negatived by the unilateral decision of the citizen. The status of an American citizen, to the former Secretary of State, was a distinguishing mark that might not be obliterated through any normal procedure of election or renunciation. Certainly equivocal actions by a naturalized citizen did not divest him of his rights as an American any more rapidly than might similar activities by a native-born American. The emphasis and weight of Marshall's opinion was firmly established on the rights, privileges, and responsibilities of *all* American citizens, and his desire to protect those benefits from judicial discretion, legislative discretion, and executive mandates.

By 1814 the Supreme Court shifted from the basic principles of the M'Ilvaine case, which had recognized expatriation at the will of the sovereign. Between 1808 and 1814 the Court's attention had been drawn to prize cases and illegal trade prosecutions predicated upon citizenship. The divergence of opinion in *The Venus*, only barely visible on the face of the opinion, disclosed a significant development in the creation of a new legal construct for the concept of citizenship. By constitutional mandate, birth within the United States conferred a type of perpetual citizenship that might be lost only under extraordinary circumstances. On the other hand, acquired citizenship through naturalization would gradually become less permanent in nature, and vulnerable to divestiture on grounds not dissimilar to the rules established for loss of domicile in international law. During the first fourteen years of Marshall's Chief Justiceship the development of a new approach to citizenship was not complete, but the evolutionary direction of the Supreme Court's jurisprudence can be seen with some clarity. Marshall's influence in the land cases was minimized by his personal interest in the resolution of the issue of alien landholding and his additional disqualification for prior service as counsel to the Fairfax proprietor; his control of the Court in prize and illegal trade matters was diminished by the jurisprudential and political differences among the justices. Not surprisingly, this field of litigation before the high court was one in which Marshall's preferences were not written into the law of the land.

CHAPTER V

International Law and the Supreme Court

EW FUNCTIONS of the United States Supreme Court are more essential to the welfare of the nation than its adjudications as a tribunal of international law, and yet this activity is perhaps the least known aspect of its jurisdiction. As the highest federal court enunciating the law of nations, the Supreme Court performs an important service in what might be termed "preventative international jurisprudence." Its decisions in the field are designed to conform the law of the United States, as far as possible, with the law and practice of international law in other sovereign nations. This judicial function does much to avoid confrontation in the halls of diplomacy, and in cases bearing directly upon national honor and self-interest it may even avoid reprisals or declared warfare between the United States and a nation offended by an alleged breach of international law.

While defending the international jurisdiction of the Supreme Court before the Virginia ratifying convention John Marshall had limited himself to the simple observation that "the Federal Judiciary . . . will be the means of preventing disputes with foreign nations."[1] Then, and in his subsequent duties as Chief Justice of the United States, Marshall considered the decision of international law cases as ancillary to the conduct of diplomacy by the executive branch of the government and the establishment of national policy by Congress and the President. Both he and his fellow judges appreciated in full measure the intimate connections between adjudications in international law and the conduct of international affairs that was assigned by the Constitution to a coordinate branch of the government. Throughout the opinions of the

---

[1] H. Johnson and C. Cullen, eds., *The Papers of John Marshall*, I (Chapel Hill, 1974), 281. See also, B. Ziegler, *The International Law of John Marshall* (Chapel Hill, 1939), 22.

early Marshall Court that are devoted to international law, there is a clear theme of establishing the law of nations[2] without trespassing upon the separate powers of the executive and legislative branches of the federal government.

Yet the mere fact that judicial power in international matters should be exercised preventatively did not deter the Supreme Court from performing its high responsibilities in this field, any more than the danger of trespassing upon the prerogatives of the President or Congress hindered them from approaching the narrow line of separation of powers established by the Constitution. Enforcement of the Embargo and Non-Intercourse laws brought the judges to a consideration of the limits of municipal authority over vessels on the high seas. The extensive prize litigation arising from the "Quasi-War" with France and the War of 1812 forced the Supreme Court into an extensive survey of the international law of war at a time when the established principles were subject to continual revision by belligerent nations seeking military and naval advantage from these alterations of the traditional law of nations. Many of the instance cases in admiralty also raised issues that could not be resolved without resort to civil law writers on international law and customs. And, as we have seen, the American concept of citizenship evolved with a full recognition of its significance in the law of nations, and with a conscientious survey of the law and practice of other nations in regard to denization and naturalization. Each of the three preceding chapters provides a basis for assessing the Supreme Court's work as the primary international tribunal of the United States, and the artificial division into chapters should not obscure the pervasive influence of international law in the areas of illegal trade, prize, marine insurance, and nationality.

The establishment of our present form of federal government worked a transformation in the international position of the States and federal government. With the vesting of diplomatic power in the executive to be exercised with the advice and consent of the Senate, the Constitution recognized the federal government as the sovereign power for international purposes. At the same time the creation of the Supreme Court of the United States was accompanied by an unqualified constitutional grant of authority in matters of international law.[3] The embarrassments of the Confederation period, coupled with a growing recognition of the weak international position allotted to the Confederation Con-

---

[2] Ziegler, *International Law of Marshall*, 27, points out that the Chief Justice's definition of the term "law of nations" and assessment of its sources appear in the prize case, Thirty Hogsheads of Sugar v. Boyle, 9 Cranch 191, at 198 (1815).

[3] Sec. 2, Art. II, and sec. 2, Art. III, Constitution of the United States.

gress, impelled the Philadelphia Convention towards the erection of a federal state that, in international affairs, would speak through one voice—that of the federal government.[4] Based upon that need for a unitary sovereignty in international matters, the Constitution, and the supplementary legislation in the Judiciary Act of 1789, conferred upon the Supreme Court the right and obligation to act as a final determiner of all international law questions within the United States. Original jurisdiction was granted to the Supreme Court in all cases involving foreign ambassadors, public ministers, and consuls. Appellate jurisdiction vested in the Court by the Constitution empowered it to review all cases arising under treaties previously made, or to be made in the future, under the authority of the United States. The Court was to have appellate jurisdiction in all cases of admiralty, and to review on appeal all matters that involved a foreign subject or citizen of a foreign state. In other words, any matter involving foreign nations or their subjects would, as a result of these provisions, ultimately find its way to the judges of the United States Supreme Court, and there in the highest international law tribunal the law of nations as construed in the United States would resolve the difficulty and provide a final determination of the litigation.

Acting upon this broad and inclusive grant of international jurisdiction to the Supreme Court, the first federal Congress provided the statutory implementation for the federal court system in the Judiciary Act of 1789.[5] This legislation empowered the federal courts to act in four general categories of cases having international aspects. First, within the jurisdiction enumerated for the district and circuit courts of the United States, there was included the power to hear actions involving aliens, limited to the usual monetary limit in diversity cases.[6] Secondly, under the grant of admiralty and maritime jurisdiction, the inferior courts were given jurisdiction of matters of prize as well as other incidental business that might have a bearing upon international law.[7] Thirdly, the Supreme Court was given original jurisdiction over causes

[4] A. McLaughlin, *The Confederation and the Constitution, 1783–1789* (New York, 1905), 134–35, 142, 147–48; C. Doren, *The Great Rehearsal* (New York, 1948), 66, 133–34, 147; M. Farrand, *The Framing of the Constitution* (New Haven, 1913), 1–12, 42–52. See also H. Johnson, "Toward a Reappraisal of the 'Federal' Government, 1783–1789," *American Journal of Legal History* VIII (1964), 314, at 323–24; J. Goebel, *Antecedents and Beginnings to 1801, Volume I, History of the Supreme Court of the United States*, ed., P. Freund (New York, 1971), 143–82, 238, 239.

[5] For a discussion of the Judiciary Act of 1789 in the light of international law functions of the Supreme Court see Goebel, *Antecedents*, 480–81.

[6] Sec. 11, 1 Stat. 78, applied to circuit court diversity jurisdiction based upon the sum of $500 in controversy.

[7] In district courts, sec. 9, 1 Stat. 76, 77 (1789); in circuit courts, sec. 21, *ibid.*, 83–84.

involving ambassadors and public ministers, while the district courts were empowered to take exclusive jurisdiction of litigation concerning consuls and vice consuls.[8] Finally, in the exercise of its appellate jurisdiction the Supreme Court was authorized to hear appeals on writs of error in matters where the validity or construction of treaties was brought into question and the decision below had been against their validity or resulted in a rejection of a claim based upon a treaty provision.[9] This last power, unlike the power of inferior courts in diversity matters involving aliens of foreign states, did not have a monetary minimum; hence appellate review was assured of all cases, no matter how small and regardless of whether the proceeding had been instituted in the State or federal courts. To the world the Supreme Court's decisions represented the final American determination in the law of nations; it acted for all intents and purposes as the highest court of a single sovereign state. Within the federal system this supremacy of the Supreme Court was insured by an extraordinary grant of power to regulate the domestic law of the United States in such a way that conflicts with the law of nations were avoided and international tranquillity was preserved.

By 1801 the Supreme Court had already established its preeminence in the field of international law and taken a strong step towards asserting its supremacy in deciding *Ware* v. *Hylton* in favor of international law and practice and by upholding the debt-recovery provisions of the 1783 peace treaty with Great Britain.[10] As Professor Goebel has shown, the preoccupation of the American public with the ratification of the Jay Treaty in March 1796 resulted in a lack of commentary, learned or otherwise, concerning the high court's opinions in *Ware* v. *Hylton*.[11] Yet this single cause that had been selected for appeal to the Supreme Court was but the tip of a large iceberg of similar matters still pending on the overcrowded dockets of the Circuit Court of the United States for the Virginia District. Coupled with the troublesome issue of title to the late Lord Fairfax's lands in the northern neck of Virginia, these cases were critical matters in the political and economic life of the Old Dominion. A cursory reading of the debates of

---

[8] Sec. 13, *ibid.*, 80–81, gave the Supreme Court exclusive original jurisdiction when foreign diplomats were parties defendant, and original but not exclusive jurisdiction when they were parties plaintiff. It should be mentioned that in the case between an alien and an American State, the Supreme Court was given original but not exclusive jurisdiction. Sec. 13, *ibid.*, 80. As to jurisdiction over consuls, see sec. 9, *ibid.*, 77. Aliens had

certain powers of removal from State courts under sec. 12, *ibid.*, p. 79.

[9] Sec. 25, *ibid.*, 85–87. Goebel, *Antecedents*, 481, notes that the provisions for proceedings on reversal were a break with tradition in that the Supreme Court might itself issue the final decision and award execution if the State court refused to do so.

[10] 3 Dall. 199–285 (1796).

[11] Goebel, *Antecedents*, 754–55.

delegates to the 1788 Virginia ratifying convention leaves little doubt that one of the rallying points for the opposition was the threat of federal tribunals enforcing the 1783 treaty provisions in Virginia.[12] Significantly, the Jay Treaty provided for a mixed commission to settle claims by British merchants against their pre-Revolutionary debtors,[13] and as one of its first decisions, the commission agreed to entertain claims even if the claimant had not exhausted his judicial remedies in the United States.[14] As a consequence many would-be litigants were willing to settle their trade credits through international channels rather than taking recourse to the uncertainties of obtaining judgment against debtors who as frequently as not were either bankrupt or migrants to the West.

Decided in 1796, *Ware* v. *Hylton* came at a time when the excesses of the French Revolution were finding their way into international law and undermining the established law and customs of nations.[15] In an age marked by opportunism in diplomacy and inconsistency in the construction of international law, the young United States committed itself to upholding the stipulations of her international treaties regardless of the political pressures encouraging disregard of those undertakings. It represented a maturity of American jurisprudence and government in that it tacitly adopted the basic principle of international law—that a coherent body of law applied equally throughout the nations of the world would, although at times inconvenient, result in international cooperation and peaceful trade that offset any temporary discomfort. In a still larger sense, it recognized that American domestic law would have to become subordinate to international law and practice, if the United States was to gain and maintain the respect of the community of nations.[16]

---

[12] J. Elliot, ed., *The Debates, Resolutions and Other Proceedings in Convention, on the Adoption of the Federal Constitution*, 3 vols. (Washington, 1827–30), III, 380–410, 413–27.

[13] H. Miller, ed., *Treaties and Other International Acts of the United States of America*, II (Washington, 1931), 249–51.

[14] Goebel, *Antecedents*, 755–56.

[15] While the eighteenth century had been a period of relative stability and strengthening of the rights of neutrals, the first fifteen years of the nineteenth century were extremely erratic in the development of international law and were marked by retaliation and reciprocity. A. Nussbaum, *A Concise History of the Law of Nations* (New York, 1947), 129–31, 178–79. Nuss-

baum points out that the United States made a contribution by reintroducing the principle of arbitration in the Jay Treaty. *Ibid.*, 213.

[16] Ziegler, *International Law of John Marshall*, 25, points to the respect the Chief Justice rendered to the *jus gentium* and how in a time of strife and expediency in the enunciation of the law of nations his pronouncements were marked by "definiteness, certainty, impartiality, and consistency . . ." He notes, *ibid.*, 33, that in Talbot v. Seeman, Marshall remarked, "It is true that a violation of the law of nations by one power does not justify its violation by another; but that remonstrance is the proper course to be pursued . . ." 1 Cranch 41 (1801).

HENRY BROCKHOLST LIVINGSTON (B. 1757–D. 1823).
Associate Justice of the Supreme Court (1806–1823).
(Library of Congress)

Unfinished Capitol, circa 1800.
(Library of Congress)

Unfinished Capitol, circa 1800.
(Library of Congress)

THOMAS TODD (B. 1765–D. 1826).
Associate Justice of the Supreme Court (1807–1826).
(Library of Congress)

GABRIEL DUVALL (B. 1752–D. 1844).
Member of Congress from Maryland (1794–1796),
Comptroller of the Treasury (1802–1811),
Associate Justice of the Supreme Court (1811–1835).
(Library of Congress)

JOSEPH STORY (B. 1779–D. 1845).
Member of Congress from Massachusetts (1808–1809),
Associate Justice of the Supreme Court (1811–1845).
(Library of Congress)

V: *International Law and the Supreme Court*

The subordination of domestic American rights to international law and the principles of comity is perhaps best illustrated by what Judge Edward Dumbauld has rightly identified as John Marshall's "most widely known case in the field of international law," *The Schooner Exchange* v. *M'Faddon*.[17] An American merchant vessel had been seized by a French privateer and after condemnation as prize was re-fitted as a man-of-war and sailed under the command of an officer in the Napoleonic navy. When she arrived at Philadelphia after having been driven to shore by the stress of weather, she was libeled by her former owner through process issued from the District Court for the Pennsylvania District. At the request of Alexander J. Dallas, United States District Attorney, the district court discharged process on the showing that the sovereign rights of France were involved and that American diplomatic relations with France might be adversely affected by the continuance of the case. On appeal to the circuit court the decree dismissing the libel was reversed and the federal prosecutor appealed to the Supreme Court of the United States where the cause was given a preference on the docket. It came up for argument just four months after the decree of the Circuit Court for the Pennsylvania District.

In opening the government's case Dallas argued that proof of the public character of the *Exchange*, coupled with proof that she was under the command of a French naval officer, should be sufficient to discharge her from the ordinary process of a United States admiralty court. Any decision to the contrary would only serve to submit the peace of the ports of the world to the whims and caprices of private individuals. "It is beautiful in theory to exclaim 'fiat Justitia—ruat coelum' but justice is to be administered with due regard to the law of nations, and to the rights of other sovereigns."[18] Citizens or subjects who felt themselves aggrieved by the acts of other sovereigns were reduced to the course of complaining to their government, which through diplomatic negotiation or the authorization of reprisals would attempt to exact satisfaction. Turning to past American practice, Dallas noted that public vessels of foreign sovereigns had not been subject to seizure and forfeiture under the Non-Intercourse Acts. On the contrary they were to be instructed to depart from American harbors, and if they persisted in those ports they were to be denied assistance in repairs and victualing.

---

[17] E. Dumbauld, "John Marshall and the Law of Nations," *University of Pennsylvania Law Review* CIV (1955), 38, at 43; 7 Cranch 116–47 (1812). Charles Warren considered the case "one of the great fundamental decisions in international law," although he notes strong public opposition to the decision. *The Supreme Court in United States History*, rev. ed., 2 vols. (Boston, 1937), I, 425–26.

[18] "Let right be done, though the heavens should fall." 7 Cranch 116, at 122, 123.

Private vessels, on the other hand, came under separate provisions which under certain circumstances might permit forfeiture and submission to the ordinary process of American admiralty courts. Similarly, the Embargo Acts excepted public vessels from their operations, and the revenue laws of the United States excepted foreign public vessels from the usual reporting requirements. Returning to the *Exchange* case, Dallas concluded that "if the courts of the United States should exercise such a jurisdiction it will amount to a judicial declaration of war."[19]

In opposition to the district attorney's position, it was argued that the United States exercised plenary authority within her territory, and that if relief were not afforded in federal courts, the owners would be without remedy.[20] Attorney-General William Pinkney urged the judges, in his replying argument, to decide the case upon "broad principles of national law and national independence" of both France and the United States.[21]

Chief Justice Marshall in delivering the Court's opinion recognized the novelty of the case, and stated that in the absence of precedents or written law on the subject the judges were forced to rely upon general principles "and on a train of reasoning founded on cases in some degree analogous to this."[22] Sovereigns entered the territories of other governments confident that the immunities belonging to their independent sovereign status would be extended to them; absent such tacit assurances no sovereign would subject himself to the power of another. Similar exemptions were understood to attach to the foreign ministers accredited to other sovereignties, either through the fiction of extraterritoriality, or through the treatment of the minister as the personal representative of his sovereign who bears the immunity his sovereign would possess if physically present in the foreign territory. By the mere act of receiving such a minister the territorial sovereign agrees to confer such an exemption upon him. Another pertinent rule was that which conferred immunity from ordinary process upon the troops of a friendly nation marching through the territory of another state with the permission of its territorial sovereign. Such troops, by virtue of his allowance of passage, carried with them a waiver of his territorial sovereign jurisdiction.

Conceding the validity of the claimant's argument that within its territorial boundaries the authority of a sovereign power was absolute, Marshall nevertheless viewed this absolute and exclusive power as being subject to self-imposed limitations:

The world being composed of distinct sovereignties, possessing equal rights and equal independence whose mutual benefit is promoted by

---

[19] *Ibid.*, 126.
[20] 7 Cranch 128–29.

[21] Pinkney's argument is in 7 Cranch 132–35.
[22] *Ibid.*, 136.

intercourse with each other and by an interchange of those good offices which humanity dictates and its wants required, all sovereigns have consented to a certain relaxation in practice, in cases under certain peculiar circumstances, of that absolute and complete jurisdiction within their respective territories which sovereignty confers.[23]

In other words while absolute and exclusive sovereignty was vested in the United States the jurisdiction of federal courts in this area would be exercised with a careful regard for international law and custom.

Applying such a standard Marshall concluded that it was improper to assume jurisdiction over the libeled French warship. He found it a universal provision in treaties between sovereign nations that public armed vessels driven into the ports of a friendly sovereign by inclement weather would be given leave to dock, repair, and refit. It was inconceivable that a sovereign who stipulated by treaty to permit the sanctuary of such a vessel should fail to agree to waive his sovereignty over her. The fact of granting the right to land carried with it the implied exception from the exercise of territorial sovereignty over the vessel. Even in the absence of treaty provisions touching upon the subject, the common law of nations clearly distinguished between the public and private vessels of a foreign nation. While individual aliens and private vessels of foreign registry who entered a sovereign's territory were amenable to the ordinary jurisdiction of his courts, as a matter of international practice national tribunals never exercised or asserted jurisdiction over the public armed vessels of a friendly nation that entered a port open for their visitation.

The delicate balance of public policy considerations shaping and influencing Marshall's opinion is somewhat obscured by the simplicity of its reasoning. The growing strategic importance of maritime commerce to the combatants in the Anglo-French wars forced unilateral changes in the rules of war concerning contraband and also encouraged admiralty courts to advance jurisdictional claims beyond those traditionally accepted in international law. Adjudications by French and British admiralty courts had worked substantial injustice to neutral American shipowners and masters. Outraged citizens demanded retribution, and the claimants in the *Exchange* case were quite correct in insisting that the federal courts were their only hope for the recovery of their property. Diplomatic channels were markedly ineffective and the likelihood of reprisals being authorized against the leading maritime powers of the world was negligible.[24] Like *Ware* v. *Hylton, Schooner*

---

[23] *Ibid.*

[24] As minister to France, Marshall had attempted to gain restitution for American ships plundered by the French, and as secretary of state he was directly concerned with diplomatic protestations to both French and British governments. A. Beveridge, *The Life of John Marshall*, 4 vols. (Boston, 1916–19), II, 277, 304–309;

Exchange v. *M'Faddon* sacrificed American domestic interests to the cause of international peace; but it also represented a denial of a forum to a citizen who had been wronged by a foreign power. While the case does not dwell upon the separation of powers between the branches of the federal government, it would appear that the Court accepted Dallas' contention that a decision for M'Faddon would be a judicial declaration of war—or at least accepted the fact that such a decree would be in the nature of a reprisal against the French government. Construed broadly or narrowly, such an order would cross the line of separation between judicial powers and political power vested in the President and Congress.

Somewhat less critical in terms of international goodwill, but more complicated in *ratio decidendi* were two causes that raised the question of the acceptance of French admiralty court instance decrees by the federal courts of the United States. The outbreak of a slave rebellion on Santo Domingo gave rise to increased restrictions upon trade to that island, and several American vessels were seized for violation of French regulations against illegal commerce with the rebels. In the instances presented to the Supreme Court, the vessels and cargoes were private American property, and after condemnation they had been purchased by private individuals. Upon arrival in the United States while in possession of those purchasers the cargoes were libeled by their former owners, presenting to American federal courts the question of the validity of the French decrees and their capacity to transfer property in the cargoes.

As we have noted previously, prize court awards were, for the most part, considered conclusive in regard to the facts they decided and as to the title to captured property. Since prize courts operated under the law of nations and that law had universal applicability in all tribunals of the civilized world, their decrees were effectual in altering property rights in vessels and goods before the court. By way of contrast, American practice in illegal trade matters, as we have indicated, was to limit the effective scope of admiralty jurisdiction to territorial waters or to ships of American registry or ownership.

The widespread success of the Santo Domingo rebellion, leading to the independence of Haiti from the mother country,[25] left the French with a difficult problem of enforcing the illegal trade laws. Ships approaching Santo Domingo to trade with the rebels were captured be-

---

IV, 495–96; L. Baker, *John Marshall: A Life in Law* (New York, 1974), 214, 262–65, 289–90.

[25] T. Ott, *The Haitian Revolution, 1789–1804* (Knoxville, 1973), 119–20, 151–69, 182, discusses the "mid-dle road" taken by the Haitian rebels, remaining within the French empire and attempting to secure a type of dominion status until independence was finally declared in 1804.

yond territorial waters, as were vessels that had completed their business and were sailing home. Because of the precarious French grip upon the island itself, the captured vessels were carried to nearby Spanish possessions and held there for safekeeping while admiralty courts in Haiti condemned them for violation of the laws of trade. In *Rose* v. *Himely*[26] an American merchant ship had been seized off the Santo Domingo coast, well beyond the traditional two-league limit, and carried into Cuba, where she remained while a Santo Domingo admiralty court decreed condemnation of the cargo. The cargo in the hands of its purchaser was subsequently taken to Charleston, where its former owner libeled it in the District Court for the South Carolina District. Although the District Court awarded the cargo to the original owner, this decree was reversed by the circuit court, and an appeal was taken to the Supreme Court. If the French decrees were valid and binding upon American courts, the purchaser under those decrees was entitled to retain possession and title; if the French decrees were void, or might be ignored by the federal courts, then the original owner might recover.

Chief Justice Marshall delivered the opinion, in which Judge Washington concurred in its entirety, and Judges Livingston, Cushing, and Chase concurred in part. Judge Johnson dissented, both from Marshall's opinion and that of the concurring judges. Newly appointed Judge Thomas Todd, although present at argument and on decision day, does not seem to have voted in the matter, although two years later he announced that he had concurred with Judge Johnson.

For the majority, if such it can be denominated, Marshall held that the French had elected to treat their rebellious subjects as non-belligerents and that the world was bound to respect that decision. Until the governments of the world, and particularly the federal government of the United States, recognized Haiti as an independent sovereign nation, the courts were required to treat the pre-existing colonial relationship as continuing. Consequently no belligerent rights were involved in the warfare in Santo Domingo, and the French courts in exercising jurisdiction over illegal trade did so as a matter of instance authority growing out of municipal regulations, and not as prize courts operating under the law of nations. Such trade regulations were strictly territorial and a "seizure for a breach of this law is to be made only within those limits over which the sovereign claimed a right to legislate."[27] Since the ship in question was seized outside the two-league limit, the condemning tribunal could not obtain jurisdiction.

Marshall also addressed and accepted an alternative argument advanced by the libelant-appellant, that the French admiralty court lacked jurisdiction to condemn property located not in its territory but

---

[26] 4 Cranch 241–93 (1808).   [27] *Ibid.*, 274.

rather in the port of a friendly nation. This, according to Marshall, depended upon the validity of the seizure itself, for capture on the high seas against the rules of international law merely made the capturing officer a maritime trespasser and vested no title in him, nor did it confer any jurisdiction upon the admiralty courts of his nation.[28] There was also a matter of notice and the owner's right to contest condemnation; and these privileges were afforded to the crew and master of a vessel that had been physically carried to the territory of the admiralty court. While he conceded that there had been a contrariety of opinion on this point, Marshall nevertheless expressed his view that since neither the ship nor her master or supercargo had been brought to Santo Domingo, the decree condemning the cargo was null and void and based upon an ex parte proceeding that the Supreme Court was not required to recognize.

Judges Livingston, Cushing, and Chase concurred with the Chief Justice on precisely the point last mentioned—that the vessel was not physically within the jurisdiction of the condemning court when the decree was entered. They expressed no opinion on the effect of the seizure on the high seas for a breach of a municipal regulation against illegal trade. In his dissenting opinion, Judge Johnson expressed his disagreement with the three concurring judges, contending that the Supreme Court in deciding *Hudson* v. *Guestier*[29] the same day as *Rose* v. *Himely* had held that condemnation while in a friendly port was a proper exercise of municipal maritime jurisdiction. In that case as then presented, seizure had been made within the two-league limit by a French revenue officer. In this respect Johnson seemed willing to concede John Marshall's premise that if the seizure on the high seas were illegal, jurisdiction would not vest in the tribunal; he based his dissent on the premise that seizure in *Rose* v. *Himely* had been legal, and thus jurisdiction was conferred on the French court in Santo Domingo, even though the vessel was not physically brought within its territory. Livingston, Cushing, and Chase were not at all concerned with the legality of the seizure, but emphasized the physical location of the corpus as a condition precedent to the exercise of *in rem* jurisdiction.

As a matter of admiralty law it would appear that Marshall and Johnson adopted the traditional position based upon the international law of prize. Capture by a belligerent nation's ship, either as an enemy ship or as a neutral vessel engaging in illegal acts, vested title in the captor at the instant of capture, permitting him to transfer ownership or possession, even before he carried the ship into port for condemna-

---

[28] In a later case, Williams v. Armroyd, 7 Cranch 423–34 (1813), the Court held that condemnation relates back to the time of seizure.

[29] 4 Cranch 293–98 (1808).

tion.[30] It was true that the assertion of a right to capture might subsequently be negatived by the decision of an admiralty prize court, but until that occurred only a recapture or ransom of the captured vessel would alter the captor's ownership. On the basis of prize law, the reasoning of Marshall and Johnson was quite sound—the validity and legality of the capture was basic to the assertion of jurisdiction in a prize court.

Judge Johnson differed from the Chief Justice in regard to the nature of the jurisdiction of the French admiralty court. He was not persuaded by Marshall's distinction between prize and instance court jurisdiction, nor did he believe that municipal laws might not be enforced upon the high seas. "Within their jurisdictional limits the rights of sovereignty are exclusive; upon the ocean they are concurrent,"[31] he proclaimed, and because of that, a wrongdoer within territorial waters might be overtaken on the high seas and seized for offenses within the territory. Prize jurisdiction, he continued, did not necessarily depend on the existence of a state of war. The decrees against illegal trade being enforced in *Rose* v. *Himely* were designed to force the reduction of the rebel army by denying them food, guns, and ammunition. The laws were therefore not merely municipal in their intention and operation but rather in the exercise of a belligerent right "strictly analogous to seizure for breach of blockade."[32] Here all the Supreme Court need do was to remain neutral, and the purchaser would retain the cargo in preference to the smuggler who broke the laws of France. "The smuggler, or the violator of neutrality, should be left to his fate."[33]

Johnson's broad and inclusive view of prize jurisdiction embraced all sovereign acts upon the high seas, which by their nature and public character might be distinguished from instance cases, which were only for the purpose of ascertaining private property interests. He accused the majority of an indistinct view of prize court jurisdiction. Since *Rose* v. *Himely* was a case involving the sovereign rights of France, it fell within the category of prize cases. A seizure, even in violation of the law of nations, vested jurisdiction in the captor's national courts, and the decree of such a tribunal was binding upon the courts of all nations. Otherwise how was lack of jurisdiction to be determined if the prize courts of the captor were divested of jurisdiction to declare the illegality of the capture by the very fact that the capture was illegal?

In this expansive view Judge Johnson was willing to extend ad-

---

[30] In The Adventure the Court had recognized the validity of a gift of a captured vessel to a third party, even before condemnation. 8 Cranch 221–29 (1814), discussed in Part II, chapter 3, pp. 477–78.

[31] Rose v. Himely, 4 Cranch 287 (1808).

[32] *Ibid.*, 288.

[33] *Ibid.*, 291.

miralty prize jurisdiction far beyond the scope assigned to it by his colleagues Marshall and Washington.[34] Yet Johnson's extreme position in this case must be reconciled with his failure to dissent in *Maley* v. *Shattuck*, an opinion announced two years earlier.[35] In *Maley* a vessel had been seized on the high seas for violation of the 1798 Non-Intercourse Act, but was restored to her Danish owner by the Supreme Court; the restoration was based in part upon the precedent of *The Charming Betsey*,[36] decided before Johnson was on the Supreme Court Bench, which established the rule that the Non-Intercourse Acts were to be strictly construed and limited in their operation on the high seas to ships of American nationality. Those previously recognized limitations on American admiralty jurisdiction in matters of municipal regulation can be conformed to Johnson's dissent in *Rose* v. *Himely* only upon the basis of the state of rebellion existing in Santo Domingo. Apparently, in Johnson's opinion, this permitted the situations to be distinguished as a matter of law. Laws against illegal trade passed to assist in the reduction of a rebellious population were, on the basis of this reasoning, far more than mere municipal regulations with a territorial limitation; they were rules established by a state engaged in warfare for its own preservation. We may assume, therefore, that Johnson's opinion in 1806 may not have been as broad as he originally expounded it; nations did not exercise concurrent powers on the high seas in all matters, but certain circumstances might justify their seizures and condemnations of vessels found on the high seas. Prize jurisdiction in Johnson's view rested not upon the existence of a formal state of declared war but rather upon military action predicated upon protection of territorial sovereignty that would entitle otherwise municipal regulations against illegal trade to be recognized in the law of nations as sovereign acts of the belligerent.

Rose v. *Himely* had been argued with the companion case of *Hudson* v. *Guestier* from February 6 to 16, 1808; the opinions were announced concurrently on March 2, and the intrinsic evidence in the opinions shows that they were discussed at the same conference of the Supreme Court.[37] The facts in *Hudson* differed from those in *Rose* only

---

[34] In later years Judge Johnson was to contend with Judge Story, arguing against Story's tendency to enlarge admiralty jurisdiction. D. Morgan, *Justice William Johnson: The First Dissenter* (Columbia, 1954), 80–82; G. Dunne, *Justice Joseph Story and the Rise of the Supreme Court* (New York, 1970), 98–102, 129–32, 200–202, 263–64. Dunne terms one difference between Story and Johnson to be the "knife edge that sometimes separated international law from purely municipal enactments." *Ibid.*, 241.

[35] Maley v. Shattuck, 3 Cranch 458–92 (1806), discussed in Part II, chapter 2, pp. 412–13.

[36] Murray v. The Charming Betsey, 2 Cranch 64–126 (1804), discussed in Part II, chapter 2, pp. 410–12.

[37] Minutes of the Supreme Court of the United States, I, RG 267, National Archives, Washington, D.C.

in the showing on the record that when the vessel was seized she was within the two-league limit from the Santo Domingan coast. As in the case of *The Sarah* in *Rose* v. *Himely* she had been carried to a Spanish port, where she remained while condemnation proceedings were held in a French admiralty court at Guadeloupe.

Delivering the majority opinion of the Court in *Hudson* v. *Guestier*,[38] Chief Justice Marshall held that seizure within territorial waters would vest jurisdiction in French admiralty courts; the only point in controversy was the physical location of the vessel in a Spanish port, and whether that would void the decree entered against her. Examining the law of nations on the subject, Marshall found it established and universally accepted that in prize matters, a vessel in the port of an allied or neutral power might nevertheless be validly condemned by the captor's national admiralty courts. In deciding whether such a rule applied with equal force to proceedings for the violation of municipal regulations, Marshall apologetically resorted to reasoning from analogy. While the traditional view was that possession of the *res* conferred admiralty jurisdiction in instance matters, it was also true that in municipal causes the mode of procedure was fixed by municipal law that could not be examined in the courts of other nations. It should be noted in passing that in *Rose* v. *Himely* the Chief Justice had touched upon the lack of notice to the crew and captain of a vessel condemned at a distance from the berth chosen by her captor, and raised the presumption that such lack of notice and opportunity to defend would taint the proceeding as ex parte and contrary to the law of nations. In *Hudson* that procedural objection seems to have been overlooked or considered irrelevant since the seizure *ab initio* was valid.

After conceding the conclusiveness of procedure upon courts of other nations, Marshall proceeded to consider the extent to which the captor's control of the vessel might be diminished by its location in the port of an ally or neutral. He felt that it was most unlikely that a territorial sovereign would take any action that would restrict the captor's control, and that in nearly all cases a petition for the release of the ship brought by the owner would be dismissed. Only if the captor so delayed proceedings in his national admiralty courts that there was good reason to anticipate that the seizure had been an illegal act, or maritime trespass, would the territorial sovereign be likely to interfere.

Judges Samuel Chase and Brockholst Livingston held to their opinions in *Rose* v. *Himely*, and persisted in their belief that if the vessel were in a port other than that of the condemning sovereign there was a lack of jurisdiction and the void decree was not binding on American courts. Upon the basis of his dissenting opinion in *Rose*,

---

[38] 4 Cranch 293–97 (1808).

Judge Johnson concurred in the majority opinion in *Hudson*, emphasizing that it was immaterial whether the case arose from a violation of municipal regulations or belligerent rights, or whether it had been made inside, or without, the territorial jurisdiction of France.

Hudson v. *Guestier* was sent back to the lower court for retrial, where, on the evidence now presented, the circuit court judge charged the jury contrary to the *Rose* rule that a capture six leagues from the coast would confer jurisdiction on the French admiralty court. Arguing in the second appeal to the Supreme Court in 1810,[39] Robert G. Harper for the original owner stressed that the point had been decided earlier in the Rose case and followed in intervening situations in *Palmer* v. *Dutilh* and *Hargous* v. *The Brig Ceres*, which had been remanded for rehearing in accordance with the opinion announced in *Rose*. Philip Barton Key and Luther Martin for the purchaser under the prize court decree argued that a nation had a right to use all the means necessary to secure obedience to her laws, and that laws of trade might be enforced beyond their territorial jurisdiction provided that the exercise of such power does not invade the exclusive rights of other nations. They pointed out that the French ordinance in question was not limited to the two-league limit, except in regard to vessels "found . . . in the territorial extent of the island."[40] Vessels cleared for ports in possession of the rebels and ships coming out of the island after trading with an interdicted port might be seized without regard to the two-league limit. This two-league limit was therefore similar in operation to the "hovering acts" of Great Britain and the United States, but a vessel that actually traded with the rebels might easily escape beyond the two-league limit by a good wind and thus avoid jurisdiction if such a narrow interpretation were given to the French ordinance. While the practicalities of enforcement were weighty arguments for the Key-Martin interpretation of the French ordinance, they were quite immaterial to the principal issue before the Supreme Court—might the French by ordinance project their jurisdiction into the high seas, and impose valid decrees of condemnation for illegal trade that would, by comity, be recognized in the United States?

The departure of Judges Cushing and Chase from the Bench before the second appeal in *Hudson* left the Chief Justice and Judges Washington, Johnson, and Todd to hear argument in association with Justice Livingston, who wrote the majority opinion. Livingston commenced by observing that he was bound by the previous opinions in *Rose* and *Hudson*, and compelled to follow the rule that trial of a seized vessel might proceed even though she was in a neutral port at the time of her condemnation. He then proceeded to examine whether,

---

[39] 6 Cranch 281–85 (1810).   [40] *Ibid.*, 283.

as it now appeared that the vessel was in fact on the high seas when seized by the French, the decision in *Hudson* would have to be altered. Livingston felt that the judgment below was correct and that seizure on the high seas was a valid exercise of French jurisdiction. His reasoning seems bottomed upon two contentions, the first of which resembles a non sequitur: "If the *res* can be proceeded against when not in possession or under the control of the court, I am not able to perceive how it can be material whether the capture were made within or beyond the jurisdictional limits of France; or in the exercise of a belligerent or municipal right."[41] Livingston's pique at having been earlier overruled on the issue of the physical situs of the *res* seems to have blinded him to Chief Justice Marshall's distinction between belligerent and municipal bases of admiralty jurisdiction. He also seems to have overlooked the correct assertions by Marshall, somewhat less consistently made by Johnson, that possession and jurisdiction over a vessel vested in the captors at the time of the seizure and that the jurisdiction of the captor's national admiralty court related back to the instant of seizure. Such possession and the appurtenant jurisdiction might be lost by recapture, or by abandonment of the captured vessel, or by carrying her into the port of a belligerent to the captor's nation, but while she was in the possession of the captor or his prize master she was to be considered subject to the admiralty jurisdiction of his national courts regardless of her physical location. In the first opinion in *Hudson*, Marshall had applied that rule to instance cases as well as prize matters.

Livingston's second basis for upholding the French admiralty court decree in *Hudson* was that undoubtedly the issue of the validity of a high-seas capture was raised in the French tribunal; the decision of the French admiralty court upholding its jurisdiction in the face of such a challenge should be treated as conclusive in American courts. Contrary to the existing practice in international law, which treated only prize court decrees as conclusive, Livingston was willing to accept at face value the purported decree or decision of the French tribunal upholding its own jurisdiction. On the basis of this standard no admiralty decree could be subject to collateral attack, and all foreign decrees were conclusive upon American courts regardless of the American court's view of the legality of the proceeding. As a final matter, Livingston failed to consider Chief Justice Marshall's concern that the proceeding before the French court not be ex parte but that the crew or master of the condemned vessel has been afforded an opportunity to defend her against condemnation. While the crew's or master's appearance would not, in and of itself, confer jurisdiction on the condemning court, it was likely to insure a challenge similar to that which Livingston

---

[41] *Ibid.*, 284.

was willing to read into the record of the French proceeding, and at the same time it would provide the American courts with assurance that the foreign decree before them for acceptance on the ground of comity was based upon a full and adversary examination of the facts of the case.

The second opinion in *Hudson* blurred Chief Justice Marshall's sharp distinction between prize and instance cases, a historical dichotomy long recognized in Anglo-American admiralty practice. It permitted American recognition of French admiralty decrees concerning illegal trade, without requiring American courts to give proper attention to matters of jurisdiction and fair trial. It did great damage to the orderly system of comity established by the Chief Justice in *Rose* v. *Himely*, causing his dissent and leaving American courts with no jurisprudential basis for reviewing French admiralty decrees and refusing to recognize those which by their patent lack of jurisdiction and disregard for the rights of the litigants offended American standards of justice.

The obeisance of the Supreme Court in 1810 to the authority of French admiralty tribunals may find justification in a desire to befriend the French Empire at a time when relations with Great Britain were badly strained, or in the alternative, in the need for judicial demonstration of willingness to condone a similar extension of American admiralty jurisdiction in the enforcement of the Non-Intercourse laws. Such public policy considerations aside, the second Hudson case must be considered one of the least laudable international law decisions of the Supreme Court in the years from 1801 to 1815.

The full impact of Livingston's opinion in the second Hudson appeal becomes obvious from a consideration of Chief Justice Marshall's synopsis of that opinion in *Williams* v. *Armroyd*.[42] An American merchant vessel after trading with the British island of Martinico had been captured on the high seas by a French privateer and seized for violation of the 1807 Milan Decree,[43] Napoleon's unilateral declaration that any ships submitting to British search or conforming to the requirements of British orders-in-council would be seized as British bottoms. The American ship was carried to the Dutch island of St. Martin, where she was held while condemnation proceedings in prize were instituted at Guadeloupe. The cargo was sold to a bona fide purchaser under St. Martin municipal law, prior to the condemnation decree at Guadeloupe. When it was brought to Philadelphia by the purchaser it was libeled by the former owner in the District Court for the Pennsylvania District.

---

[42] 7 Cranch 423–34 (1813).
[43] The second Milan decree of Dec. 11, 1807, is discussed in G. Lefebvre, *Napoleon, from Tilsit to Waterloo, 1807–1815*, H. Stockhold, trans. (New York, 1969), II, 107–34.

On a consent decree *pro forma* an appeal was taken to the circuit court where, upon submission of the French admiralty court decree, sentence was passed in favor of the purchaser, and the original owner appealed to the Supreme Court.

For the Court majority, Marshall pointed out that *Hudson* v. *Guestier* established the principle that the decree of a competent court, proceeding *in rem*, was conclusive as to the thing itself and worked a change of property. Condemnation related back to the capture and confirmed its legality, and as a result the sale at St. Martin before final condemnation did not void the purchaser's title. In answer to the argument that the Milan Decree had been declared by congressional resolution to be subversive of neutral rights and contrary to the law of nations, the Chief Justice, while agreeing that Napoleon's action was in fact a violation of the law of nations, observed that the congressional declaration did not, as it might have done, declare proceedings under the Milan Decree to be void in the United States. Given a different legislative mandate, Marshall added, the Supreme Court would have no difficulty in restoring the property to its original owner.[44] Whatever opinions the judges might entertain concerning the propriety of the French decree, as a coordinate tribunal in the administration of the law of nations it was bound to extend customary recognition to the foreign prize decree. *Stare decisis* and comity forced Marshall to deny the owner recovery in *Williams* v. *Armroyd,* but he pointed out that redress for such a wrong in international law might be obtained from Congress if that body, in the exercise of its political powers, were willing to deny recognition to the Milan Decree in the courts of the United States. As he had previously observed in *Schooner Exchange* v. *M'Faddon,* the decision concerning a French public vessel's exemption from jurisdiction announced the previous term, substantial injustice might result from the actions of belligerents who flouted traditional rules of international law; yet the judicial power of the United States, unaided by a congressional declaration of national policy, was helpless to provide a remedy through the return of condemned property subsequently found within the territory of the United States.

By 1814 the Chief Justice was convinced that Congress should take the initiative and establish national policy in most matters of international impact that might arise in the federal courts. In *Brown* v. *U.S.,*[45] a wartime case involving British-owned timber that had been

---

[44] Marshall considered the law of nations binding upon the Court, but on the other hand felt bound to follow declarations of national policy altering that law when issued by the political branches of government. Ziegler, *International Law of Marshall*, 29–30, 33–34.

[45] 8 Cranch 110–54 (1814); Judge Story's desire to extend admiralty jurisdiction to this case was probably the basis for the facetious comment

unladed from a ship prior to the declaration of war and left floating in a tidal creek until its sale to Brown after the congressional resolution declaring war, the Court was faced with another problem of public policy. The United States sought to condemn the timber as enemy property. Did title vest in the United States immediately upon the declaration of war, or was some separate and distinct legislative action required to vest title? As we shall see in the case of real property confiscation during the American Revolution,[46] the Supreme Court was willing to admit the validity of a legislative declaration to alter title even in the absence of judicial proceedings. The procedure for seizing enemy alien property was not at issue in *Brown* v. *U.S.* but rather the ramifications of the state of belligerency in regard to British-owned personal property in the United States. Did the state of war, *ipso facto*, vest title to the timber in the government of the United States? For the majority Marshall pointed out that the disposition of enemy property was a matter of policy, not of law, and that as such it was proper for the consideration of the legislature and not the executive or the judiciary. From Marshall's opinion and the Court's decree Judge Story dissented sharply with "the concurrence of one of my brethren," adhering to his opinion in the court below. He considered the timber to be subject to admiralty prize jurisdiction, and he believed that the declaration of a state of war granted to the President a power to confiscate enemy property. Story rejected any doctrine that the declaration of war, in and of itself, worked a change of ownership; rather the declaration conferred upon the President a right to confiscate in the name of the United States. Like prize jurisdiction, the power of confiscation vested in the President was inherent in the state of belligerency, and did not depend upon either express statutory or constitutional grants for its validity. Once the congressional declaration of war was passed these powers vested in the executive, subject only to limitations on their exercise by the law of nations. We may surmise that in this area, Judge Story was willing to give greater latitude to the exercise of Presidential war powers than was the majority of the Supreme Court, and on the other hand, he was willing to utilize judicial power to support the war powers of the President.[47] It is unclear to what extent he would have been willing to exercise the Supreme Court's power as a tribunal under the law of

---

that "if a bucket of water were brought into his court with a corn cob floating in it, he would at once extend the admiralty jurisdiction of the United States over it." C. Swisher, *The Taney Period, 1836–64, Volume IV, History of the Supreme Court of the United States*, ed., P. Freund (New York, 1974), 425.

[46] Smith v. Maryland, 6 Cranch 286–307 (1810), discussed at pp. 553–54, below.

[47] Dunne, *Story*, 113, attributes Story's difference with Marshall to his acceptance of the Spartan views of Cornelius van Bynkershoek.

nations as a limitation upon the actions of the President under the war powers. While Story's view of the war powers at first glance appears to be far more inclined towards executive discretion than that of his colleagues, in the final analysis it would appear to be the opening statement of a position in which the Supreme Court of the United States, by virtue of its central position as a court of international law, might become an extremely powerful force in the application of the law of nations to the conduct of the public policy of the United States. The majority position, on the contrary, recognized not only the practical political limitations to the exercise of judicial power in this manner, but also the constitutional constraints inherent in the doctrine of separation of powers.

Wartime confiscation of enemy property was no novel concern in the chambers of the Supreme Court during our period, for a series of cases raised the issue before the Court in regard to the provisions of the 1783 Peace Treaty with Great Britain, and the subsequent 1794 Treaty of Amity and Commerce, commonly referred to as the Jay Treaty. To the extent that those treaties involved the problem of alien landholding, they have been discussed in the preceding chapter, yet it is essential that we return to the same sources not only to understand the Court's approach to confiscation as a matter of international law but also to examine the constitutional and procedural problems raised by the Court's mandate to construe the international treaties and conventions entered into by the United States.

The definitive treaty of peace between the United States and her allies on one part, and Great Britain on the other, was signed on September 3, 1783, at Paris, and ratified by the Confederation Congress the following January 14. In its fourth article the parties "agreed that Creditors on either Side shall meet with no lawful Impediment to the Recovery of the full Value in Sterling Money of all bona fide Debts heretofore contracted."[48] After stipulating that Congress should recommend to the State governments restitution of all confiscated property, the fifth article stated that "it is agreed that all Persons who have any Interest in confiscated lands, either by Debts, Marriage Settlements, or otherwise, shall meet with no lawful Impediment in the Prosecution of their just Rights."[49] Supporting these two bases for recovery, the sixth article stipulated "[t]hat there shall be no future Confiscations made nor any Prosecutions commenc'd against any Person or Persons for or by Reason of the Part, which he or they may have taken in the present War, and that no Person shall on that Account suffer any future Loss or Damage, either in his Person Liberty or Property; . . ."[50]

The retrospective provision of the federal Constitution recognized

---

[48] Miller, *Treaties*, II, 154.   [49] *Ibid.*   [50] *Ibid.*, 155.

the 1783 treaty as the supreme law of the land.[51] The Supreme Court had so held in *Ware* v. *Hylton*,[52] opening federal courts to litigation by British mercantile creditors and silencing all debate over State sequestrations and other limitations upon debt recovery.

The Jay Treaty, signed at London on November 19, 1794, was designed to eliminate the differences existing between the United States and Britain, which arose in large measure from conflicting interpretations of the Peace Treaty as well as evasion of various terms in that treaty. Article 6 treated the problem of debts that were created bona fide before the Peace Treaty of 1783, and concerning which, "by the operation of various lawful Impediments since the Peace, not only the full recovery of the said Debts has been delayed, but also the Value and Security thereof, have been in several instances impaired and lessened,"[53] and concluded that they were uncollectible in the normal course of judicial proceedings in the United States. A joint commission was therefore established to ascertain the amounts remaining unpaid, and the United States government agreed to compensate British creditors in amounts to be fixed by the commission. Article 9 of the Jay Treaty, dealing with British real property in the former American colonies, provided that

> British subjects who now hold lands in the Territories of the United States, and American citizens who now hold Lands in the Dominions of His Majesty, shall continue to hold them according to the nature and Tenure of their respective Estates and Titles therein, and may grant Sell or Devise the same to whom they please, in like manner as if they were Natives; and that neither they nor their Heirs or assigns shall, so far as may respect the said Lands, and the legal remedies incident thereto, be regarded as Aliens.[54]

As to American landholding in Britain, the treaty article merely confirmed the rule of the *antenati*, as discussed above,[55] but as to American

---

[51] U.S. Constitution, Art. 6, Clause 2.

[52] See Judge Samuel Chase's opinion in Ware v. Hylton, 3 Dall. 236, in answer to Marshall's argument at bar that the Virginia sequestration statutes could not be altered by the 1783 Peace Treaty. Chase mentions not only the resolution of Congress, but also the supremacy clause of the Constitution. In briefer references to the problem Judges William Paterson, James Wilson, and William Cushing appear to have concurred with Chase. *Ibid.*, 256, 281, 282–83. Judge James

Iredell, who had dissented from Chief Justice Jay when the Ware case was argued in the Virginia Circuit Court, dissented from his colleagues in the Supreme Court, finding the congressional resolution of no import and distinguishing debts paid into the Virginia treasury so that they were denied the protection of the 1783 Peace Treaty. *Ibid.*, 276–77. See Goebel, *Antecedents*, 752–54.

[53] Miller, *Treaties*, II, 249–50.

[54] *Ibid.*, 253, 254.

[55] See Part II, chapter 4, pp. 500–506, 508–11.

land held by British subjects, it gave rise to constitutional conflict between State alienage statutes and the supremacy of the treaty provisions.

It has been shown that the Supreme Court upheld the supremacy of the 1783 treaty debt-recovery provisions in *Ware* v. *Hylton* (1796), just at the time when a substantial number of claims had been removed from judicial determination for the relatively more certain arbitration of the mixed-claims commission. Few cases of pre-Revolutionary British creditors reached the Supreme Court in our period, but they are of primary interest in regard to the light they cast upon the Court's construction of the provisions of the 1783 and 1794 treaties. The first of these cases was *Dunlop & Co.* v. *Ball*,[56] which involved the presumption in law that the expiration of twenty years after the date of a bond gave rise to the inference that it had been paid. A Virginia jury in the circuit court for that district had been so instructed, thereby resulting in denial of an action by a British mercantile firm for the collection of a pre-Revolutionary debt. For the British firm, attorney Edmund J. Lee argued that from the date of the expiration of the fee bill in December 1774 until the outbreak of hostilities the courts of Virginia were closed to business. Thereafter a series of Virginia statutes suspended execution on judgments running in favor of British creditors until at least 1784 and very likely until 1787. Even after 1787 there was persuasive evidence, both in the report of the commission under article 6 of the Jay Treaty, and in the case law of Virginia, that until 1793 it was not possible for a British merchant to collect amounts owed to him by Virginia residents.

Delivering the opinion of the Court in the Dunlop case, John Marshall lost no time in establishing the non-collectibility of British creditors' advances by actions instituted in Virginia courts between 1775 and 1793, thereby sweeping aside the debtor's contentions concerning the decade after the peace being includible in the twenty-year period in which a creditor was forced to bring his action. Marshall then considered the question he had raised in a colloquy with counsel—considering the length of the suspension during hostilities, was it not excessive to permit a creditor twenty years additional in which to bring his action? The question was not unreasonable, although it was perhaps raised with ill grace by a judge with Marshall's background of having defended Virginia debtors of British merchants in the course of his law practice. Clearly a creditor who had been subjected to long delays in his collection of outstanding obligations might be expected to act promptly upon the cessation of hostilities. The interests of justice and the need for fresh evidence demanded that debts existing since 1775

---

[56] 2 Cranch 180–85 (1804).

should be litigated as soon as possible. Applying a presumption that would allow British firms to wait until 1813 to institute action would be fraught with practical difficulties and potential injustice. Yet, concluded the Chief Justice in his opinion, "the Court think it best to adhere to old decisions,"[57] and for that reason the twenty-year-presumption rule would be followed. In *Dunlop* the British creditor might still bring action, since the years from 1775 to 1793 would be added to the twenty-year period in which presumption of payment would accrue.

Hopkirk v. *Bell*,[58] a Virginia federal circuit court case that generated two appeals to the Supreme Court, raised the question of the continued vitality of the Virginia statute of limitations of 1792,[59] as it applied to British merchants' claims. The statute provided that debts arising out of commercial transactions, a category including the promissory note executed by the defendant, were to be put into action within five years; excepted from the five-year period was any time the plaintiff resided "beyond the seas" unless he had a factor in Virginia competent to sue, in which case the statute of limitations would continue to run against him. On the record it appeared that plaintiff's firm had employed a Virginia agent since 1784, and that he was empowered to commence lawsuits on behalf of the firm. In a *per curiam* opinion the Supreme Court ruled that an agent for the collection of debts was not a factor within the terms of the Virginia statute. In addition the Virginia statute of limitations, to the extent that it impeded the collection of British debts protected by the 1783 Peace Treaty, was to be considered nullified by the ratification of the treaty. From the brief opinion we cannot be certain that the Court accepted Charles Lee's sweeping argument concerning the supremacy of treaties over State legislation, but there is no evidence that the justices disagreed with his summation: "In the case of *Ware* v. *Hylton*, 3 Dall. 199, this court, upon very solemn argument, decided, that the treaty not only repealed all the state laws which operated as impediments, but nullified all acts done, and all rights acquired, under such laws, which tended to obstruct the creditor's right of recovery."[60] By 1806 it would appear that the Court did not find it necessary to ratify this broad and all-inclusive construction of British creditors' rights under the 1783 Peace Treaty. Certainly if Lee's argument had been too broad in stating the supremacy of treaties over legislation by the American States, the Court would have been impelled to administer a strong corrective in the opinion.

A subsequent appeal in *Hopkirk* v. *Bell*,[61] decided in the 1807

---

[57] *Ibid.*, 185.
[58] 3 Cranch 454–58 (1806).
[59] An Act for the Limitation of Actions, Dec. 17, 1792, *A Collection of Such Acts of the General Assembly of Virginia . . . as are now in force* (Richmond, 1794), 114–16.
[60] 3 Cranch 454, at 457.
[61] 4 Cranch 164–65 (1807).

term of court, presented the additional fact that from the spring of 1784 until sometime in 1785, one of the partners of the plaintiff firm resided in Virginia. Once again the Supreme Court by a *per curiam* opinion held that the Virginia statute of limitations could not bar plaintiff's demand, given the facts as submitted to the Court. It will be recalled that the Court had previously held, in *Dunlop & Co.* v. *Ball*, that British creditors could not collect their debts in Virginia courts at any time prior to 1793. Article 4 of the Peace Treaty had specifically provided that there were to be no lawful impediments to the collection of those debts. The Virginia statute of limitations, by permitting the time to run against British firms who had either factors or partners resident in Virginia, created the erroneous impression that recovery was possible, and constituted a bar to recovery when those courts became available to British merchants in 1793. Mere residence in Virginia was not sufficient to toll the statute against the British firm; only residence *after* 1793 would suffice.

Higginson v. *Mein*,[62] argued and decided in the 1808 term, involved the foreclosure of a mortgage on confiscated property in the hands of a purchaser from the State of Georgia. After the loyalist mortgagor fled the State during the Revolution, the property had been confiscated under Georgia law. However it was not clear upon the record whether the bond underlying the mortgage had actually been paid, and on that basis the Supreme Court remanded the case for retrial. For the majority of the Court, John Marshall pointed out that commercial debts due to British firms and individuals had been sequestered and not confiscated under the Georgia laws. In any event confiscation of the estate of the loyalist in the land would not destroy the mortgagee's lien, which was still in existence when the 1783 Peace Treaty was signed. By virtue of articles 5 and 6 of the treaty, the mortgagee's interest was secured from State infringements. During argument Marshall had commented, "The decisions of this court have been uniform, that the acts of the states, confiscating debts, are repealed by the treaty; and if, in this case, the debt remains, does not the security remain also?"[63] Counsel for the purchaser had claimed the benefit of the presumption of payment twenty years after the date of the bond, and Marshall conceded in his opinion that the mortgagor's residence in England after 1778 would subject him to an action for judgment on the bond. Despite this, he felt that the evidence was inadequate to allow a presumption of payment to arise in the peculiar facts presented in *Higginson*.

Judge Brockholst Livingston dissented from the majority in *Higginson*, but failed to provide the reporter with his reasons for dis-

---

[62] 4 Cranch 415–20 (1808).   [63] *Ibid.*, 417.

senting. Nevertheless in the course of argument Livingston had observed that "I never heard that confiscated property has been restored by the force of the treaty. The treaty only recommends that Congress shall recommend such restitution."[64] His dissent would therefore seem to involve the applicability of the first clause of the fifth article of the treaty to *Higginson* v. *Mein*. That precatory provision refers to "Estates, Rights and Properties," while the second clause, which prohibits State action, refers to "Interest . . . either by Debts, Marriage Settlements or otherwise."[65] Was the interest of the British firm, represented by a bond and mortgage, an "estate" or was it a "debt"? Clearly the majority treated the mortgage lien as appurtenant to, and subordinate to, the bonded indebtedness; the mortgage for them obtained its vitality from the continued existence of the debt it secured. Their action in remanding the case for further consideration of the question of payment of the bond buttresses this conclusion. At the same time, the majority viewed the confiscation as working *in personam* against the loyalist mortgagor; it could not touch the mortgage lien of the British mortgagee, which subsequently came under the protection of the fourth article, and the second clause of the fifth article of the Peace Treaty.

It is difficult to view State confiscations as mere *in personam* proceedings, for the intention behind the seizure of loyalist realty was to punish the offender and at the same time to enrich the State by returning the loyalist's property to the tax rolls. Obviously an unencumbered estate held in fee simple might be confiscated (prior to the date of the Peace Treaty), without concern about other interests. But a mortgaged estate or one in which there were future interests raised delicate issues of real property law and State power to confiscate. There were also problems of notice of the confiscation proceedings to innocent parties untainted by the loyalist owner's treasonable or subversive activities. For the majority in *Higginson* identification of the mortgage lien as subordinate to the indebtedness permitted the broadest possible protection for British subjects claiming under the treaty. Their course was to identify *Higginson* as a case of indebtedness, thereby avoiding the issues of due process, notice, and *in rem* jurisdiction and their effect on the lien of a mortgagee. Livingston, on the other hand, considered confiscations as *in rem* proceedings that passed title to the purchasers and bound the entire world by their judgments; thus the mortgage lien, and all similar interests in confiscated loyalist real property, had been extinguished by the date the Peace Treaty was executed.

While the Peace Treaty was being negotiated, the debt-payment provisions and those concerning the restitution of confiscated loyalist lands at first had been closely interrelated. They were included in the

---

[64] *Ibid.*, 417–18.   [65] See Miller, *Treaties*, II, 154.

original instructions to British minister Richard Oswald, but made subject to waiver by him. When the initial proposal was submitted to the British cabinet without either provision, the government strengthened its resolve to have them included or to break off negotiations. With the appointment of Henry Strachey to the British side of the negotiating team in Paris, instructions were issued by the Cabinet requiring that the Peace Treaty include guarantees for the recovery of debts due to British subjects as well as compensation for confiscated lands of loyalists. Largely through the influence of John Adams the American commissioners acceded to the demand that the payment of pre-Revolutionary debts be insured, but their unanimous and strong opposition to compensation for confiscated lands left the British little choice but to settle for a guarantee concerning the physical safety of loyalists still remaining within American occupied territory. As a consequence of these diplomatic discussions, the recovery of trade debts emerged in the Peace Treaty as one of the principal concerns of both governments.[66] Opinions of the Supreme Court, and particularly the Marshall statement in *Higginson* v. *Mein*, gave due recognition to this emphasis upon the payment of bona fide commercial obligations arising from trade in the colonial period. At the same time they suggest some of the delicate issues of international law and federal-State relations that emerged from the treaty provisions concerning confiscated lands and lands deemed escheated by virtue of alienage. The determination of the American commissioners in resisting reimbursement for confiscations arose from their awareness of the constitutional relationship between the Confederation government and the various States; similarly, in construing treaty provisions in light of the federal system established after 1789, the Supreme Court was forced to make difficult choices and resolve the complex questions that arose in international law from the peculiar nature of the American federal Union.

The two cases before the Supreme Court in our period that involved American loyalists, *M'Ilvaine* v. *Coxe's Lessee* and *Kempe's Lessee* v. *Kennedy*,[67] both demonstrate the Supreme Court's acquiescence in State determinations of citizenship and the validity of State confiscations for treason during the American Revolution. In *M'Ilvaine* the Court observed that the 1783 Peace Treaty, in stipulating that the federal government would recommend a reconsideration of confiscations to the States, did in fact constitute Britain's recognition of the validity and legality of those confiscations. The treaty had no effect upon the sovereignty of the American States, nor did its provisions give

---

[66] R. Morris, *The Peacemakers* (New York, 1965), 296, 318, 348, 361, 367–70.

[67] 4 Cranch 209–15 (1808), and 5 Cranch 173–87 (1809).

vitality to the statutes of those States. State authority existed prior to, and independent of, any clauses in the Peace Treaty. In so reasoning the Supreme Court emphatically rejected counsel's argument that the American States were not independent until their status had been established by a Peace Treaty. Such a construction would place in issue the legitimacy of government during the war, and would be "not only inconsistent with the sovereignties of the states . . . , but its indiscriminate adoption might be productive of more mischief than it is possible . . . to foresee."[68]

Kempe's Lessee v. *Kennedy* involved lands of the wife of John Tabor Kempe, a prominent loyalist who served as the last royal attorney-general of New York. Counsel had argued that a feme covert could not commit treason while married to and living with her husband, for she was entirely within his control and direction. It was also argued that as a woman under coverture she could have no domicile other than that of her husband, and for this reason that she could not be compelled to return to New Jersey where the to-be-confiscated lands were situated. She had not fled to New York, but had resided there anterior to the outbreak of the Revolution, and hence the State of New Jersey could have no claim to her allegiance, even if, despite coverture, she were free to offer it to any State.[69] The Court's opinion was that the confiscation judgment in the New Jersey State courts was erroneous, being based upon mistakes in law on these points. Yet even though it was defective it constituted a final judgment by a court with jurisdiction to render it; absent an appeal challenging the judgment, it could not be disturbed by the Supreme Court of the United States on writ of error. Loyalists would have to exhaust their remedies in State tribunals before taking appeals to the Supreme Court. When coupled with *M'Ilvaine*, *Kempe's Lessee* leaves little doubt that loyalists who wished to claim restitution for confiscated lands would have to proceed in State courts to gain redress.

Not only did State confiscations completed before the 1783 Peace Treaty continue to be valid, but State statutes and court decisions to the extent that they determined status as citizens might result in a party's disqualification from claiming under the protection of the treaty. The principal impact of State determinations of nationality would be in regard to article 4 of the Peace Treaty, where "Creditors on either Side" were assured that they would meet no lawful impediment to the collection of debts. A loyalist who had been declared a citizen by his American State could not claim the protection of this article, since he

---

[68] 4 Cranch 215 (1808).
[69] Richard Stockton's argument on this point is a classic statement of the disabilities of a woman under coverture. 5 Cranch 174–78.

was not a *British* creditor. He might, of course, institute action on the basis of diversity of citizenship in the federal courts, or in the courts of the State claiming him as a citizen, but in either case his rights were determined by American law and not by international law as expressed in the Peace Treaty.[70]

Article 5 of the Peace Treaty also evidences the subordination of loyalist interests to those of British resident subjects. The precatory clause, binding Congress to recommend restitution to the States in regard to confiscated estates, distinguishes between "real British subjects" and "Persons resident in Districts in the Possession of his Majesty's Arms, and who have not borne Arms against the said United States."[71] In other words, loyalists who bore arms in defense of their principles were denied even the weak protection of the first clause of article 5. Undoubtedly the State court determination of bearing arms would have been as binding as its assessment of nationality. The second clause of article 5, referring to "Persons" with interests by debt, marriage settlement, or otherwise in confiscated lands, presumably protected those property rights regardless of nationality or conduct during the American Revolution.[72]

Far more significant in public interest and political impact were the cases involving realty owned or inherited by British subjects, native to and resident in the United Kingdom. In 1809 the Supreme Court held that persons claiming protection of the 1783 and 1794 treaties would have to prove at the outset their entitlement to claim rights through a predecessor in title.[73] Absent such a showing the Supreme Court would refuse to take jurisdiction under section 25 of the Judiciary Act of 1789.[74] The following year, in *Smith* v. *Maryland*,[75] the Court considered the consequences of a 1780 Maryland confiscation, which purported to appropriate a trust estate in which the equitable beneficial interest was in a British subject and resident. At bar it had been argued that the confiscation was complete before the date of the 1783 Peace Treaty, and that the Supreme Court was bound by the judgment of the Court of Appeals of Maryland on that point. This position was

---

[70] Compare the various articles in Miller, *Treaties*, II, 154–55.

[71] *Ibid.*, 154.

[72] *Ibid.*

[73] Owings v. Norwood's Lessee, 5 Cranch 344–50 (1809).

[74] Sec. 25 provided that ". . . a final judgment or decree in any suit, in the highest court of law or equity of a State in which a decision in the suit could be had, where is drawn into question the validity of a treaty . . .

of . . . the United States, and the decision is against their validity . . . or where is drawn in question the construction of any . . . treaty . . . and the decision is against that title, right, privilege or exemption specially set up or claimed by either party, under such . . . treaty . . . may be reexamined and reversed or affirmed in the Supreme Court of the United States . . ." 1 Stat. 73, at 85–86.

[75] 6 Cranch 286–307 (1810).

categorically rejected by the Supreme Court, which held that it was empowered to examine the proceedings of State courts to ascertain whether confiscations were or were not complete. Upon that determination depended the applicability of article 6, precluding *future* confiscations, and an examination of the record was incumbent upon the Court in its administration of the Peace Treaty. After such a study, the Supreme Court arrived at the conclusion that the Maryland confiscation was, in fact, completed well before the signature of the treaty, and hence recovery under the treaty was properly denied by the Maryland courts. On the other hand, it established the principle that in determining jurisdiction under section 25 of the Judiciary Act of 1789, the Supreme Court would not consider itself bound by any factual or legal determinations of State tribunals. The Court itself would be the ultimate arbiter, particularly in regard to matters where its acceptance of jurisdiction depended upon construction of State adjective law.

Fairfax's Devisee v. *Hunter's Lessee* came on for argument on February 27 and 28, 1812,[76] having been on the Court's dockets since it was originally appealed by writ of error in February 1795. John Marshall was among the counsel originally retained by the Fairfax interests and, while he was present during the argument of the case, he did not participate in the decision, and left the preparation of the opinion to his most junior colleague, Joseph Story. Lord Fairfax, the proprietor of the Northern Neck of Virginia, had died a resident and citizen of the Commonwealth in 1781, and upon his death title passed under his will to Denny Martin Fairfax, his nephew, who resided in Britain. As a consequence Denny Fairfax was subject to all of the disabilities attaching to aliens claiming land in Virginia, except as far as the 1783 and 1794 treaties with Great Britain had altered that situation. In 1789 Virginia, purporting to act pursuant to a law of 1785 (referring to the rights of the Commonwealth in the unappropriated lands of the northern neck) conveyed the lands to David Hunter, through whom the present plaintiff claimed. The Chief Justice, in conjunction with his brother, James Markham Marshall, and brother-in-law, Rawleigh Colston, had purchased the manor of Leeds from Denny Martin Fairfax in 1793 and the South Branch Manor the following year, all prior to the negotiation of the Jay Treaty.[77] Technically these lands were distinct from the waste and unappropriated lands in litigation in *Fairfax's Devisee*, but the validity of Denny Fairfax's title was of such financial importance to Chief Justice Marshall that it would have

---

[76] Argued in 1812, Fairfax's Devisee v. Hunter's Lessee, 7 Cranch 603–32 (1813), was not decided until the end of the 1813 term of Court. Minutes of the Supreme Court, II, RG 267, National Archives, Washington, D.C.

[77] Beveridge, *Life of John Marshall*, I, 203; IV, 150.

been most unwise and improper for him to participate in the decision of this case.

Judge Story's opinion for the majority does not address itself to the question of whether the 1783 Peace Treaty provisions, prohibiting future confiscations, also included subsequent escheats for alienage. Instead Story focused on the state of the title to the land.[78] He pointed out that the officers of the Commonwealth had failed to institute a proceeding of inquest of office in regard to the Fairfax title prior to the effective date of the Jay Treaty. Article 9 of the treaty stipulated that British subjects who held lands at the time of its execution would continue to hold them as if they were natives, according to the nature and tenure of their titles, and that similar security was to be afforded to American citizens who held lands in British dominions. Denny Fairfax died intestate after 1796, leaving a British heir. If he held title on November 19, 1794, the effective date of the Jay Treaty, he or his heir could not be divested of it by any subsequent action by the Commonwealth of Virginia. Judge Story, after an examination of the proceedings below and the statutes of Virginia on alienage and landholding (in order to determine the source and validity of Fairfax's title) held that an inquest of office was necessary to vest title to escheated lands in the State. Since no inquest had been instituted prior to the negotiation of the Jay Treaty, the grant to Hunter was ineffective and Fairfax's title was good and guaranteed against further State action by the supremacy of the treaty stipulation. Even though Denny Fairfax's estate may not have been inheritable by his heirs when he succeeded to Lord Fairfax's estate in 1781,[79] that incident of alienage was cured by the 1794 treaty clause that restored British subjects to the status of native-born Americans for purposes of landholding. Upon Denny Fairfax's death in or after 1796, after the commencement of litigation in *Fairfax's Devisee* but subsequent to the effective date of the Jay Treaty, title passed to his heirs or representatives in the normal course of descent and distribution. At any time after November 19, 1794, Virginia was estopped from enforcing the escheat of the Fairfax title on the ground of alienage.

So completely did Judge Story accept the principle of Supreme Court review of State court determinations limiting the right to qualify for an appeal under the treaty supremacy clause, that he did not mention the *Smith* v. *Maryland* precedent in this connection. Judge William Johnson in his dissenting opinion took pains to show that he concurred in the *Smith* rule that no State court rule could be considered binding

---

[78] 7 Cranch 618–28.

[79] At common law, if an alien held lands contrary to the law prohibiting his ownership and died in possession before being divested through action of the sovereign, the realty could not descend to his heirs but would automatically escheat to the sovereign.

in regard to the jurisdiction of the Supreme Court, even though section 25 of the Judiciary Act of 1789 limited the Court's scope of review to the federal question. Meaningful review of the federal question would be negated if the Court could not examine the underlying State-law rulings: "[W]henever a case is brought to this court . . . , the title of the parties litigant must necessarily be inquired into, and that such an inquiry must, in the nature of things, precede the consideration of how far the law, treaty, and so forth, is applicable to it; otherwise an appeal to this court would be worse than nugatory."[80]

While State courts and political orators might debate this exercise of Supreme Court jurisdiction, and insist upon the binding effect of State decisions in matters of substantive law and procedure, the Bench of the Supreme Court in 1813 was resolutely determined to make full and complete inquiry into the law and facts of each case alleged to relate to a treaty provision. State determinations, even of title to local land, would not be treated as conclusive in matters bearing upon the Supreme Court's exercise of its jurisdiction under section 25.

Judge Johnson's dissent from the majority in *Fairfax's Devisee* was predicated upon his contradictory construction of the 1794 treaty provision, particularly the phrase "now holding." While he was willing to concede, in the liberal tradition of treaty construction, that the treaty's protection would extend to all cases of a rightful possession or a legal title defeasible on the ground of alien disability, he considered Denny Fairfax's title to have been no more than a mere *scintilla juris* under the statutes and common law of Virginia; as such it did not qualify under the treaty as an interest in land. His reasoning was based upon the distinction between the descent of land to an alien, which proceeded by operation of law and hence was a matter of public record and notice (and did not require an inquest of office to effect an escheat), and passage of title to an alien by purchase which would vest a bare title in the alien subject to divestiture by a subsequent inquest of office. Judge Johnson considered a devise of realty to an alien to be similar in nature to a purchase; therefore under common law an inquest would be required. However the 1785 Virginia statute had altered the common law by asserting Virginia's title to the Northern Neck. It thus served as the equivalent of an inquest of office at common law, since as a public statute it was a matter of general knowledge. By virtue of the 1785 statute, an inquest of office was no longer required to vest title in the Commonwealth of Virginia.

Fairfax was thus a reconsideration of the issues considered in *Smith* v. *Maryland*, where the Court had permitted (in accordance with common law precedents) the escheat of inherited property without

---

[80] 7 Cranch 632 (1813).

inquest of office. British precedents also permitted an escheat without inquest of office in the case of treason convictions. Consequently there was nothing "mystical, nor anything of indispensible obligation, in this inquest of office."[81] Reduced to basic issues, Johnson's difference with the majority involved their conflicting interpretations of the Virginia law on escheat of alien lands. Johnson believed no inquest was required in the Fairfax case and that the tenuous interest held by Denny Martin Fairfax was totally extinguished by the Commonwealth's grant to David Hunter in 1789; the majority treated that grant as a nullity since it was not preceded by an inquest of office.

In Judge Story's majority opinion in *Fairfax* we find renewed evidence of the Supreme Court's deep concern that the United States be known for its adherence to international law and its respect for treaty obligations. This is obvious in light of Story's emphasis upon the need for regularity in procedure and the protection of individual rights through an inquest of office. Again the theme of due notice and the Court's abhorrence of ex parte proceedings was evident in a case concerning international law and the construction of treaties. While other nations might transgress the law of nations by their conduct and court decrees, the administration of international law in the Marshall Court was not only consonant with traditional rules but also marked by a search for fair play to the litigants. As a salutary influence towards world peace and order,[82] the law of nations was to be followed as closely as possible, the Supreme Court seeking guidance from the treatises and decisions of all civilized nations in selecting its rules of international law. Even in regard to possible future construction of the exercise of Presidential war powers, the Court gave indications that the executive might be subject to limitations imposed by the law of nations. Administration of the law of nations had become a respectable and expandable portion of the inherent constitutional jurisdiction of the Supreme Court, and the Court in turn was not reluctant to assume its formative role in the shaping of an American interpretation of the law of nations.

In construing treaties of the United States, the Court exercised great liberality in broadening the rights of the signatory powers and those claiming under them. Where necessary treaties were given immediate effect, thereby changing the case law governing matters already pending in the courts. State legislation to the extent that it proved to be contrary to treaty provisions would be declared null and void under

---

[81] *Ibid.*, 631.

[82] Quoting Chief Justice Marshall's dissenting opinion in The Venus, 8 Cranch 297 (1814), that "The law of Nations is a law founded on the great and immutable principles of equity and natural justice," Benjamin Ziegler shows the Chief Justice's efforts to expound international law with a view towards practices in the civilized nations of the world. *International Law of Marshall*, 27–28, 31.

the supremacy clause of the Constitution. Both State statutes and local case law that in any way limited rights to appeal under section 25 of the Judiciary Act of 1789 should be disregarded as binding precedent in the Supreme Court. Subordination of State municipal law to the law of nations as enunciated by the Supreme Court was well established in our period, as was the procedural safeguard that the Court kept to itself the final determination of matters of law and fact establishing its jurisdiction under section 25.

The accomplishments of the period concerning international conflicts of law are less noteworthy, primarily because of the overruling of Chief Justice Marshall's opinion in *Rose* v. *Himely*. As a consequence of the unfortunate second opinion in *Hudson* v. *Guestier* the clear-cut and pragmatic standards set forth by the Chief Justice were discarded, and the Court entered a period of servile acquiescence in the outrages against the law of nations perpetrated by France and Britain. Perhaps the judicial attitude may be justified by expedience and the realities of warfare in the Napoleonic period, but the confusion generated by these cases delayed the development of a system of comity in American international law for several decades. The Chief Justice fell back upon the separation of powers and a plea for legislative authorization of legal reprisals against foreign violations of the law of nations. While it is true that the great decisions of political policy should be left to the Congress, it is also apparent that the adjudication of American property rights in foreign tribunals of questionable jurisdiction is a matter of judicial rather than political cognizance. Divided in its view of the subject of comity, wary of the danger of antagonizing France when war with Britain was imminent, the Supreme Court was incapable of working constructively in this field.

Despite its poor showing in international conflicts of law and the extension or denial of comity, the Supreme Court made significant contributions to the growth of international law in the United States between 1801 and 1815. It consolidated the position to which it was entitled as the primary international law tribunal of the nation, and demonstrated no small degree of courage in subordinating State interests to the needs of the law of nations.[83] That progress was made at all in the light of the varying opinions of the judges is as much a tribute to the leadership and persuasive skills of the Chief Justice as it is a mark of the pressing necessity of the times that required the law of nations to be engrafted into the federal public law of the United States.

---

[83] Professor Ziegler considered John Marshall's influence to have continued in the Supreme Court at least a decade after his death in 1835, and that many of his utterances in the opinions of the Court were still being cited when Ziegler's book was written thirty years ago. *International Law of Marshall*, 23–25.

CHAPTER VI

Business Enterprise and the Supreme Court

D OUBLE SANCTIONS JUSTIFIED the exercise of Supreme Court jurisdiction in the areas of public law and maritime jurisdiction, which we have considered heretofore. On the one hand specific provisions in the federal Constitution granted extensive powers in these fields, and on the other hand two centuries of royal government and tradition supported the exercise of central authority in these areas, as well as frequent recourse to rules of natural law and international practice and comity. No such authority attached to the new and dynamic aspect of federal judicial authority inherent in the commerce clause, the contract clause, and the grant of federal jurisdiction over disputes of an interstate or international origin. Predicated upon the divisive and competitive activities of the several American States under the Articles of Confederation, and designed to minimize if not eliminate the disunity inherent in the practice of State mercantilism, the new federal Constitution made the federal government the ultimate authority in assuring the sanctity of private property on the one hand, and the enforcement of international trade practice and custom on the other. For these reasons the Supreme Court, in the first decade and a half of John Marshall's Chief Justiceship, found itself deeply involved in the task of laying the legal and constitutional foundation for the future economic prosperity of the United States.

The newly granted economic powers of the federal government threatened to generate fierce conflict between the States and the central government, raising at the same time questions of policy upon which the dominant Jeffersonian-Republican party differed sharply from the commercially oriented authors of the federal Constitution. Despite the political sensitivity of the issues of agrarianism versus commercial and industrial development, the decisions of the Supreme Court in the economic area seem to be less controlled by respect for legislative and

559

executive policy than was the case in international law litigation. The cases before the Court were of course matters of private law that required resolution for the proper operation of the federal system. The Republicans, while they did not share the economic ideology of their Federalist opponents, nevertheless were cognizant of the need for trust and security in business transactions. Simply stated, both political parties respected the role of private property in encouraging prosperity and in the political foundations of the American federal state—both were children of the Enlightenment and the political philosophy of the Lockean school.

Prior to 1801 the Supreme Court had heard nearly as many cases arising upon diversity grounds as it did in the fields of admiralty. Yet it fell to the early Marshall Court to superintend the course of law at a time when diversity cases and matters on appeal from the District of Columbia increasingly raised important issues of commercial law and business methods. The settlement of the District of Columbia and the growing importance of the city of Alexandria as a major commercial center for northern Virginia, western Maryland, and portions of central Pennsylvania increased the number of District appeals to the Supreme Court in this area of commercial law. No understanding of the Supreme Court during this period is possible without some attention to this aspect of its work. By a steady and methodical accretion of precedent, the judges laid a firm foundation upon which was to develop not only commercial prosperity, but a reasonable uniformity of mercantile rules and practices.

COMMERCIAL TRANSACTIONS

Negotiable Instruments

Perhaps the best example of the Court's work in commercial law is its attempt to minimize the severe aberrations and substantial injustice caused by the antiquated commercial law of the Commonwealth of Virginia. Forced by legislative mandate to apply Virginia law in that part of the District of Columbia that had been ceded by Virginia, the Supreme Court administered Maryland law in the county of Washington, and Virginia law in the county of Alexandria, but the commercial life in the District did not divide itself according to the bed of the Potomac River, and the duality of law in the District caused substantial litigation.

A large number of cases arising from the District of Columbia in this period involved the negotiability of promissory notes under Virginia law. Negotiability is a concept derived from the law merchant that provided legal sanction for certain types of written instruments to cir-

560

culate freely and to be accepted as vehicles for the exchange of the money that they represent. The use of these instruments was of such importance to the commercial community that it was established at an early date that defects in the transaction that gave rise to the instrument might not be pleaded in defense against the holder who attempted to redeem it. In addition, if the instrument were not surrendered to the maker when he paid his debt, he remained liable to those who innocently purchased the instrument without knowledge of the payment. Simply stated, the debt became incorporated into the instrument, permitting its free transfer in trade, and encouraging reliance upon the rules of negotiability. Negotiable instruments were transferred by indorsement, a simple signature, and therefore the endorser remained liable to his transferee and any subsequent holder, as an indemnitor for the non-payment of the instrument by the maker. The endorser's credit thus was pledged for the ultimate payment of the instrument.[1]

As a concept negotiability stands in stark opposition to the ancient rules of English common law which prohibited the transfer of a chose in action. Although those prohibitions were gradually altered in the seventeenth century, and during the early eighteenth century the law merchant was "received" into the common law of England, the status of "notes of hand," or promissory notes, remained in question until 1704. The English Promissory Note Act of that year, which did not specifically apply to the American plantations, provided that promissory notes would thereafter be treated as inland bills of exchange, and hence would take on the attributes of negotiability. While the evidence is meager, it would seem likely that most American colonies had adopted the provisions of the Promissory Note Act of 1704, either by custom and usage or legislative reception, prior to 1776.[2] Absent any work on commercial law in colonial Virginia, we cannot be certain whether Virginia considered the Promissory Note Act to be in force in the province. It is clear, however, that the independent Commonwealth of Virginia, in May 1776, passed an ordinance which provided that no English statutes would apply in the State unless they had been enacted prior to the settlement of the colony in 1607.[3] Subsequently with the return of peace, a series of revisions or restatements of Virginia law

---

[1] A good historical survey of negotiable instruments law is in J. Holden, *The History of Negotiable Instruments in English Law* (London, 1955); see also H. Johnson, *The Law Merchant and Negotiable Instruments in Colonial New York 1664–1730* (Chicago, 1963), and F. Beutel, "Colonial Sources of the Negotiable Instruments Law in the United States," *Illinois Law Review* XXXIV (1939), 137–50.

[2] Johnson, *Law Merchant*, 35–36; *The Colonial Laws of New York from the Year 1664 to the Revolution*, 5 vols. (Albany, 1894), V, 544–45.

[3] Sec. 6, Ordinance of May 1776, 9 Hening 126, at 127.

were prepared under the mandate of the General Assembly, each representing an effort to bring into one collection all English statutes deemed useful in the State, all colonial statutes that could be recovered and which were deemed to be pertinent, and such new statutes as the revisors might suggest for the modernization and improvement of the law.[4]

Upon the completion of the revisal in 1792 most of the acts contained in the revisors' reports were enacted into law by the Virginia General Assembly. Then, in what appears to have been an attempt to avoid any future confusion, the legislature provided that no English statute not enacted into law by the Assembly, regardless of its effective date, should be applicable in Virginia.[5] Since the English Promissory Note Act of 1704 was not among the statutes included in the text of the revised laws, it ceased to have any application to Virginia notes of hand, if it ever had applied to early Virginia commercial transactions. During the period 1801 to 1815 promissory notes were not negotiable instruments in Virginia or in the county of Alexandria in the District of Columbia. They were negotiable instruments under the law of Maryland, which had received the 1704 English statute,[6] and consequently negotiable instruments under the law of the county of Washington in the District of Columbia.

In attempting to resolve this problem, the Court never diverged from its policy that the statutes and highest court decisions in Virginia determined the law in the western half of the District of Columbia. Recognizing that the Virginia remedy at law was cumbersome at best for the holders of promissory notes, Marshall in *Riddle & Co.* v. *Mandeville & Jameson*[7] suggested that recourse to equity was not in conflict with Virginia law, and it would permit the court of equity to declare the respective rights of the parties without a proliferation of actions at law. Somewhat earlier the Court had spelled out an implied promise in law by one who assigned a promissory note, which would by virtue of the assignment and the privity of contract between the parties make the assignor liable to the assignee for any loss the latter

---

[4] On the revisal of statutory law in early Virginia see J. Boyd, ed., *The Papers of Thomas Jefferson*, 18 vols. to date (Princeton, 1950–), II, 305–24; S. Foard, "Virginia Enters the Union, A Legislative Study of the Commonwealth, 1789–1792" (M.A. thesis, College of William and Mary, 1966), 163–75; C. Cullen, "Completing the Revisal of the Laws in Post-Revolutionary Virginia," *Virginia Magazine of History and Biography* LXXXII (1974), 84–99.

[5] Act of Dec. 27, 1792, 1 Sheppard 199–200.

[6] See Mandeville v. Union Bank of Georgetown, 9 Cranch 9–11, at 10 (1815); Lindo v. Gardner, 1 Cranch 343–45, at 343–44 (1803); and Morgan v. Reintzel, 7 Cranch 273–76, at 273 (1812).

[7] 5 Cranch 322–33 (1809). The use of a bill in equity against a remote indorser of a promissory note had been suggested in Harris v. Johnson, 3 Cranch 311–19, at 319 (1806).

might sustain through his acceptance of the assigned note.[8] The Court hastened to state that such an implied promise in law could not be assigned to any subsequent transferee, for it was grounded in privity between the parties to the assignment. In addition such liability on the part of the assignor might not attach in the case of a gratuitous endorsement without consideration.[9] The doctrine of implied promise in law to indemnify was therefore of limited value in protecting assignees of Virginia promissory notes.

Because of the harsh consequences of the Virginia law of negotiability, the Court also spelled out a legal doctrine founded upon the assignees' reliance upon the credit of the assignors, whether immediate or remote. This potentially broader ground upon which to impose liability on assignors of promissory notes was initially set forth in *Yeaton* v. *Bank of Alexandria*,[10] which held that a banking corporation's transfer of a promissory note by endorsement, even though done within the county of Alexandria, was to be judged in accordance with the specific customs and usages of the banking trade, rather than the general law and usage of Virginia. Banks traditionally treated promissory notes as if they were inland bills of exchange, and a bank's endorsement would imply undertakings to subsequent holders that were conformable to banking usage.

Following through on this general line of reasoning the Court, in passing, noted in *Riddle & Co.* v. *Mandeville & Jameson* that "[g]eneral opinion certainly attaches credit to a note, the maker of which is doubtful, in proportion to the credit of the indorsers."[11] While the assignor's undertaking to his immediate assignee might not be assignable under Virginia law, his pledge of credit might be transferable in equity, and consequently a remote assignee might prevail against him by means of a bill in equity. Unfortunately the full rationalization for these holdings is not apparent on the face of the opinions. Clearly there is an aspect of misrepresentation on the part of an individual or banking institution that endorses a purported negotiable instrument and does not reserve its rights by appending the restriction "without recourse," even though

---

[8] Mandeville & Jameson v. Riddle & Co., 1 Cranch 290–99, at 298 (1803).

[9] Violett v. Patton, 5 Cranch 142–54, at 150–51 (1809), dealt with the problem of the alleged indorser having signed a blank sheet of paper that was subsequently filled in as a promissory note, with his name as an indorser. In his discussion Chief Justice Marshall stated that it was customary for two parties to sign promissory notes, one as principal and one as security; however it was viewed as a contract binding upon the indorser (or co-maker?) because of the benefit flowing from the payee. Marshall also indicated that the signature by Violett had secured the extension of credit and hence the paper might be considered an open letter of credit.

[10] 5 Cranch 49–57 (1809).

[11] 5 Cranch 322, at 331 (1809). As to extensions of credit and actionable misrepresentations see Lawrason v. Mason, 3 Cranch 492–96 (1806).

the law of the place of assignment, or endorsement, does not allow recourse. Notes circulate freely, and in the peculiar circumstances of the District of Columbia it might be anticipated that remote parties would rely upon an endorsement. In addition, the failure of the assignor or endorser to qualify his endorsement by adding the place of endorsement would also be some evidence of misrepresentation. There is little attention given to the form of the assignment or endorsement; if it were in accordance with the requirements of Virginia law for the transfer of bonds, it would give notice of the restrictive nature of the assignor's liability, but if it were a simple signature in accordance with mercantile custom, it would have the potentiality of deceiving remote parties.

Banking law and possible misrepresentation served to create a further foundation for the imposition of certain characteristics of negotiability upon a Virginia note of hand. In *Mandeville* v. *Union Bank of Georgetown*[12] the maker had indicated that the instrument would be negotiable at the Union Bank of Georgetown which conducted business in Washington County. Upon presentation of the note the bank extended credit and took up the note from its holder, only to have the maker claim that he had certain credits against the payee which under Virginia law could be pleaded as offsets against the amount due under the terms of the note. By this time (1815) the Supreme Court had established the conflict of laws rule concerning negotiable instruments; in *Salcum* v. *Pomeroy*[13] it held that while the law of the place of execution governed the legal relationship of the parties and the legal consequences of execution, it was the law of the place of endorsement that determined the rights acquired by endorsement. Since the note in *Mandeville* had been presented in a jurisdiction covered by Maryland law, endorsement to the bank could have been held to cut off any defenses or offsets by the maker. That simple basis for decision troubled the Court, probably because it is difficult to justify an instrument that is not negotiable in its inception taking on attributes of negotiability depending upon the place of its endorsement or assignment. Consequently Chief Justice Marshall predicated his decision upon a broader ground. By indicating that the note was negotiable at the Washington County bank the maker had authorized the bank to extend credit upon its face; it would be inequitable to permit the maker to assert offsets when the note was returned for payment under these circumstances, and permitting a discount would permit the maker to perpetrate a fraud upon the bank which had extended credit upon its representations. Marshall specifically pointed out that it was not material where the note had been endorsed, or what law governed the transaction.[14] The essence of the opinion was that the action of the maker caused the bank to rely

---

[12] 9 Cranch 9–11 (1815).   [13] 6 Cranch 221–25 (1810).   [14] *Ibid.*, 10–11.

upon his representations, and that the maker could not invoke the aid of Virginia law to the detriment of those who relied upon those representations.

Coupled with *Yeaton* v. *Bank of Alexandria, Mandeville* v. *Union Bank of Georgetown* provided a basis upon which future transfers of Virginia promissory notes at banking institutions would be governed, not by Virginia law but by the customs of the mercantile community, which treated such instruments as inland bills of exchange. Since a substantial proportion of notes circulating in the District of Columbia would either have been made negotiable at a bank, or at some point have been endorsed by a banking institution, the scope of the doctrine may have been much broader in practice than in legal theory or application.

The Court was using equitable jurisdiction to afford relief from injustices based upon the Virginia law of promissory notes, and it also resorted to the customs of banking institutions to escape the applicability of Virginia law to the transfer of promissory notes. Inherent in this latter doctrine is the inference that the parties themselves determine the perquisites of the endorsement or assignment—that the legal consequences of the transaction are not those dictated by the legislature, but those fixed by the intention of the parties. State legislation, in this view, might be considered to be merely a secondary or provisional source of law to business custom, in civil law terms dispositive rather than mandatory law, which the contracting parties were free to accept or reject.

What the Court chose to do in these cases is perhaps not as revealing as what it chose not to do. Since commercial custom and usage was reasonably uniform not only in the United States but in other nations trading with the United States, the existence of an aberration such as the Virginia law of promissory notes tended to impede the flow of commerce and make uncertain several rights of contract. A more active and adventuresome Court might well have sought and found ample justification for invalidation of the Virginia law by reference to the commerce clause and the contract clause. The moderate course of the Supreme Court would suggest extreme sensitivity to the needs of the mercantile community, but at the same time a reluctance to interfere with the establishment of State law by the tribunals and legislatures of the various States.[15] In any event the June 24, 1812, Act of Congress, making Maryland negotiable instruments law applicable to Alexandria County,[16] finally ended the Supreme Court's struggle with the perversities of Virginia negotiable instruments law.

---

[15] The methodology has been termed "classical common law" decision making by R. Bridwell and R. Whitten, *The Constitution and the Common Law* (Lexington, Mass., 1977), XV, 11–13, 62–68.

[16] 2 Stat. 755–56, at 755 (1812).

The Supreme Court's search for uniformity in the negotiable instruments law of the District of Columbia may well be considered a modest prelude to its more sweeping work after 1842 in announcing a federal common law in diversity-of-citizenship cases. The landmark case, *Swift* v. *Tyson*, decided in that year, involved a bill of exchange and the availability of latent defects in the underlying transaction to defeat the claims of a holder in due course. In *Swift*, and subsequent decisions, the Court spelled out the existence of a federal common law in commercial cases, based upon the existence of a body of international mercantile custom. Recognizing the existence of this body of usages, the courts were charged with the duty of giving effect to the reasonable anticipations of the parties, who in turn contracted with the commercial customs as their guide. Furthermore, the Supreme Court and the lower federal courts were charged by the federal Constitution with the protection of non-resident merchants against conflicting or prejudicial local customs, or the provincial biases of State court judges or juries. Consequently after *Swift* v. *Tyson* it was accepted that the federal courts would not be bound to follow State law in situations where, in diversity cases, local law conflicted with the reasonable anticipations of the parties or the general custom of merchants.

While the District of Columbia negotiable instruments cases do not adopt this extreme view of federal court authority in commercial matters, nor are they examples of Supreme Court opinion in diversity-of-citizenship cases, these early District cases do suggest that the Court was willing to exercise ingenuity and resourcefulness in bringing about uniformity in the commercial law of a territory within the exclusive control of the federal government. They may thus be considered modest precursors of *Swift* v. *Tyson*, and important to the future development of federal law in this field.

Suretyship

The transfer of negotiable instruments and the conduct of trade in a more general sense depends upon the extension of credit to the individuals involved. Consequently problems of suretyship also arise before the Supreme Court as an important part of its development of the legal basis for commercial growth. A surety is one who becomes bound to insure the performance of another's promise. If his assurance runs to the party undertaking the obligation to perform, the surety is known as an indemnitor; if it runs to the party who receives the promise to perform, the surety is known as a guarantor.[17] In either event the English statute of frauds, which had been received by nearly every

---

[17] For a discussion of suretyship see L. Simpson, *Handbook of the Law of Suretyship* (St. Paul, Minn., 1950).

American jurisdiction,[18] required that the surety's obligation be evidenced by a writing. In addition to this formal requirement, the surety's undertaking was required to be an express and unequivocal acknowledgment that he intended to become bound to answer for the actions of another. Modern courts have hesitated to say that this requirement amounted to the application of the doctrine of *strictissimi juris* to the surety's contract,[19] but whether or not the doctrine applies, it is obvious that the surety benefits from a long judicial tradition of limiting his obligation to the precise terms of his written undertaking.

Chief Justice Marshall recognized the preferred position of the surety in commercial transactions: "The law will subject a man, having no interest in the transaction, to pay the debt of another, only when his undertaking manifests a clear intention to bind himself for that debt. Words of doubtful import ought not, it is conceived, to receive that construction."[20]

Noting that merchants were in the practice of recommending each other, without anticipating that such a courtesy would subject the sponsor to liability, Marshall duly noted the exception to that rule—that if the merchant sending the recommendation was in possession of knowledge that the party mentioned was a poor credit risk, the recommendation would be considered fraudulent. The merchant who recommended another was not required to have audited the books of his beneficiary before preparing his commendation; he was expected to rely upon the general reputation of the firm in preparing his comments.[21] Even an express promise of indemnity would not give rise to a suretyship undertaking if there was a slight variance between the firm name of the addressee and the actual name of the firm that acted in reliance upon the promise.[22]

At the very time when it was discouraging technicality in pleading commercial causes,[23] the Supreme Court elected in *Grant* v. *Naylor* to rely upon a narrow and restricted interpretation of a suretyship undertaking. The demand for specificity and precision seems to have developed out of the Court's feeling that illiberality in this regard was to be preferred for policy reasons. Marshall observed:

---

[18] The English statute of frauds is 29 Car. 2, chapter 3 (1677); that its reception had not been complete, see H. Johnson, "The Prerogative Court of New York, 1686–1776," *American Journal of Legal History* XVII (1973), 95, at 110–17. See also Simpson, *Suretyship*, 115–64.

[19] Simpson, *Suretyship*, 94–100.

[20] Russell v. Clark's Executors, 7 Cranch 69–99, at 90 (1812).

[21] Citing the English case of Haycraft v. Creasey, 2 East 92, 102 English Reports (Full Reprint) 303 (K. B., 1731), in 7 Cranch 69, 94.

[22] 4 Cranch 224–36 (1808).

[23] See for example Ferguson v. Harwood, 7 Cranch 408–15 (1813), and Sheehy v. Mandeville and Jameson, 7 Cranch 208–18 (1812).

Already have so many cases been taken out of the statute of frauds, which seem to be within its letter, that it may well be doubted whether the exceptions do not let in many of the mischiefs against which the rule was intended to guard. The best judges in England have been of opinion that this relaxing construction of the statute ought not to be extended further than it has already been carried, and this court entirely concurs in that opinion.[24]

Exclusion of parole evidence in suretyship relations of this nature would result in far greater precision in contracting; mistakes would be guarded against, and businessmen would be explicit in their undertakings. This, presumably, was the intention of the Supreme Court in its decision of *Grant* v. *Naylor*.

Unlike the precision required in surety contracts by the opinion in *Grant* v. *Naylor*, general commercial contracts were interpreted in accordance with the intention of the parties, and minor deviations from the terms of the agreement might be tolerated in the interest of substantial justice. The best example of this liberal rule can be found in *U.S.* v. *Gurney*,[25] a case that was based upon an agreement for the remittance of money to the Dutch bankers for the account of the United States government. The transfers were to be made on three specified dates, and a bond to secure the performance of the contract stipulated that if the transfers were not made in accordance with the agreement the obligor would forfeit twenty percent of the amount due, which would be payable in Philadelphia, as in the case of a protested bill of exchange. Although the first and third remittances were timely, the second payment was tendered and received seventy-four days after it was due. The government claimed the twenty-percent penalty under the interpretation it placed upon the conditions of the bond.

"Contracts are always to be construed with a view to the real intention of the parties,"[26] stated Chief Justice Marshall in explaining the Court's decision in the Gurney case. The agreement was for the remittance of money to Amsterdam; the obligor had indeed made the three transfers contemplated by the contract, but the second installment was late. When that installment was tendered the United States had the option of rejecting it and demanding payment in Philadelphia in accordance with the provisions of the bond, or of accepting payment in Amsterdam. Had the government chosen the first alternative, it might properly have claimed the twenty-percent penalty. The stipulation concerning protested bills of exchange, and the fact that Pennsylvania law provided for a twenty-percent penalty in such cases, gave added weight

---

[24] 4 Cranch 235 (1808).
[25] 4 Cranch 333–46 (1808).
[26] *Ibid.*, 343. For a similar pronouncement see Cooke v. Graham's Administrator, 3 Cranch 229–35, at 234 (1805).

to this interpretation of the contract. Since the United States government had accepted late payment of the second installment in Amsterdam, it was not entitled to the penalty as liquidated damages, although it could justly claim interest from the date the installment was due until the time of its actual payment.[27]

Where bonds were to be construed in conjunction with underlying articles of agreement, they were normally subject to judicial correction if it could be shown that the bonds departed from the agreement.[28] However, the departure had to be demonstrated with clarity before a court of equity would interfere with the legal rights acquired under the bond. Thus, while bonds executed to insure the performance of agreements were subject to equitable defenses based upon mistake or departure from the agreement, clear evidence of extrinsic circumstances was required before the Supreme Court would authorize the interposition of equity to alter the "legal rights acquired under a solemn contract."[29]

Although the general rule was to construe contracts in accordance with the intentions of the parties, there were situations in which the innocent mistake of one party rendered the contract impossible of performance. Such a circumstance arose in a sales contract for Kentucky lands which contained an incorrect description of the location of the lands owned by the would-be grantor.[30] Pointing out that the seller's undertaking was to convey lands described in the agreement, and that his lack of ownership in the described lands rendered his performance impossible, the majority of the Supreme Court were of the opinion that the only remedy available to the purchaser was an award of damages for breach of the contract to convey.[31] Chief Justice Marshall delivered the opinion of the Court, as he had been "directed" to do, but dissented from the decree on the ground that the purchaser had not relied on the particular location of the land and had not claimed damages in his bill in equity.[32] He had asked, and the Kentucky District Court had awarded him a decree on that basis, that he be given the choice of the seller's lands of equal value at some other location. John Breckinridge on behalf of the purchaser argued that it was improper for a court to make an agreement for the parties, and that damages were the proper decree in this case; yet Marshall, perhaps because of

---

[27] A similar case of substantial compliance with the terms of the contract was presented in Blakeney v. Evans, 2 Cranch 185–86 (1804), where an agreement to provide labor and materials was held performed even though the contracting party did not perform it personally.

[28] Finley v. Lynn, 6 Cranch 238–52 (1810).

[29] *Ibid.*, 250.

[30] M'Ferran v. Taylor and Massie, 3 Cranch 270–82 (1806). See also Skillern's Executors v. May's Executors, 4 Cranch 137–41 (1807).

[31] 3 Cranch 270, at 282 (1806).

[32] *Ibid.*, 282.

his personal knowledge of the difficulties of locating lands in Kentucky and the lack of clarity in descriptions and conveyances, was willing to create an alternative agreement that would give the purchaser his choice of the seller's Kentucky lands and damages for any loss due to their inferior quality.

The majority opinion in *U.S.* v. *Gurney* and the opinion in *M'Ferran* seem to indicate a degree of liberality upon the part of the Chief Justice in construing contracts. Carried to an extreme this doctrine could easily have undermined the voluntary and consensual basis for contractual agreements. Yet in the two cases the Chief Justice may have had ample basis to believe that the parties claiming a breach of contract were in effect overreaching themselves and taking undue advantage of either an innocent mistake in the case of *M'Ferran* v. *Taylor and Massie*, or an inconsequential breach in the timeliness of performance in *U.S.* v. *Grundy*. Viewed in the light of Marshall's other pronouncements and the positions of the other justices, it would seem that these two cases should be limited to the facts presented in each. They represent an island of precedent rather than the mainstream of judicial support for strict enforcement of contractual agreements.

Ambiguities in contracts might be resolved by reference to local law and custom. For example, in *Pratt* v. *Law and Campbell*[33] land had been sold by dimensions, the purchaser to select from the seller's holdings those specific squares he wished to acquire within the city of Washington. The question arose whether alleys contained within the squares were to be included within the total amount of realty conveyed. The Supreme Court noted that it was customary for the purchaser of all lots in a square to take a fee simple in the alleys located in that square, but conversely, if one or more lots were not to be conveyed to him, he did not take a fee simple in the alleys but rather he held title as a tenant in common with the other landowners. As a result, the purchaser in *Pratt* was charged with the alley lands of squares only when his purchase included all lots in the square.

Enforceability of Contracts

Illegality in the consideration of a contract might render it unenforceable in the courts of the United States. This principle was enunciated by the Court in *Hannay* v. *Eve*.[34] In 1782 the captain and crew of a British armed cargo vessel, unable to reach her destination, New York, because of tempestuous weather and facing the risk of capture by American patrols, entered into an agreement to stage a mock mutiny and put into port in North Carolina. As the captain explained to the

---

[33] 9 Cranch 456–501 (1815).   [34] 3 Cranch 242–49 (1806).

crew, American legislation of 1781, to encourage mutiny and the sur-render of enemy ships, provided that the proceeds of condemnation of vessel and cargo as prize would become the property of the crew. It was agreed, however, that a portion of the proceeds would be held by the captain for the benefit of the ship's owners. The plan was carried out, the vessel was condemned, and distribution was made, but the captain declined to account to the owners for their agreed share. This suit against the captain followed, brought by the assignee of the owners to obtain the benefit of the agreement and enforce the duty owed by a captain to the owner of a vessel.

Chief Justice Marshall was fully sensitive to the moral ambiguities of the controversy. From the owner's point of view, the act of Congress was an immoral inducement to breach of fiduciary duty, and the agree-ment of captain and crew was a laudable stratagem to honor that duty. The defendant's repudiation of the agreement was an act of dishonor in morals and law. From the defendant's standpoint, the agreement was in fraud of American law and of the prize court, and the owners were ratifying the fraud in seeking the aid of the courts to benefit from it.

Marshall indicated the discomfort felt by the Court in reaching a decision:

> The essential difficulty in this cause arises from the consideration, that under the resolution of Congress, by which the vessel and cargo men-tioned in the proceedings were condemned, a sanction is claimed to a breach of trust, and a violation of moral principle. In such a case, the mind submits reluctantly to the rule of law, and laboriously searches for something which shall reconcile that rule with what would seem to be the dictate of abstract justice.[35]

In the end, however, the "rule of law" prevailed, and the Court affirmed a dismissal of the suit, leaving the parties where it found them. Even though the act of Congress was itself difficult to reconcile with "abstract justice," it was justifiable as a wartime measure, and a fraud on it would not knowingly be abetted by the courts.

Certain procedural rules aided the courts in rendering judgment upon bonds, and in insuring that no unfair dealing had taken place between the parties. When the holder of a bond based his action upon the breach of conditions contained in the bond, he was required to plead those conditions in his declaration. Additionally bond and promissory notes were subject to oyer, or a reading into the record in open court, thereby making the instrument a part of the trial record. Unless adequate excuse could be tendered for its absence, a bond or

---

[35] *Ibid.*, 247.

note would have to be brought to court and tendered as evidence in support of the action.[36] These procedural technicalities were designed to protect the maker of a bond or negotiable instrument against double liability incurred through its assignment or endorsement to a bona fide purchaser prior to the commencement of the action.

Similarly in regard to promissory notes under Virginia substantive law, the Supreme Court held that to sustain an action against an endorser the holder would normally have to enter judgment previously against the maker. However, in a situation in which the endorsed note had been accepted in payment for goods sold, failure to recover judgment against the maker of the note would not bar an action on the contract for goods sold and delivered. On the other hand, if a party to a sales contract received a promissory note in payment, he might not recover on the contract if he had transferred the note to a third party. To permit recovery under these circumstances might subject the purchaser-maker to double liability, once to the seller and once to an endorsee of the seller.[37] When the security for payment of an account was in the form of a bond, the Court required that the holder of the bond take his recovery through an action of covenant upon the bond— a security under seal was deemed to "subsume" the underlying transaction or agreement.[38] In either event, recovery upon a note or a bond would bar a subsequent action upon the underlying account or agreement.[39] These cases indicate the Supreme Court's willingness to apply Virginia law when its principles gave results conformable to the mercantile law of negotiability.

Sales Contracts

As we have noted concerning prize cases,[40] the law of sales was applied by the Court to determine the nationality of property at the time it was seized on the high seas. A group of cases arising from the seizure of the ship *Frances* and her cargo sets forth in detail some of the salient features of sales law in transatlantic trade. In the claim of James Thompson[41] the Supreme Court held that when the shipper authorized the consignee to exercise an option whether to treat the

---

[36] Hepburn & Dundas v. Auld, 1 Cranch 321–32 (1803); United States v. Arthur, 5 Cranch 257–61 (1809). In Virginia a bond with a collateral condition was not assignable. Lewis v. Harwood, 6 Cranch 82–86 (1810).

[37] Clark v. Young & Co., 1 Cranch 181–94 (1803); Harris v. Johnston, 3 Cranch 311–19 (1806). The mere possession of a note assigned to an-

other was not in itself proof of ownership. Welch v. Lindo, 7 Cranch 159–64 (1812).

[38] Young v. Preston, 4 Cranch 239–41 (1808).

[39] Sheehy v. Mandeville and Jameson, 6 Cranch 253–67 (1810).

[40] See Part II, chapter 2, pp. 449–50.

[41] 8 Cranch 335–48 (1814).

goods as his own or to sell them on the shipper's account, the title to the goods remained in the shipper until the option had been exercised. Thus seizure before the goods arrived in the United States would subject them to condemnation as British property. Similarly, in the claim of Dunham and Randolph,[42] the dispatch of goods in quantities and under conditions at variance with the American correspondent's instructions, and with the condition subsequent that the consignee could accept or reject them within twenty-four hours of their arrival, was held to result in title remaining in the British shipper when the goods were seized at sea. In French's claim,[43] the Supreme Court indicated that a contract must be shown to have subsisted between the consignor and consignee, and the shipment had to be made upon the account and risk of the consignee for title to pass upon shipment.

This line of cases makes it clear that transfer of title in sales of personal property was based upon two prerequisites: (1) a valid contract for the sale, coupled with (2) an adequate delivery, either to the purchaser or to an agent (in these cases ship captain) on his behalf.[44] Unless both conditions could be shown to exist, title remained in the shipper as did the risk of capture or loss at sea.[45]

These rules concerning sales of goods are in accord with the principles established by the Court to determine the legal adequacy of performance in the case of unilateral contracts. In those instances the contractual undertaking was satisfied only when the last step was taken to perform in accordance with the agreement. *Douglas and Mandeville v. M'Allister*[46] involved a warehousing contract that provided for the re-delivery of flour. A request for delivery followed by negotiations concerning price did not constitute a breach of contract until there had been an actual denial of the demand for re-delivery. When documents were to be tendered under the terms of a contract, it was not an adequate tender if made conditionally.[47] Although the cases in this field are too few to delineate a pattern of decision, it is clear that in conjunction with the claims in regard to the cargo of the *Frances*, they represent a conscientious effort upon the part of the Supreme Court to resolve sensitive international commercial issues conformably to principles of law developed in more normal settings.

---

[42] 8 Cranch 354–58 (1814).

[43] 8 Cranch 359–63 (1814).

[44] The Venus, 8 Cranch 253–317, at 275 (1814) is the best statement of this rule.

[45] While a chattel mortgage of personalty would not be defeated by continued possession of the mortgagor, the continued possession of a chattel by the vendor after an absolute sale was considered a fraud against creditors in spite of the fact that the sale was recorded. Hamilton v. Russell, 1 Cranch 309–18 (1803).

[46] 3 Cranch 298–300 (1806).

[47] Hepburn & Dundas v. Auld, 1 Cranch 321–32 (1803).

Public Policy and Contract Terms

The tension between the concern for commercial certainty and fair dealing and congressional mandates in the troubled area of foreign affairs could reach the breaking point, as it did in *The Mars*,[48] decided by a sharply divided Court. *The Mars* left the United States in violation of the Non-Intercourse Act of 1809, which provided that whenever a person should "load on board a ship . . . any specie, goods, wares or merchandise, with intent to export . . . the same without the United States . . . all such . . . goods . . . and also the ship . . . shall be forfeited."[49] *The Mars* was seized upon her return to the United States after having been sold to a bona fide purchaser for value. The Supreme Court upheld the forfeiture against the purchaser's claim, asserting through the opinion of Judge William Johnson that the statute was unambiguous and required the condemnation of the ship and her cargo. That the decision was harsh, Johnson freely admitted, but

> [i]n the eternal struggle that exists between the avarice, enterprise and combinations of individuals on one hand, and the powers charged with the administration of the laws on the other, severe laws are rendered necessary to enable the executive to carry into effect the measures of policy adopted by the legislature. To them belongs the right to decide on what event a divestiture of right shall take place, whether on the commission of the offense, the seizure, or the condemnation.[50]

It was clear to the majority of the Court that the forfeiture took place at the time the vessel left the United States, and consequently the formal transfer of title to the government upon seizure related back to that time. The bona fide purchaser for value of the vessel was precluded from asserting a property interest.

Judge Story, who had written the opinion in the Massachusetts Circuit Court, dissented by filing his opinion below, and two unidentified judges in the Supreme Court concurred with him in his dissent from the majority, Chief Justice Marshall being absent. As Story viewed the *Mars* cases, they raised the most delicate policy issues. On the one hand a decision for the claimants would strike "at the root of almost all the forfeitures in rem which the legislature has provided to guard the revenue laws from abuse,"[51] but on the other hand

---

[48] United States v. Brigantine Mars, 8 Cranch 417–18 (1814); United States v. 1960 Bags of Coffee, 8 Cranch 398–416 (1814). The two cases were argued jointly and the reasoned opinion of the Court was reported under the latter title.

[49] 2 Stat. 506 (1809).

[50] 8 Cranch 398, at 405 (1814).

[51] *Ibid.*, 406.

if the secret taint of forfeiture be indissolubly attached to the property, so that at any time and under any circumstances within the limitations of law, the United States may inforce their right against innocent purchasers, it is easy to foresee that great embarrassments will arise to the commercial interests of the country; and no man, whatever may be his caution or diligence, can guard himself from injury and perhaps ruin.[52]

Resorting to the common law of forfeitures, which he held applicable to the provisions of the Non-Intercourse Act of 1809, Story demonstrated that in all cases of forfeiture for personal offenses, title did not pass to the English crown until there had been seizure and prosecution, or an inquest of office found. Carefully distinguishing certain English precedents that might be authority for a contrary position, Story maintained that no absolute title had vested in the United States until the actual seizure was made. It was improper to use the doctrine of relation[53] to consider the time of the offense, and in any event, it was a long established rule of construction that the doctrine of relation should not be utilized when its effect would be to injure an innocent party or destroy a lawful vested interest.

Looking to the vast extent of commercial transfers the favor with which navigation and trade are fostered in modern times, and the extreme difficulty of ascertaining latent defects in title, it seems difficult to resist the impression that the present is a case which requires the application of the milder view of the law.[54]

The decision concerning the *Mars* demonstrates at once the fidelity with which the Supreme Court supported the legislative and executive branches in the administration of the Non-Intercourse and Embargo laws, and the degree to which that policy might clash with an evolving jurisprudence in the field of business and commercial transactions which required certainty in contract and openness in dealing.

BUSINESS ORGANIZATIONS AND VESTED RIGHTS

Modes of organizing business activity had begun to change in the early years of John Marshall's Chief Justiceship, but the corporate form had not been utilized to any considerable degree except in the fields of banking and insurance underwriting. Joint ventures remained the preferred organization for land speculations, and partnerships served

---

[52] *Ibid.*
[53] As to the doctrine of relation

concerning deeds see Wood v. Owings & Smith, 1 Cranch 239–52 (1803).
[54] 8 Cranch 398, at 416 (1814).

the mercantile world as they had for centuries before.[55] From 1801 to 1815 there was a gradual development of Supreme Court case law concerning partnerships, based upon the Supreme Court's appellate jurisdiction over the federal judicial system. For example, in *Harrison* v. *Sterry*[56] and *Clark's Executors* v. *Van Riemsdyk*,[57] the Court was confronted with the problems of a partner's authority to bind his firm in ordinary transactions, and the firm's ratification of a partner's acts by its failure to repudiate them when an opportunity arose to do so.

The most revealing discussion of the nature of corporations occurs in *Korn & Wisemiller* v. *Mutual Assurance Society*,[58] which involved the relationship of the shareholders-subscribers of a mutual fire insurance company to the corporation. The defendant-shareholders, who resided in the city of Alexandria, refused to pay the assessment made by the Virginia corporation, contending that the cession of the county of Alexandria had suspended their insurance coverage, and therefore cancelled their obligation to pay assessments. They further contended that the new mode of assessing and evaluating properties, instituted by a corporate charter amendment in 1804, was prejudicial to their interests and freed them from their contract to pay assessments. These claims to exemption were denied by the Supreme Court, which pointed out that a change of political authority, although it might alter the mode of contracting thereafter, could not alter valid, pre-existing private contracts. As far as the change of the assessment method was concerned, the Court observed, "Every member, in fact, stands in the peculiar situation of being partly both sides, insurer and insured."[59] Those who had joined in the formation of the Mutual Assurance Society were bound to abide by its rules and regulations until such time as they might withdraw from participation by the methods prescribed in the charter. The relationship between shareholder-subscriber and the Society was not necessarily based upon benefits accruing to the individual or the corporation; hence a subscriber might be expected to pay his assessment even if his insurance had lapsed. The pooling of funds and the collegiality of obligations ran not only to the corporation but to fellow shareholders.

This tells us much about the Marshall Court's view of corporations in particular, and other forms of joint venture in general. Indeed the then current judicial view of corporations may be seen in the

---

[55] J. Hurst, *The Legitimacy of the Business Corporation in the Laws of the United States, 1780–1970* (Charlottesville, 1970), 13–19.

[56] 5 Cranch 289–302 (1809).

[57] 9 Cranch 153–64 (1815). In Hall v. Leigh, 8 Cranch 50–52 (1814), the

Court declined to treat a relationship as a joint venture when separate instructions were received and executed in regard to a shipment of goods.

[58] 6 Cranch 192–202 (1810).

[59] *Ibid.*, 201.

Mutual Assurance Society case—did not all corporations rest as much upon the contractual undertakings of shareholders as upon their corporate charters from the legislature? Did not the separate shareholders serve as sureties for the obligations of the corporation, and were they not bound for its actions undertaken in the normal course of business? Similarly, could not the officers of the corporation be viewed, as the Court did in *Van Ness* v. *Forrest*,[60] as trustees for the corporation, and in turn for its shareholders? Corporate activity was therefore based partly upon a legislative charter or grant, partly upon contractual privity between the shareholders themselves and among them and the corporation, and finally upon fiduciary ties between shareholders, corporation, and officers of the corporation. Although the corporation might trace its origin to the charter, its functions and legal status were defined by a multifaceted and complex series of relationships among the individuals who served as its shareholders, directors, and officers.

The status of corporations also arose in procedural cases involving citizenship for purposes of diversity jurisdiction in the federal courts. While full treatment can be postponed until chapter 8, it will be helpful at this point to examine briefly the substantive aspects of *Bank of the U.S.* v. *Deveaux*.[61] A Georgia statute imposed a tax upon the Georgia branch of the Bank, and upon the refusal of the Bank officials to pay the assessment, cash belonging to the Bank had been seized. The Bank brought action in the federal circuit court, and the Georgia officials pleaded in bar that the court did not have jurisdiction. Being a body corporate and politic, the Bank, they contended, could neither sue nor be sued in the federal courts, for it was not a citizen within the terms of the Judiciary Act.[62] To this plea the Bank of the U.S. demurred, and on the joinder in demurrer judgment was given for the defendants. From that judgment an appeal was taken to the Supreme Court, where Chief Justice Marshall delivered the majority opinion.

Marshall conceded at the outset that a corporation as a mere legal entity could neither sue nor be sued, unless the rights of its members might be exercised in their corporate name. The general understanding previously appeared to be that it was possible for corporations to litigate in federal courts, and while no specific decision had been made on the point, a number of previous cases supported that position. Under English law it was not uncommon that corporations might be treated as residents of cities for certain purposes, and in *Mayor of London* v. *Wood*[63] the judges had held that the courts might look

---

[60] 8 Cranch 30–35 (1814).
[61] 5 Cranch 61–92 (1809).
[62] The jurisdictional statute is sec.

11, Act of Sept. 24, 1789, I Stat. 73, at 78, 79.
[63] 12 Modern 669–89, 88 Eng. Rep. 1592–1603 (K.B., 1702).

beyond the corporation to seek the identity of the individuals composing it. Upon that basis the federal courts might, while considering a challenge to their jurisdiction, look beyond the corporation to seek the identity of the individual corporate members. Here the controversy was "substantially between aliens, suing by a corporate name, and a citizen [of Georgia], or between citizens of one state suing by a corporate name, and those of another state."[64] Counsel for the Georgia officials in the instant case had employed a "course of acute, metaphysical and abstruse reasoning,"[65] Marshall observed, in raising this hitherto unknown objection to federal diversity jurisdiction.

Although the Deveaux case finds its primary importance in the field of federal jurisdiction, it nevertheless demonstrates the Supreme Court's use of "residence" cases from English law to reason by analogy to "citizenship" cases based upon diversity-of-state-citizenship in the federal union. The implication might be that citizenship in a State was similar to, or perhaps even identical with, the concepts of residence or domicile in English jurisprudence. Were the analogy pressed further in subsequent cases, as unfortunately it was not, the result might have been recognition of a federal citizenship based upon formal acceptance into the body politic by birth or naturalization, coupled with a State "citizenship" founded upon acquisition of domicile either by birth, free choice, or presumption of law in the case of persons under disabilities. Viewed in this light the *Deveaux* opinion may represent an otherwise unarticulated view of citizenship in the federal union, one that would be not incompatible with the Marshallian concept of the federal Union, but at the same time, a position that was far from widespread in the antebellum Republic.

An examination of the new corporate forms and other modes of business organization drew the Court into the examination of vested property rights and their protection against growing legislative incursions at both State and federal levels. The cases that were most significant in developing the doctrine of vested rights were rather remote from

---

[64] 5 Cranch 61, at 91. Marshall's opinion proceeds upon the basis of efficacy and loose constitutional construction. "A constitution, from its nature, deals in generals, not in details. Its framers cannot perceive minute distinctions which arise in the progress of the nation, and therefore confine it to the establishment of broad and general principles." *Ibid.*, 87. The underlying reason for federal tribunals was to make impartial justice available in certain actions, among them cases between citizens of differing States. Hence actions by corporations falling within that category are within the spirit of the Constitutional mandate. *Ibid.*

[65] *Ibid.*, 88. Marshall conceded that this type of reasoning had been "ably employed," but nevertheless rejected the argument.

the normal flow of commercial activity. In constitutional impact none was more important than *Fletcher* v. *Peck*,[66] which resolved the famous Yazoo land controversy. While *Fletcher* did not involve a corporation it was concerned with a joint venture that had acquired title to lands under a subsequently repealed legislative land grant. Two other cases, *Terrett* v. *Taylor*[67] and *Town of Pawlet* v. *Clarke*,[68] involved title to glebe lands under colonial grants from Virginia and New Hampshire. Corporate forms as such were not at issue, but the cases dealt with land granted to localities to serve a mutually beneficial purpose in the respective towns and parishes.

The background of legislative corruption and speculative land fever that gave rise to *Fletcher* v. *Peck* has been recounted in Part I.[69] Its place in the evolution of the principle of vested property rights is what must attract our consideration at this point. As Chief Justice Marshall viewed the attempted repeal of the Yazoo land grants, the action by the reformed legislature of Georgia violated "certain great principles of justice, whose authority is universally acknowledged."[70] Although the titles granted to the original speculators who were directly involved in the bribery might be subject to rescission by judicial decree, it was apparent to him that strong policy considerations precluded the same challenge to the title held by bona fide purchasers for value as the pleadings acknowledged the plaintiffs to be. "Titles which, according to every legal test, are perfect, are acquired with that confidence which is inspired by the opinion that the purchaser is safe."[71] He concluded, "All titles would be insecure, and the intercourse between man and man would be very seriously obstructed,"[72] if the pretensions of Georgia were allowed. Although the peculiar circumstances of the Yazoo grants were unlikely to recur, Marshall was unwilling to endorse the hazardous constitutional principle underlying the repealing statute, "that a legislature may, by its own act, devest the vested estate of any man whatever, for reasons which shall, by itself, be deemed sufficient."[73] Marshall strongly suggested that the nature of society and government required some limitations upon legislative power, but where could those limitations be found if the property of an individual citizen, honestly acquired, might be taken without compensation?

After evaluating the repealing act in terms of Anglo-American

---

[66] 6 Cranch 87–148 (1810).

[67] 9 Cranch 43–55 (1815).

[68] 9 Cranch 292–338 (1815).

[69] See Part I, chapter 10, pp. 336–45. See also C. Haskins, "The Yazoo Land Companies," in American Historical Association *Papers*, V, Part IV, 393–437 (1891); C. McGrath, *Yazoo: Law and Politics in the New Republic* (Providence, 1966).

[70] 6 Cranch 87, at 133 (1810).

[71] *Ibid.*, 133–34.

[72] *Ibid.*

[73] *Ibid.*, 134.

concepts of property and constitutional government, the Chief Justice proceeded to show that a land grant was a form of contract, and a contract in turn was protected against State action by the federal Constitution. The framers of the Constitution and the people who ratified it "in adopting that instrument, have manifested a determination to shield themselves and their property from the affects of those sudden and strong passions to which men are exposed."[74] The repealing clause was repugnant to the contract clause, and it was also in the nature of an ex post facto law since it worked a forfeiture of Fletcher's estate for a crime committed not by him, but by a remote predecessor in title.

Vested rights theory continued to limit State legislative initiative in the five years following *Fletcher* v. *Peck*. Judge Story's opinions in *Terrett* v. *Taylor* and *Town of Pawlet* v. *Clarke* involved colonial land grants that had been nullified by subsequent State statutes. In *Terrett* the overseers of the poor in the county of Alexandria of the District of Columbia sought to sell glebe lands possessed as part of a church's endowment that had been bestowed upon the Alexandria parish of the then Church of England. Prior to the Revolution the glebe lands had been enjoyed by the parish and the profits from the land had been used for the support of the parsons and for various charitable purposes. In 1784 the parishes of the Episcopal Church were incorporated under a Virginia State statute, but the incorporation was revoked in 1786, at which time parishes were authorized to appoint trustees to administer their property. As Judge Story approached the various questions presented on appeal, the initial issue was whether the Virginia legislature might, on its own action, cancel a charter granted by a previous General Assembly. He indicated that at English common law the proper procedure for the revocation of a corporate charter was by means of a judicial proceeding in *quo warranto*. Legislative revocation of the charter was quite another, and novel, procedure. Not pausing to resolve that issue, Story pointed out that even if the charter might be revoked by legislative action, it was questionable whether the parish might be divested of title to the glebe lands. Such a doctrine would uproot almost every land title in Virginia, and be "utterly inconsistent with a great and fundamental principle of a republican government, the right of the citizens to the free enjoyment of their property legally acquired."[75] The congregation had taken title to the glebe lands, and acquired a vested interest therein "that the legislature can repeal statutes creating private corporations or confirming to them property already acquired by them under the faith of previous laws, . . . without the consent or default of the corporators, we are not prepared to admit."[76] Invoking principles

---

[74] *Ibid.*, 138. [75] 9 Cranch 43, at 50–51 (1815). [76] *Ibid.*, 52.

of natural justice, the "fundamental laws of every free government," the spirit and letter of the federal Constitution and the case law in "respectable judicial tribunals,"[77] Story held the Virginia legislation's giving glebe lands to the overseers of the poor to be totally invalid.

A contrasting set of facts awaited the Court in *Town of Pawlet* v. *Clarke*, where no Anglican congregation had been legally established in the colonial period, and no benefit had been derived from the royal grant of glebe lands contained in the 1761 town charter of Pawlet. Only after independence did a small group of Episcopalians gather together for the conduct of services, and thereby attempt to establish a claim to the glebe lands. After a detailed discussion of the mode of erecting parishes in the Church of England, Judge Story held that a mere voluntary association of Anglicans did not constitute a parish. Before they acquired rights to a glebe, they would have to be legally recognized and established as a parish, and the title to the parcel would then vest in the parson, to be "inherited" by his successor in office. Because no parish establishment had occurred under the royal government, title to the land remained in abeyance, and hence the Crown before 1776 or its successor, the State of Vermont, might with the consent of the town of Pawlet dispose of the title to the glebe lands. This the State of Vermont had done in 1794 by its statute that vested title in the town of Pawlet.

Although Judge Story refrained in the majority opinion[78] from holding that the town of Pawlet had taken title in 1761 subject to a trust for the church, Johnson in his concurring opinion[79] was clear in asserting that title had passed immediately to the town upon the execution of the royal grant. The application of the trust was subject to the will of the whole population of the town, and until there was a legally constituted Anglican congregation in Pawlet, nothing prevented the legislature from making an appropriation of the property. While Johnson's opinion avoided what he considered the overly elaborate discussion of ecclesiastical law in Story's opinion, the position taken by Johnson serves to cloud the issue of vesting. If in fact legal title had passed to the town in 1761 there was no need for a legislative act in 1794 to accomplish the same purpose. It should of course be noted that while Judge Story claimed that no interest passed to the town or a church in 1761, he nevertheless conditioned the validity of Crown or State re-grants of the same land upon the concurrence of the town of Pawlet. Consequently it would seem that he recognized some inchoate equitable right in the town of Pawlet, even though he was not willing to concede that it held legal title, as a trustee or otherwise.

---

[77] *Ibid.*   [78] 9 Cranch 292, at 322–37 (1815).   [79] *Ibid.*, 337–38.

The emergence of a doctrine of vested property rights has long been recognized by students of American constitutional history, but the intimate relationship between this development and the Supreme Court's work in the fields of commercial law and business transactions has been largely overlooked. For the effective conduct of business and trade, contractual relationships had to be rendered more precise. Principles of privity of contract had to be refined. The extension of credit was to be bolstered by the development of legal liability for misrepresentation, quite distinct from the traditional undertakings of sureties. Security of title, based in part upon vested property rights, was but another legal foundation for the economic and commercial growth of the United States.

THE BANKRUPTCY ACT OF 1800 AND STATE INSOLVENCY ACTS

English common law had traditionally dealt harshly with those who failed to satisfy judgments outstanding against them. Should the sheriff fail to seize property in sufficient quantity to satisfy the judgment debtor's obligation, it was possible for the creditor to move to the more rigorous sanction of imprisonment for debt,[80] leaving his debtor languishing in the local jail until such time as his obligation under the judgment was fulfilled. Although imprisonment for debt was not as common in America as it had been in England, it nevertheless became a problem in the colonial period, and hapless debtors were gradually extended the privilege of being released from prisons through the operation of colonial insolvency laws.[81] These acts, which were for the most part continued after independence, provided for the transfer of the debtor's assets to a trustee, whereupon the prisoner would be discharged from confinement upon a court order and allowed to leave the jail for the healthier imprisonment of remaining within the "jail liberties," usually the boundaries of the town in which the jail was located. The former prisoner's property was, of course, held for the benefit of his creditors. Insolvency acts provided but limited relief to the wealthier merchants and entrepreneurs whose trade crossed provincial boundaries. Discharge under the insolvency acts of one colony

---

[80] J. Goebel, Jr., ed. *The Law Practice of Alexander Hamilton*, 2 vols. to date (New York, 1964–), I, 96–99.

[81] P. Coleman, *Debtors and Creditors: Insolvency, Imprisonment for Debt, and Bankruptcy, 1606–1900* (Madison, 1974); E. Ryan, "Imprisonment for Debt: Its Origins and Repeal," *Virginia Magazine of History and Biography* XLII (1934), 53–58.

did not serve as a discharge in other colonies, and this situation persisted into the nineteenth century.[82]

In construing State insolvency acts the Supreme Court tended to adopt a liberal view designed to advance the beneficent intention of the legislature. The intent of the States in enacting insolvency laws was to provide for the release of the imprisoned debtor and the preservation of his health; it was not intended to provide additional security for the payment of the judgment debt.[83] Trustees of an insolvent debtor were not to be allowed to meddle with his intangible property unless specifically authorized to do so.[84] Trustees in insolvency took title by an assignment in law, and if their insolvent could not have brought action on diversity grounds in the federal courts, they were precluded from doing so regardless of their residence.[85] Certain equitable considerations entered into the Supreme Court's opinions in insolvency cases. For example, where the mortgage of realty was challenged as a fraud against other creditors, the Supreme Court considered compliance with the recording acts as strong evidence of open dealing that could not prejudice unsecured creditors. A clear distinction was made between a bona fide conveyance or mortgage, and one made to avoid the operation of the insolvency laws.[86]

Interstate and foreign trade rendered a system of nationwide bankruptcy a necessary complement to State insolvency laws, and provision for a uniform law of bankruptcy had been made in the federal Constitution. Discharge in a federal bankruptcy proceeding would remove the threat of prosecution by creditors throughout the United

---

[82] The New York Moot discussed this question in 1770 and rendered an opinion that out-of-colony creditors were precluded from suing the insolvent in their jurisdictions only if they had personally appeared in the insolvency proceeding in his colony of residence. See H. Johnson, "John Jay: Colonial Lawyer" (Ph.D. diss., Columbia University, 1965), 179–81. In Reily v. Lamar, Beall and Smith, 2 Cranch 344–57 (1804), the Supreme Court held that in regard to the cession of the District of Columbia, a Maryland resident of the District might not take advantage of Maryland insolvency laws after the transfer of jurisdiction; insolvency laws were to benefit residents of the enacting State, and when the purported insolvent became a resident of the District of Columbia he lost the benefit of those provisions. Of course in most other respects Maryland law continued to apply in the ·County of Washington where the insolvent resided.

[83] Simms and Wise v. Slacum, 3 Cranch 300–11 (1806). Fraud in obtaining the discharge would not vitiate the order of discharge from prison. On the other hand if the discharging magistrate participated in the fraud or was himself interested in the insolvent's estate, the discharge would be void.

[84] Turner v. Fendall, 1 Cranch 117–37 (1801).

[85] Sere and Laralde v. Pitot, 6 Cranch 332–38 (1810).

[86] United States v. Hooe, 3 Cranch 73–92 (1805); Bank of Alexandria v. Herbert, 8 Cranch 36–39 (1814).

States; at the same time the retention of State insolvency laws, to the extent they were not repugnant to federal legislation, would permit cheaper and more expeditious relief to financially distressed individuals who had creditors in only one State. Despite the apparent need for a federal bankruptcy statute, the first act dealing with the problem was not enacted by Congress until April 1800. Repealed in December 1803, it made its impression upon the case law of the United States Supreme Court.[87]

The 1800 Federal Bankruptcy Act provided that certain acts involving the concealment of assets, the secret removal of property, departing from the jurisdiction of the courts of one's place of residence, and similar acts, were to be considered acts of bankruptcy. Upon the petition of a creditor and proof before a commissioner of bankruptcy, an individual found to have committed an act of bankruptcy would be declared a bankrupt and his property would be transferred to an assignee in bankruptcy for administration. At a time not more than twelve months after the issuance of the commission in bankruptcy, the creditors of the bankrupt were to be assembled by the assignee, and a first dividend was to be paid them out of the bankrupt's estate; within the succeeding six months the second and final dividend was to be paid, whereupon the bankrupt was to be awarded a certificate of discharge.

Although the general procedures for the administration of bankrupts' estates were not particularly complicated, the Bankruptcy Act of 1800 made some significant alterations in the common law that might have raised problems for the Supreme Court had the law enjoyed a longer period of effectiveness. For example, an assignment in bankruptcy was declared to bar the entail that might attach to the bankrupt's realty, as if there had been a fine and recovery to eliminate the interests of subsequent takers in tail.[88] Chattels over which the bankrupt exercised the power of sale or disposition were considered to be his property and subject to seizure by the assignee in bankruptcy.[89] Even bonds or notes due and payable by the bankrupt at some future date might be considered outstanding charges against his estate and included in the group of claims after being discounted for their future maturity dates.[90] Section 61 of the Bankruptcy Act specifically provided that it would not repeal any State insolvency laws then in force or to be thereafter en-

---

[87] Act of April 4, 1800, An Act to establish a uniform System of Bankruptcy throughout the United States, 2 Stat. 19–36; Act of December 19, 1803, An Act to repeal an Act intituled, "An Act to establish a uni-form system of Bankruptcy throughout the United States," 2 Stat. 248.

[88] Sec. 11, 2 Stat. 24 (1800).
[89] Sec. 27, 2 Stat. 28 (1800).
[90] Sec. 39, 2 Stat. 32 (1800).

acted, except as those laws might relate to persons clearly within the purview of the Bankruptcy Act.[91]

The most significant case to come before the Supreme Court under the provisions of the Bankruptcy Act was that of *United States* v. *Fisher*.[92] This raised the problem of the priority of the United States as a claimant in bankruptcy proceedings. The preference provision in the statute itself did not specify the nature of the government's priority in cases of bankruptcy; rather it reserved to the United States those preferences that then existed in favor of the government. Historically the traditional preference in regard to the collection of customs had been broadened in 1797 to include internal revenue collections and funds held by other persons indebted to the United States. The Fisher case involved the bankrupt endorser of a bill of exchange held by the United States government, and the United States claimed a preference over the claims of the endorser's other creditors in bankruptcy. Alexander J. Dallas, the United States Attorney for Pennsylvania, argued that the term "other persons" included all individuals who were indebted to the government; Jared Ingersoll countered that the preference existed only in the case of revenue collections and not for normal commercial debts. Furthermore, Ingersoll argued that the broadening of the statutory preference to include commercial debts was unconstitutional. By such a construction, judgments, liens, and mortgages might be set aside by the prerogatives of the United States. The Bankruptcy Act would thus become an impairment of the obligations of contract. In any event, such a construction was expressly authorized neither by the Constitution nor by the legislative language, and it was neither necessary nor proper to carry into execution the particular enumerated powers.

In reply Dallas urged that while it was the Court's duty to declare a statute unconstitutional if it conflicted with the Constitution, yet it was not proper for the Court to consider the inconvenience, the inexpedience, or the lack of policy inherent in the act; that was within the province of Congress. Congress had the power to collect revenue, and if it determined that a broad preference such as that provided in the 1797 statute was necessary, then it was not fitting that the Supreme Court should declare that policy unconstitutional.

Delivering the opinion of the Court, Chief Justice Marshall examined the 1797 act for the collection of revenue in its entirety, and concluded that Congress had intended a broad construction of the term "other persons," and that Fisher's assignor in bankruptcy fell within that category. The language was clear and principles of construction used in cases of ambiguous language need not be resorted to. No funda-

---

[91] 2 Stat. 36 (1800).   [92] 2 Cranch 358–405 (1804).

mental rights were overthrown by the 1797 statute or the Bankruptcy Act, and when mere convenience was argued to defeat a political regulation the Court was required to assume that Congress had considered the policy aspects of the question when it enacted the statute. Moving on to the issues concerning the "necessary and proper" clause, the Chief Justice rejected the contention that no law was authorized by the Constitution that was not indispensably necessary to give effect to the enumerated power. Such a rule of construction would, in his opinion, "produce endless difficulties."[93] "Congress must possess the choice of means, and must be empowered to use any means which are in fact conducive to the exercise of a power granted in the constitution."[94] Since the federal government was to pay the debt of the Union, it must be authorized to do so by expeditious methods, including the negotiation of bills of exchange. It followed that Congress might take steps to insure that such remittances were secured from the failure of endorsers such as Fisher's assignor.

From Marshall's opinion, his fellow Virginia judge, Bushrod Washington, dissented. He contended that the term "other persons" in the 1797 statute was restricted by the other sections and clauses of the statute, and also limited by the preamble, which spoke only of the collection of the public revenues. In addition the Court's interpretation of the Bankruptcy Act provisions made the property rights of individuals uncertain. To adopt the view of the majority "would not only be productive of the most cruel injustice to individuals, but would tend to destroy, more than any other act I can image, all confidence between man and man. The preference claimed . . . is of a nature against which the most prudent man cannot guard himself."[95] The parallel between this aspect of Washington's dissent and Judge Story's dissent in *U.S. v. 1960 Bags of Coffee*[96] indicates that the judges were alive to the interests of stability and certainty in commercial relations as they debated the forfeiture provisions of the Non-Intercourse acts on one hand, and the preference under the Bankruptcy Act of 1800 on the other. Secret forfeitures and hidden priorities in favor of the federal government were to be treated with suspicion and distrust.

CONCLUSION

While it cannot be claimed that the work of the Supreme Court in the fields of commercial law, business organization, or insolvency and bankruptcy was either novel or far-reaching in its significance, it is

---

[93] *Ibid.*, at 390.
[94] *Ibid.*

[95] *Ibid.*, 402.
[96] Discussed above at pp. 574–75.

clear that these private law adjudications of the Court take on new meaning when viewed in constitutional terms. Latent in these opinions are doctrines of legality, preferences for certainty and stability in property law, and a willing acceptance of the economic unity of the American nation. The Supreme Court in *United States* v. *Fisher* established a basis for the liberal construction of the necessary and proper clause. In *Korn & Wisemiller* v. *Mutual Assurance Society* it laid a foundation for its view of a corporation, not as a mere creation of the State but as a complex legal entity to which its shareholder-subscribers were tied by bonds of contract and fiduciary duty, and which gained an existence separate from the laws and government under which it was created. The doctrine of vested property rights, inherited from an earlier period in the Court's history, was enhanced and solidified in *Fletcher* v. *Peck* and the glebe land cases. Clearly this was a time of building slowly and steadily towards the great constitutional decisions that were to follow. Even though erected with small stones, the foundations of power were extremely well laid.

CHAPTER VII

Public Land Policy and the Supreme Court

ALTHOUGH COMMERCIAL LITIGATION formed a significant and growing proportion of the Supreme Court's business from 1801 to 1815, it was nevertheless dwarfed in economic magnitude by the great cases involving real property and public land grants. While this might be anticipated in the caseload of a court that, like the Supreme Court, dealt with the problems of a society and economy that remained predominantly agrarian, the number of cases in the early Marshall Period is nevertheless noteworthy. Quite possibly the greater investment security afforded by the federal Constitution, coupled with general economic recovery after 1788, encouraged foreign investment in American land companies. In any event there were extremely large amounts of money and land involved in this litigation before the Court, and it is to those cases that we must now turn our attention.

Independence found the States in the midst of a widespread preoccupation with the investment opportunities in wilderness lands.[1] It also left Americans with a colonial legacy of two distinctive land systems that were destined to shape the future land policy at both federal and State levels. The predominant system was based upon the township system of colonial New England, and applied to federal territorial holdings in furtherance of the principles of the 1787 Northwest Ordinance.[2] The New England colonial system was designed to encourage dense and cooperative settlement; land grants were made to groups of associated individuals who sought to establish not only their individual farms but

---

[1] William Priest wrote, "Were I to characterize the United States, it would be by the appellation of the land of speculation." *Travels in the United States of America* (London, 1802), 132.

[2] See M. Jensen, "The Creation of the National Domain, 1781–1784," *Mississippi Valley Historical Review* XXVI (1939–40), 323–42.

also towns with the essential public institutions of schools and churches.[3] By way of contrast the Virginia system of land grants, based upon individual initiative in locating vacant lands and securing their survey, encouraged large grants to wealthy investors who did not intend to settle the lands or to exert more than a nominal effort to attract actual settlers.[4] Within the Virginia land grant system, which was characteristic of both the southern and the Middle Atlantic colonies, there were some protections against the engrossment of large tracts of desirable land,[5] but for the most part the colonies that applied the Virginia system of land grants tended to have widely dispersed settlements and their most desirable lands were usually held by politically prominent investors.

So many colonial and Revolutionary leaders were involved in pre-Revolutionary land companies in Ohio and Kentucky that it has been suggested that the frustration of their efforts by the royal proclamation of 1763 may well have been a leading cause of the American Revolution.[6] While this contention can no longer be accepted without qualification, it nevertheless is accurate to say that the leading men throughout the Revolutionary and early national period of American history were deeply and pecuniarily interested in both State and federal land policies. George Washington had early and continuing interests in Ohio River Valley lands;[7] Judge James Wilson wrecked his career on the Supreme Court through his speculations in western lands and the consequent insolvency that haunted his last days;[8] Chief Justice John Marshall while he presided over the deliberations of the Supreme Court

---

[3] For discussions of New England towns, their organization, land policies and family relationships, see R. Akagi, *The Town Proprietors of the New England Colonies* (Philadelphia, 1924); S. Powell, *Puritan Village: The Formation of a New England Town* (Garden City, N.Y., 1963); P. Greven, *Four Generations: Population, Land and Family in Andover, Massachusetts* (Ithaca, 1970); and K. Lockridge, *A New England Town: The First Hundred Years, Dedham, Massachusetts, 1636–1736* (New York, 1970). The provisions for the establishment of churches may be seen in Town of Pawlet v. Clarke, 9 Cranch 282 (1815), discussed in Part II, chapter 6, p. 581.

[4] For a discussion of the Virginia treasury warrant system as applied in Kentucky, see H. Johnson and C. Cullen, eds., *The Papers of John Marshall*, I (Chapel Hill, 1974), 100–104.

[5] In general these involved the size and shape of the land surveyed. The preference was for square or rectangular tracts with only a limited portion on navigable waterways. See discussion at pp. 601–602, below.

[6] T. Abernethy, *Western Lands in the American Revolution* (New York, 1959), 20, 100–101; H. Adams, "Washington's Interest in Western Lands," *Johns Hopkins University Studies* III, No. 1 (January 1885); on the pre-Revolutionary operations of the Transylvania Company see A. Henderson, "A Pre-Revolutionary Revolt in the Old Southwest," *The Mississippi Valley Historical Review* XVII (1914), 198 et seq.; J. Boyd and R. Taylor, eds., *The Susquehanna Company Papers*, 12 vols. (Ithaca, 1930–71), II, xxxiii–xlii, et seq.

[7] Abernethy, *Western Lands*, 20, 103–105.

[8] C. Smith, *James Wilson* (Chapel Hill, 1956), 376–88.

had extensive holdings in the former Fairfax proprietary in Virginia, and in the North American Land Company investments in western New York State.[9] Indeed Marshall earlier had been active in the acquisition and patenting of Kentucky lands in association with his father, Colonel Thomas Marshall of Kentucky.[10] Beyond the substantial earnings of his law practice, the bulk of the Chief Justice's estate may be said to have been derived from wise and circumspect investments in undeveloped lands.

Clearly the subject of public land policy was one legal matter that touched upon private interests in high political places; as such it was subject to political debate[11] and at times used for partisan advantage. Yet the establishment of definite rules of public policy in this field was absolutely essential, not only to quiet titles long subject to doubt but also to encourage both domestic and international faith in the integrity of the federal and State governments.

Historically public policies towards land distribution had been conditioned by the twin considerations of the need for density of settlement in frontier areas and a conflicting tendency towards large grants to absentee owners, made for the purpose of adding non-tax revenues to the public treasury. Until the end of the Indian menace by the conclusion of the War of 1812, density of settlement was as important as it had been in the seventeenth century, but the reduced circumstances of the American States and the federal government, brought on by the economic drain of the Revolution and the depression that followed, resulted in growing recourse to large grants made to syndicated land companies. As a result, the early Marshall Court presided over a series of cases appealed from State and lower federal courts, and raised in the first instance by one of the largest land booms in American history. These cases resulted in a group of decisions concerning land policy that would serve as precedents for later adjudications in the federal courts. They also injected into the tawdry land litigation a sense of regularity and evenhanded equity that was all too often lacking in the opinions of the State courts, which increasingly fell under the influence of popular and legislative majorities ranged in opposition to the large land companies.

The conflicting public goals of settlement promotion and treasury

---

[9] A. Beveridge, *The Life of John Marshall*, 4 vols. (Boston, 1916–19), I, 196, II, 203–11; L. Baker, *John Marshall: A Life in the Law* (New York, 1974), 79–81, 293–98; Johnson and Cullen, eds., *Marshall Papers*, II (Chapel Hill, 1977), 140–49.

[10] Johnson and Cullen, *Marshall Papers*, I, 100–104.

[11] One of the most scholarly criticisms of the Virginia land policy can be found in the Virginia version of Blackstone's *Commentaries*, edited by St. George Tucker, 5 vols. (Philadelphia, 1803), II, Appendix, notes A., C., and especially D.

enrichment were well exemplified in the early land case of *Huidekoper's Lessee* v. *Douglass,* which has been discussed previously in terms of its contribution to the issue of States' rights and national authority.[12] We must now return to that case for an examination of its place in the law of public lands as enunciated by the Supreme Court. It will be recalled that the litigation involved a Pennsylvania statute of 1792 that imposed a settlement requirement upon the grantees of public lands, but at the same time provided relief from that condition if the grantee was prevented from settling, despite continuing efforts, because of hostile military action. After the Holland Land Company had made large investments in western Pennsylvania public lands, based upon this supposed waiver of the settlement requirement, the Pennsylvania legislature attempted to call into question the validity of the company's title. Frustrated in its efforts to protect the squatters by judicial unwillingness to deny the company's rights, the legislature and its Jeffersonian Republican majority bided its time. Finally, in 1800, the Pennsylvania Supreme Court held that only the exercise of "persistent efforts" to settle warranted lands would protect the company's title.[13] Thereafter the Holland Land Company mounted a series of ejectment actions against the settlers, with sufficient success that an alarmed legislature passed an 1802 statute, authorizing a special court to be assembled at Sunbury to consider the validity of the company's claims. When that court met it left the issue of settlement to the jury, thereby indicating that the matter was one of fact to be tried *de novo* upon the facts proved in each case.

Faced with the likelihood of continued and onerous litigation in State courts, the Holland Land Company took two alternative routes to stabilizing its position in Pennsylvania lands. First it appointed Harm Jan Huidekoper as its agent, and Huidekoper proceeded to follow a moderate policy designed to quiet settler discontent by making realistic compromises of pending land cases.[14] Secondly, the company turned to the Pennsylvania legislature in an effort to secure some recognition of its purported titles, and failing in that attempt, it resorted to the federal courts to protect its interests.[15] Three ejectment actions were instituted in the United States Circuit Court at Philadelphia,[16] the last

---

[12] 3 Cranch 1–73 (1805). The case is discussed at length in Part I, chapter 10, pp. 317–23.

[13] Commonwealth v. Tench Coxe, 4 Dall. 170–205 (1800).

[14] P. Evans, *The Holland Land Company* (Buffalo, 1924), 112–76; N. Tiffany, *Harm Jan Huidekoper* (Cambridge, 1904), 95–116, 131.

[15] After rejecting a resolution denying federal court jurisdiction, the Pennsylvania legislature appropriated

money for the defense of the settlers. Evans, *Holland Land Company,* 146–48; C. Smith, ed., *Pennsylvania Laws,* IV (Philadelphia, 1810), 199.

[16] Two cases in the April 1804 term of the circuit court went without a decision when the judges disagreed on the law. See Huidekoper v. Burrus, 12 Fed. Cas. 840 (No. 6848) (Cir. Ct. Pa. 1804), and Huidekoper v. McClean, 12 Fed. Cas. 848 (No. 6852) (Cir. Ct. Pa. 1804). Another case,

of which, *Huidekoper's Lessee* v. *Douglass,* was destined for appeal to the Supreme Court of the United States. Judge Richard Peters of the district court and Associate Justice Bushrod Washington had disagreed concerning the legal construction of the proviso concerning hostilities that prevented settlement. Based upon that division of opinion *Huidekoper's Lessee* was appealed to the Supreme Court under the new certified-question provision of the Judiciary Act of 1802.[17]

The questions certified were three in number. First, did the proviso excuse a warrantee from performing as required by the settlement condition? Secondly, if there were prevention but the warrantee persisted in his efforts, what title did he receive? And finally, was the Commonwealth of Pennsylvania the only party that might take advantage of non-compliance with the settlement requirement?[18] The ambiguous phraseology of the statute was thus brought before the Supreme Court for construction. Section 9 of the act, the clause in immediate issue, read as follows:

> No warrant or survey, to be issued or made in pursuance of this act, for lands lying north and west of the rivers Ohio and Alleghany [*sic*], and Conewango creek, shall vest any title in or to the lands therein mentioned, unless the grantee has, prior to the date of such warrant, made, or caused to be made, or shall, within the space of two years next after the date of the same, make, or cause to be made, an actual settlement thereon, by clearing, fencing and cultivating, at least two acres for every hundred acres contained in one survey, erecting thereon a messuage for the habitation of man, and residing, or causing a family to reside thereon, for the space of five years next following his first settling of the same, if he or she shall so long live; and that in default of such actual settlement and residence, it shall and may be lawful to and for this Commonwealth to issue new warrants to other actual settlers for the said lands, or any part thereof, reciting the original warrants, and that actual settlements and residence have not been made in pursuance thereof, and so often as defaults shall be made, for the time and in the manner aforesaid, which new grants shall be under and subject to all and every the regulations contained in this act. Provided always, nevertheless, That if any such actual settler, or any grantee, in any such original or suc-

---

Huidekoper v. Stiles, 12 Fed. Cas. 850 (No. 6853) (Cir. Ct. Pa. 1804), was decided on other grounds. This litigation was both dangerous and expensive. See Evans, *Holland Land Company* 151–52; R. Ferguson, *Early Western Pennsylvania Politics* (Pittsburgh, 1938), 198.

[17] The disagreement at circuit is not reported but it is mentioned in the report of the jury charge after the return of the Supreme Court's mandate. See Huidekoper's Lessee v. Douglass, 12 Fed. Cas. 847 (No. 6851) (Cir. Ct. Pa. 1805). The certification of questions is based upon 2 Stat. 156 (1802), and is discussed at Part II, chapter 10, p. 628.

[18] 3 Cranch 1, at 8–10.

ceeding warrant, shall, by force of arms of the enemies of the United States, be prevented from making such actual settlement, or be driven therefrom, and shall persist in his endeavours to make such actual settlement as aforesaid, then, in either case, he and his heirs shall be entitled to have and to hold the said lands, in the same manner as if the actual settlement had been made and continued.[19]

As the Chief Justice noted,[20] the statute was ambiguous in setting forth the requirements for settlement and residence. Settlement was to be made within two years after the date of the warrant, and the occupation was to continue for five years after settlement. Clearly five years' residence could not be accomplished within the two years after the issuance of the warrant. The logical conclusion, supported by other verbiage in the section, was that a settlement within two years followed by five years' residence was required for title to vest under the warrant. As to the proviso exempting from the settlement requirement those lands that were affected by hostile military action, it was clear that the provisions were contradictory if applied equally to actual settlers, to those driven off the land, and to those who persisted in efforts to make a settlement. The "plain and natural" method of construction was to apply the terms of the proviso to the description of persons to whom they are adapted, referring each to each, *reddendo singula singulis*. As applied to the actual settler who had been driven from his lands and the warrantee who had been prevented from making a settlement, the proviso did not require residence as a condition to his taking title, but merely persistence in his efforts during the two years immediately following the issuance of the warrant. Neither residence nor settlement beyond the two-year period was required to vest title in the warrantee.

Turning to the policy considerations that had been urged before the Supreme Court, Marshall conceded that settlement of the country was one of the intentions of the Pennsylvania legislature in passing the 1792 act; however, it was equally apparent that the fiscal advantages of land sales had not been ignored in the minds of the legislators: "At any rate, if the legislature has used words, dispensing with residence, it is not for the court to say they could not intend it."[21] There was also the contractual situation created by the 1792 law and the issuance of warrants under its provisions: "This is a contract; and although a state is a party, it ought to be construed according to those well established principles, which regulate contracts generally."[22] The Chief Justice then

---

[19] Smith, ed., *Pennsylvania Laws*, III, 506. The full text is also reprinted in 3 Cranch 1–8; sec. 9, *ibid.*, 5–6.

[20] The opinion in 3 Cranch 65–71 closely follows the reasoning of Chief Justice Shippen's dissent in Attorney General v. The Grantees, which was printed in the margin of counsel's argument in the Supreme Court of the United States. See 3 Cranch 29–31.

[21] *Ibid.*, 70.

[22] *Ibid.*

observed that had an individual citizen behaved as the Pennsylvania legislature did in this instance, he would be estopped from reclaiming title by a suit in equity: "All those principles of equity, and of fair dealing, which constitute the basis of judicial proceedings, require that courts should lean against such a construction."[23]

Marshall's exegesis into contract law may be taken as a leitmotif of the contract clause which would appear with fuller orchestration five years later in *Fletcher* v. *Peck*. In the absence of a fuller discussion of the act of the Pennsylvania legislature creating the Sunbury court, we cannot be certain of the Chief Justice's view of that procedure. However, it seems likely that Pennsylvania's overreaching the normal boundaries of legislative activity and the abandonment of the property rights of the Holland Land Company to the uncertainties of private litigation and legislative discretion was profoundly disturbing to his sense of the sanctity of private property.

The paragraphs concerning contractual relationships between the Commonwealth of Pennsylvania and the Holland Land Company occur at the end of the opinion, and follow statutory construction of material that standing alone effectively disposes of the issues raised by the certified questions. In terms of substantive law the contract paragraphs may well be considered obiter dicta; yet they may serve the purpose of introducing the constitutional issue of obligation of contract, thereby justifying the Supreme Court's procedural departure in this case. Normally the construction of a State statute by the highest court of the State was considered to be binding upon the federal courts—including the Supreme Court. However, in the case of constitutional claims entwined with State law, or questions involving Supreme Court jurisdiction in international law, State court holdings avoiding the federal issues were not necessarily conclusive upon the federal courts, but might be reconsidered by those tribunals.[24] Since *Huidekoper* involved the title to land, jurisdiction and venue in the federal system were exercised exclusively by the Circuit Court of the United States for Pennsylvania.[25] In accordance with section 34 of the Judiciary Act of 1789, the law governing the decisions of the Pennsylvania Circuit Court was to be that of Pennsylvania,[26] and clearly Pennsylvania statutes were to be given the construction prevailing in Pennsylvania's highest appellate court. Perhaps it was to bring *Huidekoper* into the federal arena that the Supreme Court, speaking by Chief Justice Marshall, invoked the "private law of contract," spelling out an equitable estoppel against the Commonwealth of Pennsylvania. In the decisions concerning the trans-

---

[23] *Ibid.*, 70–71.
[24] See discussion in Part II, chapter 5, pp. 553–54, concerning Smith v. Maryland. 6 Cranch 286 (1810).

[25] The best statement of the rule is in the later case of Massie v. Watts, 6 Cranch 148–70 (1810).
[26] I Stat. 73 at 92.

ferability of promissory notes in the District of Columbia, the Chief Justice had laid down a series of precedents concerning misrepresentations in business transactions,[27] and it might be that similar policy considerations and views of federalism were also involved in *Huidekoper*. Yet it was one thing for a Supreme Court to exercise plenary jurisdiction over the District of Columbia, and quite another exercise of federal judicial power to impose sanctions to secure equity and fair dealing in business transactions occurring entirely within one sovereign State. Even when diversity jurisdiction was involved the early Marshall Court did not make this sort of departure from its usual moderate approach to matters of federal court jurisdiction and procedure.

On balance, the opinion in *Huidekoper* demonstrates a position concerning jurisdiction that transcends the Marshall Court's own holdings. It is possible that the majority's sense of outrage at Pennsylvania's political intrusions upon the sanctity of private property led to the decision and that the paragraphs concerning the contractual situation arose from those feelings. On the other hand, the judges may have wished to hint at the limitations that the contract clause of the federal Constitution placed upon State legislative action. That they did so without mentioning the constitutional foundation for such a power is unfortunate, for absent the constitutional connection, it is unclear why the Supreme Court of the United States failed to follow the precedents of the Supreme Court of Pennsylvania. As it stands on the record, the opinion in *Huidekoper* leaves the impression that in this case the Supreme Court of the United States assumed the duty of regulating all contractual relationships and protecting all contracting parties against unfair dealings. That position was totally inconsistent with the other opinions of the Court, and as a practical matter, the Huidekoper case has remained an isolated precedent in this regard.

These ambiguities in *Huidekoper* also serve to provide new insight into *Fletcher* v. *Peck*,[28] which arose in a federal court on the basis of diversity of citizenship, and was the leading public land case to come before the Marshall Court in the years from 1801 to 1815. While *Fletcher* needs little further discussion than that which has been given previously in this volume, it is helpful to examine the Yazoo case as a public lands adjudication that was in line with and developed from the uncertain precedents in *Huidekoper*. As in *Huidekoper*, the Court in *Fletcher* was deeply concerned with the equities involved when State governments used their sovereign power to the detriment of adverse contracting parties. It was inequitable and subversive of property rights

---

[27] See Part II, chapter 6, pp. 563–65.

[28] 6 Cranch 87–148 (1810). See Part I, chapter 10, pp. 337–53, and Part II, chapter 6, pp. 579–80.

for legislatures to consider themselves independent of the normal rules of contractual duty and fair dealing, observed Chief Justice Marshall in his opinion for the Court. To Marshall and his judicial colleagues the very mention of the legislative power to divest property rights without just reason and adequate compensation warranted its immediate rejection. Sweeping governmental power over private property was not only contrary to Anglo-American law but also disruptive of stability in a Republic where sovereignty resided in the people and individual property was the main foundation of social and political order.[29]

Distinguishing between normal political acts of legislation and those legislative resolutions, grants, and statutes that transferred rights of property, Marshall held that the repeal of a statute that was in the nature of a contract could not divest rights acquired under the statute.[30] He then commented that if property might be seized without compensation after having been fairly acquired, then where might one seek after the limits upon legislative power and discretion?[31] Those "rules of property which are common to all the citizens of the United States, and . . . those principles of equity which are acknowledged in all our courts"[32] were violated by the 1796 Georgia repealing act. Even were Georgia an independent State there would be grounds for questioning the constitutionality of her repudiation in *Fletcher*.

Fletcher thus shares with *Huidekoper* the common theme that the American States, when dealing with property rights, were bound by an internal law—a common constitutional limitation—that was independent of any federal jurisdiction or the operation of the supremacy clause of the federal Constitution. There was, as the Chief Justice mentioned in *Fletcher*, a commonality of property rules which, at the very least, prevented legislative takings without compensation. These cases thus reaffirmed the existence of a doctrine throughout the United States concerning the sanctity of vested property rights and their insulation from legislative appropriation; that doctrine in turn was based upon American concepts of limited government and a tradition of limited legislative and executive authority.

Having affirmed the capacity of the State law and constitution to render justice in the Fletcher case, the Supreme Court then went beyond *Huidekoper* to spell out the federal relationship that brought the con-

---

[29] As to Marshall's thought see R. Faulkner, *The Jurisprudence of John Marshall* (Princeton, 1968), 22–33. While Judge William Johnson's position has not received a similar vigorous analysis, it is clear that while he differed from Marshall's reasoning in Fletcher he concurred with the holding of that case because he felt the revocation of the land grants violated natural law. See D. Morgan, *Justice William Johnson: The First Dissenter* (Columbia, S.C., 1954), 207–15.

[30] 6 Cranch 135–39 (1810).
[31] *Ibid.*, 135.
[32] *Ibid.*, 134.

tract clause of the federal Constitution to bear upon the legislative discretion of the State of Georgia. Sound principles of constitutional policy led the people of the United States, in their adoption of the Constitution, to demonstrate "a determination to shield themselves and their property from the effects of those sudden and strong passions to which men are exposed. The restrictions on the legislative power of the states are obviously founded in this sentiment; and the constitution of the United States contains what may be deemed a bill of rights for the people of each State."[33]

Clearly the Georgia repealing statute of 1796 violated the principle of the federal contract clause and federal supremacy; but it was even more basically defective in its disregard for the common system of the American States and the consequent respect for private property that inhered in the nature of limited constitutional government. The Chief Justice referred not to *federal law*, but to a *common American law* of property and constitutional limitations. The federal Constitution did not create private property rights, nor did it make federal courts the exclusive protectors of American private ownership of land; it merely implemented the common constitutional rights that Americans gained from State law, and raised them to the dignity of federally guaranteed constitutional principles. As such, the rights of contract and of property ownership became part of the supreme law of the land, thereafter to be subject to the dual control of State courts enforcing their own law and ultimately the federal courts.

A similar emphasis upon State law protecting property rights may be found in *Fairfax's Devisee* v. *Hunter's Lessee*,[34] the alienage case appealed on constitutional question grounds from the adverse decision of the Virginia Court of Appeals. Delivering the opinion on behalf of the Court, Judge Story held that English common law precedents concerning alien lands would, in the absence of specific legislative language, apply to Virginia's attempted seizure of the Fairfax proprietary lands. As we have seen previously,[35] the Fairfax case was a significant aspect of the Court's work in the field of international law, yet it has added importance as an example of the Court's applying common law precedents to construe the land policy statutes of Virginia, and as a yardstick by which to determine the validity of Virginia's attempt to escheat the lands of Lord Fairfax's alien devisee, Denny Martin Fairfax.

Judge Story's re-examination of the Virginia law in the Fairfax case re-emphasizes the problem of threshold questions that touched upon the Supreme Court's jurisdiction and powers. In dealing with the conclusive effect of the Virginia Court of Appeals holding, Story would

---

[33] *Ibid.*, 138.
[34] 7 Cranch 603–32 (1813).

[35] The case is discussed at length in Part II, chapter 5, pp. 554–57.

appear to have considered that court's statement of Virginia law to have had an adverse effect upon a federal treaty right. Hence the nature of the federal union required a *de novo* consideration of Virginia land law. As in the other land cases, *Huidekoper* and *Fletcher*, the *Fairfax* opinion carefully traced the public policy of Virginia, spelling out in detail the State law governing inquests of office in the escheat of alien land titles. As Justice Story observed:

> That an inquest of office should be made in cases of alienage, is a useful and important restraint upon public proceedings. No part of the United States seems to have been more aware of its importance, or more cautious to guard against its abolition, than the Courts of Virginia. It prevents individuals from being harassed by numerous suits introduced by litigious grantees. It enables the owner to contest the question of alienage directly by a traverse of the office. It affords an opportunity for the public to know the nature, the value, and the extent of its acquisitions *pro defectu hæredis*; and *above all it operates as a salutary suppression of that corrupt influence which the avarice of speculation might otherwise urge upon the legislature.* The common law, therefore, ought not to be deemed to be repealed, unless the language of a statute be clear and explicit for this purpose. [Emphasis added][36]

At the same term in which the Supreme Court handed down its opinion in *Fairfax's Devisee* it was presented with another case involving property rights which was determined by the precedent of *Fletcher* v. *Peck*. This was *New Jersey* v. *Wilson*,[37] a federal question case brought up on appeal from the New Jersey State courts, which had upheld a State statute repealing a tax exemption claimed to run with the land covered by a colonial land grant. In 1758 the province of New Jersey met with the Delaware Indians to extinguish the tribe's titles to the southern portion of the province, thereby opening it to settlement. Consideration for the cession of Indian claims was in the form of the creation of a tribal reservation, upon which the province agreed by legislative act not to impose any form of taxation. The remainder of the Delaware tribe entered upon the reservation, but in 1801 they requested permission of the State legislature to sell the reservation lands. Acting upon this petition the legislature empowered the tribe to sell the lands, and in 1803 they did so, transferring title to the plaintiffs below. Neither the statute authorizing sale nor the deed of transfer mentioned the tax exemption attached to the land; however, in October 1804 the New Jersey State legislature repealed the 1758 statute conferring the exemption, and officers of the State proceeded to assess the plaintiffs for tax arrears.

---

[36] 7 Cranch 622–23.   [37] 7 Cranch 164–67 (1812).

Examining the record, Chief Justice Marshall found that there had been a valid contract between the Delaware Indians and New Jersey, and that part of the consideration for the tribe's cession of southern New Jersey had been the tax exemption granted to them in regard to the reservation lands. While the exemption was for their benefit, according to the Chief Justice, it was also annexed by its terms to the land itself, and not to the persons of the Indians. Only if the exemption attached to the land would it enhance the reservation's value in case of subsequent sale. Marshall conceded that New Jersey could have insisted upon the surrender of the tax exemption as a condition for its agreement to the transfer of the land, but it had not done so, and consequently the purchaser succeeded to the privileges and immunities attached to the land. Standing in the place of the original grantees the plaintiff was entitled to the benefit of their contract, and the 1804 statute repealing the exemption was contrary to the contract clause of the federal Constitution.[38]

The decision in *New Jersey* v. *Wilson* cannot be dismissed without some consideration of its differences from *Fletcher* v. *Peck*, upon which the Court might have made a distinction. *Fletcher* involved a State grant made in 1795 and repealed in 1796; in its inception and its repeal, the right involved had been subject to the terms of the federal Constitution. The colonial grant in *New Jersey* v. *Wilson* not only predated the Constitution but was made by provincial authorities in the name of the sovereign as well as on behalf of the province. There was thus a problem of the devolution of responsibility and sovereignty. Were the contracts made by the provincial legislature and grants thereunder made in the name of the king binding upon the States that succeeded to the royal sovereignty? Or were they federal diplomatic obligations which descended through the Confederation Congress to the federal government under the Constitution? Presumably under the *Wilson* precedent this did not matter, for the Court treated the case as if the State of New Jersey was the party bound by the 1758 agreement, and hence the federal contract clause as a limitation on State actions was applicable. In treating the contract as one between a State and private individuals, Marshall obscured the question of the legal status of the Indians, leaving that constitutional problem for resolution nearly two decades later.[39] He also failed to develop the question of whether the plaintiff's rights arose by virtue of the contract alone, and thus, being in existence when the federal Constitution was ratified, came within its protections; the contrary view might be that the plaintiff's rights, and those of his Indian grantors, were determined by the law in existence at the time of the

---

[38] *Ibid.*
[39] In Cherokee Nation v. Georgia,

5 Peters 1–79 (1831), and Worcester v. Georgia, 6 Peters 515–97 (1832).

1758 grant. At that time the province of New Jersey was presumably in the position to repeal the tax exemption feature at any time, subject only to the exercise of the royal veto over the repealing legislation. These were fundamental problems inherent in an exclusive reliance upon contract clause language, and some reference to the common law of property doctrine set forth in *Huidekoper* might have strengthened the Supreme Court's opinion in the Wilson case. A doctrine of vested rights created by individual consent not only pre-dated the federal contract clause, but might, in conditions such as presented in *Wilson*, have proved a more flexible and effective constitutional instrument.

Taken together the decisions in *Huidekoper, Fletcher*, and *Fairfax v. Hunter* suggest the need to reconsider the role of common law in the American federal system, and particularly its availability as a Supreme Court instrument for the limitation of State deprivations of private property.[40] Such a concept of universal common law, dimly reflecting the "custom of the realm" in Dr. Bonham's Case,[41] was a part of Anglo-American legal tradition, although a repudiated segment of English constitutional law. Yet its place in the federal system, if it did indeed have a place in the federal government, could only be justified by a paramount need to secure the sanctity of private property as a buttress for the liberties of all American citizens. That such a theme should be expostulated at a time when the Supreme Court struck down the contention that there was a federal common law of crimes,[42] and during the period when the Court expended considerable effort to avoid declaring that commercial law was applicable uniformly throughout the United States,[43] including the District of Columbia, is an event worthy of serious attention. There can be little doubt that the Supreme Court in the early years of Marshall's presidency treated private property rights within the States as a matter of constitutional concern. While barely hinting at the future evolution of the contract clause as a federal shield for private property, the Court was willing to set forth constitutional reasons why the States themselves were bound to give due recognition and protection to the vested rights of their citizens. Those constitutional reasons were extraconstitutional, in the sense that they preceded the Constitution and did not grow out of the provisions drafted by the Philadelphia Convention. At the same time they were tacitly

---

[40] In Green v. Liter, 8 Cranch 229–51 (1814), Judge Story cited English precedents in support of the proposition that no actual possession, or seizin, was required of the grantee when he received title from the Crown in the form of a patent. This principle was applied to Virginia grants of land in Kentucky prior to 1792.

[41] 8 Coke Rep. 107a–121b, 77 Eng. Rep. 638–58 (C.B., 1609; K.B., 1610).

[42] See discussion of the Federal common law of crimes in Part II, chapter 8, pp. 633–46.

[43] See Part II, chapter 6, pp. 560–66.

recognized by the federal Constitution, the State constitutions, and (in our period) by the express acceptance of constitutional guarantees by the Supreme Court.

The emergence of constitutional doctrine in this area overshadows the routine development and enunciation of rules and precedents concerning State public land law. Foremost among the land cases coming before the Supreme Court on diversity grounds were those from the newly formed State of Kentucky. These may be briefly summarized as an illustration of the manner in which the Supreme Court either interpreted the land law of the State, or developed new rules based upon prior State practice.[44] In *Marshall* v. *Currie* the Court followed Kentucky law and Virginia practice in accepting the accuracy of an entry even though two of the four corners were marked by trees identified only by initials.[45] Recognizing "the laxity of the rules upon which the rights of individuals depended under the land law of Virginia" Judge Johnson, for the Court, confessed to "the necessity of liberality in deciding upon the validity of entries," in "anxiety to save the early estates acquired in that country."[46] In *Bodley* v. *Taylor* the Supreme Court again followed a liberal interpretation, taking judicial notice of the conditions of settlement and the unlettered status of many locators of land.[47] There Chief Justice Marshall cited with approval the rule of the Kentucky courts that only required that an entry have such "reasonable certainty which would enable a subsequent locator, by the exercise of a due degree of judgment and diligence, to locate his own lands on the adjacent residuum."[48]

Similarly, in *Bodley*, Marshall followed the Kentucky precedent that settlements were considered to be in the form of squares of 400 acres, and in addition that settlements were places of public notoriety since they were actually inhabited, as distinguished from pre-emption lands, which might be indistinguishable from vacant land. Surveying methods and the accuracy of Kentucky entries again came before the Supreme Court in *Massie* v. *Watts*; Marshall referred once more to the difficulties involved in obtaining specificity in entries and surveys, and stated that the principles laid down by Virginia and Kentucky courts should be considered expositions of the land statutes. The rule of con-

---

[44] In an appeal from the Federal Circuit Court in Tennessee Marshall wrote, "In cases depending on the statutes of a state, and more especially in those respecting titles to land, this Court adopts the construction of the state where that construction is settled, and can be ascertained." Polk's Lessee v. Wendell, 9 Cranch 87–102, at 98 (1815).

[45] 4 Cranch 172–77 (1807). The appellant, Humphrey Marshall, was the Chief Justice's cousin and brother-in-law.

[46] *Ibid.*, 176–77.

[47] 5 Cranch 191–234 (1809).

[48] *Ibid.*, 224.

struction to be followed was that if "by any reasonable construction of an entry, it can be supported, the courts will support it."[49] The entry in question was construed to include the principle of rectilinear surveys, by which it was assumed that adjacent boundaries would run at right angles to each other. These opinions demonstrate a desire to adhere closely to Kentucky precedents in cases involving the labyrinth of early land titles.[50] As the Chief Justice observed in *Bodley* v. *Taylor*:

> The very extraordinary state of land title in that country [Kentucky] has compelled its judges, in a series of decisions, to rear up an artificial pile [of precedents] from which no piece can be taken, by hands not intimately acquainted with the building, without endangering the structure, and producing a mischief to those holding under it, the extent of which may not be perceived.[51]

Since the Kentucky precedents tended, in cases of doubt, to protect property acquired under the land laws,[52] both Marshall and his colleagues found little difficulty in following those local laws. Only when extraordinary action was taken to dispossess patentees of their lands was the Court willing to supersede State law and customs.

State procedures and precedents were studied closely in the course of the Supreme Court's determination of land cases. One of the first cases that confronted John Marshall when he took his place on the bench was *Wilson* v. *Mason*,[53] which raised complicated issues concerning Virginia land granting practices. The defendant, a successor in interest to the original claimant, based his title upon a survey that varied from the description entered by virtue of George Mason's treasury warrant. As Marshall pointed out, the Virginia act of 1779, which established the treasury warrant system and under which, incidentally, he and his father had acquired over 400,000 acres of Kentucky land,[54] provided very precise steps to be taken in the acquisition of land. The date of the warrant itself did not confer any priority, he observed, except when two entries of the same date were entered against the same land; in such instances the earlier warrant would have precedence. Except in that limited circumstance, the party who first made an entry upon vacant land was entitled to survey it and obtain a patent. No-

---

[49] 6 Cranch 165 (1810).

[50] On the other hand entries which were clearly incorrect would not support a valid title. Finley v. Williams, 9 Cranch 164–72 (1815).

[51] 5 Cranch 191, at 234.

[52] As to quantity description see Vowles v. Craig, 8 Cranch 371–81 (1814); Taylor v. Brown, 5 Cranch 234–56, at 249–50 (1809). Taylor v. Brown also demonstrates an effort to overcome several technical defects in a survey conducted under the colonial military bounty law of Virginia. *Ibid.*, 234–56.

[53] 1 Cranch 45–103 (1801).

[54] Johnson and Cullen, *Marshall Papers*, I, 100–104.

where in the statute, according to Marshall, was there an indication that the legislature intended a survey to substitute for a warrant, nor was there any indication that a survey would confer title in the absence of a properly registered entry.[55] It was the entry of a tract of vacant land with the appropriate surveyor that conferred an equitable property right upon the entrant. Upon a valid survey the entry might mature into a legal estate in the land, evidenced by a duly executed patent. Accuracy in the description at the entry, coupled with a survey conforming to the entry, was what the Court sought in awarding priority of title.

Marshall's decision in *Wilson* gains significance since it was a case of first impression. Virginia courts had not construed the 1779 land statute, and thus the Supreme Court was compelled to consider the statute unaided by State precedents.[56] As a practical matter the opinion doubtless had more general acceptance because of John Marshall's personal knowledge of this aspect of the Virginia land system. At the same time, had Virginia courts subsequently adopted a contrary construction of the 1779 act, the Supreme Court would have been obliged to follow the State court rules in this regard. Until that time the rule established by the Supreme Court was binding upon the lower federal courts as well as persuasive with the Kentucky State tribunals that heard land matters.

The precise role of the Supreme Court in public land law is difficult to determine from these few cases. It is clear that the judges considered property rights a fundamental part of the constitutional system of the American Republic, both in its federal character and in regard to its constituent States. To that extent they were willing to invoke not only the contract clause of the federal Constitution but also the common American law of property. This they found in the laws of the various States, and they used both judicial instruments to compel a modicum of regularity and responsibility from the State legislatures and courts. At the same time, when construing statutes that set forth State land policies, the Court felt itself bound by the law of the situs in which the land was located. Federal law thus followed State law, where it was codified or clearly explicated by the State courts, except where that law was deemed at odds with the Constitution or enmeshed with a substantial claim of a federal right. Given the temper of the times and the restrictions imposed by the Constitution and judicial practice upon the powers of the federal courts, it is remarkable that the Supreme Court had such a significant impact upon the land policies of the States.

---

[55] The procedure of requiring entries apparently originated with the 1779 law; in the colonial period surveys were made upon the basis of land warrants without any intervening entry being filed or recorded. Taylor v. Brown, 5 Cranch 234.

[56] 1 Cranch 45, at 94–95.

FEDERAL LAND POLICY

Frontier warfare served to limit westward migration in the time period between the American Revolution and John Marshall's appointment as Chief Justice. Consequently, only one case, which resulted in a short *per curiam* opinion, deals with federal land grants in the West.[57] Federal land policies, as they came to the attention of the Supreme Court, developed not on the headwaters of the Ohio or Mississippi but rather on the more proximate banks of the Potomac River in the District of Columbia. The Residency Bill of 1790[58] established the new capital district under the direction of Commissioners for the District of Columbia, and those officials were charged with land sales as well as the evolution of plans for the city and the governmental office buildings that would be required when the functions of the federal government were transferred from Philadelphia to Washington. Since the Residency Bill made no appropriation of money for the conduct of the Commissioners' work, it was apparent at the outset that the sale of public lands within the District would be the primary funding source for the settlement.

Not surprisingly the District Commissioners looked kindly upon the purchase offers made by the Revolutionary financier, Robert Morris of Philadelphia.[59] They also welcomed Morris' two future associates in Washington land development, James Greenleaf and John Nicholson.[60] When the three formed a partnership to invest in Washington city real estate, it seemed an auspicious sign for the prompt economic development of the new Federal City. Yet the syndicate and the Commissioners shared an overly optimistic view concerning the extent of foreign and domestic interest in this particular real estate opportunity, and prob-

---

[57] Matthews v. Zane's Lessee, 5 Cranch 92–99 (1809), held that once a federal land office was established for a district, the authority of all other land offices for that district terminated. Any entries made or surveys filed in the old district were of no legal effect.

[58] An Act for establishing the temporary and permanent seat of the government of the United States, July 16, 1790, 1 Stat. 130 (1790).

[59] An early attempt to sell lots at a public auction had been a failure and it was at this time that James Greenleaf evidenced his interest in the purchase of large tracts. W. Bryan, *His-*

tory of the National Capital, 2 vols. (New York, 1914), I, 123, 146, 214.

[60] Biographical sketches of Morris may be found in C. Ver Steeg, *Robert Morris, Revolutionary Financier* (Washington, 1954); E. Young, *Forgotten Patriot: Robert Morris* (New York, 1950); and E. Oberholtzer, *Robert Morris: Patriot and Financier* (New York, 1905). The collected papers of Robert Morris as Financier have begun to appear. E. Ferguson, ed., *The Papers of Robert Morris*, 2 vols. to date (1973–). Concerning James Greenleaf, see A. Clark, *Greenleaf and Law in the Federal City* (Washington, 1901).

lems developed shortly after the purchases had been made with provision for installment payments over a period of one to three years. Straitened financial conditions hampered the syndicate in raising funds to meet the installments, and their circumstances were made worse by the failure of their Dutch agents to market a substantial portion of this Washington real estate to European buyers.[61] In many ways the syndicate had taken upon itself the task of becoming a participant in the economic development of the farmland and swamps of Washington into a city suitable for the reception of governmental officials and their families. Its acceptance of this quasi-public responsibility, along with the reputation of Robert Morris, may well have caused the District Commissioners, in their dealings with purchasers, to be less cautious than they might otherwise have been. At any rate, the insolvency of the financier caused substantial damage to this development program and jeopardized the transfer of the capital to Washington. It also threw into doubt those land titles that had been acquired through the Morris, Nicholson, and Greenleaf partnership, and brought before the Supreme Court a group of cases concerning Washington city lots.

The case of *O'Neale* v. *Thornton*[62] raised the issue of the resale of certain lots concerning which Morris and Greenleaf had defaulted in paying the purchase price. Under a 1793 Maryland statute covering the sale of lands in the District of Columbia,[63] upon default the Commissioners of Washington had the power to advertise such lands for sale and to sell them at auction, applying the proceeds to the purchase price, the costs of the sale, and the interest. The balance was to be paid to the original purchasers. Morris and Greenleaf, having failed to make payment as required by their contract, were subjected to such a sale, and William O'Neale purchased certain of the lots in question, giving his promissory note. O'Neale then defaulted in making his payment, and the Commissioners advertised the lots for another sale under the same statutory provision. The property was then sold to one Andrew Ross, apparently for less than the amount due by the Morris syndicate to the Commissioners. The surviving commissioner, William Thornton, sued O'Neale for the deficiency. In the circuit court O'Neale claimed that the resale by the Commissioners to Ross was a disaffirmance of their sale to him; consequently, the promissory note was void for failure of consideration. This argument the circuit court rejected, and O'Neale appealed to the Supreme Court.

---

[61] The intricate transactions can be followed in Bryan, *History of the National Capital*, I, 215–35, 258, 281, 298; Clark, *Greenleaf and Law*, 71–75, 85–86, 113, 135–43.

[62] 6 Cranch 53–70 (1810).

[63] Chapter 58, Laws of 1793, *Laws of Maryland Made and Passed at a Session of the Assembly . . .* , F. Green, printer (Annapolis, 1793).

The 1793 Maryland statute provided that

> on sales of lots in the said city by the said commissioners, or any two of them, under terms or conditions of payment being made therefor at any day or days after such contract entered into, if any sum of the purchase-money or interest shall not be paid, for the space of thirty days after the same ought to be paid, the commissioners, or any two of them, may sell the same lots at vendue, in the city of Washington, at any time after sixty days' notice of such sale in some of the public newspapers of Georgetown and Baltimore town, and retain, in their hands, sufficient of the money produced by such *new* sale, to satisfy all principal and interest due on the *first* contract, together with the expenses of advertisements and sale; and the *original* purchaser, or his assigns, shall be entitled to receive from the said commissioners, at their treasury, on demand, the balance of the money which shall have been actually received by them, or under their order, on the said *second* sale; and all lots so sold shall be freed and acquitted of all claim, legal and equitable, of the *first* purchaser, his heirs and assigns.[64]

The italicization, contained in William Cranch's 1813 edition of the Supreme Court reports, provides the key to the construction problem that faced the Chief Justice. If successive sales on defaults were authorized, O'Neale's equity might be foreclosed; but if, as his counsel argued, only one sale was authorized, the sale to Ross was a disaffirmance of O'Neale's title and relieved him of liability on the note.

Examining the Maryland statute, the Chief Justice observed, "Men use a language calculated to express the idea they mean to convey."[65] It was apparent to him that the legislature had in mind only two sales, the initial grant by the Commissioners, and the second instituted by them upon the default of the first grantee. The power of reselling the land was restricted by the words that conferred it. No legislator would have drawn the law without mentioning intermediate sales, had he contemplated a continuing power in the Commissioners. In addition the Chief Justice noted that the sale had followed shortly after the enactment of the statute, suggesting that the legislature had in contemplation this particular sale of a large tract of realty, with no anticipation that the component lots would decline in value. This situation persuaded the Maryland legislature to provide a prompt summary remedy in the event of default, but no special powers for a contingency not contemplated.

In misconstruing their powers and reselling a second time by summary process, the Commissioners put themselves in the position of being unable to continue their contract with O'Neale, and he, by pleading lack of consideration to the note, confirmed the title of the pur-

---

[64] The quoted section is reproduced in 6 Cranch 56.   [65] *Ibid.*, 68.

chaser under the sale. Thus while not deciding whether the second sale at auction conveyed good title, Marshall ruled that, if the evidence was believed, the Commissioners' action abrogated the transaction with O'Neale, including his obligation to pay on the promissory note. On this reasoning Marshall returned the case to the circuit court for a new trial. In terms of land policy, *O'Neale* v. *Thornton* demonstrates a tendency on the part of the Court to favor the normal procedures of common law and equity in the foreclosure of mortgage liens; while statutory alterations might be tolerated in specific circumstances, the Court was unwilling to countenance broad construction of such statutes.

While the Morris syndicate made extensive purchases from the District Commissioners, it also had dealings with one of the original proprietors of Washington real estate, Daniel Carroll of Duddington. These transactions developed from contracts entered into between Carroll and James Greenleaf, based upon the transfer of certain of Carroll's lands to Greenleaf, conditioned upon Greenleaf's building a house upon each of the twenty lots within three years after the date of the contract. With the formation of the syndicate Morris and Nicholson shared in the benefit of this land contract, but it was only a short time before the terminal date of the construction period that Robert Morris requested an extension of time in which to complete the houses. At the same time he asked Carroll for the conveyance of title to the lots involved, pointing out the risks the syndicate would take in erecting a block of twenty houses upon land it did not own. Not only did Carroll refuse to transfer title to the land, but he also refused to extend the time for compliance with the condition. This left the syndicate with the choice of abandoning contracts for land, some of which they had already contracted to sell, or constructing the required number of houses at breakneck speed. Morris elected the second course, and by the time his deadline was past, twenty houses had been built, although only six were ready for occupancy. Amidst public celebration and a barbecue hosted by the financier, the "completion" of the houses was celebrated; Daniel Carroll was present, but despite his seeming acquiescence he later refused to convey title to the lots, claiming that uninhabitable houses could not be tendered in satisfaction of the land contract conditions. Shortly after the barbecue, Robert Morris was compelled to make an assignment for the benefit of his creditors, and it fell to Henry Pratt and others acting as his trustees to sue Carroll for specific performance of the agreement to convey.[66] The trustees did not bring their action until seven years after Daniel Carroll's May 1797 re-entry of the premises.

In the Circuit Court for the District of Columbia the bill brought

---

[66] See Clark, *Greenleaf and Law*, 126–40, 189–90.

by Morris' trustees was dismissed, and the trustees appealed to the Supreme Court. In delivering the Court's opinion[67] the Chief Justice rejected defendant Carroll's contention that he could not convey to the plaintiffs until such time as the District Commissioners awarded him his moiety of the land granted to the Commissioners by the Maryland act erecting the District. Marshall indicated that since Carroll was under a contractual obligation to convey to Greenleaf he had a duty to take such steps as were in his power to secure the necessary division of the public lands. When in February 1796 Robert Morris paid a portion of the purchase price and demanded deeds to the twenty lots, to be held in escrow pending completion of the houses, this was in accordance with the apparent expectation of the parties. This failure to convey, in Marshall's view, was a probable cause for Morris' failure to complete the houses. Had an action for specific performance been brought at that time, the plaintiff would most likely have prevailed. However, the Chief Justice pointed out that time was of the essence in this agreement, and equity could not relieve when it was impossible to place the parties in the situation they would have occupied had their performance been timely. He concluded that "the Plaintiffs are too late to be entitled to the aid of this Court."[68]

Pratt and his fellow trustees had also claimed that the construction of the houses was a satisfactory compliance with the condition, and therefore that Carroll should be ordered to convey title. Marshall rejected this argument, pointing out that "completed houses" meant buildings suitable for habitation. The structures erected by the Morris syndicate were mere shells, with brick walls and roofs, but without interior amenities. Except for the six buildings actually finished on the interior, he held that the construction condition had not been met. This then raised for Marshall the question of whether the contract was severable. He held it to be so based upon Greenleaf's undertaking to reconvey to Carroll any lot not built upon within the required time. As a consequence, Carroll was ordered to convey to Morris' trustees those lots upon which houses had been completed under the agreement. In return the Morris syndicate was to pay £100 for each lot left unimproved, in accordance with the original Greenleaf-Carroll contract. Additionally, Marshall left it to the election of the Morris trustees whether they would press the claim for the land in the lower court, and assume the duty of paying the £100 per unimproved lot, or simply abandon the claim.

Pratt v. *Carroll* is more useful as a demonstration of the Supreme Court's facility in equitable matters than as a case delineating land policy for the District of Columbia. Yet the facts of the case reveal

---

[67] Pratt v. Carroll, 8 Cranch 471–78 (1814).   [68] *Ibid.*, 476.

many of the underlying difficulties in the Commissioners' scheme for the development of the District. In failing to partition the land between themselves and the original proprietors, including Daniel Carroll, the Commissioners delayed the time for conveying title to lots that would be allocated to them as part of the public domain. At the same time they embarrassed the proprietors and those who had purchased under them. Part of the uncertainty in *Pratt* v. *Carroll* involved the question of which lots would be assigned to Carroll in the division of the District. James Greenleaf had, of course, agreed with the Commissioners for the purchase of those lots that would be assigned to them in the same area. Having made agreements with both Carroll and the Commissioners, Greenleaf was secure in the knowledge that eventually he would obtain title to the square in question. Yet future ownership was a poor foundation upon which to base an expensive construction project for the development of another's land.

Further complicating factors were present in the construction conditions, imposed by the Commissioners with a view towards accelerating the physical growth of the city itself, and insuring adequate housing and facilities for the government personnel that would arrive with the transfer of government. Clearly it was in the best interest of those who purchased Washington lots to see the city grow rapidly; at the same time construction costs were high, and doubtless the isolated situation of the District and its general lack of population made labor difficult to obtain at any price. In retrospect the short period of time allowed to the investors for the improvement of their lands seems to have been more effective in generating litigation and jeopardizing land titles than it was in encouraging the construction of dwellings, hotels, and other buildings within the city of Washington. Paradoxically, a scheme for the rapid development of Washington through conditional grants with construction requirements actually worked to hamper building activity by subjecting titles to question and challenge by adverse parties. No better illustration of the sorry state of affairs can be found than the Supreme Court case of *Pratt* v. *Law and Campbell*,[69] a tangled group of cases combined for appeal to the Supreme Court at its February 1815 term.

Thomas Law was an early and enthusiastic investor in Washington real estate, having been convinced of the potential value of city property through the efforts of the Morris syndicate. As a result he purchased, with a down payment to be followed by other installments, the right to select from the syndicate's future allocation of lots, a total amount of real estate not to exceed 2.4 million square feet. The Morris syndicate stipulated to convey this property to Law as soon as they had received their allocations, and to secure their performance, agreed to

---

[69] 9 Cranch 456–502 (1815).

mortgage their Washington holdings to Law. On December 4, 1794, an agreement was executed which incorporated these provisions, as well as a stipulation by Thomas Law that he would construct a brick building at least two stories in height upon every third lot acquired under the contract. Subsequently Law selected some 2 million square feet of land, but failed to designate the remaining 400,000 square feet or to release the mortgage on the Morris syndicate land that had been pledged as security for their performance. It was in this condition that the Morris insolvency assignment found the parties.[70]

Included among the land selected by Law were certain lots covered by the Morris syndicate's agreement with Daniel Carroll, then not paid for, and subject to the building conditions imposed by Carroll upon the remainder of the syndicate's lands. Thus the delay in securing title deeds from Carroll and the syndicate's disagreement with Carroll concerning the construction provision in their agreement hampered the syndicate from complying with Law's request for the conveyance of certain lots in settlement of his agreement to purchase the remaining 400,000 square feet. Law also disagreed with Morris and his colleagues concerning the inclusion of alleys within the total amount of land to be granted to him in accordance with his selection of the 2 million square feet. The squares in the city had been laid out in a group of lots that were accessible not only from the platted streets but also by means of alleys running between the lots into the interior of the square, thereby providing communication with service entrances of buildings to be built upon the lots. The Morris syndicate insisted that the land covered by the platted alleys was properly chargeable to the Law allotment, while Law maintained that the alleys were not to be included within his 2 million square feet.

The legal labyrinth of what Judge William Johnson termed "this intricate and voluminous case"[71] was further complicated by the filing of an attachment against the lands mortgaged to Law by a judgment creditor, and a competing attachment in favor of Thomas Law.[72] While these attachments, and the question of whether an equitable interest in land was subject to attachment, formed the main concern of counsel arguing before the Supreme Court, they need not concern us at this point.

Judge Johnson held that in computing the amount of property selected by Thomas Law it was proper to include all alleys situated in squares wholly allocated to Law, since in such cases the title to the

---

[70] See Clark, *Greenleaf and Law*, 94, 100, 104–109, 264, Bryan, *History of the National Capital*, 1: 295–96.

[71] At 9 Cranch 486.

[72] These attachments arose from the case of Campbell v. Morris, 3 H. & McH. 535 (Maryland, 1797).

alleys would pass to Law. However, where the squares contained one or more lots owned by some third party, the alleys should be excluded from the agreement by which Law was to receive title in fee simple. The existence of a variety of easements over the alleys would, in the latter case, contradict the existence of a fee simple in the alleys.

As to the conveyance of title conditioned upon Law's compliance with the building conditions, Johnson pointed out that no matter what the legal or equitable considerations may have been in 1796, twenty years later it was clear that the tender of the fee burdened with the building condition had been acquiesced in by Law and could no longer be challenged. Turning to the building condition, and Law's failure to comply within the time prescribed, Johnson indicated that the Morris syndicate had initially failed to convey property in the quantity specified in the agreement. On them should fall the consequences of the circumstances produced by their own default. Furthermore, Law had progressed on his construction work based upon similar stipulations concerning building made in contracts between the Morris syndicate and Daniel Carroll on one hand, and the syndicate's agreement with the Commissioners on the other. After observing that it would be impossible to determine the connection between Morris' failure and Thomas Law's building program, Johnson decided that the construction requirement should be removed from consideration in the case, since its impact upon the performance of the parties was impossible to assess with accuracy. The only equitable remedy available to Law was the award of that portion of the purchase price that was not covered by transfers of land in accordance with his agreement. In regard to the mortgaged property, Judge Johnson decided that while the land had been sold under an execution in favor of William Campbell, Campbell was equitably entitled to only the amount of the syndicate's indebtedness to him. The remaining proceeds from the land should be applied to compensate James Greenleaf for the loss he sustained in paying Morris and Nicholson's bills of exchange payable to a third party.

Pratt v. *Law and Campbell* provides some measure of the difficult issues that would face the federal courts in future years because of speculative land operations within the city of Washington. Sustained by elaborate interlocking credit arrangements and burdened with unrealistic construction requirements, the land system within the District of Columbia was a fertile source of litigation in the federal courts.[73]

---

[73] From this weed-infested field would grow several other Supreme Court cases calling for an explanation of the decision in Pratt v. Law and Campbell. See Greenleaf v. Cook, 2 Wheat. 13 (1817). Chief Justice Marshall's investments in Washington lots are explored in H. Johnson, "The Tribulations of Conway Robinson: John Marshall's 'Washington Lotts'," *Virginia Magazine of History and Biography* LXXIX (1971), 427–35.

CHAPTER VIII

Jurisdiction and Procedure of Federal Courts and the Federal Common Law of Crimes

THE JURISDICTION and procedure of courts long remained among the most arcane and archaic areas of the law; at the same time they may well be the most significant because of the emphasis that the Anglo-American legal system has placed upon formality and regularity. Although the ghosts of the forms of common law actions did not rule as strongly in John Marshall's America as they did in Frederic William Maitland's England nearly a century later, they nevertheless left their mark upon the availability of remedies and the classification of actions. In most of the American State courts, and in federal tribunals as well, the ancient distinction between actions at law and suits in equity persisted, continuing professional debate over the availability of equitable remedies within the common law system. While it would be unproductive to dwell upon the minutiae of federal practice issues reported by Judge Cranch in the years from 1801 to 1815, it is nevertheless necessary to examine the Supreme Court's work in these technical fields if we are to understand the internal development of the federal court system, including the Supreme Court itself.

Professor Goebel has demonstrated that the Supreme Court under Chief Justices Jay and Ellsworth had succeeded in adapting the common law method of appeal by writ of error to the requirements of practice in the fields of equity and admiralty jurisdiction.[1] The Judiciary Act of 1789 prescribed review by writ of error, but the Supreme Court ruled that parties seeking review in chancery and admiralty matters might annex a large supporting schedule of documents, thereby permitting full consideration of the record below by the judges of the reviewing

---

[1] J. Goebel, *Antecedents and Beginnings to 1801, Volume I, History of the Supreme Court of the United States*, ed., P. Freund (New York, 1971), 686–706.

court as on the traditional appeal. Early in Marshall's Chief Justiceship this judicial gloss upon the Judiciary Act requirements was rendered academic by the statutory authorization of appeal as the system of review in equity and admiralty. Nevertheless it demonstrated how a Supreme Court, determined to exercise its jurisdiction in traditional ways, might overcome limitations imposed upon its practice by congressional statute.

Traditionally Anglo-American courts had controlled their own procedures and worked within broadly defined jurisdictional lines. The American Revolution, however, left a legacy of opposition to centralized authority as well as suspicion of the judicial branch, which had served as a prop for the royal prerogative in the critical years before independence.[2] The result was a series of popular demands for limitations upon judicial power enforced by legislative control or constitutional restraints. Historically the weakness of federal authority under the Articles of Confederation had been highlighted by the embarrassing De Longchamps affair, and the inability of the Federal Court of Appeals in Cases of Prize and Capture to enforce its appellate decisions against the various States.[3] Constitutional revision at the Philadelphia Convention of 1787 did much to strengthen the federal Union, but it did not end the nagging fear of centralized judicial authority. Consequently the judicial system established under the new federal Constitution was one of severely limited jurisdiction. Those limitations were found in the Constitution itself, in the Judiciary Act of 1789 which gave life to a federal court system dependent upon Congress for its jurisdiction, and in the Process Acts of 1789 and 1792. Each of these documents bore the clear marks of compromise between effective court structure on the one hand and the dominant political mood of suspicion on the other.[4]

Americans of the anti-Federalist persuasion felt that local and State governments were controlled more easily than a remote national government; consequently State and local courts were preferable to

---

[2] *Ibid.*, 83–100. See also C. Ubbelohde, *The Vice Admiralty Court and the American Revolution* (Chapel Hill, 1960), and D. Lovejoy, "Rights Imply Equality: The Case Against Admiralty Jurisdiction in America, 1769–1776," *William and Mary Quarterly*, 3rd Series, XVI (1959), 460–82.

[3] On the De Longchamps case, in which an assault upon a French consul was permitted to go unpunished in Pennsylvania courts, see E. Dickinson, "The Law of Nations as Part of the National Law of the United States," *University of Pennsylvania Law Review* CI (1952), 26–56, at 36. The inability of the Federal Court of Appeals in cases of prize to enforce its decrees is discussed in J. Jameson, ed., *Essays in the Constitutional History of the United States During the Formative Period* (New York, 1891), 1–45, at 14, and H. Bourguignon, *The First Federal Court: The Federal Appellate Prize Court of the American Revolution, 1775–1787* (Philadelphia, 1977), 297–318.

[4] See generally, Goebel, *Antecedents*, 457–58, 504, 510, 540, 546–48.

federal tribunals. Familiar procedures in State courts were to be preferred over differing adjective law in the courts of sister States or the
uncertainties of a new federal procedure to be uniformly applied. As a
result section 2 of the Process Act of 1789 required federal courts to
follow State procedures in common law cases tried before them.[5]
Similarly, section 34 of the Judiciary Act of 1789[6] required State law
be followed by federal courts trying common law cases within the various
States. Provincialism on the one hand, and the ongoing debate over
the nature of federalism on the other, shaped the constitutional and
legislative charters for the federal court system and the United States
Supreme Court. As a member of the Virginia ratifying convention, a
student of the federal Constitution, and an active practitioner in the
federal courts after 1790, Chief Justice Marshall was well acquainted
with the limitations upon jurisdiction; it was within this political framework that he and his fellow judges began to lay the foundations of
judicial power.

ORIGINAL JURISDICTION

"The courts of the United States are all of limited jurisdiction,"
Chief Justice Marshall wrote in 1809, "and their proceedings are erroneous, if the jurisdiction be not shown upon them."[7] His words
renewed, in another context, the position taken six years before when
the Supreme Court denied its own jurisdiction in *Marbury* v. *Madison*.[8]
The mandamus case not only perpetuated judicial review in federal
jurisprudence but it also demonstrated the technique for determining
the legitimacy of judicial jurisdiction. The federal judge sought the well-
spring of federal judicial power in Article III of the Constitution; its
terms were paramount, and its limitations upon jurisdiction were absolute in the absence of constitutional amendment.[9]

Federal judicial power was limited in scope, and it was also designed to perform those restricted functions that were essential to
national well-being. The Supreme Court itself was required to serve as
an agency for restricting its own jurisdiction within constitutional and
legislative guidelines, and it also exercised that function for the inferior
federal courts through the process of appellate supervision. In *Marbury*
the Supreme Court rejected legislative accretions to its constitutional
original jurisdiction. This self-denial was not simply a political ex-

---

[5] 1 Stat. 276. See also Buddicum v.
Kirk, 3 Cranch 293–98 (1806), and
Beale v. Thompson and Maris, 8
Cranch 70–71 (1814).
[6] 1 Stat. 92. See also Bodley v.
Taylor, 5 Cranch 191–234 (1809).

[7] In Kempe's Lessee v. Kennedy, 5
Cranch 185 (1809).
[8] 1 Cranch 137–80 (1803).
[9] *Ibid.*, 176–78.

pedient to embarrass Thomas Jefferson while avoiding public humiliation should the Court's mandate be ignored; quite the contrary, the
acceptance and self-denying enforcement of limitations upon jurisdiction asserted the Court's authority to control its jurisdiction and practice.
Furthermore, when the Court in *Marbury* accepted the finite constitutional and legislative restrictions upon its institutional growth, it
deflected political attacks that might be mounted against judicial ag-
grandizement. Insulated from criticism on these grounds the Court
could concentrate upon shaping its appellate procedures and ordering
its original jurisdiction in such a way that it served the great functions
that the Founding Fathers had intended—it was the highest court for
the enforcement of international law, it superintended judicial enforcement of federal supremacy, and it heard appeals in cases adjudicating
disputes between individuals, States, and nations tried in the first instance in neutral federal courts.

Marbury revolved around the availability of mandamus as an
original writ from the Supreme Court, and the Court's holding that
original jurisdiction conferred by the federal Constitution might not be
supplemented by congressional action short of constitutional amendment.[10] In resolving the uncertainties[11] concerning the availability of the
prerogative writ of mandamus as a function of the Court's original
jurisdiction *Marbury* was a renewed affirmation of the inviolability of
the constitutional basis of the Supreme Court's original jurisdiction.
Limited though that power might be under the provisions of Article III,
it served two fundamental federal purposes—it provided a neutral forum
for the adjudication of disputes between the various American States,
and a tribunal to hear cases involving diplomatic officers accredited to
the United States. The denial of mandamus jurisdiction in *Marbury*
was therefore not destructive of the Supreme Court's powers but rather
still another shield of protection of its original jurisdiction from the
incursions of legislative or executive power.

The Burr conspiracy prosecution, discussed at length above,[12]
gave rise to the case of *Ex Parte Bollman* and *Ex Parte Swartwout*,[13]
requesting the issuance of writs of habeas corpus ad subjiciendum by the
Supreme Court to deliver two prisoners committed by the United States
Circuit Court for the District of Columbia, and awaiting trial for trea-

---

[10] The limitation of Supreme Court
mandamus to matters of appellate
jurisdiction rests upon Marshall's discussion in Marbury, and upon M'Intire v. Wood, 7 Cranch 504–506
(1813), which considered the mandamus power in the federal circuit
courts.

[11] Precedents prior to 1801 cast
some doubt upon the Court's power
to issue writs of mandamus. See
Goebel, *Antecedents*, 785–86.

[12] See Part I, chapter 9, pp. 247–91.

[13] 4 Cranch 75–136 (1807).

son. The Supreme Court awarded the writ, but Judge William Johnson dissented from the majority, claiming that the petition requested the aid of the Supreme Court in the exercise of its original jurisdiction. On the basis of *Marbury* v. *Madison* he felt that the application should be denied, for no grant of original habeas corpus jurisdiction was set forth in Article III.[14] Viewed in this light, section 14 of the Judiciary Act of 1789 conferring habeas corpus powers upon the Court was just as unconstitutional as section 13, which granted mandamus authority.

The majority in *Ex Parte Bollman* characterized the petition as one addressed to the appellate jurisdiction of the Supreme Court. Speaking for the majority Chief Justice Marshall cited the distinction made in *Marbury* (where there was no prior judicial proceeding) between original and appellate jurisdiction—that appellate jurisdiction "revises and corrects the proceedings in a cause already instituted, and does not create that cause"[15]—and stated that in that light *Ex Parte Bollman* was clearly an appellate case. The decision to imprison an individual was a judicial act.[16] It necessarily preceded an application for his release upon habeas corpus, and hence the grant of the writ of habeas corpus and subjiciendum was a mode of revising (as on an appeal) a judicial decision in favor of imprisonment.

One of the most far-reaching decisions in this field in the early Marshall Period was that of *Strawbridge* v. *Curtiss*,[17] which sharply limited a litigant's access to the federal courts on diversity grounds. The formal pleading of diversity of citizenship had become encrusted with the barnacles of technical nicety since the Court's 1798 decision in *Bingham* v. *Cabot II*,[18] but it remained undetermined whether in actions that concerned joint parties a shared citizenship by one plaintiff and one defendant would divest the federal courts of jurisdiction. *Strawbridge* laid down the rule that complete diversity must exist, and three years later its holding was cited with approval in *Hope Insurance Company* v. *Boardman*[19] despite John Quincy Adams' able argument at the bar that "[t]he effect of that decision [*Bingham* v. *Cabot II*] has been to exclude many cases upon nice questions of pleading which would

---

[14] *Ibid.*, 103. It should be noted that Judge Johnson felt that individual judges might issue *habeas corpus* writs where the request involved an ambassador or minister. However in those cases he believed the power came from the constitutional grant of original jurisdiction rather than from the grant in the Judiciary Act of 1789. *Ibid.*, 106, 107.

[15] I Cranch 137, at 175; 4 Cranch 75 at 100–101 (1807).

[16] 4 Cranch 101.

[17] 3 Cranch 267–68 (1806). The Strawbridge precedent was limited to the case of joint plaintiffs, but in regard to them it was required that each of them have different State citizenship than that of the defendants.

[18] 3 Dall. 382 (1797). See discussion in Goebel, *Antecedents*, 586–88.

[19] 5 Cranch 57–61 (1809).

otherwise have been clearly within the jurisdiction of the courts of the United States."[20]

Yet the Supreme Court under Chief Justice Marshall seems to have preferred strict standards for the allegations of diversity, and to have applied the requirements of the Judiciary Act of 1789 in a way that diversity jurisdiction was required to be shown on the face of the pleadings before the court might proceed.[21] The rule in *Strawbridge* was broadened to include corporations and their shareholders in *Bank of the United States* v. *Deveaux,* where the Supreme Court rent the corporate veil asunder by insisting that no diversity could exist if the opponent could demonstrate that one of the Bank's shareholders was a citizen of his (the opponent's) State.[22] Judgment would not cure the failure to allege jurisdiction, and even if the erring plaintiff prosecuted the case, his mistake might be taken advantage of, and the case dismissed upon appeal.[23] Jurisdictional amount, in diversity cases and other matters, was subject to appellate determination by the Court, and the findings of lower courts were persuasive, but not binding upon the Supreme Court.[24]

The Deveaux case deserves special attention, for while it restricted diversity jurisdiction by requiring complete diversity between shareholders and adversary, it also enlarged the class of persons who might gain access to the federal courts. Although the Constitution refers to "citizens" as that group which may claim status to sue on diversity

---

[20] *Ibid.,* 58.

[21] See Abercrombie v. Dupuis, 1 Cranch 343 (1803); Wood v. Wagnon, 2 Cranch 9 (1804); and Hepburn v. Ellzey, 2 Cranch 445–53 (1804). While litigation between aliens was not cognizable before federal courts, in salvage cases based on *in rem* or *quasi in rem* jurisdiction, the Supreme Court upheld jurisdiction. Mason v. Le Blaireau, 2 Cranch 240 (1804); Montalet v. Murray, 4 Cranch 46–47 (1807). The Bingham rule had also been applied to applications for removal to the federal courts. See Goebel, *Antecedents,* 593.

[22] 5 Cranch 91–92 (1809). However citizens of the same State might claim diversity if they were nominal parties for others entitled to assert it. Browne v. Strode, 5 Cranch 303 (1809).

[23] Capron v. Noorden, 2 Cranch 126–27 (1804).

[24] United States v. Brig Union, 4 Cranch 216–18 (1808). In civil appeals to the Supreme Court various jurisdictional amounts were established by statute. Generally the amount specified in the declaration determined the jurisdictional sum if plaintiff did not prevail, while the judgment amount applied if he was successful at trial. Cooke v. Wilson, 5 Cranch 13–15 (1809); Wise & Lynn v. Columbia Turnpike Co., 7 Cranch 276 (1812). In an action upon a penal bond it was the Court's opinion that the penalty should be ignored in establishing the jurisdictional amount. United States v. M'Dowell, 4 Cranch 316–17 (1808). The value of the estate passing under the terms of the will was the standard in probate proceedings. Carter's Heirs v. Cutting, 8 Cranch 251–53 (1814). Should the jurisdictional amount not appear on the face of the papers submitted upon appeal, the parties would be given time to prove the amount of affidavits. Rush v. Parker, 5 Cranch 287–88 (1809).

grounds in federal courts, it was unclear whether a corporation was a "citizen" or whether that term was properly restricted to natural persons in possession of full political and civil rights. In *Deveaux* the Court held that the uncontroverted averments in the pleadings to the effect that all of the officers, directors, and shareholders were citizens of a State other than that of the defendant, would be adequate to confer diversity jurisdiction upon the federal courts. While it has been argued that the Deveaux case expands diversity jurisdiction to parties not contemplated by the Founding Fathers,[25] it also may be said that the Court adapted its constitutional and statutory constructions to accord with the altered nature of business organizations in early-nineteenth-century America.[26] In terms of diversity jurisdiction, corporations might sue or be sued in federal courts, but they or their opponents might divest the court of jurisdiction by showing a failure of complete diversity as required by the *Strawbridge* precedent. For this reason it would seem that the *Deveaux* holding that corporations might in effect be "citizens" was of limited value in antebellum jurisprudence.

APPELLATE JURISDICTION

Within the galaxy of federal circuit courts the Circuit Court for the District of Columbia was a star of first magnitude. Although it had all of the powers of the other circuit courts, it had jurisdiction over all crimes and offenses committed within the District (whether or not they were violations of federal law) and authority in all cases of law and equity.[27] In 1801 Congress gave the Supreme Court power to review any final judgment, order, or decree of the Circuit Court for the District that exceeded $100 in value.[28] This the Supreme Court, in *Curtiss* v. *Georgetown Turnpike Company*,[29] held to be a more ample grant of appellate jurisdiction than was given in regard to all other circuits by the various judiciary acts. This broader jurisdiction was shown in *Carter's Heirs* v. *Cutting*,[30] where the high court reviewed upon appeal the appellate decision of the Circuit Court for the District of Columbia in a probate matter. Normally a case decided in a district court, re-

---

[25] C. Warren, "Corporations and Diversity of Citizenship," *Virginia Law Review* XIX (1933), 669; W. McGovney, "A Supreme Court Fiction," *Harvard Law Review* LVI (1943), 853, at 876–77.

[26] The rule as to nominal plaintiffs in Browne v. Strode, discussed in Part II, chapter 8, note 22, and the holding in Chappedelaine and Cloiseverre v. Decheneux, 4 Cranch 306–16 (1808), that alien executors of a deceased

plaintiff's estate could maintain an action against a defendant residing in decedent's domiciliary State, seem also to reflect this utilitarian approach to the problem of diversity jurisdiction.

[27] Sec. 3, 5, Act of Feb. 2, 1801, 2 Stat. 103, at 105, 106.

[28] 2 Stat. 106 (1801).

[29] 6 Cranch 233–37 (1810).

[30] 8 Cranch 251–53 (1814).

viewed upon writ of error by the appropriate circuit court, was not subject to still further appellate review by the Supreme Court.[31]

The Court's appellate jurisdiction over civil cases in the District of Columbia was solidly based upon the 1801 federal act concerning the District.[32] In *Young* v. *Bank of Alexandria* this authority was maintained even against a 1792 Virginia banking charter, by which the Bank of Alexandria was granted exemption from appeals in all causes initiated and won by the bank.[33] Clearly the procedural relief from appellate review was a right that might have been asserted as a privilege against the sovereign power of the Commonwealth of Virginia. Yet the Supreme Court held that under section 8 of the 1801 statute that established the authority of federal courts in the District, there were appeals by writ of error from the decisions of the Circuit Court of the United States for the District of Columbia. Considering the 1801 Act, Chief Justice Marshall observed:

> The words of the act of Congress being as explicit as language can furnish, must comprehend every case not completely excepted from them. . . . The act incorporating the bank professes to regulate, and could regulate, only those courts which were established under the authority of Virginia. It could not affect the judicial proceedings of a court of the United States, or of any other state.[34]

He distinguished between those corporate rights upon which depended the validity of the corporations acts, and which were of general obligation and presumably binding upon all successor and superior sovereignties, and those which were merely procedural in nature. Rights directly concerning the procedure of courts, "those peculiar remedies which may be bestowed"[35] on a corporation by its charter, could be

---

[31] United States v. Goodwin, 7 Cranch 108–12 (1812); United States v. Gordon, 7 Cranch 287 (1813).

[32] An Act concerning the District of Columbia, Feb. 27, 1801, 1 Stat. 103–108.

[33] Young v. Bank of Alexandria, 4 Cranch 384–98 (1808).

[34] *Ibid.*, 397. Similarly, in Wilson v. Mason, 1 Cranch 45–103, at 91–92 (1801), the Court sustained its jurisdiction to review a United States District Court review of a *caveat* in a Kentucky land title case. Virginia, whose law governed title, severely limited judicial review in land cases.

[35] *Ibid.* The transfer of sovereignty over the Counties Alexandria and Washington in the future District of Columbia raised a number of similar problems. It was held that letters of administration taken out in the courts controlling the future County of Washington prior to the cession were not effective within the District of Columbia. Fenwick v. Sear's Administrators, 1 Cranch 259–82 (1803). An executor of the estate of a resident of Alexandria, appointed prior to the cession, would have to obtain new letters of appointment. Dixon's Executors v. Ramsay's Executors, 3 Cranch 319–24 (1806). We have previously noted that the insolvency laws of Maryland ceased to operate in the District upon the date of cession. See discussion of Reily v. Lamar, Beall and Smith, 2 Cranch 344–57 (1804), in Part II, chapter 6, note 77.

exercised and claimed upon in the courts of the sovereign power that granted them.

Marshall's opinion in *Young* v. *Bank of Alexandria* demonstrates a judicial tendency to leave untrammeled the right of Congress to regulate District of Columbia courts. On this policy ground the decision makes good sense, but when considered against the background of a developing sensitivity to vested property rights, the *Young* decision leaves several questions unanswered. As a successor in sovereignty over the county of Alexandria, did not the United States assume to itself the obligations contained in the 1792 Virginia charter of the bank? Did the transfer of sovereignty work a forfeiture of property rights vested under corporate charters? Even if the freedom from prolonged litigation through appeals might be considered to be of a procedural character, might it not be said to have tangible value to which standards of due process and compensation under the Fifth Amendment might attach? Marshall's distinction between the classes of privilege contained in the Virginia charter might have successfully cloaked these deeper questions of constitutionality, leaving those points to be developed at more auspicious times and in more suitable appeals. Yet it is obvious that in the Young case the Supreme Court chose to overlook the property aspects of the case and to focus its attention upon the legislative powers of Congress to make laws for the District of Columbia and to regulate the jurisdiction of the federal courts.

The Supreme Court's review of criminal cases in the District of Columbia courts was seemingly not as extensive as its appellate authority in civil actions. In *United States* v. *More*[36] the Court denied its own jurisdiction over criminal appeals from the Circuit Court for the District of Columbia. However, as we have seen, it did assert its appellate authority over those criminal matters in *Ex Parte Bollman* and *Ex Parte Swartwout*.[37] During this early period, appellate review was available on habeas corpus rather than by writ of error, and, on questions of law, by a certificate of division in the circuit court.[38]

Appeals from the District of Columbia made important contributions to the development of the law of marine insurance, negotiable instruments, insolvency, and real property. To the extent that there was a federal common law of the United States, it existed in the District of Columbia. The unique situation of the District, ceded to the federal government by two independent sovereign States, created special problems of conflict of laws and the persistence of private rights. When the

---

[36] 3 Cranch 159–74 (1805).
[37] 4 Cranch 101–37 (1807). See discussion in Part II, chapter 8, notes 13, 14.
[38] See United States v. Sanges, 144 U.S. 310, at 319–23 (1892), for a history of Supreme Court review in federal criminal cases. Not until 1898 was the writ of error made available in capital cases. *Ibid.*, 321.

Supreme Court in the future would be called upon to adjudicate questions concerning the newly acquired territories and the Indian tribes, the earlier resolution of parallel questions concerning the Federal City would ease the path of judicial exploration. Furthermore, in appeals from the District, the Supreme Court was engaged in examining the nature of federal sovereignty in the absence of supportive State governmental activity, and without the federalist limitations upon national authority inherent under the Constitution of the United States.[39] Because of these qualitative differences in appeals from the District of Columbia, as well as their quantitative impact upon the early Marshall Court (representing 35 percent of its appellate caseload), it is impossible to overstate the significance of the District of Columbia to the evolution of the early Supreme Court.

By way of qualification, however, it is necessary to note that the Court in asserting its appellate jurisdiction over the District of Columbia was implementing the intentions of Congress as embodied in the 1801 statute concerning the District. There the legislators expressed the policy that the Supreme Court should enjoy a general superintendence of the civil litigation arising in the Federal City. An entirely different circumstance existed in regard to the Northwest Territory, established by congressional ordinance before the establishment of the new federal government under the Constitution. Presented with the question of its appellate jurisdiction over the General Court of the Northwest Territory, the Supreme Court held that the territorial court was clearly a federal court, and hence subject to congressional control.[40] However, it declined to exercise appellate authority to review the decisions of the General Court, since Congress in erecting the territorial court had not provided a mode of appellate review, nor had the Supreme Court been authorized to review those territorial decisions by virtue of the new federal Constitution or the various judiciary acts. This decision in *Clark* v. *Bazadone* provides further evidence that all of the Supreme Court's appellate jurisdiction was the product of a constitutional grant as implemented by legislative action; absent one or the other of these vital elements, the Court refused to expound a theory of residual superintendence of federal courts as a foundation for its jurisdiction. Absent congressional action there was, in the Court's opinion, no inherent appellate jurisdiction in the Supreme Court.

---

[39] It should be noted that of all the federal circuit courts only those of the District of Columbia had resident circuit judges. They met quarterly, rather than on the semiannual schedule of the other circuit courts, and sec. 1 of the Act concerning the District of Columbia required them to apply Virginia law in Alexandria County and Maryland law in Washington County. See 1 Stat. 103–105, 105–106 (1790).

[40] Clark v. Bazadone, 1 Cranch 212–14 (1803).

The quasi-independent status of the future States of Maine and Kentucky resulted in some statutory modification of the usual procedure of allocating one circuit court per State, and making circuit court boundaries contiguous with those of the various States. The Judiciary Act of 1789 gave the district court established in Kentucky all of the jurisdiction of a federal circuit court, with appeals to run to the Supreme Court on the same basis as appeals from the circuit courts.[41] On the other hand, the district court established for Maine, while given circuit court powers, was left subject to appellate supervision from the Massachusetts circuit court.[42] This traditional relationship was disturbed by ambiguities in the Judiciary Act of 1803, which provided that appeals from district courts exercising circuit court powers should lie to the Supreme Court in cases of equity, admiralty, and prize. Following the uncertain congressional lead, the Supreme Court in *The Sloop Sally* v. *United States* upheld its appellate jurisdiction in maritime matters, but in *United States* v. *Weeks* it continued the established jurisdiction of the Circuit Court for the Massachusetts District in common law cases.[43]

Appeals from the federal district court in Kentucky ran to the Supreme Court of the United States under the Judiciary Act of 1789, and continued to do so until 1815 despite the independent existence of Kentucky as a State of the Union since 1792. This form of appellate supervision was used as the basis for the 1804 establishment of the District Court for the Territory of Orleans.[44] In *Morgan* v. *Callender* the Supreme Court upheld the validity of this jurisdictional arrangement,[45] thereby confirming the right of Congress to eliminate circuit courts from the appellate structure at such times and under such conditions as the legislators deemed appropriate. As a result of the precedent established in regard to semi-independent Kentucky, it proved possible for Congress to apply flexible appellate rules in regard to the western territories. This in turn made it possible to administer law in federal lands without requiring the creation of an intermediate appellate court for each territory, and conversely, it allowed the accretion of both dis-

---

[41] Secs. 1, 10, 1 Stat. 73, at 77–78 (1789).

[42] Sec. 10, 1 Stat. 78.

[43] Sec. 2 of the Act in addition to the Act intituled, "An Act to amend the judicial system of the United States," Mar. 3, 1803, 2 Stat. 244, provided for appeals from district courts to run to circuit courts having authority in their district. In conjunction with the Maine provisions in the 1789 Judiciary Act, this could have been construed to mean that the Maine District Court was to hear appeals from its own decisions. United States v. Weeks, 5 Cranch 1 (1809); Sloop Sally v. United States, 5 Cranch 372–74 (1809).

[44] An Act erecting Louisiana into Two Territories and providing for the temporary government thereof, Mar. 26, 1804, 2 Stat. 283–89, at 285–86.

[45] 4 Cranch 370 (1808).

trict court and circuit court jurisdiction into the hands of territorial district judges.[46] For the time being the problem of circuit-riding Supreme Court justices was limited to the original States east of the Appalachian Mountain range.

The two sources of appellate jurisdiction already discussed—that deriving from sections 9, 11, and 13 of the Judiciary Act of 1789, and that based upon section 5 of the 1801 Act concerning the District of Columbia—apply to cases that either originated in federal courts or that were transferred to those tribunals on the basis of diversity of citizenship under section 12 of the 1789 Judiciary Act. Yet to be discussed is the most important aspect of appellate jurisdiction—the Supreme Court's authority under section 25 of the Judiciary Act of 1789 to review

> [1] a final judgment or decree in any suit, in the highest court of law or equity of a State in which is drawn in question the validity of a treaty or statute of, or an authority exercised under the United States, and the decision is against their validity; [2] or where is drawn in question the validity of a statute of, or an authority exercised under any State, on the ground of their being repugnant to the constitution, treaties, or laws of the United States, and the decision is in favour of such their validity, [3] or where is drawn in question the construction of any clause of the constitution, or of a treaty, or statute of, or commission held under the United States, and the decision is against the title, right, privilege or exemption specially set up or claimed by either party . . .[47]

This so-called federal-question appellate jurisdiction was bottomed upon two constitutional provisions. Most immediately, it drew upon Article III, Section 2, Clause 1 for its validity: "The judicial Power shall extend to all Cases, in Law and Equity, arising under this Constitution, the Laws of the United States and Treaties made, or which shall be made, under their Authority."

As Chief Justice Marshall was to observe in *Cohens* v. *Virginia* in 1821,[48] this clause conferred upon the federal courts a jurisdiction based not upon the status of the parties but rather upon the character of the action. A broad conferral of jurisdiction, this clause was not limited to federal court cases in its application, but logically included also those decisions of the State courts that fell within the category described.

Supplementing this grant in Article III of the Constitution, the "supremacy clause" of Article VI declared the Constitution, laws, and

---

[46] The normal structure of separate district and circuit courts was established in the States of Kentucky, Ten- nessee, and Ohio by the Act of Feb. 24, 1807, 2 Stat. 420–21.

[47] 1 Stat. 85–87 (1789).

[48] 6 Wheat. 264–450 (1821).

treaties of the United States to be the supreme law of the land, and
that the judges of every State should be bound thereby, regardless of
any contrary constitutional rules or statutes of the various States. Unless Article VI might be assumed to be self-executing, Article III,
Section 2 had to be construed as conferring appellate jurisdiction upon
the Supreme Court in "federal question" matters. Indeed in enacting
the Judiciary Act of 1789 and making provision for such review, Congress had accepted this connection between supremacy on one hand,
and "federal question" jurisdiction of the Supreme Court on the other.
Yet as the Supreme Court would soon learn after its 1816 decision in
Martin v. *Hunter's Lessee*,[49] there was intense opposition to the jurisdiction of the Supreme Court in this area.

During the years from 1801 to 1815 the Supreme Court exercised
forbearance and restraint in asserting its authority under section 25 of
the Judiciary Act of 1789. In *Gordon* v. *Caldcleugh*[50] the justices refused jurisdiction where the State courts had acted favorably on the
request of a party who relied upon alienage and the removal provisions
of section 12 of the 1789 Judiciary Act. Pointing to section 25 as applying only to those cases where rights claimed under federal statutes had
been *denied*, the Court declined to grant section 25 review. However,
where both parties in a claim for title to land claimed title under the
same federal act, the Supreme Court held that the party wronged by
the adverse decision of the State court might take a section-25 appeal.[51]
Clearly the party seeking review under section 25 would have to show
that he had raised a "federal question" and that it had been decided
against his claim. *Owings* v. *Norwood's Lessee* made it clear that the
status of the plaintiff or defendant in the action, and his right to claim
under a federal treaty, was the only basis upon which section-25 jurisdiction would be exercised.[52] In *Owings* the defendant claimed the
benefit of a pre-Revolutionary mortgage executed in favor of a British
creditor. He asserted that his interest was under the protection of the
1794 Anglo-American treaty even though he did not derive his title
from the British mortgagee. His position was that since the treaty protected the interest of the mortgagee, it divested the title of the plaintiff
and hence defeated his ejectment action. For the Supreme Court, Chief
Justice Marshall stated that when an individual's title was not affected
by the treaty, he might not claim it as a basis for a section-25 appeal.

As a consequence of *Gordon* v. *Caldcleugh, Matthews* v. *Zane*, and

---

[49] 1 Wheat. 304–81 (1816). See C.
Warren, "Legislative and Judicial Attacks on the Supreme Court," *American Law Review* XLVII (1913), 5
et seq., for an account of the opposition.

[50] 3 Cranch 268–70 (1806).
[51] Matthews v. Zane, 4 Cranch 382–
83 (1808).
[52] 5 Cranch 344–50 (1809).

Owings v. *Norwood's Lessee*, it became clear that only a limited class of litigants were entitled to a section-25 appeal. They were required to (1) have a claim to rights under the federal Constitution, or under the statutes or treaties of the United States, and (2) show that a decision of a State or federal court denied those rights as claimed. Yet restricting the class of litigants who might qualify for section-25 relief did not imply subservience or fear of State judicial and political power. Quite the contrary, for in *Owings*, while in the process of denying an attempt to use section 25 for purposes of collateral attack, Chief Justice Marshall gave a forthright explanation for the existence of Article III, Section 1 of the Constitution and section 25 of the Judiciary Act: "The reason for inserting that clause in the constitution was, that all persons who have real claims under a treaty should have their causes decided by the national tribunals. It was to avoid the apprehension as well as the danger of state prejudices."[53] Appeals under section 25 were established for the highest national purposes, and the Chief Justice was not willing to have this intention blurred by allowing promiscuous use of section 25 by litigants not entitled to claim under its provisions.

Alert to the dangers of permitting section 25 to become a conduit for otherwise unauthorized appeals to the federal Supreme Court, John Marshall and his associates were equally cognizant of the likelihood that technicalities of procedure and precedent might emasculate the "federal question" review power. *Smith* v. *Maryland*, one of the wartime land confiscation cases discussed previously,[54] raised the latter problem with immediacy. The Maryland Court of Appeals had already held that the act of the Maryland legislature immediately transferred title out of the British aliens, and that no further steps were necessary to vest title in the State of Maryland. Consequently the 1783 Peace Treaty and its prohibition against *future* confiscations could not apply to the Smith case. Furthermore, it had become a custom, if not a precedent, in the Supreme Court, to accept as binding the decisions of the highest courts of the States concerning real property situated in the States where the decisions were rendered.

The logical problem inherent in *Smith* v. *Maryland* was set forth by Judge Bushrod Washington, who delivered the opinion of the Court: "[T]he whole difficulty in this case depends upon that part of it which involves the construction of certain state laws, and that the operation and effect of the treaty, which constitutes the residue of the case, is obvious so soon as that construction is settled."[55] While the Court would hear the argument of counsel as to the construction of the State

---

[53] *Ibid.*, 348.
[54] See discussion in Part II, chapter 5, pp. 553–54.

[55] 6 Cranch 304 (1810).

statute, and give proper attention to the determinations of the State legislature and the construction of the highest court of the State involved, "still, if, according to the true construction of the state laws, this court should be of opinion that the acts of confiscation left something to be done . . . which was not done at the time the treaty was made, . . . we must say that, in this case, the construction of the treaty was drawn into question. . . ."[56] In other words once an appellant had established *prima facie* qualification under section 25, the Supreme Court would proceed to an independent examination of the facts that might give rise to a "federal question." Neither legal precedents nor State court constructions would preclude it from making the necessary review and resolving the jurisdictional questions raised by the party claiming the protection of the Constitution or the laws or treaties of the United States.

While it cannot be said that the early Marshall Court's work in regard to section-25 appeals was of great political concern, nor that it involved direct clashes with the legislatures of the various States,[57] it is nevertheless true that the potentialities of section-25 review were tested in the years from 1801 to 1815. The Court evidenced a genuine commitment to uphold its authority in matters pertaining to treaty obligations, a field of legitimate concern because of the central position of the Supreme Court as the highest American tribunal of international law. Ultimately that concern would lead to a direct confrontation with the Commonwealth of Virginia in *Martin* v. *Hunter's Lessee*. Less definite was the extent to which the Supreme Court might exert itself to protect section-25 jurisdiction in domestic matters dealing with federal constitutional rights and claims of privilege under congressional statutes. For our period at least, the primacy of federal statutes over State legislation and precedents was permitted to remain vague.

While the full potentiality for section-25 review remained in the future, a direct and important conflict took place in 1809 between the Supreme Court and the authority of a State legislature. *United States* v. *Peters*[58] arose on the basis of prize litigation in the Pennsylvania State Court of Admiralty during the American Revolution. This case was subsequently reversed upon appeal to the Federal Court of Appeals in Prize Causes. After the establishment of the new federal court system

---

[56] *Ibid.*, 305. By 1813 the logic of Judge Washington's opinion was so generally accepted that it was not discussed in Fairfax's Devisee v. Hunter's Lessee. 7 Cranch 602–32 (1813).

[57] From 1802–15, thirteen cases reached the Supreme Court on writs of error to State courts. The opinion concerning their lack of political significance is advanced in Warren, "Legislative and Judicial Attacks on the Supreme Court," *American Law Review* XLVII (1913), 5.

[58] 5 Cranch 115–41 (1809).

under the new Constitution, and after District Judge Peters entered a decree ordering payment according to the prize court's ruling, the Pennsylvania legislature prohibited the State tribunals from effectuating the appellate court's sentence, and passed a similar resolution inhibiting the federal district court judge from enforcing the decree. The successful party in the Federal Court of Appeals then brought a petition for mandamus to the Supreme Court, asking that District Judge Richard Peters show cause why he should not enforce the prize court's decree. In his return Judge Peters cited the State statute as his prudential reason for non-compliance. Chief Justice Marshall in his most magisterial tone observed,

> If the legislatures of the several states may, at will, annul the judgments of the courts of the United States, and destroy the rights acquired under those judgments, the constitution itself becomes a solemn mockery, and the nation is deprived of the means of enforcing its laws by the instrumentality of its own tribunals. So fatal a result must be deprecated by all.[59]

In a rather sweeping assertion of supervisory power, Marshall continued that if the supervision of the jurisdiction of the federal courts was vested in the "supreme judicial tribunal of the nation,"[60] then the Pennsylvania legislature had no constitutional power to interfere with the proceedings in the United States District Court for Pennsylvania. He then held that the proceeds of the prize litigation were held by David Rittenhouse not as treasurer for the Commonwealth of Pennsylvania but in his individual character as a stakeholder for the litigants. Consequently the case was in no way an action brought against a sovereign State and hence under the ban of the Eleventh Amendment. The Supreme Court issued a peremptory mandamus to Judge Peters, ordering that the proceeds of the litigation be paid in accordance with the decree of the Federal Court of Appeals.

The Peters case made patent the underlying tendency in *Smith* v. *Maryland*—the Supreme Court would hold the determination of federal court jurisdiction in its own hands, subject only to the legislation of Congress and the mandate of the federal Constitution. Indeed it had been litigation and political conflicts such as that presented in the Peters case that originally brought on the pressure for constitutional reform that resulted in the Philadelphia Convention. While Chief Justice Marshall may have been overly effusive in asserting the Supreme Court's

---

[59] *Ibid.*, 136.   [60] *Ibid.*

supervisory authority in *Peters*, he was nevertheless surely right in stressing the subordination of State legislation to the federal Constitution and statutes passed by Congress, including procedures for questioning a federal court's judgment.[61]

APPELLATE PRACTICE IN THE SUPREME COURT

The major development in appellate practice before the Supreme Court during our period was the regularization of admiralty and chancery appeals effectuated by section 2 of the Judiciary Act of 1803.[62] The 1789 Judiciary Act had stipulated that all appeals to the Supreme Court were to be taken by writ of error, but as Professor Goebel has shown in the previous volume, this restriction upon the scope and method of appeal had been broadened by a loose construction of the requirements for a statement of the case in regard to admiralty and chancery matters.[63] The extended record permitted under this judicial gloss upon the statute of 1789 was adequate for most purposes that would be achieved by the civil law appeal; however the 1803 enactment authorized for the first time the right of the Supreme Court to accept new evidence in admiralty and prize cases. In addition the extended record in chancery and admiralty causes was made a required part of appeals to the Supreme Court by virtue of express provision of the 1803 statute.

Conflicts in opinion between the two-judge circuit courts came under consideration in the Judiciary Act of 1802, which provided for the submission of certified questions to the Supreme Court in situations where circuit court judges differed.[64] This new procedure was examined in *Ogle* v. *Lee*, where the Court was requested to pass upon the entire case rather than limiting the scope of its inquiry to the points raised in the certified questions.[65] This the Court declined to do, giving a unanimous opinion that only issues upon which the circuit court was divided would be considered. Other matters might subsequently be brought up in the normal procedure by writ of error after judgment. Although *Ogle* v. *Lee* is only a *per curiam* opinion it is of significance since it reaffirmed the Court's reliance upon the writ of error as the principal mode of appeal in common law matters.

---

[61] See Wilson v. Mason, 1 Cranch 45–103 (1803), discussed in Part II, chapter 8, note 34.

[62] Act of Mar. 3, 1803, 2 Stat. 244.

[63] Goebel, *Antecedents*, 686–706. In Hawthorne v. United States the Supreme Court upheld its statutory authority to take new evidence while hearing an appeal in admiralty. 7 Cranch 107–108 (1812).

[64] 2 Stat. 159 (1802), superseding sec. 2 of the Judiciary Act of 1793, 1 Stat. 334. Possibly the new procedure was based upon the procedure in the Virginia State courts, of adjourning cases for difficulty to the next sitting of the General Court where the judges met *en banc*.

[65] 2 Cranch 33 (1804).

A certain degree of flexibility and ingenuity was demonstrated by the Court in developing appellate procedures. *Barton v. Petit and Bayard* presented the delicate problem of a case where the resolution of the issues involved the examination of a writ of execution arising from a separate and distinct piece of litigation.[66] Since the writ did not originate with the *Barton* action, it was not part of the *Barton* record, and hence not before the Supreme Court on writ of error. While the Court declined to act upon the suggestion that it might take judicial notice of the existence of the execution, it did fashion a writ termed a special writ of certiorari, directed to the circuit court in which the execution was a matter of record. Elsewhere we have seen the writ of habeas corpus ad subjiciendum used as an appellate procedure in criminal cases,[67] and in *Barton* a new form of certiorari was utilized to enable litigants to prove points made in appellate practice before the Court. The writ of error was found inadequate to review an order enjoining the execution of judgment in a common law action, but the Supreme Court authorized the use of a mandamus nisi in the nature of a procedendo to accomplish the same purpose.[68]

Pendency of an appeal left the subject matter of the litigation undetermined, and an alteration of the law during the course of the appeal might alter the law of the case. In *United States* v. *The Schooner Peggy*[69] the 1800 Convention with France was concluded while an appeal of the vessel's condemnation was before the Supreme Court. She was restored to her owner in accordance with the stipulations of the treaty even though an earlier decision or failure to appeal would have left the owner without legal rights to the vessel. When the Non-Intercourse Act of 1806 was permitted to expire without a statutory reservation of the forfeitures accrued under the legislation, the Supreme Court held that all pending libels under the Act were to be dismissed, even if the ships and cargo had been sold and the proceeds held subject to the lower court's order.[70]

Not infrequently the Supreme Court was asked to review the exercise of discretion by lower federal courts. It applied the rule of decision that matters in the discretion of trial courts were not reviewable by writs of error. Refusal to permit the amendment of pleadings,[71] denial of a new trial or a request to re-institute a cause after dismissal or

---

[66] 7 Cranch 288–90 (1813).

[67] In *Ex Parte* Bollman and *Ex Parte* Swartwout, discussed in Part II, chapter 8, notes 15, 16.

[68] Livingston v. Dorgenois, 7 Cranch 577–89 (1813).

[69] 1 Cranch 103–10 (1801).

[70] Yeaton v. United States, 5 Cranch 281–84 (1809); Schooner Rachel v. United States, 6 Cranch 329–30 (1810).

[71] Marine Insurance Company of Alexandria v. Hodgson, 6 Cranch 206–21 (1810); Sheehy v. Mandeville & Jameson, 6 Cranch 253–67 (1810).

default judgment, all were held non-reviewable by writ of error,[72] as was the trial court's refusal to permit a continuance.[73] While it was not reversible error for a court to refuse a jury instruction on an abstract point of law,[74] trial courts were required to provide instructions upon the legal construction of facts that might be found by juries.[75] Despite the frequency of appeals concerning discretion, it would seem that the practicing bar did not possess adequate guidelines to frame their exceptions to trial court actions. Certainly the parameters of reviewable discretion in the trial court were matters of considerable doubt in this period.

THE LOWER FEDERAL COURTS

In enunciating the parameters of its own jurisdiction the Supreme Court established broad classes of judicial power which were equally applicable to the federal circuit and district courts. Consequently much of the preceding discussion applies to the appellate jurisdiction and procedures of the lower courts. However, in other situations the Supreme Court resolved issues limited in their scope to the district and circuit courts, and it is to those cases that we must now turn to discover not only the Court's supervisory work concerning those courts but also to determine how appellate jurisdiction and procedure in the lower courts affected the flow of cases to the Supreme Court itself. Naturally no survey of the lower federal courts can be definitive without an exhaustive study of the surviving records and the printed opinions of those tribunals—a subject well beyond the scope of this work, but one that will be receiving attention by virtue of the project of the Judicial Conference of the United States, which is designed to prepare histories of each of the federal circuits. Pending the completion of that work, the discussion that follows must be used as a guide to the development of the lower federal courts in the years from 1801 to 1815.

By the time Chief Justice Ellsworth took office in 1796, the assignment of circuit-riding duties to Supreme Court justices had ceased to be a matter of political controversy.[76] The repeal of the Judiciary Act of 1801 in an atmosphere of partisan mistrust, however, raised again the possibility of hostilities between Congress and the Court on this issue.

---

[72] Resler v. Sheehee, 1 Cranch 110–17 (1801); Henderson v. Moore, 5 Cranch 11–13 (1809); Marine Insurance Company v. Young, 6 Cranch 206–21 (1810); Welch v. Mandeville, 7 Cranch 152–56 (1812).

[73] Wood & Bemis v. Young, 4 Cranch 237–38 (1808).

[74] Hamilton v. Russell, 1 Cranch 309–18 (1803); Marine Insurance Co. of Alexandria v. Young, 5 Cranch 187–91 (1809).

[75] Smith v. Carrington, 4 Cranch 62–73 (1807); Maryland Insurance Company v. Woods, 6 Cranch 29–51 (1810).

[76] Goebel, *Antecedents*, 554–69, provides the details.

Rising like a phoenix from the ashes of the 1789–92 debates, the case of *Stuart* v. *Laird* posed the question of the constitutionality of the assignment of Supreme Court justices to serve on the circuit courts.[77] At the bar it was urged that while this custom had been acquiesced in by the Supreme Court from 1789 to 1801, it had been abolished by the Judiciary Act of the latter year, and its revival brought the constitutional question to the forefront. For the Court Judge William Paterson delivered an opinion that upheld the right of the Congress to establish the jurisdiction of the inferior federal courts and to transfer a cause from one tribunal to another. Paterson pointed out that the practice of the Court itself, and the judges' acquiescence in their assignment to circuit duties, had fixed the construction of the Constitution in that regard. "Of course, the question is at rest, and ought not now to be disturbed."[78]

Maritime matters were of continual concern to the lower federal courts, and Supreme Court decisions concerning jurisdiction in this area were significant in delineating the permissible scope of judicial activity by the district and circuit courts. The traditional view of prize and admiralty jurisdiction, set forth in *United States* v. *La Vengeance*,[79] was that transactions entered into upon navigable waters were within the admiralty jurisdiction of the federal courts, even if some common law proceeding were available as a remedy. *La Vengeance* was followed by the Supreme Court in the 1808 decision of *United States* v. *The Schooner Betsy and Charlotte*.[80] Ostensibly these cases advance a broad view of civil admiralty jurisdiction, but if they are examined closely they prove to be rather restricted in their application. Both involved forfeitures brought on by violations of federal statutes. The *La Vengeance* was alleged to have violated the act prohibiting the exportation of arms and munitions, and the *Betsy and Charlotte* purportedly breached the 1806 Non-Intercourse law. Both were proceedings *in rem* against the vessels and their cargo. The *in rem* nature of the forfeiture actions was the basis upon which the Supreme Court had denied trial by jury to the owners. In other words, an *in rem* proceeding was by its nature a matter of admiralty concern, and hence subject to

---

[77] 1 Cranch 299–309 (1803). This was a motion to enforce a forthcoming bond that had been filed in the Virginia Circuit Court established under the 1801 Judiciary Act. It had been returned to the circuit court constituted under the 1802 Judiciary Act. In opposition to the claimant under the bond, it was objected that it was returnable at a different circuit court, hence the action should have been dismissed.

[78] *Ibid.*, 309. Subsequently it was held that if the assigned Supreme Court Justice were absent, the District Court Judge might hold a valid circuit court for his district. Pollard and Pickett v. Dwight, 4 Cranch 421–33 (1808).

[79] 3 Dall. 297–301 (1796).

[80] 4 Cranch 443–52 (1808).

civil law procedures that did not include jury trial. However, as we have seen in *Peisch* v. *Ware*, an *in rem* salvage case, the "saving clause" might be applied even to such an action. Apparently it was not the nature of the action that gave exclusive admiralty jurisdiction to the federal courts but rather the fact that Congress had provided express sanctions for the enforcement of its laws, and these were to be applied in federal courts exercising admiralty and maritime jurisdiction.[81]

Territorial limitations upon admiralty jurisdictions were graphically presented in the prize case of *Brown* v. *United States,* which arose from the government's seizure of timber owned by a British merchant that was seized at the opening of the War of 1812 while it was floating in the waters of a tidal creek.[82] Evidence at bar showed that when the tide receded the timber was resting upon the muddy bottom of the creek, and based upon this showing, Chief Justice Marshall and the majority of the judges held that the seizure had been made upon land, and thus was not a matter of prize jurisdiction. Judge Story dissented, relying upon his earlier opinion as circuit justice in the Circuit Court for Massachusetts. He had held there that the seizure of enemy property, either on the sea, or near the coast, or on coastal land, was a proper basis for prize adjudication. Judge Story's position was based upon a broadening of the "navigable from the sea" standard embodied in the Judiciary Act of 1789. Subsequently in *De Lovio* v. *Boit*,[83] he advanced the principle that maritime contracts, regardless of the place of execution, and maritime torts on the high seas or in harbors where the tide ebbs and flows, were within the admiralty jurisdiction of the federal courts. While the uncertainties concerning maritime jurisdiction were not to be resolved before 1815, it does appear that tentative steps had been taken to construe the grant of admiralty power to the federal courts, and that the Marshall Court in this early period was extremely cautious in expanding admiralty jurisdiction beyond its traditional English limits.

Some minor points of practice enunciated during this early period of the Marshall Court deserve passing mention. The problem of injunctive relief in federal courts against State judgments, and of State injunctive relief against judgments of the federal courts, was resolved by a prohibition against both forms of injunction.[84] While the potentialities for conflict and litigation on these grounds were not substantially diminished by these holdings, nevertheless the fundamental rule of non-

---

[81] On *in rem* admiralty jurisdiction see discussion in Part II, chapter 3, pp. 476–77.

[82] 8 Cranch 110–54 (1814). See discussion in Part II, chapter 2, pp. 451–52.

[83] 7 Fed. Cas. 418 (No. 3776) (Cir. Ct. Mass. District 1815).

[84] Diggs & Keith v. Wolcott, 4 Cranch 179–80 (1807); M'Kim v. Voorhis, 7 Cranch 279–81 (1812).

interference that prevails to the present day was based upon these opinions.

English procedural rules were followed by the Supreme Court in its holding that courts of law and equity might exercise concurrent jurisdiction in actions for dower.[85] The Supreme Court distinguished between local actions to establish title to realty that were cognizable only in the federal court of the situs,[86] and transitory actions based upon contractual rights or fraudulent practices concerning realty, which might be heard in any federal court having power under diversity rules or federal question jurisdiction.[87] As we have noted in the chapter on international law, the Supreme Court accepted the binding nature of foreign condemnations in prize matters, but it reserved the right to inquire into the jurisdiction of the tribunal issuing the decree.[88] A foreign prize decree was treated only as evidence of its own correctness, and not of the facts upon which the decree was based. In regard to matters of domestic conflict of laws, in *Mills* v. *Duryee*[89] the Court declared that judgments entered by the courts of one State of the Union were required to be accepted as conclusive evidence of debt by the courts of every other State. The opinion specifically rejected the contention at bar that all the full faith and credit clause required was that out-of-state judgment be treated as prima facie evidence of the facts upon which the sister State judgment was based.

These instances of Supreme Court action concerning the jurisdiction of the lower federal courts provide some insight into the work of the Court towards a balanced and symmetrical arrangement of federal and State courts in the administration of justice. There is a noticeable reluctance to overextend federal jurisdiction beyond its necessary limits, and a deft sensitivity on the part of the Supreme Court judges which precludes the delivery of opinions that might be construed as serving the interests of the federal judiciary to the detriment of the States. Furthermore there is a clear preference for upholding only those jurisdictional powers that are absolutely essential to the constitutional functions of the federal courts within the Union. Restraint and orderly growth were the hallmarks of judicial enunciations in these vital areas.

FEDERAL CRIMINAL LAW AND THE COMMON LAW OF CRIMES

When John Marshall became Chief Justice the state of federal criminal law was the subject of much acrimonious debate, arising in

---

[85] Herbert v. Wren, 7 Cranch 366–82 (1813).

[86] Massie v. Watts, 6 Cranch 148–70 (1810).

[87] Bodley v. Taylor, 5 Cranch 191–234 (1809).

[88] Part II, chapter 5, pp. 534–43.

[89] 7 Cranch 481–87 (1813).

part from partisan use of criminal prosecutions to stifle opposition opinion, and in part from ambiguities in the federal Constitution concerning the source of criminal law at the federal level. In the first volume of this *History* Professor Goebel has traced with characteristic care and precision the events leading up to the passage of the controversial Sedition Act of 1798, and the unhappy sequel of prosecutions for criminal libel against opposition editors and authors.[90] For our purposes it is sufficient to note here that the Sedition Act was permitted to expire on March 3, 1801, but its death did not abate the legacy of political and constitutional debate over the more fundamental question concerning the nature of the criminal jurisdiction that had been vested in the federal courts by the Constitution.[91] While the new administration of Thomas Jefferson was not above the use of criminal libel prosecutions to stifle the Federalist press,[92] the expiration of the Sedition Act did much to remove the question of criminal law from the political arena into the courts of justice. The most pressing issue became the applicability of the English common law of crimes to federal law, which would supply the federal courts with extensive criminal jurisdiction that had not been conferred either by constitutional provision or congressional action.

Substantial areas of criminal law, left untouched by congressional statutory provisions, had traditionally been enforced in English and American colonial courts as inherent attributes of sovereignty. By the time of the Declaration of Independence, criminal law throughout the American colonies tended to parallel closely English criminal law,[93] and it was argued that as a sovereign power the United States had criminal jurisdiction over common law offenses not prohibited by federal statute. Supplementing this theory that criminal jurisdiction over common law offenses was an inherent attribute of sovereignty, there was the possibility of construing section 34 of the Judiciary Act of 1789 as applying the State criminal law (which included English common law crimes) to federal criminal prosecutions. While Virginia's revision of her colonial statutes had substantially eliminated the possibility of the survival of a common law of crimes,[94] few other American States had followed suit, and nearly all had adopted the law of their province as it existed at the beginning of the Revolution or at the Declaration

---

[90] Goebel, *Antecedents*, 608–51.

[91] Legislative debate on the repeal of the 1801 Judiciary Act kept the issue of common law crimes before the national consciousness. *Annals of Congress*, 7th Cong., 1st sess., 583, 596, 611–14.

[92] L. Levy, *Jefferson and Civil Liberties: The Dark Side* (Cambridge, Mass., 1963), 61–62.

[93] See generally, J. Goebel and T. Naughton, *Law Enforcement in Colonial New York* (New York, 1944).

[94] See the discussion in Part II, chapter 6, pp. 561–63.

of Independence.[95] This meant that substantial portions of the English common law of crimes were effective within the United States at the State level. That residuum of non-statutory authority available to State prosecutors might conceivably be held applicable to federal criminal prosecutions under the mandate of section 34.[96]

At the outset it is essential to note the extremely restricted sphere of criminal jurisdiction that had been granted to the federal courts by specific acts of Congress. The Act of April 30, 1790,[97] initiated legislation on criminal matters, establishing five general categories of cases:

1. The constitutional offense of treason was given statutory substance, and supplemented by a crime of misprision of treason.
2. Certain offenses against international law, such as physical assault or civil law actions against a foreign diplomat, were prohibited.
3. Crimes committed upon the high seas, and outside the jurisdiction of a State—such as willful murder, robbery, piracy, mutiny, or cooperation with pirates—were made federal offenses.
4. Certain criminal acts committed in a "fort, dock-yard, magazine, or in any other place or district of country [*sic*], under the sole and exclusive jurisdiction of the United States," were prohibited.
5. Penalties were imposed for the protection of the governmental authority of the United States—including prohibitions against perjury, the bribery of judges in federal courts, the release of federal prisoners, and the counterfeiting of federal notes and currency.[98]

Clearly a strong argument could be made that the 1790 Crimes Act set forth only those criminal sanctions that were absolutely necessary to the exercise of the constitutional functions of the federal government. Yet it is by no means obvious that the enumeration of one or more crimes falling within these "federal" categories was indicative of a legislative intent to exclude all other crimes not specifically mentioned. Viewed in the light of the Marshall Court's jurisdiction opinions, discussed previously in this chapter, the question was whether the Court's demand for specific legislative grants of jurisdiction would apply to the criminal law field, or whether some more expansive view of federal judicial power—suggested by the property-oriented opinions in

---

95 For a good summary of the Revolutionary reception statutes, see J. Smith, *Cases and Materials on the Development of Legal Institutions* (St. Paul, Minn., 1965), 469–83.

96 The applicability of sec. 34 to criminal matters was questionable at this time. In United States v. Burr,

Chief Justice Marshall had limited its scope to civil matters. 4 Cranch 75 (1807). See also Commonwealth v. Schaffer, 4 Dall. (Pa)., Appendix, xxvi.

97 I Stat. 112–19.

98 *Ibid.*

United States v. *1960 Bags of Coffee* and *United States* v. *Fisher*—would prevail.

Subsequent to 1790 the most significant expansion of federal criminal jurisdiction was through statutes prohibiting offenses against international law and in statutory enunciation of maritime crimes bordering upon treason. In the Neutrality Act of 1794 American citizens were prohibited from accepting commission from any foreign prince or state, from enlisting in military service against the United States or her allies, and from augmenting the force of a foreign privateer or launching a military expedition against a friendly nation.[99] The Logan Act of January 30, 1799,[100] made it illegal for an unauthorized American citizen to engage in discussions with a foreign power concerning disputes or controversies between the power and the United States. Each of these statutes grew out of particular difficulties brought on by President Washington's Neutrality Proclamation in the first instance, and by the "Quasi-War" with France that followed after the failure of the XYZ Mission. They have been discussed elsewhere[101] and need not detain us at this point, except for the purpose of illustrating the international thrust of the legislation and its relevance to diplomatic affairs.

Federal jurisdiction over maritime activities deemed criminal in nature also expanded slightly after 1790, as evidenced by the 1800 prohibition against American citizens owning or serving upon vessels engaged in the international slave trade.[102] In 1804 Congress prohibited the willful casting away, burning, or other form of destruction on the high seas of a vessel by one not its owner.[103] The same provision penalized the destruction of a vessel by its owner for the purpose of obtaining an insurance settlement. Finally in 1805 the commission of certain crimes, including treason, on a foreign armed vessel within one league of American shores, was prohibited and prosecutions were brought within the cognizance of the federal courts.[104] Backed by traditional rules of maritime law and enjoying the support of the mercantile community, these statutes served purposes readily identifiable with the constitutional authority of the federal government, and its obligation to protect its citizens and their property from violence or loss upon the high seas and in territorial waters. Since marine insurance was a large interstate business in the early years of the Republic, it can also be said that the prohibitions against participation in the slave trade and

---

[99] 1 Stat. 381–84 (1794). An express prohibition against Americans accepting privateering commissions against the United States or a friendly nation was enacted in 1797. 1 Stat. 520.

[100] 1 Stat. 613 (1799).
[101] See Part II, chapter 2, pp. 409–10.
[102] 2 Stat. 70–71 (1800).
[103] 2 Stat. 290 (1804).
[104] 2 Stat. 339–42, at 339 (1805).

against the destruction of vessels might be intended to encourage inter-state commerce and protect underwriters from unnecessary risks and fraudulent practices.

Supplementing these few criminal statutes were a variety of penalties in administrative statutes, designed to enforce compliance with the revenue or navigation laws or similar legislation. Some examples are fines assessed against masters and mates of vessels failing to make the necessary reports to customs officers, fines and penalties against postmasters and their clerks for demanding excessive postage, a capital penalty against an employee of the United States mint or his suborner, who embezzled precious metals.[105] Citizens who failed to pay the carriage tax were penalized by a double assessment; those using unstamped paper were fined under the provisions of the 1797 Stamp Act, and individuals who traded with the Indians without a federal license were subjected to forfeiture of the goods involved.[106] We have previously examined at length the system of forfeitures applicable to violations of the various Non-Intercourse Acts and the Embargo laws.[107] Even with the broader view of criminal law that would include such administrative misdemeanors within its purview, the federal statutory law of crimes remained closely tied to the delegated powers of the federal government. Indeed the mixture of civil and criminal sanctions within the revenue and navigation laws tends to stress the limitation of federal court jurisdiction to specific constitutional purposes.

This brief review of federal criminal law from the vantage point of an attorney or judge in March 1801 tends to highlight the narrow scope of federal criminal jurisdiction. The single statute that had made a substantial departure from the pattern was the Sedition Act of 1798, which provided penal sanctions against those who would

> unlawfully combine or conspire together, with intent to oppose any measure or measures of the government of the United States which are or shall be directed by proper authority, or to impede the operation of any law of the United States, or to intimidate or prevent any person holding a place or office in or under the government of the United States, from undertaking, performing or executing his trust or duty; . . .[108]

Counseling or procuring a riot, unlawful assembly or combination, was also declared illegal, and the second section of the Act provided fines and imprisonment for those who would

---

[105] 1 Stat. 246–51, at 250 (1792).
[106] 1 Stat. 373–75 (1794); 1 Stat. 137–38 (1790); 1 Stat. 329–32 (1793); 1 Stat. 527–32 (1797).

[107] In Part II, chapter 2, pp. 409–10, 415–19.
[108] 1 Stat. 596–97, at 596.

cause or procure to be written, printed, uttered or published . . . any false, scandalous and malicious writing or writings against the government of the United States, . . . either house of the Congress . . . , or the President, . . . with intent to defame the said government, . . . or to stir up sedition within the United States, . . .[109]

Evidence regarding the enactment of the Sedition Act would indicate its origin in the fear that the common law crime of seditious libel would not be within the jurisdiction of the federal courts, and the statutory language shows an effort to include the broad provisions of the common law crime. However that may be, it is obvious that the Sedition Act represented a sharp departure from the normal pattern of federal criminal legislation. It was subject to attack upon two fundamental grounds. First, it served no federal purpose specifically enunciated in the Constitution, and secondly, it upset the pre-existing balance between federal and State powers. The other federal criminal statutes were designed to "fill in" the interstices left by State legislation and international law, and to provide national law where it was absolutely necessary and proper to secure federal purposes. Hitherto when State law was both applicable and adequate, Congress had refrained from legislative action, but most American States either had specific statutory prohibitions against seditious libel or they prosecuted such offenses under common law precedents. The Sedition Act for the first time provided penalties at the federal level for crimes also punishable under State law.

Significantly, both political parties used seditious libel prosecutions against their opponents when they had the opportunity to do so, but at first they differed in their choice of tribunals. The Jeffersonians attempted to use State courts for this purpose,[110] while the Federalists had earlier passed the Sedition Act to bring the seditious libel prosecutions within the jurisdiction of federal courts. Republican preference for State jurisdiction in this field paralleled the choice of State courts for the enforcement of the Non-Intercourse and Embargo Acts. However when State remedies proved inadequate, either because courts and juries were hostile, or because State substantive and procedural law was ineffective, the Jeffersonians like their Federalist predecessors were willing to resort to the common law of crimes to justify federal prosecutions.[111] In retrospect it is obvious that the common law of crimes

[109] Ibid.

[110] William Dickenson, a Federalist editor, was prosecuted in a Pennsylvania State court. Philadelphia Aurora, May 17, 1806. See also People v. Croswell, 3 Johnson's Cases (New York), 337 (1804), discussed at length in Goebel, Law Practice of Hamilton, I, 775–884; and Respublicae v. Dennie, 4 Yeates (Pa.), 267 (1805).

[111] The use of common law indictments in embargo cases may be seen in reports published in the Richmond Enquirer, June 2, 1809; see also T.

was a potent political weapon wielded by the party in power against its opposition; as such it was tainted with the aura of political self-interest and marked the frontier line at which the equal administration of justice was pitted in battle with the savagery of political ruthlessness.

When John Marshall administered the Presidential oath to Thomas Jefferson, the broad question of a federal common law of crimes had not been presented to the Supreme Court, although it had been debated at length in the press, in pamphlet literature, and in the impeachment trial of Senator William Blount of Tennessee.[112] Not only did the lack of authoritative precedent leave the criminal jurisdiction of federal courts in doubt, but it also left unanswered the pressing question of the role of the federal judiciary in the political life of the nation. The legal and constitutional issues concerning the common law of crime were intimately connected to the practical consideration that political leaders could, and did, use the doctrine of common law crime to stifle the opposition press and perpetuate themselves in office. While these two aspects of the subject may be readily distinguished for purposes of academic study, it is apparent that any legal resolution of the problem was bound to be influenced by practical political considerations.

Before the Supreme Court struck down the doctrine of the common law of crimes in its 1812 holding in *United States* v. *Hudson and Goodwin*[113] the result was far from predictable. Immediately after Marshall became Chief Justice it was clear that both he and Judge Bushrod Washington favored the doctrine,[114] and that Judge Samuel Chase had declared himself in opposition to it.[115] When Judge William Johnson joined the Bench in 1804 it might well have been assumed that his views of federalism and legislative power would have inclined him towards a strict statutory basis for criminal liability.[116] In his circuit court opinion in *Hudson and Goodwin*, Judge Brockholst Livingston had declared himself in opposition to the doctrine, but his fellow Republican Joseph Story might even then have been identified as favoring a federal common law in this field.[117] Certainly after the decision in *Hudson and Goodwin*, Story not only used the doctrine in his circuit court opinions but he also lobbied for a statutory enactment that

---

Jefferson to A. Gallatin, Aug. 11, 1808, Worthington L. Ford, ed., *Writings of Jefferson*, IX (New York, 1897), 202.

[112] *Annals of Congress*, 5th Cong., 3rd sess., 2264–65, 2319; M. Borden, *The Federalism of James A Bayard* (New York, 1955), chapter 5; R. Walters, *Alexander James Dallas* (Philadelphia, 1953), 108–10.

[113] 7 Cranch 32–34 (1812).

[114] As to Marshall see R. Faulkner,

The Jurisprudence of John Marshall (Princeton, 1969), 87–89; *Address of the Minority in the Virginia Legislature* (Richmond, 1799).

[115] United States v. Worrall, 2 Dall. 384 (1798).

[116] D. Morgan, *Justice William Johnson* (Columbia, S.C., 1954), 77–80.

[117] G. Dunne, *Justice Joseph Story and the Rise of the Supreme Court* (New York, 1970), 108–109.

would recognize the existence of common law crimes as federal offenses.[118] We may conclude that while the general consequence of Republican appointments to the Supreme Court was the declining popularity of the doctrine, nevertheless there were strongly held views among the judges that might persuade the majority to favor either position.

Given the uncertain alignment of judges during the early years of his Presidency, it is not surprising that Thomas Jefferson sought to limit seditious libel prosecutions to matters that might be punished in State courts. Federal district attorneys were consistently discouraged from prosecuting these cases in federal courts, and the President tacitly reaffirmed this policy in his second Inaugural Address in 1805.[119] However his attention was diverted from these concerns by the mobilization of governmental power to combat the Burr expedition in the first instance and to prosecute the participants thereafter. In the midst of these tumultuous times, District Judge Pierpont Edwards of Connecticut asked the federal grand jury to consider the publications of several Federalist newspapers in Connecticut, including the *Connecticut Courant* issued by Barzillai Hudson and George Goodwin.[120] Claiming that his views represented those of a majority on the Supreme Court, Judge Edwards instructed the jurors to refer to the common law of crimes in their consideration of these editors and their possible prosecution for seditious libel. True bills were returned and the cases were brought to trial in September 1807 before President Jefferson's instructions to dismiss the indictments were received in Connecticut. The lack of witnesses and the absence of a Supreme Court circuit justice to replace William Paterson delayed trial to April 1808, at which time Judge Brockholst Livingston and Judge Edwards divided in opinion on the question of a federal common law of crimes, and the issue was certified to the Supreme Court in October 1808.

In the intervening year the Republican party's opposition to the doctrine had been weakened by the practical difficulties that the Jefferson administration had experienced in enforcing the Embargo. The

---

[118] Dunne, *Story*, 168, 240.

[119] J. Daveiss, "Sketch of the Political Profiles of Three Presidents," in *A View of the President's Conduct Concerning the Conspiracy of 1806* (Frankfort, Kentucky, 1807), 59n–60n; Ford, ed., *Writings of Jefferson*, VIII (New York, 1897), 346.

[120] Proceedings in the circuit court can be traced in United States Circuit Court for the District of Connecticut, Docket Book, Case 33, 34 (April 1806), and Docket Book and Case Papers (September 1806), Federal Records Center, Waltham, Mass.; Records of the Supreme Court, Appellate Case Papers, Case No. 395, RG 267, National Archives, Washington, D.C.; *The Witness* (Litchfield, Connecticut), Apr. 30, 1806; and Hampden, *A Letter to the President of the United States Touching the Prosecutions under his Patronage, before the Circuit Court in the District of Connecticut* (New Haven, 1808). See also *Dictionary of American Biography*, III, 44.

prosecution in *United States* v. *Smith*,[121] a Virginia case in the federal circuit court heard and decided by Chief Justice Marshall two months before *Hudson and Goodwin* appeared on the Supreme Court docket, illustrates this changing Republican attitude towards common law crimes. While the indictment in the case is missing from the files, Marshall's decision and the court minutes would indicate that, in addition to proceeding for the assessment of a fine and a forfeiture under the Embargo Acts, the government also pressed for criminal sanctions based upon the doctrine of common law crimes. Strictly construing the statute relied upon by the government, Marshall held that since a fine and forfeiture had been prescribed by Congress, it would have to be regarded as the exclusive penalty in this case. He specifically refrained from "deciding the question whether an indictment can be supported in this court on common law principles."[122]

Despite its limitations as a precedent, the *Smith* decision may be evidence of a change of position on the part of the Chief Justice. Although Marshall was not willing to deny the existence of a common law of crimes at the federal level, he was willing to limit the use of the principle to offenses not prohibited by statute. Once a statutory penalty had been imposed, it eliminated the common law on the subject as a residual basis for prosecution. Yet before his elevation to the Supreme Court Bench, in defending the Sedition Act, Marshall had claimed that the statute was harmless since it only codified the common law criminal rules on seditious libel.[123] Did the common law crime of seditious libel continue to exist along with the Sedition Act? Marshall's holding in *United States* v. *Smith* answered that question in the negative, although it is most likely Marshall in 1798 had believed that the two foundations for prosecutions were co-existent.

When *Hudson and Goodwin* was finally argued before the Supreme Court in March 1812 the charged political situations of the Burr trial, the Embargo prosecutions and the Sedition Act animosities were past history. Clearer and more present dangers were obvious in the form of seditious libel prosecutions by the Republican administration, particularly if the threatened war with Great Britain were to become reality. In his opinion for the majority of the Court, Judge Johnson observed, "Although this question is brought up now for the first time

---

[121] The progress of the unreported case, United States v. Smith, can be traced in the United States Circuit Court, District of Virginia, Order Book No. 7, 206–207, 235, 267–68; and Richmond *Enquirer*, Dec. 17, 22, 1808; June 2, 6, 1809. On the Embargo see L. Sears, *Jefferson and the Embargo* (Durham, N.C., 1927) and W. Jennings, *The American Embargo, 1807–1809* (Iowa City, 1921). See also discussion in Part II, chapter 2, pp. 415–33.

[122] Richmond *Enquirer*, June 6, 1809.

[123] *Address of the Minority in the Virginia Legislature.*

to be decided by this court, we consider it as having been long since settled in public opinion."[124]

Prosecutions based upon the common law of crimes had long ago been abandoned in Johnson's view, and in addition he held that the doctrine of a federal common law was inconsistent with the nature of the federal Union. Since the federal government was created through concessions by the States, in Johnson's opinion

[t]he judicial power of the United States is a . . . power to be exercised by courts organized for the purpose, and brought into existence by . . . the legislative power of the Union. . . . All . . . courts created by the general government possess no jurisdiction but what is given them by the power that creates them, and can be vested with none but what the power ceded to the general government will authorize them to confer.[125]

While couched in terms of federalism, it is obvious that Judge Johnson's opinion in *Hudson and Goodwin* drew heavily upon the rich body of precedent discussed earlier in this chapter which held that in the absence of statutory authorization, the federal lower courts lacked any jurisdiction and the Supreme Court was severely limited in the exercise of its appellate jurisdiction. Equally clear is the conformity of the *Hudson and Goodwin* rule with the legislative history of federal criminal law, excepting of course the Sedition Act, which had been attacked on constitutional grounds. Judge Johnson clearly inferred that Congress in granting criminal jurisdiction to the federal courts was limited by those national powers that had been delegated to the federal government by the States. If there remained a common law of crimes in the various States, then it obviously could not have been granted to the federal government by ratification of the Constitution.

Johnson conceded that there was some basis for the argument that a sovereign political body upon its creation was vested with the means to sustain its existence.[126] However, even if that principle were admitted, he nevertheless felt that federal courts might not, in the absence of statutory authorization, punish all acts detrimental to the peace and dignity of the United States. The only exception to this general rule would be the power of courts to fine for contempt or contumacy or to enforce their orders.[127] Those, Johnson allowed, were powers implied in the act of creating courts; however no criminal juris-

---

[124] 7 Cranch 32, at 32.
[125] *Ibid.*, 33.
[126] This may have been in answer to an assertion of this nature made in a grand jury charge delivered by Chief Justice Oliver Ellsworth in South

Carolina in 1799. The charge is printed in the Boston *Independent Chronicle*, June 10–13, 1799. See Johnson's opinion at 7 Cranch 33.
[127] *Ibid.*, 34.

diction in common law causes might be exercised as an implied power of the federal courts. Judge Johnson's opinion specifically declines to consider whether Congress might confer common law criminal jurisdiction upon the inferior federal courts.

While an effort was made to make the *Hudson* rule all inclusive, its acceptability decreases as one moves away from the specific fact situation of the case. In eliminating the doctrine of common law crime from the domestic prosecution of miscreants in federal courts, it was most effective. However it left unaffected vast areas of maritime and international law,[128] as well as crime within the federal districts and territories that were not subject to constitutional limitations inherent in the federal-State relationship. The implication of *Hudson and Goodwin* is that there was no common law of crimes, subject only to Judge Johnson's concession that in federal matters covered by delegated powers there might be a valid congressional grant of common law jurisdiction. Yet the authority of the United States Supreme Court as a tribunal of international law neither was a product of congressional legislation nor was it subject to limitation by federal-State constitutional relations. Our reading of *Rose* v. *Himely* and *Hudson* v. *Guestier* would suggest, however,[129] that even in the field of international law, the Supreme Court would defer to the policy of Congress and the executive before taking action to assert its jurisdiction.[130]

In addition to the questionable authority of *Hudson and Goodwin* in the field of international law, the opinion raised conceptual problems and administrative difficulties in regard to the District of Columbia and other places within the exclusive jurisdiction of the United States. District Judge Richard Peters observed in 1816 that all of the lesser crimes could be committed with impunity in those territories since they were not covered by congressional statutes and in the wake of *Hudson and Goodwin* they were not punishable under the doctrine of common law crime.[131] The complex situation arising in the District of Columbia may be taken as illustrative of the other federal territories. As we have seen, the 1801 congressional statute concerning the District had received into the law of the District the laws of Maryland and Virginia as they existed at the time sovereignty was transferred. While Virginia's revision of her law had done much to eliminate common law crimes in that State, the Maryland law contained no similar statutory break with the

---

[128] See Part II, chapter 5, p. 529.

[129] United States v. Henfield, 11 Fed. Case. (No. 1099) (Cir. Ct. Pa. 1793), might be cited as precedent for a common law of crimes derived from the law of nations. See also F. Wharton, *State Trials of the United States during the Administrations of Washington and Adams* (Philadelphia, 1849), 59 66, 84.

[130] See Part II, chapter 5, pp. 533–41.

[131] W. Crosskey, *Politics and the Constitution in the History of the United States*, 2 vols. (Chicago, 1953), II, 782.

colonial period.[132] Even before *Hudson and Goodwin* there would have been confusion, not unlike the differences between the counties of Alexandria and Washington concerning the assignment, or endorsement, of promissory notes. Narrowly limited to its facts *Hudson and Goodwin* need not have applied to a federal territory such as the District of Columbia, since it arose in Connecticut where the State possessed its own criminal statutes and its own common law of crimes. Problems of delegation of power to the federal government, and the grant of judicial power by Congress to the federal courts, ever present in the minds of the judges when they decided *Hudson and Goodwin*, were not germane to the issue of a common law of crimes in the District of Columbia. On the other hand, the broad doctrine of *Hudson and Goodwin* was declared applicable to all circuit courts of the United States, and no exception was made for the District of Columbia circuit. In another context, the Supreme Court had held that the laws of Maryland and Virginia applied in the District not by virtue of their enactment by those States but rather because they had been adopted by Congress as rules of decision within the District. Hence if Congress was precluded from passing legislation recognizing a federal common law of crimes because of constitutional limitations upon federal authority, then it could not by adopting Virginia or Maryland law make the doctrine of common law crimes from those jurisdictions applicable in the District of Columbia.

Blurring the distinction between territories of exclusive federal jurisdiction and the authority of circuit courts sitting in States of the Union was the product of a doctrinaire and sweeping application of federal rules to non-federal circumstances. As a consequence the District of Columbia, the newer federal territories, and areas within the States subject to exclusive federal jurisdiction were left with the meager provisions of the 1790 Crimes Act and its even more restricted supplementary legislation. That a result so detrimental to law and order should have followed from *Hudson and Goodwin* is a matter of some surprise, in spite of the bitter and acrimonious political and constitutional debates that had occurred over the doctrine of common law crimes, and the practical difficulties that had been presented in efforts to enforce the Embargo. In retrospect the Hudson and Goodwin case may be seen as an early victory for civil liberties in the federal courts, requiring that henceforth statutory notice and definiteness be required as a prerequisite to the imposition of criminal prohibitions and penalties.

In 1816 the *Hudson and Goodwin* rule was mentioned in a case involving a maritime tort of forcibly rescuing a vessel taken as prize

---

[132] See discussion of Reily v. Lamar, in Part II, chapter 4, pp. 519–21; and Bank of Alexandria, in Part II, chapter 6, pp. 560–62.

by two American privateers.[133] The rescue had taken place on the high seas, and since it did not fall within any statutory prohibitions, it had been prosecuted in the Massachusetts Circuit Court on common law crime indictments. The lower court judges divided in opinion on whether the circuit court had common law jurisdiction, and on the certification of the question, the Supreme Court dismissed the indictment on the precedent of *Hudson and Goodwin*. Judge Story felt that the case did not fall within the *Hudson and Goodwin* rule; both Judge Washington and Judge Livingston expressed a wish to hear the case argued in regard to the 1813 precedent. Judge Johnson, who wrote the majority opinion in favor of the defendant, indicated that since the Attorney General declined to argue the cause, and no counsel appeared for defendant, the Court obliged to reaffirm their opinion in *Hudson and Goodwin*. The net effect of *United States* v. *Coolidge* was to strengthen the likelihood that the *Hudson and Goodwin* rule was applicable to all criminal prosecutions under the authority of the United States, and to limit severely the powers of the federal courts over maritime crimes and torts.

Chief Justice Marshall's position in regard to federal common law crimes is not discernible from the Supreme Court opinions in *Hudson and Goodwin* or *United States* v. *Smith*, although in the latter instance his refusal to permit prosecutions at common law when there was a statutory remedy might indicate a growing sentiment against the doctrine of common law crimes. Whatever his personal opinion might have been, he was unable to maintain the unity of opinion in the Supreme Court. While *Hudson and Goodwin* was announced without dissent, it subsequently came under heavy attack in the circuit courts by Judge Story.[134] The comments by Judges Washington and Livingston in *United States* v. *Coolidge* indicated their willingness to consider the application of the *Hudson and Goodwin* rule to maritime crimes. In these cases, as in the Supreme Court's determinations concerning foreign prize decrees, the unanimity of the Court was badly broken. Marshall's silence may well have been an effort on his part to refrain from a further division of the Court; yet it is not unlikely that he may have moved in

---

[133] United States v. Coolidge, 1 Wheat. 415–17 (1816); additional details on the case may be obtained from Docket 4, Circuit Court, District of Massachusetts, Federal Records Center, Waltham, Mass., and Appellate Case Files, Case No. 671, RG 267, National Archives.

[134] United States v. Bigelow and Jenkins, an unreported case in Ap-

pellate Case Files, Case No, 730, RG 267, National Archives. See also *The Trial of George Travers on indictment for the murder of James McKin and on the indictment for the murder of Thomas Hasey . . . before the Circuit Court of the United States Held in Boston, Dec. 27, 1814* (Boston, 1815), 90.

the direction of accepting a modified and limited version of the *Hudson and Goodwin* rule by 1815. His opinion in *United States* v. *Smith* was a pre-*Hudson* precedent for the restrictive use of the doctrine of common law crimes. More broadly, his opinions concerning the civil jurisdiction of the Supreme Court and the inferior federal courts were clearly aimed at constraining federal judicial activity within the express grants made by the federal Constitution and congressional action. While the public policy considerations of *Hudson and Goodwin* may have given Marshall cause to hesitate, it was not a case with which he might differ so strongly as to make dissent the only conscionable recourse. With the *Hudson and Goodwin* precedent, the initiative of making law for the federal territories, including the District of Columbia, passed to the Congress. The removal of the Supreme Court from the support of the federal common law of crimes doctrine would do nothing but strengthen the Court within the government and in the eyes of the American people.

CONCLUSION

The jurisdiction of the Supreme Court, and of federal courts in general, was clarified and consolidated in the period from 1801 to 1815. Relying upon a narrow and restrictive view of the constitutional and statutory foundations of judicial power, the Court avoided direct conflict with the legislative and executive branches of the government and actively sought from those political branches the policy guidance it needed in fields of international law. At the same time the Supreme Court enhanced the authority of all federal courts in the areas of their authorized jurisdiction, insuring that in matters most closely touching upon the nature of the federal Union and international law, the ultimate decision rested in the hands of the federal judiciary. The special circumstances making the District of Columbia an exclusive federal jurisdiction gave the Supreme Court a unique opportunity to shape a distinctly federal jurisprudence for that District and to develop rules that might later serve in newly acquired federal territories. Regularization of appeals in matters of admiralty and chancery, and the Court's reservation of the right to determine "jurisdictional" facts in reviewing federal questions under section 25 of the 1789 Judiciary Act, insured the Court of an effective and ample appellate jurisdiction in vital areas touching upon international law, maritime affairs, and federal supremacy. In the years to follow, these foundations of jurisdiction would be used for broader and more obvious national purposes, but their establishment in this period represents one of the outstanding achievements of Marshall's jurisprudence and leadership.

CHAPTER IX

Conclusion

I N THIS SECOND PART of the volume the reader's attention has been
focused upon the internal development of the Supreme Court as
evidenced by the reported opinions of the Court, and upon detailed
points of law contained in those opinions. The cases have been analyzed
not only in terms of "black letter law" but also for the light they throw
upon the internal operations of the Court as well as for information
concerning the place of the Court in the governance of the American
States and the federal Union. Neither of these latter two matters have
been analyzed from this standpoint by previous scholars, and as a consequence the received knowledge of the Court's history from 1801 to
1815 has been to view it as a power struggle between Thomas Jefferson
and the political branches of government on one side and John Marshall
and the judges of the Supreme Court on the opposing side. With a
firm fixation upon the fascinating political events of these times, scholars
have often lost contact with the legal developments that are important
in and of themselves and also as additional evidence of what happened
in American government and constitutional development in the decade
and a half we have considered.

Constitutions, even when they are written documents, have an
internal dynamic that influences the future evolution of constitutional
theory and practice. Our Constitution of 1787 was no exception to this
rule; its internal dynamic was favorable to strong executive leadership,
coupled with a vagueness about judicial power with a potential to encourage the expansion of judicial authority. At the same time the very
form of the Constitution demonstrated a strong commitment to a Revolutionary tradition which, based on colonial experience, preferred legislative power to both executive or judicial strength. In the legislature the
voice of the franchised citizenry was most clearly heard and most
responsibly effectuated. The arrangement of the articles of the Consti-

tution, with the legislative power set forth first, followed by that of the executive, and finally by the judiciary, suggests a wish to set forth the authority of the federal government as being predominantly legislative, and to imply a degree of subordination in the constitutional status of both the President and the federal judges. If we are to construe the Constitution in these terms, the Supreme Court was least equal among the three branches of the federal government. Indeed, it has been readily apparent through its history that the Court, because it lacks both political power and an electoral mandate, is quite ineffectual to frustrate the determined will of the President and Congress and certainly powerless to withstand constitutional amendment as the mandate of the American people.

It is in the nature of American constitutional theory, particularly judicial review and the rule of law, that we must seek the authority (rather than the power) of the Supreme Court. As the agency for the decision of cases touching upon the concerns of the Union, the Court of necessity must pass upon the constitutional conformity of given State or federal action. In this sense the Court may be viewed as an arbiter, between the various States, the States and the federal government, the States and foreign nations or nationals, and between the citizens of the various States or foreign nations. Performance of its arbitral functions requires impartiality, for its power (if there be any) rests not upon the coercive attributes of sovereignty but rather upon the dual moral suasions of reasonability and internal and international tranquillity.

This stance of impartiality was severely undermined by the Supreme Court's activities from 1798 through 1801. Whether certain excesses in judicial behavior, particularly in the Sedition Act trials, may be attributed to a temporary Federalist hysteria resulting in a departure from the party's fundamental commitment to popular government,[1] or whether as viewed in this volume, the extreme Federalist and colonial views of judicial behavior were not suitable to a bipartisan political system, may be subject to debate. What seems quite obvious is the fact that in 1801 some substantial adjustments had to be made in the institutional and functional relationships between the Court, Congress, and the President, as well as in the popular and juristic view of the proper function of judges in the federal government. The major contribution of the Marshall Court to American government during this period was its adaptation to changed circumstances and its maintenance of an impartiality that served to detach it from political controversy and to

---

[1] This is the well-documented view of S. Presser, "A Tale of Two Judges: Richard Peters, Samuel Chase and the Broken Promise of Federalist Jurisprudence," *Northwestern University Law Review* LXXIII (1978), 26–111.

remove it from the dangers it faced from the politically powerful legislative and executive branches of government.

This period, as a time of transition, cannot be considered without giving some thought to the preceding decades of American history, nor can a reader fully understand the years from 1801 to 1815 without some knowledge of the golden era of constitutional adjudication from 1819, with the Dartmouth College[2] case and *M'Culloch* v. *Maryland*[3] to 1824 and *Gibbons* v. *Ogden*.[4] While neither period has been discussed in any detail in this volume, it is apparent from what has been said that the Court before 1801, despite its partisan political inclinations, was a weak branch of the federal government. Yet by 1815 it had established itself on a sufficiently steady foundation and could begin the task of considering both the broader federal applications of the contract clause and the elasticity of the "necessary and proper" clause. The discussion in Part II is an effort to explain how these changes in circumstances occurred.

Any study of the Supreme Court so limited in time cannot be construed more broadly than the limits of its parameters. It has been shown that the unanimity of opinion among the judges, prevailing through a major part of this period, began to break down after 1812, and that both the rule of seniority and the limitations upon dissenting opinions had less importance thereafter. Similarly, the Court in this period demonstrated great caution in challenging the will of the legislature and President, and extrapolated an impressive case law on the separation of powers. It might well be argued that in later years the Marshall Court departed from some, and perhaps all, of the practices that have been described here. Yet during this segment of its history, the Court appears to have been treading the cautious and circumspect path that has been delineated.

Men and their institutions are mirrors of their past, hemmed in by their heritage and reluctant adaptors to changed conditions and circumstances. In 1801 the Supreme Court was already molded by its short history, but also faced with the "Revolution of 1800," a political and constitutional event of vastly greater import than either the Federalist judges or the Jeffersonian-Republican legislators could imagine. Neither understood or practiced the principle of separation of powers as we know it today, and judicial restraint in approaching "political questions" was largely undiscovered until *Marbury* and the later Embargo cases. Each branch feared the other, not only because of the past but also by virtue of possible hostilities in the future. Viewed in this light the much discussed personal animosity between Chief Justice Marshall and President Jefferson may be placed into the perspective of

---

[2] 4 Wheat. 518 (1819).   [3] 4 Wheat. 316 (1819).   [4] 9 Wheat. 1 (1824).

being but one aspect of the redefinition of the role of the Supreme Court in a new political environment.[5] Whatever the personal relationship may have been between the President and the Chief Justice, it is apparent that in enforcing the Embargo and Non-Intercourse laws and in other less obvious cases, the Supreme Court, following its developing sense of the rule of law and separation of powers, upheld legislative action except in instances where constitutional rights of citizens were threatened.

Ultimately historians must attempt to answer the difficult questions of causation in the chronology of events. Yet the events leading to the institutional metamorphosis of the Supreme Court in the period 1801 to 1815 defy classification in regard to cause and effect. Obviously the threat of impeachment and the inchoate power of Congress to alter— and even abolish, as in 1802—the jurisdiction of the lower federal courts and, in appellate matters of the Supreme Court itself, were strong influences upon the moderation of the judges' behavior and the jury charges in the years after 1801. To that degree, it can be said that the Republican ascendancy was effective in bringing about change in judicial activities. And yet well before the two judicial impeachments were returned by the House of Representatives the Court had begun to make transitions, in *Marbury* v. *Madison*[6] and *Stuart* v. *Laird*,[7] which presaged the development of a full-scale concept of rule of law and a deep-seated respect for the primacy of legislative power as well as for the concept of separation of powers. As the years wore on towards 1815, it became clear that Republican fears of entrenched Federalist judges frustrating the will of the electorate were ill founded. This not only aborted the efforts at judicial impeachment, but also blunted legislative efforts to curb judicial power. Co-existence in this troublesome time resulted in a new respect between the branches of government, and a more realistic allocation of the powers of government between the Court, Congress, and the President.

In spite of these changes in the status and posture of the Supreme Court, one can see from this part the remarkable flexibility and dynamism that was inherent in the constitutional position of the Court. In international law matters it not only exercised broad authority, but it was also the final arbiter of threshold considerations bearing upon its jurisdiction. During the period under discussion the important fields of maritime law, prize cases, and marine insurance matters were important aspects of the business before the lower federal courts and the Supreme

---

[5] For expressions of Jefferson's attitude towards Marshall see Part I, chapter 5, p. 141; chapter 7, p. 208; chapter 8, pp. 289–91. The evidence of Marshall's feelings about Jefferson is sparse for the period 1801–15 due to a small amount of surviving Marshall correspondence for these years.

[6] 1 Cranch 137 (1803).

[7] 1 Cranch 299 (1803).

IX: *Conclusion*

Court. Each of these areas, and virtually every other decision of the Supreme Court, may be analyzed in terms of the ability of the Court to influence its own institutional growth by the determination of matters brought before it for adjudication, and to break away from precedent in situations where national policy so demanded, as in the areas of international law and prize cases. Ultimately the exercise of ordinary judicial functions, so often ignored by earlier constitutional historians who looked for landmark cases, was the vehicle for the Court's growth in the early Marshall years. For these reasons Part II of this volume has paid particular attention to "private law" cases, as well as the great themes of "public law" for which the Supreme Court has been recognized in these years. All of the opinions of the Court must be viewed not merely as the static conclusion of an adjudicative process, but also as the means by which the Supreme Court developed in institutional strength and exercised a restrained but effective degree of self-determination.

TABLE 1.

OPINIONS BY JUDGES DELIVERING OPINIONS, 1801–15

	Marshall	Cushing	Paterson	Chase	Washington	Johnson	Livingston	Todd	Duvall	Story	Seriatim & Per Curiam	TOTALS
1801	4										1	5
1803	10		1								6	17
1804	8	1									5	14
1805	17										4	21
1806	17				1						8	26
1807	11					1					7	19
1808	19	1		1		1					6	28
1809	31	2			1		2				9	45
1810	23				2	2	3				10	40
1812	18				4	3	1	1	1	1	3	32
1813	19				4	4	6		1	7	6	47
1814	14				6	6	4	1	2	10	3	46
1815	18				3	3	5			8	1	38
TOTALS	209	4	1	1	21	20	21	2	4	26	69	378

TABLE 2.

OPINIONS IN ORIGINAL JURISDICTION CASES, AND APPELLATE JURISDICTION CASES, BY CIRCUIT COURT OF ORIGIN, 1801–15

	ORIG. JURIS.	N.H.	MASS.	CONN.	R.I.	VT.	N.Y.	N.J.	PA.	DEL.	MD.	VA.	N.C.	S.C.	GA.	KY.	TENN.	OHIO	LA.	D.C.	STATE APPEALS	TOTALS
1801				1			1									1				2		5
1803	1										1	1			1					12	1	17
1804			2		1				2		1	1	2		1					4		14
1805			2						2		1	3			2	1				10	1	22
1806			1						1		2	3			2	3	1			11	2	26
1807	1			1	1	1			4			1			4	4				2		19
1808				1	1			1	3	2	2	1		2	4	3				7	1	28
1809			2		1			1	1		3	1		2	1	6		1		24	2	45
1810			1			1			2		9	2			1	2			3	16	3	40
1812			1	3	2	1	1		2		1	2			1	1	1			15	1	32
1813			1		1				2	1	12	1		2	1	1	3	1	4	13	3	46
1814		1	9		10						9	2		2	1	2				8	2	46
1815		1	3	2	5	2	3			1	1	2			4	3	4		1	5	1	38
TOTALS	2	2	22	8	22	5	5	2	19	4	42	20	2	8	23	27	9	2	8	129	17	378

TABLE 3.

OPINIONS ON NATIONALITY AND STATUS OF PERSONS, BY JUDGE AND TERM OF COURT, 1801–15

	Marshall	Cushing	Paterson	Chase	Washington	Johnson	Livingston	Todd	Duvall	Story	Seriatim & Per Curiam	TOTALS
1801												0
1803												0
1804	1											1
1805	2										1	3
1806	1											1
1807												0
1808		1				1						2
1809	1											1
1810	2				1							3
1812												0
1813	2									1	1	4
1814	2				1							3
1815	1									1		2
TOTALS	12	1			2	1				2	2	20

TABLE 4.

OPINIONS ON INTERNATIONAL LAW, EXCLUSIVE OF PRIZE CASES,
BY JUDGE AND TERM OF COURT, 1801–15

	Marshall	Cushing	Paterson	Chase	Washington	Johnson	Livingston	Todd	Duvall	Story	Seriatim & Per Curiam	TOTALS
1801												0
1803												0
1804	1											1
1805												0
1806											1	1
1807											1	1
1808	1	1										2
1809	1											1
1810	1											1
1812	1											1
1813							1			1		2
1814												0
1815	2											2
TOTALS	7	1					1			1	2	12

TABLE 5.

OPINIONS IN ADMIRALTY AND MARINE INSURANCE CASES, BY JUDGE AND TERMS OF COURT, 1801–15

	Marshall	Cushing	Paterson	Chase	Washington	Johnson	Livingston	Todd	Duvall	Story	Seriatim & Per Curiam	TOTALS
1801	2											2
1803	1										1	2
1804	5											5
1805	2										2	4
1806	5										2	7
1807	4											4
1808	8			1							1	10
1809	4	2					1				1	8
1810	7						2				4	13
1812	2				1	1						4
1813	12				1	1	2			1	3	20
1814	10				5	4	3		1	5	1	29
1815	5				2	4	2		1	3	0	17
TOTALS	67			1	9	10	10		2	9	15	125

TABLE 6.

OPINIONS ON THE LAW MERCHANT, EXCLUSIVE OF BILLS AND NOTES,
BY JUDGE AND TERM OF COURT, 1801–15

	Marshall	Cushing	Paterson	Chase	Washington	Johnson	Livingston	Todd	Duvall	Story	Seriatim & Per Curiam	TOTALS
1801												0
1803	1											1
1804												0
1805	2											2
1806	2											2
1807												0
1808	1											1
1809	4											4
1810												0
1812								1				1
1813							1					1
1814						2	1					3
1815						1						1
TOTALS	10					3	2	1				16

TABLE 7.

OPINIONS ON BILLS AND NOTES, BY JUDGE AND TERM OF COURT, 1801–15

	Marshall	Cushing	Paterson	Chase	Washington	Johnson	Livingston	Todd	Duvall	Story	Seriatim & Per Curiam	TOTALS
1801												0
1803	3										1	4
1804												0
1805	1											1
1806	1											1
1807	1											1
1808												0
1809	3										1	4
1810	3											3
1812	3											3
1813							2					2
1814	1											1
1815	1											1
TOTALS	17						2				2	21

TABLE 8.

OPINIONS RELATED TO BUSINESS ENTERPRISE, BY JUDGE AND TERM OF COURT, 1801–15

	Marshall	Cushing	Paterson	Chase	Washington	Johnson	Livingston	Todd	Duvall	Story	Seriatim & Per Curiam	TOTALS
1801												0
1803	2											2
1804	4											4
1805	7											7
1806	4										2	6
1807	2										1	3
1808	3										1	4
1809	7											7
1810	5					1					1	7
1812	3											3
1813	1						2			3		6
1814	1						1					2
1815	1									1		2
TOTALS	40					1	3			4	5	53

TABLE 9.

OPINIONS ON REAL PROPERTY LAW, BY JUDGE AND TERM OF COURT, 1801–15

	Marshall	Cushing	Paterson	Chase	Washington	Johnson	Livingston	Todd	Duvall	Story	Seriatim & Per Curiam	TOTALS
1801												0
1803												0
1804												0
1805	2										1	3
1806	1											1
1807											4	4
1808	5	1				1						7
1809	3				1							4
1810	2										1	3
1812	2				1						1	4
1813	3						1			1	1	6
1814	1									1		2
1815	4					1					2	7
TOTALS	23	1			2	2	1			4	8	41

TABLE 10.

OPINIONS ON PUBLIC LANDS, BY JUDGE AND TERM OF COURT, 1801–15

	Marshall	Cushing	Paterson	Chase	Washington	Johnson	Livingston	Todd	Duvall	Story	Seriatim & Per Curiam	TOTALS
1801	1											1
1803												0
1804												0
1805	1											1
1806	1											1
1807						1						1
1808												0
1809	4											4
1810	2										1	3
1812												0
1813	1								1			2
1814								1				1
1815	3									1		4
TOTALS	13					1		1	1	1	1	18

TABLE 11.

OPINIONS IN CONSTITUTIONAL LAW, BY JUDGE AND TERM OF COURT, 1801–15

	Marshall	Cushing	Paterson	Chase	Washington	Johnson	Livingston	Todd	Duvall	Story	Seriatim & Per Curiam	TOTALS
1801												0
1803	1		1									2
1804		1										1
1805	2											2
1806	1										2	3
1807	1										1	2
1808		1										1
1809	4										1	5
1810	1				1						2	4
1812	1					1		1				3
1813	1					2	1			1		5
1814									1			1
1815										2		2
TOTALS	12	2	1		1	3	1	1	1	3	6	31

662

TABLE 12.

OPINIONS ON COURTS AND PROCEDURE, BY JUDGE AND TERM OF COURT, 1801–15

	Marshall	Cushing	Paterson	Chase	Washington	Johnson	Livingston	Todd	Duvall	Story	Seriatim & Per Curiam	TOTALS
1801	2										1	3
1803	2		1								3	6
1804	2										4	6
1805	6										2	8
1806	5				1						3	9
1807	5										1	6
1808	4										2	6
1809	16	1					1				6	24
1810	13				1		1				4	19
1812	4				2	1		1		1	3	12
1813	4				2	2				3	3	14
1814	2									3	1	6
1815	5				1		1			1		8
TOTALS	70	1	1		7	3	3	1		8	33	127

TABLE 13.

OPINIONS ON CONFLICT OF LAWS, BY JUDGE AND TERM OF COURT, 1801–15

	Marshall	Cushing	Paterson	Chase	Washington	Johnson	Livingston	Todd	Duvall	Story	Seriatim & Per Curiam	TOTALS
1801	1											1
1803												0
1804	1											1
1805												0
1806	2											2
1807	1											1
1808	1										1	2
1809	1											1
1810	1											1
1812	1											1
1813												0
1814												0
1815												0
TOTALS	9										1	10

Table of Cases

Table of Statutes

673

TABLE OF STATUTES

About the Index

READERS HAVING RECOURSE to this index should be alert to certain compromises that have been made between comprehensiveness in indexing and the publishing economies to be obtained through brevity. Essentially, the index is designed to serve the user in locating elusive items that cannot be found through other aids. The separate tables of cases and statutes have been provided as a substitute for indexing those materials. When a case is particularly important to the career of an individual, the case is cross-referenced under his name in the index. The reader may then locate the case by use of the Table of Cases. In addition to this supportive use of the two tables of authorities, the index presumes that for large bodies of material related to the subject matter of chapters, readers will first read the appropriate chapters rather than having resort to the index. Consequently, the reader should have initial resort to the table of contents to locate materials that might be expected to fall within the broad outline of chapter contents. Only where materials occur in places that might be unusual, or where a degree of cross-referencing seemed useful, were broad subjects included in this index.

The index to individuals promised to become prolix unless certain limitations were imposed. No effort has been made to identify or include in the index every party-litigant; only parties claiming substantial historical significance other than their participation in cases have been included. On the other hand, since this volume is intended for scholars of legal and constitutional history, counsel appearing before the Court are indexed as are judges in both federal and state courts. Constitutional law students may object to the rather cursory sub-topic indexing under the names of individual judges of the United States Supreme Court. To this the authors plead the defense that the volume treats the work of the Court, and hence the career and thought of each judge on the Court; even diligent use of an exhaustive index would not be a substitute for a careful reading of the book. For those readers unwilling to do so, it is suggested that the topics included in the main index, used in conjunction with entries under a judge's name, will provide a fairly accurate guide to specific materials concerning that individual.

Subject matter indexing has occurred most heavily in the area of private law, the major public law issues for the most part having been subsumed in chapter groupings. The chronological arrangement of Part I limited the need for extensive indexing of the major historical events of the Jefferson and Madison administrations. Certain segments of the volume would lend themselves to tedious geographical indexing, but that temptation has been spurned.

The authors hope that this index will serve well the interests of those who will consult it for an understanding of the Supreme Court of the United States from 1801 to 1815, and of those who seek information concerning the state of public and private law during that period.

680

Index

A NOTE ON THE BOOK

This book is set in Linotype Times Roman. Composition by Maryland Linotype Company, Baltimore, Maryland. Printed and bound by The Kingsport Press, Kingsport, Tennessee. Paper is Troy Book Vellum manufactured by Miami Paper Corporation, West Carrollton, Ohio.

Woodcut of seal of the Supreme Court by Fritz Kredel.

Typography and binding design by
WARREN CHAPPELL